KT-172-962

**Darwin and
the Top End**
Pages 270–281

**Northern and
Outback Queensland**
Pages 252–261

**South of
Townsville**
Pages 238–251

Brisbane
Pages 222–237

Sydney
Pages 64–159

**The Blue Mountains
and Beyond**
Pages 168–185

• Cairns

**The South Coast and
Snowy Mountains**
Pages 186–193

QUEENSLAND

• Brisbane

**NEW
SOUTH
WALES**

• Port Augusta

• Adelaide

• Sydney

**CANBERRA
AND ACT** •

VICTORIA
• Melbourne

Tasmania
Pages 456–475

Canberra and ACT
Pages 194–211

TASMANIA
• Hobart

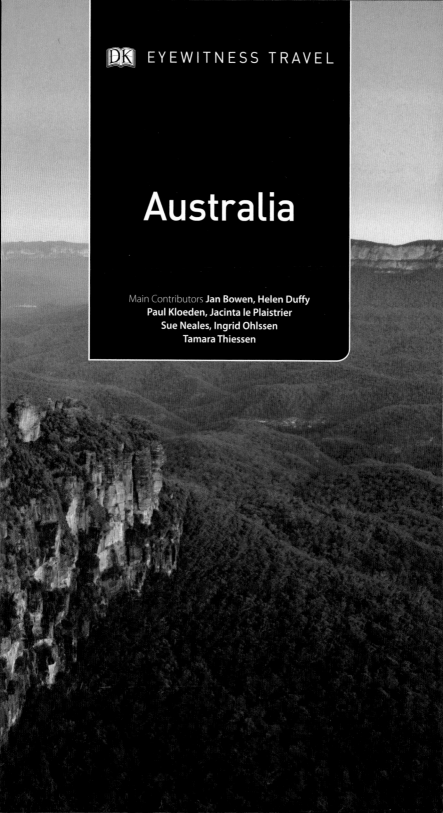

DK EYEWITNESS TRAVEL

Australia

Main Contributors **Jan Bowen, Helen Duffy**
Paul Kloeden, Jacinta le Plaistrier
Sue Neales, Ingrid Ohlssen
Tamara Thiessen

DK | Penguin Random House

Produced by Duncan Baird Publishers
London, England

Managing Editor Zoë Ross

Managing Art Editors Vanessa Marsh (with
Clare Sullivan and Virginia Walters)

Editor Rebecca Miles

Commissioning Designer Jill Mumford

Designers Dawn Davis-Cook, Lucy Parissi

Consultant Helen Duffy

Main Contributors Jan Bowen, Helen Duffy,
Paul Kloeden, Jacinta le Plaistrier, Sue Neales,
Ingrid Ohlsson, Tamara Thiessen.

Photographers Max Alexander, Alan
Keohane, Dave King, Rob Reichenfeld,
Peter Wilson.

Illustrators Richard Bonson, Jo Cameron,
Stephen Conlin, Eugene Fleury, Chris Forsey,
Steve Gyapay, Toni Hargreaves, Chris Orr,
Robbie Polley, Kevin Robinson, Peter Ross,
John Woodcock.

Printed and bound in China

First published in the UK in 1998 by Dorling
Kindersley Limited
80 Strand, London WC2R 0RL

18 19 20 21 10 9 8 7 6 5 4 3 2 1

**Reprinted with revisions 1999, 2000,
2001, 2002, 2003, 2005, 2006, 2008,
2010, 2012, 2014, 2016, 2018**

Copyright 1998, 2018 © Dorling Kindersley
Limited, London
A Penguin Random House company

ISBN 978 0 2413 0593 5

MIX
Paper from
responsible sources
FSC™ C018179
www.fsc.org

Aboriginal Painting

**The information in this
DK Eyewitness Travel Guide is checked regularly.**

Every effort has been made to ensure that this book is as up-to-date as possible
at the time of going to press. Some details, however, such as telephone numbers,
opening hours, prices, gallery hanging arrangements and travel information are
liable to change. The publishers cannot accept responsibility for any consequences
arising from the use of this book, nor for any material on third party websites, and
cannot guarantee that any website address in this book will be a suitable source of
travel information. We value the views and suggestions of our readers very highly.
Please write to: Publisher, DK Eyewitness Travel Guides, Dorling Kindersley,
80 Strand, London, WC2R 0RL, UK, or email: travelguides@dk.com.

◀ **Title page** Sunset at the Three Sisters, Blue Mountains National Park, New South Wales **Front cover image** The Bay of Fires at
Binalong Bay in Northeastern Tasmania **Back cover image** Bronte beach in Sydney

Contents

The Twelve Apostles in Port Campbell National Park, seen from the Great Ocean Road

Sydney Opera House

HOW TO USE THIS GUIDE

This guide helps you to get the most from your visit to Australia. *Introducing Australia* maps the whole country and sets it in its historical and cultural context. The 17 regional chapters, including *Sydney*, describe important sights with maps, pictures and illustrations, as well as introductory features

on subjects of regional interest. Suggestions on restaurants, accommodation, shopping and entertainment are in *Travellers' Needs*. The *Survival Guide* has tips on getting around the country. The cities of Sydney, Melbourne and Brisbane also have their own *Practical Information* sections.

Sydney

The centre of Sydney has been divided into four sightseeing areas. Each area has its own chapter which opens with a list of the sights described. All the sights are numbered and plotted on an *Area Map*. Information on each sight is easy to locate within the chapter as it follows the numerical order on the map.

1 Area Map
Sights are numbered on a map. Sights in the city centre are also shown on the Sydney Street Finder (*see pp152–9*). Melbourne also has its own Street Finder (*see pp418–25*).

A locator map shows where you are in relation to other areas of the city centre.

Sights at a Glance lists the chapter's sights by category: Historic Streets and Buildings, Museums and Galleries, Parks and Gardens etc.

All pages relating to Sydney have orange thumb tabs.

2 Street-by-Street Map
This gives a bird's-eye view of the heart of each sightseeing area.

A suggested route for a walk covers the more interesting streets in the area.

Stars indicate sights that no visitor should miss.

3 Detailed Information on each Sight
All the sights in Sydney are described individually. Useful addresses, telephone numbers, opening hours and other practical information are provided for each entry. The key to all the symbols used in the information block is shown on the back flap.

ADELAIDE AND THE SOUTHEAST

The Southeast is a region rich with pine forests, wineries and a spectacular coastline. The state capital, Adelaide, is a vibrant city, whose surrounding hills abound with vineyards from the Barossa to McLaren Vale. To the east, the great Murray River meanders from the Victoria border down to the Southern Ocean. Just off the Fleurieu Peninsula lies Kangaroo Island, a haven for wildlife.

Australia Area by Area

Apart from Sydney, Australia has been divided into seven chapters. Within the chapters the regions are further divided into 16 areas. The most interesting towns and places to visit are numbered on an *Regional Map* at the beginning of each chapter.

1 Introduction
The landscape, history and character of each region is described here, showing how the area has developed over the centuries and what it offers to the visitor today.

Exploring Adelaide and the Southeast

Each area of Australia can be identified quickly by its own colour coding, which is shown on the inside front cover.

2 Regional Map
This shows the main road network and gives an illustrated overview of the whole area. All interesting places to visit are numbered and there are also useful tips on getting around the region.

3 Detailed Information
All the important towns and other places to visit are described individually. They are listed in order, following the numbering on the *Regional Map*. Within each town or city, there is detailed information on important buildings and other sights.

For all the top sights, a visitors' checklist provides the practical information needed to plan your visit.

Ayers House

4 Australia's Top Sights
Historic buildings are dissected to reveal their interiors; museums and galleries have colour-coded floorplans; the national parks have maps showing facilities and trails. Major towns have maps, with sights picked out and described.

Story boxes explore specific subjects further.

INTRODUCING AUSTRALIA

DISCOVERING AUSTRALIA

The following tours have been designed to take in as many of Australia's highlights as possible. In a country as large as Australia, some long-distance travel is inevitable and driving times may be longer than readers are used to. However, the itineraries endeavour to keep travel distances realistic. To begin with there are three two-day city tours, covering Sydney, Melbourne and Perth. The itineraries for Sydney and Melbourne can easily be combined by anyone travelling between the two. Extra suggestions are provided for those who wish to extend their visit, or take in other nearby sights. The city tours are followed by 14 days on the East Coast, five days in the Red Centre and ten days on the West Coast. These tours can be combined with trips to southern and northern Australia. Pick, combine and follow your favourite tours, or simply dip in and out and be inspired.

10 Days on the West Coast – Perth to Exmouth

- Explore the boutiques and restaurants of colourful **Northbridge** in Perth.
- Wonder at the mysterious landscape of the Pinnacles in **Nambung National Park**.
- Discover all about the local shipwrecks at **Geraldton**'s WA Museum.
- Peer into **Hamelin Pool** and learn about million-year-old stromatolites.
- Snorkel on Ningaloo Reef in the **Cape Range National Park**.
- Swim with whale sharks off the coast of **Exmouth**.

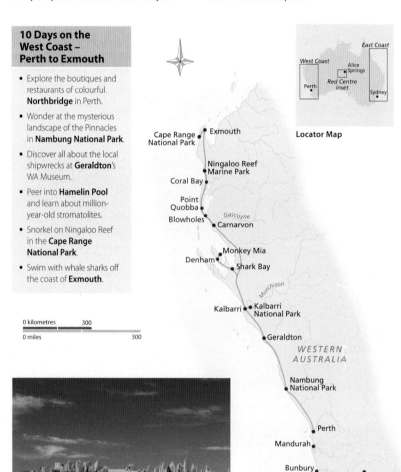

Locator Map

West Coast

East Coast

Alice Springs

Perth Red Centre inset

Sydney

Exmouth

Cape Range National Park

Ningaloo Reef Marine Park

Coral Bay

Point Quobba

Blowholes

Gascoyne

Carnarvon

Monkey Mia

Denham

Shark Bay

Murchison

Kalbarri Kalbarri National Park

Geraldton

WESTERN AUSTRALIA

Nambung National Park

Perth

Mandurah

Bunbury

Busselton Katanning

0 kilometres   300

0 miles   300

The Pinnacles
This extraordinary landscape of limestone pillars can be found in Nambung National Park, on the western coast of Australia.

◀ View of Sydney, New South Wales by Thomas Baines (1820–1875)

Key

━━━ 14 Days on the East Coast
━━━ 5 Days in the Red Centre
━━━ 10 Days on the West Coast

0 kilometres   200

0 miles   200

5 Days in the Red Centre

- Find yourself a long way from anywhere in **Alice Springs** and visit the excellent galleries in town.

- Enjoy a spectacular sunset at **Uluṟu-Kata Tjuṯa National Park**. Try to capture Uluṟu's famous colour changes with your camera.

- Walk or cycle around the base of **Uluṟu**, marvelling at the colours and textures of the great rock.

- Embark on the Valley of the Winds walk at **Kata-Tjuṯa** and stroll among the giant boulders.

Byron Bay Lighthouse This iconic structure was erected on the easternmost point of the Australian mainland in 1901.

14 Days on the East Coast – Sydney to Cairns

- Tour the **Sydney Opera House** or admire it from aboard a ferry from **Circular Quay**.

- Visit one of **Sydney's beaches** and embark on a clifftop walk.

- Lounge on the beautiful beaches of the East Coast, such as **Byron Bay** and **Port Macquarie**.

- Wander around laid-back **Brisbane** and picnic in the Botanic Garden.

- Look for platypuses in **Eungella National Park**.

- Visit **Townsville's** aquarium and tour nearby **Magnetic Island**.

- Set off from **Cairns** to dive on the spectacular **Great Barrier Reef**.

2 Days in Sydney

This vibrant, beautiful city boasts museums, galleries and world-class restaurants, as well as iconic landmarks and tempting beaches.

- **Arriving** Sydney Airport, located about 10 km (6 miles) south of the city, is the main gateway. To reach the centre you can take a bus, train or taxi.

- **Moving on** The drive from Sydney to Melbourne takes just under 9 hours; the flight time is 1 hour and 35 minutes. If you have a lot of time on your hands, you could also catch a train. To reach Canberra from Sydney will take about 3 hours by car, just under an hour by plane, and just over 4 hours by train.

Day 1
Morning A couple of days in this city give you enough time to take in the main sights. On your first morning, visit the **Art Gallery of New South Wales** *(pp114–17)*; don't miss the Aboriginal and Torres Strait Islander art on display. Next, wander down through the **Royal Botanic Gardens** *(pp110–11)*, a peaceful oasis containing a vast variety of plants and trees. Continue past the Sydney Opera House, to **Circular Quay** *(pp78–89)*. There are several lunch spots here, especially in The Rocks and beyond the Overseas Passenger Terminal.

Dome of the Queen Victoria Building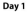

Afternoon Tour the **Sydney Opera House** *(pp88–9)* or visit the **Museum of Contemporary Art** *(p82)*, where you can enjoy a breathtaking view from the café. If you are feeling active, walk over the **Sydney Harbour Bridge** *(pp84–5)* or challenge yourself to the BridgeClimb. Explore **The Rocks** *(pp80–81)* and stay in the area for dinner.

Day 2
Morning Take a ferry from Circular Quay to one of the many harbour bays, coves and beach areas around Sydney *(pp148–9)*. Consider a trip to **Manly** *(p130)*, where you can swim in the sea, relax in a café or learn to surf. Then, either take the ferry back or walk to Spit Bridge before jumping on a bus to **Sydney Town Hall** *(p97)*.

Afternoon If you're a keen shopper, head to George Street and visit the **Queen Victoria Building** *(p94)*, as well as the **Westfield Sydney** *(p93)* shopping centre, home to big department stores such as David Jones and Myer.

If relaxing in leafy surroundings is more appealing, flop on the grass in **Hyde Park** *(p97)* after checking out the Anzac Memorial, or walk down to **Darling Harbour** *(pp100–101)*. Relax with a cup of tea in the tranquillity of the **Chinese Garden of Friendship** *(pp102–3)*, then visit the excellent interactive **Powerhouse Museum** *(pp106–7)*. For dinner, choose somewhere in **Chinatown** *(p103)* or, if you feel like treating yourself, admire the view from the restaurant in **Sydney Tower** *(p95)*. If you find you've still got energy to burn, head over to **Darlinghurst** *(pp120–29)* to check out Sydney's small bar scene, before walking down the infamous King's Cross strip.

> **To extend your trip…**
> Spend a day lounging on world-famous **Bondi Beach** *(p131)*; alternatively, walk from Bondi to **Coogee** *(p149)* along the clifftop. If beach life doesn't appeal, head to the **Blue Mountains** *(pp170–73)* for a couple of days, or spend a day tasting wines in the splendid **Hunter Valley** *(pp178–9)*. There is also the option of driving from Sydney to the capital city of **Canberra** *(pp194–209)*, in the Australian Capital Territory.

2 Days in Melbourne

Considered the most European of Australia's cities, Melbourne offers many gardens and parks to relax in, fascinating cultural events and some excellent tourist sights.

- **Arriving** Melbourne has two airports: Tullamarine and Avalon. Tullamarine is the main hub and closer to the city. To reach the city from Tullamarine, take the SkyBus or a taxi; the airport bus meets all flights from Avalon.

The iconic Sydney Opera House and Circular Quay

Statue of Charles La Trobe in Melbourne's State Library of Victoria

Day 1
Morning Join a walking tour of Melbourne's laneways and **arcades** (pp392–3), and discover cafés, boutiques and colourful street art. There is usually the option to include lunch in the tour; if not, just stop somewhere along the way that takes your fancy.

Afternoon Visit the **Ian Potter Centre: National Gallery of Victoria** (closed Mon; p407), which has an excellent collection of Australian art, or spend some time at the nearby **Immigration Museum** (p392), where you can learn more about the varied communities that make up modern Melbourne. It may well be raining by now, so jump on the free **City Circle Tram** (p416) as it travels around the Central Business District. In the evening, explore the suburb of **Fitzroy** (p400) and stop for dinner in Gertrude Street.

Day 2
Morning Head to the **Queen Victoria Market** (closed Mon & Wed; p390), and sample some of the delicious foods on offer. If the weather's nice, buy some picnic provisions and make your way to the **Royal Botanic Gardens** (pp402–3) for lunch.

Afternoon Stop in at the **Old Melbourne Gaol** (pp398–9), where Ned Kelly was hanged and where his death mask can still be seen, and learn more about the justice handed out here. Ned Kelly's armour is kept at the **State Library of Victoria**

(p389). Those travelling with children may prefer to head to the **Melbourne Museum** (p399) with its wonderful Forest Gallery and dinosaur skeletons. In the evening, tuck into an Italian meal on **Lygon Street** (p399).

> **To extend your trip…**
> Arrange a day trip south of Melbourne to see the penguins at **Phillip Island** (p446) or to the **Yarra Valley** (p447) to taste Victoria's famous wines. If you have more time, consider driving the **Great Ocean Road** (pp432–3) to **Adelaide** (pp344–53) or jumping on a ferry to explore **Tasmania** (pp456–75).

2 Days in Perth

This relaxed city is almost as close to Southeast Asia as it is to Sydney. Those in search of culture, beaches, interesting day trips and a laid-back atmosphere won't be disappointed.

- **Arriving** Perth Airport has an international and a domestic terminal. The Connect shuttle bus will drop you off at your accommodation in Perth or Fremantle; alternatively, you can take a taxi or a bus to the city centre.

Day 1
Morning Wander through **Central Perth** (pp306–9), exploring its arcades and malls, then head down to the Swan River to see the **Swan Bells** (p309). From here, make your way to **Kings Park** (p310), where you can take a guided walk, enjoy the view and have lunch.

Afternoon Double back through the city to the **Perth Cultural Centre** (p308), where you'll find the Art Gallery of Western Australia (closed Tue), the Perth Institute of Contemporary Art (PICA; closed Mon) and the Western Australian

Museum – Perth. Spend the evening in lively **Northbridge** (p308), where there is a range of restaurants and bars.

Day 2
Morning Explore the port city of **Fremantle** (pp314–15). Wander the streets admiring the 19th-century architecture and stopping in any shops or galleries that catch your eye. Don't miss Fremantle's oldest building, the **Round House** (p314). Alternatively, jump on a ferry to **Rottnest Island** (pp312–13), where you can hire a bike, look for quokkas, see the sights and take advantage of the beautiful white-sand beaches.

Afternoon If you've spent the morning on Rottnest Island, be sure to spend at least some time in Fremantle, admiring the city's historic buildings before finding somewhere to enjoy an evening meal. Take in a tour of **Fremantle Prison** (p315) and visit the **Shipwreck Galleries** of the **Western Australian Museum** (p314).

> **To extend your trip…**
> Visit Perth's **Sunset Coast** (pp310–11), where you can enjoy places like **Cottesloe Beach**, with its relaxed atmosphere and attractive beaches. Or head out to the **Swan Valley** wineries (p310).

The Bell Tower: Home of the Swan Bells, by the Swan River in Perth

14 Days on the East Coast – Sydney to Cairns

- **Airports** Arrive at Sydney Airport and depart from Cairns Airport.

- **Transport** A car is essential for this trip, although it is possible to take buses up the coast and amend and extend the itinerary as necessary.

- **Booking ahead** If planning a tour to Fraser Island and/or the Whitsunday Islands, consider arranging this in advance.

Days 1 and 2: Sydney
See the city itinerary on pages 12–13.

Day 3: Newcastle
Leave the busy streets of Sydney behind and head north, to the quieter, more down-to-earth city of **Newcastle** (p177). Once there, visit the excellent **Newcastle Region Art Gallery** (closed Mon) to see its remarkable collection of Australian art, then make your way to the restored **Fort Scratchley** (closed Tue), where you can learn about what took place in this town during World War II.

Day 4: Port Macquarie
From Newcastle, continue north along the Pacific Highway to **Port Macquarie**

The pedestrian Goodwill Bridge in Brisbane, leading to the Queensland Cultural Precinct

(p183), a popular holiday destination with some attractive beaches. En route, you could leave the main road to visit **Crowdy Bay National Park** (p182), where fishing is a popular activity.

Day 5: Coffs Harbour
The journey north to **Coffs Harbour** (p182) will take you past a number of lovely sandy beaches, including **Nambucca Heads** (p183) and the surf spot of **Third Headland Beach** (p182). Coffs Harbour itself is one of the most popular tourist destinations in New South Wales and has lots of activities available, including horseriding, diving and surfing.

Days 6 and 7: Byron Bay
Travel through quaint **Grafton** (p182) on your way north and

stop for a walk along the river or, in season (Oct), to admire the jacaranda trees in bloom. **Byron Bay** (p183), the easternmost point on the Australian mainland, draws backpackers, holidaymakers and people on weekend trips to the beach. Spend an afternoon admiring the views, relaxing on the golden sand, swimming in the sea and trying your hand at a range of watersports.

Days 8 and 9: Brisbane
Cross into Queensland and pass through a series of small surf communities until you reach **Surfers Paradise Beach** (p243). If you enjoy pulsating nightlife, then consider extending your stay here. When you reach **Brisbane** (pp222–37), be sure to visit the **City Botanic Gardens** (pp228–9) and the **Queensland Cultural Precinct** (pp232–3), where you'll find the Queensland Museum & Science Centre and the Queensland Art Gallery and Gallery of Modern Art (QAGOMA). A popular trip outside the city centre is to the **Lone Pine Koala Sanctuary** (p234), where you can enjoy a cuddle with one of these irresistible critters.

Day 10: Hervey Bay
The Sunshine Coast stretches north of Brisbane as far as **Noosa** (p243). On your way there, you may want to stop at **Australia Zoo** (p242), made famous by the late Steve Irwin.

Whale-watching boat returning to Hervey Bay Marina, Queensland

For practical information on travelling around Australia see pp556–63

The golden sands and clear waters of idyllic Magnetic Island

Most people come to **Hervey Bay** (p245) to travel on to Fraser Island, but if time is limited, note that it's possible to see whales from here too (Aug–Oct). Take the passenger ferry to **Fraser Island** (p246), the world's largest sand island, for a quick visit.

> **To extend your trip…**
> Organize a day trip to Fraser Island from Hervey Bay, either joining an organized tour or hiring a 4WD. Alternatively, travel further up the coast and embark on a boat trip around the **Whitsunday Islands** (p250).

Day 11: Rockhampton
This section of the journey will take you through the attractive town of **Bundaberg** (p245), home of Australia's most

Mount Hypipamee crater, Atherton Tablelands

famous rum, before you reach **Rockhampton** (p248), a pleasant town with a number of heritage buildings from the 19th century. This is a good place to break your journey north. Visit the **Aboriginal Dreamtime Cultural Centre** (closed Sat & Sun), then stop by the spire marking the fact that the Tropic of Capricorn runs through the town. If you have time to spare, visit the caves at **Mount Etna National Park** (p248), 25 km (15 miles) north of town. This is where the endangered ghost bat nests.

Day 12: Mackay and Eungella National Park
The next stretch of highway is mostly uninteresting until you reach the town of **Mackay** (p250), where you can admire a number of Art Deco buildings and enjoy a little beach time. From Mackay, travel west to **Eungella National Park** (p250) and engage in some platypus spotting (dusk and dawn are the best times for this activity).

Day 13: Townsville and Magnetic Island
Townsville (p251) is Queensland's second-largest city, and there's an excellent aquarium here, **Reef HQ** (p251), as well as a number of museums. Most people, however, choose to press on to **Magnetic Island** (p251) and stay there. Enjoy the beaches and good walking opportunities, or organize a tour of the island by 4WD.

> **To extend your trip…**
> If you're an experienced scuba diver, head to nearby **Ayr** (p250), the jumping-off point for the SS *Yongala* wreck dive.

Day 14: North via the Atherton Tablelands to Cairns
Continue to drive up the coast until you reach the town of Innisfail, then make your way inland to the **Atherton Tablelands** (p259). Stop in this incredibly fertile farming area to enjoy the temperate climate and the beautiful scenery and to buy locally grown fruit and vegetables from numerous roadside stalls. Drop back down to the coast into **Cairns** (p258), where you can visit the **Flecker Botanic Gardens**, and consider taking part in some of the many activities on offer. There are a number of restaurants here, or buy some street food at the night market.

> **To extend your trip…**
> Stay in Cairns for a few extra days and explore the **Great Barrier Reef** (pp216–21). If snorkelling and diving are not for you, take the Kuranda Scenic Railway north to **Kuranda** (p258). There is also the option to head north to visit **Port Douglas** (p257), **Daintree National Park** (p257) and **Cape Tribulation** (p257).

5 Days in the Red Centre

- **Airports** Alice Springs Airport is 15 km (9 miles) out of town. The Alice Wanderer Airport Transfers Shuttle meets flights, or you can take a taxi to your hotel.

- **Transport** A car is essential for this trip. It can be picked up and dropped off in Alice Springs.

- **Booking ahead** When visiting Uluṟu, be sure to book your accommodation at Yulara well in advance.

Day 1: Alice Springs
This circular tour begins and ends in **Alice Springs** (pp286–7). There are several art galleries to visit here, as well as a number of sights to suit most interests. Those keen to find out more about the local fauna should head to the **Alice Springs Desert Park**; history buffs can pay a visit to the **Telegraph Station Historical Reserve** and the **Royal Flying Doctor Service Visitor Centre** (pm only Sun).

Day 2: Uluṟu-Kata Tjuṯa National Park
The drive from Alice Springs to **Uluṟu-Kata Tjuṯa National Park** (pp290–93) is a long one. Most people take the Stuart and Lassiter highways, but there are also some 4WD routes. En route, don't confuse Mount Conner for your first glance of Uluṟu. Check into your accommodation, then drive out to see Uluṟu at sunset.

Day 3: Uluṟu (Ayers Rock)
Make your way to **Uluṟu** (p292) and consider following one of the walking trails, such as the Base Walk (about 3 to 4 hours). For a quicker lap around it, hire a bicycle. Don't forget to visit the **Uluṟu-Kata Tjuṯa Cultural Centre** (p293) while you're here to learn more about the park and the area's history.

Day 4: Kata Tjuṯa (The Olgas)
Consider visiting Uluṟu again, then travel on to **Kata Tjuṯa** (pp292–3), formerly known as The Olgas. There are a couple of walking trails here, the shorter Walpa Gorge Walk and the Valley of the Winds Walk, which takes about 3 hours. If you can, stay to see the sunset.

Day 5: Alice Springs
This is another long day of driving, so stop at one of the roadhouses along the way, then relax and wash the red dust off you in Alice Springs (see Day 1).

> **To extend your trip…**
> Drive to **Kings Canyon** (p289) and embark on the 6-km (4-mile) Rim Walk. The scenery is breathtaking, but be sure to walk early in the morning or in the afternoon rather than in the heat of the day. It is also possible to arrange a one-way car rental from Alice Springs, and drive either south, towards **Adelaide** (pp348–53), or north, to **Darwin** (pp274–7) and **Kakadu National Park** (pp280–81).

Entrance to Alice Springs Desert Park, in the Northern Territory

10 Days on the West Coast – Perth to Exmouth

- **Airports** Arrive and depart from Perth Airport.

- **Transport** A one-way hire car is essential for this trip, and a domestic flight required from Exmouth to Perth.

- **Booking ahead** If you want to stay at Monkey Mia, book your accommodation well in advance.

Days 1 and 2: Perth
See the city itinerary on p13.

> **To extend your trip…**
> Head south for a few days to visit the wineries in **Margaret River** (pp318–19), climb the **Gloucester Tree** (p319) and explore the Timber Towns, such as **Pemberton** (p319) and **Manjimup** (p319).

Day 3: Nambung National Park
The Pinnacles, a landscape of limestone columns that formed underground and were revealed by the winds, is the main attraction in **Nambung National Park** (p328). Drive along the 3-km (2-mile) Pinnacles Drive, taking the time to get out of your car and wander around.

The distinctive shape of Uluṟu (Ayers Rock), in Uluṟu-Kata Tjuṯa National Park

Erupting geyser at the Blowholes, north of Carnarvon

Day 4: Kalbarri via Geraldton

On your journey north, stop in **Geraldton** *(pp328–9)* to visit the **WA Museum – Geraldton**, which features an excellent gallery dedicated to the area's shipwrecks. From here, continue on to Kalbarri.

Day 5: Kalbarri National Park

Kalbarri National Park *(p329)* can be explored either on foot or by bicycle. In addition to beautiful beaches, it offers a series of vertiginous cliffs, gorges and lookouts. It's also possible to join a canoe tour down the Murchison River.

Day 6: Monkey Mia

Leave the Northwest Coastal Highway and head for Denham. Stop at **Shark Bay World Heritage and Marine Park** *(pp330–31)* to admire the ancient stromatolites of **Hamelin Pool** and visit nearby **Shell Beach** to see how shells were once used as building material. You can either choose to base yourself in **Denham** *(p330)* or, if you're not an early riser, press on to Monkey Mia.

Day 7: Carnarvon and the Blowholes

Get up early to witness the 8am dolphin-feeding session at the small beach of **Monkey Mia** *(p331)*, then head back the way you came to rejoin the highway and drive to **Carnarvon** *(p329)*, where you can take a tour of one of the fruit plantations. In the afternoon, drive the 70 km (43 miles) to see the **Blowholes** *(p329)*. If you're camping and don't mind roughing it a little, Point Quobba is a lovely spot to spend the night.

Day 8: Ningaloo Reef Marine Park

A great spot to experience **Ningaloo Reef Marine Park** *(p332)* is the small seaside town of Coral Bay, since its still waters allow snorkellers to enjoy the reef from close to the shore. It's also possible to fish, dive and whale-watch here in season.

> **To extend your trip…**
> There are a number of station stays in this area, so consider spending a couple of nights experiencing life in the Outback.

Days 9 and 10: Exmouth and the Cape Range National Park

There is not much to see in **Exmouth** *(p332)* itself, so head instead to one of the nearby beaches or go straight to the **Cape Range National Park** *(p332)*, where you can do some walking or take advantage of the superb snorkelling. If you enjoy camping, consider staying overnight in the park, but be aware that facilities are limited. At present only a handful of pitches can be booked in advance; the rest are allocated on a first-come-first-served basis at the entrance gate to the park. Spend the morning in the park, then make your way to the airport for the flight back to Perth.

> **To extend your trip…**
> In season (Mar–May), arrange to go swimming or **snorkelling with whale sharks** *(p332)*. You could also consider carrying on north to **Broome** *(p334)* or **Darwin** *(pp274–7)*, or driving west to visit **Karijini National Park** *(p333)*.

Cliffs in Kalbarri National Park, Western Australia

Putting Australia on the Map

Australia lies in the southern hemisphere and covers 7,692,024 sq km (2,969,907 sq miles) of land. A continent, it is bordered by the Pacific Ocean to the east and the Indian Ocean to the west. More than 80 per cent of its 24 million people reside along the coastline with its more hospitable climate. The capital, Canberra, is in the Australian Capital Territory (ACT), but the most populous city is Sydney. Tasmania, an island state, lies 240 km (150 miles) off the southern tip of the country, across the Bass Strait.

Key

━━ Highway

━━ Major road

─── Railway

▬▬ State border

Southeast Asia and the Pacific Rim

For additional map symbols *see back flap*

Arafura Sea

Torres Strait
Cape York

Arnhem Land

Gulf Of Carpentaria

Groote Eylandt

Mornington Island

Cooktown

0 kilometres 250
0 miles 250

Cairns

Tennant Creek

NORTHERN
TERRITORY

Mount Isa

P a c i f i c

Townsville

Proserpine

Mackay

Great Barrier Reef

QUEENSLAND

Flinders

O c e a n

Alice
Springs

Longreach

Rockhampton

Blackall

Hervey Bay

Diamantina

Fraser Island

Charleville

Maroochydore

Coober
Pedy

Lake Eyre

Toowoomba

Brisbane

Coolangatta

SOUTH
AUSTRALIA

Moree

Bourke

Coffs Harbour

Lake Torrens

Broken
Hill

Darling

NEW
SOUTH
WALES

Lake Gairdner

Ceduna

Dubbo

Whyalla

Maitland Newcastle

Murray

Sydney

Port Lincoln

Adelaide

Mildura

Wollongong

Wagga Wagga

Canberra

Kangaroo Island

VICTORIA

STRALIAN
APITAL
TERRITORY

Melbourne

Geelong

King Island

Bass Strait

Flinders Island

Tasman Sea

Devonport

Launceston

TASMANIA

Hobart

A PORTRAIT OF AUSTRALIA

Australia is the world's oldest continent, inhabited for more than 60,000 years by Aborigines. It was settled by the British during their maritime heyday, in 1788, and since then has transformed from a colonial outpost into a nation with a population of more than 24 million people. For visitors, its ancient, worn landscape contrasts with the vitality and youthful energy of its inhabitants.

Covering an area as large as the United States of America or the entire European continent, Australia's landscape is highly diverse, encompassing the dry Outback, the high plateaus of the Great Dividing Range, the lush woods of Tasmania, the rainforests and coral reefs of the tropical north and almost 36,000 km (22,300 miles) of mainland coastline. The Great Dividing Range forms a spine down eastern Australia, from Queensland to Victoria, separating the fertile coastal strip from the dry and dusty interior.

Dominating the vegetation is the eucalypt, known as the "gum tree", of which there are some 500 varieties.

Australian trees shed their bark rather than their leaves, the native flowers have no smell and, with the exception of the wattle, bloom only briefly.

Australia has a unique collection of fauna. Most are marsupials, such as the kangaroo and koala. The platypus and echidna are among the few living mammals that both lay eggs and suckle their young. The dingo, Australia's first introduced species, arrived from Southeast Asia more than 5,000 years ago and is considered the country's native dog.

Australia's antiquity is nowhere more evident than in the vast inland area known as the Outback.

Sydney Opera House, jutting into Sydney Harbour

◄ The spectacular Twelve Apostles rock formation in Port Campbell National Park, Western Victoria

Ancient, eroded landscape of the Olgas, part of Uluṟu-Kata Tjuṯa National Park in the Northern Territory

Once a huge inland sea, its later aridity preserved the remains of the creatures that once inhabited the area. Some fossils found in Western Australia are 350 million years old – the oldest forms of life known on earth.

The Aborigines

The indigenous inhabitants of Australia, the Aborigines and Torres Strait Islanders, today constitute 3 per cent of the national population, living in rural and very remote areas, as well as within the cities.

The early days of European colonialism proved disastrous for the Aborigines. Thousands were killed in hostilities or by

Aboriginal Australian

unfamiliar diseases. During the 1850s, many Aborigines were confined to purpose-built reserves in a misguided attempt to overcome widespread poverty. Since the 1950s there have been serious efforts to redress this lack of understanding. Conditions are improving, but even today, in almost every aspect of life, including health care, education and housing, Aborigines are worse off than other Australians. In 1992, a milestone occurred when the High Court overturned the doctrine of *terra nullius* – that Australia belonged to no one at the time of British settlement. The Native Title Act followed, which, in essence, states that where Aborigines could establish unbroken occupancy of an area, they could then claim that land as their own.

Most Australians support this reconciliation and are increasingly aware of the rich heritage of the Aborigines. The Aboriginal belief in the Dreamtime *(see pp34–5)* may never be completely assimilated into the Australian consciousness,

The kangaroo, a famous icon of Australia

but an understanding of ancestral beings is an invaluable guide to traditional lifestyles. Aboriginal painting is now respected as one of the world's most ancient art forms and modern Aboriginal art began to be taken seriously in the 1970s. Aboriginal writers have also come to the forefront of Australian literature. Younger Aborigines are beginning to capitalize on this new awareness to promote equal rights and, with Aboriginal cultural centres being set up throughout the country, it is unlikely that Australia will dismiss its native heritage again.

Society

Given Australia's size and the fact that early settlements were far apart, Australian society is remarkably homogeneous. Its citizens are fundamentally prosperous and the way of life in the major cities and towns is much the same however many miles divide them. It takes a keen ear to identify regional accents.

However, there is some difference in lifestyle between city dwellers and the country people. Almost 90 per cent of the population lives in the fast-paced cities along the coast and has little more than a passing familiarity with the Outback. The major cities preserve pockets of colonial heritage, but the overall impression is modern, with new buildings reflecting the country's youth. In contrast, the rural communities tend to be slow-moving

Wine barrels lining the wall of a winery's cellar in Australia, ageing the contents before they are bottled for release

and conservative. For many years, Australia was said to have "ridden on the sheep's back", a reference to wool being the country's main money-earner. However, the wool industry is no longer dominant. Much of Australia's relatively sound economy is now achieved from coal, iron ore and wheat, and as the largest diamond producer in the world. Newer industries such as tourism and wine making are also increasingly important. Australians are generally friendly and relaxed, with a self-deprecating sense of humour. On the whole, Australia has a society without hierarchies, an attitude generally held to stem from its convict beginnings. Yet, contrary to widespread belief, very few Australians have true convict origins. Within only one generation of the arrival of the First Fleet in 1788, Australia had become a nation of immigrants.

Isolated Outback church in Silverton, New South Wales

Originally hailing almost entirely from the British Isles, today one in three Australians comes from elsewhere. Australia's liberal postwar immigration policies led to an influx of survivors from war-torn Europe, most notably Greeks, Italians, Poles and Germans.

The emphasis shifted towards the end of the 20th century and today the majority of new immigrants hail from Southeast Asia, China and India. Although some racism does exist, this blend of nations has, on the whole, been a successful experiment and Australia is justifiably proud to have one of the most harmonious multicultural communities in the world.

Indonesian satay stall at Parap Market in Darwin in the Northern Territory

Politics

Since 1901, Australia has been a federation, with its central government based in the purpose-built national capital, Canberra. Each state also has its own government. The nation inherited the central parliamentary system from England, and there is a two-party system consisting of the left (Labor) and the right (a coalition of Liberal and National Parties). The prime minister is the head of federal government, while the heads of state governments are premiers. Australia is a self-governing member of the British Commonwealth and retains the British monarch as its titular head of state. At present, the national representative of the monarch is the Governor-General, but the nation is involved in an ongoing debate about its future as a republic. There is opposition from those who argue that the system currently in place has led to one of the most stable societies in the world, while others believe that swearing allegiance to a British monarch has little meaning for the current population, many of whom are immigrants from other parts of the world. A referendum in November 1999 saw the monarchy retained with some 55 per cent of the votes.

The nation's character has always been shaped by its sparsely populated island location, far distant from its European roots and geographically closer to Southeast Asia.

The Parliamentary area next to Lake Burley Griffin in Canberra

Today there is a growing realization that the country must look to the Pacific region for its future. Closer ties with Asia, such as business and trade with Indonesia, China and Japan, have been forged.

Art and Culture

Blessed with a sunny climate and surrounded by the sea, outdoor leisure is high on the list of priorities for Australians – going to the beach is almost a national pastime. Australians are also mad about sport: four codes of football, cricket, tennis and golf are high on the national agenda.

Poster for *Mad Max: Fury Road*, which won many technical Oscars

Yet despite this reputation, Australians actually devote more of their time and money to artistic pursuits than they do to sporting ones, and as a result the national cultural scene is very vibrant. It is no accident that the Sydney Opera House is one of the country's most recognizable symbols. The nation is probably best known for its opera singers, among whom have been two of the all-time greats, Dame Nellie Melba and Dame Joan Sutherland. Opera Australia and the Australian Ballet, both based in Sydney, are acknowledged for

Australian Rules football match in Melbourne

their high standards. Every state also has its own thriving theatre company and symphony orchestra. Major art galleries abound throughout the country, from the many excellent state galleries exhibiting international works to a multitude of small private galleries exhibiting local and contemporary Australian and Aboriginal art.

The Australian film industry has also come into its own since the 1970s. Prominent Australian films such as *Mad Max* (1979), *Crocodile Dundee* (1985), *Moulin Rouge!* (2001), *Happy Feet* (2006) and the multiple-Oscar-winning *Mad Max: Fury Road* (2015) have won international acclaim, as well as awards.

This is not to say that Australia's cultural pursuits are entirely high-brow. Low-budget television soap operas such as *Neighbours* have become high-earning exports. Rock bands such as AC/DC also have an international following.

In almost all aspects, it seems, Australia lives up to its nickname of "the lucky country" and it is hard to meet an Australian who is not thoroughly convinced that this young and vast nation is now the best country on earth.

Young boogie boarder

Australia's Landscape

Geological stability has been largely responsible for creating the landscape of the earth's oldest, flattest and driest inhabited continent. Eighty million years ago, Australia's last major bout of geological activity pushed up the Great Dividing Range, but since then the continent has slept. Mountains have been eroded down, making it difficult for rain clouds to develop. Deserts have formed in once lush areas and today more than 70 per cent of the continent is arid. However, with some of the oldest rocks on earth, its landscapes are anything but uniform, and include rainforests, tropical beaches, glacial landforms, striking coastlines and flood plains.

Australia's drift towards the equator has brought a northern monsoon climate, as in Kakadu National Park *(see pp280–81)*.

Cradle Mountain *(see p471)* in southwest Tasmania was created by geological upheaval, glaciation and erosion. Here jagged mountain ranges, ravines and glacial lakes have formed a landscape that is quite unique in Australia.

Kata Tjuṯa (The Olgas)

Geological remnants of an immense bed of sedimentary rock now almost covered by sand from erosion, Kata Tjuṯa's weathered domes may once have been a single dome many times the size of Uluṟu *(see pp290–93)*.

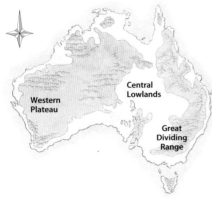

There are three main geological regions in Australia: the coastal plain including the Great Dividing Range; the Central Lowlands; and the Western Plateau. The Great Dividing Range is a relatively new feature in geological terms. It contains Australia's highest mountains, deep rivers, spectacular gorges and volcanic landforms. The Central Lowlands subsided when the continental margins on either side rose up – a result of rifting caused by continental drift. The Western Plateau contains many of Australia's large deserts and is composed of some of the most ancient rocks in the world.

Western Plateau

Central Lowlands

Great Dividing Range

The area to the east of Queensland was flooded at the end of the last Ice Age, creating ideal conditions for a coral reef. The Great Barrier Reef *(see pp216– 21)* now forms one of the world's most stunning sights.

The Nullarbor Plain *(see p371)* was created by the upthrust of an ancient sea floor. Today, sheer cliffs drop away from this desert landscape dotted with sinkholes and plunge into the sea below, creating one of Australia's most startling coastlines.

The Australian Continent

The Australian continent finally broke away from its last adjoining landmass, Antarctica, 40 million years ago and embarked on a long period of geographical isolation. During this time Australia's unique flora and fauna evolved and flourished *(see pp28–9)*. Aboriginal people lived undisturbed on this continent for at least 40,000 years, developing the land to their own needs, until the arrival of Europeans in 1770 *(see pp50–55)*.

Two hundred million years ago, the area of land that is now continental Australia was attached to the lower half of the earth's single landmass, Pangaea.

Between 200 and 65 million years ago, Pangaea separated to form two supercontinents, Gondwanaland in the south and Laurasia in the north.

Fifty million years ago, Gondwanaland had broken up into the various southern continents with only Antarctica and Australia still attached.

Today, the drifting of the continents continues and Australia is moving northwards towards the equator at the rate of 8 cm (3 in) a year.

Flora and Fauna

Forty million years of isolation from other major land masses have given Australia a collection of flora and fauna that is unique in the world. Low rainfall and poor soil has meant meagre food sources, and animals and plants have evolved some curious adaptations to help them cope. Surprisingly, these adverse conditions have also produced incredible biodiversity. Australia has more than 20,000 species of plants, and its rainforests are among the richest in the world in the number of species they support. Even its desert centre has 2,000 plant species and the world's greatest concentration of reptile species.

The platypus lives in an aquatic environment like a fish, suckles its young like a mammal, lays eggs and has the bill of a duck.

The lush rainforest is a haven for many endemic species of flora and fauna.

Epiphytes, ferns and vines abound around this rainforest creek.

At least 30 species of spinifex cover many of Australia's desert plains.

Rainforests

The east coast rainforests are among the most ancient ecosystems on earth. At least 18,000 plant species exist here. Some trees are more than 2,500 years old, and many are direct descendants of species from Gondwana *(see p27)*.

Arid Regions

The vast reaches of Australia's arid and semiarid regions teem with life. Desert plants and animals have developed unique and specific behavioural and physical features to maximize their survival chances in such harsh conditions.

The golden bowerbird of the rainforest builds spectacular bowers out of sticks as a platform for its mating displays. Some bowers reach well over 2 m (6.5 ft) in height.

The boab (baobab) tree sheds its leaves in the dry season to survive.

Spinifex grass, found across the desert, stores water and needs frequent exposure to fire to thrive.

The Wollemi pine was discovered in 1994 and caused a sensation. It belongs to a genus thought to have become extinct between 65 and 200 million years ago.

The thorny devil feeds only on ants and can consume more than 3,000 in one meal.

Mammals

Australian mammals are distinctive because the population is dominated by two groups that are rare or non-existent elsewhere. Monotremes, such as the platypus, are found only in Australia and New Guinea, and marsupials, represented by 180 species here, are scarce in other parts of the world. In contrast, placental mammals, highly successful on other continents, have been represented in Australia only by bats and rodents, and more recently by dingos. Mass extinctions of larger placentals occurred 20,000 years ago.

Red kangaroos are the most common of many species of this marsupial found in Australia.

The dingo was introduced into Australia by migrating humans c. 5,000 years ago.

Eucalypt trees provide food for possums and koalas.

Moist fern groundcover shelters a variety of small mammals and insects.

This coral garden is home to many molluscs, crustaceans and brightly coloured fish.

Open Woodland

The woodlands of the eastern seaboard, the southeast and southwest are known as the Australian bush. Eucalypt trees predominate in the hardy vegetation that has developed to survive fire, drought and poor-quality soil.

Sealife

Australia's oceans are poor in nutrients but rich in the diversity of life they support. Complex ecosystems create beautiful underwater scenery, while the shores and islands are home to nesting seabirds and giant sea mammals.

Koalas feed only on nutrient-poor eucalypt leaves, and have evolved low-energy lives to cope, such as sleeping for 20 hours a day.

Seagrass beds have high-saline conditions which attract many sea creatures. Shark Bay shelters the highest number of sea mammals in the world (see pp330–31).

Kookaburras are very efficient breeders: one of the young birds is kept on in the nest to look after the next batch of hatchlings, leaving both parents free to gather food.

The Australian sealion is one of two seal species unique to Australia. Its extended breeding cycle helps it contend with a poor food supply.

World Heritage Areas of Australia

UNESCO's World Heritage Convention was adopted in 1972 to protect areas of universal cultural and natural significance. Nineteen groups of sites in Australia are inscribed on the World Heritage List and include unusual landforms, ancient forests and areas of staggering biodiversity, as well as 12 historic convict sites and the Sydney Opera House. Several of the sites (including Kakadu National Park, Willandra Lakes, the Tasmanian wilderness and Uluṟu-Kata Tjuṯa National Park) are also listed for their Aboriginal cultural heritage.

Fossil sites in Riversleigh *(see p261)* and Naracoorte chart Australia's important evolutionary stages.

Purnululu National Park *(see p335)*

Kakadu National Park is a landscape of wetlands and tropical splendour. Art sites document the interaction between Aborigines and the land *(see pp280–81)*.

Northern Territory

The Ningaloo Coast *(see p332)*

Western Australia

South Australia

Australian Fossil Mammal Site at Naracoorte *(see p359)*

Shark Bay is home to a vast colony of sea mammals. The bay's stromatolites (algae-covered rocks) are the oldest form of life known on earth *(see pp330–31)*.

Uluṟu-Kata Tjuṯa National Park contains two major Aboriginal sites *(see pp290–93)*. The world's largest monolith is an extraordinary geological phenomenon in the flat desert plains.

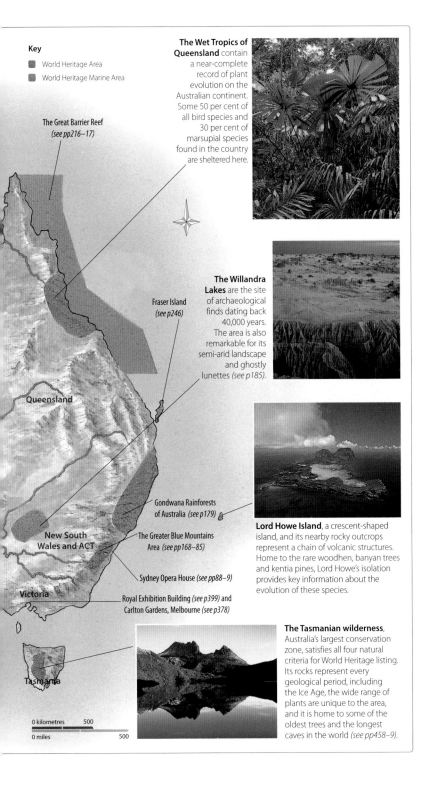

Key

World Heritage Area

World Heritage Marine Area

The Great Barrier Reef *(see pp216–17)*

Fraser Island *(see p246)*

Queensland

Gondwana Rainforests of Australia *(see p179)*

New South Wales and ACT

The Greater Blue Mountains Area *(see pp168–85)*

Sydney Opera House *(see pp88–9)*

Victoria

Royal Exhibition Building *(see p399)* and Carlton Gardens, Melbourne *(see p378)*

Tasmania

0 kilometres 500

0 miles 500

The Wet Tropics of Queensland contain a near-complete record of plant evolution on the Australian continent. Some 50 per cent of all bird species and 30 per cent of marsupial species found in the country are sheltered here.

The Willandra Lakes are the site of archaeological finds dating back 40,000 years. The area is also remarkable for its semi-arid landscape and ghostly lunettes *(see p185)*.

Lord Howe Island, a crescent-shaped island, and its nearby rocky outcrops represent a chain of volcanic structures. Home to the rare woodhen, banyan trees and kentia pines, Lord Howe's isolation provides key information about the evolution of these species.

The Tasmanian wilderness, Australia's largest conservation zone, satisfies all four natural criteria for World Heritage listing. Its rocks represent every geological period, including the Ice Age, the wide range of plants are unique to the area, and it is home to some of the oldest trees and the longest caves in the world *(see pp458–9)*.

The Australian Outback

The Outback is the heart of Australia and one of the most ancient landscapes in the world. It is extremely dry – rain may not fall for several years. Dramatic red rocks, ochre plains and purple mountains are framed by brilliant blue skies. Development is sparse: "towns" are often no more than a few buildings and facilities are basic. There may be hundreds of miles between one petrol station and another. The Outback isn't easy to explore, but it can be a rewarding experience. Make sure you are well equipped (*see p562*), or take an organized tour.

Locator Map

The Australian Outback

Camels were brought to Australia in the 1870s from the Middle East, as a means of desert transport. The Outback is now home to the only wild camels in the world. Camel safaris for tourists are available in many places.

Saltbush, which gets its name from its ability to withstand saline conditions, is a typical form of vegetation.

Outback Life

The enduring image of Australia's Outback is red dust, solitary one-storey shacks and desert views as far as the eye can see. Although small areas of the Outback have seen towns spring up over the past 100 years, and many interstate roads are now suitable for most vehicles, this image remains true to life across vast stretches of the interior landscape. Most of the Outback remains pioneering country far removed from the modern nation.

Camping in the bush is one of the highlights of any trip into Australia's Outback, whether independently or with an organized tour. You will need a camping permit, a swag (canvas-covered bed roll), a mosquito net and a good camping stove to eat and sleep in relative comfort under the stars.

The film industry has long been a fan of the Outback's vast open spaces and dramatic colours. Films such as the 1994 comedy *The Adventures of Priscilla, Queen of the Desert* made spectacular use of the Red Centre's sparse and dusty landscape.

Australian "hotels" in Outback areas often operate only as public houses, re-named hotels to counteract Australia's once strict licensing laws.

Pioneers and Explorers

Many European explorers, such as Edward Eyre and John Stuart, ventured into the Outback during the 19th century. The most infamous expedition was Robert O'Hara Burke's from Victoria to the Gulf of Carpentaria *(see p57)*. Ironically, it was the rescue missions due to his inexperience which brought about the pioneers' most significant investigations of Australia's interior.

Robert O'Hara Burke
1820–61

The Birdsville Races in Queensland are the biggest and best of the many horse races held in the Outback, where locals gather to bet and socialize.

A solitary building set against vast areas of open desert landscape can be an evocative landmark in the Outback.

Opal mining in towns such as Coober Pedy *(see p372)* is one source of the Outback's wealth. Tourists need a miner's permit, available from state tourist offices, to hunt for gems.

Aboriginal Culture

Far from being one homogeneous race, at the time of European settlement in the 18th century, the estimated 750,000 Aborigines in Australia had at least 300 different languages and a wide variety of lifestyles, depending on where they lived. The tribes of northern coastal areas, such as the Tiwis, had most contact with outsiders, especially from Indonesia, and their culture was quite different from the more isolated Pitjantjatjaras of Central Australia's deserts or the Kooris from the southeast. However, there were features common to Aboriginal life and these have passed down the centuries to present-day traditions.

Men's Dreaming by Clifford Possum Tjapaltjarri

Aboriginal artifacts and tools, decorated in traditional ornate patterns

Traditional Aboriginal Lifestyles

For tens of thousands of years, the Aborigines were a race of hunters leading a nomadic existence. They made light-weight, versatile tools such as the boomerang, and built temporary mud dwellings. The extent of their wanderings differed from region to region. People who lived in areas with a plentiful supply of food and water were relatively more static than those in areas where such essentials were scarce.

Through living in small groups in a vast land, Aboriginal society came to be broken up into numerous clans separated by different languages and customs. Even people with a common language would live apart in extended family groups, consisting of a husband, wife, aunts, uncles and all their children to share the responsibilities of daily life. Groups would come together from time to time to conduct religious ceremonies, arrange marriages and settle inter-clan disputes. Trade was an important part of social life. Shell, ochre and wood were some of the goods exchanged along trade routes that criss-crossed the entire country.

The nomadic way of life largely ended when English settlers claimed vast tracts of land, but other aspects of traditional life have survived. In Aboriginal communities, senior members are still held in great respect, and are responsible for maintaining laws and meting out punishments to those who break them or divulge secrets of ancient rituals. Such rituals are part of the Aboriginal belief system called "Dreamtime".

The Dreamtime

The Dreamtime (or Dreaming) is the English term for the Aboriginal system of laws and beliefs. Its basis is a rich mythology about the earth's creation. "Creation ancestors" such as giant serpents are believed to have risen up from the earth's core and roamed the world, creating valleys, rivers and mountains. Other progenitors caused the rain and sun, and created the people and wildlife. Sites where ancestral beings are thought to have emerged from the earth are sacred and are still used as the locations for ceremonies and rituals today.

The belief in the Dreamtime is, in essence, a religious ideology for all Aborigines, whatever their tribe, and forms the basis of Aboriginal life. Every Aborigine is believed to

The Boomerang

Contrary to popular belief, not all boomerangs will return to the thrower. Originally, "boomerang" simply meant "throwing stick". They were used for hunting, fighting, making fire, stoking the coals when cooking and in traditional games. A hunter did not normally require a throwing stick to return since its purpose was to injure its target sufficiently to enable capture. Over time, intricate shapes were developed that allowed sticks to swirl in a large arc and return to the thrower. The returning boomerang is limited to games, killing birds and directing animals into traps. Light and thin, with a deep curvature, its ends are twisted in opposite directions. The lower surface is flat and the upper surface convex.

Aboriginal boomerang

have two souls – one mortal and one immortal, linked with their ancestral spirit (or totem). Each family clan is descended from the same ancestral being. These spirits provide protection: any misfortune is due to disgruntled forebears. As a consequence, some clan members have a responsibility for maintaining sacred sites. Anyone failing in these duties is severely punished.

Each Dreamtime story relates to a particular landscape; as one landscape connects with another, these stories form a "track". These "tracks" are called Songlines and criss-cross the Australian continent. Aborigines are able to connect with other tribes along these lines.

Aborigines painted with white paint to ward off evil spirits

Aboriginal Song and Dance

Aboriginal songs tell stories of Dreamtime ancestors and are intrinsically linked to the worship of spirits – the words of songs are often incomprehensible due to the secrecy of many ancestral stories. Simple instruments accompany the songs, including the didgeridoo, a 1-m- (3-ft-) long wind instrument with a deep sound.

Aborigines also use dance as a means of communicating with their ancestors. Aboriginal dance is experiencing a cultural renaissance, with new companies performing both traditional and new works.

Aboriginal Issues

Although few Aborigines now maintain a traditional nomadic lifestyle, the ceremonies, creation stories and art that make up their culture remain strong.

The right to own land has long been an issue for present-day Aborigines; they believe that they are responsible for caring for the land entrusted to them at birth. The Land Rights Act of 1976 has done much to improve these rights. The Act established Aboriginal Land Councils which negotiate between the government and Aborigines to claim land for its traditional owners *(see pp62–3)*. Where Aboriginal rights have been established, that land cannot be altered in any way. In areas of large Aboriginal

Decorating bark with natural ochre stains

inhabitance, the government has also agreed that white law can exist alongside black law, which allows for justice against Aboriginal offenders to be meted out according to tribal law. In many cases, this law is harsh and savage, but it allows for Aborigines to live by their own belief system.

The revival of Aboriginal art was at the forefront of seeing Aboriginal culture in a more positive light by Australians. Aboriginal artists such as Emily Kame Kngwarreye combine traditional materials such as bark and ochre with acrylics and canvas, while telling Dreaming stories in a modern idiom.

Many Aborigines have now moved away from their traditional lifestyle and live within the major cities, but they remain distinctly Aboriginal and generally choose to live within Aboriginal communities. Within designated Aboriginal lands *(see pp266–7)*, many still follow bush medical practices and perform traditional rituals.

It cannot be denied that Aborigines are still disadvantaged in comparison with the rest of Australians, particularly in terms of housing, health, employment, education and life expectancy. But growing awareness of, and respect for, their culture and traditions is gradually leading to a more harmonious coexistence.

Aborigines performing a traditional dance at sunset

Aboriginal Art

As traditionally nomadic people with little interest in decorating their temporary dwellings, Aborigines often expressed their creativity on landscape features such as rocks and caves *(see pp51–2)*. Many art sites are thousands of years old, although they have often been re-painted over time to preserve the image. Rock art reflects daily Aboriginal life as well as religious beliefs. Some ancient sites contain representations of now extinct animals; others depict human figures with blue eyes, strange weapons and horses – evidently the arrival of Europeans. Aboriginal art is also seen in everyday objects – utensils and accessories such as belts and headbands.

Bark painting, such as this image of a fish, has disappeared from southern areas, but still flourishes in Arnhem Land and on Melville and Bathurst islands.

Cave rock was a popular "canvas" for traditional Aboriginal art, particularly when tribes took cover during the rainy season.

The outline style of rock engraving was developed most fully in the Sydney-Hawkesbury area, due to vast areas of soft Hawkesbury sandstone. More than 4,000 figures have been recorded, often gigantic in size – one whale engraving is more than 20 m (65 ft) long. Groups of engravings can cover more than 1 ha (2.5 acres).

Figures showing the human anatomy are often depicted in basic but exaggerated, stylized forms.

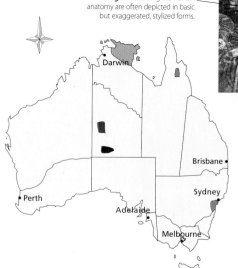

Major Aboriginal Art Sites

- Arnhem Land, Northern Territory
- Central Desert
- Uluṟu-Kata Tjuṯa National Park
- Laura, Queensland
- Melville and Bathurst islands
- Sydney-Hawkesbury area

Quinkans are stick-like figures found in far north Queensland's Laura region. They represent spirits that are thought to emerge suddenly from rock crevices and startle people, to remind them that misbehaviour will bring swift retribution.

Burial poles are an example of how important decoration is to Aborigines, even to commemmorate death. These brightly coloured Tutini burial poles belong to the Tiwi people of Melville and Bathurst islands *(see p278)*.

The crocodile image personifies the force of nature, as well as symbolizing the relationship between humans and the natural environment. Both are common themes within Aboriginal art.

Bush Plum Dreaming (1991) by Clifford Possum Tjapaltjarri is a modern example of ancient Aboriginal techniques used by the Papunya tribe.

"X-ray art", such as this figure at Nourlangie Rock in Kakadu National Park *(see pp280–81)*, shows the internal and external anatomy of living subjects, including a range of animals.

Arnhem Land Rock Art

Arnhem Land is the 90,000-sq km (34,750-sq mile) Aboriginal territory which stretches from east of Darwin to the Gulf of Carpentaria (see pp266–7). Magnificent rock art "galleries" in this region date from 16,000 BC (see p51) – some of the oldest Aboriginal art in the country.

Totemic art at Uluru *(see pp290–93)* is thought to portray the beings in Aboriginal culture who are believed to have created the rock.

Australian Artists and Writers

The first Europeans to paint Australia were those who arrived on the *Endeavour (see pp54–5)*, but it was not until the prosperity generated by the 1850s gold rushes that art gained any public recognition. There had been colonial artists, of whom Conrad Martens (1801–78) was the best known, but in a country where survival was the most immediate problem, art was not a high priority. The first writings were also journals of early settlers; it was 100 years before Australia could claim the beginnings of a literary tradition, when Rolf Boldrewood (1826–1915) wrote *Robbery Under Arms* (1888), a heroic tale of the bush.

Artist Sir Russell Drysdale

Artists

The so-called "Heidelberg School", named after an area around Melbourne, was the first distinctive Australian school of painting at the end of the 19th century. Its mainstays included Tom Roberts (1856–1931), Charles Conder (1868–1909), Frederick McCubbin (1855–1917) and Arthur Streeton (1867–1943). The group drew strongly on the *plein air* methods of the French Impressionists to capture the distinctive light and openness of the Australian landscape. Then, in the early 1900s, Hans Heysen captured the national imagination with his delicately coloured gum trees and his view of the Australian landscape. Sir Sidney

Kelly in Spring (1956), one of Sir Sidney Nolan's "Ned Kelly" series

Nolan (1917–92), best known for his "Ned Kelly" series of the 1940s based on the country's most notorious bushranger *(see p398)*, also produced landscape paintings which propelled Australian art on to the international scene for the first time.

The best known of the talented Boyd family, Arthur Boyd (1920–99), is another great on the Australian art scene; his "Half-Caste Bride" series catapulted him into the art world in 1960.

Probably the greatest interpreter of Australia's Outback is Sir Russell Drysdale (1912–81), whose paintings depict the harshness of this landscape. Brett Whiteley (1939–92) is a more recent talent whose sensual work reflects his view of the world.

Winner of the Archibald Prize for portraiture, William Dobell (1899–1970) is often regarded as the figurehead of the Sydney Modernist movement. He achieved some level of notoriety when, in 1944, two fellow artists mounted a legal challenge to the granting of the Archibald for his portrait of Joshua Smith, claiming it was "not a portrait but a caricature". The action was unsuccessful, but all Dobell's further work generated publicity for the wrong reasons. Possibly the most popularly recognized Australian artist is Ken Done. Often dismissed for blatant commercialism, his brilliantly coloured work has achieved sales of which most artists only dream.

The most significant collection of Australian art can be seen at Canberra's National Gallery *(see pp206–7)*.

Toberua (1994) by Ken Done

The Antipodeans

Formed in Melbourne in 1959, the Antipodeans consisted of seven of Australia's best-known modern artists, all born in the 1920s: Charles Blackman, Arthur Boyd, David Boyd, John Brack, Robert Dickerson, John Perceval and Clifton Pugh. The aim of the group was to support figurative painting rather than abstraction. The group denied that they were creating a national style and the name Antipodeans was adopted to avoid too narrow a focus on Australia, as the group aimed for international recognition at exhibitions in London. Ironically, it later came to apply to Australian art in general.

Portrait of Miles Franklin by Marie McNiven

Writers

Much of Australian fiction is concerned with the difficulties Europeans experienced in a harsh land, or the relationship between white settlers and Aborigines. The themes can be traced back to an early Australian novelist, Henry Handel Richardson, the pseudonym of Ethel Richardson (1870–1946). Her trilogy, *The Fortunes of Richard Mahoney* (1929), was published to great acclaim. Contemporary novelist David Malouf (born in 1934) explores these issues in *Remembering Babylon* (1993), winner of the Prix Baudelaire, and *Conversations at Curlow Creek* (1996).

One of Australia's most celebrated novelists is Patrick White (1912–90), who won the Nobel Prize in 1973 with

Film poster of *Schindler's List*, based on *Schindler's Ark*

The Eye of the Storm. Two-time Booker Prize-winner Peter Carey (born in 1943) celebrated Australia's most famous bush-ranger in *The True History of the Kelly Gang* (2000).

Louisa Lawson (1848–1920), is credited with Australia's first feminist journal, *Dawn,* written between 1888 and 1905. At the same time, another feminist, Miles Franklin (1879–1954), defied traditional women's roles of the time by pursuing an independent life in Australia, England and the USA. Her life was documented in several autobiographies.

For descriptions of pre- and postwar Sydney life in the slums, the novels of Ruth Park (born in 1922), such as *Harp in the South* (1948) and *Fence around the Cuckoo* (1992), are unbeatable. Novelist Thomas Keneally (born in 1935) won the 1982 Booker Prize with *Schindler's Ark*.

Tim Winton (born 1960) draws inspiration from the Australian landscape in lauded novels such as *Cloudstreet* and *Breath*.

Aboriginal writer Sally Morgan (born 1951) put indigenous Australian writing on the map with her 1988 autobiography *My Place*.

Writer and journalist Richard Flanagan (born 1961), from Tasmania, won the 2014 Booker Prize for *The Narrow Road to the Deep North*.

Poets

Australia's early poets were mostly bush balladeers, articulating life in the Australian bush. "The Man from Snowy River" and "Clancy of the Overflow" by A B "Banjo" Paterson (1864–1941) are classics and have been immortalised in song and film. Writing from the late 1800s until his death in 1922,

Henry Lawson similarly wrote some enduring bush verse, but his poetry also had a more political edge. His first published poem in the *Bulletin* literary magazine in 1887 was the rallying "Song of the Republic". One of Australia's leading poets, Les Murray (1938–), is known as the "bush bard" for his writing on bush life.

Poets such as Judith Wright (1915–2000) and Oodgeroo Noonuccal (1920–93), have powerfully expressed the anguish of Aboriginal people.

Henry Lawson

Playwrights

Australia's most prolific contemporary playwright is David Williamson, born in 1942. A satirist exploring middle-class life and values, Williamson has been an international success and several of his plays, such as *Dead White Males* (1995), have been performed both in London and New York.

Ray Lawler gained renown in 1955 with *Summer of the Seventeenth Doll*, which challenged the deep-rooted Australian concept of male friendship. The play has been adapted as an opera, with music by Australian composer Richard Meale.

Other notable contemporary playwrights are Nick Enright, Stephen Sewell, Michael Gow and Louis Nowra.

The Wines of Australia

Grapes and wine have been produced in Australia virtually since European settlement in 1788 *(see pp54–5)*. The first vineyards were planted in Sydney in 1791 and over the next 40 years vines were planted in the Hunter Valley (1827), the Barossa at Jacobs Creek (1847), the Yarra Valley (1930), and Adelaide (1937). John and Elizabeth Macarthur became Australia's first commercial wine producers with a small vintage in 1827 from their Sydney farm *(see p131)*. In the 1960s, with the introduction of international grape varieties, such as Chardonnay, small oak-barrel maturation and modern wine-making technology, the wine industry really developed. Since the 1990s Australia has earned an excellent reputation for high-quality wines and there are more than 1,500 wineries operating today.

Locator Map
▪ *Major wine-producing regions of Australia*

0 kilometres 500
0 miles 500

Leeuwin Estate winery in Margaret River, Western Australia *(see pp318–19)* is one of the nation's largest producers of top-quality table wines, including Chardonnay and Cabernet Sauvignon.

● Perth

Adelaide

The Father of Australian Wine

James Busby is often regarded as the father of the Australian wine industry. Scottish-born, he arrived in Sydney in 1824. During the voyage to Australia he wrote the country's first wine book, detailing his experiences of French vineyards. He established a property at Kirkton in the Hunter Valley, New South Wales, and returned to Europe in 1831, collecting 570 vine cuttings from France and Spain.

James Busby

These were cultivated at Kirkton and at the Sydney and Adelaide Botanic Gardens. In 1833, having founded Australia's first wine-producing region, he emigrated to New Zealand.

Mount Hurtle winery produces distinctive white table wines. It is located in one of South Australia's main wine regions, McLaren Vale *(see pp342–3)*.

Wine Regions of Australia

Since signing a trade agreement with the European Union, Australia has had to implement a new classification system for its wine-producing regions. The whole of Australia has 28 wine zones, which can be whole state (Tasmania) or parts of states (Western Victoria). Within these zones are 61 wine regions, such as the Barossa (see pp360–61), with the main ones listed below. Some of the up-and-coming areas in Australia are Mudgee and Orange (NSW), and Geelong (VIC).

① South Burnett
② Granite Belt
③ Hastings River
④ Hunter Valley
⑤ Mudgee
⑥ Orange
⑦ Cowra
⑧ Lachlan Valley
⑨ Canberra
⑩ Gundagai
⑪ Hilltops
⑫ Sydney
⑬ Shoalhaven
⑭ Southern Highlands
⑮ Riverina

⑯ Murray Darling
⑰ Swan Hill
⑱ Rutherglen Glenrowan
King Valley
⑲ Yarra Valley
⑳ Mornington Peninsula
㉑ Geelong
㉒ Tasmania
㉓ Sunbury
㉔ Macedonl
㉕ Pyrenees
㉖ Grampians
㉗ Coonawarra
㉘ Mount Benson
㉙ Padthaway

㉚ Langhorne Creek
㉛ McLaren Vale
㉜ Adelaide Hills
㉝ Eden Valley
㉞ Barossa
㉟ Clare Valley
㊱ Kangaroo Island
㊲ Esperance
㊳ Great Southern
㊴ Pemberton
㊵ Manjimup
㊶ Margaret River
㊷ Swan District
㊸ Perth Hills

Balmoral House is part of the Rosemount Estate in the Upper Hunter Valley (see pp166–7). The house gives its name to the winery's excellent Balmoral Shiraz.

Visiting a Winery

Wine tourism is increasingly popular in Australia and information and maps are readily available at information bureaux. Most wineries are open daily (but you should ring ahead to avoid disappointment) and if they charge for tastings it will be refunded against a purchase from the "cellar door". Winery restaurants are also popular and some have barbeques and entertainment for children while others have a wine-food paired menu. With strict drink-drive laws it may be better to take a guided tour – these can be by bus or limousine.

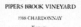

PIPERS BROOK VINEYARD
1988 CHARDONNAY
Tasmania

Pipers Brook in Tasmania was established in 1973 and is home to the acclaimed Kreglinger Wine Estates.

Surfing and Beach Culture

Australia is the quintessential home of beach culture, with the nation's beaches ranging from sweeping crescents with rolling waves to tiny, secluded coves. Almost all Australians live within a two-hour drive of the coast, and during the hot summers it is almost second nature to make for the water to cool off. The clichéd image of the sun-bronzed Australian is no longer the reality it once was thanks to increased sun protection awareness, but popular beaches are still packed with tanned bodies basking on golden sands or frolicking in deep blue waves. Fines levied for inappropriate behaviour mean that the atmosphere is calm and safe at all times. Surfing has always been a national sport, with regular carnivals and competitions held on the coastline. There are also opportunities for beginners to try their hand at this daring sport.

The sun-bleached hair and dangerously deep tans have gone, but surfing is ever popular.

Surf carnivals attract hundreds of spectators, who thrill to races, "iron man" competitions, dummy rescues and spectacular lifeboat displays.

Surfer in Action

Riding the waves is a serious business. Wetsuit-clad "surfies" study the surfing reports in the media and think nothing of travelling vast distances to reach a beach where the best waves can be found.

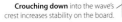

Crouching down into the wave's crest increases stability on the board.

Where to Surf

The best surfing to be found in Australia is on the New South Wales coast (*see pp182–3*), the southern Queensland coast, especially the aptly named Surfer's Paradise and the Sunshine Coast (*pp242–3*) and the southern coastline of Western Australia (*pp316–17*). Tasmania also has some fine surfing beaches on its northwestern tip (*pp470–71*). Despite superb north Queensland beaches, the Great Barrier Reef stops the waves well before they reach the mainland. In summer, deadly marine stingers (box jellyfish) here make surf swimming impossible in many areas, unless there is a stinger-proof enclosure.

Surf lifesaving is an integral part of the Australian beach scene. Trained volunteer lifesavers, easily recognized by their red and yellow swimming caps, ensure that swimmers stay within flag-defined safe areas and are ready to spring into action if someone is in trouble.

Beach Activities

Australian beaches are not only the preserve of surfers. Winter temperatures are mild in most coastal areas, so many beach activities are enjoyed all year. Weekends see pleasure boats of all sizes competing in races or just out for a picnic in some sheltered cove. The sails of windsurfers create swirls of colour on gusty days. Kite-flying has become an art form, with the Festival of the Winds a September highlight at Sydney's Bondi Beach *(see p44)*. Arts-focused Sculptures by the Sea exhibitions are popular at Cottesloe, WA, and on the Bondi-to-Bronte coast walk in Sydney.

Festival of the Winds

Takeaway snack food at the beach is an Australian tradition, since many sunlovers spend entire days by the ocean. Fish and chips, kebabs and burgers are on sale at beach cafés.

Surfboards, once made out of wood, are now built of light fibreglass, often in bright colours, improving speed and visibility.

The Australian crawl revolutionized swimming throughout the world in the 1880s. For most Australians, swimming is an everyday sport, learned at a very early age.

Safety

Beaches are safe provided you follow a few guidelines:
- Always swim "between the flags".
- Don't swim alone.
- Note signs warning of strong currents, blue bottles or stingers.
- If you get into difficulty, do not wave but signal for help by raising one arm straight in the air.
- Use factor 50+ sunscreen and wear a shirt and hat.

AUSTRALIA THROUGH THE YEAR

The seasons in Australia are the opposite of those in the northern hemisphere. In the southern half of the continent spring comes in September, summer is from December to February, autumn runs from March to May, while winter begins in June. In contrast, the tropical climate of the north coast is more clearly divided into wet and dry seasons, the former between November and April. Australia's vast interior has a typical desert climate – baking hot days and cool nights. The weather throughout Australia is reliable enough year-round to make outdoor events popular all over the country.

Spring

With the warm weather, the profusion of spring flowers brings gardens and national parks to life. Food, art and music festivals abound in cities. Footballers finish their seasons, cricketers warm up for summer matches and the horse-racing fraternity gets ready to place its bets.

Australian Football League Grand Final in September

of the Torres Strait Islanders are celebrated through dance, song and art.

Floriade (mid-Sep–mid-Oct), Canberra. Magnificent flower festival in Commonwealth Park (see p199).

Tulip Time Festival (two weeks from mid-Sep), Bowral. The Corbett Gardens are carpeted with flowers (see p190).

Carnival of Flowers (date varies), Toowoomba. Popular floral festival including spectacular garden and flower displays (see p244).

October

Melbourne Fringe Festival (mid-Sep–early Oct, dates vary), The arts festival showcases hundreds of events, such as live performances, films, visual arts, multi-media exhibits and comedy shows.

Australian Rugby League Grand Final (first Sun), Sydney. National event.

Floriade, the spring flower festival in Canberra

Leura Garden Festival (early October), Blue Mountains. Village fair and garden shows (see p174).

Melbourne International Arts Festival (two weeks, mid- to late Oct), Dance, theatre, music and visual arts events.

Melbourne Marathon (date varies). Fun run through the city.

Carlton Italian Festa (Sun, date varies), Melbourne. Street carnival through the city's Italian district (see p399).

September

Mudgee Wine Festival (date varies). Includes bush dances as well as wine (see p181).

Festival of the Winds (Sun, date varies), Bondi Beach (see p43). Multicultural kite-flying festival; music, dance.

Royal Melbourne Show (last two weeks). Agricultural exhibitions, rides and displays.

Australian Football League Grand Final (last Sat in Sep), Melbourne (see p401).

Torres Strait Cultural Festival (mid-Sep, even-numbered years), Thursday Island. The spiritual traditions

Festival of the Winds, Australia's annual kite-flying festival

Rose and Rodeo Festival
(last weekend), Warwick.
Australia's oldest rodeo
attracts riders from all over
the world *(see p244)*.
Jacaranda Festival *(last week)*,
Grafton. Australia's oldest flower
festival features a Grand Float
procession through the town
(see p182).
Maldon Folk Festival *(late Oct/
early Nov, weekend before
Melbourne Cup)*. Folk music
concerts in this Victorian
country town.

The Melbourne Cup, Australia's annual
thoroughbred horse race

November
Sculpture by the Sea *(date varies,
around last week Oct/first week Nov)*,
Sydney. Great outdoor sculptures
can be seen at Bondi beach.
The High Country Festival
(late Oct–early Nov), Mansfield.
Horse races, parades, markets,
arts and cultural exhibitions.
Melbourne Cup *(first Tue)*.
Australia's most popular
horse race virtually brings
the nation to a halt.

Summer

The beginning of the school
holidays for Christmas marks
the start of the summer in
Australia and the festivities
continue until Australia Day
on 26 January. Summer also
brings a feast for sport lovers,
with tennis, surfing events
and a host of cricket matches.
Arts and music lovers make
the most of organized festivals.

Santa Claus celebrating Christmas on Bondi Beach, Sydney

December
Carols by Candlelight *(24 Dec)*,
Melbourne. Top musicians
unite with locals to celebrate
Christmas.
Christmas at Bondi Beach
(25 Dec). Holiday-makers hold
parties on the famous beach
(see p131).
Sydney to Hobart Yacht Race
(26 Dec). Sydney Harbour teems
with yachts setting off for
Hobart *(see p464–5)*.
Boxing Day Test Match *(26 Dec)*,
Melbourne.
New Year's Eve *(31 Dec)*, Sydney
Harbour. Street parties and
firework displays.

January
Hanging Rock Picnic Races
(1 Jan & 26 Jan). Premier country
horse racing event *(see p441)*.
Festival of Sydney *(second
week–end Jan)*. City throngs
during this cultural festival.
Australian Open *(last two
weeks)*, Melbourne. Australia's
popular Grand Slam tennis
tournament.
Country Music Festival *(last
two weeks)*, Tamworth. Australia's
main country music festival,
culminating in the Golden
Guitar Awards *(see p181)*.
Midsumma Festival *(mid-Jan–
first week Feb)*, Melbourne. This
annual Gay and Lesbian festival
includes street parades.
Tunarama Festival *(last
weekend)*, Port Lincoln. Tuna
tossing competitions and
fireworks *(see p370)*.

Australia Day Concert
(26 Jan), Sydney. This free
outdoor concert is part of the
celebrations for the birth of
the nation *(see p60)*.
Chinese New Year *(late Jan or
early Feb)*, Sydney and Melbourne.
Cricket Test Match, Sydney.
**Leeuwin Estate Winery Music
Concert** *(Jan–Feb)*, Margaret
River. Concert attracting stars
(see p318).

Fireworks in Sydney for the Australia
Day celebrations

February
**Perth International Arts
Festival** *(three weeks from mid-
Feb)*. Australia's oldest arts fest.
Adelaide Fringe *(mid-Feb–
mid-Mar)*. Second-largest fringe
festival in the world.
Adelaide Festival *(late Feb–
mid-Mar)*. Festival of theatre,
dance, music, writing and art.

Australian Grand Prix, held in Melbourne in March

Autumn

After the humidity of the summer, autumn brings fresh mornings and cooler days that are tailor-made for outdoor pursuits such as bushwalking, cycling and fishing, as well as outdoor festivals. There are numerous sporting and cultural events to tempt the visitor. Many of the country's wineries open their doors during the harvest season and hold gourmet food and wine events. Anzac Day (25 April) – the day in 1915 when Australian and New Zealand forces landed at Gallipoli – has been observed annually since 1916 and is a national holiday on which Australians commemorate their war dead.

Yarra Valley wine

March
Gay and Lesbian Mardi Gras Festival *(varies)*, Sydney. Flamboyant street parades and events.
Day on the Green *(weekends in Mar)*. Concerts at Rochford Winery in the Yarra Valley attracts international performers.
Begonia Festival *(first two weeks)*, Ballarat. Begonia displays in the Botanical Gardens *(see p439)*.
Moomba Festival *(second week)*, Melbourne. International aquatic events on the Yarra River *(see pp404–5)*.
Australian Celtic Festival *(second weekend)*, Glen Innes. Traditional Celtic events celebrate the town's British heritage *(see p180)*.

Australian Formula One Grand Prix *(mid-Mar)*, Melbourne. Top Formula One drivers compete, while the city celebrates with street parties *(see p407)*.
St Patrick's Day *(17 Mar or Sun before)*, Sydney. Pubs serve green beer, and a family festival is held at Prince Alfred Park.
International Flower and Garden Show *(late Mar–early Apr)*, Melbourne. Spectacular floral event held in the beautiful Exhibition Gardens *(see p399)*.

April
Melbourne International Comedy Festival *(end Mar– early Apr)*. Comedy acts from around the world perform indoors and out.

Royal Easter Show *(week preceding Good Fri)* Sydney. Agricultural shows, funfair rides, local arts and crafts displays and team games.
Rip Curl Pro Surfing Competition *(Easter weekend)*, Bells Beach. Pros and amateurs take part in this premier competition *(see p433)*.
Easter Fair *(Easter weekend)*, Maldon. An Easter parade and a colourful street carnival takes over this quaint country town *(see p436)*.
Bright Autumn Festival *(last week Apr–early May)*, Bright. Winery tours, art exhibitions and street parades *(see p451)*.
Anzac Day *(25 Apr)*. Australia's war dead and war veterans are honoured in services throughout the country.

May
Aussie Wine Month *(all month)*, Nationwide. This is the country's biggest national celebration of the diversity, quality and regionality of Australian wines.
Kernewek Lowender Cornish Festival *(mid- to late May)*, Little Cornwall. A biennial celebration of the area's Cornish heritage which began with the copper discoveries of the 1860s *(see p367)*.
Vivid Sydney *(late May–mid Jun)*. Light installations and projections on landmark buildings.

Anzac Day ceremony along Canberra's Anzac Parade

Racing in Alice Springs' Camel Cup

Winter

Winter in the east can be cool enough to require warm jackets, and it is often icy in Victoria and Tasmania. Many festivals highlight the change of climate in celebration of freezing temperatures. Other events, such as film festivals, are arts-based and indoors. The warm rather than sweltering climate of the Outback in winter offers the opportunity for pleasurable outdoor events.

June

Three-Day Equestrian Event (first weekend), Adelaide. Spectacular riding skills are displayed by the world's best horses and riders.

Sydney Film Festival (two weeks mid-Jun). The latest blockbuster film releases are combined with retrospectives and showcases.

Laura Dance & Cultural Festival (odd-numbered years), Cape York. Celebration of Aboriginal culture.

July

Yulefest (throughout Jun, Jul, Aug), Blue Mountains. Hotels, guesthouses and some restaurants celebrate a mid-winter "traditional Christmas" with log fires and all the usual yuletide trimmings.

Brass Monkey Festival (throughout Jul), Stanthorpe. Inland Queensland turns the freezing winter temperatures into an opportunity for celebration (see p244).

Alice Springs Show (first weekend). Agricultural and historical displays are combined with arts, crafts and cookery demonstrations at this popular event.

Cairns Show (mid-Jul). A cultural celebration of historical and contemporary life in the Australian tropics (see p258).

Camel Cup (mid-Jul), Alice Springs. Camel racing on the dry Todd River.

Melbourne International Film Festival (last week Jul–mid-Aug). The largest and most popular film festival.

Almond Blossom Festival (end Jul–early Aug), Mount Lofty. Includes almond cracking.

August

City to Surf Race (second Sun), Sydney. A 14-km (9-mile) fun run from the city centre (usually Hyde Park) to Bondi Beach.

Shinju Matsuri Festival (last weekend–first week Sep), Broome. Pearl festival.

The Archibald, Wynne and Sulman Prizes Exhibition (late Jul–early Sep), Sydney. Held at the Art Gallery of NSW, these are the nation's favourite and most prestigious art awards for painting, with critics' and people's choice awards.

Mount Isa Rodeo (mid-Aug). Largest rodeo (see p261).

Henley-on-Todd Regatta (third Sat), Alice Springs. Races in bottomless boats along the dry Todd River.

Melbourne Writers' Festival (late Aug–early Sep). This event presents the best writers from Australia and around the world in a 10-day programme.

Dragon Boat race, part of the Shinju Matsuri in Broome

The Climate of Australia

This vast country experiences a variable climate. Three-quarters of its land is desert or scrub and has low, unreliable rainfall. The huge, dry interior is hot year-round during the day but can be very cold at night. The southern half of Australia, including Tasmania, has warm summers and mild winters. Further north, seasonal variations lessen and the Top End has just two seasons: the dry, and the wet, with its monsoon rains and occasional tropical cyclones.

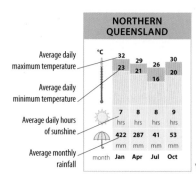

NORTHERN QUEENSLAND

Average daily maximum temperature

Average daily minimum temperature

Average daily hours of sunshine

Average monthly rainfall

°C	Jan	Apr	Jul	Oct
max	32	29	26	30
min	23	21	16	20
sunshine	7 hrs	8 hrs	8 hrs	9 hrs
rainfall	422 mm	287 mm	41 mm	53 mm

NORTH OF PERTH

°C	Jan	Apr	Jul	Oct
max	33	34	28	33
min	26	22	14	22
sunshine	8 hrs	9 hrs	7 hrs	9 hrs
rainfall	160 mm	30 mm	0 mm	1 mm

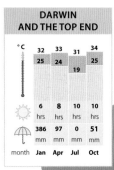

DARWIN AND THE TOP END

°C	Jan	Apr	Jul	Oct
max	32	33	31	34
min	25	24	19	25
sunshine	6 hrs	8 hrs	10 hrs	10 hrs
rainfall	386 mm	97 mm	0 mm	51 mm

THE RED CENTRE

°C	Jan	Apr	Jul	Oct
max	36	27	19	31
min	21	12	4	14
sunshine	10 hrs	10 hrs	9 hrs	10 hrs
rainfall	43 mm	10 mm	8 mm	18 mm

PERTH AND THE SOUTHWEST

°C	Jan	Apr	Jul	Oct
max	29	24	17	21
min	17	14	9	12
sunshine	10 hrs	7 hrs	5 hrs	8 hrs
rainfall	8 mm	43 mm	170 mm	56 mm

THE YORKE AND EYRE PENINSULAS

°C	Jan	Apr	Jul	Oct
max	32	26	18	26
min	19	13	7	13
sunshine	10 hrs	6 hrs	5 hrs	7 hrs
rainfall	15 mm	18 mm	18 mm	23 mm

ADELAIDE AND THE SOUTHEAST

°C	Jan	Apr	Jul	Oct
max	30	23	15	23
min	16	13	7	11
sunshine	10 hrs	6 hrs	4 hrs	7 hrs
rainfall	20 mm	46 mm	66 mm	43 mm

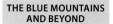

THE BLUE MOUNTAINS AND BEYOND

°C	Jan	Apr	Jul	Oct
high	26	23	16	23
low	18	13	9	15
sun	6 hrs	5 hrs	6 hrs	7 hrs
rain	95 mm	138 mm	110 mm	67 mm

SOUTH OF TOWNSVILLE

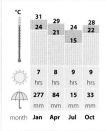

°C	Jan	Apr	Jul	Oct
high	31	29	24	28
low	24	21	15	22
sun	7 hrs	8 hrs	8 hrs	9 hrs
rain	277 mm	84 mm	15 mm	33 mm

CANBERRA AND ACT

°C	Jan	Apr	Jul	Oct
high	28	19	11	20
low	13	7	1	6
sun	9 hrs	7 hrs	5 hrs	8 hrs
rain	48 mm	41 mm	46 mm	56 mm

BRISBANE

°C	Jan	Apr	Jul	Oct
high	29	26	20	27
low	21	16	9	16
sun	8 hrs	7 hrs	7 hrs	8 hrs
rain	163 mm	94 mm	56 mm	64 mm

SYDNEY

°C	Jan	Apr	Jul	Oct
high	26	22	16	22
low	18	14	8	13
sun	7 hrs	6 hrs	6 hrs	7 hrs
rain	89 mm	135 mm	117 mm	71 mm

THE SOUTH COAST AND SNOWY MOUNTAINS

°C	Jan	Apr	Jul	Oct
high	24	21	14	22
low	19	15	8	15
sun	7 hrs	5 hrs	6 hrs	6 hrs
rain	85 mm	140 mm	122 mm	75 mm

EASTERN VICTORIA

°C	Jan	Apr	Jul	Oct
high	27	19	12	21
low	12	10	4	8
sun	8 hrs	6 hrs	4 hrs	7 hrs
rain	40 mm	52 mm	45 mm	59 mm

TASMANIA

°C	Jan	Apr	Jul	Oct
high	22	17	11	17
low	12	9	4	8
sun	8 hrs	5 hrs	4 hrs	6 hrs
rain	48 mm	48 mm	53 mm	58 mm

WESTERN VICTORIA

°C	Jan	Apr	Jul	Oct
high	25	18	10	17
low	11	9	3	9
sun	7 hrs	5 hrs	5 hrs	6 hrs
rain	38 mm	50 mm	77 mm	70 mm

MELBOURNE

°C	Jan	Apr	Jul	Oct
high	26	20	13	19
low	14	11	6	9
sun	8 hrs	5 hrs	4 hrs	6 hrs
rain	48 mm	58 mm	48 mm	66 mm

THE HISTORY OF AUSTRALIA

Australia is a young nation in an ancient land. It is a nation of immigrants, past and present, forced and free. The first European settlers occupied a harsh country; they explored it, exploited its mineral wealth and farmed it. In so doing, they suffered at the hands of nature, as well as enduring depressions and wars. Out of all this, however, has emerged a modern and cosmopolitan society.

The first rocks of the Australian landscape began to form some four-and-a-half billion years ago. Over time many older rocks were covered by more recent rocks, but in places such as the Pilbara region of Western Australia erosion has exposed a landscape 3,500 million years old *(see pp334–5)*. About 500 million years ago Australia, together with South America, South Africa, India and the Antarctic, formed a supercontinent known as Gondwanaland. This landmass moved through a series of different climatic zones; today's desert interior was once a shallow sea *(see pp26–7)*.

The First Immigrants

Australia was first settled by Aboriginal people who arrived by sea from Asia more than 60,000 years ago. On landing, they quickly adapted to the climatic and geographical conditions. Nomadic hunters and gatherers, the Aborigines moved with the seasons and spread across the continent, reaching Tasmania 35,000 years ago. They had few material possessions beyond the tools and weapons required for hunting and obtaining food. The early tools, known today as core tools, were very

simple chopping implements, roughly formed by grinding stone. By 8,000 BC Aborigines had developed the sophisticated returning boomerang *(see p34)* and possibly the world's first barbed spear. So-called flaked tools of varying styles were in use 5,000 years later, finely made out of grained stones such as flint to create sharp cutting edges.

Beneath the apparently simple way of life, Aboriginal society was complex. It was based on a network of mainly nomadic bands, comprising between 50 and 100 people, bound by kin relationships, who lived according to strictly applied laws and customs. These laws and beliefs, including the spiritual significance of the land, were upheld through a tradition of song, dance and art *(see pp34–7)*. With no centralized or formal system of government, individual groups were led by prominent, generally older men, who were held in great respect. Across the continent there were more than 200 languages spoken and approximately 800 dialects. In many respects, Aboriginal life was also very advanced: excavations at Lake Mungo provide fascinating evidence of ancient burial rituals, including what is

43,000–38,000 BC Tools found in a grave pit beside Nepean River are among the oldest firmly dated signs of human occupation in Australia	**35,000 BC** Aborigines reach Tasmania	*Diprotodon 20,000 BC*		**13,000** End of Ice Age
60,000 BC	**50,000 BC**	**40,000 BC**	**30,000 BC**	**20,000 BC**	**10,000 BC**
170–60,000 BC Aborigines thought to have reached Australia	**42,000 BC** Aboriginal engravings at Olary, South Australia	**25,000 BC** Woman is cremated at Lake Mungo – the world's oldest known cremation	**20,000 BC** Humans live in the Blue Mountains despite Ice Age. Remains of the largest marsupial, Diprotodon, date back to this period

◄ *Desmond, A New South Wales Chief (about 1825) by Augustus Earle* believed to be the world's oldest cremation 25,000 years ago (*see p185*).

Theories of a Southern Land

In Europe, the existence of a southern land was the subject of debate for centuries. As early as the 5th century BC, with the European discovery of Australia some 2,000 years away, the mathematician Pythagoras speculated on the presence of southern lands necessary to counterbalance those in the northern hemisphere. In about AD 150, the ancient geographer Ptolemy of Alexandria continued this speculation by drawing a map showing a landmass enclosing the Atlantic and Indian oceans. Some scholars went so far as to suggest that it was inhabited by "antipodes", a race of men whose feet faced backwards. Religious scholar St Augustine (AD 354–430) declared categorically that the southern hemisphere contained no land; the contrary view was heretical. But not all men of religion agreed: the 1086 *Osma Beatus*, a series of maps illustrating the

Woodcut of an "antipodean man" (1493)

works of the monk Beatus, showed the hypothetical land as a populated region.

It was not until the 15th century, when Europe entered a golden age of exploration, that these theories were tested. Under the patronage of Prince Henry of Portugal (1394–1460), known as Henry the Navigator, Portuguese sailors crossed the equator for the first time in 1470. In 1488 they sailed around the southern tip of Africa, and by 1502 they claimed to have located a southern land while on a voyage to explore South America. The Italian navigator, Amerigo Vespucci, described it as Paradise, full of trees and colourful birds. The location of this land is not clear but it was definitely not Australia.

In 1519 another Portuguese expedition set off, under the command of Ferdinand Magellan, and was the first to circumnavigate the world. No drawings of the lands explored survive, but subsequent maps show Tierra del Fuego as the tip of a landmass south of the Americas. Between 1577 and 1580 the Englishman Sir Francis Drake also circumnavigated the world, but his maps indicate no such land. Meanwhile, maps prepared in Dieppe in France between 1540 and 1566 show a southern continent, Java la Grande, lying southeast of Indonesia.

First known map of Australia known as the *Dauphin Chart*, 1530–36

5,000 BC Dingo is the first domesticated animal to reach Australia from Southeast Asia	**500 BC** Pythagoras speculates on existence of southern lands	**AD 150** Ptolemy believes the southern land encloses the Atlantic and Indian oceans	**450** Macrobius, in his *Dream of Scorpio*, envisages uninhabited southern land
5,000 BC	**1,000 BC**	**AD 1**	**1000**
		400 St Augustine declares south to be all ocean and rejects idea of antipodeans	**1086** Beatus, on his *Mappa mundi*, shows a southern land inhabited by a monster with one large foot

Copperplate print of a dingo

Abel Tasman's Dutch discovery ships

The Dutch Discovery

By the 17th century Portugal's power in Southeast Asia was beginning to wane, and Holland, with its control of the Dutch East Indies (Indonesia), was the new power and responsible for the European discovery of Australia.

Willem Jansz, captain of the ship *Duyfken*, was in search of New Guinea, a land thought to be rich in gold, when he sailed along the Cape York Peninsula in 1606. He found the coast inhospitable. In 1616 Dirk Hartog, commanding the *Eendracht*, was blown off course on his way to the East Indies. He landed on an island off Western Australia and nailed a pewter plate to a pole *(see p330)*.

Dutch navigator Abel Tasman charted large parts of Australia and New Zealand between 1642 and 1644, including Tasmania which he originally named Van Diemen's Land in honour of the Governor-General of the East Indies. It became Tasmania in 1855.

The Dutch continued to explore the country for 150 years, but although their discoveries were of geographic interest they did not result in any economic benefit.

The Forgotten Spaniard

In 1606, the same year that Willem Jansz first set foot on Australian soil, Luis Vaez de Torres, a Spanish Admiral, led an expedition in search of "Terra Australis". He sailed through the strait which now bears his name between Australia and New Guinea *(see p256)*. His discovery, however, was inexplicably ignored for 150 years. He sent news of his exploration to King Felipe III of Spain from the Philippines but died shortly after. Perhaps his early death meant that the news was not disseminated and the significance of his maps not realized.

Bronze relief of Luis Vaez de Torres

The First Englishman

The first Englishman to land on Australian soil was the privateer William Dampier in 1688. He published a book of his journey, *New Voyage Round the World*, in 1697. Britain gave him command of the *Roebuck*, in which he explored the northwest Australian coast in great detail. His ship sank on the return voyage. The crew survived but Dampier was court martialled for the mistreatment of his subordinates.

Portrait of William Dampier

1577–80 Sir Francis Drake circumnavigates the world but indicates no austral region beneath South America

Sir Francis Drake

Dampier's compass

1688 William Dampier lands on Australian soil

1200

1300 Marco Polo describes a southern land which is later added to the imaginary Terra Australis on Renaissance maps

1400

Hartog's plate

1616 Dirk Hartog sails from Amsterdam and lands on the western shore of Australia, nailing a pewter plate to a pole

1600

1756 Final Dutch voyage of the *Buis* to Australia

The Colonization of Australia

By the mid-18th century Britain had taken over as the world's main maritime power. In 1768 Captain James Cook set off to find Australia in the *Endeavour* and in 1770 King George III formally claimed possession of the east coast, named New South Wales. Overcrowding of jails and the loss of American colonies in the War of Independence led the British to establish a penal colony in the new land. The First Fleet, consisting of two men-of-war and nine transport ships, arrived in Sydney Cove on 26 January 1788. The initial settlement consisted of 750 convicts, approximately 210 marines and 40 women and children. Faced with great hardship, they survived in tents, eating local wildlife and rations from Britain.

Captain James Cook *(c.1800)*
The English navigator charted eastern Australia for the first time between 1770 and 1771.

Boat building at the
Government dockyard

Aborigines depicted
observing the new
white settlement.

Britain Takes Possession
In 1770 the Union Jack was raised on the east coast of Australia, and Britain finally claimed possession of this new-found land.

A View of Sydney Cove
This idyllic image, drawn by Edward Dayes and engraved by F Jukes in 1804, shows the Aboriginal peoples living peacefully within the infant colony alongside the flourishing maritime and agricultural industries. In reality, by the end of the 18th century they had been entirely ostracized from the life and prosperity of their native land. The first settlement was founded at Port Jackson, renamed Sydney Cove.

Sir Joseph Banks
Aboard the *Endeavour* with Captain Cook, botanist Joseph Banks was responsible for the proposal of Botany Bay as the first penal settlement.

First Fleet Ship
This painting by Francis Holman (c.1787) shows three views of the *Borrowdale*, one of the fleet's three commercial store ships.

Scrimshaw
Engraving bone or shell was a skilful way to pass time during long months spent at sea.

Buildings looked impressive but were poorly built.

Convict housing

Governor Phillip's House, Sydney
This grand colonial mansion, flanked by landscaped gardens, was home to Australia's first government.

Barracks housing
NSW Rum Corps

Prison Hulks
Old ships, unfit for naval service, were used as floating prisons to house convicts until the mid-19th century.

1768 Captain James Cook sets out from England for Tahiti on his ship, the *Endeavour*

1775 British over-crowding of jails and prison hulks

Aborigine Bennelong

1788 Aborigine Bennelong is captured and held for five months, then taken to England to meet King George III

1770

1780

1790

1770 Cook discovers the east coast of Australia and takes possession for Britain

1779 Botanist Joseph Banks recommends Botany Bay for penal settlement

Merino sheep

1797 John Macarthur introduces merino sheep from the Cape of Good Hope
(see p131)

Exploring the Coastline

Once the survival of the first settlement was assured, both the government and the free settlers began to look beyond its confines. Faced with a vast, unknown continent and fuelled by desires for knowledge and wealth, they set out to explore the land. The 19th century was a period of exploration, discovery and settlement.

Between 1798 and 1799 the English midshipman Matthew Flinders and surgeon George Bass charted much of the Australian coastline south of Sydney. They also circumnavigated Tasmania, known at that time as Van Diemen's Land *(see p53).* In 1801 Flinders was given command of the sloop *Investigator* and explored the entire Australian coastline, becoming the first man to successfully circumnavigate the whole continent.

John Batman and local Aboriginal chiefs

William Wentworth and William Lawson forged a successful route across the Blue Mountains *(see pp172–3).* In 1824 explorers Hamilton Hume and William Hovell opened up the continent further when they travelled overland from New South Wales to Port Phillip Bay, the present site of Melbourne.

Between 1828 and 1830 Charles Sturt, a former secretary to the New South Wales Governor, led two expeditions along Australia's inland river systems. On his first journey he discovered the Darling River. His second expedition began in Sydney and followed the Murray River to the sea in South Australia. This arduous task left Sturt, like many such explorers before and after him, suffering from ill health for the rest of his life.

Exploring the Interior

Inland New South Wales was opened up for settlement in 1813, when Gregory Blaxland,

Sturt's party shown being attacked by Aborigines on their journey to the Murray River

New Colonies

Individual colonies began to emerge across the continent throughout the 19th century. First settled in 1804, Tasmania became a separate colony in 1825; in 1829 Western Australia became a colony with the establishment of Perth. Originally a colony of free settlers, a labour shortage led to the westward transportation of convicts.

In 1835 a farmer, John Batman, signed a contract with local Aborigines to acquire 250,000 ha (600,000 acres) of land where Melbourne now stands *(see p385).* His action resulted in a rush for land in the area.

1798–9 Matthew Flinders and George Bass circumnavigate Tasmania	**1808** Major Johnston leads an insurrection against rum being abolished as currency	**1825** Van Diemen's Land (later Tasmania) becomes a separate colony		**1840–41** Sheep farmer Edward John Eyre is the first European to cross the Nullarbor Plain

E J Eyre

1800	**1810**	**1820**	**1830**	**1840**

1801–3 Flinders circumnavigates Australia	**1804** Hobart Town is established			**1833** Port Arthur opens as a penal establishment. It remains in use until 1877
	1813 The first currency, the "holey dollar" and "dump", is introduced			**1829** Western Australia is annexed, using convicts for cheap labour

Holey dollar and dump, made from Spanish coins

A typical colonial house in Hobart Town (now Hobart), Tasmania, during its early days in 1856

The settlement was recognized in 1837, and the separate colony of Victoria was proclaimed in 1851, at the start of its gold rush *(see pp58–9)*. Queensland became a separate colony in 1859. South Australia was established in 1836 as Australia's only convict-free colony. Based on a theory formulated by a group of English reformers, the colony was funded by land sales which paid for public works and the transportation of free labourers. It became a haven for religious dissenters, a tradition that still continues today.

Crossing the Continent

Edward John Eyre, a sheep farmer who arrived from England in 1833, was the first European to cross the Nullarbor Plain from Adelaide to Western Australia in 1840.

In 1859 the South Australian government, anxious to build an overland telegraph from Adelaide to the north coast, offered a reward to the first person to cross the continent from south to north. An expedition of 20 to 40 men and camels left Melbourne in 1860 under the command of police officer Robert O'Hara Burke and surveyor William Wills. Burke, Wills and two other men travelled from their base camp

The Rum Rebellion

In 1808, the military, under the command of Major George Johnston and John Macarthur *(see p131)*, staged an insurrection known as the Rum Rebellion. At stake was the military's control of the profitable rum trade. Governor William Bligh (1754–1817), target of a mutiny when captain of the *Bounty*, was arrested after he tried to stop rum being used as currency. The military held power for 23 months until government was restored by Governor Lachlan Macquarie.

William Bligh

at Cooper Creek to the tidal mangroves of the Flinders River which they mistook for the ocean, before heading back south. They returned to the base camp only hours after the main party, who now believed them dead, had left. Burke and Wills died at the base camp from starvation and fatigue.

The crossing from south to north was finally completed by John McDouall Stuart in 1862. He returned to Adelaide sick with scurvy and almost blind.

The return of Burke and Wills to Cooper Creek in 1860

1851 Gold discovered near Bathurst, New South Wales, and at Ballarat and Bendigo, Victoria *(see pp58–9)*

1862 John Stuart is the first explorer to cross from south to north Australia

1872 Overland telegraph from Adelaide to Darwin, via Alice Springs

1873 Uluru (Ayers Rock) first sighted by Europeans

1899 Australians fight in the Boer War

1850 | **1860** | **1870** | **1880** | **1890**

1854 Eureka Stockade *(see p58)*

1853 Last convicts transported to Tasmania

1868 Last transportation of convicts to Australia arrive in Western Australia

1876 Last full-blooded Tasmanian Aborigine, Truganini, dies *(see p473)*

1880 Ned Kelly hanged *(see p455)*

Death mask of Ned Kelly

The 1850s Gold Rush

Gold was discovered near Bathurst in New South Wales and at Ballarat and Bendigo in Victoria in 1851. Established towns were almost deserted as men from all over the country, together with immigrants from Europe and China, rushed to the gold fields. Some became extremely wealthy, while others returned empty-handed. By the 1880s, Australia was a prosperous country and cities were lined with ornate architecture, some of which was constructed by the last waves of convict labour. Despite gold found in Western Australia in the 1890s, however, the final decade of the 19th century was a period of depression, when wool prices fell, Victoria's land boom collapsed and the nation suffered a severe drought.

Edward Hargraves
In 1851 Hargraves made his name by discovering gold in Bathurst, New South Wales.

Panning dish

Lamp

Pick axe

Gold Mining Utensils
Mining for gold was initially an unskilled and laborious process that required only a few basic utensils. A panning dish to swill water, a pick axe to loosen rock and a miner's lamp were all that were needed to commence the search.

Digging for Gold
Edwin Stocqueler's painting Australian Gold Diggings *(1855) shows the varying methods of gold mining and the hard work put in by thousands of diggers in their quest for wealth. As men and their families came from all over the world to make their fortune, regions rich in gold, in particular Victoria, thrived. Previous wastelands were turned into tent settlements and gradually grew into impressive new cities.*

Eureka Stockade
In 1854 an insurrection took place just outside the town of Ballarat when miners rebelled against costly licences and burned them at a stockade (see p438).

Might versus Right *(c.1861)*
ST Gill's painting depicts the riots on the Lambing Flag gold fields in New South Wales in 1861. Chinese immigrants, who came to Australia in search of gold, were met with violent racism by European settlers who felt their wealth and position were in jeopardy.

Tent villages covered the Victoria landscape in the 1850s.

Gold panning was the most popular extraction method.

Prosperity in Bendigo
The buildings of Williamson Street in Bendigo *(see p436)* display the prosperity that resulted from gold finds in Victoria.

Chinese Miners' Medal
Racism against the Chinese eventually subsided. This medal was given by the Chinese to the district of Braidwood, Victoria, in 1881.

Miners wore hats and heavyweight trousers to protect them from the sun.

The sluice was a trough which trapped gold in its bars as water was flushed through.

Gold Prospecting Camel Team
Just as the gold finds dried up in Victoria, gold was discovered in Western Australia in the 1890s. Prospectors crossed the continent to continue their search.

Souvenir handkerchief of the Australian Federation

Unwanted immigrants were tested in obscure languages such as Gaelic. Between 1901 and 1910 there were nine different governments led by five different prime ministers. None of the three major political groups, the Protectionists, the Free Traders and the Labor Party, had sufficient support to govern in its own right. By 1910, however, voters were offered a clear choice between two parties, Labor and Liberal. The Labor Party won a landslide victory and since then the Australian government has come solely from one of these two parties.

Federal Beginnings

Australia entered the 20th century on an optimistic note: the federation of its six colonies formed the Australian nation on 1 January 1901. Within the federation, there was one matter on which almost everyone agreed: Australia would remain "European" with strong ties to Britain. One of the first acts of the new parliament was to legislate the White Australia Policy. The Immigration Restriction Act required anyone wishing to emigrate to Australia to pass a dictation test in a European language.

World War I

When Britain entered World War I in 1914, Australia followed to defend the "mother land". Most Australians supported the war, but they would not accept conscription or compulsory national service.

Enlisting poster

Australia paid a very high price for its allegiance, with 64 per cent of the 331,781 troops killed or wounded. Memorials to those who fought and died are found throughout the country, ranging from the simple to the impressive such as the Australian War Memorial in Canberra (see pp204–5). World War I was a defining moment in Australia's history. Anzac Day, rather than Australia Day, is felt by many to be the true national day. It commemorates the landing of the Australian and New Zealand Army Corps at Gallipoli in Turkey on 25 April 1915, for their unsuccessful attempt to cross the Dardanelles and

Labor government publicity poster

1901 The Commonwealth of Australia comes into being. The White Australia Policy becomes law with the passage of the Immigration Restriction Bill

Australia's national flag

1919 Postwar immigration includes the Big Brother movement, which welcomes adolescents

1921 Edith Cowan becomes the first woman MP in the country

1900 **1905** **1910** **1915** **1920**

1902 Women's suffrage is granted in Australia

1912 Walter Burley Griffin is chosen to design Canberra (see p195)

1914–18 Australia takes part in World War I

1920 Qantas is formed as a local airline

QANTAS

Qantas logo

link up with the Russians. This was the first battle in which Australian soldiers fought as a national force and, although a failure, they gained a reputation for bravery and endurance. It is an event that many believe determined the Australian character and saw the real birth of Australia.

Between the Wars

During the 1920s, Australia, boosted by the arrival of some 300,000 immigrants, entered a period of major development. In 1920 Qantas (Queensland and Northern Territory Aerial Service Ltd) was formed, which was to become the national airline, and made its first international flight in 1934. Building of the Sydney Harbour Bridge began in 1923 (see pp84–5). Australia's population reached 6 million in 1925, but this new optimism was not to last.

In 1929 Australia, along with much of the world, went into economic decline. Prices of wool and wheat, major export earners, fell dramatically. By 1931, a third of the country was unemployed. People slept in tents in

Celebrating the opening of Sydney Harbour Bridge

city parks; swagmen (workers with their possessions on their backs) appeared as men left cities in search of work in the country.

Prices began to increase again by 1933 and manufacturing revived. From 1934 to 1937 the economy improved and unemployment fell. The following year, however, Australia again faced the prospect of war.

World War II

Though World War II was initially a European war, Australians again fought in defence of freedom and the "mother land". However, when Japan entered the war, Australians felt for the first time that their national security was at risk. In 1942 Darwin, Broome and Townsville were bombed by the Japanese, the first act of war on Australian soil. The same year two Japanese midget submarines entered Sydney Harbour.

Britain asked for more Australian troops but for the first time they were refused: the men were needed in the Pacific. This was a major shift in Australian foreign policy away from Britain and towards the USA.

Swagmen during the Great Depression

1923 Vegemite first produced

Jar of Vegemite

1927 First federal parliament held in Canberra in temporary Parliament House

1932 Sydney Harbour Bridge opens

1929 The Great Depression hits Australia, bringing great hardship

1928 Royal Flying Doctor service starts

1933 Western Australia produces a referendum in favour of secession from Britain, but parliament rejects it

1939–45 Australia takes part in World War II

1941 Australian War Memorial opens in Canberra

1925 **1930** **1935** **1940** **1945**

First Australian car

1948 Holden is the first car produced that is entirely made in Australia

Australians fought alongside the Americans in the Pacific and nearly 250,000 US troops spent time in Australia during the war. This led, in 1951, to the signing of Australia's first defence treaty with a foreign country: the ANZUS treaty between Australia, New Zealand and the United States.

Again, war affected most Australian communities and towns. Nearly one million of Australia's seven million population went to fight: 34,000 were killed and 180,000 wounded.

Poster promoting travel and tourism in 1950s Australia

Postwar Immigration

The proximity of the fighting in World War II left Australia feeling vulnerable. The future defence of the country was seen to be dependent upon a strong economy and a larger population.

The postwar immigration programme welcomed not only British immigrants but also Europeans. Almost two million immigrants arrived in Australia in the 20 years

following World War II, 800,000 of whom were not British. In 1956, the status of "permanent resident" allowed non-Europeans to claim citizenship. In 1958, the dictation entry test was abolished. Yet until 1966 non-Europeans had to have 15 years' residence before gaining citizenship, as opposed to five years for Europeans.

The Menzies Era

From 1949 until 1966, Prime Minister Robert Menzies "reigned", winning eight consecutive elections. The increasing population and international demand for Australian raw materials during this time provided a

British migrants arriving in Sydney in 1967 as part of the postwar wave of immigration

Mabo and Beyond

In 1982, Edward Koiki (Eddie) Mabo, a Torres Strait Islander, took action against the Queensland government claiming that his people had ancestral land rights. After a ten-year battle, the High Court ruled that Aborigines and Torres

Edward Koiki Mabo

Strait Islanders may hold native title to land where there has been no loss of traditional connection. This ended the concept of *terra nullius* – that Australia belonged to no one when Europeans arrived there – and acknowledged that Aborigines held valid title to their land. Subsequent legislation has provided a framework for assessing such claims.

1955 Australian troops sent to Malaya

Neville Bonner

1958 Immigration dictation test abolished

1971 Neville Bonner becomes Australia's first Aboriginal MP

1976 "Advance Australia Fair" becomes national anthem

1979 Severe droughts in the country last three years

1981 Preference given to immigrants with family members already in Australia. Increase in Asian immigration

| 1955 | 1960 | 1965 | 1970 | 1975 | 1980 | 1985 |

1965 Australian troops sent to Vietnam as part of their National Service

1956 Melbourne hosts the Olympic Games

1966–72 Demonstrations against the Vietnam War

1967 Referendum on Aborigines ends legal discrimination

1973 Sydney Opera House opens (see pp88–9)

Sydney Opera House

1983 Bob Hawke elected as prime minister

1983 America's Cup victory

1986 Proclamation of Australia Act breaks legal ties with Britain

Vietnam War protestors in Australia, focusing on Vietnam Air Force chief Nguyen Cao Kỳ

In 1972, the Labor Party, under Edward Gough Whitlam, was elected on a platform of social reform. It abolished conscription, introduced free university education and health care through public hospitals, lowered the voting age from 21 to 18 and gave some land rights to Aborigines. In 1974, an immigration policy without any racial discrimination was adopted.

high standard of living. Menzies understood his people's desire for peace and prosperity, and gave Australians conservatism and stability. He did, however, also involve them in three more wars, in Korea (1950), Malaya (1955) and Vietnam (1965). Vietnam was the first time Australia fought in a war in which Britain was not also engaged.

Social Unrest and Change

Opposition to conscription and the Vietnam War increased in the late 1960s and led to major demonstrations. At the same time there was concern for issues such as Aboriginal land rights and free education. In 1967, a constitutional referendum was passed by 90.8 per cent of the voters, ending the ban on Aboriginal inclusion in the national census. It also gave power to the federal government to legislate for Aborigines in all states, ending state discriminations.

Prime Minister Whitlam hands over Aboriginal land rights in 1975

The Changing Economic and Political Landscape

The unprecedented dismissal of the Whitlam Labor administration in 1975 ushered in an era of social and political reform. Free education and universal health care were wound back, the nation dealt with recession in the 1980s and 1990s and avoided the worst of the global financial crisis in the 2000s due to economic stimulus packages. The election of Kevin Rudd as prime minister in 2007 marked a return to government for the Labor party after 11 years under Liberal leader John Howard. The new government's first act was a formal apology to indigenous Australians for the pain of past mistreatment. Rudd was toppled as Labor leader in 2010 by Julia Gillard, the country's first female prime minister. Closer ties with Asia saw China emerge as Australia's biggest trading partner, with the nation's natural mineral resources and agriculture products in high demand.

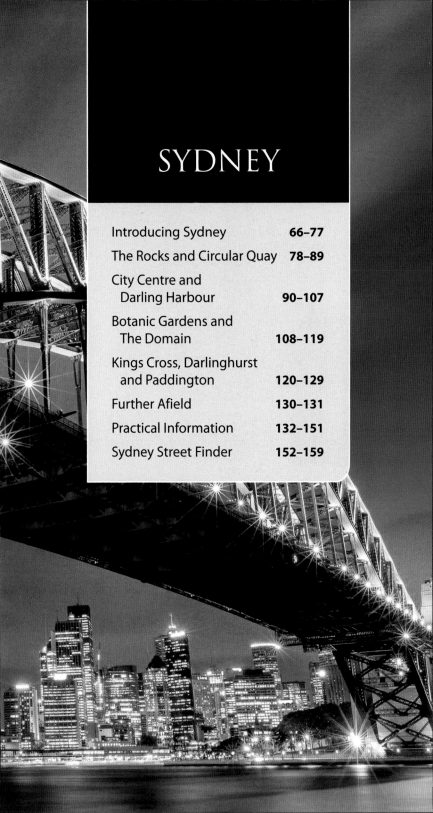

SYDNEY

Central Sydney

This guide divides the centre of Sydney into four distinct areas, and the majority of the city's main sights are contained in these districts. The Rocks and Circular Quay are the oldest part of inner Sydney. The City Centre is the central business district, and to its west lies Darling Harbour, which includes Sydney's well-known Chinatown. The Botanic Gardens and The Domain form a green oasis almost in the heart of the city. To the east are Kings Cross and Darlinghurst, the hub of café culture, and Paddington, an area that still retains its charming 19th-century character.

The Lord Nelson Brewery Hotel is a traditional pub in The Rocks (see p482), which first opened its doors in 1834. Its own specially brewed beers are available on tap.

Queen Victoria Building is a Romanesque former produce market, built in the 1890s. It forms part of a fine group of Victorian buildings in the City Centre (see p94). Now a shopping mall, it retains many of its original features, including its ornate roof statues.

Key

▨ Major sight

▢ Other buildings

0 metres 250
0 yards 250

◀ The Sydney Harbour Bridge, the central business district and the Opera House

Greater Sydney

Fort Denison

Palm Beach

Hornsby

Mona Vale

Penrith

Blacktown

Chatswood

Manly

Glenbrook

Parramatta

Burwood

CENTRAL SYDNEY

Bondi

Bankstown

Sydney Airport

Maroubra

Campbelltown

Sutherland

Cronulla

0 km 10

0 miles 10

Farm Cove

ROYAL BOTANIC GARDENS

BOTANIC GARDENS AND THE DOMAIN

Art Gallery of New South Wales

Kings Cross

KINGS CROSS, DARLINGHURST AND PADDINGTON

MOORE PARK

Kippax Lake

ALLIANZ STADIUM

SYDNEY CRICKET GROUND

THE ENTERTAINMENT QUARTER

CENTENNIAL PARK

The Art Gallery of New South Wales *(see pp114–15)* is the city's premier art gallery, set amid the Botanic Gardens and The Domain district. It houses an excellent collection of early and contemporary Australian, Aboriginal and European art.

Elizabeth Bay near Potts Point is a picturesque bay with fine views across Sydney Harbour. It is situated in the heart of colonial Sydney, at the northern end of the Kings Cross, Darlinghurst and Paddington area *(see pp124–5).*

Sydney's Best: Museums and Galleries

Sydney is well endowed with museums and galleries, and, following the current appreciation of social history, much emphasis is placed on the lifestyles of past and present Sydneysiders. Small museums are also a feature of the Sydney scene, with a number of historic houses recalling the colonial days. Most of the major collections are housed in architecturally significant buildings – the Classical façade of the Art Gallery of NSW makes it a city landmark, while the MCA or Museum of Contemporary Art has given new life to a 1950s Art Deco-style building at Circular Quay.

The Museum of Sydney includes *The Edge of the Trees*, an interactive installation *(see p96)*.

The Museum of Contemporary Art is Australia's only museum dedicated to exhibiting national and international contemporary art *(see p82)*.

The Rocks and Circular Quay

City Centre and Darling Harbour

The National Maritime Museum is the home port for HMB *Endeavour*, a replica of the vessel that charted Australia's east coast in 1770, with Captain Cook in command *(see pp104–5).*

| 0 metres | 500 |
| 0 yards | 500 |

The Powerhouse Museum, set in a former power station, uses both traditional and interactive displays to explore Australian innovations in science and technology *(see pp106–7).*

The Art Gallery of New South Wales includes colonial watercolours in its Australian collection, which, to avoid deterioration, are only shown for a few weeks each year. Charles Meere's *Australian Beach Pattern* (1940) is one of them *(see pp114–17)*.

Elizabeth Bay House is elegantly furnished to reflect the 1840s period, when the Colonial Secretary Alexander Macleay lived in the house that ultimately caused his bankruptcy *(see p124)*.

Botanic Gardens and The Domain

Kings Cross, Darlinghurst and Paddington

The Hyde Park Barracks were originally built by convicts for their own incarceration. They were later home to poor female immigrants. Exhibits recall the daily life of these occupants *(see p118)*.

The Sydney Jewish Museum documents the history of the city's Jewish community. Exhibits include reconstructed scenes, such as George Street in 1848, a Jewish business area *(see p125)*.

The Australian Museum is where visitors can discover the Earth's age, find out about meteorites, volcanic activity, mining and more with its stunning display of rocks and minerals *(see pp98–9)*.

Sydney's Best: Architecture

For such a young city, Sydney possesses a great diversity of architectural styles. They range from the simplicity of Francis Greenway's Georgian buildings (*see p177*) to Jørn Utzon's Expressionist Sydney Opera House (*see pp88–9*). Practical colonial structures gave way to elaborate Victorian edifices such as Sydney Town Hall. The same passion for detail is seen in Paddington's terraces. Later, Federation warehouses and bungalows introduced a uniquely Australian style.

Colonial convict structures were simple with shingled roofs, based on the English homes of the first settlers. Cadman's Cottage is an example of this style (*see p82*).

Contemporary architecture abounds in Sydney, including Governor Phillip Tower. The Museum of Sydney is at its base (*see p96*).

The Rocks and Circular Quay

Colonial Georgian buildings include St James' Church (*see p119*). Francis Greenway's design was adapted to suit the purposes of a church.

Contemporary Expressionism's main emphasis is roof design and the silhouette. Innovations were made in sports stadiums and museums, such as the Australian National Maritime Museum (*see p104–5*).

American Revivalism took up the 1890s vogue of arcades connecting many different streets. The Queen Victoria Building is a fine example (*see p94*).

City Centre and Darling Harbour

Victorian architecture abounds in the city. Sydney Town Hall includes a metal ceiling, installed for fear that the organ would vibrate a plaster one loose (*see p97*).

Designed by Frank Gehry, the Dr Chau Chak Wing Building for the University of Technology, Sydney, is affectionately known as the "crumpled paper bag". It challenges construction norms, achieving a fluidity of form with 320,000 bricks that were laid by hand.

Modern Expressionism includes one of the world's greatest examples of 20th-century architecture. The construction of Jørn Utzon's Sydney Opera House began in 1959. Despite the architect's resignation in 1966, it was opened in 1973 *(see pp88–9).*

Early Colonial's first buildings, such as Hyde Park Barracks *(see p118),* were mainly built for the government.

tanic Gardens
d The Domain

Australian Regency was popular during the 1830s. The best-designed villas were the work of John Verge. The beautiful Elizabeth Bay House is considered his masterpiece *(see p124).*

**Kings Cross,
Darlinghurst and
Paddington**

Colonial Grecian and Greek Revival were the most popular styles for public buildings designed during the 1820–50 period. The Darlinghurst Court House is a particularly fine example *(see p125).*

Victorian iron lace incorporated filigree of cast-iron in prefabricated patterns. Paddington's verandas are fine examples of this 1880s style *(see pp126–7).*

Colonial military buildings were both functional and ornate. Victoria Barracks, designed by engineers, is a fine example of a Georgian military compound *(see p128).*

0 metres   500

0 yards   500

Sydney's Best: Parks and Reserves

Sydney is almost completely surrounded by national parks and intact bushland. There are also a number of national parks and reserves within Greater Sydney itself. Here, the visitor can gain some idea of how the landscape looked before the arrival of European settlers. The city parks, too, are filled with plant and animal life. The more formal plantings of both native and exotic species are countered by the indigenous birds and animals that have adapted and made the urban environment their home. One of the highlights of a trip to Sydney is the huge variety of birds to be seen, from large birds of prey such as sea eagles and kites, to the shyer species such as wrens and tiny finches.

Garigal National Park is made up of rainforest and moist gullies, which provide shelter for superb lyrebirds and sugar gliders.

Lane Cove National Park is an open eucalypt forest dotted with grass trees, as well as fine stands of blue gums and apple gums. The rosella, a type of parrot, is common in the area.

North Arm Walk is covered in spring with grevilleas and flannel flowers blooming profusely.

Bicentennial Park is situated at Homebush Bay. The park features a mangrove habitat and attracts many water birds, including pelicans.

Barangaroo Reserve is the location of an old industrial site. It has been transformed into a 6-ha (-acre) harbour foreshore park, landscaped with 75,000 native trees and shrubs, rocky outcrops, walking trails and picnic spots.

Hyde Park is situated on the edge of the city centre (see p97). The park provides a peaceful respite from the hectic streets.

Middle Head and Obelisk Bay are dotted with gun emplacements, tunnels and bunkers built in the 1870s to protect Sydney from invasion. The superb fairy wren lives here, and water dragons can at times be seen basking on rocks.

North Head is covered with coastal heathland, with banksias, tea trees and casuarinas dominating the cliff tops. On the leeward side, moist forest surrounds tiny, secluded harbour beaches.

Grotto Point's paths, winding through the bush to the lighthouse, are lined with bottlebrushes, grevilleas and flannel flowers.

Bradleys Head is a nesting place for the ringtail possum. Noisy flocks of rainbow lorikeets are also often in residence. The views across the harbour to Sydney are spectacular.

South Head contains unique plant species such as the sundew.

Nielsen Park is inhabited by the kookaburra, easily identified by its call, which sounds like laughter.

The Domain features palms and Moreton Bay figs. The Australian magpie, with its black and white plumage, is a frequent visitor (see p113).

Moore Park is filled with huge Moreton Bay figs which provide an urban habitat for the flying fox.

Centennial Park contains open expanses and groves of paper-bark and eucalypt trees. Black swans may be seen on the lake, but the brushtail possum is a shy creature that comes out only at night (see p129).

0 kilometres _____ 4

0 miles _____ 2

Garden Island to Farm Cove

Sydney's vast harbour, also named Port Jackson after a Secretary in the British Admiralty who promptly changed his name, is a drowned river valley which was transformed over millions of years. Its intricate coastal geography of headlands and secluded bays can sometimes confound even lifelong residents. This waterway was the lifeblood of the early colony, with the maritime industry a vital source of wealth and supply. The legacies of recessions and booms can be viewed along the shoreline: a representation of a nation where an estimated 80 per cent of the population cling to the coastal cities, especially in the east.

The city skyline is a result of random development. The 1960s' destruction of architectural history was halted, and towers now stand amid Victorian buildings.

Two harbour beacons, known as "wedding cakes" because of their three tiers, are solar powered and equipped with a fail-safe back-up service. There are around 350 buoys and beacons now in operation.

The barracks for the naval garrison date from 1888.

Garden Island marks a 1940s construction project with 12 ha (30 acres) reclaimed from the harbour.

Sailing on the harbour is a pastime not exclusively reserved for the rich elite. Of the several hundred thousand pleasure boats registered, some are available for hire while others take out groups of inexperienced sailors.

Mrs Macquaries Chair is a carved rock seat by Mrs Macquaries Road *(see p112)*. In the early days of the colony this was the site of a fruit and vegetable garden which was farmed until 1805.

| 0 metres | | 250 |
| 0 yards | | 250 |

The Andrew (Boy) Charlton Pool is a favourite bathing spot for inner-city residents, and is named after the 16-year old who won an Olympic gold medal in 1924. It was erected in 1963 on the Domain Baths' site, which had a grandstand for 1,700.

Woolloomooloo Finger Wharf was a disembarkation point when most travellers arrived by sea.

Locator Map
See Street Finder, map 2

Harry's Café de Wheels, a snack van, has been a Sydney culinary institution for more than 50 years. Photographs of celebrity customers are pinned to the van, attesting to its fame.

The Royal Botanic Gardens display both flowering and non-flowering plants. Here the first trees were planted by the new European colonists; some of these trees survive today *(see pp110–11).*

Farm Cove has long been a mooring place for visiting naval vessels. The land opposite, now the Botanic Gardens, has been continuously cultivated for over 200 years.

Sydney Cove to Walsh Bay

It is estimated that over 70 km (43 miles) of harbour foreshore have been lost as a result of the massive land reclamation projects carried out since the 1840s. That the 13 islands existing when the First Fleet arrived in 1788 have now been reduced to just eight is a startling indication of rapid and profound geographical transformation. Redevelopments around the Circular Quay and Walsh Bay area from the 1980s have opened up the waterfront for public use and enjoyment, acknowledging it as the city's greatest natural asset. Sydney's environmental and architectural aspirations recognize the need to integrate city and harbour.

Conservatorium of Music

The Sydney Opera House was designed to take advantage of its spectacular setting. The roofs shine during the day and seem to glow at night. The building appears as a visionary landscape to the onlooker *(see pp88–9)*.

1857 Man O'War Steps

Government House, a Gothic Revival building, was home to the state's governors until 1996.

Harbour cruises regularly depart from Circular Quay, taking visitors out and about both during the day and in the evening. They are an incomparable way to see the city and its waterways.

The Sydney Harbour Bridge was also known as the "Iron Lung" at the time of its construction. During the Great Depression it provided on-site work for approximately 1,400, while others worked in specialist workshops *(see pp84–5)*.

| 0 metres | 250 |
| 0 yards | 250 |

The Rocks, settled by convicts and troops in 1788, is one of Sydney's oldest neighbourhoods. Rich in heritage, many of its old sandstone buildings have been restored and house speciality and craft shops.

Locator Map
See Street Finder, maps 1 & 2

The Tank Stream, the colony's first water supply, now runs underground and spills into the quay.

Cahill Expressway

Circular Quay, originally and more accurately known as Semi-Circular Quay, was the last and arguably greatest convict-built structure. Tank Stream mudflats were filled in to shape the quay, and sandstone from The Rocks formed the sea wall.

The Wharf Theatre resides on a pier that took six years to build, mostly due to the diversion of labour and materials during World War I. The theatre was opened in 1984.

The wharves were completed in 1922.

Imports and exports to and from the city were stored in these wharves until 1977.

The wharves' design included a rat-proof sea wall around the port. This was an urgent response to the 1900 bubonic plague outbreak, attributed to rats on the wharves.

THE ROCKS AND CIRCULAR QUAY

Circular Quay, once known as Semi-Circular Quay, is often referred to as the "birthplace of Australia". It was here, in January 1788, that the First Fleet landed its human freight of convicts, soldiers and officials, and the new British colony of New South Wales was declared. Sydney Cove became a rallying point whenever a ship arrived bringing much-needed supplies from "home". The Quay and The Rocks are focal points for New Year's Eve festivities. The area is packed during the annual Vivid festival, when many of the buildings are bathed in colour for a spectacular light show when the winter sun goes down. The Rocks area offers visitors a taste of Sydney's past, but it is a far cry from the time, little more than 120 years ago, when most inhabitants lived in rat-infested slums, and gangs ruled its streets. Now scrubbed and polished, The Rocks forms part of the colourful promenade from the Sydney Harbour Bridge to the spectacular Sydney Opera House.

Sights at a Glance

Museums and Galleries
1. Susannah Place
2. Museum of Contemporary Art
4. Sailors' Home
5. The Rocks Discovery Museum
11. National Trust Centre
15. Justice and Police Museum

Theatres and Concert Halls
17. *Sydney Opera House pp88–9*

Historic Streets and Buildings
3. Cadman's Cottage
6. Campbell's Storehouses
7. *Sydney Harbour Bridge pp84–5*
8. Hero of Waterloo
10. Sydney Observatory
13. Macquarie Place
14. Customs House
16. Writers' Walk

Churches
9. Garrison Church
12. St Philip's Church

See also Street Finder map 1

For keys to symbols *see back flap*

Street-by-Street: The Rocks

Named for the rugged cliffs that were once its dominant feature, this area has played a vital role in Sydney's development. In 1788, the First Fleeters under Governor Phillip's command erected makeshift buildings here, with the convicts' hard labour used to establish more permanent structures in the form of rough-hewn streets. The Argyle Cut, a road carved through solid rock using just hammer and chisel, took 18 years to build, beginning in 1843. By 1900, The Rocks was overrun with disease; the street now known as Suez Canal was once Sewer's Canal. Today, the area is still rich in colonial history and colour.

❽ Hero of Waterloo
Lying beneath this historic pub is a tunnel originally used for smuggling.

❿ ★ Sydney Observatory
The first European structure on this prominent site was a windmill. The present museum holds some of the earliest astronomical instruments brought to Australia.

❾ Garrison Church
Columns in this church are decorated with the insignia of British troops stationed here until 1870. Australia's first prime minister was educated next door.

LOWE

Hero of Waterloo ↑

WATSON ROAD
ARGYLE STREET
TRINITY AVENUE
UPPER FORT STREET
BRADFIELD HIGHWAY
CUMBERLAND STREET
GLOUCESTE
HIGHWAY
PLAYFA
HARRINGTON STREET
ARGYLE STREE
GEORGE STREET

Argyle Cut

Suez Canal

❷ ★ Museum of Contemporary Art
Australian and international art is displayed in a Classical building. A café housed in a modern extension offers superb views of the harbour.

Walkway along Circular Quay West foreshore

❺ The Rocks Discovery Museum
Key episodes in The Rocks' history are illustrated by this museum's collection of maritime images and other artifacts.

Locator Map
See Central Sydney map pp66–7

The Rocks Market is a hive of activity every weekend, offering an eclectic range of craft items and jewellery utilizing Australian icons from gum leaves to koalas *(see p137).*

❸ ★ Cadman's Cottage
John Cadman, government coxswain, resided in what was known as the Coxswain's Barracks with his family. His wife Elizabeth was also a significant figure, believed to be the first woman to vote in New South Wales, a right she insisted on.

The Overseas Passenger Terminal is where some of the world's luxury cruise liners berth during their stay in Sydney.

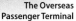

| 0 metres | | 100 |
| 0 yards | | 100 |

Key

— Suggested route

Old-fashioned Australian goods at the corner shop, Susannah Place

❶ Susannah Place

58–64 Gloucester St, The Rocks.
Map 1 B2. **Tel** (02) 9241 1893.
🚌 Sydney Explorer, Circular Quay routes from Elizabeth St. 🚆 Circular Quay, Wynyard. **Open** 2–5pm daily.
Closed Good Fri, 25 Dec. 🚫 ✅
🌐 sydneylivingmuseums.com.au

This terrace of four brick and sandstone houses dating back to 1844 has a rare history of continuous domestic occupancy from the 1840s through to 1990. It is now a museum examining the living conditions of its former inhabitants. Rather than re-creating a single period, the museum retains the renovations carried out by different tenants.

Built for Edward and Mary Riley, who arrived from Ireland with their niece Susannah in 1838, these houses have basement kitchens and backyard outhouses. Piped water and sewerage were probably added by the mid-1850s.

The terrace escaped the wholesale demolitions that occurred after the outbreak of bubonic plague in 1900, as well as later clearings of land to make way for the Sydney Harbour Bridge *(see pp84–5)* and the Cahill Expressway. In the 1970s it was saved once again when the Builders Labourers' Federation imposed a "green ban" on The Rocks, temporarily halting all redevelopment work which was destructive to cultural heritage.

❷ Museum of Contemporary Art

Circular Quay West, The Rocks. **Map** 1 B2. **Tel** (02) 9245 2400. 🚌 Sydney Explorer, Circular Quay routes from Elizabeth St. 🚆 Circular Quay. **Open** 10am–5pm daily (to 9pm Thu). **Closed** 25 Dec. ♿ ✅ 🌐 mca.com.au

When Sydney art collector John Power died in 1943, he left his entire collection and a financial bequest to the University of Sydney. In 1991 the collection, which by then included works by Hockney, Warhol, Lichtenstein and Christo was transferred to this 1950s Art Deco-style building at Circular Quay West. As well as showing its permanent collection, the museum hosts exhibitions by local and overseas artists. The MCA Store sells distinctive gifts by Australian designers.

❸ Cadman's Cottage

110 George St, The Rocks. **Map** 1 B2. 🚌 Circular Quay routes from Elizabeth St. 🚆 Circular Quay. **Closed** to the public.

Built in 1816 as barracks for the crews of the governor's boats, this sandstone cottage is Sydney's oldest surviving dwelling. Visitors can walk around the small, historic site, but cannot enter the building.

The cottage is named after John Cadman, a convict who was transported in 1798 for horse-stealing. By 1813, he was coxswain of a timber boat and later, coxswain of government craft. He was granted a full pardon and in 1827 he was made boat superintendent and moved to the four-room cottage that now bears his name.

Cadman married Elizabeth Mortimer in 1830, another ex-convict who was sentenced to seven years' transportation for the theft of one hairbrush. They lived in the cottage until 1845. Cadman's Cottage was built on the foreshore of Sydney Harbour. Now, as a result of successive land reclamations, it is set well back from the water's edge.

The Art Deco-style Museum of Contemporary Art, with the adjoining modern extension

❹ Sailors' Home

106 George St, The Rocks. **Map** 1 B2. 🚌 Sydney Explorer, Circular Quay routes from Elizabeth St. Ⓣ Circular Quay.

Built in 1864 as lodgings for visiting sailors, the first and second floors here were dormitories, but these were later divided into 56 cubicles or "cabins" which were arranged around open galleries and lit by four enormous skylights. At the time it was built, the Sailors' Home was a welcome alternative to the many seedy inns and brothels in the area, saving sailors from the perils of "crimping". "Crimps" would tempt newly arrived men into bars providing much sought-after entertainment. While drunk, the sailors would be sold on to departing ships, waking miles out at sea and returning home in debt.

Sailors used the home until 1980. It now houses the private Billich Gallery, with works by surreal artist Charles Billich.

❺ The Rocks Discovery Museum

Kendall Lane, The Rocks. **Map** 1 B2. **Tel** (02) 9240 8680. 🚌 Sydney Explorer, Circular Quay routes from Elizabeth St. Ⓣ Circular Quay. **Open** 10am–5pm daily. **Closed** Good Fri, 25 Dec. ♿ 🖥 therocks.com.au

This fascinating museum, in a restored 1850s sandstone coach house, is home to a unique collection of archaeological artifacts and images that detail the story of The Rocks from the pre-European days to the present. There are four permanent exhibitions which are highly interactive, making use of touch screens and audio and visual technology. Some of the artifacts were found at the archaeological site on Cumberland Street.

The Rocks Discovery Museum has been developed in close consultation with local Aboriginal groups, so that their story of the area is properly told.

Terrace restaurants at Campbell's Storehouses on the waterfront

❻ Campbell's Storehouses

7–27 Circular Quay West, The Rocks. **Map** 1 B2. 🚌 Sydney Explorer, Circular Quay routes from Elizabeth St. Ⓣ Circular Quay. ♿

Robert Campbell, a prominent Scottish merchant in the early days of Sydney, purchased this land on Sydney Cove in 1799. In 1802 he began constructing a private wharf and storehouses in which to house the tea, sugar, spirits and cloth he imported from India. Campbell was the only merchant operating in Australia who managed to infiltrate the monopoly held by the British East India Company. The first five sandstone bays were built between 1839 and 1844. A further seven bays were built between 1854 and 1861. The full row of storehouses were finally completed in 1890, including a brick upper storey. Part of the old sea wall and 11 of the original stores are still standing. The pulleys that were used to raise cargo from the wharf can be seen near the top of the preserved buildings.

The area fell into disrepair during the first half of the 20th century. However, in the 1970s the Sydney Cove Redevelopment Authority finalized plans and began renovating the site. Today the bond stores contain a range of fine restaurants catering to all tastes, from contemporary Australian to Chinese and Italian. Their virtually unimpeded views across Circular Quay towards the Sydney Opera House (see pp88–9) and Sydney Harbour Bridge (see pp84–5) make these

outdoor eating establishments very popular with local business people and tourists alike.

❼ Sydney Harbour Bridge

See pp84–5.

The historic Hero of Waterloo Inn, built in the 19th century

❽ Hero of Waterloo

81 Lower Fort St, The Rocks. **Map** 1 A2. **Tel** (02) 9252 4553. 🚌 311. **Open** 10am–11:30pm Mon–Wed, 10am–midnight Thu–Sat, 10am–10pm Sun. **Closed** Good Fri, 25 Dec. ♿ limited.

This picturesque old inn is especially welcoming in the winter with its log fires.

Built in 1844, this was a favourite drinking place for the nearby garrison's soldiers. Some sea captains were said to use the hotel to recruit. Patrons who drank too much were pushed into the cellars via a trapdoor. Tunnels then led to the wharves and on to waiting ships.

❼ Sydney Harbour Bridge

Completed in 1932, the construction of the Sydney Harbour Bridge was an economic feat, given the depressed times, as well as an engineering triumph. Prior to this, the only links between the city centre on the south side of the harbour and the residential north side were by ferry or a circuitous 20-km (12-mile) road route which involved five bridge crossings. The single-span arch bridge, colloquially known as the "Coathanger", took eight years to build, including the railway line. The bridge was manufactured in sections on the latter-day Luna Park site. Loans for the total cost of approximately 6.25 million old Australian pounds were eventually paid off in 1988.

The 1932 Opening
The ceremony was disrupted when zealous royalist Francis de Groot rode forward and cut the ribbon, in honour, he claimed, of King and Empire.

The deck, 59 m (194 ft) above sea level, was built from the centre.

The arch spans 503 m (1,650 ft) and supports the weight of the bridge deck.

City Centre

Harbour Bridge Pylon Lookout

Building the foundations

Beginning the arch

Building the Bridge
Planted in solid sandstone, the foundations are 12 m (39 ft) deep. The arch was built in halves with steel cable restraints initially supporting each side. Once the two halves met, work began on the deck.

Joining the arch

Deck under construction

Anchoring tunnels are 36 m (118 ft) long and dug into rock at each end.

Support cables were slackened over a 12-day period, enabling the two halves to join.

Temporary attachment plate

The Bridge Design
The steel arch of the bridge supports the deck, with hinges at either end bearing the bridge's full weight and spreading the load to the foundations. The hinges allow the structure to move as the steel expands and contracts in response to wind and extreme temperatures.

BridgeClimb

Thousands of people have enjoyed the spectacular bridge-top views after a 3.5-hour guided tour up ladders, catwalks and finally the upper arch of the bridge. A 2.5-hour "Express Climb" is also available.

Over 150,000 vehicles cross the bridge each day, about 15 times as many as in 1932.

Bridge Workers

The bridge was built by 1,400 workers, 16 of whom were killed in accidents during construction.

North Shore

Maintenance

Painting the bridge has become a metaphor for an endless task. Approximately 30,000 litres (6,593 gal) of paint are required for each coat, enough to cover an area equivalent to 60 soccer pitches.

The vertical hangers support the slanting crossbeams which, in turn, carry the deck.

Father of the Bridge

Chief engineer Dr John Bradfield shakes the hand of the driver of the first train to cross the bridge. Over a 20-year period, Bradfield supervised all aspects of the bridge's design and construction. At the opening ceremony, the highway linking the harbour's south side and northern suburbs was named in his honour.

Paying the Toll

The initial toll of sixpence helped pay off the construction loan. The toll is now collected electronically and is used for maintenance and to pay for the 1992 Sydney Harbour Tunnel.

A Flagpole on the Mudflats

The modest flagpole on Loftus Street, near Customs House, flies a flag, the Union Jack, on the spot where Australia's first ceremonial flag-raising took place. On 26 January 1788, Captain Arthur Phillip hoisted the flag to declare the foundation of the colony. A toast to the king was drunk and a musket volley fired. On this date each year, the country marks Australia Day with a national holiday *(see p45)*. In 1788, the flagpole was on the edge of mudflats on Sydney Cove. Today, due to land reclamations, it is set back from the water's edge.

The Founding of Australia by Algernon Talmage

❾ Garrison Church

Cnr Argyle & Lower Fort sts, Millers Point. **Map** 1 A2. **Tel** (02) 9247 1071. 📷 311. **Open** 9am–6pm daily. 🔼 Sun: 9:30am, 4pm. ♿ **W** churchillanglican.com

Officially named the Holy Trinity Church, this was the colony's first military church.

Henry Ginn designed the church and, in 1840, the foundation stone was laid. In 1855, it was enlarged to hold up to 600 people. Regimental plaques hanging along interior walls recall the church's military associations. A small cabinet displays Australian military and historical items.

East window, Garrison Church

Other features to look out for are the brilliantly coloured east window and the carved red cedar pulpit.

❿ Sydney Observatory

Observatory Hill, Watson Rd, The Rocks. **Map** 1 A2. **Tel** (02) 9921 3485. 📷 Sydney Explorer, 311. **Open** 10am–5pm daily. Night viewings call to book. **Closed** 25 Dec. ♿ **W** maas.museum/sydney-observatory

In 1982 this domed building, which had been a centre for astronomical observation and research for almost 125 years, became the city's astronomy museum. It has interactive displays and games, along with night sky viewings; it is essential to book for these.

The building began life in the 1850s as a time-ball tower. At 1pm daily, the ball on top of the tower dropped to signal the correct time. At the same time, a cannon was fired at Fort Denison. This custom continues today *(see p112)*.

During the 1880s Sydney Observatory became known around the world when some of the first astronomical photographs of the southern sky were taken here. From 1890 to 1962 the observatory mapped some 750,000 stars as part of an international project that resulted in an atlas of the entire night sky.

⓫ National Trust Centre

Observatory Hill, Watson Rd, The Rocks. **Map** 1 A3. **Tel** (02) 9258 0123. 📷 Sydney Explorer, 311. **Open** 9am–5pm Tue–Fri. Gallery: **Open** 11am–5pm Tue–Sun. **Closed** pub hols. ♿ 📷 🖥 **W** nationaltrust. org.au

The buildings that form the headquarters of the National Trust of Australia, date from 1815, when Governor Macquarie chose the site for a military hospital. Today they house a café, a National Trust shop and the S H Ervin Gallery, with changing exhibitions throughout the year, designed to explore the richness and diversity in Australian art.

⓬ St Philip's Church

3 York St (enter from Jamison St). **Map** 1 A3. **Tel** (02) 9247 1071. 📷 311. **Open** 9am–5pm Mon–Fri. **Closed** 26 Jan. 📷 Phone first. 🔼 Sun: 8:30am, 10:15am (children's), 6pm. **W** churchillanglican.com

The square tower of this Victorian Gothic church dwarfed by modern edifices was a local landmark when it was first built.

The original 1793 church burned down and was replaced in 1810. Construction of the current building, designed by Edmund Blacket, began in 1848. Work was disrupted in 1851, when the stonemasons left for the gold fields, but by 1856 the church was finally completed.

A peal of bells was donated in 1888 to mark Sydney's centenary, and they still announce the services each Sunday.

Interior and pipe organ of St Philip's Church

⑬ Macquarie Place

Map 1 B3. 🚌 Circular Quay routes from Elizabeth St.

Governor Macquarie created this park in 1810 on what was once the vegetable garden of the first Government House. The sandstone obelisk, designed by Francis Greenway *(see p177)*, was erected in 1818 to mark the starting point for all roads in the colony. The gas lamps recall the fact that this was also the site of the city's first street lamp in 1826.

Also in this area are the remains of the bow anchor and cannon from HMS *Sirius*, flagship of the First Fleet. The statue of Thomas Mort, a 19th-century industrialist, is today a marshalling place for somewhat kamikaze bicycle couriers.

⑭ Customs House

31 Alfred St, Circular Quay. **Map** 1 B3. **Tel** (02) 9242 8551. 🚌 Circular Quay routes from Elizabeth St, Sydney Explorer. **Open** 8am–midnight Mon–Fri, 10am–midnight Sat, 11am–5pm Sun. **Closed** Good Fri, 25 Dec. ♿ 🅿️ ✏️ 🆆 **sydneycustomshouse.com.au**

Colonial architect James Barnet designed this 1885 sandstone Classical Revival building on the same site as a previous Customs House. Its recalls the bygone days when trading ships berthed at Circular Quay. The building stands near the mouth of Tank Stream, the fledgling colony's freshwater supply. Among its many fine features are tall veranda columns of polished granite, a finely sculpted coat of arms and a clock face, added in 1897, which features a pair of tridents and dolphins.

Detail from Customs House

A complete refurbishment was completed in 2005. Facilities include a City Library with a reading room and exhibition space, and an open lounge area with an international newspaper and magazine salon, Internet access and bar. On the roof, Café Sydney offers great views.

Montage of criminal "mug shots", Justice and Police Museum

⑮ Justice and Police Museum

Cnr Albert & Phillip sts. **Map** 1 C3. **Tel** (02) 9252 1144. 🚌 Circular Quay routes from Elizabeth St. 🚆 Circular Quay, Martin Pl. **Open** 10am–5pm Sat & Sun (open daily in Jan & NSW school hols). **Closed** Good Fri, 25 Dec. 🎫 📷 ♿ limited. 🆆 **sydneyliving museums.com.au**

The buildings housing this museum originally comprised the Water Police Court, designed by Edmund Blacket in 1856, the Water Police Station, designed by Alexander Dawson in 1858, and the Police Court, designed by James Barnet in 1885. Here the rough-and-tumble underworld of quayside crime, from the petty to the violent, was dealt swift and, at times, harsh justice. The museum exhibits illustrate that turbulent period, as they re-create legal and criminal history.

Formalities of the late-Victorian legal proceedings can be easily imagined in the fully restored courtroom. Menacing implements from knuckledusters to bludgeons are displayed as the macabre relics of notorious crimes. Other interesting aspects of policing, criminality and the legal system are highlighted in special changing exhibitions. The museum powerfully evokes the realities of Australian policing and justice.

⑯ Writers' Walk

Circular Quay. **Map** 1 C2. 🚌 Circular Quay routes from Elizabeth St. 🚆 Circular Quay.

This series of plaques is set in the pavement at regular intervals between East and West Circular Quay. It gives the visitor the chance to ponder the observations of famous Australian writers, both past and present, on their home country, as well as the musings of some noted literary visitors.

Each plaque is dedicated to a particular writer, consisting of a personal quotation and a brief biographical note. Australian writers in the series include the novelists Miles Franklin and Peter Carey, poets Oodgeroo Noonuccal and Judith Wright *(see pp38–9)*, humorists Barry Humphries and Clive James, and the influential feminist writer Germaine Greer. Among the international writers included who have visited Sydney are Mark Twain, Charles Darwin and Joseph Conrad.

Strolling along a section of the Writers' Walk at Circular Quay

⑰ Sydney Opera House

No other building on earth looks like the Sydney Opera House. Popularly known as the "Opera House", it is, in fact, a complex of theatres and halls linked beneath its famous shells. Its birth was long and complicated. Many of the construction problems had not been faced before, resulting in an architectural adventure which lasted 14 years. Today it is Australia's most popular tourist attraction, as well as one of the world's busiest performing arts centres, hosting nearly 2,000 performances for more than 1.4 million attendees every year. The forecourt is a spectacular outdoor performance space in its own right, often hosting festivals and concerts.

★ Joan Sutherland Theatre
The venue's second-largest theatre is home to Opera Australia, as well as the Australian Ballet.

Detail of Possum Dreaming *(1988)*
The mural in the Joan Sutherland Theatre foyer is by Michael Tjakamarra Nelson, an artist from the central Australian desert.

Opera House Walkway
Extensive public walkways around the building offer the visitor views from many different vantage points.

KEY

① **The Joan Sutherland Theatre's** ceiling and walls are painted black to focus attention on the stage.

② **The Monumental Steps** and forecourt are used for outdoor performances.

③ **The Playhouse**, seating almost 400, is ideal for intimate productions, but is also able to present plays with larger casts.

Northern Foyers
The Utzon Room and the large northern foyers of the Opera Theatre and Concert Hall have spectacular views over the harbour and can be hired for conferences, lunches, parties and weddings.

★ **Concert Hall**
This is the largest hall, with seating for 2,690. Its high vaulted ceiling, white birch timber and brush box panelling provide a majestic setting for performances including music concerts, talks and comedy events.

VISITORS' CHECKLIST

Practical Information
Bennelong Point. **Map** 1 C2.
Tel (02) 9250 7111.
sydneyoperahouse.com
Box office: (02) 9250 7777.
Open tours and performances.
Closed Good Fri, 25 Dec.
limited (02) 9250 7777.
9am–5pm, call (02) 9250 7250; for disabled visitors: noon daily.
TTY for hearing impaired 133 677, then ask for 9250 7250.

Transport
Sydney Explorer, Circular Quay routes from Elizabeth St.
Circular Quay.

★ **The Roofs**
Although apocryphal, the theory that Jørn Utzon's arched roof design came to him while peeling an orange is enchanting. The highest point is 67 m (221 ft) above sea level.

Detail of Utzon's Tapestry *(2004)*
Jørn Utzon's original design for this Gobelin-style tapestry, which hangs floor to ceiling in the Utzon Room, was inspired by the music of Carl Philipp Emanuel Bach.

CITY CENTRE AND DARLING HARBOUR

George Street, Australia's first thoroughfare, was originally lined with mud and wattle huts, but following the gold rush shops and banks came to dominate the area. The removal of buses and traffic and construction of a light rail line to run through a pedestrianized George Street is revitalizing the city's heart. Hyde Park, on the edge of the city centre, was once a racecourse.

Today it is a peaceful oasis. The country's industrial age began in Darling Harbour in 1815 with the opening of a steam mill, but later the area became rundown. In the 1980s, it was the site of low-rise, tourism-focused redevelopment, followed by another wave of redevelopment from 2016, including new entertainment facilities, high-rises and hotels, and pedestrian walkways.

Sights at a Glance

Museums and Galleries
7 Museum of Sydney
10 Australian Museum pp98–9
15 Australian National Maritime Museum pp104–5
18 Powerhouse Museum pp106–7

Cathedrals and Synagogues
8 St Mary's Cathedral
11 Great Synagogue
13 St Andrew's Cathedral

Parks and Gardens
9 Hyde Park
17 Chinese Garden

Historic Streets and Buildings
1 Queen Victoria Building
3 Strand Arcade
4 Martin Place
5 Sydney Tower p95
6 Lands Department Building
12 Sydney Town Hall
20 Chinatown

Entertainment
2 State Theatre
14 Sea Life Sydney Aquarium, Wild Life Sydney Zoo and Madame Tussaud's
16 King Street Wharf

Markets
19 Paddy's Markets

See also Street Finder maps 1, 3 and 4

0 metres 250
0 yards 250

◄ Bird sculptures at the Harbourside Shopping Centre in Darling Harbour

For keys to symbols see back flap

Street-by-Street: City Centre

Sydney is a city in transformation. Vibrant by day, traditionally the streets would empty when the workers and shoppers retreated to the suburbs at night. A booming population and the growing appeal of city living is driving a renaissance in the city centre, however, with an emerging night scene that revolves around wine bars, restaurants, theatres and cultural events. Rapid development of high-rise apartments has been accompanied by the biggest infrastructure projects in the city in a century. The removal of buses and cars from George Street and the introduction of light-rail modern trams running its length by 2019 will enable the pedestrianization of the city's major boulevard.

❶ ★ Queen Victoria Building
Taking up an entire city block, this 1898 former produce market was lovingly restored in 1986 and is now a shopping mall.

❷ State Theatre
A gem from the golden age of movies, this 1929 cinema was once hailed as "the Empire's greatest theatre". It now hosts live concerts too.

The Queen Victoria Statue was found after a worldwide search in 1983 ended in a small Irish village. It had lain forgotten and neglected since being removed from the front of the Irish Parliament in 1947.

To Sydney
Town Hall

0 metres   100
0 yards   100

Key

— Suggested route

Marble Bar was once a landmark bar in the 1893 Tattersalls hotel. It was re-erected in the basement of the Sydney Hilton in 1973, and again in 2005 when the hotel was rebuilt.

❸ Strand Arcade
A reminder of the late 19th century Victorian era when Sydney was famed as a city of elegant shopping arcades, this faithfully restored example is said to have been the finest of them all.

Locator Map
See Central Sydney map pp66–7

MLC Centre

❹ ★ Martin Place
Martin Place's 1929 Art Deco Cenotaph is the site of annual Anzac Day war remembrance services including the solemn dawn service.

Theatre Royal

Westfield Sydney, one of the city's main shopping centres, features the David Jones and Myer department stores (*see p137*), speciality shops and a large food court.

Hyde Park's northern end

❺ ★ Sydney Tower
The tower tops the city skyline, giving a bird's eye view of the whole of Sydney. It rises 309 m (1,000 ft) above the ground and can be seen from as far away as the Blue Mountains.

❶ Queen Victoria Building

455 George St. **Map** 1 B5. **Tel** (02) 9264 9209. 🚇 Town Hall. **Open** 9am–6pm Mon–Wed, 9am–9pm Thu, 9am–6pm Fri & Sat, 11am–5pm Sun; 11am–5pm public hols. ♿ *See Shopping pp136–41.* 🌐 qvb.com.au

French designer Pierre Cardin called the Queen Victoria Building "the most beautiful shopping centre in the world". Yet this ornate Romanesque building, better known as the QVB, began life as the Sydney produce market. Completed to the design of City Architect George McRae in 1898, the dominant features are the central copper dome and the glass roof which lets in a flood of natural light.

Ornately decorated Gothic foyer of the State Theatre

The market closed at the end of World War I. By the 1950s, the building was threatened with demolition.

Refurbished at a cost of over A\$75 million, the QVB reopened in 1986 as a shopping gallery with more than 190 shops. A wishing well incorporates a stone from Blarney Castle, a sculpture of Islay, Queen Victoria's dog and a statue of the queen herself.

Inside the QVB, suspended from the ceiling, is the Royal Clock. Designed in 1982 by Neil Glasser, it features part of Balmoral Castle above a copy of the four dials of Big Ben. Every hour, a fanfare is played with a parade depicting various English monarchs.

❷ State Theatre

49 Market St. **Map** 1 B5. **Tel** (02) 9373 6655. 🚇 Town Hall, Martin Place. Box office: **Open** 9am–5:30pm Mon–Fri. **Closed** Good Fri, 25 Dec. ♿ 🎭 (book ahead). 🌐 statetheatre.com.au

When it opened in 1929, this cinema was hailed as the finest that local craftsmanship could achieve. The State Theatre is one of the best

Roof detail, Queen Victoria Building

examples of ornate period cinemas in Australia. Its Baroque style is evident in the foyer, with its high ceiling, mosaic floor, marble columns and statues. The auditorium is lit by a 20,000-piece chandelier. The beautiful Wurlitzer organ (under repair) rises from below stage before performances. The theatre is now one of the city's special events venues.

❸ Strand Arcade

412–414 George St. **Map** 1 B5. **Tel** (02) 9265 6800. 🚇 Wyatt Place, Wynyard. **Open** 9am–5:30pm Mon–Wed & Fri, 9am–9pm Thu, 9am–8pm Sat, 11am–4pm Sun. **Closed** 25, 26 Dec, some public hols. ♿ *See Shopping pp136–41.* 🌐 strandarcade.com.au

Victorian Sydney was a city of grand shopping arcades. The Strand, joining George and Pitt streets and designed by English

Pitt Street entrance to the majestic Strand Arcade

architect John Spencer, was the finest of all. Opened in April 1892, it was lit by natural light pouring through the glass roof and the chandeliers, each carrying 50 jets of gas as well as 50 lamps.

After a fire in 1976, the building was restored to its original Victorian splendour. Now visitors can enjoy its shopping and beautiful coffee shops.

❹ Martin Place

Map 1 B4. 🚌 George St & Elizabeth St routes. 🚇 Martin Place.

This plaza was opened in 1891 and made a traffic-free precinct in 1971. It is busiest at lunchtime as city workers enjoy their sandwiches while watching free entertainment in the amphitheatre near Castlereagh Street.

Every Anzac Day *(see p46)* the focus moves to the Cenotaph at the George Street end. Past and present service personnel attend a dawn service and wreath-laying ceremony, followed by a march along Elizabeth Street. The shrine, by Bertram MacKennal, was unveiled in 1929.

On the southern side of the Cenotaph is the façade of the Renaissance-style General Post Office, considered to be the finest building by James Barnet, colonial architect in 1866.

A stainless steel sculpture of upended cubes, the Dobell Memorial Sculpture, is a tribute to Australian artist William Dobell, created by Bert Flugelman in 1979.

🟑 Sydney Tower

With a design capable of withstanding earthquakes and extreme wind, Sydney Tower was conceived as part of the original 1970s Centrepoint shopping centre, but was not completed until 1981. About one million people per year admire the stunning views. On the podium level, visitors enjoy a multimedia journey around Australia in the 4D Cinema Experience. Those with a head for heights can also venture outside the tower on a SKYWALK tour.

VISITORS' CHECKLIST

Practical Information
100 Market St. **Map** 1 B5. **Tel** 1800 258 693. **Open** May–Sep: 9am–9:30pm; Oct–Apr: 9am–10pm
Last entry: 1 hr before closing.
🚻 ♿ 🚫 🚻 📷
w sydneytowereye.com.au

Transport
🚌 Sydney Explorer, all city routes.
🚌 Darling Harbour. 🚉 St James, Martin Place, Town Hall.

Sydney Tower Eye Observation Deck
Views from Level 4 stretch north to Pittwater, Botany Bay to the south, west to the Blue Mountains, and along the harbour out to the open sea.

The 30-m (98-ft) spire completes the total 309 m (1,000 ft) of the tower's height.

The water tank holds 162,000 l (35,500 gal) and acts as an enormous stabilizer on very windy days.

Skywalk

Level 4: Sydney Tower Eye

Level 3: Private event space

Level 2: Buffet restaurant

Level 1: A la carte restaurant

The turret's nine levels, with room to hold almost 1,000 people at a time, include two revolving restaurants, a coffee shop and the Observation Level.

The windows comprise three layers. The outer has a gold dust coating. The frame design prevents panes falling outwards.

The 56 cables weigh seven tonnes each. If laid end to end, they would reach from New Zealand to Sydney.

The shaft is designed to withstand wind speeds expected only once in 500 years, and earthquakes.

The stairs are two separate, fireproofed emergency escape routes with 1,504 steps.

Double-decker lifts can carry up to 2,000 people per hour. At full speed, a lift takes only 40 seconds to ascend the 76 floors to the Observation Level.

The 4D Cinema Experience is a virtual reality ride across Australia, with a 180° cinema, 3D technology and special effects.

Construction of Turret
The nine turret levels were erected on the roof of the base building, then hoisted up the shaft using hydraulic jacks.

SKYWALK
Visitors can take a 45-minute tour on a platform around the turret's exterior.

❻ Lands Department Building

23 Bridge St. **Map** 1 B3. 🚌 325, George St routes. **Open** one day a year. ♿
🌐 sydneylivingmuseums.com.au

Designed by colonial architect James Barnet, this three-storey Classical Revival edifice dates from 1877–90. Pyrmont sandstone was used for the exterior, as it was for the GPO building.

All the decisions about the subdivision of much of rural eastern Australia were made in the offices within. Statues of explorers and legislators who "promoted settlement" fill 23 of the façade's 48 niches; the remainder are still empty. The luminaries include the explorers Hovell and Hume, Sir Thomas Mitchell, Blaxland, Lawson and Wentworth, Ludwig Leichhardt, Bass, Matthew Flinders and botanist Sir Joseph Banks.

The imposing sandstone edifice of the Lands Department Building

❼ Museum of Sydney

Cnr Phillip & Bridge sts. **Map** 1 B3. **Tel** (02) 9251 5988. 🚌 Circular Quay routes. 🚢 Circular Quay, Martin Pl. **Open** 10am–5pm daily. **Closed** Good Fri, 25 Dec. 🅿️ 🍴 ♿ 🛍️ 🌐 sydneylivingmuseums.com.au/museum-of-sydney

Situated at the base of Governor Phillip Tower, the Museum of Sydney is a modern museum built on a historic site and details the history of Sydney from 1788 to the present. Its many attractions include the archaeological remains of the colony's first Government House, as well as exhibits that explore the evolution of Sydney over two centuries and honour the original Cadigal people.

Indigenous Peoples

This gallery explores the culture, history, continuity and place of Sydney's original inhabitants. The collectors' chests hold everyday items like flint and ochre. In the square outside the complex, the *Edge of the Trees* sculptural installation symbolizes the first contact between the Aborigines and Europeans. Inscribed in the wood are signatures of First Fleeters and the names of botanical species.

History of Sydney

Outside the museum, a paving pattern outlines the site of the first Government House. The original foundations, below street level, can be seen through a window. A segment of wall has now been reconstructed using the original sandstone.

The Colony display on Level 1 focuses on Sydney during the critical decade of the 1840s: convict transportation ended, the town officially became a city and then suffered economic depression. On Level 2, 20th-century Sydney is explored against a panorama of images.

❽ St Mary's Cathedral

St Marys Rd. **Map** 1 C5. **Tel** (02) 9220 0400. 🚌 Elizabeth St routes. 🚢 St James, Martin Pl. **Open** 6:30am–6pm Mon–Fri, 6:30am–7pm Sat–Sun. Crypt: **Open** 10am–4pm Mon–Fri (adm). ♿ with advance notice. 📷 by arrangement. 🌐 stmaryscathedral.org.au

Although Catholics arrived with the First Fleet, Mass was initially prohibited as it was feared priests would provoke civil strife among the colony's Irish Catholics. It was not until 1820 that the first Catholic priests were officially appointed and services were permitted. In 1821, Governor Macquarie laid the foundation stone for St Mary's Chapel on the first land granted to the Catholic Church in Australia.

The initial section of this Gothic Revival-style cathedral was opened in 1882 and completed in 1928, but without the twin southern spires originally proposed by the architect William Wardell. By the entrance are statues of Australia's first cardinal, Moran, and Archbishop Kelly, who laid the stone for the final stage in 1913. They were sculpted by Bertram MacKennal, also responsible for the Martin Place Cenotaph (*see p93*). The crypt's terrazzo mosaic floor took 15 years to complete.

The stunning gold-coloured sandstone interior of St Mary's Cathedral

❾ Hyde Park

Map 1 B5. Elizabeth St routes.

Hyde Park was named after its London equivalent by Governor Macquarie in 1810. The fence around the park marked the outskirts of the township. Once an exercise field for garrison troops, it later incorporated a racecourse and a cricket pitch. Though much smaller today than the original park, it is still a quiet haven in the middle of the bustling city centre, with many notable features.

The 30-m (98-ft) high Art Deco Anzac Memorial commemorates Australians who have died for their country. Opened in 1934 it now includes a military exhibition downstairs.

Sandringham Garden, filled with mauve wisteria, is a memorial to kings George V and George VI, opened by Queen Elizabeth II in 1954.

The bronze and granite Archibald Fountain commemorates the French and Australian World War I alliance. It was completed by François Sicard in 1932 and donated by J F Archibald, one of the founders of the popular *Bulletin* literary magazine.

The *Emden* Gun, on the corner of College and Liverpool Streets, commemorates a World War I naval action. HMAS *Sydney* destroyed the German raider *Emden* off the Cocos Islands on 9 November 1914, and 180 crew members were taken prisoner.

Candelabra in the Great Synagogue

❿ Australian Museum

See pp98–9.

⓫ Great Synagogue

187 Elizabeth St, entrance at 166 Castlereagh St. **Map** 1 B5. **Tel** (02) 9267 2477. Elizabeth St routes. St James. **Open** services & tours only. by arrangement. **Closed** public and Jewish hols. noon Thu, 1st & 3rd Tue. **greatsynagogue.org.au**

The longest established Jewish Orthodox congregation in Australia assembles in this synagogue (consecrated in 1878). Although Jews had arrived with the First Fleet, worship did not commence until the 1820s. With its carved porch columns and wrought-iron gates, the synagogue is perhaps the finest work of Thomas Rowe, architect of Sydney Hospital (*see p117*). The interior features a stunning panelled ceiling.

⓬ Sydney Town Hall

483 George St. **Map** 4 E2. **Tel** (02) 9265 9333. Town Hall. **Open** 8am–6pm Mon–Fri. **Closed** pub hols. **sydneytownhall.com.au**

The steps of Sydney Town Hall have been a favourite meeting place since it opened in 1869. Walled burial grounds originally covered the site. It is a fine example of High

Grand Organ in the 19th-century Centennial Hall

Victorian architecture. The original architect, J H Wilson, died during its construction, as did several of the architects who followed. The vestibule, an elegant salon with stained glass and a crystal chandelier, is the work of Albert Bond. The clock tower was completed by the Bradbridge brothers in 1884. From 1888–9, other architects designed Centennial Hall, with its imposing 19th-century Grand Organ with over 8,500 pipes.

Some people believe this became Sydney's finest building by accident, as each architect strove to outdo similar buildings in Manchester and Liverpool. Today, it makes a good venue for concerts.

⓭ St Andrew's Cathedral

Sydney Square, cnr George & Bathurst sts. **Map** 4 E3. **Tel** (02) 9265 1661. Town Hall. **Open** contact the cathedral for opening times and tours. **sydneycathedral.com**

While the foundation stone for the country's oldest cathedral was laid in 1819, the building was not consecrated until 1868. The Gothic Revival design, by Edmund Blacket, was inspired by York Minster in England. Inside are memorials to Sydney pioneers, a 1539 Bible and beads made from olive seeds collected in the Holy Land.

The southern wall includes stones from London's St Paul's Cathedral, Westminster Abbey and the House of Lords.

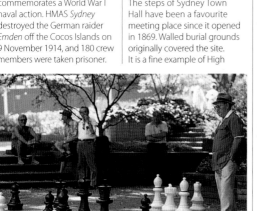

Game in progress on the giant chessboard in Hyde Park

⑩ Australian Museum

The Australian Museum, the nation's leading natural science museum, was founded in 1827 and was the first established museum of Australian natural history. The main building, an impressive sandstone structure with a marble staircase, faces Hyde Park. Architect Mortimer Lewis was forced to resign his position when building costs began to far exceed the budget. Construction was completed in the 1860s by James Barnet. The collection provides a journey across Australia and the near Pacific, covering biology, and natural and cultural history. The museum's changing programme of events includes expert talks, workshops, "Dinosnore" sleepovers and behind-the-scenes looks at some of its 18 million objects.

Original Museum Entrance
The façade features massive Corinthian square pillars or piers.

Chapman Mineral Collection

Planet of Minerals
This section features a walk-through recreation of an underground mine with a display of gems and minerals.

Rhodochrosite   Cuprite

Crystal Hall Entrance
This glass entrance walkway on William Street, which appeared on the architect's original plan, opened in 2015.

Education Centre

★ First Australians
From dreaming to the struggle for self-determination and land rights, this exhibit tells the stories of Australia's first peoples.

Ground floor

Historic original entrance

Museum Guide

First Australians and the Long Gallery are on the ground floor. Mineral and rock exhibits are on Level 1. Birds and Insects can be found on Level 2, along with Kidspace, Surviving Australia and Dinosaurs.

The Long Gallery, on the ground floor, provides insights into 100 famous Australians.

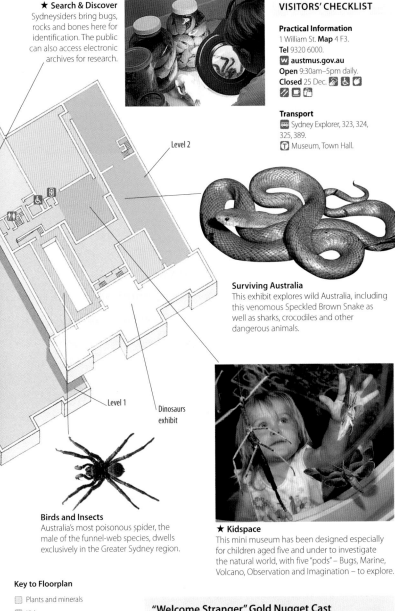

★ **Search & Discover**
Sydneysiders bring bugs, rocks and bones here for identification. The public can also access electronic archives for research.

Level 2

Level 1

Dinosaurs exhibit

Surviving Australia
This exhibit explores wild Australia, including this venomous Speckled Brown Snake as well as sharks, crocodiles and other dangerous animals.

Birds and Insects
Australia's most poisonous spider, the male of the funnel-web species, dwells exclusively in the Greater Sydney region.

★ **Kidspace**
This mini museum has been designed especially for children aged five and under to investigate the natural world, with five "pods" – Bugs, Marine, Volcano, Observation and Imagination – to explore.

Key to Floorplan

- Plants and minerals
- Kidspace
- Birds and insects
- First Australians
- The Long Gallery
- Search & Discover
- Dinosaurs exhibition
- Surviving Australia
- Temporary exhibition space
- Non-exhibition space

"Welcome Stranger" Gold Nugget Cast

In 1869, the largest gold nugget ever found in Australia was discovered in Victoria. It weighed 71.06 kg (156 lb). The museum holds a cast of the original in a display examining the impact of the gold rush, when the Australian population doubled in ten years.

◄—— 67.5 cm (26 1/2 in) wide ——►

Street-by-Street: Darling Harbour

Darling Harbour was New South Wales' bicentennial gift to itself. The original 1988 urban redevelopment transformed what was once a busy industrial centre and international shipping terminal catering for the developing local wool, grain, timber and coal trades into a low-rise tourism and entertainment precinct, complete with the Australian National Maritime Museum and Sydney Aquarium. In 2013, a $3-billion reinvention of the area commenced, combining stunning high-rise architecture with innovative, pedestrian-friendly walkways and open spaces at ground level. The first landmark building, the sprawling International Convention Centre (ICC) opened in December 2016, followed by luxury hotels, residential towers and new shopping facilities.

Harbourside offers restaurants and cafés with superb views over the water to the city skyline. There is also a wide range of speciality shops, selling unusual gifts, souvenirs and other items.

ICC Sydney is a world-class convention, exhibition and entertainment precinct including an 8,000-seat theatre, all housed in a strikingly modern glass-rendered complex.

The Tidal Cascades sunken fountain was designed by Robert Woodward, also responsible for the El Alamein Fountain (see p124). The double spiral of water and paths replicates the patterns of the cockle shells once plentiful on the rocks at the water's edge.

Chinese Garden of Friendship ↗

The Chinese Garden of Friendship is a haven of peace and tranquillity in the heart of Sydney. Its landscaping, with winding pathways, waterfalls, lakes and pavilions, offers an insight into the rich culture of China.

Pyrmont Bridge opened in 1902 to service the busy harbour. It is the world's oldest swingspan bridge and opens for vessels up to 14 m (46 ft) tall. The monorail track above the walkway opens up for even taller boats.

Locator Map
See Central Sydney map pp66–7

Swingspan supports for Pyrmont Bridge are sunk 10 m (33 ft) below the harbour floor.

The Star Casino

⑮ ★ Australian National Maritime Museum
Compelling exhibits detail the nation's seafaring history before and after European settlement.

The HMAS *Vampire* destroyer (1959) is the largest in the vessel fleet moored outside the museum.

King Street Wharf →

Wharf for harbour cruise departures

⑭ ★ Sea Life Sydney Aquarium
The aquatic life of Sydney Harbour, the open ocean and the Great Barrier Reef is displayed in massive tanks which can be seen from underwater walkways.

Cockle Bay Wharf is vibrant and colourful, and is an exciting food and entertainment precinct.

```
0 metres        100
0 yards         100
```

Key

— Suggested route

⓮ Sea Life Sydney Aquarium, Wild Life Sydney Zoo & Madame Tussaud's

Aquarium Pier, Darling Harbour. **Map** 4 D2. **Tel** 1800 614 069. 🚌 Sydney Explorer. 🚢 Darling Harbour. Ⓣ Town Hall. 🚊 Paddy's Markets. Aquarium: **Open** 9:30am–7pm daily. Zoo: **Open** Apr–Sep: 9:30am–5pm; Oct–Mar: 9:30am–6pm. Madame Tussaud's: **Open** 9:30am–7pm. Last adm: 1 hr before closing. 🚻 📷 🅿 🖥
Ⓦ sydneyaquarium.com.au
Ⓦ sydneywildlifeworld.com.au
Ⓦ madametussauds.com.au

These fascinating attractions are adjacent to one another on Darling Harbour, with good discounts to be had by buying a multi-attraction ticket.

The aquarium's themed zones include more than 13,000 animals from 700 marine and freshwater species in 6 million litres of water. One of the highlights is Shark Valley's 100 m (110 yd) of acrylic underwater tunnels, allowing close views of sharks, stingrays and many types of fish. Other exhibits include a Great Barrier Reef display, dugongs and a raft ride through an exhibit simulating a rugged sub-Antarctic environment with a colony of king and gentoo penguins. Wild Life Sydney Zoo offers an authentic Australian wildlife experience, with more than 100 native species in 10 different habitats. Highlights include the koalas in Gum Tree Valley and the kangaroo walkabout.

Madame Tussaud's is another fun destination, with life-size wax figures of the famous and powerful, including sporting heroes, historical figures, actors, musicians and celebrities from Australia and around the world.

A tang fish in the Great Barrier Reef display

⓯ Australian National Maritime Museum

See pp104–5.

⓰ King Street Wharf

Lime St, between King and Erskine sts. **Map** 4 D1. 🚊 Paddy's Markets. 🚌 Sydney Explorer. 🚢 Darling Harbour. 🚻 ♿ 🖥 📷 🅿 Ⓦ kingstreet wharf.com.au

Merchant bankers and city workers from nearby offices flock to this harbourside venue, which combines a modern glass-and-steel shrine to café society with a working wharf. Passengers arrive and depart in style on harbour cruises, ferries and water taxis, or on foot from the city. The complex is flush with bars and restaurants that vie for the best views. Midway along the wharf is the Pumphouse boutique brewery, with more than 40 beers. This is not just a party circuit, there are also low-rise residential apartments set back from the water.

Night lights at King Street Wharf, Darling Harbour

⓱ Chinese Garden of Friendship

Darling Harbour. **Map** 4 D3. **Tel** (02) 9240 8888. 🚌 Sydney Explorer. Ⓣ Town Hall. 🚊 Paddy's Markets. 🚢 Darling Harbour. **Open** 9:30am–5:30pm daily (Apr–Sep: 5pm). **Closed** Good Fri, 25 Dec. 🅿 ♿ about 60 per cent.
Ⓦ chinesegarden.com.au

The Chinese Garden was built in 1984. It is a tranquil refuge from the city streets. The garden's design was a gift to Sydney from its Chinese sister city of Guangdong. The Dragon Wall, in the lower section beside the lake, has glazed carvings of two

Structuralist design of the Aquarium Pier, the home of Sea Life Sydney Aquarium, Wild Life Sydney Zoo and Madame Tussaud's

For hotels and restaurants in this area see pp482–3 and pp504–7

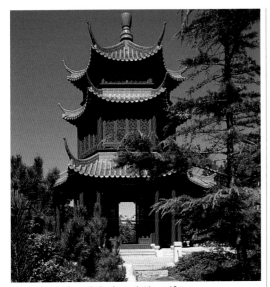

Twin Pavilion in the Chinese Garden, decorated with carved flowers

dragons, one representing Guangdong province and the other the state of New South Wales. The lake is covered with lotus and water lilies for much of the year and a rock monster guards against evil. On the other side of the lake is the Twin Pavilion. Waratahs (New South Wales' floral symbol) and flowering apricots are carved into its woodwork in Chinese style, and are also planted at its base.

A tea house at the top of the stairs in the Tea House Courtyard serves Chinese and Western light refreshments.

⑱ Powerhouse Museum

See pp106–7.

⑲ Paddy's Markets

Cnr Thomas & Hay sts, Haymarket. **Map** 4 D4. **Tel** 1300 361 589. Sydney Explorer. Town Hall. Paddy's Markets. **Open** 9am–6pm Wed–Sun & public hols Mon. **Closed** 25 Apr, 25 Dec. *See also Shopping pp136–41.* paddysmarkets.com.au

The Haymarket district, near Chinatown, is home to Paddy's Markets, Sydney's oldest and best-known market. It has been in this area, on a number of sites, since 1869 (with only one five-year absence). The origin of the name is uncertain, but is believed to have come from either the Chinese who originally supplied much of its produce, or the Irish who were among their main customers.

Once the shopping centre for the inner-city poor, Paddy's Markets is now an integral part of the Market City Shopping Centre, which includes cut-price fashion outlet stores, an Asian food court and a cinema complex. Yet despite this transformation, the familiar clamour, smells and chaotic bargain-hunting atmosphere of the original marketplace remain. Every weekend the market is filled with up to 800 stalls selling everything from fresh produce to electrical products, homewares, leather goods, and pets such as rabbits and puppies.

⑳ Chinatown

Dixon St Plaza, Sydney. **Map** 4 D4. George St routes. Town Hall. Paddy's Markets.

Originally concentrated around Dixon and Hay streets, Chinatown is now expanding to fill Sydney's Haymarket area, stretching as far west as Harris Street, south to Broadway and east to Castlereagh Street. It is home to a pulsating mix of restaurants, noodle bars, hawker food stalls and quirky gift shops that stay open until late. It is the preferred destination of many of the city's top chefs in search of a late-night meal long after their own kitchens have closed.

For years, Chinatown was little more than a run-down district at the edge of the city's produce markets, where many Chinese immigrants worked at traditional businesses. Today, Dixon Street, its main thoroughfare, features spruced-up public spaces with more trees, seating, lighting and artworks, while still retaining its character and heritage.

Chinatown is a distinctive area that hosts vibrant festivals and Friday night markets. There are many excellent greengrocers, herbalists and butchers' shops with wind-dried ducks hanging in their windows. Asian jewellers, clothes shops and confectioners fill the lively arcades.

Traditional archway entrance to Chinatown in Dixon Street

⑮ Australian National Maritime Museum

Bounded as it is by the sea, Australia has a history inextricably linked to maritime traditions. The museum displays material in a broad range of permanent and temporary thematic exhibits, many with interactive elements. As well as artifacts relating to the enduring Aboriginal maritime cultures, the exhibits survey the history of European exploratory voyages in the Pacific, the arrival of convict ships, successive waves of migration, water sports and recreation, and naval life. Historic vessels on show at the wharf include a flimsy Vietnamese refugee boat, sailing, fishing and pearling boats, a navy patrol boat and a World War II commando raider.

Museum Façade
The billowing steel roof design by Philip Cox suggests both the surging sea and the sails of a ship.

Eora Indigenous Gallery – First People
This gallery traces the seafaring traditions of both the Aboriginal peoples and the Torres Strait Islanders.

The Tasman Light was used in a Tasmanian lighthouse.

★ Navigators
This 1754 engraving of an East Indian sea creature is a European vision of the uncharted, exotic "great south".

The *Sirius* anchor is from a 1790 wreck off Norfolk Island.

Mini Mariners Play! adjoins the USA Gallery and is a dedicated, maritime-themed play space for children under five.

Main entrance (sea level)

The Navy exhibit examines naval life in war and peace, as well as the history of colonial navies.

The USA Gallery honours enduring maritime links between the US and Australia. American traders stopped off in Australia on their way to China.

Museum Guide

The Watermarks, Navy and Linked by the Sea: USA Gallery exhibits are located on the main entrance level (sea level). The Eora – First People, Navigators, Passengers and Commerce sections are found on the first level.

Key to Floorplan

- ☐ Navigators and Eora – First People
- ☐ Passengers
- ☐ Mini Mariners Play!
- ☐ Navy
- ☐ USA Gallery
- ☐ Temporary exhibitions
- ☐ Non-exhibition space

★ On the Waterfront
The museum's heritage fleet – including boats, seafarers' memorial anchors and sculptures, among many other vessels and items of note – takes pride of place on the waterfront.

VISITORS' CHECKLIST

Practical Information
2 Murray St, Darling Harbour.
Map 3 C2. **Tel** 9298 3777.
Open 9:30am–5pm daily
(Jan: to 6pm). **Closed** 25 Dec.
⬛ (special exhibitions, destroyer, submarine and *Endeavour*). ♿
⬛⬛⬛ⓦ anmm.gov.au

Transport
🚌 Sydney Explorer.
Ⓣ Town Hall. 🚌 Convention, Pyrmont Bay. 🚢 Pyrmont Bay Wharf.

Upper level

Gallery One

A replica of Captain *Cook's Endeavour* is based at the museum.

Lighthouse
Sailors were guided by this 1874 lighthouse for over a century. It was rebuilt complete with original kerosene lamp.

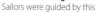

Action Stations
Experience the compelling history of the Royal Australian Navy by exploring the drama and danger of navy life in this interactive exhibition.

★ Vampire
The museum's largest vessel is the 1959 Royal Australian Navy destroyer, whose insignia is shown here. Tours of "The Bat" are accompanied by simulated battle action sounds.

HMAS *Onslow* (Oberon-class submarine)

VAMPIRE

AUDAMUS

The Wharf for Visiting Vessels has welcomed many ships, including a replica of the 17th-century Dutch East India Company flagship *Batavia*.

⑱ Powerhouse Museum

This former power station, completed in 1902 to provide power for Sydney's tramway system, was redesigned to cater for the needs of an interactive, hands-on museum. Revamped, the Powerhouse opened in 1988. The early collection was held in the Garden Palace where the 1879 international exhibition of invention and industry from around the world was held. Few exhibits survived the devastating 1882 fire, and today's huge and ever-expanding collection was gathered after this disaster. The building's monumental scale provides an ideal context for the epic sweep of ideas encompassed within: everything from the realm of space and technology to the decorative and domestic arts. The museum emphasizes Australian innovations and achievements, celebrating both the extraordinary and the everyday.

What's It Like to Live in Space?
Find out how astronauts live and work in space and experience weightlessness in the zero gravity space lab.

★ Transport
See the vehicles that carry us from the cradle to the grave, including a pram, a hearse and everything inbetween: a penny farthing bicycle, boats and even flying machines.

Level 2

Level 1

Strasburg Clock
This fascinating timepiece operates for six minutes every day, before the hour.

Key to Floorplan

- Temporary exhibitions
- Social History and Design
- Science and Technology
- Non-exhibition space

Ecologic
Discover the science behind global warming and what can be done to prevent it.

Museum Guide

The museum houses more than 20 exhibitions on four levels, descending from Level 4. The shop, café, entrance, Boulton & Watt Engine, Robert Stephenson's Locomotive No. 1 and temporary exhibits are on Level 3. Level 2 has thematic exhibits. Level 1 has displays on space and transport, as well as interactive technology displays.

VISITORS' CHECKLIST

Practical Information
500 Harris St, Ultimo.
Map 4 D4.
Tel 9217 0111. **Open** 10am–5pm
daily. **Closed** 25 Dec. 🚭 ♿ 📷
📷 📹 W **maas.museum/
powerhouse-museum**

Transport
🚌 501. 🚠 Darling Harbour. 🚉
Central. 🚇 Paddy's Markets.

Level 4

Level 3

Main entrance

★ **Boulton & Watt Engine**
The oldest surviving rotative steam engine in the world, it powered a London brewery for 102 years from 1875. It is regularly put into operation in the museum.

Icons
Explore what makes an object iconic through more than 70 rarely displayed items, such as this Regency settee and matching armchairs, designed by Thomas Hope, London, in about 1802.

★ **Locomotive No. 1**
Robert Stephenson built this locomotive in England in 1854. It hauled the first train in New South Wales in 1855. Using models and voices, the display re-creates a 19th-century day trip for a group of Sydneysiders.

The Neville Wran Building,
a 1980s addition, is based on the design of grand exhibition halls and railway stations of the 19th century.

BOTANIC GARDEN AND THE DOMAIN

This tranquil part of Sydney can seem a world away from the bustle of the city centre. It is rich in the remnants of Sydney's convict and colonial past: the site of the first farm and the boulevard-like Macquarie Street where the barracks, hospital, church and mint – bastions of civic power – are among the oldest surviving public buildings in Australia. This street continues to assert its dominance today as the location of the state government of New South Wales.

The Domain, an open, grassy space, was originally set aside by the colony's first governor for his private use. Today it is filled with joggers and touch footballers sidestepping picnickers and sunbathers. In January, during the Festival of Sydney, it hosts free outdoor concerts. The Royal Botanic Garden has for almost 200 years collected, grown, researched and conserved plants from Australia and the rest of the world. The result is a parkland of great diversity and beauty.

Sights at a Glance

Historic Streets and Buildings
2 Conservatorium of Music
3 Government House
8 State Library of New South Wales
9 Parliament House
10 Sydney Hospital
11 The Mint
12 Hyde Park Barracks Museum

Museums and Galleries
6 Art Gallery of New South Wales pp114–17

Churches
13 St James' Church

Islands
5 Fort Denison

Monuments
4 Mrs Macquaries Chair

Parks and Gardens
1 Royal Botanic Garden pp110–11
7 The Domain

See also Street Finder, maps 1 and 4

0 metres 250
0 yards 250

For keys to symbols *see back flap*

❶ Royal Botanic Garden

The Royal Botanic Garden, a 30-ha (75-acre) oasis in the heart of the city, occupies a superb position, wrapped around Farm Cove at the harbour's edge. Established in 1816 as a series of pathways through shrubbery, it is the oldest living scientific institution in the country and houses an outstanding collection of plants from Australia and overseas. A living museum, the gardens are also the site of the first farm in the fledgling colony. Fountains, statues and monuments are today scattered throughout. The diversity is amazing: there are thousands of trees, stands of bamboo, a cactus garden, a rainforest walk, one of the world's finest collections of palms, a herb garden and a garden containing rare and threatened plant species.

Locator Map
See Central Sydney map pp66–7

★ Palm Grove
Begun in 1862, this cool summer haven is one of the world's finest outdoor collections of palms. There are about 180 species in the grove.

★ Herb Garden
Herbs from around the world used for a wide variety of purposes – culinary, medicinal and aromatic – are on display here. A sensory fountain and a sundial modelled on the celestial sphere are also features.

KEY

① **Conservatorium of Music** (see p112).

② **Government House (1897)**

③ **The Fleet Steps** met those disembarking from ships in Farm Cove.

④ **Mrs Macquaries Chair,** where the governor's wife liked to watch the harbour, is marked by a rock ledge seat (see p112).

⑤ **Mrs Macquaries Road**

⑥ **Andrew (Boy) Charlton Pool** is a popular spot for inner-city swimming and sunbathing.

⑦ **Wollemi Pine**

★ The Calyx
A gift from the NSW government to the Garden for its 200th birthday in 2016, this magnificent structure is regularly reinvented with changing horticultural exhibitions, displays and events.

Macquarie Wall
In 1810, work began on this 290-m- (950-ft-) long wall intended to separate the convict domain from the town's "respectable Class of Inhabitants". Only a small section remains standing today.

VISITORS' CHECKLIST

Practical Information
Mrs Macquaries Rd. **Maps** 1 & 2.
Tel 9231 8111.
🔲 rbgsyd.nsw.gov.au
Open from 7am daily (Nov–Feb: to 8pm; Mar: 6:30pm; Apr & Sep: 6pm; May & Aug: 5:30pm; Jun & Jul: 5pm; Oct: 7:30pm).
The Calyx **Open** 10am–4pm daily.
Sydney Fernery and Succulent Garden **Open** 9am–4:30pm daily.
♿ 📷 daily (not Jan–Feb, public hols). Tours: 9231 8125.

Transport
🚌 Sydney Explorer, 200, 441.
🚢 Circular Quay. 🚇 Martin Place, St James, Circular Quay.

Choragic Monument (1870)
This sandstone replica of the marble monument by Lysicrates in Athens was sculpted by Walter McGill.

★ Australia's First European Farm
Some oblong beds in the Middle Garden follow the direction of the first furrows ploughed in the colony.

National Herbarium of New South Wales
Over one million dried plant specimens document biological diversity. Discovery and study of new plants aims to slow down the extinction rate of entire species.

0 metres 200
0 yards 200

❷ Conservatorium of Music

Macquarie St. **Map** 1 C3. **Tel** (02) 9351 1222. 🚌 Sydney Explorer, Circular Quay routes. 🚇 Martin Place. **Open** 8am–6pm Mon–Sat, public areas only. Phone for details of concerts. ♿ **Closed** public holidays, Easter Sat, 24 Dec–2 Jan. 📞 phone 0404 256 256 for details. 🌐 **music.sydney.edu.au**

When it was finished in 1821, this striking castellated Colonial Gothic building was meant to be the stables and servants' quarters for Government House, but construction of the latter was delayed for almost 25 years. That stables should be built in so grand a style, and at such great cost, brought forth cries of outrage and led to bitter arguments between the architect, Francis Greenway *(see p177)*, and Governor Macquarie – and a decree that all future building plans be submitted to London.

Between 1908 and 1915 "Greenway's folly" underwent a dramatic transformation. A concert hall, roofed in grey slate, was built on the central courtyard and the building in its entirety was converted for the use of the Sydney Conservatorium of Music.

The café holds lunchtime concerts during the school term and an upper level with great harbour views. "The Con" continues to be a training ground for future musicians and a great place to visit.

Resting on the carved stone seat of Mrs Macquaries Chair

❸ Government House

Royal Botanic Garden (Macquarie St entrance). **Map** 1 C3. **Tel** (02) 9228 4111. 🚌 Sydney Explorer, Circular Quay routes. 🚇 Circular Quay. House **Open** 10:30am–3pm most Fri–Sun & 26 Jan (guided tour only; ID required). **Closed** Good Fri, 25 Dec. Garden **Open** 10am–4pm daily. 📷 every 30 mins. 🌐 **governor.nsw.gov.au/government-house**

The official residence of the governor of New South Wales, this is one of Australia's oldest buildings. Erected between 1837 and 1845, the turreted Gothic Revival edifice overlooks the harbour and Sydney Opera House from within the Royal Botanic Garden. The eastern terrace has hosted lavish receptions and entertainment since 1862. A fine collection of 19th- and early 20th-century furnishings and decorations is housed in the ground-floor state rooms, while the upstairs rooms have been used as the private quarters of the Governor, Queen Elizabeth II and other members of the royal family and visiting heads of state. The grand interior features exquisite hand-painted stencilled ceilings and a significant collection of portraits.

❹ Mrs Macquaries Chair

Mrs Macquaries Rd. **Map** 2 E2. 🚌 Sydney Explorer, 111. ♿ 📷

The scenic Mrs Macquaries Road winds along much of what is now the city's Royal Botanic Garden, from Farm Cove to Woolloomooloo Bay and back again. The road was built in 1816 at the instigation of Elizabeth Macquarie, wife of the Governor. In the same year, a stone bench, inscribed with details of the new road and its commissioner, was carved into the rock at the point where Mrs Macquarie would often stop and admire the view.

Rounding the cove to the west leads to Mrs Macquaries Point. These lawns are a popular picnic spot with Sydneysiders, particularly at sunset.

❺ Fort Denison

Sydney Harbour. **Map** 2 E1. **Tel** (02) 9247 5033. 🚌 Circular Quay. **Open** daily tours: for prices and times call 1300 072 757, or visit 🌐 **national parks.nsw.gov.au**. **Closed** 25 Dec. 📷 📷 📷 🌐 **fortdenison.com.au**

First named Rock Island, this prominent, rocky outcrop in Sydney Harbour was also dubbed "Pinchgut", probably because of the meagre rations given to convicts who were confined there as punishment.

In 1796, convicted murderer Francis Morgan was hanged on the island in chains. His body was left to rot on the gallows for three years as a warning to the other convicts.

Between 1855 and 1857, the Martello tower (the only one in Australia), gun battery and

Conservatorium of Music at the edge of the Royal Botanic Garden

For hotels and restaurants in this area see pp482–3 and pp504–7

barracks that now occupy the island were built as part of Sydney's defences. The site was renamed after the governor of the time. The gun, still fired at 1pm each day, helped mariners to set their ships' chronometers accurately.

Today the island is the perfect setting for watching harbour activities, such as the New Year fireworks displays *(see p45)*.

❻ Art Gallery of New South Wales

See pp114–17.

❼ The Domain

Art Gallery Rd. **Map** 1 C4. 🚌 Sydney Explorer, 111, 411. ♿

Once the governor's private park, this public grass space attracts thousands to open-air summer concerts and festival events. Since the 1890s, it has hosted Sydney's version of Speakers' Corner. Today, it is popular with joggers and office workers playing touch football or relaxing in their lunch hours.

View of Sydney Harbour from The Domain

❽ State Library of New South Wales

Macquarie St. **Map** 1 C4. **Tel** (02) 9273 1414. 🚌 Sydney Explorer, Elizabeth St routes. 🚇 Martin Place. **Open** 9am–8pm Mon–Thu, 9am–5pm Fri, 10am–5pm Sat & Sun. **Closed** most public hols, Mitchell Library closed Sun. ♿ 📷 📖 📸 🌐 sl.nsw.gov.au

The state library is housed in two separate buildings connected by a passageway and a glass bridge. The older building, the Mitchell

Mosaic replica of the Tasman Map, State Library of New South Wales

Library wing (1910), is a majestic sandstone edifice facing the Royal Botanic Garden *(see pp110–11)*. Huge stone columns supporting a vaulted ceiling frame the impressive vestibule. On the vestibule floor is a mosaic replica of an old map illustrating the two voyages made to Australia by Dutch navigator Abel Tasman in the 1640s *(see p53)*. The two ships of the first voyage are shown off the south coast, the two from the second voyage are seen to the north-west. The original Tasman Map is held in the Mitchell Library as part of its collection of historic Australian paintings, books, documents and pictorial records.

The Mitchell wing's vast reading room, with its huge skylight and oak panelling, is just beyond the main vestibule. There is also an attractive contemporary structure that faces Macquarie Street *(see pp118–19)*. This area houses the State Reference Library. Beyond the Mitchell wing is the Dixson Gallery, housing cultural and historical exhibitions which change regularly.

Outside the library, facing Macquarie Street, is a statue of the explorer Matthew Flinders, who first ventured into central Australia *(see pp56–7)*. On the windowsill behind him is a statue of his travelling companion, his cat, Trim.

❾ Parliament House

Macquarie St. **Map** 1 C4. **Tel** (02) 9230 2111. 🚌 Sydney Explorer, Elizabeth St routes. 🚇 Martin Place. **Open** 9am–5pm Mon–Fri. **Closed** public hols. ♿ 📷 (02) 9230 3444 to book. 🌐 parliament.nsw.gov.au

The central section of this building, which houses the State Parliament, is part of the original Sydney Hospital built from 1811–16 *(see p117)*. It has been a seat of government since 1829 when the newly appointed Legislative Council first held meetings here. The building was extended twice during the 19th century and again during the 1970s and 1980s. The current building contains the chambers for both houses of state parliament, as well as parliamentary offices.

Parliamentary memorabilia is on view in the Jubilee Room, as are displays showing Parliament House's development and the legislative history of the state.

The corrugated iron building with a cast-iron façade tacked on at the southern end was a prefabricated kit from England. In 1856, this dismantled kit became the chamber for the new Legislative Council. Its packing cases were used to line the chamber; the rough timber can still be seen.

Malby's celestial globe, Parliament House

❻ Art Gallery of New South Wales

Established in 1871, the art gallery has occupied its present imposing building since 1897. Designed by the Colonial Architect W L Vernon, the gallery doubled in size following building extensions in 1988. Two equestrian bronzes by Gilbert Bayes (1872–1953) – *The Offerings of Peace* and *The Offerings of War* – greet the visitor on entry. The gallery itself houses some of the finest works of art in Australia, with permanent collections of Australian, Aboriginal, European, Asian and Contemporary art. The Yiribana Gallery is among the largest in the world to exclusively exhibit Aboriginal and Torres Strait Islander art and culture. Free guided tours take place daily, covering Aboriginal art, highlights of the collection or major exhibitions.

Lower Level 3

Mars and the Vestal Virgin *(1638)*
This oil on canvas by Parisian painter Jacques Blanchard (1600–38) depicts Mars' encounter with a Vestal Virgin, who subsequently gave birth to Romulus and Remus, founders of Rome.

★ **Pukumani Grave Posts** *(1958)*
Carved by the Tiwi people of Melville Island (north of Australia), these posts represent qualities of the deceased whose grave they solemnly surrounded.

Sofala *(1947)*
Russell Drysdale's visions of Australia show "ghost" towns laid waste by devastating natural forces such as drought.

Ground Level

Gallery Guide

There are five levels. The Upper and Ground levels, plus Lower Level 1 host temporary exhibitions. The Ground Level also has European and Australian works. On Lower Level 2 are the Contemporary galleries, which house the most extensive collection of modern art in the country. The Yiribana Aboriginal Gallery is on Lower Level 3.

For hotels and restaurants in this area see pp482–3 and pp504–7

Banks of the Marne *(c. 1888)*
This landscape painting by the post-Impressionist artist Paul Cézanne is a highlight of the gallery's collection of modern art.

Lower Level 2

Guardians, Tang Dynasty
These 7th-century Chinese figures are part of a collection highlighting different traditions, periods and cultures from the many countries of Asia.

Natives on the Ouse River, Van Diemen's Land *(1838)*
English-Australian artist John Glover was dubbed the father of Australian landscape painting for his bright depictions of the Van Dieman's Land bush (now Tasmania).

Lower Level 1

Mars and the Vestal Virgin

The sandstone entrance was added in 1909.

★ **The Golden Fleece** *(1894)*
Also known as *Shearing at Newstead*, this work by Tom Roberts marks the coming of age of Australian Impressionist art.

Key to Floorplan

☐ Australian Art
☐ European Art
☐ Asian Art
☐ Modern Gallery (20th-Century European Art)
☐ Contemporary Art
☐ Domain Theatre
☐ Yiribana Aboriginal Gallery
☐ Temporary exhibition space
☐ Non-exhibition space
☐ Photography Gallery

Exploring the Art Gallery's Collection

The gallery's early focus was on Australian and British art, and these areas continue to be well represented. Aboriginal art began to be added to the collection during the 1940s, with strong acquisition programmes in recent decades. The Contemporary galleries are an exciting addition, with both international and Australian pieces on display. The gallery stages major temporary exhibitions, and the annual Archibald, Wynne and Sulman prizes always entertain and usually stir controversy.

Chaucer at the court of Edward III, a Ford Madox Brown painting of 1847–51

Grace Cossington Smith's *The curve of the Bridge* (1928–9)

Australian Art

Among the most important colonial works is John Glover's *Natives on the Ouse River, Van Diemen's Land* (1838), an idealized image of Aboriginal people in a landscape unsullied by European contact. The old wing holds paintings from the Heidelberg School of Australian Impressionism. Charles Conder's *Departure of the Orient – Circular Quay* (1888) and Tom Roberts's *The Golden Fleece – Shearing at Newstead* (1894) hang alongside works by Frederick McCubbin and Arthur Streeton. The Gallery's paintings by Sidney Nolan exploit

myths of early Australian history and range from *Boy in Township* (1943) to *Burke* (c. 1962).

There is a strong collection of Australian Modernism, including *The Curve of the Bridge* (1928–9) by Grace Cossington Smith, There are also fine holdings by Thea Proctor, William Dobell, Russell Drysdale, Arthur Boyd and Brett Whiteley *(see p38)*, among others.

Yiribana Aboriginal Gallery

The Yiribana Gallery is the home of the Aboriginal and Torres Strait Islander collection, celebrating indigenous Australia's enduring cultural heritage and myriad contemporary expressions. The earliest work in the collection, by Tommy McRae, dates back to the late 19th century, yet the stories, ceremonies and figures depicted in many of the works are testament to the oldest continuous culture in the world. Contemporary artists have generated a renaissance of indigenous visual art that has transfigured Australia's cultural landscape and is celebrated in this Gallery.

European Art

The scope of the European collection ranges from Medieval to modern art. British art from the late 19th to the early 20th century forms an outstanding component. Among the Old Masters are some significant Italian works that reflect Caravaggio's influence. There are also several notable works from the Renaissance in Sienese and Florentine styles.

The Visit of the Queen of Sheba to King Solomon (1884–90) by Edward Poynter has been on display since 1892. Ford Madox Brown's *Chaucer at the Court of Edward III* (1847–51) is the most commanding work in the Pre-Raphaelite collection.

Impressionists and Post-Impressionists are represented by Pissarro, Monet, Kandinsky, Braque and many others.

Photography

With a collection of over 5000 works, Australian photography forms a major part of the gallery. From 19th-century material by Charles Kerry and Charles Bayliss, to 20th-century Pictorialism by Harold Cazneaux, Norman C Deck and many others, the collection then traces the development of modernist photography through the work of Olive Cotton, Max Dupain and their peers. Major international figures like Eadweard Muybridge, Robert Mapplethorpe, Dorothea Lange, Man Ray and Cindy Sherman also feature.

Brett Whiteley's vivid *The balcony 2* from 1975

Asian Art

The Asian collections offer one of the largest pan-Asian displays of art in the southern hemisphere, including exquisite calligraphy, traditional and modern paintings, textiles, porcelain and an extraordinary legacy of Buddhist art. The galleries occupy two levels; the lower level displays the art of East Asia – China, Korea and Japan; the upper level displays the art of South and Southeast Asia and changing exhibitions. The upper gallery is housed within a white glass pavilion, inspired by floating lanterns typically found in Asia. The lower one includes a fully operational Japanese tearoom.

Amitabha Buddha, dating from between the late 8th and the mid-9th centuries

Contemporary Art

The Art Gallery of NSW has a long-standing history of collecting the art of its day. In 1979, it was the first Australian art museum to appoint a curator of contemporary art. This collection encompasses works in all media by artists from Australia and across the globe, including Fiona Hall, Bill Henson, Anish Kapoor, Louise Bourgeois and Ai Weiwei. The Gallery holds Australia's most comprehensive representation of art from the 1960s to the present day. From pivotal new acquisitions to collection favourites, the gallery's rotating exhibitions have a sense of experimentation and energy, offering visitors fresh perspectives on the art of our time.

Il Porcellino, the bronze boar in front of Sydney Hospital

⑩ Sydney Hospital

Macquarie St. **Map** 1 C4. **Tel** (02) 9382 7111. 🚌 Sydney Explorer, Elizabeth St routes. 🚆 Martin Place. **Open** daily. 📷 for tours. ♿ 📱 book in advance.

This imposing collection of Victorian sandstone buildings stands on the site of what was once the central section of the original convict-built Sydney Hospital. It was known locally as the Rum Hospital because the builders were paid by being allowed to import rum for resale. Both the north and south wings of the Rum Hospital survive as Parliament House *(see p113)* and the Sydney Mint. The central wing was demolished in 1879 and the new hospital, which is still operational, was completed in 1894.

The Classical Revival building boasts a Baroque staircase and elegant stained-glass windows in its central hall. Florence Nightingale approved the design of the 1867 nurses' wing. In the inner courtyard, there is a brightly coloured Art Deco fountain (1907), somewhat out of place among the surrounding heavy stonework.

At the front of the hospital sits a bronze boar called *Il Porcellino*. It is a replica of a 17th-century fountain in Florence's Mercato Nuovo. Donated in 1968 by an Italian woman whose relatives had worked at the hospital, the statue is an enduring symbol of

Stained glass at Sydney Hospital

the friendship between Italy and Australia. Like his Florentine counterpart, *Il Porcellino* is supposed to bring good luck to all those who rub his snout. Coins tossed in the pool at his feet for luck and fortune are collected for the hospital.

⑪ The Mint

10 Macquarie St. **Map** 1 C5. **Tel** (02) 8239 2288. 🚌 Sydney Explorer, Elizabeth St routes. 🚆 St James, Martin Place. **Open** 9am–5pm Mon–Fri. **Closed** Good Fri, 25 Dec. ♿ ground floor only. 📱 🌐 **sydneylivingmuseums.com.au/the-mint**

The gold rushes of the mid-19th century transformed colonial Australia *(see pp58–9)*. The Sydney Mint opened in 1854 in the south wing of the Rum Hospital in order to turn recently discovered gold into bullion and currency. This was the first branch of the Royal Mint to be established outside London, but it was closed in 1927 as it was no longer competitive with the mints in Melbourne *(see p391)* and Perth *(see p309)*. The Georgian building then went into decline after it was converted into government offices. The Mint's artifacts are now in the Powerhouse Museum *(see pp106–7)*. The head office of the Historic Houses Trust of NSW is now located here and you can look through the front part of the building.

⑫ Hyde Park Barracks Museum

Queens Square 10, Macquarie St.
Map 1 C5. **Tel** (02) 8239 2311.
🚌 Sydney Explorer, Elizabeth St
routes. 🚆 St James, Martin Place.
Open 10am–5pm daily. **Closed**
Good Fri, 25 Dec. 🏛 ♿ ground
floor only. 🎧 on request. 📷
🌐 **sydneylivingmuseums.com.au**

Described by Governor
Macquarie as "spacious" and
"well-aired", the beautifully
proportioned barracks are the
work of Francis Greenway and
are considered his masterpiece
(see p177). They were completed
in 1819 by convict labour and
designed to house 600 convicts.
Until that time convicts had
been forced to find their own
lodgings after their day's work.

Replica convict hammocks on the third
floor of Hyde Park Barracks

Subsequently, the building then
housed, in turn, young Irish
orphans and single female
immigrants, before it later
became courts and legal offices.

Refurbished in 1990, the
barracks reopened as a museum
on the history of the site and its
occupants. The displays include
a room reconstructed as convict
quarters of the 1820s, as well as
pictures, models and artifacts.
Many of the objects recovered
during archaeological digs at
the site and now on display
survived because they had
been dragged away by rats
to their nests; today the rodents
are acknowledged as valuable
agents of preservation.

The Greenway Gallery on
the first floor holds varied
exhibitions on history and
culture. Hyde Park Barracks is
one of 11 Australian convict
locations listed as UNESCO
World Heritage sites for their
outstanding universal value.

Macquarie Street

*Named after Governor Lachlan Macquarie, this
street was designed as a ceremonial thoroughfare from the harbour to Hyde Park. It houses
some of Australia's main architectural treasures,
as well as New South Wales Parliament House,
home of the State Government.*

The Mitchell Library
wing's portico (1906) has
Ionic columns.

This wing of the
library was built
in 1988 and
connected to
the old section
by a glass
walkway.

Parliament House was
once the convict-built Rum
Hospital's northern wing.

1. State Library of NSW *(1906–41)*

2. Parliament House *(1811–16)*

The roof of The Mint
has now been
completely restored to
replicate the original
wooden shingles in
casuarina (she-oak).

The Mint, like its twin,
Parliament House, has an
unusual double-colonnaded,
two-storeyed veranda.

**Hyde Park
Barracks Café**

4. The Mint *(1816)*

⑬ St James' Church

179 King St. **Map** 1 B5. **Tel** (02) 8227 1300. Ⓣ St James, Martin Place. **Open** 10am–4pm Mon–Fri, 9am–1pm Sat, 7:30am–4pm Sun. ♿ Concerts: 1:15pm Wed (free). 🅦 **sjks.org.au**

This fine Georgian building, constructed by convict labour, was originally designed as a courthouse in 1819. The architect, Francis Greenway, had to build a church instead when plans to construct a cathedral on George Street were abandoned. Greenway designed a simple yet elegant church. Consecrated in 1824, it is the city's oldest church. Many additions were carried out, including designs by John Verge in which the pulpit faced the high-rent pews, while convicts and the military sat directly behind the preacher where the service was inaudible. A Children's Chapel was created in 1929. Prominent members of early 19th-century society, many of whom died violently, are honoured with marble tablets. These tell the stories of luckless explorers, the governor's wife dashed to her death from her carriage, and shipwreck victims.

Detail from the Children's Chapel mural in the St James' Church crypt

---

The lamps hanging over the gateways of Parliament House are reproductions of the 19th-century gas lamps that used to stand here.

The entrance stairs of Pyrmont sandstone have set the tone for all renovations. The stone, quarried in colonial times, must be matched exactly.

Arcaded stone verandas with ornate balustrading

Arched sandstone bridges

Locator map

Corrugated iron and cast-iron façade

3. Sydney Hospital (1868–94)

The Land Titles Office, a W L Vernon building from 1908, has a Classical form with some fine Tudor Gothic detailing.

The stained-glass windows in St James' Church are mostly 20th century. Those in the Chapel of the Holy Spirit represent air, earth, fire and water.

Copper spire

Georgian sandstone façade

Statue of Prince Albert

5. Hyde Park Barracks Museum (1817–19)

6. Land Titles Office (1908–13)

7. St James' (1820)

KINGS CROSS, DARLINGHURST AND PADDINGTON

Sydney's densely populated Kings Cross and Darlinghurst districts are still remembered for their 1920s gangland associations. However, an exciting scene of restaurants and wine bars has added a touch of sophistication to Kings Cross, long known as Sydney's red-light district. Darlinghurst comes into its own every March, during the flamboyant Gay and Lesbian Mardi Gras parade. The Victorian terraces of Paddington are still admired for their wrought-iron "lace" verandas. Paddington is also famed for its fine restaurants, galleries and antiques shops. On Saturdays, people flock to Paddington Markets, spilling out into the pubs and cafés of the surrounding area.

Sights at a Glance

Historic Streets and Buildings
2 Victoria Street
3 Elizabeth Bay House
6 Old Gaol, Darlinghurst
7 Darlinghurst Court House
8 Five Ways
9 Paddington Village
10 Juniper Hall
11 Paddington Town Hall
12 Victoria Barracks
14 Paddington Street
16 The Entertainment Quarter

Parks and Gardens
4 Beare Park
15 Centennial Park

Museums and Galleries
5 Sydney Jewish Museum

Monuments
1 El Alamein Fountain

Markets
13 Paddington Markets

See also Street Finder, maps 2, 5 and 6

0 metres   500
0 yards   500

◀ Colourful Victorian terrace houses in the Sydney suburb of Paddington   **For keys to symbols** *see back flap*

Street-by-Street: Potts Point

The substantial Victorian houses filling the streets of this old suburb are excellent examples of the 19th-century concern with architectural harmony. New building projects were designed to enhance rather than contradict the surrounding buildings and general streetscape. Monumental structures and fine details of moulded stuccoed parapets, cornices and friezes, even the spandrels in herringbone pattern, are all integral parts of a grand suburban plan. (This plan included an 1831 order that all houses cost at least £1,000.) Cool, dark verandas extend the street's green canopy of shade, leaving an impression of cold drinks enjoyed on summer days in fine Victorian style.

The McElhone Stairs were preceded by a wooden ladder that linked Woolloomooloo Hill, as Kings Cross was known, to the estate far below.

Horderns Stairs

These villas, from the Georgian and Victorian eras, can be broadly labelled as Classical Revival and are fronted by leafy gardens.

VICTORIA STREET

TUSCULUM STREET

MANNING

Kings Cross Station

HUGHES STREET

② ★ Victoria Street
From 1972–4, residents of this historic street fought a sometimes violent battle against developers wanting to build high-rise towers, motels and blocks of flats.

MACLEAY STREET

Werrington, a mostly serious and streamlined building, also has flamboyant Art Deco detailing which is now hidden under brown paint.

ELIZABE

Tusculum Villa was just one of a number of 1830s houses subject to "villa conditions". All had to face Government House, be of a high monetary value and be built within three years.

Challis Avenue is a fine and shady complement to nearby Victoria Street. This Romanesque group of terrace houses has an unusual façade, with arches fronting deep verandas and a grand ground floor colonnade.

Locator Map
See Street Finder, map 2

Rockwall, a symmetrical and compact Regency villa, was built to the designs of the architect John Verge in 1830–37.

Landmark Hotel

Del Rio is a finely detailed high-rise apartment block. It clearly exhibits the Spanish Mission influence that filtered through from California in the first quarter of the 20th century.

The Arthur McElhone Reserve

❸ ★ **Elizabeth Bay House**
A contemporary exclaimed over the beauty of the 1830s garden: "Trees from Rio, the West Indies, the East Indies, China…the bulbs from the Cape are splendid."

Art Deco Birtley Towers

0 metres   50
0 yards   50

Key

— Suggested route

Elizabeth Bay was part of the original land grant to Alexander Macleay. He created a botanist's paradise with ornamental ponds, quaint grottoes and promenades winding all the way down to the harbour.

El Alamein Fountain, commemorating the World War II battle

❶ El Alamein Fountain

Fitzroy Gardens, Macleay St, Potts Point. **Map** 2 E5. 🚌 311.

This fountain in the shape of a dandelion in the heart of the Kings Cross district has a reputation for working so spasmodically that passers-by often murmur facetiously, "He loves me, he loves me not." Built in 1961, it commemorates the Australian army's role in the siege of Tobruk, Libya, and the battle of El Alamein in Egypt during World War II. At night, when it is brilliantly lit, the fountain looks surprisingly ethereal.

❷ Victoria Street

Potts Point. **Map** 5 B2. 🚌 311, 324, 325, 389.

At the Potts Point end, this street of 19th-century terrace houses, interspersed with a few incongruous-looking high-rise blocks, is, by inner-city standards, almost a boulevard. The gracious street you see today was once at the centre of a bitterly fought conservation struggle, one which almost certainly cost the life of a prominent heritage campaigner.

In the early 1970s, many residents, backed by the "green bans" put in place by the Builders' Labourers Federation of New South Wales, fought to prevent demolition of old buildings for high-rise

development. Juanita Nielsen, heiress and publisher of a local newspaper, vigorously took up the conservation battle. On 4 July 1975, she disappeared without trace. An inquest into her disappearance returned an open verdict, and the case that captivated Sydney and dominated the front pages of newspapers remains unsolved.

As a result of the actions of the union and residents, most of Victoria Street's superb old buildings still stand.

❸ Elizabeth Bay House

7 Onslow Ave, Elizabeth Bay. **Map** 2 F5. **Tel** (02) 9356 3022. 🚌 Sydney Explorer, 311. **Open** 10am–4pm Fri–Sun & Australia Day. **Closed** Good Fri, 25 Dec. 🎫 📷 ♿ ground floor. 🖥 sydneylivingmuseums.com.au

Elizabeth Bay House contains the finest colonial interior on display in Australia. It is a potent expression of how the depression of the 1840s cut short the 1830s' prosperous optimism. Designed in Greek Revival style by John Verge, it was built for Colonial Secretary Alexander Macleay, from 1835–39. The oval saloon with its dome and cantilevered staircase is recognized as Verge's masterpiece. The exterior is less satisfactory, as the intended colonnade and portico were not finished owing to a crisis in Macleay's financial affairs. The present

Juanita Nielsen

portico dates from 1893. The interior is furnished to reflect Macleay's occupancy from 1839–45, and is based on inventories drawn up in 1845 for the transfer of the house and contents to his son, William Sharp. He took the house in return for paying off his father's debts, leading to a rift that was never resolved.

Macleay's original 22-ha (55-acre) land grant was sub-divided for flats and villas from the 1880s to 1927. In the 1940s, the house itself was divided into 15 flats. In 1942, the artist Donald Friend saw the ferry *Kuttabul* hit by a torpedo from a Japanese midget submarine from his flat's balcony.

The house was restored and opened as a museum in 1977. It is a property of the Historic Houses Trust of NSW.

The sweeping staircase under the oval dome, Elizabeth Bay House

❹ Beare Park

Ithaca Rd, Elizabeth Bay. **Map** 2 F5. 🚌 311.

Originally a part of the Macleay Estate, Beare Park is now encircled by a jumble of apartment blocks.

A refuge from hectic Kings Cross, it is one of only a few parks serving a populated area. Shaped like a natural amphitheatre, the park has glorious views of Elizabeth Bay.

The family home of J C Williamson, a famous theatrical entrepreneur who came to Australia from America in the 1870s, formerly stood at the eastern extremity of the park.

For hotels and restaurants in this area see pp482–3 and pp504–7

Star of David in the lobby of the Sydney Jewish Museum

❺ Sydney Jewish Museum

148 Darlinghurst Rd, Darlinghurst. **Map** 5 B2. **Tel** (02) 9360 7999. Sydney, Bondi & Bay Explorer, 311, 389. **Open** 10am–4pm Sun–Thu, 10am–2pm Fri. **Closed** Sat, Jewish hols. **W** sydneyjewishmuseum.com.au

Sixteen Jewish convicts were on the First Fleet, and many more were to be transported before the end of the convict era. As with other convicts, most would endure and some would thrive, seizing all the opportunities the colony had to offer.

The Sydney Jewish Museum relates stories of Australian Jewry within the context of the Holocaust. The ground floor display explores present-day Jewish traditions and culture within Australia. Ascending the stairs to the mezzanine levels

1–6, the visitor passes through chronological and thematic exhibitions which unravel the tragic history of the Holocaust.

From Hitler's rise to power and *Kristallnacht*, through the evacuation of the ghettos and the Final Solution, to the ultimate liberation of the infamous death camps and Nuremberg Trials, the harrowing events are graphically documented. This horrific period is recalled using photographs and relics, some exhumed from mass graves, as well as audiovisual exhibits and oral testimonies.

Holocaust survivors act as guides and their presence, bearing witness to the recorded events, lends considerable power and moving authenticity to the exhibits in the museum.

❻ Old Gaol, Darlinghurst

Cnr Burton & Forbes sts, Darlinghurst. **Map** 5 A2. **Tel** (02) 9339 8744. 333, 378, 380, 389. **Open** 9am–5pm Mon–Fri. **Closed** public hols. 11am, 1pm, 2pm & 3pm.

Originally known as the Woolloomooloo Stockade and later as Darlinghurst Gaol, this complex was also home to the National Art School. It was constructed over a 20-year period from 1822.

Surrounded by walls almost 7 m (23 ft) high, the cell blocks radiate from a central round-house. The jail is built of stone

quarried on the site by convicts, which was then chiselled by them into blocks.

No fewer than 67 people were executed here between 1841 and 1908. Perhaps the most notorious hangman was Alexander "The Strangler" Green, after whom Green Park, outside the jail, is thought to have been named. Green lived near the park until public hostility forced him to live inside the jail.

Some of Australia's most noted artists, including Frank Hodgkinson, Jon Molvig and William Dobell, trained or taught at the art school which was established here in 1921.

The former Governor's house, Old Gaol, Darlinghurst

❼ Darlinghurst Court House

197 Oxford St at Taylor Square, Darlinghurst. **Map** 5 A2. **Tel** 1300 679 272. 378, 380, 382. **Open** Feb–Dec: 10am–4pm Mon–Fri. **Closed** Jan, mid-Dec, public hols.

Abutting the grim old gaol, to which it is connected by underground passages, and facing tawdry Taylor Square, this unlikely gem of Greek Revival architecture was begun in 1835 by colonial architect Mortimer Lewis. He was only responsible for the central block of the main building with its six-columned Doric portico with Greek embellishments. The side wings were not added until the 1880s.

The Court House is still used by the state's Supreme Court, mainly for criminal cases, and these are open to the public.

Beare Park, a quiet inner-city park with harbour views

Street-by-Street: Paddington

Paddington began to flourish in the 1840s, with the construction of the Victoria Barracks. A village emerged around the workers' cottages, and rapid development followed, with narrow Victorian terraces crowding the streets. Hard hit by the Great Depression, the area became run down and slum-like. A 1947 plan proposing mass demolition to build blocks of flats was thwarted by an influx of post-war European migrants who found the area convenient and affordable. The 1960s saw the restoration of homes and gentrification of this bohemian suburb.

❽ ★ Five Ways
This shopping hub was established in the late 19th century on the busy Glenmore roadway trodden out by bullocks.

Duxford Street's terrace houses in toning pale shades constitute an ideal of town planning: the Victorians preferred houses in a row to have a pleasingly uniform aspect.

"Gingerbread" houses can be seen in Broughton and Union streets. With their steeply pitched gables and fretwork bargeboards, they are typical of the rustic Gothic Picturesque architectural style.

The London Tavern opened for business in 1875, making it the suburb's oldest pub. Like many of the pubs and delicatessens in this well-serviced suburb, it stands at the end of a row of terraces.

Key

— Suggested route

The Korban Flaubert design and sculpture studio is housed in this strikingly modern building. It was designed to hold Australian and international contemporary sculpture and paintings. Suitable access gates and a special in-house crane enabled the movement of large-scale artworks.

Locator Map
See Central Sydney map pp66–7

Paddington's streets are a treasure trove of galleries, bars and restaurants. A wander through the area should prove an enjoyable experience.

Warwick, built in the 1860s, is a minor castle lying at the end of a row of humble terraces. Its turrets, battlements and assorted decorations, in a style somewhat fancifully described as "King Arthur", even adorn the garages at the rear.

Windsor Street's terrace houses are, in some cases, a mere 4.5 m (15 ft) wide.

Street-making in Paddington's early days was often an expensive and complicated business. A cascade of water was dammed to build Cascade Street.

⓮ ★ Paddington Street
Under the established plane trees, some of Paddington's finest Victorian terraces exemplify the building boom of 1860–90. Over 30 years, 3,800 houses were built in the suburb.

0 metres 50
0 yards 50

Pretty cast-iron balcony, the typical architecture of Paddington

8 Five Ways

Cnr Glenmore Rd & Heeley St. **Map** 5 C3. 389.

At this picturesque intersection, where three streets cross on Glenmore Road, a shopping hub developed by the tramline that ran from the city to Bondi Beach *(see p131)*. On the five corners stand 19th- and early 20th-century shops, one now a restaurant.

Much of the architecture in Paddington features decorative cast-iron "lacework" balconies, using mixed Victorian and Classical Revival styles. Streets lined with pretty houses make this one of Sydney's most desirable areas.

9 Paddington Village

Cnr Gipps & Shadforth sts. **Map** 5 C3. 333, 378, 380, 382.

Paddington began its life as a working-class suburb of Sydney. The community mainly consisted of the carpenters, quarrymen and stonemasons who supervised the convict gangs that built the Victoria Barracks in the 1840s.

The 19th-century artisans and their families occupied a tight huddle of spartan houses crowded into the area's narrow streets. A few of these houses still remain. Like the barracks, these dwellings and surrounding shops and hotels were built of locally quarried stone.

The terraces of Paddington Village are now a popular address with young, up-and-coming Sydneysiders.

10 Juniper Hall

250 Oxford St. **Tel** (02) 9357 5222. **Map** 5 C3. 333, 378, 380, 382. **Open** check website for exhibition dates. **juniperhall.com.au**

The emancipist gin distiller Robert Cooper built this superb example of colonial Georgian architecture for his third wife, Sarah. He named it after the main ingredient of the gin that made his fortune.

Completed in 1824, the two-storey home is the oldest dwelling still standing in Paddington. It is probably also the largest and most extravagant house ever built in the suburb. It had to be: Cooper already had 14 children when he declared that Sarah would have the finest house in Sydney. Once resident in the new house, he subsequently fathered 14 more.

Juniper Hall was saved from demolition in the mid-1980s and has been restored. It is now home to the annual Moran Art Prize and holds exhibitions through the year.

11 Paddington Town Hall

Cnr Oxford St & Oatley Rd. **Map** 5 C3. 333, 378, 380, 382. **Closed** to the public except the cinema. **palacecinemas.com.au**

Paddington Town Hall was completed in 1891. A design competition was won by local architect J E Kemp. The Classical Revival building still dominates the area. No longer a centre of local government, the building now houses a cinema, library and a large ballroom.

Paddington Town Hall

The archway at the Oxford Street entrance to Victoria Barracks

12 Victoria Barracks

Oxford St. **Map** 5 B4. **Tel** (02) 8335 5330. 378, 380, 382. Museum: **Open** 10am–1pm Thu (last adm noon), 10am–4pm first Sun of the month. Sun. **Closed** Dec–Jan. Parade & tour: 10am Thu. **armymuseumnsw.com.au**

Victoria Barracks is the largest and best-preserved group of late Georgian architecture in Australia, covering almost 12 ha (30 acres). They are widely considered to be one of the best examples of a military barracks in the world.

Designed by the colonial engineer Lieutenant Colonel George Barney, the barracks were built between 1841 and 1848 using local sandstone quarried by convict labour. Originally intended to house 800 men, they have been in continuous use ever since and still operate as a centre of military administration.

The main block is 225 m (740 ft) long and has symmetrical two-storey wings with cast-iron verandas flanking a central archway. The perimeter walls have foundations 10 m (40 ft) deep in places. A former gaol block now houses a military museum. The tour leaves sharp at 10am on Thursdays.

13 Paddington Markets

395 Oxford St. **Map** 6 D4. **Tel** (02) 9331 2923. 378, 380, 382. **Open** 10am–4pm Sat. **Closed** 25 Dec. *See Shopping p137.* **paddingtonmarkets.com.au**

This market, which began in 1973 as Paddington Bazaar, takes place every Saturday, come rain or shine, in the grounds of Paddington Village Uniting Church. It is probably the most colourful in Sydney – a place to meet and be seen as much as to shop. Stallholders come from all over the world and young designers, hoping to launch their careers, display their wares. Other offerings are jewellery, pottery and other arts and crafts, as well as new and second-hand clothing. Whatever you are looking for you are more than likely to find it here.

Paddington Street terrace house

⓮ Paddington Street

Map 6 D3. 🚌 333, 378, 380, 382.

With its huge plane trees shading the road and fine terrace houses on each side, Paddington Street is one of the oldest and loveliest of the suburb's streets.

Paddington grew rapidly as a commuter suburb in the late 19th century and most of the terraces were built for renting to Sydney's artisans. They were decorated with iron lace, Grecian-style friezes, worked parapets and cornices, pilasters and scrolls.

By the 1900s, the terraces became unfashionable and people moved out to newly emerging "garden suburbs". In the 1960s, however, their architectural appeal came to be appreciated again and the area was reborn.

Paddington Street now has a chic atmosphere where small art galleries operate out of quaint and grand shopfronts.

⓯ Centennial Park

Map 6 E5. **Tel** (02) 9339 6699.
🚌 Clovelly, Coogee, Maroubra, Bronte, Randwick, City, Bondi Beach & Bondi Junction routes, Bondi Explorer Bus.
Open permanently, but cars permitted only between sunrise and sunset. ♿
🅿 💷 🚻 see website for details.
ⓦ centennialparklands.com.au

Entering this 220-ha (544-acre) park through one of its sandstone and wrought-iron gates, the visitor may wonder how such an extensive and idyllic place has survived so close to the centre of the city. Formerly a common, Centennial Park was dedicated "to the enjoyment of the people of New South Wales forever" in 1888 as part of the centenary of the foundation of the colony. On 1 January 1901, 100,000 people gathered here to witness the Commonwealth of Australia come into being, when the first Australian federal ministry was sworn in by the first governor-general (*see p60*).

The park boasts landscaped lawns, a rose garden, statues and a coordinated series of walks. Once the source of the city's water supply, the swamps are home to many species of waterbirds. Picnickers, painters, runners, cyclists, skaters and horse-riders all share this vast park. Equipment hire is available, as well as barbecues and a scenic café and restaurant. An adjacent golf course with a large driving range, and tennis courts offer even more sporting opportunities.

⓰ The Entertainment Quarter

Lang Rd, Moore Park. **Map** 5 C5.
Tel 8117 6700. 🚌 339, 355.
Open most retail shops: 10am–10pm; markets: 8am–2pm Wed & Sat.
ⓦ eqmoorepark.com.au

There is a vibrant atmosphere in the Entertainment Quarter, which is located next door to the working studios that produced some very famous movies, such as *The Matrix* and *Moulin Rouge*.

There are 16 cinema screens showing the latest movies, and at the La Premiere cinema you can enjoy your movie with wine and cheese, sitting on sofas. Four live-entertainment venues, including Sydney's premier comedy venue, regularly feature the latest local and international acts. You can also enjoy bungy trampolining, bowling or seasonal ice-skating, and children love the play areas. There are many restaurants, cafés and bars offering a range of snacks, meals and drinks.

On Wednesdays and Saturdays, you can savour fresh produce, and enjoy workshops and cooking demonstrations, at the EQ Produce Markets. More than 100 stalls feature regional products, with many offering free tastings.

Shops are open until late every day, and there is a good selection of products. There is plenty of undercover parking and the Entertainment Quarter is a pleasant stroll from the Paddington end of Oxford Street.

The lush green expanse of Centennial Park

Further Afield

Beyond Sydney's inner city, the harbour foreshore is home to secluded beaches, cultural and historic sights and scenic outlooks, including those afforded by Taronga Zoo's spectacular setting. The vibrant Barangaroo precinct brings a stunning headland park, as well as diverse dining and shopping on the city's edge. Among Sydney's beachside playgrounds are Manly to the north and Bondi south of the harbour. Further west at Parramatta, sights recall and evoke early European settlement.

Sights at a Glance

❶ Ku-ring-gai Chase National Park
❷ Manly
❸ Taronga Zoo
❹ Bondi Beach
❺ Luna Park
❻ Sydney Olympic Park
❼ Parramatta

Key

▨ Central Sydney
▬ Highway
▬ Major road

Sights within Greater Sydney

0 km ___ 5
0 miles ___ 5
10 km = 6 miles

To the right of Manly wharf are shops, restaurants and bars on the adjacent pier and, on the left, the tranquil harbour-side beach known as Manly Cove. **Manly Sea Life Sanctuary** is at the far end of Manly Cove, where visitors can see sharks, giant stingrays and other species in an underwater viewing tunnel.

The Corso is a lively pedestrian thoroughfare that leads to Manly's ocean beach.

❶ Ku-ring-gai Chase National Park

McCarrs Creek Rd, Church Point.
ℹ️ Kalkari Discovery Centre (02) 9472 9300. **Open** 9am–5pm daily. **Closed** 25 Dec.

Ku-ring-gai Chase National Park lies on Sydney's northernmost outskirts, 30 km (19 miles) from the city, and covers 15,000 ha (37,000 acres). It is bounded to the north by Broken Bay, at the mouth of the Hawkesbury River, with its eroded valleys formed

during the last Ice Age. Sparkling waterways and golden beaches are set against the backdrop of the national park. Picnicking, bushwalking and windsurfing are popular here.

The Hawkesbury River curls around an ancient sandstone landscape rich in Aboriginal rock art. The national park has hundreds of Aboriginal art sites, the most common being rock engravings thought to be 2,000 years old.

❷ Manly

🚢 Manly. Manly Sea Life Sanctuary: West Esplanade. **Tel** 1800 199 742 or 1800 614 069. **Open** 9:30am–5pm daily. **Closed** 25 Dec. ♿ 🅿️
ⓦ manlysealifesanctuary.com.au

If asked to suggest a single excursion outside the city, most Sydneysiders would nominate the 11-km (7-mile) ferry ride from Circular Quay to Manly. This narrow stretch of land lying between the harbour and the ocean was named by Governor Phillip, even before Sydney got its name, for the impressive bearing of the Aboriginal men.

❸ Taronga Zoo

Bradley's Head Rd, Mosman. **Tel** (02) 9969 2777. 🚢 from Circular Quay. 🚌 247 from Wynard. **Open** 9:30am–5pm daily (May–Aug & 31 Dec: to 4:30pm). ♿ 🅿️ 🍴 ⓦ 🐾
ⓦ taronga.org.au

Taronga opened in 1916 in its idyllic harbourside location, with sweeping views across the water. The protection and preservation of endangered creatures is at the heart of the zoo's prolific conservation programmes. Free daily presentations include the engaging Free Flight Bird Show.

❹ Bondi Beach

🚌 380, 382, 381.

This long crescent of golden sand has long drawn the sun and surf set (see pp148–9). The word *bondi* is Aboriginal for "water breaking over rocks". Surfers visit from far and wide in search of the perfect wave.

People also seek out Bondi for its trendy seafront cafés and cosmopolitan milieu as much as for the world-famous beach.

Brass band playing on The Corso, Manly's esplanade

Crescent-shaped Bondi Beach, Sydney's most famous beach, looking towards North Bondi

The pavilion, built in 1928 as changing rooms, is now a busy venue for festivals, plays, films and arts and crafts displays.

❺ Luna Park

1 Olympic Dr, Milsons Point. **Tel** (02) 9922 6644. ⓣ Milsons Point. 🚌 209, 230. **Open** daily. Check website for up-to-date entry times. ♿🚻 🚻🖥️🅦 lunaparksydney.com

The amusement park with its famous smiling face entrance has been a popular destination since 1935. Entry is free, with passes required for the rides and entry into Coney Island. Coney Island is the world's last operating example of a true 1930s fun house, and the gentle Ferris Wheel is popular for panoramic views of the harbour, especially as the sun sets.

❻ Sydney Olympic Park

Sydney Olympic Park. **Tel** 9714 7888. ⓣ Olympic Park. Visitors' Centre: cnr Showground Rd & Herb Elliott Ave; **Open** 9am–5pm daily. **Closed** Good Fri, 25 Dec, 26 Dec, 1 Jan. 🎫♿🖥️ 🚲🅦 sydneyolympicpark.com.au

Host to the 27th Olympic Games in 2000, Sydney Olympic Park is at Homebush Bay. The interactive ANZ Stadium Explore Tour gives a taste of some of the stadium's best-loved sporting

moments. In summer, pack a picnic and bring a rug for the free Movies by the Boulevard.

Other facilities include the Aquatic Centre with a waterpark, an archery range and a Tennis Centre. There is an arena that hosts concerts by major Australian and international acts.

❼ Parramatta

🚆 Parramatta. 🚌 Parramatta. ℹ️ 346a Church St (02) 8839 3311.

The fertile soil of this Sydney suburb resulted in its foundation as Australia's first rural settlement, celebrating its first wheat crop in 1789. **Elizabeth Farm**, dating from 1793, is the oldest surviving home in Australia. Once the home of John Macarthur, the farm played a major role in breeding merino sheep, so

vital to the country's economy *(see p55)*. The house is now a museum, detailing the lives of its first inhabitants until 1850.

Old Government House in Parramatta Park is the oldest intact public building in Australia, built in 1799. The Doric porch, added in 1816, is attributed to Francis Greenway *(see p177)*. Inside is a collection of early 19th-century furniture. **St John's Cemetery** on O'Connell Street is the final resting place of many First Fleet settlers *(see p54)*.

🏛️ Elizabeth Farm

70 Alice St, Rosehill. **Tel** (02) 9635 9488. **Open** 10am–4pm Wed–Sun (daily in Jan & NSW school hols). **Closed** Good Fri, 25 Dec. ♿ 🚻 🚲 🖥️

🏛️ Old Government House

Parramatta Park (entry by Macquarie St). **Tel** (02) 9635 8149. **Open** daily. **Closed** Good Fri, 25 Dec. ♿ 🚻

Drawing room in Old Government House in Parramatta

GETTING AROUND SYDNEY

The best way to see the city's sights and attractions is on foot, coupled with public transport. Buses and trains serve the suburbs and outlying areas as well as the inner city. The Sydney Light Rail links the downtown area to the inner west, while a new line out to south-eastern suburbs will open in 2019. Passenger ferries provide a fast and scenic means of travel between the city and the many harbourside suburbs. An Opal smartcard makes it easy to pay for travel on all forms of public transport. Transport NSW has an excellent online and mobile trip planner for public transport; the Infoline is the telephone version of the service.

Driving in Sydney

Driving is not the ideal way to get around Sydney: the roads are confusing, traffic is congested and parking can be dear. If using a car, avoid peak hours (about 7:30–9:30am and 4–7:30pm).

Overseas visitors can use their usual driving licences to drive in Sydney.

Parking in Sydney is strictly regulated, with fines for any infringements. There are many car parks in and around the city. Also look for blue and white "P" signs or metered parking zones.

Taxis

Taxis are plentiful in the city: there are many taxi ranks and taxis are often found outside large hotels. Meters indicate the fare plus any extras, such as booking fees and waiting time. A 20 per cent night tariff applies from 10pm. Book wheelchair-accessible taxis with any major taxi company. Uber is also available via the app.

Sydney by Bicycle

Cycling is permitted on all city and suburban roads, but stay in designated cycling tracks or areas with light motor traffic. Helmets are compulsory by law. Cyclists can find GPS-based ride routes from **Bicycle New South Wales**.

Cycling in Centennial Park

Walking

Take care when walking around the city. Vehicles are driven on the left. For safety, only cross the roads at designated crossings. Push-button crossings with walk signals or countdown timers are found at traffic lights. Pedestrian crossings are marked by thick white stripes across the road.

Tickets

Travelling on public transport requires a pre-paid Opal card or Opal single-trip ticket. Opal cards can be used on all public transport but not for private, sightseeing and Fast Ferry services including to Fort Denison.

The Opal card has to be pre-loaded with money, from $10 for adults, $5 for children. There is no charge for the card itself. Register the card online to check balances, top up and block it if it is lost. It can be topped up wherever cards are sold (including convenience stores and newsagents) or at top-up machines at stations and wharves. Users must tap on and off each journey; the tap pad shows the remaining balance. After eight paid journeys in a week (running Mon–Sun), remaining journeys are half-price. When daily and weekly fare caps are reached, travel is free for the rest of the day or week. The daily and weekly fare caps for adults are $15 and $60 respectively, half that for children and concession. There is a $2.50 fare cap on Sundays.

Opal single-trip tickets for trains, ferries and light rail are available from ticket machines at selected stations and wharves. Opal single trip bus tickets can be purchased from the driver on board, except on pre-pay bus services, which includes all city centre buses.

DIRECTORY

Useful Information

Bicycle New South Wales
Tel (02) 9704 0800.
W bicyclensw.org.au

Opal
Tel 13 65 25. W opal.com.au

Sydney & Bondi Explorer
W theaustralianexplorer.com.au

Sydney Buses
W sydneybuses.info

Sydney Buses Transit Shop Circular Quay
Opposite Wharf 5. **Map** 1 B3.
Tel (02) 9244 1990.

Sydney Trains
W sydneytrains.info

Transport Infoline and Mobile App
Tel 13 15 00.
W transportnsw.info
W transportnsw.info/apps

For Hire light
Taxi licence number
Taxi company name
Driver's photo licence

Travelling by Bus

Government-owned Sydney buses provide a punctual service that links up conveniently with the city's rail and ferry systems. As well as covering city and suburban areas, there are the excellent privately owned sightseeing bus routes – the Sydney Explorer and the Bondi Explorer. The **Transport Infoline** can advise you on routes, fares and journey times for all Sydney buses. Armed with the map printed on the inside back cover of this book and an Opal card, you can enjoy travelling about the city without the difficulties and expense of city parking.

Using Sydney Buses

Sydney Buses operates an extensive network with comfortable, modern buses covering more than 300 routes across the city and suburbs. Route numbers and journey destinations are displayed on the front, back and left side of all Sydney buses. An "X" or "E" in front of the number means that it is an express bus; an "L" indicates limited stops. Red buses with routes starting with "M" are high-capacity metro buses that cover routes used by large numbers of commuters. Buses also feature electronic displays that scroll to show the areas the bus travels through. When you see your bus approaching, raise your arm to signal to the driver that you want the bus to stop. Most buses have stepless entries, which allow less mobile passengers and people with strollers to board with ease. Buses also have priority seating areas at the front for disabled, elderly or less mobile passengers.

Single-journey Opal tickets can be purchased on board regular buses from the driver on routes outside the city centre but not on pre-paid services. Try to have coins ready as drivers are not always able to change large notes. You will be given a ticket valid for that journey only. Buses with a "pre-pay" sign require you to have an Opal card or single Opal ticket before you board. You must have pre-paid tickets to board buses in the city centre. Opal cards are available at main bus stops, convenience stores and newsagents. You must tap your Opal card on and off using the touch pad located inside the bus doors at the start and end of your journey. Your remaining

Opal reader, which should be tapped with the card at the start and end of each journey

Opal balance will be displayed. You do not need to tap on and off single Opal tickets bought from the driver on board.

When you wish to alight, press one of the stop buttons well before the bus reaches your stop. The doors are electronic and can only be opened by the drivers.

Note that eating, drinking and smoking are prohibited on buses.

Bus Stops

Bus stops are indicated by yellow and black signs with a profile of a bus. Below this symbol, the numbers of all buses along the route are clearly listed. Large circular light blue signs with a capital "B" on them also indicate major bus stops and interchanges.

Timetables are usually found at main bus stops. They are also available at Sydney Buses Transit Shops, as well as on Transport NSW online and mobile sites. Public holidays usually follow the Sunday timetable.

Sightseeing by Bus

Two Sydney bus routes run by **Sydney Explorer**, the open-top double-decker Sydney Explorer and the Bondi Explorer, offer flexible sightseeing with commentaries in several languages. The Sydney Explorer covers a 32-km (20-mile) circuit and stops at 26 of the city's most popular attractions. The Bondi Explorer travels through a number of Sydney's eastern suburbs with 10 stops, taking in much of the area's coastal scenery.

The red Sydney Explorer buses run daily every 15 to 20 minutes, the Bondi route every 30 minutes. The advantage of these services is that you can explore at will, getting on and off as often as you wish for the duration of your ticket validity. Explorer bus stops are clearly marked. One- and two-day tickets are available for hop-on/hop-off travel on both Explorer routes and can be bought when boarding a bus. Tickets are also available from most hotels, information kiosks and some newsagents.

Sightseeing on the open-top Sydney Explorer bus

Travelling by Train

The key link between the city and suburbs, Sydney's railway network also serves much of the central business district and reaches out to Newcastle and the Hunter region to the north, Bathurst to the west, Kiama and Bomaderry to the south and Goulburn to the southeast. Sydney Trains operates seven major suburban lines. The City Circle loop stops at Central, Town Hall, Wynyard, Circular Quay, St James and Museum stations. Most suburban lines pass through Central and Town Hall.

DIRECTORY

Train Companies

NSW TrainLink
Central Railway Station,
Platform 1, Sydney Terminal.
Map 4 E5. **Tel** 132232.
W nswtrainlink.info

Sydney Light Rail
Tel 131500.
W transportnsw.info

Sydney Trains Information
Central Railway Station
Map 4 E5. **Tel** 131500.
Circular Quay Railway Station
Map 1 B3. **Tel** (02) 9224 3553.
W sydneytrains.info

Pedestrian concourse outside Central Railway Station

Finding Your Way Around Sydney Trains

The state government-owned Sydney Trains network is mainly used by commuters and covers the city and surburban Sydney. It is an efficient, economical and easy way to travel to and from the suburbs such as Parramatta. **Sydney Trains Information** has details of services and timetables.

Trains run from 4:15am until about midnight, when buses replace train services at railway stations. When using trains at night: use carriages near the train guard, marked by a blue light.

Using the Sydney Trains Route Map

Sydney Trains lines are numbered and colour-coded and route maps are displayed at all stations and in train carriages. Distances shown on the map are not to the correct scale. Train stations are signposted with a white capital T in an orange circle.

Country and Inter-Urban Trains

NSW TrainLink manages the inter-city and regional train network in the state. Find trip information and book online at NSW TrainLink's website. Its main retail centre is at Central Station, and some travel agents and backpacker accommodation can book tickets.

Inter-urban trains run to several areas, including Blue Mountains *(see pp172–5)*, Wollongong *(see p190)* and Newcastle *(see p177)*.

Using the Sydney Light Rail

The **Sydney Light Rail** network provides easy access to some of the most popular areas at the south of the city, including

Paddy's Markets, Chinatown, Darling Harbour and the Sydney Fish Market. A new line through George St and to southeastern suburbs is to open in 2019.

Services on the 23-stop inner west line from Central to Dulwich Hill are frequent – every 10–15 minutes during the day and night. A service linking Central Station and The Star casino operates 24 hours a day, every day. Services to stations beyond The Star run from 6am until 11pm daily, with extended hours on Fridays and Saturdays.

You must have an Opal card or single-trip Opal ticket to use the Light Rail network. Single-trip tickets are available from Opal ticket machines at most Light Rail stations. You must tap your Opal card or ticket on and off at the start and end of your journey, using the readers on each station platform.

The Sydney Light Rail

The Sydney Light Rail is designed to link Central Railway Station with Glebe and the inner west, via Darling Harbour. These efficient and environmentally friendly trains offer a quicker and quieter means of travelling around parts of the city. Light Rail stations are indicated by a white capital L in a red circle.

Travelling by Ferry and Water Taxi

For more than a century, Sydney ferries have been a picturesque, as well as a practical, feature of the Sydney scene. Travelling by ferry is both a pleasure and an efficient way to journey between Sydney's various harbour suburbs. Sightseeing cruises are operated by various private companies, including whalewatching excursions beyond the harbour. Water taxis can be a convenient and fast alternative, although they are more expensive.

A water taxi on Sydney Harbour

Water Taxis

Small, fast taxi boats are available for hire to carry passengers around the harbour. You can flag them down like normal road cabs. Try King Street Wharf or Circular Quay, near the Overseas Passenger Terminal.

Water taxis will pick up and drop off passengers at any navigable pier. However, they are not cheap. Rates vary, depending on the distance. Fare estimates are available online. A short trip such as Darling Harbour to Circular Quay costs about $70–90 for a short, 10-minute journey for two to four people, and $10 for each additional passenger.

Sydney ferries coming and going at Circular Quay Ferry Terminal

Using Sydney's Ferries

There is a steady line of Sydney Ferries crossing the harbour every day between 6am and midnight. They service most of Sydney Harbour, Manly and stops along the Parramatta River.

The state-government owned ferry network operated by Harbour City Ferries has seven lines covered by the Opal network. A number of private lines and Fast Ferry services also operate but require a separate ticket. The **Transport NSW** website has trip-planning information including timetables and fares.

While most ferry routes start or end at Circular Quay, you can board and disembark at any stop along the route. Electronic destination boards at the entrance to each wharf indicate the wharf from which your ferry will leave. You will need an Opal card or single-journey Opal ticket to use the Transport NSW ferry network.

Manly's ferry terminal is serviced by regular ferries and the Fast Ferry service that runs during peak hours on weekdays. Fast Ferry tickets can be bought online or at the ticket office at Wharf 6 Circular Quay or Pier 26, shop 2B, at Darling Harbour.

Sightseeing by Ferry

Sydney Ferries' wide network offers an affordable alternative to commercial harbour cruises. Although there is no commentary, a ferry trip is a very cost-effective and pleasant way to experience Sydney Harbour.

Tour operators offer sightseeing cruises from Circular Quay and Darling Harbour, as well as hop-on/hop-off tickets and two- to four-hour whale-watching cruises (Jun–Oct). Travel to Fort Denison in the middle of the harbour is only available through **Captain Cook Cruises**, with tickets sold at Circular Quay.

DIRECTORY

Ferry Companies

Captain Cook Cruises
Tel (02) 9206 1111 or 1800 804 943.
W captaincookcruises.com.au

Manly Fast Ferry
Tel (02) 9583 1199.
W manlyfastferry.com.au

Sydney Ferries and Transport NSW
Tel 131500.
W transportnsw.info

Water Taxi Companies

H2O Water Taxis
Tel 1300 420 829.
W h2owatertaxis.com.au

Water Taxis Combined
Tel (02) 9555 8888.
W watertaxis.com.au

Electronic destination board for all ferries leaving Circular Quay

SHOPPING IN SYDNEY

For many travellers, shopping can be as much of a voyage of discovery as sightseeing. The variety of shops in Sydney is wide and the quality of goods is high. The city has two good quality department stores, many elegant arcades and shopping galleries, as well as popular weekly and monthly markets. The range of merchandise available is vast and local talent is promoted. But the most interesting shopping doesn't stop at the city centre; there are several "satellite" alternatives within close proximity.

A jumble of bric-a-brac in a typical Sydney junk shop

Shopping Hours

Most shops are open from 9 or 10am to 5:30pm every day, though some may close early on Saturdays and Sundays. High-end boutiques open from 10am to 6pm. On Thursdays, most shops stay open until 9pm. Most shops in Chinatown are open late every evening and on Sundays.

How to Pay

Major credit cards are accepted almost everywhere, although very small stores may require a minimum purchase of A$10–20 before accepting electronic payment. Department stores will usually exchange goods or give you a refund if you are not satisfied or change your mind, provided you have kept your receipt. Other stores will only refund if an item is faulty or not as described. A 10 per cent Goods and Services Tax (GST) is included in the marked price, and the amount is indicated separately on the receipt.

Sales

Many shops conduct sales all year round. The big department stores of **David Jones** and **Myer** have two gigantic and chaotic clearance sales every year. The post-Christmas sales start on 26 December and last into January. The other major sale time starts in June in the lead up to the end of the financial year.

Tax-free Sales

Duty-free shops are found in the city as well as at Kingsford Smith Airport *(see p554)*. You can save 10 per cent on goods such as perfume, jewellery and watches, and up to 30 per cent on alcohol at duty-free shops but you must show your passport and onward ticket. Some stores will deliver your goods to the airport to be picked up on departure. Duty-free items must be kept in their sealed bags until you depart.

You can claim back the GST paid on most goods for purchases with a combined value of A$300 or more, at the airport under the Tourist Refund Scheme.

Chifley Tower, with the Chifley Plaza shopping arcade at its base

Arcades and Malls

Arcades and shopping malls in Sydney range from the ornately Victorian to modern marble and glass. The Queen Victoria Building *(see p94)* is Sydney's most palatial shopping space. Four levels contain more than 200 shops.

The elegant Strand Arcade *(see p94)* was originally built in 1892. Jewellery, lingerie, high fashion, antiques and fine cafés are its stock in trade.

Pitt Street Mall has several shopping centres including **MidCity** and **Westfield Sydney**, the city's largest mall, featuring department, up-market and speciality stores.

The Galeries houses the Kinokuniya bookstore, which sells Australian and American imprints, as well as Chinese and Japanese language books.

Both the **MLC Centre** and nearby **Chifley Plaza** cater to the prestige shopper, as do the

Gleebooks, popular with students and Glebe locals *(see pp138–9)*

luxury stores in nearby King and Castlereagh streets. Gucci, Cartier and Tiffany & Co. are just some of the shops found in this area.

Harbourside Shopping Centre has shops selling souvenirs, jewellery and Australiana, along with a range of waterfront restaurants.

Further afield, the **Westfield Bondi Junction** complex is only a 15-minute train ride from the centre of Sydney. It offers more than 440 stores, as well as bars, restaurants and an 11-screen cinema. The **Birkenhead Point Outlet Centre**, a 20-minute bus ride from the city in Drummoyne, has numerous stores selling well-known brands at discounted prices.

Best of the Department Stores

The spring floral displays and Christmas windows at **David Jones** are legendary, as is the luxurious perfumery and cosmetics hall on the ground floor. The store spreads out in two buildings, across the road from each other on Market and Elizabeth streets. The food hall is famous for its gourmet fare and fine wines. **Myer** has a ground floor packed with makeup and accessories, including a large MAC counter. Both stores sell women's clothing, lingerie, menswear, baby goods, children's clothes, toys, stationery, kitchenware, furniture, china, crystal and silver.

Part of the spring floral display in David Jones department store

Canopy over the harbourside Rocks Market

Markets

Scouring markets for the cheap, the cheerful and the unusual has become a popular pastime in Sydney.

Balmain Market, held each Saturday, includes interesting works by a number of local artists. The **Bondi Beach Market** on Sundays is known for its trendy second-hand clothing. The Saturday **Glebe Market** is a treasure-trove for the junk shop enthusiast and canny scavenger. The market is bright and popular with the inner-city grunge set.

The Rocks Markets features a foodie market in Jack Mundey Place (9am–3pm Fri) and the bigger, bustling weekend market sprawling on to nearby George Street (10am–5pm Sat & Sun), with stalls selling clothes, bags, one-off pieces of jewellery, artworks, prints and more.

Sydney Fish Market is the place to go for fresh seafood. You can choose from more than 100 species, both live and prepared. Above the market, the Sydney Seafood School offers lessons in preparing and serving seafood. The **Carriageworks Farmers Markets** include a fresh produce market with a focus on local and unusual produce and an artisans market with creative arts and crafts. They are held in a historic railway workshop a short walk from Redfern train station.

Other good markets are Paddy's Markets *(see p103)*, Chinatown's Friday night market *(see p103)*, Fox Studio Markets and Paddington Markets *(see pp128–9)*.

(see p103), Chinatown's Friday night market *(see p103)*, Fox Studio Markets and Paddington Markets *(see pp128–9)*.

DIRECTORY

Arcades and Malls

Birkenhead Point Outlet Centre
19 Roseby Street, Drummoyne.
w birkenheadpoint.com.au

Chifley Plaza
2 Chifley Square. **Map** 1 B4.
w chifleyplaza.com.au

The Galeries
500 George St (crn Park St).
Map 4 E2. w thegaleries.com

Harbourside Shopping Centre
Darling Harbour. **Map** 3 C2.
w harbourside.com.au

MidCity
Pitt St Mall. **Map** 4 E2.
w midcityshopping.com.au

MLC Centre
19–29 Martin Place. **Map** 1 B4.
w mlccentre.com.au

Westfield
500 Oxford St, Bondi Junction.
Tel (02) 9947 8000;
Cnr Pitt St & Market St, Sydney.
Tel (02) 8236 9200. **Map** 4 E2.

Department Stores

David Jones
Cnr Market & Castlereagh sts.
Map 1 B5.
w davidjones.com.au

Myer
436 George St. **Map** 1 B5.
w myer.com.au

Markets

Balmain Market
Cnr Darling St & Curtis Rd,
Balmain.

Bondi Beach Market
Bondi Beach Public School,
Campbell Parade, North Bondi.

Carriageworks Farmers Markets
245 Wilson St, Eveleigh.
w carriageworks.com.au

Glebe Market
Glebe Public School, Glebe Point
Rd, Glebe. **Map** 3 B5.

Sydney Fish Market
Cnr Pyrmont Bridge Rd & Bank St,
Blackwattle Bay. **Map** 3 B2.
w sydneyfishmarket.com.au

The Rocks Markets
George St, The Rocks. **Map** 1 B2.
w therocks.com

Specialist Shopping in Sydney

Sydney offers an extensive range of gift and souvenir ideas, from unset opals and jewellery to Aboriginal art and hand-crafted souvenirs. Museum shops, such as at the Museum of Sydney (see p96) and the Art Gallery of NSW (see pp114–17), often have specially commissioned items that make great presents or reminders of your visit.

One-offs

Specialist shops abound in Sydney – some practical, some eccentric, others simply indulgent. **Wheels & Doll Baby** designs clothes that mix 1950s chic, rock'n'roll and Hollywood glamour. **The Hour Glass** stocks traditional watches, while in the creative hub of Newtown, you will find unique leather goods, including handbags, wallets and belts, from **Leo Monk**. Or head to **Yoshi Jones**, where you can pick up unique Australian designs with a Japanese aesthetic. Vintage silk kimonos are unpicked, cut by hand and upcycled into innovative styles. **R.M. Williams** offers classic stockman's gear including boots, belts, clothes and accessories.

For antiques and quirky artisan homewares, try **Elements I Love**.

Australiana

Australiana has become more than just a souvenir genre; it is now an art form in itself.

The **Ken Done Gallery** has distinctive prints by artist Ken Done on a selection of posters, prints, scarves and books at his small gallery story. **Australia the Gift**, opposite Wynyard Station, sells a huge range of items, from leather, clothing and wool, to mugs, magnets and quirky tea-bag holders. The **Art Gallery of NSW** store stocks a wide range of Australian art books, prints, posters and giftware. The Queen Victoria Building (see p94) is dominated by shops selling Australiana: souvenirs, antiques, art and crafts.

The small shop at the Australian Museum (see pp98–9) sells slightly unusual gift items, such as native flower presses, bark paintings and Australian animal puppets, puzzles and games, as well as a collection of jewellery made from Australian minerals and products featuring Aboriginal designs.

Books

The large **Dymocks** store on George St sells guide books and maps on Sydney. For more eclectic browsing, try **Abbey's Bookshop**, **Ariel** and **Gleebooks**, while **Berkelouw Books** has three floors of new, second-hand and rare books. **The Bookshop Darlinghurst** specializes in gay and lesbian fiction and non-fiction. The State Library of NSW (see p113) bookshop has a good choice of Australian books, particularly on history.

Music

Several specialist music shops of international repute can be found in Sydney. **Red Eye Records** is for the streetwise, with its collectables, rarities, alternative music and concert tickets. **Mojo Record Bar** sells vinyl records at the front and drinks out the back in its themed small bar space. **Birdland** has a good stock of blues, jazz, soul and avant-garde. **The Recordstore** specializes in vinyl records of many styles, including breakbeat, drum 'n' bass, dubstep and hip hop. **Suzie Q Coffee + Records** sells an eclectic mix of second-hand LPs, and **Utopia Records** in hard rock and heavy metal. Australia's largest classical and jazz music specialist, **Fish Fine Music**, is found in the QVB.

Aboriginal Art

Traditional paintings, fabric, jewellery, boomerangs, carvings and cards can be bought at the **Aboriginal and Pacific Art**.

You can find souvenirs representing Aboriginal Australia at several shops in the Harbourside Shopping Centre, Darling Harbour. The **Coo-ee Aboriginal Art Gallery** boasts a large selection of limited edition prints, hand-printed fabrics, books and Aboriginal music.

The **Kate Owen Gallery** features three large floors of Aboriginal art, with friendly, knowledgeable staff who are happy to share their expertise. Works by urban indigenous artists can be found at the **Boomalli Aboriginal Artists' Cooperative**.

Opals

Sydney offers a variety of opals in myriad settings. **Opal Minded**, a family-owned business founded by a second-generation opal miner, creates its pieces using opals sourced from its own mines in Queensland. At **Opal Fields** you can view a collection of opalized fossils, before buying from the wide range of gems. **Giulian's** has unset opals, including blacks from Lightning Ridge, whites from Coober Pedy and boulder opals from Quilpie.

Jewellery

Long-established Sydney jewellers with 24-carat reputations include **Fairfax & Roberts** and **Hardy Brothers**. World-class pearls are found in the waters off the northwestern coast of Australia. Rare and beautiful examples can be found at **Paspaley Pearls**.

The Family Jewels has been attracting jewellery buyers to its main Paddington store since the 1980s. **Dinosaur Designs** made its name with colourful, chunky resin jewellery, while at **Love & Hatred**, jewelled wrist cuffs, rings and crosses recall lush medieval treasures.

Jan Logan is an iconic Australian jewellery designer, with stores in Melbourne, Hong Kong and London, as well as Sydney. Choose from beautiful and unusual contemporary pieces, otherwise the shop also carries antiques.

DIRECTORY

One-offs

Elements I Love
124 James St,
Leichhardt. **Map** 5 B3.
Tel 9560 3067.

The Hour Glass
142 King St.
Map 1 B5.
Tel 9221 2288.

Leo Monk
417 King St, Newtown.
Tel 9557 5728.

R.M. Williams
Level 3, Westfield Sydney,
Pitt St. **Map** 4 E2.
Tel 8246 9136.

Wheels & Doll Baby
259 Crown St,
Darlinghurst.
Map 5 A2.
Tel 9361 3286.

Yoshi Jones
Level 1, 249 King St,
Newtown.
Tel 9550 1663.

Australiana

Art Gallery of NSW
Art Gallery Road,
The Domain.
Map 2 D4.
Tel 9225 1700.

Australia the Gift
312 George St.
Map 1 B4.
Tel 9223 4066.

Ken Done Gallery
Level 2, 1 Hickson Rd.
Map 1 B2.
Tel 8274 4599.
W **kendone.com.au**

Books

Abbey's Bookshop
131 York St.
Map 1 A5.
Tel 9264 3111.

Ariel
42 Oxford St,
Paddington.
Map 5 B3.
Tel 9332 4581.

Berkelouw Books
19 Oxford St, Paddington.
Map 5 B3.
Tel 9360 3200.
Also at: 70 Norton St,
Leichhardt.
Tel 9560 3200.
W **berkelouw.com.au**

**The Bookshop
Darlinghurst**
207 Oxford St,
Darlinghurst.
Map 5 A2.
Tel 9331 1103.

Dymocks
424 George St.
Map 1 B5.
Tel 9235 0155.
One of several branches.

Gleebooks
49 Glebe Point Rd, Glebe.
Map 3 B5.
Tel 9660 2333.

Music

Birdland
Level 4, 428 George St.
Map 1 B4.
Tel 9231 1188.

Fish Fine Music
Level 2, Queen Victoria
Building.
Map 1 B5.
Tel 9264 6458.

Mojo Record Bar
Basement Level,
73 York St.
Map 1 A4.
Tel 9262 4999.

The Recordstore
255B Crown St,
Darlinghurst.
Map 5 A2.
Tel 9380 8223.

Red Eye Records
143 York St.
Map 1 A5.
Tel 9267 7440.

**Suzie Q Coffee +
Records**
1/18 Hutchinson St,
Surry Hills. **Map** 5 A3.
Tel 9332 2739.

Utopia Records
Lower Ground Floor,
511 Kent St (entrance on
Bathurst St). **Map** 1 A5.
Tel 9571 6662.

Aboriginal Art

**Aboriginal and
Pacific Art**
2 Danks St,
Waterloo.
Tel 9699 2211.

**Boomalli Aboriginal
Artists' Cooperative**
55–59 Flood St,
Leichhardt.
Tel 9560 2541.

**Coo-ee Aboriginal
Art Gallery**
31 Lamrock Ave,
Bondi Beach.
Tel 9300 9233.

Kate Owen Gallery
680 Darling St,
Rozelle.
Tel 9555 5283.

Opals

Giulian's
98 Harrington St.
Map 1 B3.
Tel 9252 2051.
Also at: Four Seasons
Hotel, 199 George St.
Map 1 B3.
Tel 9247 5630.

Opal Fields
Shop 14, Level 2,
Queen Victoria Building.
Map 1 B5.
Tel 9264 6660.

Opal Minded
55 George Street,
The Rocks.
Map 1 B2.
Tel 9247 9885.

Jewellery

Dinosaur Designs
Level 1,
Strand Arcade.
Map 1 B5.
Tel 9223 2953.
One of two branches.

Fairfax & Roberts
19 Castlereagh St.
Map 1 B5.
Tel 9232 8511.

The Family Jewels
48 Oxford St, Paddington.
Map 5 B3.
Tel 9331 6647.
W **thefamilyjewels.
com.au**
One of several branches.

Hardy Brothers
60 Castlereagh St.
Map 1 B5.
Tel 8262 3100.

Jan Logan
36 Cross St,
Double Bay.
Tel 9363 2529.

Love & Hatred
Strand Arcade.
Map 1 B5.
Tel 9233 3441.

Paspaley Pearls
2 Martin Place.
Map 1 B4.
Tel 9232 7633.

Clothes and Accessories

Australian style was once an oxymoron. Sydney now offers a plethora of chic shops as long as you know where to look. Top boutiques sell both men's and women's clothing, as well as accessories. The city's "smart casual" ethos, particularly in summer, means there are plenty of luxe but informal clothes available.

Australian Fashion

A number of Sydney's fashion designers have attained a global profile, including **Alex Perry** and **Akira Isogawa**. Perry's glamorous and breathtaking creations are often seen on the red carpet.

Young jeans labels such as **Sass & Bide** (women only) have also shot to fame, with celebrities wearing their denims. Nearby is **Scanlan & Theodore**, a stalwart of the Australian fashion scene.

Other shops are **Dragstar**, with its selection of retro women's and children's clothing, such as bright sundresses and minis. The quirky **Tigerlily** has locally designed casual, beach and swimwear, while **Zimmermann** offers women's and girls' clothes and is famous for its swimwear. **Camilla** is the place to go for Camilla Frank's vibrant, playful and luxurious free-flowing designs. Head to **Farage Women** for tailored business wear.

High-street clothing can be found in and around Pitt Street Mall and Bondi Junction. Here you will find both international and homegrown fashion outlets. **Sportsgirl** sells funky clothing that appeal to both teens and adult women. The **Witchery** stores are a favourite among women for their stylish designs, as is **Country Road**, known for its classically tailored work and weekend wear. **Just Jeans** doesn't just sell jeans; it stocks the latest trends for men and women.

General Pants has funky street labels for men and women, with denim a speciality. Surry Hills is the place for discount and vintage clothing; check out **Zoo Emporium**. New designers try out their wares in Bondi, Glebe and Paddington markets (see p137).

International Labels

Many Sydney stores sell designer imports. For the best ranges, visit **The Corner Shop**, an eclectic boutique that stocks a carefully chosen selection of clothing and accessories from emerging fashion names. **Cosmopolitan Shoes** stocks labels such as Dolce & Gabbana, Sonia Rykiel, Dior and Jimmy Choo. **Hype DC** also offers all the latest ranges. For classic tailored suits and shoes, head to the King Street store of German fashion house **Hugo Boss**. For quality men's shoes, try **Aquila** in Chifley Plaza.

Luxury Brands

Many visitors like to shop for international designer labels such as **Gucci** and **Prada**. You will find both in Westfield Sydney, plus **Chanel** and **Jimmy Choo** in nearby Castlereagh Street and local design queen **Leona Edmiston** in Chifley Plaza. The Queen Victoria Building (see p94) is home to **Bally**, and Martin Place has designer A-listers such as **Armani**. Louis Vuitton is just around the corner, while **Girls with Gems** is in Double Bay.

Surf Shops

For the latest surf gear, head to Bondi, where the streets are lined with shops selling clothing, swimwear as well as boards of all sizes to buy and hire. Surfers and novices should check out **Between the Flags** for boards, as well as **Bondi Surf Co**. Besides selling its own beachwear label, **Rip Curl** also sells Australian brands such as Tigerlily and Billabong. **Surfection** and **The Big Swim** are popular surf and swimwear shops packed with bikinis and the latest performance brands and accessories.

Clothes for Children

Department stores, **David Jones** and **Myer** (see p137), are one-stop shops for children's clothes, from newborn to teenage.

Size Chart

Women's clothes

Australian	6	8	10	12	14	16	18	20
American	4	6	8	10	12	14	16	18
British	6	8	10	12	14	16	18	20
Continental	38	40	42	44	46	48	50	52

Women's shoes

Australian	6–6½	7	7½–8	8½	9–9½	10	10½–11
American	5	6	7	8	9	10	11
British	3	4	5	6	7	8	9
Continental	36	37	38	39	40	41	42

Men's suits

Australian	44	46	48	50	52	54	56	58
American	34	36	38	40	42	44	46	48
British	34	36	38	40	42	44	46	48
Continental	44	46	48	50	52	54	56	58

Men's shirts

Australian	44	38	39	41	42	43	44	45
American	34	15	15½	16	16½	17	17½	18
British	34	15	15½	16	16½	17	17½	18
Continental	44	38	39	41	42	43	44	45

Men's shoes

Australian	7	7½	8	8½	9	10	11	12
American	7	7½	8	8½	9½	10½	11	11½
British	6	7	7½	8	9	10	11	12
Continental	39	40	41	42	43	44	45	46

Look out for good quality Australian labels such as Seed, Pavement and Bardot Junior, which have standalone stores in some shopping centres too.

Accessories

The team behind **Dinosaur Designs** are some of Australia's most celebrated designers. They craft chunky bangles, necklaces and rings, and also bowls, plates and vases, from jewel-coloured resin. **Chilli Coral**, sells home decor and gifts including Australian-made Samantha Ronson bowls, Bison tableware, vintage bottles and handmade jewellery. At the **Art Gallery of NSW** (see p138) you can find brooches and bags featuring designs by Australian artists such as Brett Whiteley. In her plush store, **Jan Logan** sells exquisite jewellery, using all kinds of precious and semi-precious stones.

Australian hat designer **Helen Kaminski** uses fabrics, raffia, straw, felt and leather to make hats and bags. In a different style altogether, **Crumpler** use high-tech fabrics to make bags that will last a century. **Andrew McDonald**'s little studio shop in the beautiful Strand Arcade brings to life handcrafted shoes for men and women.

DIRECTORY

Australian Fashion

Akira Isogawa
12A Queen St, Woollahra.
Map 6 E4. **Tel** 9361 5221.

Alex Perry
Level 2, Strand Arcade.
Map 1 B5. **Tel** 9233 6555.

Camilla
132a Warners Ave, Bondi.
Tel 9130 1430.

Country Road
Ground level, Queen Victoria Building. **Map** 1 B5.
Tel 9261 2009.

Dragstar
535A King St, Newtown.
Map 1 B4. **Tel** 9550 1243.

Farage Women
Shops 79, Level 1 Strand Arcade. **Map** 1 B5.
Tel 9233 1272.

General Pants
Ground level, Westfield Sydney, Pitt St Mall. **Map** 4 E1. **Tel** 8275 5160.

Just Jeans
Shop 56, Mid City Centre, Pitt St Mall. **Map** 4 E2.
Tel 9223 1696.

Sass & Bide
132 Oxford St, Paddington. **Map** 5 B3.
Tel 9360 3900.

Scanlan & Theodore
122 Oxford St, Paddington. **Map** 5 B3.
Tel 9380 9388.

Sportsgirl
Street level, Westfield Sydney, 188 Pitt St.
Map 1 B5. **Tel** 9223 8255.

Tigerlily
Pitt Street Mall, Westfield Sydney. **Map** 1 B5.
Tel 9221 1665.

Witchery
Shop 3, Met Centre, 273 George St. **Map** 1 B4.
Tel 9252 8450.

Zimmermann
2–16 Glenmore Rd, Paddington. **Map** 5 B3.
Tel 9357 4700.

Zoo Emporium
180B Campbell St, Surry Hills. **Tel** 9380 5990.

International Labels

Aquila
Shop 8, Chifley Plaza, Chifley Square. **Map** 1 B4.
Tel 9223 9568.

The Corner Shop
Shop 55, Level 1, Strand Arcade. **Map** 1 B5.
Tel 9221 1788.

Cosmopolitan Shoes
Shop 1, 5 Knox St, Double Bay. **Tel** 9362 0510.

Hugo Boss
97 King St. **Map** 1 B5.
Tel 9223 9211.

Hype DC
Shop 55, Queen Victoria Building. **Map** 1 B5.
Tel 9262 7444.

Luxury Brands

Armani
4 Martin Place. **Map** 1 B4.
Tel 8233 5888.

Bally
Ground floor, Queen Victoria Building.
Map 1 B5. **Tel** 9267 3887.

Chanel
70 Castlereagh St.
Map 1 B5.
Tel 1300 242 635.

Girls with Gems
Shop 15, 28–34 Cross St, Double Bay.
Tel 9328 3056.

Gucci
Level 3, Westfield Sydney. **Map** 1 B5.
Tel 1300 442 878.

Jimmy Choo
41 Castlereagh St, MLC Centre. **Map** 1 B4.
Tel 8666 0606.

Leona Edmiston
Shop 20, Chifley Plaza.
Map 1 B4.
Tel 9230 0322.

Louis Vuitton
365 George St. **Map** 1 B5.
Tel 1300 883 880.

Prada
Level 3, Westfield Sydney.
Map 1 B5. **Tel** 9231 3929.

Surf Shops

Between the Flags
152–158 Campbell Parade, Bondi Beach.
Tel 9365 5611.

The Big Swim
74 Campbell Parade, Bondi Beach.
Tel 9130 1511.

Bondi Surf Co.
80 Campbell Parade, Bondi Beach.
Tel 9365 0870.

Rip Curl
82 Campbell Parade, Bondi Beach.
Tel 9130 2660.

Surfection
31 Hall St, Bondi Beach.
Tel 9130 1051.

Clothes for Children

David Jones
Cnr Elizabeth & Market sts.
Map 1 B5.
Tel 9266 5544.

Myer
436 George St.
Map 1 B5.
Tel 9238 9111.

Accessories

Andrew McDonald
2nd Floor, Strand Arcade.
Map 1 B5.
Tel 8084 2595.

Art Gallery of NSW
Art Gallery Rd, The Domain. **Map** 2 D4.
Tel 9225 1700.

Chilli Coral
401 Crown St, Surry Hills.
Map 5 A3. **Tel** 8021 7869.

Crumpler
Ground floor, Strand Arcade. **Map** 1 B5.
Tel 9222 1300.

Dinosaur Designs
See pp138–9.

Helen Kaminski
Shop 3, Four Seasons Hotel, 199 George St.
Map 1 B3.
Tel 9251 9850.

Jan Logan
36 Cross St, Double Bay.
Tel 9363 2529.

ENTERTAINMENT IN SYDNEY

Sydney has the standard of entertainment and nightlife you would expect from a cosmopolitan city. Everything from opera and ballet at Sydney Opera House to outdoor productions in the Royal Botanic Gardens is on offer. The ICC at Darling Harbour and large venues at Homebush host major concerts. Venues such as the Capitol, the Lyric Theatre and the Theatre Royal host the latest musicals, while

Sydney's many smaller theatres stage fringe productions, modern dance and musical events. Pub rock thrives in the inner city and beyond; and there are nightspots for comedy, dance and alternative music. Movie buffs are well catered for with film festivals, art-house films and foreign titles, as well as the latest Hollywood blockbusters. Free outdoor entertainment is popular, especially in the summer.

The Sydney Theatre on Hickson Road, Walsh Bay

Information

For details of events in the city, check the online listings calendars provided by the City of Sydney via **Tourism NSW**, as well as the online versions of major news outlets. Daily newspapers also carry cinema, and often arts and theatre, advertisements. The most comprehensive listings appear in the *Sydney Morning Herald*'s "Spectrum" section every Saturday. The *Daily Telegraph* has good entertainment coverage most days.

Tourism NSW information kiosks have free guides and the quarterly *What's on in Darling Harbour*. Kiosks are found at Town Hall, Circular Quay and Martin Place. *Where Magazine* is available at the airport and the **Sydney Visitor Centre** at The Rocks. You can also try whatson.cityofsydney.nsw.gov.au or timeout.com/sydney.

Music fans are well served by free online guides, including www.themusic.com.au, www.thebrag.com and www.inthemix.com.au. Many venues have leaflets about forthcoming attractions, while the major

venues have information and event listings on their websites.

Buying Tickets

Some of the most popular shows in Sydney can sell out months in advance. While it is better to book ahead, it is still worth calling or checking websites to see if tickets are available on the day.

You can buy tickets from the box office, online or by phone. Buying online, either through major ticket agencies or from the venue's own website, is the easiest way to purchase tickets.

Tickets can be mailed to you, sent to your phone, or emailed to print yourself. Tickets can also be collected from the box office half an hour before the show.

Buying tickets from touts is not advisable, as you could be denied access to the event. It is legal, though, as long as tickets are not sold for more than the original cost. Try second-hand marketplace www.gumtree.com.au if events are sold out. Be wary of electronic tickets, though, since unscrupulous touts can sell the same e-ticket to multiple customers.

Choosing Seats

If booking online, you will be able to look at a seating plan and choose your seat. Matinees and weekday performances are often cheaper than weekends and evenings.

You can generally select the price category or seating area; some events give you the option to choose your seat, while others offer you the best available at the time.

The annual Gay and Lesbian Mardi Gras Festival's dog show *(see p46)*

Booking Agencies

Sydney has two main ticket agencies: **Ticketek** and **Ticketmaster**. Between them, they represent all the major entertainment and sporting events. The quickest and easiest way to check ticket availability and book is via the agencies websites. Both agencies have outlets throughout NSW and the ACT. Opening times vary between agencies and outlets, but they usually follow business hours. Phone bookings can be made via the call centres until late evening, but it is often hard to get through when popular shows go on sale. For Internet bookings, visit their website.

Agencies accept cash, Visa, MasterCard and Amex. Some agencies do not accept Diners Club. Booking fees apply per ticket and a service and delivery fee applies per transaction (even if tickets are sent electronically). There are no refunds (unless a show is cancelled) or exchanges.

A busker at Circular Quay

Discount Tickets and Free Entertainment

Tuesday is budget-price day at most cinemas. Some independent cinemas have special prices on other days. The Sydney Symphony Orchestra and Opera Australia *(see p144)* offer a special Student Rush price to full-time students under 28 but only if surplus tickets are available. These can be bought on the day of the performance, from the box office at the venue. The Belvoir also sets aside tickets for unemployed and student patrons for various performances, usually matinees and midweek.

Outdoor events are especially popular in Sydney, and many are free *(see pp44–7)*. Sydney Harbour is a splendid, although crowded, setting for the New Year's Eve fireworks, with a 9pm display for families, as well as the midnight display. Arrive early to secure a spot. The Sydney Festival in January is a huge extravaganza

The Spanish firedancers *Els Comediants* at the Sydney Festival

of performance and visual art. Various outdoor venues in the Rocks, Darling Harbour and in front of the **Sydney Opera House** *(see pp88–9)* feature numerous events. The most popular free events are December's Christmas Carols and January's symphony and opera concerts, held in the Domain. Also popular is the Vivid Festival of Light, Music and Ideas, which takes place every evening for more than three weeks in May–June at various locations around the city.

Disabled Visitors

Many older venues were not designed with the disabled visitor in mind, but this has been redressed in most newer buildings, and most venues set aside accessible seats. It is best to phone the box office beforehand to request special seating and

Publicity shot of the Australian Chamber Orchestra *(see p144)*

other needs or call **Ideas Inc**, who have a list of Sydney's most wheelchair-friendly venues. The Sydney Opera House has disabled parking, wheelchair access and a loop system in the Concert Hall for the hearing impaired. The website of **Easy Access Australia**, is another source of information for seniors and people with disabilities.

DIRECTORY

Useful Numbers

Easy Access Australia
W easyaccessaustralia.com.au

Ideas Inc
Tel 1800 029 904.
W ideas.org.au

Sydney Opera House
Information Desk
Tel (02) 9250 7111.
Disabled Parking Information
Tel (02) 9250 7185.

Sydney Visitor Centre
Tel 8273 0000 or 9281 2244.
W sydney.com

Tourism NSW
W visitnsw.com

Ticket Agencies

Ticketek
Tel 13 28 49.
W ticketek.com.au

Ticketmaster
Tel 136 100.
W ticketmaster.com.au

Performing Arts and Cinema

Sydney has a wealth of orchestral, choral, chamber and contemporary music from which to choose, and of course every visitor should enjoy a performance of some kind at the Sydney Opera House. There is also a stimulating range of musicals, classic plays and Shakespeare by the Sea, as well as contemporary, fringe, experimental theatre and comedy. Prominent playwrights include David Williamson, Debra Oswald, Brendan Cowell, Stephen Sewell and Louis Nowra. Australian film-making has also earned an excellent international reputation. A rich variety of both local and foreign films are screened throughout the year.

Classical Music

Much of Sydney's orchestral music and recitals are the work of the famous **Sydney Symphony Orchestra (SSO)**. Numerous concerts are given, mostly in the Sydney Opera House Concert Hall (see pp88–9), the **City Recital Hall** and the **Sydney Town Hall**.

The **Australian Chamber Orchestra** also performs at the Opera House and City Recital Hall, and has won high acclaim for its creativity. The **Australia Ensemble** is the resident chamber music group at the University of New South Wales.

Many choral groups and ensembles book St James' Church (see p119) for their performances because of its atmosphere and acoustics. Formed in 1973, the respected **Sydney Youth Orchestra** stages performances in major concert venues. The **Australian Youth Choir** is booked for many private functions, but if you are lucky, you may catch one of their major annual performances.

Comprising the 120-strong Sydney Philharmonia Symphonic Choir and the 40-member Sydney Philharmonia Motet Choir, the **Sydney Philharmonia Choirs** are the city's finest.

One of Sydney's most impressive vocal groups is the **Café of the Gate of Salvation**, which has been described as an "Aussie blend of a capella and gospel".

Originally specializing in chamber music, **Musica Viva** now presents string quartets, jazz, piano groups, percussionists, soloists and international avant-garde artists as well.

Synergy is one of Australia's foremost percussion quartets. Its innovative performance style spans traditional and contemporary percussion from around the world.

Comedy

The **Comedy Store** is known for its line-up of performances by local and visiting comics in an intimate setting with a bar. It hosts shows most nights each week and is the premier smaller venue for the popular **Sydney Comedy Festival**. Monday is comedy night at **The Old Manly Boatshed**, where both local and visiting comics perform. Tuesday is also comedy night at the **Harold Park Hotel**, where special events and entertainment is offered most nights of the week.

Dance

The **Australian Ballet** has two seven-week Sydney seasons at the Opera House: one in March/April, the other in November/December. **Sydney Dance Company** is the city's leading modern dance group. Productions are mostly staged at the Sydney Opera House.

Bangarra Dance Theatre uses traditional Aboriginal and Torres Strait Islander dance and music as its inspiration. The startling and original **Legs on the Wall** are a physical theatre group, brilliantly combining circus and aerial techniques with dance and narrative, often performed while suspended from skyscrapers.

Opera

In 1956, the Australian Opera (now called **Opera Australia**) was formed. It presented four Mozart productions in its first year. But it was the opening of the Sydney Opera House in 1973 that heralded new public interest. Opera Australia's summer season is held from early January to early March; the winter season from June to the end of October. Every year at the popular Opera in The Domain, members of Opera Australia perform excerpts from famous pieces.

Theatre

Sydney's larger, mainstream musicals are staged at the **Theatre Royal**, the opulent **State Theatre** (see p94) and the **Capitol Theatre**. **The Star** entertainment and casino complex boasts two theatres, the Showroom, and the first-rate Lyric Theatre for musical productions and stage shows.

Smaller venues also offer a range of interesting plays and performances. These include the **Seymour Centre**, the **Belvoir** and the **Ensemble Theatre**. The **Griffin Theatre** at The Stables specializes in works by new Australian playwrights, while the **Parade Theatre** at the National Institute of Dramatic Arts (NIDA) showcases work by NIDA's students. The well-respected **Sydney Theatre Company (STC)** stages an impressive line-up of shows featuring acclaimed and emerging actors at its Walsh Bay theatres, including **The Wharf**, as well as at the Sydney Opera House.

The **Bell Shakespeare Company** productions always feature an evocative interpretation of the Bard. **Shakespeare Australia** performs The Wind in the Willows in the Royal Botanic Gardens every year in January.

The **Sydney Festival** provides an enjoyable celebration of original, often edgy theatre, dance, music and visual arts.

Film

The city's main commercial cinema is the **Event Cinemas** complex. A similar Hoyts-run multiplex can be found in the Fox Studios Entertainment Quarter (see p129). Indian vegetarian restaurant **Govinda's** has a boutique movie room with comfortable reclining chairs, cushioned floors and lounges, and it offers a value combination ticket including buffet dinner and movie.

Cinephiles flock to **Palace Cinemas** on Norton Street and **Dendy Opera Quays** cinema at Circular Quay. **Cinema Paris** shows arthouse and indie films, as well as many Bollywood productions. The **Chauvel Cinema** in the Paddington Town Hall has long been the spiritual home of Australian film culture, screening the best of independent and world cinema.

Most mainstream cinemas offer half-price tickets on Tuesday, while Palace does so on Monday. The Sydney Film Festival is one of the highlights of the city's calendar (see p47). The main venue is the State Theatre. The **Flickerfest International Short Film Festival** is held at the Bondi Pavilion at Bondi Beach in January. In February, **Tropfest** holds an outdoor screening of short films.

Run by Queer Screen, the **Mardi Gras Film Festival** starts mid-February for 15 days.

DIRECTORY

Classical Music

Australia Ensemble
Tel 9385 4874.
W ae.unsw.edu.au

Australian Chamber Orchestra
Tel 8274 3888.
W aco.com.au

Australian Youth Choir
W niypaa.com.au

Café of the Gate of Salvation
W cafeofthegateof salvation.com.au

City Recital Hall
Angel Place. **Map** 1 B4.
Tel 8256 2222.
W cityrecitalhall.com

Musica Viva
Tel 8394 6666.
W musicaviva.com.au

Sydney Philharmonia Choirs
Tel 8274 6200.
W sydney philharmonia.com.au

Sydney Symphony Orchestra
Tel 8215 4600.
W sydneysymphony. com

Sydney Town Hall
483 George Street.
Map 4 E2.
Tel 9265 9333.
W sydneytownhall. com.au

Sydney Youth Orchestra
Tel 9251 2422.
W syo.com.au

Synergy
Tel 9663 5532.
W synergy percussion.com

Comedy

Comedy Store
Entertainment Quarter, Driver Ave, Moore Park.
Map 5 C5. **Tel** 9357 1419.
W comedystore.com.au

Harold Park Hotel
78A Ross St, Glebe.
Tel 9660 4745.
W haroldparkhotel. com.au

The Old Manly Boatshed
40 The Corso, Manly.
Tel 9977 4443.
W oldmanlyboatshed. com.au

Sydney Comedy Festival
Tel 9519 9231.
W sydneycomedy festival.com.au

Dance

Australian Ballet
Tel 1300 369 741.
W australianballet. com.au

Bangarra Dance Theatre
Tel 9251 5333.
W bangarra.com.au

Legs on the Wall
Tel 9560 9479.
W legsonthewall. com.au

Sydney Dance Company
Tel 9221 4811.
W sydneydance company.com

Opera

Opera Australia
Tel 9318 8200.
W opera.org.au

Theatre

Bell Shakespeare Company
Tel 8298 9000. W bell shakespeare.com.au

Belvoir
25 Belvoir St, Surry Hills.
W belvoir.com.au

Capitol Theatre
13 Campbell St, Haymarket.
Map 4 E4. W capitol theatre.com.au

Ensemble Theatre
78 McDougall St, Kirribilli.
Box office: **Tel** 9929 0644.
W ensemble.com.au

Griffin Theatre
10 Nimrod St, Kings Cross.
Map 5 B1. **Tel** 9361 3817.
W griffintheatre.com.au

Parade Theatre
215 Anzac Parade, Kensington. **Map** 5 B4.
W nida.edu.au

Seymour Centre
Cnr Cleveland St & City Rd, Chippendale.
W seymourcentre.com

Shakespeare Australia
Tel 03 8676 7511 or 1300 122 344. W shakespeare australia.com.au

The Star
80 Pyrmont St, Pyrmont.
Map 3 B1. **Tel** 9777 9000.
W star.com.au

State Theatre
49 Market St. **Map** 1 B5.
W statetheatre.com.au

Sydney Festival
Tel 8248 6500. W sydney festival.org.au

Sydney Theatre Co
Tel 9250 1999. W sydney theatre.com.au

Theatre Royal
MLC Centre, King St.
Map 1 B5. **Tel** 1300 723 038 (Ticketmaster).
W theatreroyal.net.au

The Wharf
Pier 4, Hickson Rd, Walsh Bay. **Map** 1 A1.
Tel 9250 1777. W sydney theatre.com.au

Film

Chauvel Cinema
Paddington Town Hall, 249 Oxford St, Paddington.
Map 5 C3. W palace cinemas.com.au

Cinema Paris
Entertainment Quarter, Driver Ave, Moore Park.
Map 5 C5. **Tel** 9332 1633.
W hoyts.com.au

Dendy Opera Quays
Shop 9/2, East Circular Quay. **Map** 1 C2. **Tel** 9247 3800. W dendy.com.au

Event Cinemas
505–525 George St.
Map 4 E3. **Tel** 9273 7300.
W eventcinemas.com.au

Flickerfest
W flickerfest.com.au

Govinda's
112 Darlinghurst Rd, Darlinghurst. **Map** 5 B1.
W govindas.com.au

Mardi Gras Festival
W queerscreen.org.au

Palace Cinemas
Palace Norton Street Cinema 99 Norton St, Leichhardt. W palace cinemas.com.au

Tropfest
W tropfest.com

Music Venues and Nightclubs

Sydney attracts some of the biggest names in modern music all year round. Venues range from the cavernous Allphones Arena to small and noisy back rooms in pubs. Visiting international DJs frequently play sets at Sydney clubs. Some venues cater for a variety of music tastes – rock and pop one night, jazz, blues or folk the next. There are several free online gig guides available, including www.themusic.com.au, www.thebrag. com.au and www.inthemix.com.au which tell you what is on.

Getting In

Tickets for major shows are available through booking agencies such as Ticketek and Ticketmaster (see p142). Prices vary considerably, depending on the shows that are going to take place. You may pay from A$30 to A$70 for a gig at the Metro, but over A$150 for seats for a concert by major international touring acts. **Moshtix** also sells tickets for smaller venues across Sydney and their website gives a good idea of the various venues and what is on. Buying online also prevents you from having to queue early for tickets from the door.

You can also pay at the door on the night at most places, unless the show is sold out. Nightclubs often have a cover charge, but some venues will admit you free before a certain time in the evening or on weeknights.

Most venues serve alcohol, so shows are restricted to those at least 18 years of age. This is the usual case unless a gig is specified "all ages". It is advisable that people under 30 years old carry photo identification, such as a passport or driver's licence, because entry to some establishments is very strict. You are also not allowed to carry any kind of bottle into most nightclubs or other venues. Similarly, any cameras and recording devices are usually prohibited.

Be guided by the style of the artist and their audience, but be aware that flip flops are generally not welcome and are considered a safety hazard. Wear thin layers, which you can remove when you get hot, instead of a coat, and avoid carrying a big bag, because many venues do not have a cloakroom.

Rock, Pop and Hip Hop

Pop's big names and famous rock groups perform at the **Enmore Theatre**, **ICC Sydney**, **Qudos Bank Arena**, **Hordern Pavilion** and sports grounds such as the Allianz Stadium at Moore Park and ANZ Stadium at **Sydney Olympic Park** (see p131) in Homebush Bay. More intimate locations include the **State Theatre** (see p94), **Factory Theatre** and Sydney's best small live music venue, **The Metro Theatre**. Hip hop acts usually play in rock venues rather than in nightclubs. You are almost as likely to find a crew rapping as a band strumming and drumming at The Metro Theatre or the **Palace Hotel**. It is not unusual to catch a punk, garage or electro-folk band at **The Bald Faced Stag** on Parramatta Road. Classic pub rock is played by some of Australia's best-loved musicians at **The Bridge Hotel** in Rozelle.

Pub rock is a constantly changing scene in Sydney. Listings appear on venue websites and online gig guides, as well as in the street press (see p142). Music stores are also full of flyers for gigs at The Metro Theatre, where international and Australian acts perform every week. These shows usually sell out very quickly.

Jazz, Folk and Blues

For many years, the first port of call for any jazz, funk, groove or folk enthusiast has been **The Basement**. Visiting luminaries play some nights, talented local musicians others, and the line-ups now also include popular world music and hip-hop bands. **505**, in Surry Hills, features live jazz, blues, reggae, gypsy, latin, funk and folk styles Monday to Saturday. Experimental jazz is offered on Fridays and Saturdays at the **Seymour Centre** (see p145). **Leadbelly Newtown** offers dinner-and-show deals, as well as show-only tickets, and has been drawing an excellent roster of jazz, blues and roots talent. Marrickville's **Camelot Lounge** presents jazz, folk, blues, cabaret and world music, while the **Cat & Fiddle Hotel** in Balmain is the place to go for acoustic music on weekends. **Gaelic Club** features traditional Irish musicians on Friday nights.

House, Breakbeats and Techno

Sydney's long-time super club, **Home Sydney** in Cockle Bay, features three levels and a gargantuan sound system. Friday night is the time to go, as the DJs present a pulsating mix of house, trance, drum and bass and breakbeats. A mainstream crowd flocks to the nearby **Bungalow 8** on King Street Wharf. Once the sun has set, house DJs turn the place into a club. At **Pacha**, in the Ivy complex, you can experience hallucinatory burlesque with international artists every Saturday night. There are bands or DJs at the **World Bar** in Kings Cross every night.

For something a little more hip, try **Candy's Apartment** on Bayswater Road, or join the student and backpacker crowd at **Side Bar Sydney**, where you'll find DJs and live music in the nightclub seven nights a week. The **Arthouse Hotel** hosts regular burlesque, cabaret, DJ and club nights in the 1836 heritage School of Arts Building next to the Hilton Hotel. In the heart of The Rocks district, resident DJs and guest musicians get the crowd on the dance floor with uplifting nu-disco and house beats at **The Argyle**, which also hosts themed party nights and boasts five bars over two levels. Or sample the low-ceilinged **Chinese Laundry** on Sussex Street, which you'll find tucked under the gentrified pub, Slip Inn.

Gay and Lesbian Pubs and Clubs

Sunday night is the big night for many of Sydney's gay community, although there is plenty of action throughout the week. A number of venues have a gay or lesbian night on one night of the week and attract a mainstream crowd on the other nights. The **Bank Hotel** in Newtown presents live bands for free Thursdays to Saturdays from 8pm until late upstairs at Waywards. **The Polo Lounge**, on the top floor of the Oxford Hotel, has great views of the city's skyline. Catch live music at the first-floor supper club.

ARQ on Flinders Street is the largest of the gay clubs, with pounding commercial house music. The main dance floor is overlooked by a mezzanine for watching the writhing mass of bodies below. **Midnight Shift** on Oxford Street is for men only, and **Stonewall** is a lively gay bar with nightly entertainment over three levels, including DJs, dancers and drag shows.

The **Colombian** is the best of the Oxford Street bars, with a mock Central American jungle and large windows that open out to the street. The **Oxford Hotel** and its upper-level cocktail bar **Gingers** are popular too. There's always something on in the main bar and visiting acts often perform in its basement level underground bar. The **Imperial Hotel** has drag shows on most nights of the week. The **Oxford Art Factory** in Darlinghurst has live music as well as burlesque and cabaret evenings.

DIRECTORY

Rock, Pop and Hip Hop

The Bald Faced Stag
345 Parramatta Rd, Annandale. **Tel** 9560 7188.
W baldfacedstag.com.au

The Bridge Hotel
119 Victoria Rd, Rozelle. **Tel** 9810 1260.

Enmore Theatre
130 Enmore Rd, Newtown. **Tel** 9550 3666/9519 9331.
W enmoretheatre.com.au

Factory Theatre
105 Victoria Rd, Marrickville. **Tel** 9550 2990. W factorytheatre.com.au

Hordern Pavilion
Driver Ave, Moore Park.
Map 5 C5. **Tel** 9921 5333.
W playbillvenues.com

ICC Sydney
14 Darling Drive, Darling Harbour. **Tel** 9215 7100.
W iccsydney.com.au

The Metro Theatre
624 George St.
Map 4 E3. **Tel** 9550 3666.
W metrotheatre.com.au

Moshtix
Tel 1300 438 849.
W moshtix.com.au

Palace Hotel
730–742 George St, Haymarket. **Map** 4 E4.
Tel 9212 2111.
W palacehotelsydney.com.au

Qudos Bank Arena
Sydney Olympic Park, Homebush Bay. **Tel** 8765 4321. W qudosbankarena.com.au

State Theatre
49 Market St. **Map** 1 B5.
Tel 9373 6852.
W statetheatre.com.au

Sydney Olympic Park
Homebush Bay. **Tel** 9714 7888. W sydneyolympicpark.com.au

Jazz, Folk and Blues

505
280 Cleveland St, Surry Hills. W venue505.com

The Basement
29 Reiby Place. **Map** 1 B3.
Tel 9251 2797. W thebasement.com.au

Camelot Lounge
Cnr 103 Railway Pde & 19 Marrickville Rd, Marrickville. **Tel** 9550 3777.
W camelotlounge.com

Cat & Fiddle Hotel
456 Darling St, Balmain.
Tel 9810 7931.
W catandfiddle.com.au

Gaelic Club
64 Devonshire St, Surry Hills. **Tel** 9212 1587.
W gaelicclubsydney.com

Leadbelly Newtown
42 King St, Newtown.
Tel 9557 7992.
W theleadbelly.com.au

Seymour Centre
Cnr Cleveland St & City Rd, Chippendale.
W seymourcentre.com

House, Breakbeats and Techno

The Argyle
18 Argyle St, The Rocks.
Map 1 B2. **Tel** 9247 5500.
W theargylerocks.com

Arthouse Hotel
275 Pitt St. **Map** 1 B5.
Tel 9284 1200. W arthousehotel.com.au

Bungalow 8
The Promenade, 3 Lime St, King St Wharf. **Tel** 9299 4660. W kingstreetwharf.com.au

Candy's Apartment
22 Bayswater Rd, Kings Cross. **Map** 5 B1. **Tel** 9380 5600. W candys.com.au

Chinese Laundry
111 Sussex St. **Map** 1 A3.
Tel 8295 9999. W chineselaundryclub.com.au

Home Sydney
101 Cockle Bay Wharf, Darling Harbour. **Map** 4 D2. W homesydney.com

Pacha
Level 1, Ivy, 330 George St.
Map 1 B4. **Tel** 9240 3006.

Side Bar Sydney
509 Pitt Street. **Map** 4 D5.
Tel 9288 7888. W sidebarsydney.com.au

World Bar
24 Bayswater Rd, Kings Cross. **Map** 5 C1.
W theworldbar.com

Gay and Lesbian Clubs and Pubs

ARQ
16 Flinders St, Taylor Square.
Map 5 A2. **Tel** 9380 8700.
W arqsydney.com.au

Bank Hotel
324 King St, Newtown.
Tel 8568 1900.
W bankhotel.com.au

Colombian
Cnr Oxford and Crown Sts, Surry Hills. **Map** 5 A2.
Tel 9360 2151.
W colombian.com.au

Gingers
Level 1, 134 Oxford St, Darlinghurst. **Map** 5 A2.
Tel 9331 3467.

Imperial Hotel
35 Erskineville Rd, Erskineville. **Tel** 9516 1766.

Midnight Shift
85 Oxford St, Darlinghurst.
Map 5 A2. **Tel** 9358 3848.
W themidnightshift.com.au

Oxford Art Factory
38–46 Oxford St, Darlinghurst. **Map** 5 A2.
Tel 9332 3711.
W oxfordartfactory.com

Oxford Hotel
134 Oxford St, Darlinghurst.
Map 5 A2. **Tel** 9331 3467.
W theoxfordhotel.com.au

The Polo Lounge
Level 2, 134 Oxford St, Darlinghurst. **Map** 5 A2.
Tel 9331 3467.

Stonewall
175 Oxford St, Darlinghurst.
Map 5 A2. **Tel** 9360 1963.
W stonewallhotel.com

Sydney's Beaches

Being a city built around the water, it is no wonder that many of Sydney's recreational activities involve the sand, sea and sun. There are many harbour and surf beaches in Sydney, most of them accessible by bus *(see p133)*. Even if you're not a swimmer, the beaches offer a chance to get away from it all for a day or weekend and enjoy the fresh air and relaxed way of life.

Scuba diving at Gordons Bay

Swimming

You can swim at either harbour or ocean beaches. Harbour beaches are generally smaller and sheltered. Popular ones are Camp Cove, Shark Bay and Balmoral Beach.

At the ocean beaches, surf lifesavers in their red and yellow or blue caps are on duty. Swimming rules are strongly enforced. Surf lifesaving carnivals are held throughout the summer. **Surf Life Saving Australia**'s **Beachsafe** website has information on facilities, the weather and lifesaving services.

The beaches can become polluted, especially after heavy rain. The **Beach Watch and Harbour Watch Info Line** provides information.

Surfing

Surfing is more a way of life than a leisure activity for some Sydneysiders. If you're a beginner, try Bondi, Bronte, Palm Beach or Collaroy.

Two of the best surf beaches are Maroubra and Narrabeen. Bear in mind that local surfers know one another well and do not take kindly to "intruders"

who drop in on their waves. To hire a surfboard, try Bondi Surf Co on Campbell Parade, Bondi Beach, or Aloha Surf on Pittwater Road, Manly. If you would like to learn, there are two schools: **Manly Surf School** and **Lets Go Surfing** at Bondi Beach. They also hire out boards and wetsuits.

Windsurfing and Sailing

There are locations around Sydney suitable for every level of windsurfer. Boards can be hired from **Balmoral Sailing School**.

Good spots include Palm Beach, Narrabeen Lakes, La Perouse, Brighton-Le-Sands and Kurnell Point (for beginner and intermediate boarders) and Long Reef Beach, Palm Beach and Collaroy (for more experienced boarders).

One of the best ways to see the harbour is while sailing. A sailing boat, including a skipper, can be hired for the afternoon from the **East Sail** sailing club. The sailing club has two-day courses and also hires out sailing boats and motor cruisers to experienced sailors.

Scuba Diving

There are some excellent dive spots around Sydney, especially in winter when the water is clear, if a little cold. Favoured spots are Shelly Beach, Gordons Bay and Camp Cove.

Pro Dive Coogee offers a range of courses, escorted dives, introductory dives, and hire equipment. **Dive Centre Manly** also runs courses, hires equipment and conducts boat dives seven days a week.

DIRECTORY

Balmoral Sailing School
Balmoral Park, The Esplanade, Mosman, Balmoral Beach. **Tel** 9960 5344. W sailingschool.com.au

Beachsafe
W beachsafe.org.au

Beach Watch/Harbour Watch
W environment.nsw.gov.au/beach

Dive Centre Manly
10 Belgrave St, Manly. **Tel** 9977 4355. W divesydney.com.au
Also at Bondi and City.

East Sail
d'Albora Marinas, New Beach Rd, Rushcutters Bay. **Tel** 9327 1166. W eastsail.com.au

Lets Go Surfing
128 Ramsgate Ave, North Bondi. **Tel** 9365 1800.
W letsgosurfing.com.au

Manly Surf School
North Steyne Rd, Manly. **Tel** 9932 7000. W manlysurfschool.com.au

Pro Dive Coogee
27 Alfreda St, Coogee. **Tel** 9665 6333. W provdivesydney.com

Surf Life Saving NSW
Tel 9471 8000.
W surflifesaving.com.au

Rock baths and surf lifesaving club at Coogee Beach

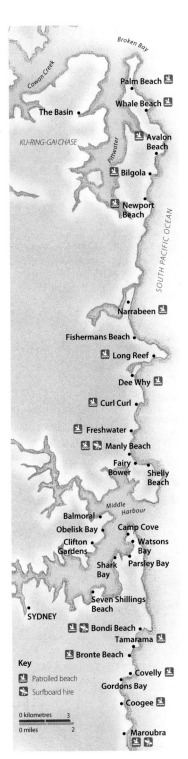

Top 30 Beaches

These beaches have been selected for their safe swimming, water sports, facilities available or their picturesque setting.

	Swimming Pool	Surfing	Windsurfing	Fishing	Scuba Diving	Picnic/Barbecue	Restaurant/Café
Avalon	★	★	★	★		★	
Balmoral	★	★	★	★	★	★	
The Basin	★					★	
Bilgola							
Bondi Beach	★	★		★	★	★	★
Bronte	★	★		★	★	★	★
Camp Cove					★		
Clifton Gardens	★		★	★	★	★	
Clovelly				★	★	★	★
Coogee	★		★	★	★	★	★
Curl Curl	★	★		★			
Dee Why	★	★		★	★	★	★
Fairy Bower					★		
Fishermans Beach		★	★	★	★		
Freshwater	★	★		★	★	★	
Gordons Bay				★	★		
Long Reef		★	★	★	★		
Manly Beach	★			★	★	★	★
Maroubra		★	★	★	★	★	★
Narrabeen	★	★		★		★	
Newport Beach	★	★	★	★		★	
Obelisk Bay							
Palm Beach	★	★	★	★		★	★
Parsley Bay						★	
Seven Shillings Beach	★					★	
Shark Bay	★					★	★
Shelly Beach					★	★	★
Tamarama		★	★	★	★	★	★
Watsons Bay	★				★		★
Whale Beach	★	★	★	★		★	★

Fishing in Sydney

Surprisingly for a thriving city port, there is a wide variety of fish to be caught. From the rocks and headlands of the northern beaches, such as Palm Beach and Bilgola, tuna, whiting and blenny abound. The Narrabeen Lakes offer estuary fishing, with a population of flathead and bream. The sheltered Middle Harbour has many angling spots. Even recreational fishing requires a licence, and NSW Recreational Fishing Fee must be paid by everyone.

Triplefin blenny

SPORTING SYDNEY

Throughout Australia sport is a way of life, and Sydney is no exception. On any day you'll see locals on golf courses at dawn, running on the streets keeping fit, or having a quick set of tennis after work. At weekends, during summer and winter,

there is no end to the variety of sports you can watch. Thousands gather at the Allianz Stadium and Sydney Cricket Ground (SCG) when a big game is on while, for those who are unable to make it, sport reigns supreme on weekend television.

Cricket

During the summer months Test cricket and one-day internationals are played at the Sydney Cricket Ground (SCG). Shorter Twenty20 evening games have a fun and exciting atmosphere. It is advisable to book well in advance (through **Ticketek**) for Test matches and for all the one-day international matches, or check online to see if tickets are available on the day.

Australia versus the All Blacks

Rugby League and Rugby Union

The popularity of rugby league knows no bounds in Sydney. This is what people refer to as "the footy". There are three major competition levels: local, State of Origin – which matches Queensland against New South Wales – and international Tests. The "local" competition fields teams from all over Sydney as well as Newcastle, Canberra, Brisbane, Melbourne, the Gold Coast, Far North Queensland and Auckland, New Zealand.

These matches are held all over Sydney, but the ANZ Stadium at Sydney Olympic Park is by far the biggest venue. Tickets for State

of Origin and Test matches often sell out immediately. Call Ticketek to check availability.

Rugby union is the second most popular football code. Again, matches at Test level sell out very quickly. For some premium trans-Tasman rivalry, catch a Test match between Australia's "Wallabies" and the New Zealand "All Blacks". Phone Ticketek for details.

Golf and Tennis

Golf enthusiasts need not do without their round of golf. There are many courses throughout Sydney where visitors are welcome at all times. These include **Moore Park**,

St Michael's and Warringah golf courses. It is sensible to phone beforehand for a booking, especially at weekends.

Tennis is another favoured sport. Courts available for hire can be found all over Sydney. Many centres also have floodlit courts available for night time. Try **Cooper Park** or **Parkland Sports** Centre.

Playing golf at Moore Park, one of Sydney's public courses

Australian Rules Football

Although not as popular as in Melbourne, "Aussie Rules" has a strong following in Sydney. The local teams, Sydney Swans and Greater Western Sydney Giants, play their home games at the SCG and Spotless Stadium at Homebush.

Rivalry between the Sydney supporters and their Melbourne counterparts is always strong. Fans from the south arrive to cheer on their teams. Tickets for regular competition rounds can usually be bought on the day of the game or through Ticketek and **Ticketmaster**.

Basketball

Basketball is a popular spectator and recreational sport. Sydney has male and female teams competing in the National Basketball League. The games, held at the Sydney Sports Centre at Homebush have much of the pizzazz,

One-day cricket match between Australia and the West Indies, SCG

Aerial view of the Allianz Stadium at Moore Park

colour and excitement of American basketball. Tickets can be purchased by phone or on the Internet from Ticketek.

Cycling and Inline Skating

Sydney boasts excellent, safe locations for the whole family to go cycling. One of the most frequented is Centennial Park (see p132). You can hire bicycles and safety helmets from **Centennial Park Cycles** and also from **Inner City Cycles** in Glebe, where you can hire out equipment by the day or by the week.

Another popular pastime in summer is inline skating. **Rollerblading Sydney** hires equipment and runs tours starting at Milsons Point to all parts of Sydney. They offer private and group lessons. Or keep both feet firmly on the ground and watch skateboarders and inline skaters practising their moves at the ramps at Bondi Beach (see p149).

An inline skater enjoying a summer evening on the city's streets

Horse Riding

For a leisurely ride, head to Centennial Park or contact the **Centennial Parklands Equestrian Centre**. They will give you details of the four riding schools that operate in the park. **Shellby Equestrian Centre** conducts trail rides through Ku-ring-gai Chase National Park (see p130).

Further afield, you can enjoy the magnificent scenery of the Blue Mountains (see pp172–3) on horseback. The **Megalong Australian Heritage Centre** has trail rides from one hour to an overnight ride. All levels of experience are catered for.

Horse riding in one of the parks surrounding the city centre

Adventure Sports

Sydney offers a wide range of adventure sports for those seeking a more active and thrill-filled time. You can participate in guided bushwalking, mountain biking, canyoning, rock climbing and abseiling expeditions in the nearby Blue Mountains National Park. The **Blue Mountains Adventure Company** runs one-day or multi-day courses and trips for all standards of adventurer.

SYDNEY STREET FINDER

The page grid superimposed on the *Area by Area* map below shows which parts of Sydney are covered in this *Street Finder*. Map references given for all sights, shops and entertainment venues in Sydney described in this chapter refer to the maps in this section. All the major sights are clearly marked so they are easy to locate. The key, set out below, indicates the scale of the maps and shows what other features are marked on them, including railway stations, bus terminals, ferry boarding points, taxi ranks, emergency services, post offices and tourist information centres. Map references are also given for hotels *(see pp482–3)* and restaurants *(see pp504–7)*.

Sydney Harbour Bridge
(see pp84–5) viewed from
North Sydney Olympic Pool

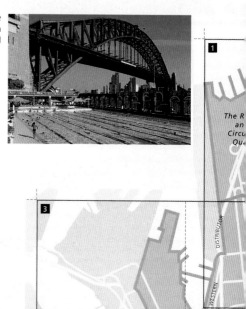

Key

- Major sight
- Place of interest
- Other building
- Ferry boarding point
- Main railway station
- Bus station
- Sydney Trains station
- Light Rail station
- *i* Tourist information
- Hospital with casualty unit
- Police station
- Golf course
- Church
- Mosque
- Synagogue
- Highway
- Railway line
- Ferry route
- Pedestrianized street
- Tunnel

Scale of Map Pages

| 0 metres | 250 |
| 0 yards | 250 |

| 0 metres | 500 |
| 0 yards | 500 |

Sundial in the Royal Botanic Gardens *(see pp110–11)*

Statues on the Art Deco Anzac Memorial in Hyde Park *(see p97)*

A bright, colourful coffee shop in Surry Hills, Sydney

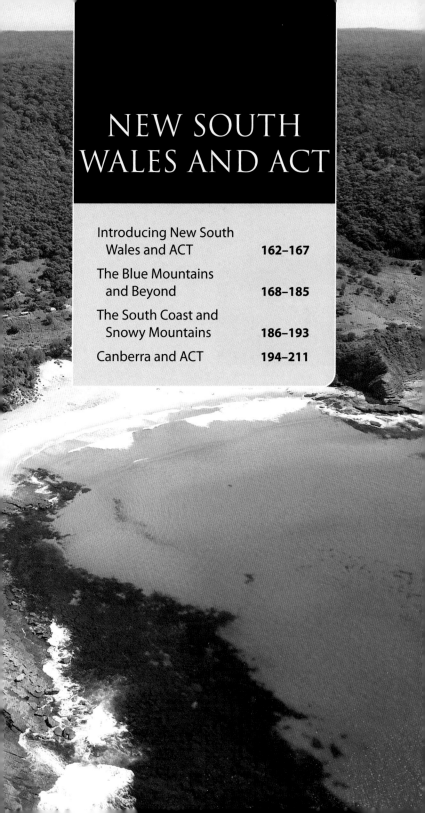

NEW SOUTH WALES AND ACT

New South Wales and ACT at a Glance

This southeastern corner of the continent, around Sydney Cove, was the site of the first European settlement in the 18th century and today it is the most densely populated and varied region in Australia, and home to its largest city, Sydney *(see pp64–159)*, as well as Canberra, the nation's capital. It also contains the country's highest mountain, Mount Kosciuszko. In the east there are farmlands and vineyards, the Blue Mountains and the ski resorts of the Snowy Mountains. To the far west is a desert landscape. The coastline is tropically warm in the north, cooler in the south.

Locator Map

Broken Hill *(see p185)* is one of the few 19th-century mining towns in Australia that continues to survive on its mineral resources. It is also the location of the Royal Flying Doctor Service headquarters, and guided tours detailing the history of the service are popular with visitors.

Broken Hill

Bc

The Blue Mountains and Beyond *(see pp168–85)*

Griffith

Wagga Wa

0 kilometres 100

0 miles 100

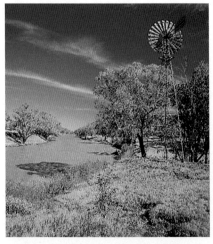

◀ Aerial view of South Era Beach, part of the Royal National Park

Bourke's major attraction is its remote location. Irrigated by the Darling River, the town is also a successful agricultural centre *(see p185)*. A lift-up span bridge crosses the river.

Tamworth is the heart of Australian country music. The Big Golden Guitar Tourist Centre and Coffee Shop is fronted by the city's iconic large golden guitar *(see p181)*.

Tenterfield's School of Arts building has a proud history as the site of Sir Henry Parkes' Federation speech in 1889, which was followed, 12 years later, by the founding of the Commonwealth of Australia *(see p60)*. A museum in the town details the event.

Moree

Armidale

Tamworth

Dubbo

Taree

Parkes

Maitland

Orange

Newcastle

Lithgow

Windsor ● Gosford

nberra and ACT
ee pp194–211)

Penrith

Camden

Sydney

Goulburn

Wollongong

nberra ●

Nowra-Bomaderry

The South Coast and
Snowy Mountains
(see pp186–93)

The Three Sisters rock formation is the most famous sight within the Blue Mountains National Park *(see pp172–3)*. At night it is floodlit for a spectacular view.

Windsor is one of the best preserved 19th-century towns in the state *(see p176)*. The Macquarie Arms Hotel is considered to be the oldest operational hotel in Australia.

Canberra was designed as the new national capital in 1912 by architect Walter Burley Griffin. Anzac Parade offers fine views of New Parliament House, atop Capital Hill *(see pp198–9)*.

Mount Kosciuszko, in Kosciuszko National Park, is Australia's highest mountain. Panoramic views of the Snowy Mountains can be found at the Mount Kosciuszko Lookout, accessible via a walking trail or a chairlift *(see pp164–5)*.

The Snowy Mountains

The Snowy Mountains stretch 500 km (310 miles) from Canberra to Victoria. Formed more than 250 million years ago, they include Australia's highest mountain, Mount Kosciuszko, and the country's only glacial lakes. In summer, wildflowers carpet the meadows; in winter, snow gums bend beneath the cold winds. The Snowy Mountains are preserved within the Kosciuszko National Park and are also home to two of Australia's largest ski resorts, Thredbo and Perisher. The Snowy Mountains Scheme dammed four rivers to supply power to much of inland eastern Australia *(see p187)*.

The Snowy Mountains are home to the Kosciuszko National Park which was declared a World Biosphere Reserve by UNESCO in 1997.

The Snowy River rises below Mount Kosciuszko and is now dammed and diverted to provide hydroelectricity for Melbourne and Sydney as part of the Snowy Mountains Scheme.

Blue Lake is a spectacular glacial lake, one of only a few in the country, which lies in an ice-carved basin 28 m (90 ft) deep.

Seaman's Hut, built in honour of a skier who perished here in 1928, has saved many lives during fierce blizzards.

The Alpine Way offers a spectacular drive through the mountains, best taken in spring or summer, via the Thredbo River Valley.

Geehi River

Snowy River

Perisher Valley •

Mount Kosciuszko ▲
2,228 m (7,310 ft)

Alpine Way

Thredbo

Prominent Peaks of the Snowy Mountains

Mount Kosciuszko is Australia's highest mountain, and may be approached by gentle walks across alpine meadows from Thredbo or from Charlottes Pass. Mount Townsend is only slightly lower but, with a more pronounced summit, is often mistaken for its higher and more famous neighbour.

Charlottes Pass marks the start of the summit walk to Mount Kosciuszko. It was named after Charlotte Adams, who, in 1881, was the first European woman to climb the peak.

Dead Horse Gap is a striking pass named after a group of "brumbies" (wild horses) that perished in a snowdrift here during the 19th century.

0 metres   5

0 yards   5

Key

▬▬▬ Major road

═══ Minor road

■ ■ Walking trail

Downhill and cross-country skiing and snowboarding are popular in the Snowy Mountains between June and September.

VISITORS' CHECKLIST

Practical Information

ℹ️ Snowy Region Visitors Centre, Kosciuszko Road, Jindabyne (02) 6450 5600.
🅦 **snowymountains.com.au**
Perisher Valley: 🅦 **perisher. com.au** Charlotte Pass:
🅦 **charlottepass.com.au**
Yarrangobilly: **Open** 9am–5pm daily. ♿ 📷 🅿️

· **Wilsons Valley** ⛺

Lake Jindabyne

Jindabyne ⛺

edbo River

Mowamba River

Thredbo River was once known as the Crackenback River by stockmen who thought the ranges rising on either side of the valley were steep enough to break a man's back.

Flora and Fauna

The Snowy Mountains are often harsh, windswept and barren, yet myriad flowers, trees and wildlife have evolved to survive all seasons. Almost all species here are unique to the alpine regions of Australia.

Silver snow daisies, with their white petals and yellow centres, are the most spectacular of all the alpine flowers en masse.

Mountain plum pine is a natural bonsai tree, which grows slowly and at an angle. The pygmy possum feeds on its berries.

Sphagnum moss surrounds the springs, bogs and creeks in the highest regions, and helps to protect primitive alpine plants.

Corroboree frogs live only in the fragile sphagnum moss bogs of the region.

Mountain pygmy possums live under the snow, high up in the mountains.

The Yarrangobilly Caves, about 130 km (80 miles) north of Thredbo, are a system of 70 limestone caves formed 750,000 years ago. They contain magnificent white columns, cascading frozen waterfalls and delicate underground pools.

Brown and rainbow trout, both introduced species, thrive in the cool mountain streams.

Wines of New South Wales and ACT

New South Wales and ACT were the cradle of Australian wines. A small consignment of vines was on board the First Fleet when it landed at Sydney Cove in January 1788 (*see pp54–5*), and this early hope was fulfilled in the steady development of a successful wine industry. New South Wales is now the home of many fine wineries with an international reputation. The state is currently in the vanguard of wine industry expansion, planting new vineyards and developing established districts to meet steadily rising domestic and export demand.

Locator Map

New South Wales wine region

Banderra Estate Sand Hills Vineyard in the Lachlan Valley near Forbes produces both traditional and modern wines. Shiraz reds along with classic dry whites, such as Chardonnay, are particularly good.

Falls Wines' Canowindra vineyard, near Cowra, produces premium fruit for the winery's range of Chardonnay, Semillon, Cabernet Sauvignon, Shiraz and Merlot wines.

De Bortoli is a family-owned winery in the Riverina district. Its speciality wines, such as Dry Botrytis Semillon, are matched by its consistently reasonable prices.

Charles Sturt University Winery is a major innovator of winemaking techniques and viticultural science. The university has a second winery at its campus in the Orange region.

Parkes

Molong

Forbes

Orange

Lachlan River

Cowra

West Wyalong

Ardlethan

Griffith

Narrandera

Wagga Wagga

Yas

Lake Burrinjuck

Gundagai

CANBERRA

Tumut

Tumbarumba

Albury

Kiandra

Murray River

Lake Eucumbene

Cooma

Key

- Hastings River
- Upper Hunter Valley
- Lower Hunter Valley
- Mudgee
- Orange
- Lachlan Valley
- Gundagai
- Cowra
- Hilltops
- Riverina
- Tumbarumba
- Canberra ACT
- Shoalhaven Coast and Southern Highlands

Mudgee's high altitude and red soil produces intense red wines.

The Hunter Valley was Australia's first successful wine region and still thrives today.

Wine Regions

There are eight wine zones in NSW which contain 23 regions. The Hunter Valley area is the most well known and justly famous for Semillon, Chardonnay, Shiraz and Cabernet Sauvignon. The cooler climate in Orange produces highly prized wines and the Riverina produces great dessert-style wines.

Key Facts

Location and Climate

The climate in New South Wales ranges from Mediterranean-style to subtropical, tempered by varying altitudes and local topography. Valleys which trap regular rainfall and a range of nutritious soils all benefit the state's wine production. Sydney's position as Australia's premier gateway city means that NSW's wineries are among the most accessible, especially those of the upper and lower Hunter Valley.

Grape Varieties

The principal varieties are Chardonnay and Semillon for white, Shiraz and Cabernet Sauvignon for reds. Other local grape varieties include Pinot Noir, Verdelho, Chambourcine and Riesling.

Good Producers

Tyrrells; Lake's Folly; McWilliams; Montrose; Rosemount; Rothbury; Wyndham; Brokenwood; Cassegrain; Drayton; De Bortoli; Reynolds; Clonakilla.

THE BLUE MOUNTAINS AND BEYOND

Think of mid- to northern New South Wales and vibrant colours spring to mind. There are the dark blues of the Blue Mountains; the blue-green seas of the north coast; the verdant green of the rainforests near the Queensland border; and the gold of the wheat fields. Finally, there are the reds and yellows of the desert in the far west.

Ever since English explorer Captain James Cook claimed the eastern half of Australia as British territory in 1770 and named it New South Wales, Sydney and its surroundings have been at the forefront of Australian life.

On the outskirts of Sydney, at Windsor and Richmond, early convict settlements flourished into prosperous farming regions along the fertile Hawkesbury River. The barrier of the Blue Mountains was finally penetrated in 1812, marking the first spread of sheep and cattle squatters north, west and south onto the rich plains beyond. In the middle of the 19th century came the gold rush around Bathurst and Mudgee and up into the New England Tablelands, which led to the spread of roads and railways.

Following improved communications in the late 19th and early 20th centuries, northern New South Wales now contains more towns, a denser rural population and a more settled coastline than anywhere else in the country. Fortunately, all this development has not robbed the region of its natural beauty or assets. From the grand and daunting wilderness of the Blue Mountains to the blue waters and surf of Byron Bay, the easternmost point in Australia, the region remains easy to explore and a delight to the senses. It is most easily divided into three parts: the coastline and mild hinterland, including the famous Hunter Valley vineyards; the hills, plateaus and flats of the New England Tablelands and Western Plains with their rivers, national parks and thriving farming areas; and the remote, dusty Outback, west of the vast Great Dividing Range.

The combination of urban civilization, with all the amenities and attractions it offers, and the beautiful surrounding landscape, make this region a favourite holiday location with locals and tourists all year round.

Cape Byron lighthouse on Australia's most easterly point

◀ Hanging Rock, in the Blue Mountains National Park

Exploring the Blue Mountains and Beyond

Distances can be long in mid- to northern New South Wales, so the extent of any exploration will depend on the time available. Within easy reach of Sydney are historic gold rush towns such as Windsor and those between Bathurst and Mudgee, the cool retreats of the Blue Mountains, and the gentle, green hills of the Hunter Valley and its vineyards. The north coast and its hinterland are best explored as part of a touring holiday between Sydney and the Queensland capital, Brisbane, or as a short break to the beaches and fishing areas around Port Macquarie, Forster and Coffs Harbour.

Key

The Blue Mountains and Beyond

West of the Divide *pp184–5*

Impressive Three Sisters rocks in the Blue Mountains National Park

Sights at a Glance

The lighthouse at Cape Byron, Byron Bay – mainland Australia's easternmost point

Getting Around

An extensive rail and bus network up the north coast and to major towns such as Coffs Harbour, Byron Bay and Armidale makes this region very accessible. However, a car is still the best way to see the natural highlights of the area. Highways are good, although rarely dual carriageway, with the exception of the coastal Princes Hwy and parts of the Hume Hwy. Other routes are the New England Hwy to the Northern Tablelands, the Newell Hwy to Moree and the Great Western Hwy through the Blue Mountains to Bathurst.

0 kilometres   50

0 miles   50

Key

▬▬ Highway
▬▬ Major road
∷∷∷ Minor road
── Scenic route
╌╌╌ Main railway
── Minor railway
▭▭ State border

Extensive green vineyards of the Hunter Valley

❶ Blue Mountains National Park

The landscape of the Blue Mountains was more than 250 million years in the making as sediments built up then were eroded, revealing sheer cliff faces and canyons. Home to Aboriginal communities for an estimated 14,000 years, the rugged terrain proved, at first, a formidable barrier to white settlers *(see p174)*, but since the 1870s it has been a popular holiday resort. The mountains get their name from the release of oil from the eucalyptus trees which causes a blue haze. Excellent drives and walking trails allow for easy exploration of the region.

Mount Wilson
A basalt cap, the result of a now extinct volcano, provides the rich soil for the gardens of this attractive summer retreat.

Flora and Fauna in the Blue Mountains

Many species of flora and fauna that are unique to Australia can be easily seen in the Blue Mountains. For example, the superb lyrebird is a fan-tailed bird found in the forests, distinguishable by its high-pitched cry.

Possum The sassafras (*Doryphora sassafras*) tree is one of the species of the warm temperate rainforest and produces tiny white flowers. The shy brushtail possum seeks shelter in the woodlands by day and forages at night.

Jenolan Caves
Nine spectacular limestone caves are open to the public; stalactites and stalagmites can be seen in beautiful and striking formations.

Key

▬ Major road
▭ Minor road
▬▪ Railway

0 km   5
0 miles   5

For hotels and restaurants in this area see pp483–4 and pp507–9

Mount Tomah Botanic Garden
Cool-climate species from around the world
are grown here, including rhododendrons
from the Himalayas.

WINDSOR

ount Toman
0 m (3,280 ft)

Springwood

32

Lawson

• Woodford

Glenbrook •

SYDNEY

Wentworth Falls
This waterfall is evidence of a
massive slip in the escarpment.
Pockets of rainforest thrive along
its edges.

Leura
Elegant old residences such as the
Leura Mansion are features of this
pretty village.

KEY

① **Katoomba** is the largest town in
the vicinity of the national park and
has a full range of accommodation
for tourists.

② **The Leuralla Toy and Railway
Museum** is home to the southern
hemisphere's largest collection of
toys, trains and related memorabilia.

③ **The Cathedral of Ferns** is an area
of green foliage set amid streams,
resembling tropical rainforest.

Three Sisters
Erosion formed this spectacular rock formation. Aboriginal legend
has it that it is in fact three sisters, imprisoned by their father to
protect them from a bunyip (a mythical swamp creature).

For keys to symbols *see back flap*

Exploring the Blue Mountains

The Blue Mountains, reaching 1,100 m (3,600 ft) above sea level at their highest point, at first made the early colonists virtual prisoners of the Sydney Cove area. Many settlers were convinced that plains suitable for grazing and crops would be found beyond the mountains, but attempts to reach the imagined pastures repeatedly failed. In 1813, however, three farmers, Gregory Blaxland, William Lawson and William Charles Wentworth, set out on a well-planned mission, following the ridge between the Grose and Cox rivers, and emerged successfully on the western side of the mountains. The construction of roads and a railway made the mountains an increasingly attractive destination, and resorts and country homes were soon established. In 1959, the Blue Mountains National Park was gazetted, ensuring the preservation of the large tracts of remaining wilderness.

🏛 Norman Lindsay Gallery and Museum

14 Norman Lindsay Crescent, Faulconbridge. **Tel** (02) 4751 1067. **Open** 10am–4pm daily. **Closed** 25 Dec. 🅿 ♿ 🆆 **normanlindsay.com.au**

Norman Lindsay, one of Australia's most recognized artists, inspired considerable controversy during his lifetime with his sumptuous nudes and risqué novels. Born in 1879, he bought his mountain retreat in 1913 and set about producing an enormous body of work, much of which reflects his rejection of the moral and sexual restraints of his era.

His beautifully preserved home is now a gallery for his many paintings, cartoons, mythological garden sculptures and children's books. There is a whole room devoted to *The Magic Pudding*, a perennial favourite. There is also a re-creation of the interior of his original studio, and a peaceful garden set amid the mountain bushland.

Leura

ℹ Echo Point, Katoomba. **Tel** 1300 653 408. 🚢 first Sun of the month.

This small town on the Great Western Highway, with its European gardens and Art Deco architecture, recalls the elegance of life in the 1920s. Its secluded, tree-lined main street is a magnet for fine art galleries, cafés, shops, up-market restaurants and the Leuralla Toy and Railway Museum.

Six km (3.5 miles) from Leura, Everglades House is an Art Deco fantasy of curves, balconies and rose-pink walls. The Everglades gardens are considered classic examples of cool-climate design from the 1930s. They include a shaded alpine garden, a grotto pool, rhododendron stands and peacocks roaming around the grounds. Some other gardens in the area are opened to the public during the Leura Garden Festival each October *(see p44)*.

Visitors can get an overview of the surrounding landscape by taking the Cliff Drive to Katoomba. The lookout at Sublime Point, at the end of Sublime Point Road, also provides startling views across the Jamison Valley.

Scenic Skyway ride over the Blue Mountains from Katoomba

Katoomba

ℹ Echo Point, Katoomba. **Tel** 1300 653 408. 🆆 **visitbluemountains.com.au**

Katoomba is the bustling tourism centre of the Blue Mountains and a good base from which to explore the mountains. However, it still manages to retain a veneer of its gracious former self, when it first attracted wealthy Sydneysiders in need of mountain air during the 1870s. The Paragon Café, with its dark-wood panelling and mirrored walls, is a reminder of these glory days, as are the imposing guesthouses with their fresh air and beautiful views across the Jamison Valley.

Within a few minutes' drive of the town are the region's most popular attractions. Echo Point is home to a large information centre and lookout, with views across to the imposing bulk of Mount Solitary and the most famous of icons, the Three Sisters *(see pp172–3)*. A short walk leads down to this striking rock formation, while further on the Giant Staircase – steps hewn out

Picturesque tree-lined Main Street in Leura

For hotels and restaurants in this area see pp483–4 and pp507–9

of the rock face – curls around its eastern side. Beyond the Staircase is the Leura Forest, which is a warm temperate rainforest.

On the western side of town the world's first glass-floor Skyway, 270 m (885 ft) above the valley floor, departs regularly. The Scenic Skyway traverses 205 m (670 ft) above the mountains, while the Scenic Railway offers a nerve-wracking plummet down a mountain gorge. Reputed to be the steepest rail track in the world, it was originally built in the 1880s to transport miners down to the valley's rich coal deposits.

Blackheath

4,100. Govetts Leap Rd.
Tel 1300 653 408.

Blackheath is a small village that offers a quieter prospect than many of the busy mountain towns further east. The excellent standard of restaurants and accommodation available in the town often induces visitors to stay one or two nights here, rather than make the return to Sydney the same day. But the real draw of this area is the chance to explore the mist-enshrouded rifts and ravines of the beautiful Grose Valley.

The best place to start is the Heritage Centre, 3 km (2 miles) from Blackheath along Govetts Leap Road. Displays document the geological, Aboriginal and European histories of the region and local flora and fauna, while park officers are available to offer advice on the best walks in the area. Govetts Leap, with its heady views across Grose Valley, provides a point of orientation and is the starting place for a number of tracks. A clifftop track leads off in a southerly direction past Bridal Falls, the highest waterfalls in the Blue Mountains, and through stretches of exposed mountain heathland.

A steep and arduous 8-hour return trek into the valley leads to Blue Gum Forest. Walk through the dense covered forest with towering blue-gum eucalyptus trees. The Grand Canyon is a destination only for the fit – this 5-hour walk, through deep gorges and

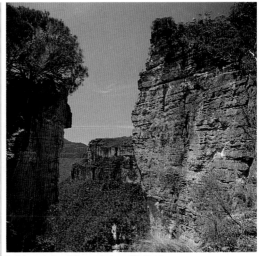
Eroded gorge in Grose Valley, near the town of Blackheath

sandstone canyons, sheds some light on the geological mysteries of the mountains.

Jenolan Caves

Jenolan Caves Rd. **Tel** (02) 6359 3911.
Open 9am–5pm daily. to small section of Orient and Chifley caves.
jenolancaves.org.au

The Jenolan Caves lie southwest of the mountain range. The Great Western Highway passes the grand old hotels of Mount Victoria before a south turn is taken at Hartley, the centre of the first grazing region established by Blaxland, Lawson and Wentworth from 1815 onwards. The southern stretch of the road, cutting across the escarpment of Kanimbla Valley, is one of the most scenic in the mountains. The Jenolan Caves

Limestone formations in the Jenolan Caves

were first discovered in 1838 and are remarkable for their complexity and accessibility. More than 300 subterranean chambers were formed in a limestone belt that was deposited more than 300 million years ago. The nine caves open to the public have a variety of delicate limestone formations, pools and rivers, including the ominously named Styx River.

Mount Tomah Botanic Garden

Bells Line of Road. **Tel** (02) 4567 3000.
Open 9am–5:30pm daily (from 9:30am Sat, Sun & public holidays). **Closed** 25 Dec. **bluemountains botanicgarden.com.au**

Mount Tomah lies along the Bells Line of Road, a quiet but increasingly popular route with tourists to the area.

Tomah takes its name from an indigenous word for "fern". The Botanic Garden was set up as an annex to Sydney's Royal Botanic Garden (see pp110–11) in order to house species that would not survive the coastal conditions. Of special interest are the southern hemisphere plants which developed in isolation once Australia broke away from Gondwanaland (see p27).

The overall layout of the gardens is a feat of engineering, and the views across Grose Valley are breathtaking.

❷ Windsor

🚉 1,850. 🚌 🚍 🚍 ℹ️ Hawkesbury Valley Way, Clarendon (02) 4560 4620.
ⓦ hawkesburytourism.com.au

Windsor was named by Governor Macquarie and this well-preserved colonial settlement is one of the five "Macquarie towns". Established on the banks of the Hawkesbury River in 1794, the town provided farmers with both fertile land and the convenience of river transport.

In the centre of town, St Matthew's Church, designed by Francis Greenway, is a fine example of Georgian colonial architecture and is considered to be his most successful work. Other buildings of interest include the Macquarie Arms, which claims to be Australia's oldest hotel, and the **Hawkesbury Museum**, set in a Georgian residence. The museum chronicles Windsor's early colonial history.

🏛️ **Hawkesbury Museum**
8 Baker St, Windsor. **Tel** (02) 4560 4655. **Open** 10am–4pm Wed–Mon. **Closed** Good Fri, 25 Dec. 🖼️

Environs
One of the other five "Macquarie towns" is Richmond, which lies 6 km (3.5 miles) west of Windsor.

St Matthew's Church in Windsor, designed by Francis Greenway

This attractive settlement was established five years earlier, in 1789. The farmstead of Mountainview, built in 1804, is one of the oldest surviving homes in the country.

❸ Gosford

🚉 155,000. 🚌 🚍 🚍 🚢
ℹ️ 1300 130 708, (02) 4343 4444.
ⓦ visitcentralcoast.com.au

Gosford is the principal town of the popular holiday region known as the Central Coast, and provides a good base for touring the surrounding area. The rural settlements that once dotted this coastline have now evolved into one continuous beachside suburb, stretching as far south as Ku-ring-gai Chase National Park (see p130). Gosford itself sits on the calm northern shore of Brisbane Waters, an excellent spot for sailing and other recreational activities. The nearby coastal beaches are renowned for their great surf, clear lagoons and long stretches of sand. The beaches here are so numerous that it is still possible to find a deserted spot in any season except high summer. The **Forest of Tranquility – Australian Rainforest Sanctuary** is located in a valley of subtropical and temperate rainforest. There are undercover picnic areas, play areas, barbecue facilities, a kiosk and Function Centre, in addition to 5 km (3 miles) of beautiful rainforest walks.

A kangaroo at the Forest of Tranquility

The **Australian Reptile Park** is home to many types of reptiles, including crocodiles, massive goannas, snakes and other species. The park offers wildlife shows such as crocodile feeding, venomous snake and spider milking and a picnic area where you can hand-feed the friendly kangaroos that share the grassy space.

Memorial Park, located in the town of The Entrance, is a short drive north of Gosford. See dozens of pelicans vying for fish from the human feeders at the free pelican feeding show that takes place at 3:30pm daily on

Entrance to the Australian Reptile Park in Gosford

For hotels and restaurants in this area see pp483–4 and pp507–9

the waterfront. The show also provides visitors with an entertaining and educational commentary about the area's pelicans, birds and marine life.

🎫 **Forest of Tranquility – Australian Rainforest Sanctuary**
Ourimbah Creek Rd, Ourimbah.
Tel (02) 4362 1855. **Open** 10am–4pm Sat & Sun (last adm 2pm). **Closed** 25 Dec. 🅿️ ♿ limited. 🌐 forestof tranquility.com

🎫 **Australian Reptile Park**
Pacific Hwy, Somersby. **Tel** (02) 4340 1022. **Open** 9am–5pm daily. **Closed** 25 Dec. 🅿️ ♿ 🌐 reptilepark.com.au

Environs
There are several national parks within a short distance of Gosford. Bouddi National Park is one of the most diverse reserves in the state, with sandstone cliffs, secluded beaches and coastal heaths blanketed in wildflowers. Also worth a visit is the Bulgandry Aboriginal site in Brisbane Waters National Park, which has rock engravings of human and animal figures dating back thousands of years.

❹ Newcastle
🏙️ 140,000. ✈️ 🚉 🚌 🚌
🌐 visitnewcastle.com.au

One visitor to Newcastle, Australia's second-oldest city, remarked in the 1880s: "To my mind the whole town appeared to have woke up in fright at our arrival and to have no definite ideas of a rendezvous whereat to rally." The chaos to which he referred was largely the result of the city's reliance on coal mining and vast steel works. Building progressed with no planning as profits rose.

Today this chaos only adds to Newcastle's charm. The city curls loosely around a splendid harbour and its main streets rise randomly up the surrounding hills. Industry is still the mainstay, but this does not detract from the city's quaint beauty. The main thoroughfare of Hunter Street has many buildings of diverse architectural styles. The Courthouse follows a style known as Late Free

Italianate post office in Newcastle

Classical; the Court Chambers are High Victorian; the post office was modelled on Palladio's Basilica in Venice and the town's cathedral, Christ Church, is an elaborate and impressive example of Victorian Gothic.

The modern **Newcastle Region Art Gallery** houses works by some of the country's most prominent 19th- and 20th-century artists, including the Newcastle-born William Dobell, Arthur Boyd and Brett Whiteley (*see pp38–9*).

Queens Wharf is the main attraction of the harbour fore-shore. It was redeveloped during the 1980s as part of a bicentennial project. There are splendid views from its

promenade areas and outdoor cafés. On the southern side of the harbour, Nobbys Lighthouse sits at the end of a long causeway; the vista back over old Newcastle makes the brief walk worthwhile.

Further on lies **Fort Scratchley**, built originally to repel the coal-seeking Russians in the 1880s. Despite constant surveillance, the fort did not open fire until the 1940s, when the Japanese shelled Newcastle during World War II. Good surfing beaches lie on either side of the harbour's entrance.

🏛️ **Newcastle Region Art Gallery**
Cnr Darby & Laman sts. **Tel** (02) 4974 5100. **Open** 10am–5pm Tue–Sun.
Closed 25 Dec, Good Fri.
🌐 nag.org.au

🏰 **Fort Scratchley**
Nobbys Rd. **Tel** (02) 4974 2027. **Open** 10am–4pm Wed–Mon (last tour 2:30pm). **Closed** Good Fri, 25 Dec. 📷 paid. ♿ 🌐 fortscratchley.com.au

Environs
Four times the size of Sydney Harbour (*see pp78–107*), Lake Macquarie lies 20 km (12 miles) south of Newcastle. The lake's vast size facilitates nearly every kind of watersport imaginable. On the western shore, at Wangi Wangi, is Dobell House, once home to the renowned local artist, William Dobell.

Francis Greenway, Convict Architect

Australian $10 notes once bore the portrait of the early colonial architect Francis Greenway. This was the only currency in the world to pay tribute to a convicted forger. Greenway was transported from England to Sydney in 1814 to serve a 14-year sentence for his crime. Under the patronage of Governor Lachlan Macquarie, who appointed him Civil Architect in 1816, Greenway designed more than 40 buildings, of which 11 still survive today. He received a full King's Pardon in 1819, but soon fell out of favour because he charged exorbitant fees for his architectural designs while still on a government salary. Greenway eventually died in poverty in 1837.

Francis Greenway (1777–1837)

❺ A Tour of the Hunter Valley

The first commercial vineyards in Australia were established on the fertile flats of the Hunter River in the 1830s. Originally a specialist area for fortified wines, Tyrell's helped shift the focus towards new, high-quality modern wines. February and March are busy months with the Harvest Festival taking place from March to April and the Jazz in the Vines festival in October. With beautiful scenery and more than 150 wineries, mostly open daily, the Hunter Valley is one of the top tourist destinations in New South Wales.

③ **Lake's Folly** Max Lake started this vineyard in the 1960s, successfully growing Cabernet Sauvignon grapes in the Hunter Valley for the first time since the 1900s.

④ **Hope Estate** Cask Hall was the vision of the late wine writer Len Evans. The vineyard's wines are now world famous, as are its concerts.

⑤ **Tyrrells' Vineyards** The Tyrrell family has been making wine here since 1858. An outdoor tasting area gives views over the vineyards.

⑥ **Brokenwood**
The first vintage was picked here in 1973, and this winery has attracted a loyal following ever since.

⑦ **Tamburlaine**
A small private producer – wines are available only from the winery or through winery membership.

⑧ **Lindemans** This is one of the best-known wineries in the Hunter Valley, producing legendary Semillon and Shiraz wines.

⑨ **McWilliams Mount Pleasant Winery** Phil Ryan, the legendary winemaker, ran this winery for many years. It is home to the Mount Pleasant Elizabeth Semillon, one of Australia's best quality white wines.

⑩ **Petersons Winery**
This small family winery is known for its unique experimentation with champagne-style wine production in the Hunter Valley.

① **Rothbury** An early morning champagne breakfast and hot-air balloon flight over the Hunter Valley from this town are a luxurious way to start a day touring the wineries.

② **The Hunter Valley Wine Society** This group organizes wine tastings from many local vineyards and offers excellent advice for the novice. Shiraz and Semillon are the two most recognizable Hunter Valley styles.

0 kilometres   5

0 miles   5

Key

▬▬ Tour route

── Other road

Tips for Drivers

Tour length: 60 km (37 miles). While there are no limits on the numbers of wineries that can be visited, three or four in one day will give time to taste and discuss the wines leisurely. Don't forget Australia's strict drink-driving laws (see p561).

Starting point: Cessnock is the gateway to the Hunter Valley and is home to its major visitors' centre.

Stopping-off points: Apart from the picnic areas and restaurants at the wineries, Pokolbin has plenty of cafés, a general store and a bush picnic area. The Mount Bright lookout gives a panoramic view over the region.

Panoramic mountain view from Barrington Tops

❻ Barrington Tops World Heritage Area

🚉 Gloucester. 🛈 27 Denison St, Gloucester (02) 6558 5252. **Open** daily. 🌐 visitgloucester.com.au

Flanking the north of the Hunter Valley is the mountain range known as the Barringtons. One of the highest points in Australia, its high country, the "Barrington Tops", reaches 1,550 m (5,080 ft), and light snow is common in winter. The rugged mountains, cool-climate rainforest, gorges, cliffs and waterfalls make Barrington Tops a paradise for hikers, campers, birdwatchers and climbers. Its 280,000 ha (690,000 acres) of forest, with 1,000-year-old trees, are protected by the Barrington Tops National Park. The rainforest was declared a World Heritage Area in 1986 and a Wilderness Area in 1996 as part of the Gondwana Rainforests of Australia (formerly the Central Eastern Rainforest Reserves) (see pp30–31).

Spinning wheel from the Armidale Folk Museum

Barrington Tops is a favourite weekend escape for Sydney-siders. Tourist operators organize environmentally friendly 4WD trips into the heart of the wild forests, with camping along the Allyn River, hiking trails at Telegherry and Jerusalem Creek and swimming in the rock pool at Lady's Well.

Barrington Tops is best reached through Dungog or from Gloucester.

❼ Armidale

🏙 22,000. 🚆 🚌 🚍 🛈 82 Marsh St (02) 6770 3888. **Open** daily. 🌐 armidaletourism.com.au

Lying in the heart of the New England Tablelands, Armidale is a sophisticated university city surrounded by some of the state's most magnificent national parks, while concerts, plays, films and lectures fill its many theatres, pubs and university halls.

Some 35 buildings in Armidale are classified by the National Trust, testament to the land booms of the 19th century, including the town hall, court-house and St Peter's Anglican Cathedral. The **New England Regional Art Museum** holds the A$20 million Howard Hinton and Chandler Coventry collections, with many works by Australian artists, including Tom Roberts and Norman Lindsay (see p38). To the east of Armidale is the 90-ha (220-acre) **Oxley Wild Rivers National Park**, containing the 220-m (720-ft) high Wollomombi Gorge, one of the highest waterfalls in Australia.

🏛 New England Regional Art Museum
106 Kentucky St. **Tel** (02) 6772 5255. **Open** 10am–4pm Tue–Sun. **Closed** 1 Jan, Good Fri, 25 Dec. 📷 ♿ 🌐 neram.com.au

🌳 Oxley Wild Rivers National Park
188 W North St, Walcha. **Tel** (02) 6777 4700. **Open** Mon–Fri. ♿ limited. 🌐 nationalparks.nsw.gov.au

One of the incredible views across Gibraltar Range National Park

❽ Gibraltar Range National Park

Gwydir Hwy. **Tel** (02) 6739 0700. **Open** daily. 🏕 only for camping and facilities. ♿ 🅦 **nationalparks. nsw.gov.au**

Situated 70 km (43 miles) east of Glen Innes, Gibraltar Range National Park is known for its giant rocky tors towering 1,200 m (4,000 ft) above sea level, surrounded by heath and swamp land. The area is at its most beautiful in the summer, when wildflowers such as waratahs and Christmas bells bloom. The park also has good walking trails and camping facilities.

Gibraltar Range National Park is linked to Washpool National Park by a 40-km (25-mile) World Heritage walk. Washpool has visitor facilities at Coombadjha Creek but wilderness walking is its main feature.

Glen Innes and its surrounding villages of Glencoe, Ben Lomond and Shannon Vale are known as Australia's "Celtic Country". Settled by Scottish, Welsh, Irish and Cornish immigrants in 1852, the area's heritage is celebrated by the

annual Australian Celtic Festival *(see p46)*. The town's Standing Stones are a traditional monument to all Celtic settlers.

Sapphire mining remains a major industry. Public digging ("fossicking") for sapphires, topaz, garnet and beryl is still possible near the mining villages of Emmaville and Torrington. Glen Innes hosts a gem and mineral fair each September.

❾ Tenterfield

🏘 3,500. ✈ 🚌 🚍 🛈 157 Rouse St (02) 6736 1082. 🅦 **tenterfield tourism.com.au**

The rural town of Tenterfield, to the north of the New England Tablelands, occupies a special place in Australian history. Often described as the "Birthplace of Our Nation", it was at the town's School of Arts building on 24 October 1889 that local politician and towering figure of 19th-century Australian politics, Sir Henry Parkes, made his

Plaque celebrating Henry Parkes' speech

historic "One Nation" speech. The address explained his vision of all the colonies in Australia uniting to form one country. Parkes' Tenterfield address led to a popular movement of support, resulting in Australian Federation on 1 January 1901 *(see p60)*. The School of Arts was the first building to be acquired by the New South Wales National Trust because of its political and historic importance.

Other historic buildings in this small town include the Victorian mansion Stannum House, the bluestone saddlers' shop (made famous in the song "Tenterfield Saddler"), and the restored courthouse with its glass ceiling.

Also not to be missed are Bald Rock and Boonoo Boonoo, which are about 40 km (25 miles) north of Tenterfield. Bald Rock is the second biggest monolith in Australia after Uluru *(see pp290–93)* and the largest exposed granite rock, dating back to the Lower Triassic period which was over 200 million years ago. It is 750 m (2,460 ft) long and approximately 200 m (650 ft) high. It offers magnificent views of volcanic ranges to the east, Girraween National Park in Queensland to the north and Mount McKenzie to the south. Boonoo Boonoo Falls cascade 210 m (690 ft) into the gorge below, ideal for swimming, and surrounded by rainforest bathed in moisture from the falls.

Tenterfield's School of Arts building

⑩ Inverell

🏔 11,000. ✈ 🚌 🚉 ℹ️ Water Towers Complex, Campbell St (02) 6728 8161. 🌐 inverell.com.au

Inverell is known as "Sapphire City" because so many of the world's sapphires are mined in the area. Many of the buildings in the main street were built during the 1880s mining boom and are well preserved. The **Inverell Pioneer Village** features buildings gathered from around the district and relocated to create this tourist theme town.

Just south of Inverell lies the mighty Copeton Dam. White-water rafting below the dam on the wild Gwydir River is an exhilarating experience.

🚌 **Inverell Pioneer Village**
Tingha Rd, Inverell. **Tel** (02) 6722 1717. **Open** 10am–4pm Tue–Sun. **Closed** Good Fri, 25 Dec. 🐾 ♿
🌐 inverellpioneervillage.org.au

⑪ Tamworth

🏔 36,000. ✈ 🚉 🚌 ℹ️ The Big Golden Guitar, 2 The Ringers Rd (02) 6767 5300. 🌐 visittamworth.com

Tamworth is a thriving rural city at the centre of fertile agricultural plains. Yet despite its history, fine old buildings and claim to fame as the first Australian city with electric street lighting, it remains best known as Australia's country music capital.

Every January, thousands of country music fans and performers flock here for the Country Music Festival, which includes country music, blue grass, busking, bush ballads,

harmonica playing and the Golden Guitar Awards *(see p45)*. Reflecting the city's main interest there is the Big Golden Guitar Tourist Centre, fronted by a large golden guitar, the Gallery of Stars, where Australia's country music greats are immortalized in wax, and the Hall of Fame Museum in Peel Street dedicated to musicians who have made a major contribution to the industry and the Country Music Hands of Fame cornerstone.

Tamworth's other source of fame is as the equestrian centre of Australia. The Quarter Horse Association and Appaloosa Association are based here, and rodeos and show-jumping events are held here.

⑫ Mudgee

🏔 8,500. 🚌 🚉 Lithgow. ℹ️ 84 Market St (02) 6372 1020. 🌐 visitmudgeeregion.com.au

Mudgee is a magnificent old rural town with gardens and grand buildings, many of which are protected by the National Trust.

Situated on the banks of the Cudgegong River, the town was first settled by William Lawson, who discovered its good grazing country in 1821. The settlement was surveyed and planned in 1824 by Robert Hoddle. The design was so successful that he copied Mudgee's grid layout 14 years later for Melbourne *(see pp386–7)*. Don't miss the Regent Theatre on Church Street, the many churches, banks and civic buildings on Market Street, the railway station

Sheep grazing under a tree in the Mudgee region

and the restored West End Hotel that now houses the excellent Colonial Inn Museum.

Mudgee is also famous for its surrounding wineries and the Mudgee Wine Festival held each September *(see p44)*. From the local countryside come foods such as yabbies (crayfish), trout, lamb, peaches and asparagus.

Environs
During the 1850s and 1860s, gold was discovered to the south of Mudgee, bringing thousands of hopeful prospectors to the region *(see pp58–9)*. The villages of Hill End, Hargraves, Windeyer and Sofala once had populations of more than 20,000 each, but became ghost towns once the boom was over. Hill End is the most famous of these and is now classed as a Living Historic Site with almost all of its buildings dating back to the 1870s. The creeks of Windeyer continued to yield alluvial gold until the 1930s. Panning for gold in the river is a popular tourist activity.

One of Australia's most famous writers, Henry Lawson, hailed from the region *(see p39)*, and Gulgong, a quaint gold rush village famous for being depicted on the original A$10 note, contains the **Henry Lawson Centre**.

🏛 **Henry Lawson Centre**
147 Mayne St, Gulgong. **Tel** (02) 6374 2049. **Open** 10am–3:30pm Mon–Sat, 10am–1pm Sun. **Closed** Good Fri, 25 Dec. 🐾 🌐 henrylawson gulgong.org.au

Golden Guitar Tourist Centre, fronted by a huge golden guitar

Northern New South Wales Coastline

The northern New South Wales coastline is known for its mix of natural beauty, mild climate and good resorts. Australia's most easterly mainland point, Byron Bay, is an attractive, up-market resort which is enhanced by its unspoiled landscape and outstanding beaches. Elsewhere, clean and isolated beaches directly abut rainforest, with some national parks and reserves holding World Heritage status *(see pp30–31)*. Sugar cane and bananas are commonly grown in the region.

④ Red Cliff Beach

Adjacent to the beautiful Yuraygir National Park, Red Cliff is one of several sandy, isolated beaches in the immediate vicinity.

⑤ Moonee Beach

A creek meandering through bush country to the ocean offers perfect opportunities for safe swimming, picnics and camping.

⑥ Urunga

Two rivers, the Bellingen and the Kalang, reach the ocean in this picturesque beach resort. Its safe waters make it a particularly popular holiday site for families.

Coffs Harbour is one of the most popular tourist destinations in New South Wales. Surrounded by excellent beaches, there is also an attractive man-made harbour and a range of top-quality tourist facilities.

⑨ Arakoon

This picturesque headland is part of a state recreation area. Nearby is Trial Bay Gaol, a progressive 19th-century prison that re-opened during World War I to house prisoners of war from various countries.

⑦ Third Headland Beach

Like its neighbour Hungry Head Beach, 5 km (3 miles) north, Third Headland is a popular surfing beach with strong waves hitting the headland cliffs.

Grafton is a quaint 19th-century rural town, with elegant streets and riverside walks. The town is best known for its abundance of jacaranda trees, whose striking purple blooms are celebrated in a festival each October *(see p45)*.

⑫ ★ Crowdy Bay

Part of a national park, Crowdy Bay's lagoons, forests and swamps are abundant with native wildlife. Coarse-fishing is a popular activity from the sea's edge.

Dor

• **Taree**
Newcastle
Sydney

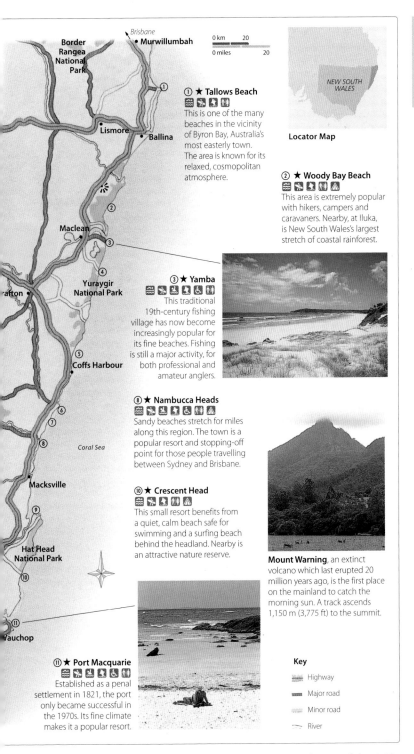

Brisbane
Murwillumbah

Border Ranges National Park

0 km   20
0 miles   20

Lismore
Ballina

Locator Map

NEW SOUTH WALES

① ★ Tallows Beach

This is one of the many beaches in the vicinity of Byron Bay, Australia's most easterly town. The area is known for its relaxed, cosmopolitan atmosphere.

② ★ Woody Bay Beach

This area is extremely popular with hikers, campers and caravaners. Nearby, at Iluka, is New South Wales's largest stretch of coastal rainforest.

Maclean

Yuraygir National Park

afton

③ ★ Yamba

This traditional 19th-century fishing village has now become increasingly popular for its fine beaches. Fishing is still a major activity, for both professional and amateur anglers.

Coffs Harbour

⑧ ★ Nambucca Heads

Sandy beaches stretch for miles along this region. The town is a popular resort and stopping-off point for those people travelling between Sydney and Brisbane.

Coral Sea

⑩ ★ Crescent Head

This small resort benefits from a quiet, calm beach safe for swimming and a surfing beach behind the headland. Nearby is an attractive nature reserve.

Macksville

Hat Head National Park

Mount Warning, an extinct volcano which last erupted 20 million years ago, is the first place on the mainland to catch the morning sun. A track ascends 1,150 m (3,775 ft) to the summit.

Wauchop

⑪ ★ Port Macquarie

Established as a penal settlement in 1821, the port only became successful in the 1970s. Its fine climate makes it a popular resort.

Key

- ⚏ Highway
- ⚏ Major road
- ⚏ Minor road
- ⚏ River

West of the Divide

In stark contrast to the lush green of the Blue Mountains and the blue waters of the New South Wales coastline, the western region of the state is archetypal of Australia's Outback. This dusty, dry landscape, parched by the sun, is an understandably remote area, dotted with a few mining towns and national parks. Dubbo and Wagga Wagga are the main frontier towns, but anything beyond is commonly referred to as "Back o' Bourke" and ventured into by only the most determined of tourists. Even the most adventurous should avoid the area in high summer.

Locator Map

■ West of the Divide
□ The Blue Mountains pp168–83

Sights at a Glance

⓭ Dubbo
⓮ Lightning Ridge
⓯ Bourke
⓰ Broken Hill
⓱ Willandra National Park
⓲ Wagga Wagga

Key

═══ Major road
═══ Minor road
– – Track
══ Main railway
══ Regional border

0 kilometres 200
0 miles 200

⓭ Dubbo

🏙 39,500. ✈ 🚌 🚍 🚆 🛈 cnr Newell Hwy & Macquarie St (02) 6801 4450. 🆆 **dubbotourism.com.au**

Dubbo is located at the geographical heart of the state and is the regional capital of western New South Wales. The area was first noted for its rich agricultural potential in 1817 by explorer John Oxley, sited as it is on the banks of the Macquarie River. The city has since grown into a rural centre producing $45 million worth of food and agricultural goods annually.

Dubbo also has a strong colonial history and period architecture. Among the more interesting buildings are the 1876 Dubbo Museum, with its ornate ceilings and cedar staircase, the 1890 Italianate courthouse and the 1884 Macquarie Chambers, with their Tuscan columns and terracotta tiles.

At the **Old Dubbo Gaol**, visitors can hear the tragic story of Jacky Underwood, an Aborigine hung for his part in the Breelong massacre of 1900, when eleven white settlers were killed. Dubbo magistrate Rolf Boldrewood drew on the characters of the gaol's inmates to write the classic novel *Robbery Under Arms (see p38)*.

The most popular sight in Dubbo is the large **Taronga Western Plains Zoo**, 5 km (3 miles) from the town. The

Rhinoceros in Western Plains Zoo

zoo's emphasis is on breeding endangered species. Visitors can see over 1,000 animals.

🏛 **Old Dubbo Gaol**
Macquarie St. **Tel** (02) 6801 4460. **Open** 9am–4:30pm daily. **Closed** Good Fri, Dec 25. 🅿 🆆 **olddubbogaol.com.au**

🦁 **Taronga Western Plains Zoo**
Obley Rd. **Tel** (02) 6881 1400. **Open** 9am–4pm daily. ♿ 🔋 📷 🆆 **taronga.org.au**

⓮ Lightning Ridge

🏙 5,000. ✈ 🚍 🛈 Morilla St (02) 6829 1670.

Lightning Ridge is a small mining village and home of the treasured black opal – a rare dark opal shot with red, blue and green. Gem enthusiasts from around the world come to try their luck on the opal fields. The town is also famous for its hearty welcome to visitors, unusual within mining communities, and its mine tours, plethora of opal shops and hot bore spas.

⑮ Bourke

🏔 3,000. ✈ 🚌 🚃 ℹ Kidman Way
(02) 6872 1321. Ⓦ **visitbourke.com**

Situated on the Darling River, part
of Australia's longest river system,
Bourke is a colourful town that
was once the centre of the
world's wool industry. It still
produces 25,000 bales per year.

Bourke's heyday is evident in
the colonial buildings and the
old weir, wharf, lock and lift-up
span bridge which recall the
days of the paddlesteamer
trade to Victoria (see p435).
The town's cemetery tells
something of Bourke's history:
Afghan camel drivers who
brought the animal to Australia
from the Middle East in the
19th century are buried here.

⑯ Broken Hill

🏔 21,000. ✈ 🚉 🚌 🚃 ℹ cnr
Blende and Bromide sts (08) 8080
3560. Ⓦ **visitbrokenhill.com.au**

The unofficial centre of Outback
New South Wales, Broken Hill
is a mining city perched on
the edge of the deserts of
inland Australia. The town was
established in 1883, when vast
deposits of zinc, lead and silver
were discovered in a 7-km
(4-mile) long "Line of Lode" by
the then-fledgling company,
Broken Hill Pty Ltd. Broken Hill
has since grown into a major
town and BHP has become
Australia's biggest corporation.

Broken Hill's now declining
mining industry is still evident;
slag heaps are piled up, there
are more pubs per head than
any other city in the state and
streets are named after metals.

Mungo World Heritage Area

Lake Mungo is an area of great
archaeological significance.
For 40,000 years, it was a 10-m
(33-ft) deep lake, around
which Aborigines lived. The
lake then dried up, leaving its
eastern rim as a wind-blown
sand ridge known as the
Walls of China. Its age was
determined in the 1960s when
winds uncovered an Aboriginal
skeleton known as Mungo
Man. Lake Mungo has been
protected as part of the
Willandra Lakes World Heritage
Area since 1981 (see pp30–31).

Walls of China sand ridges

Surprisingly, Broken Hill also
has more than 20 art galleries
featuring desert artists. The
city is also the base of the
Royal Flying Doctor Service
(see p261) and School of the Air.

To the northwest of Broken
Hill is **Silverton**, once a thriving
silver mining community and
now a ghost town. It is popular
as a location for films, such as
Mad Max and *Priscilla, Queen
of the Desert*.

⑰ Willandra National Park

ℹ 200 Yambil St, Griffith (02) 6966
8100. **Open** daily. **Closed** in wet
weather. 🅿 ♿ to homestead.
Ⓦ **nationalparks.nsw.gov.au**

Willandra National Park, on
the edge of a riverine plain,
has significant wildlife and
historic values. The park covers
part of the once prosperous
Willandra Sheep Station and
contains the homestead and
shearing complexes of the
former station. The homestead
overlooks peaceful Willandra
Creek, where grasslands and
creek beds are home to
kangaroos, emus and ground-
nesting birds.

⑱ Wagga Wagga

🏔 57,000. ✈ 🚉 🚌
ℹ Tarcutta St, 1300 100 122.
Ⓦ **tourismwaggawagga.com.au**

Named by its original
inhabitants, the Widadjuri
people, as "a place of many
crows", Wagga Wagga has
grown into a large, modern
city serving the surrounding
farming community. It has won
many accolades for its wines
and the abundance of gardens
has earned it the title of "Garden
City of the South".

The large Botanic Gardens
and the Wagga Historical
Museum are well worth a
visit. The Widadjuri track is
a popular walk along the
Murrumbidgee River banks.

Environs

The gentle town of **Gundagai**,
nestling beneath Mount
Parnassus on the banks of the
Murrumbidgee River, has been
immortalized in the bush ballad
"Along the Road to Gundagai".
More tragic is Gundagai's place
in history as the site of
Australia's greatest natural
disaster when floods swept
away the town in 1852.

Historic pub in the ghost town of Silverton, near Broken Hill

For hotels and restaurants in this area see pp483–4 and pp507–9

THE SOUTH COAST AND SNOWY MOUNTAINS

Although the busiest highway in Australia runs through southern New South Wales, the area remains one of the most beautiful in the country. Its landscape includes the Snowy Mountains, the surf beaches of the far south, the historic Southern Highland villages and the farming towns of the Murray and Murrumbidgee plains.

Ever since European settlers crossed the Blue Mountains in 1812 *(see p174)*, the southern plains of New South Wales around Goulburn, Yass and Albury have been prime agricultural land. Yet the wilderness of the Snowy Mountains to the east and the steep escarpment which runs the length of the beautiful South and Sapphire coasts, from Wollongong to the Victoria border, has never been completely tamed. Today, the splendour of southern New South Wales is protected by a number of large national parks.

The great Snowy Mountains offer alpine scenery at its best. In summer, the wildflower-scattered meadows, deep gorges and cascading mountain creeks seem to stretch endlessly into the distance; in winter, the jagged snow-capped peaks and twisted snow gums turn this summer walking paradise into a playground for keen downhill and cross-country skiers.

The area also has a long and colourful cultural heritage: Aboriginal tribes, gold diggers and mountain cattlemen have all left their mark here. During the 1950s and 1960s, the region became the birthplace of multicultural Australia, as thousands of European immigrants came to work on the Snowy Mountains Scheme, an engineering feat which diverted the flow of several rivers to provide hydroelectricity and irrigation for southeastern Australia.

But southern New South Wales is more than just landscapes; civilization is never far away. There are excellent restaurants and hotels along the coast, Wollongong is an industrial city and the gracious towns of the Southern Highlands offer historic attractions.

Snowy Mountains landscape in autumn

◀ Bucolic landscape around the Thredbo River, in the Snowy Mountains

Exploring the South Coast and Snowy Mountains

The Great Dividing Range, which runs from the Blue Mountains (see pp172–5) down to the Snowy Mountains and into Victoria, divides the region into three areas. There is the coastal strip, a zone of beautiful beaches, which starts at Wollongong and runs south for 500 km (310 miles) to Eden, hemmed in by the rising mountain range to its west. On the range lie the Southern Highlands, Mount Kosciuszko and the Snowy Mountains. West of the range are the farming plains of the Murrumbidgee River.

Waterfall in the beautiful Morton National Park

Golden inlet at Ben Boyd National Park, on the southern tip of New South Wales

Getting Around

A car is essential to do full justice to this region, with the Hume Hwy providing excellent access to the Southern Highlands and the western farming towns. Wollongong and the southern beaches are linked from Sydney to the Victoria border by the coastal Princes Hwy. From Canberra, the Monaro Hwy is the best route to the Snowy Mountains. From Bega to the east or Gundagai and Tumut in the west, take the Snowy Mountains Hwy. A train service between Sydney and Canberra stops at the Southern Highlands and Hume Hwy towns, while the coastal resorts are serviced by buses from both Sydney and Melbourne.

0 kilometres 25

0 miles 25

Sights at a Glance

1 Royal National Park
2 Wollongong
3 The Southern Highlands
4 Goulburn
5 Morton National Park
6 Cooma and the
    Snowy Mountains

Key

▬▬ Highway
▬▬ Major road
▭▭▭ Minor road
▬▬ Scenic route
⌐⌐ Main railway
▬▬ Minor railway
▬▬▬ State border
△ Summit

Snowy landscape near Thredbo Village

Imposing 19th-century architecture in Cooma

For keys to symbols *see back flap*

❶ Royal National Park

🚆 Loftus, then tram to Audley (Sun public hols only). 🚌 Bundeena from Cronulla. 🅸 Sir Bertram Stevens Drive, Audley (02) 9542 0648. ✇ **nationalparks.nsw.gov.au**

Designated a national park in 1879, the "Royal" is the oldest national park in Australia and the oldest in the world after Yellowstone in the USA. It covers 16,500 ha (37,000 acres) of spectacular landscape.

To the east, waves from the Pacific Ocean have undercut the sandstone and produced coastal cliffs, interspersed by creeks, waterfalls, lagoons and beaches. Sea eagles and terns nest in caves at the Curracurrang Rocks. Heath vegetation on the plateau merges with woodlands on the upper slopes and rainforest in the gorges. The park is ideal for bushwalking, swimming and bird-watching.

❷ Wollongong

🅰 280,000. 🚆 🚌 🚍 🅸 93 Crown St (02) 4267 5910. ✇ **visitwollongong.com.au**

The third largest city in the state, Wollongong is situated on a coastline of beautiful surf beaches. Mount Kembla and Mount Keira provide a backdrop to the city. Originally a coal and steel industrial city – the BHP steel mill at Port Kembla is still a major employer – Wollongong is fast building a reputation as a leisure centre. Northbeach is the most famous of its 17 surf beaches. Flagstaff Point, with its lighthouse, boat harbour, beach views and seafood restaurants, is popular with visitors. Fresh seafood is also on offer at the fish market in Wollongong harbour. The city boasts Australia's largest regional art gallery, and the Nan Tien Temple, the largest Buddhist temple in the southern hemisphere, built for the region's Chinese community.

Figure in
Nan Tien Temple

❸ The Southern Highlands

🚌 🚆 Bowral, Moss Vale, Mittagong, Bundanoon. 🅸 62–70 Main St, Mittagong 1300 657 559 or (02) 4871 2888. ✇ **southern-highlands. com.au**

Quaint villages, country guesthouses, homesteads and beautiful gardens are scattered across the lush landscape of the Southern Highlands. The region has been a summer retreat for Sydneysiders for almost 100 years. Villages such as Bowral, Moss Vale, Berrima and Bundanoon are also ideal places in the winter for pottering around antiques shops, dining on hearty soups, sitting by open fires and taking bushwalks and country drives. The region's gardens are renowned for their blaze of colours in the spring and autumn. The Corbett Gardens at Bowral are a showpiece during its Tulip Festival (see p44). Bowral is also home to the **Bradman Museum**, where a fascinating collection of photos and cricketing memorabilia commemorates the town's famous son, cricketer Sir Donald Bradman. Bradman is said to have first showed signs of greatness as a child, hitting a golf ball against a water tank stand with a stump-wide strip of wood.

Visiting the village of Berrima is like stepping back in time. The settlement, now home to an abundance of antiques and craft shops, is one of the most unspoilt examples of a small Australian town of the 1830s.

Popular walks in the area include Mount Gibraltar, Carrington Falls, the magnificent Fitzroy Falls at the northern tip of Morton National Park and the majestic Kangaroo Valley. The five Wombeyan Caves, west

Fishing boats moored along Wollongong Harbour

For hotels and restaurants in this area see pp484–5 and pp509–10

Impressive peak of Pigeon House in Morton National Park

of the town of Mittagong, form an imposing underground limestone cathedral.

🏛 Bradman Museum
St Jude St, Bowral. **Tel** (02) 4862 1247.
Open 10am–5pm daily. **Closed** 25 Dec. 🅿️ 🚻 🖥 **W** bradman.com.au

Sandstone house in Goulburn

❹ Goulburn
🏙 24,500. 🚉 🚌 🚌 **i** 201 Sloane St (02) 4823 4492. **W** igoulburn.com

Goulburn is at the heart of the Southern Tablelands, with its rich pastoral heritage. Proclaimed in 1863, the town's 19th-century buildings, such as the courthouse, post office and railway station, are testament to the continuing prosperity of the district.

The Big Merino, a giant, hollow concrete sheep, marks Goulburn as the "fine wool capital of the world".

Environs
The town of **Yass** is known for its fine wool and cool-climate wines. Worth a visit is the historic Cooma Cottage, now owned by the National Trust. It was once the home of Australian explorer Hamilton Hume, between 1839 and 1873.

❺ Morton National Park
🚉 Bundanoon. 🚌 Fitzroy Falls.
i Fitzroy Falls (02) 4887 7270.
W nationalparks.nsw.gov.au/
morton

Morton National Park stretches along the rugged hinterland from north of the Shaolhavern Valley to the Ulladulla area. Fitzroy Falls are at the northern end of the park. At Bundanoon, magnificent sandstone country can be explored.

To the south, views of the coastline and Budawang wilderness can be found in Little Forest Plateau and the top of Pigeon House Mountain.

❻ Cooma and the Snowy Mountains
🏙 8,000. ✈ 🚌 🚌 **i** 119 Sharp St (02) 6450 1742. **W** visitcooma.com.au

Colourful Cooma has a rich history as a cattle, engineering and ski town. During the construction of the Snowy Mountains Scheme (see p187), Cooma was also the weekend base for the thousands of immigrants working up in the mountains during the week. Stories surviving from this era include tales of frontier-like shootouts in the main street, interracial romances and bush mountain feats. However, Cooma is now a sleepy rural town that acts as the gateway to the Snowy Mountains and the southern ski slopes.

The modern resort town of Jindabyne on Lake Jindabyne is home to the Kosciuszko National Park information centre, a myriad of ski shops and lodges, and plenty of nightlife. The two major ski resorts are Thredbo Village along the Alpine Way and the twin resort of Perisher Blue, linked by the ski tube train to Lake Crackenback and the Blue Cow ski fields. Take the chairlift from Thredbo in summer to walk to the summit of Australia's highest mountain, Mount Kosciuszko (see p164), or simply to stroll among the wildflowers and snow gums in the alpine meadows. Another recommended walk is to Blue Lake and the Cascades from Dead Horse Gap. Lake Eucumbene and the Thredbo and Eucumbene rivers offer excellent fly-fishing.

Environs
The ghost settlement of **Kiandra** has a marked historic walking trail detailing the gold rush era in the town (see pp58–9). Nearby is the gentle ski resort of Mount Selwyn and the spectacular Yarrangobilly Caves with their underground walks set among limestone stalactites and stalagmites.

Resort town of Jindabyne in the Snowy Mountains

The South Coast

From Nowra to the border with Victoria, the south coast of New South Wales is a magical mix of white sand beaches, rocky coves and coastal bush covered with spotted gums and wattles, and alive with a variety of birds. The coastline is rich in Aboriginal sites, fishing villages and unspoilt beach settlements. The 400 km (250 miles) of coast are divided into three distinct areas – the Shoalhaven Coast to the north, the Eurobodalla ("Land of Many Waters") Coast in the centre and the Sapphire Coast in the far south.

Ulladulla is a small fishing village flanked by the dovecote-shaped peak of Pigeon House Mountain in the Morton-Budawang National Park. A bushwalk offers breathtaking coastal views.

⑦ ★ **Horseshoe Bay Beach, Bermagui** 🚌 🔼 Writer Zane Grey brought fame to this tiny game fishing town with his tales of marlin fishing.

Central Tilba is a delightful historic farming village, backed by the 800-m (2,600-ft) Mount Dromedary. The town itself is famous for its weatherboard cottages and shops, now housing some of the region's finest cafés and arts and crafts shops, and its cheese and wine. The cheese factory and wineries are all open to visitors.

Nowra is the town centre of the beautiful Shoalhaven Coast, near the mouth of the Shoalhaven River. The name means "black cockatoo" in the local Aboriginal language. Nearby are the resorts of Culburra and Shoalhaven Heads, adjacent to Seven Mile Beach National Park.

⑩ ★ **Merimbula Beach** 🚌 🔼 The tourist centre of the Sapphire Coast is famous for its oysters, deep-sea fishing and surrounding white sandy beach.

⑪ ★ **Eden** 🚌 🔼 🏔 Set on the deep Twofold Bay, this was once a whaling station. It is now the centre of whale-watching on the south coast during spring. It is also a major tuna fishing town and centre for the local timber industry.

0 kilometres   25

0 miles   25

Deua National Park

Moruya

Bodalla

Ce Ti

Bega

Orbost

Sydney

Nowra

orton
ional
ark

rra

Ulladulla

NEW SOUTH WALES

Locator Map

① ★ Shoalhaven Heads

At the mouth of the Shoalhaven River, this beach resort is at the heart of a popular holiday area. Sailing and windsurfing on the river are popular activities among the locals.

② ★ Jervis Bay

This is one of the most beautiful natural harbours in Australia, famous for its naval bases, national park, tiny settlements of Husskinson and Vincentia, and some of the whitest beaches and crystal clear waters in the world.

③ Wreck Bay

This area, within Jervis Bay National Park, abounds with Aboriginal history. The cultural centre offers walkabout tours of local bushlife and archaeology. Nearby Cave Beach is one of the region's most popular for its secluded location.

④ Lake Conjola

This lake, 10 km (6 miles) north of Ulladulla, is one of many lakes in the region popular with canoeists. Camp sites are also available.

Key

- ⌗ Highway
- ▬ Major road
- ▭ Minor road
- ⌇ River

⑥ Batemans Bay

The Clyde River enters the sea here, marking the start of the Eurobodalla coastline with its rivers, lakes and chain of heavenly quiet beaches popular with Canberrans.

⑧ Mimosa Rocks

This coastal park, just off the south coast road, offers exceptional bushwalking opportunities and idyllic beaches. Secluded camp sites, with minimum facilities, are popular with families and anglers.

⑨ Tathra Beach

This tiny fishing village and holiday haven includes a maritime museum, housed in a 150-year-old wharf building.

⑫ Ben Boyd National Park

Camping, bushwalks and fine beaches are all features of this park. Temperate rainforests begin to take over the landscape in the surrounding region. The ascent to Mount Imlay offers panoramic views of the coast.

⑤ ★ Pebbly Beach

Set within Murramarang National Park, this beach is famous for its tame kangaroos that visit the beach and camp ground, particularly at dusk and dawn.

CANBERRA AND AUSTRALIAN CAPITAL TERRITORY

Located within New South Wales, some 300 km (185 miles) southwest of Sydney, Canberra is Australia's capital and its political heartland. The city was planned in 1908 as the new seat of federal parliament to end rivalry between Sydney and Melbourne. The surrounding Australian Capital Territory (ACT) features bush and mountain terrain.

Canberra was once little more than a sheep station on the edge of the Molonglo River. American architect Walter Burley Griffin won an international competition to design the city. He envisaged a spacious, low-level, modern city, with its major buildings centred on the focal point of Lake Burley Griffin. Canberra (its name is based on an Aboriginal word meaning "meeting place") is a city of contradictions. It consists of more than just politics, diplomacy and monuments. Lacking the traffic and skyscrapers of Australia's other main cities, it has a serenity and country charm suited to strolling around the lake, bush driving and picnicking.

Canberra is the national capital and the centre of political and administrative power in Australia, yet it is also a rural city, ringed by gum trees, with the occasional kangaroo seen hopping down its suburban streets. The city holds the majority of the nation's political, literary and artistic treasures, and contains important national institutions such as the High Court of Australia, the Australian National University and the Australian War Memorial, but it has a population of fewer than 400,000. These contradictions are the essence of the city's attraction. Canberra's hidden delights include Manuka's elegant cafés, excellent wines and sophisticated restaurants. Special events include the annual spring flower festival, Floriade, which turns the north shore of the lake into a blaze of colour, and the spectacular hot-air ballooning festival in April.

Outside the city lie the region's natural attractions. Tidbinbilla Nature Reserve is home to wild kangaroos, wallabies, emus, koalas and platypuses. The Murrumbidgee River is excellent for canoeing, and the wild Namadgi National Park has bush camping, Aboriginal art sites, alpine snow gums and mountain creeks for trout fishing.

Hot-air ballooning festival over Lake Burley Griffin, near the National Library of Australia

◀ Entrance to Parliament House at Capital Hill, Canberra

Exploring Canberra and ACT

Central Canberra lies around Lake Burley Griffin, framed by the city's four hills – Black Mountain and Mount Ainslie to the north and Capital Hill and Red Hill to the south. Most of Canberra's main sights are accessible from the lake. Scattered throughout the northern suburbs are other places of interest such as the Australian Institute of Sport. To the south lies the wilderness and wildlife of Namadgi National Park.

The city of Canberra nestled around Lake Burley Griffin

Sights at a Glance

Historic Streets and Buildings
② Royal Australian Mint
③ Government House
⑤ Yarralumla
⑦ Civic Square
⑧ Australian War Memorial pp204–5
⑩ Telstra Tower
⑭ Mugga-Mugga

Parks and Gardens
① Red Hill
⑨ Australian National Botanic Gardens
⑱ Namadgi National Park p211

Modern Architecture
④ Parliament House pp202–3

Museums and Galleries
⑥ National Gallery pp206–7
⑫ Australian Institute of Sport
⑬ National Museum of Australia
⑯ Canberra Deep Space Communication Complex

Aquariums and Nature Reserves
⑪ National Zoo and Aquarium
⑰ Tidbinbilla Nature Reserve

Rivers
⑮ Murrumbidgee River

0 kilometres 1
0 miles 1

Getting Around

Many of the sights around Lake Burley Griffin are within walking distance of each other. The Canberra Day Tours Explorer Bus also travels between attractions. The city centre's layout can make driving difficult, but to explore the bush suburbs a car is essential as there is no suburban train system. Most of the sights in ACT are within half an hour's drive of the city.

Key

- Street-by-Street area *pp198–9*
- ④ Metroad (city) route
- Highway
- Major road
- Minor road
- Territory boundary

Australian Capital Territory

Hall
Uriarra Crossing
Lake Ginninderra
CANBERRA
Canberra
Queanbeyan
Royalla
Googong Reservoir
Tharwa
Cotter River
Orroral River
Williamsdale
Namadgi National Park
Naas River
Murrumbidgee River

0 kilometres 20
0 miles 20

For additional map symbols *see back flap*

The Parliamentary Triangle

Canberra's major monuments, national buildings and key attractions are all situated around Lake Burley Griffin within the Parliamentary Triangle. Designed to be the focal point of Canberra's national activities by the architect Walter Burley Griffin *(see p201)*, the Parliamentary Triangle has Capital Hill at its apex, topped by Parliament House. Commonwealth Avenue and Kings Avenue fan out from Capital Hill, cross the lake and end at Parkes Way. Running at a right angle from the base of the triangle is Anzac Parade, which leads to the Australian War Memorial *(see pp204–5)* and completes the basic symmetry of Burley Griffin's plan.

④ ★ Parliament House
Completed in 1988, this is one of the world's most impressive parliamentary buildings.

KEY

① **The High Court of Australia** is the highest court of justice in the country.

② **Kings Avenue**

③ **Capital Hill**

④ **Museum of Australian Democracy** was the first parliamentary building in Canberra. Built in 1927, it was the centre of Australian politics until 1988, when Parliament House became the home of federal government. It is open to the public.

⑤ **Questacon** is an action-packed science and technology centre with hundreds of hands-on displays.

⑥ **The National Library** is the country's largest and includes Captain Cook's original journals.

⑦ **Commonwealth Avenue**

⑧ **The Captain Cook Memorial Jet** in Lake Burley Griffin spurts water to a height of 147 m (480 ft).

⑨ **Commonwealth Park** is ablaze with colour during September and October when it is home to the city's annual spring flower festival, Floriade *(see p45)*.

⑩ **Parkes Way**

⑪ **St John the Baptist Church and Schoolhouse** were built in 1844 and are two of Canberra's oldest buildings.

⑫ **The Australian American Memorial** was given to Australia by the United States as a thank you for the Pacific alliance during World War II *(see pp61–2)*.

⑥ ★ National Gallery of Australia
This impressive art gallery contains an excellent collection of Australian colonial and Aboriginal art, as well as many significant European works.

Blundells Cottage
Built in 1858, this is a fine example of an early colonial cottage typical of remote farming life of the time.

Lake Burley Griffin
This artificial lake was created by damming the Molonglo River in 1963. The water feature was central to Walter Burley Griffin's elegant design for Canberra.

CANBERRA

Lake Burley
Griffin

Locator Map

0 metres 500
0 yards 500

❽ ★ Australian War Memorial
The nation's tribute to its 102,000 war dead is also a remarkable museum.

Anzac Parade
Eleven memorials line the boulevard, commemorating Australia's war efforts in the 20th century.

Exploring the Parliamentary Triangle

Canberra, with its still lake and impressive national monuments and institutions, can at first glance appear cold and somewhat forbidding to visitors. But venture inside the various buildings dotted around Lake Burley Griffin within the Parliamentary Triangle, and a treasure trove of architecture, art, history and politics will be revealed. The lake itself, surrounded by gardens, cycle paths and outdoor sculptures and memorials, is a picturesque location for relaxing picnics and leisurely strolls. Exploring the entire Parliamentary Triangle can take one or two days. It is, however, more easily tackled by dividing it into two parts, taking in first the north and then the south of the lake.

🏛 Museum of Australian Democracy

King George Terrace, Parkes.
Tel (02) 6270 8222. **Open** 9am–5pm daily. **Closed** 25 Dec. 🖼 🚻 📷 🖥
W moadoph.gov.au

Built in 1927 as the first parliamentary building in the new national capital, Old Parliament House was the centre of Australian politics for more than 60 years. It was replaced by the new Parliament House in 1988 *(see pp202–3)*.

This building has witnessed many historic moments: Australia's declaration of war in 1939; news of the bombing of Australia's northern shores by the Japanese in 1942; the disappearance and presumed drowning of Prime Minister Harold Holt in 1967 and the dismissal of the Whitlam government by Sir John Kerr in 1975 *(see pp62–3)*.

Today the building is home to the Museum of Australian Democracy, which includes several historical exhibitions. Visitors can explore the Kings Hall, the old House of Representatives and Senate chambers, and see the peephole in the wall of the prime minister's office, discovered during renovations. The National Portrait Gallery's main collection is also held in the museum.

Blundells Cottage

🏚 Blundells Cottage

Wendouree Drive, Parkes.
Tel (02) 6272 2902. **Open** 10–11:30am, noon–4pm Sat. **Closed** 25 Dec. 🖼
W natcap.gov.au

This small sandstone farmhouse was built in 1858 by the Campbell family, owners of a large farming property at Duntroon Station, for their head ploughman. It was later occupied by bullock driver George Blundell, his wife, Flora, and their eight children.

This excellent example of a colonial cottage conveys the remoteness of early farming life. The cottage once looked out over sheep paddocks, but these were flooded by Lake Burley Griffin *(see pp198–9)*.

🏛 National Capital Exhibition

Commonwealth Park. **Tel** (02) 6272 2902. **Open** 9am–5pm Mon–Fri, 10am–4pm Sat & Sun. **Closed** 25 Dec–2 Jan and public hols (except Australia Day). 🚻 📷 🖥
W natcap.gov.au

The rotunda housing the National Capital Exhibition, north of Lake Burley Griffin at Regatta Point, is recommended as a starting point for any tour of Canberra. Inside are models, videos and old photographs showing the history and growth of Canberra as the federal capital of Australia. These provide a good orientation of the city.

From the windows of the rotunda is a clear view of Lake Burley Griffin, the Parliamentary Triangle and the Captain Cook Memorial Jet and Globe and the National Carillon. The jet fountain and bronze, copper and enamel globe on the edge of the lake were part of the 1970 bicentennial commemoration of the claiming of the east coast of Australia by British navy officer Captain James Cook in 1770 *(see p54)*. The elegant fountain lifts a column of water

Neo-Classical façade of the Museum of Australian Democracy and its impressive forecourt

147 m (480 ft) out of the lake from 11am until 2pm, provided the weather is not too windy. The National Carillon has 55 bronze bells and there are regular recitals.

🏛 National Library of Australia

Parkes Place, Parkes. **Tel** (02) 6262 1111. **Open** 10am–8pm Mon–Thu, 10am–5pm Fri & Sat, 1:30–5pm Sun. **Closed** Good Fri, 25 Dec, public hols. 🚹 📷 📧 🅦 **nla.gov.au**

This five-storey library, an icon of 1960s architecture, is the repository of Australia's literary and documentary heritage. Containing more than 7 million books, as well as copies of most newspapers and magazines published in Australia, thousands of tapes, manuscripts, prints, maps and old photographs, it is the nation's largest library and leading research centre. There are also historic items in a rotating display such as Captain Cook's original journal from his *Endeavour* voyages.

Leonard French stained glass

The building, designed by Sydney architect Walter Bunning (1912–1977) and completed in 1968, includes some notable works of art. Foremost are the modern stained-glass windows by Australian architect and artist Leonard French (1928–), made of Belgian chunk glass and depicting the planets. There are also the Australian life tapestries by French artist Mathieu Mategot.

🏛 Questacon – The National Science and Technology Centre

Cnr King Edward Terrace & Parkes Place, Parkes. **Tel** (02) 6270 2800. **Open** 9am–5pm daily. **Closed** 25 Dec. 🚹 🅦 **questacon.edu.au**

With 200 hands-on exhibits in six different galleries arranged around the 27-m- (90-ft-) high cylindrical centre of the building, science need never be dull again. A must for anyone visiting Canberra, Questacon demonstrates that science can be fascinating, intriguing, fun and an everyday part of life.

Visitors can freeze their shadow to a wall, play a harp with no strings, experience an earthquake and feel bolts of lightning. You can also enjoy giant slides and a roller coaster simulator, and there are regular science demonstrations and special lectures.

🏛 High Court of Australia

Parkes Place, Parkes. **Tel** (02) 6270 6811. **Open** 9:45am–4:30pm Mon–Fri, noon–4pm Sun. **Closed** public hols. 🚹 📧 🅦 **hcourt.gov.au**

British and Australian legal traditions are embodied in this imposing lakeside structure, opened in 1980 by Queen Elizabeth II. The High Court is centred on a glass public hall, designed to instil respect for the justice system. Two murals by artist Jan Sensbergs look at the Australian constitution, the role of the Federation and the significance of the High Court. There are three courtrooms, and chambers for the Chief Justice and six High Court judges. Sittings are open to the public.

On one side of the ramp at the entrance is a sculpture of a waterfall made out of granite. It is intended to convey how the decisions of this legal institution trickle down to all Australian citizens.

Jan Sensbergs mural in the High Court

🏛 St John the Baptist Church and Schoolhouse Museum

Constitution Ave, Reid. **Tel** (02) 6248 8399. **Open** 10am–noon Wed, 2–4pm Sat, Sun. **Closed** Good Fri, 25 Dec. 🚹 🚻
🅦 **stjohnscanberra.org**

Built in 1844 of local bluestone and sandstone, the Anglican church of St John the Baptist and its adjoining schoolhouse are Canberra's oldest surviving buildings. They served the pioneer farming families of the region. Memorials on the walls of the church commemorate many early settlers, including statesmen, scientists and scholars.

Within the schoolhouse is a museum containing various 19th-century memorabilia.

Walter Burley Griffin

In 1911, the Australian government, then located in Melbourne, decided on Canberra as the best site for a new national capital. An international competition for a city plan was launched, and the first prize was awarded to a 35-year-old American landscape architect, Walter Burley Griffin. Influenced by the design of Versailles, his plan was for a garden city, with lakes, avenues and terraces rising to the focal point of Parliament House atop Capital Hill. On 12 March 1913, a foundation stone was laid by Prime Minister Andrew Fisher, but bureaucratic arguments and then World War I intervened. By 1921, little of Canberra had begun to be constructed, and Burley Griffin was dismissed from his design post. He stayed in Australia until 1935, when, reduced to municipal designs, he left for India. He died there in 1937, although his original vision lives on in the ever-expanding city of Canberra.

Walter Burley Griffin

❶ Red Hill

Via Mugga Way, Red Hill.

One of the highlights of a visit to Canberra is a drive to the top of Red Hill, which offers excellent views over Lake Burley Griffin, Parliament House, Manuka and the embassy suburb of Yarralumla (see p204). Behind Red Hill stretch the southern suburbs of Canberra, with the beautiful green of the Brindabella Ranges to the west.

An alternative view of Canberra, offering a better understanding of Walter Burley Griffin's carefully planned city design, can be seen from the top of Mount Ainslie, on the north side of the lake behind the Australian War Memorial (see pp204–5).

Panoramic view of Canberra from Red Hill

❷ Royal Australian Mint

Denison St, Deakin. **Tel** (02) 6202 6999 or 1 300 652 020. 🚌 30, 31. **Open** 8:30am–5pm Mon–Fri, 10am–4pm Sat–Sun, public hols. **Closed** Good Fri, 25 Dec. 📷 10am & 2pm Mon–Fri. ♿ 🖥 ramint.gov.au

The Royal Australian Mint is the sole producer of Australia's circulating coin currency. It has produced over 11 billion circulating coins and today has the capacity to mint over two million coins per day, or over 600 million per year. The Mint is dedicated to commemorating Australia's culture and history through its numismatic programme.

❸ Parliament House

Parliament House is the meeting place of Australia's Parliament and the centre of Australia's democracy. Opened in 1988, the building on Capital Hill is the third home of the Federal Parliament since 1901. The building is set on a 32-ha (80-acre) site and is the focal point of Canberra. Its architecture reflects Australia's commitment to open government.

House of Representatives Chamber
This chamber accommodates the 150 elected members of the House of Representatives.

KEY

① **Members' Hall**

② **The steel flagpole** reaches a height of 81 m (256 ft) and weighs 220 tonnes.

③ **The Great Veranda** is clad with white Italian marble cut from a single cliff face. Its grand design marks both the ceremonial and the public entrance for Parliament House.

④ **The Commonwealth coat of arms** above the entrance features an emu and kangaroo in the skeleton-like style of Aboriginal rock paintings.

★ **The Great Hall**
This hall is used for state functions. The 20-m (65-ft) tapestry is based on an Arthur Boyd painting.

When touring the Mint you can see the history of Australian currency as well as how coins are made. You can even view the coins coming directly off the presses.

❸ Government House

Dunrossil Drive, Yarralumla. **Tel** (02) 6283 3533. **Open** two days a year – phone ahead to check. 🚐 📷 obligatory.

Government House has been the official residence of the Governor General, the representative of the monarch in Australia, since 1927. The house was once part of a large sheep station called Yarralumla, which was settled in 1828, and is now where heads of state and the Royal Family stay when visiting Australia. The house is closed to the public, except on special open days; however, a lookout point on Lady Denman Drive offers good views of the residence and the large gardens.

Elegant façade and front grounds of Government House

★ **Entrance Foyer**
The 48 grey-green, marble pillars are designed to be reminiscent of a eucalypt forest.

VISITORS' CHECKLIST

Practical Information
Capital Hill. **Tel** (02) 6277 7111. **Open** 9am–5pm daily (later on days parliament is sitting). **Closed** 25 Dec. 📷 In-depth paid tours 10am, 1pm, 3pm; free tours 9.30am, 11am, noon, 2pm, 3.30pm. ♿ 📷 📼 **aph.gov.au**

Transport
🚌 1, 934.

Forecourt
The Aboriginal mosaic, red gravel and pool represent Australia's landscape and native inhabitants.

Entrance

❺ Yarralumla

Yarralumla. **Tel** (02) 6205 0044
(Canberra Visitors' Centre). 🚌 901, 31.
🏛 for embassy open days. ♿
variable. 📷

The suburb of Yarralumla, on
the edge of Capital Hill, is home
to more than 80 of Australia's
foreign embassies and
diplomatic residences. A drive
through the tree-lined streets
gives a fascinating view of the
architecture and cultures of
each country represented, as
embodied in their embassies and
grand ambassadorial residences.

The traditional style of the Chinese Embassy in Yarralumla

Distinctive buildings include
the vast Chinese Embassy at
No. 15 Coronation Drive, with
its red columns, dragon statues
and pagoda-shaped roofs.

On Moonah Place, the Indian
Embassy has pools, a shallow
moat and a white temple
building in the Mogul architectural style, with a gold spire on

❻ Australian War Memorial

The Australian War Memorial was built to
commemorate all Australians who have died
while serving their country. The Roll of Honour
and the symbolic Tomb of the Unknown
Australian Soldier serve as a reminder of the
horror and sadness of war. The Anzac Hall is the
stage for sound and light shows, one of which
recreates a bombing raid over Germany.

Façade of the Australian War Memorial

★ **Roll of Honour**
Names of all the 102,600 Australians killed
in action are written on bronze panels in
the cloisters.

KEY

① **Eternal flame**

② **The Pool of Reflection** is a
peaceful place where families can
mourn their loved ones. Rosemary
planted by the pool symbolizes
remembrance.

③ **Orientation Gallery**

④ **First World War Gallery**

⑤ **Aircraft Hall**

⑥ **Second World War Gallery**

Entrance

top. The High Commission of Papua New Guinea on Forster Crescent is built as a Spirit House, with carved totem poles outside; the Mexican Embassy on Perth Avenue boasts a massive replica of the Aztec Sun Stone.

Just across Adelaide Avenue is The Lodge, the official residence of the Australian prime minister and his family.

❻ National Gallery of Australia

See pp206–7.

❼ Civic Square

Civic Centre. 🚌 many routes.

The commercial heart of Canberra is the Civic Centre, on the north side of Lake Burley Griffin close to the northwest corner of the Parliamentary Triangle *(see pp198–9)*. It is the centre of many administrative, legal and local government functions in Canberra, as well as having the highest concentration of offices and private sector businesses. It is also the

Ethos statue, Civic Square

city's main shopping area. The central Civic Square, as envisaged by Walter Burley Griffin in his original city plan, is a common meeting place and relaxing area. It is dominated by the graceful bronze statue of Ethos, by Australian sculptor Tom Bass, located at the entrance of the ACT Legislative Assembly. In the adjacent Petrie Plaza is a traditional carousel, a much-loved landmark among the citizens of Canberra.

Hall of Memory
Adorning the golden dome is one of the world's largest mosaics, built in part by war widows.

Anzac Hall

VISITORS' CHECKLIST

Practical Information
Treloar Crescent, Campbell.
Tel (02) 6243 4211.
W awm.gov.au
Open 10am–5pm daily.
Closed 25 Dec. 🦽 📷 📱 🖥

Transport
🚌 10, 81, 910, 981.

Stained-glass Windows
The figures on these windows represent the personal, social and fighting skills of all Australians during wartime.

★ Tomb of the Unknown Soldier
Beneath this red marble slab is buried an unknown Australian soldier who died during World War I. He symbolizes all Australians who have been killed while serving their country.

❻ National Gallery of Australia

Australian society is diverse, multicultural and vibrant, and the 160,000 works of art owned by the National Gallery of Australia reflect the spirit of the country. The NGA opened in 1982, and the core of its collection consists of Australian art, from European settlement to present day, by some of its most famous artists, such as Tom Roberts, Arthur Boyd, Sidney Nolan and Margaret Preston *(see p38)*. The oldest art in Australia is that of its indigenous inhabitants *(see pp36–7)*, and the Aboriginal & Torres Strait Islander art collection offers fine examples of both ancient and contemporary works. The gallery's Asian and international collections are also growing. Modern sculptures are on display in the gardens.

Level 2

Level 1
Entrance

★ **In a Corner on the MacIntyre** *(1895)*
Tom Roberts' depiction of this country's bushland is painted in the fractured light style of the Australian School of Impressionism.

Sandringham Beach *(c.1933)*
This dynamic painting by Clarice Beckett exudes a leisurely feel that captures Australia's passion for the beach as a place of relaxation and recreation.

Sculpture Garden

The National Gallery makes the most of its picturesque, lakeside gardens as the site for an impressive collection of sculptures, from classical, such as Aristide Maillol's *The Mountain*, to modern. Two of the best known and loved contemporary sculptures in the garden are *Cones* by Bert Flugelman and *The Pears* by George Baldessin.

The Mountain by Aristide Maillol

Gallery Guide

The National Gallery is easily visited within two hours, although an excellent one-hour tour of the highlights is offered twice daily. On the lower level is the largest Aboriginal art collection in the world and the Impressionism to Pop collections. Also highly recommended, on the upper level, is the extensive Australian art collection. Touring "blockbuster" art shows are featured at the gallery at least twice per year.

Blue Poles *(1952)*
When this work by US artist Jackson Pollock was bought for $1.2 million in 1973 it outraged conservative Australians, who claimed that it looked like it had been painted by a child or a drunk.

Orde Poyntan Gallery

★ **The Aboriginal Memorial** *(1988)*
These log poles by the Ramingining people honour all Aborigines who have died during white settlement.

Level 1

Main entrance

Key to Floorplan
- Australian Art
- Indian and Southeast Asian Art
- Aboriginal & Torres Strait Islander Art
- Sculpture Gallery
- Impressionism to Pop
- Pacific Art
- Melanesian Art
- Temporary exhibition space
- Non-exhibition space
- Children's Gallery
- East Asian Art

Rock Garden section of the Australian National Botanic Gardens

⑨ Australian National Botanic Gardens

Clunies Ross St, Acton. **Tel** (02) 6250 9588. **Open** 8:30am–5pm daily. **Closed** 25 Dec. ♿ 📷 🖥
🌐 anbg.gov.au

On the slopes of Black Mountain, the Australian National Botanic Gardens hold the finest scientific collection of native plants in the country. Approximately 90,000 plants of more than 5,000 species are featured in its displays.

The Rainforest Gully, one of the most popular attractions, features plants from the rainforests of eastern Australia. One fifth of the nation's eucalypt species are found on the Eucalypt Lawn. The Aboriginal Trail is a self-guided walk that details how Aborigines have utilized plants over thousands of years.

⑩ Telstra Tower

Black Mountain Drive, Acton. **Tel** 1800 806 718 or (02) 6219 6120. **Open** 9am–10pm daily. 🚇 ♿ 🖥
🌐 telstratower.com.au

Known affectionately by locals as "the giant syringe", Telstra soars 195 m (640 ft) above the summit of Black Mountain. The tower houses state-of-the-art communications equipment, such as television transmitters and cellular phone bases. The tower also features an exhibition on the history of telecommunications in Australia, from its first telegraph wire in Victoria in 1854 to the 21st century.

There are three viewing platforms at different levels offering spectacular 360° views of Canberra and the surrounding countryside. There is also a revolving restaurant. In 1989, Black Mountain Tower, as it was originally called, was made a member of the World Federation of Great Towers, which includes such buildings as the Empire State Building in New York.

⑪ National Zoo and Aquarium

Lady Denman Drive, Scrivener Dam. **Tel** (02) 6287 8400. **Open** 9:30am–5pm daily. **Closed** 25 Dec. 🚇 ♿ 📷 by arrangement. 🖥 🏨
🌐 nationalzoo.com.au

A wonderful collection of Australia's fish, from native freshwater river fish to brilliantly coloured cold sea, tropical and coral species are on display in the National Zoo and Aquarium. This is Australia's only combined zoo and aquarium. There are about 20 aquariums on show, including a number of smaller tanks containing freshwater and marine animals. They have some eight different species of shark on display.

The 9-ha (22-acre) landscaped grounds of the adjacent **Zoo** have excellent displays of numerous native animals including koalas, wombats, dingoes, fairy penguins, Tasmanian devils, emus and kangaroos. As well as the native residents of the zoo there are many favourites from all over the world, including several big cats (the zoo has the largest collection of big cats in the country), primates, two giraffes and African antelopes.

The zoo also organizes "Meet a Cheetah" encounters. Under the supervision of a keeper, you will enter the cheetah enclosure and actually be able to touch and pat the animals. For even more close encounters, there is the two-hour ZooVenture tour, which would appeal to those animal lovers who want to enjoy a more hands-on behind-the-scenes kind of experience. Both this tour and "Meet a Cheetah" have age and height restrictions, and must be booked well ahead of your visit.

Kangaroo in the National Zoo

⑫ Australian Institute of Sport

Leverrier Crescent, Bruce. **Tel** (02) 6214 1010. 🚌 7, 980. **Open** for tours only: 10am, 11:30am, 1pm, 2:30pm daily. **Closed** 25 & 26 Dec. 🚇 ♿ 📷 obligatory.
🌐 experienceais.com

Australian Olympic athletes are often on hand to show visitors around the world-class Australian Institute of Sport (AIS). This is the national centre of Australia's sports efforts. Here you can see where the athletes sleep, train and eat. You can see how your fitness levels compare and test your sporting skills. There is also an exhibition of interactive sports displays, the Sportex exhibition, which includes themes such as "Heroes and Legends" and "How do you measure up?" Athletes can take visitors on guided tours around the amazing facilities. A shop and a café are also open to visitors.

The *Harvest of Endurance* scroll, depicting the 1861 Lambing Flat Riots, in the National Museum of Australia

⑬ National Museum of Australia

Lawson Crescent, Acton Peninsula. **Tel** (02) 6208 5000 or 1800 026 132. 🚌 7, 81, 934, 981. **Open** 9am–5pm daily. **Closed** 25 Dec. ♿ 📷 by arrangement. 🎟 (special exhibitions). 🅿 📷 🌐 nma.gov.au

Established by an Act of Parliament in 1980, the National Museum of Australia moved to its permanent home on the Acton Peninsula in early 2001. It shares its location with the Australian Institute of Aboriginal and Torres Strait Islander Studies. The innovative, purpose-built facility quickly became an architectural landmark. Its unique design was inspired by the idea of a jigsaw puzzle.

Before beginning a tour of the museum, visitors can experience an audiovisual introduction to the museum in the Circa, a novel rotating cinema. A huge, three-dimensional map of Australia is visible from three floors. Using digital animation and interactive media stations, it helps to place the displays in their geographical context.

The permanent exhibitions explore the people, events and issues that have shaped and influenced the country. The museum's aim is to be a focus for sharing stories and promoting debate, and interactive displays involve visitors by inviting their contributions.

The **First Australians** gallery is the largest permanent exhibition and relates the stories and experiences of Aboriginal and Torres Strait Islander people. It not only illuminates their history but also deals frankly with contemporary social issues. Displays include Central Australian desert art, stone tools and Aboriginal jewellery made from Tasmanian seashells and a Torres Island outrigger canoe. In the **Landmarks** gallery, discover how Australia's cities, towns and communities have developed throughout history. The displays explore the ways people have engaged with landscapes, flora, fauna and technologies to build the Australia we recognise today.

The **Journeys** exhibition reviews how immigration has shaped the country. Since 1788 more than 10 million people have arrived in Australia as immigrants, and this gallery uses individual stories, as well as objects from the museum's collection, to look at the remarkable diversity of the Australian experience.

One of the more moving exhibitions is **Eternity**, in which the personal stories of 50 Australians are brought to life. The intention of this unique display is to explore history through emotion. "Your Story", an interactive exhibit, allows visitors to record their own stories,

Untitled by Charlie Alyungurra, in the First Australians gallery

which then become part of the collection.

The museum also acknowledges the significance of the land in Australia's identity. In **Old New Land**, the relationship between people and the environment is examined.

The landscaping of the museum is also notable and includes the striking Garden of Australian Dreams, which incorporates many symbols of Australian culture. The Backyard Café spills out into the innovative garden.

In addition, the museum hosts a range of temporary exhibitions. There are also children's galleries and performance spaces, as well as a television broadcast studio.

The Mermaid Coffin by Gaynor Peaty, in Eternity

Further Afield in the ACT

More than 70 per cent of the Australian Capital Territory is bushland. A one-day tour along Tourist Drive 5 provides an opportunity to see native animals in the wild, swim in the majestic Murrumbidgee River, visit a deep-space tracking station, and relax in the lovely gardens of the historic Lanyon Homestead.

Interior of the small stone cottage at Mugga-Mugga

⑭ Mugga-Mugga

8 Narrabundah Lane, Symonston. **Tel** (02) 6235 5677. **Open** 1:30–4:30pm Sat–Sun. **Closed** late Dec–mid-Jan. ♿

One of Canberra's earliest historic sites, Mugga-Mugga reflects the social and material history of a rural working-class family who worked on Duntroon Estate. The site's main feature is a small stone cottage built for the estate's head shepherd in the 1830s. It has been adapted over time, but is still furnished with household items that belonged to the Curley family who moved to Mugga-Mugga in 1913. A galvanized iron garage near the cottage houses an exhibition on the issue of Federation (see p60).

⑮ Murrumbidgee River

ℹ️ ACT Parks and Conservation Service 13 2281.

The Murrumbidgee River meets the Cotter River at Casuarina Sands, a beautiful place to fish and canoe. Nearby is Cotter Dam, good for picnics, swimming and camping.

On the bank of the Murrumbidgee River south of Canberra is **Lanyon Homestead**, a restored 1850s home.

On the same property is the Sidney Nolan Gallery, which features the Ned Kelly series of paintings (see p38).

🏠 **Lanyon Homestead**
Tharwa Drive, Tharwa. **Tel** (02) 6235 5677. **Open** 10am–4pm Tue–Sun. **Closed** Good Fri, 24 & 25 Dec. ♿ 🅿️ 🖥️

⑯ Canberra Deep Space Communication Complex

Via Paddys River Rd (Tourist Drive 5). **Tel** (02) 6201 7880. **Open** 9am–5pm daily. **Closed** 25 Dec. ♿ 🖥️ 📷 🅿️ by arrangement. 🌐 **cdscc.nasa.gov**

Canberra Deep Space Communication Complex is managed by the Commonwealth Scientific and Industrial Research Organization (CSIRO) and the American NASA organization. It is one of only three such deep-space tracking centres in the world linked to the NASA control centre in California. The complex has six satellite dishes, the largest of which measures 70 m (230 ft) in diameter and weighs a hefty 3,000 tonnes.

Visitors to the Space Centre can see a piece of moon rock 3.8 billion years old, examine an astronaut's space suit, learn about the role of the complex during the Apollo moon landings and see pictures sent back from Mars, Saturn and Jupiter.

Emu at Tidbinbilla Nature Reserve

⑰ Tidbinbilla Nature Reserve

Via Paddys River Rd (Tourist Drive 5). **Tel** 13 2281 or (02) 6205 1233. **Open** 9am–5pm daily (to 4:30pm in winter). **Closed** 25 Dec. 📷 ♿ limited. 📷 🌐 **tidbinbilla.act.gov.au**

The tranquil Tidbinbilla Nature Reserve, with its 5,450 ha (13,450 acres) of forests, grasslands, streams and mountains, is a paradise for wildlife lovers. Kangaroos and their joeys bask in the sun, emus strut on the grassy flats, platypuses swim in the creeks, koalas thrive on the eucalypt branches and bower birds and superb lyrebirds can be seen in the tall forests.

The reserve is set at the end of a valley. Visitors hike up to Gibraltar Rock or take a night stroll with a ranger to see sugar gliders and possums. The Birrigai Time Trail is a 3-km (2-mile) walk through various periods of history. The visitors' centre features Aboriginal artifacts and pioneer relics.

Tracking dishes known as "antenna" at the Canberra Space Complex

⓲ Namadgi National Park

Namadgi National Park covers almost half of the Australian Capital Territory. It is a beautiful, harsh landscape of snow, mountains, river valleys and Aboriginal rock art. Only 35 km (22 miles) south of Canberra, Namadgi is remote and solitary. Many days could be spent exploring the park, but even a day's walking will reward you with breathtaking views of the country.

Corin Dam stores high-quality water from the Cotter River, sourced in the Bimberi Wilderness.

Booromba Rocks

Visitors' Centre
Trail maps of the park and information on ranger-guided walks are available here.

Nursery Swamp

Boboyah Pine Forest

Orroral Bush Camp Site
Camping out in this wild, bush setting amid the wildlife is an experience not to be missed.

Mount Clear is one of three camping grounds in the park.

Yankee Hat
Ancient Aboriginal rock art thought to date back thousands of years has been discovered in this area.

Key

▬ Major road

▬ Minor road

– – Walking trail

〰️ River

For keys to symbols *see back flap*

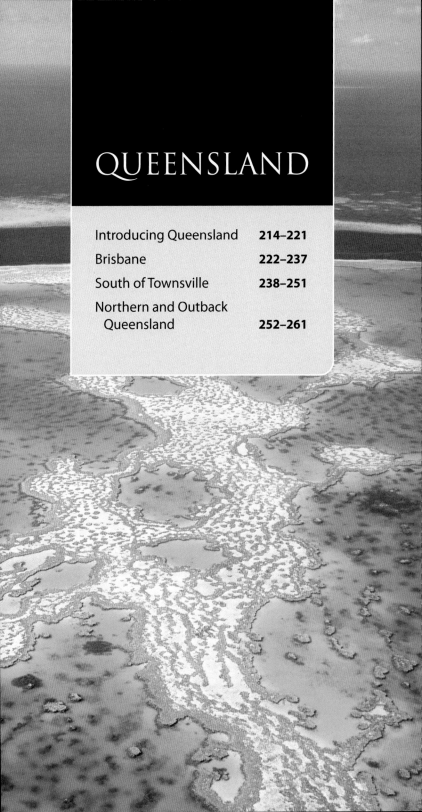

QUEENSLAND

Queensland at a Glance

Australia's second-largest state encompasses some 1,727,000 sq km (667,000 sq miles) and is the country's most popular tourist destination, after Sydney, due to its tropical climate. Brisbane, the state capital, is a modern city, with skyscrapers looking out over the Brisbane River. The southern coastline is a haven for surfers and is the region that most typifies the nation's beach culture. Further north is the Great Barrier Reef, one of the natural wonders of the world. Inland, cattle stations and copper mines generate Queensland's wealth. The Far North remains remote and unspoiled, with rainforests and savannah land abundant with native wildlife.

Weipa

Northern and Outback Queensland
(see pp252–61)

Mount Isa   Cloncurry

Hughenden

Mount Isa is one of Queensland's largest inland cities and revolves almost entirely around its copper, zinc and lead mining industries *(see p261)*.

Longreach

0 km   100

0 miles   100

Charlev

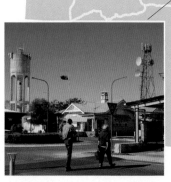

Longreach is in the heart of Queensland's Outback, and its most popular sight is the Stockman's Hall of Fame, documenting Australia's Outback history. Longreach is also the site of Qantas' original hangar *(see p261)*.

Cunnamulla

◀ The spectacular coral islands of the Great Barrier Reef

Locator Map

Cairns is Queensland's most northerly city and is a popular boarding point for touring the Great Barrier Reef. The city's hub is its esplanade, lined with cafés *(see p258)*.

The Great Barrier Reef is the largest coral reef in the world. Hundreds of islands scatter the coastline, but only a few are developed for tourists, who come here to dive among the coral and tropical fish *(see pp216–21)*.

Maryborough has many typical "Queenslander" houses, known for their wide verandas shading residents from the tropical sun *(see p245)*.

irns

Townsville

arters
wers

Bowen

Mackay

Emerald

Rockhampton

Gladstone

South of Townsville *(see pp238–51)*

Bundaberg

Maryborough

Gympie

Caloundra

Toowoomba

Brisbane

Brisbane, the state capital, is a highly modern yet relaxing city *(see pp222–37)*. Skyscrapers blend with older edifices, such as the impressive City Hall.

Surfers Paradise is the vibrant centre of the Gold Coast and more than lives up to its name. Chic hotels, pulsating nightclubs, high fashion stores and beach poseurs can all be found here *(see p243)*.

The Great Barrier Reef

Coral reefs are among the oldest and most primitive forms of life, dating back at least 500 million years. Today, the Great Barrier Reef is the largest reef system in the world, covering 2,000 km (1,250 miles) from Bundaberg to the tip of Cape York and an area of approximately 350,000 sq km (135,000 sq miles). Between the outer edges of the reef and the mainland, there are more than 2,000 islands and almost 3,000 separate reefs, of differing types. On islands with a fringing reef, coral can be viewed at close hand, although the best coral is on the outer reef, about 50 km (30 miles) from the mainland.

Locator Map

The channel of water between the inner reef and Queensland's mainland is often as deep as 60 m (200 ft) and can vary in width between 30 km (20 miles) and 60 km (40 miles).

Coral is formed by tiny marine animals called polyps. These organisms have an external "skeleton" of limestone. Polyps reproduce by dividing their cells and so becoming polyp colonies.

Fringing reefs surround islands or develop off the mainland coast as it slopes away into the sea.

Typical Section of the Reef

In this typical section of the Great Barrier Reef, a deep channel of water runs close to the mainland. In shallower water further out are a variety of reef features including coral cays, platform reefs and lagoons. Further out still, where the edge of the continental shelf drops off steeply, is a system of ribbon reefs.

Platform reef

Coral cays are sand islands, formed when reef skeletons and other debris such as shells are exposed to the air and gradually ground down by wave movement into fine sand.

Platform reefs form in shallow water, growing outwards in a circle or oval rather than upwards in a wall.

Queensland's tropical rainforest is moist and dense, thriving on the region's heavy, monsoon-like rains and rich soil.

How the Reef was Formed

The growth of coral reefs is dependent on sea level, as coral cannot grow above the water line or below 30 m (100 ft). As sea level rises, old coral turns to limestone, on top of which new coral can build, eventually forming barrier reefs. The Great Barrier Reef consists of thousands of separate reefs and is comparatively young, most of it having formed since the sea level rose after the end of the last Ice Age. An outer reef system corresponds with Queensland's continental shelf. Reef systems nearer the mainland correspond with submerged hills.

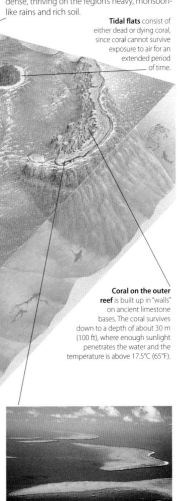

Tidal flats consist of either dead or dying coral, since coral cannot survive exposure to air for an extended period of time.

Coral on the outer reef is built up in "walls" on ancient limestone bases. The coral survives down to a depth of about 30 m (100 ft), where enough sunlight penetrates the water and the temperature is above 17.5°C (65°F).

Coral grows on the continental shelf

Forested hills

1 Approximately 18,000 years ago, during the last Ice Age, waters were low, exposing a range of forested hills. Coral grew in the shallow waters of the continental shelf.

Coral starts building upwards as waters rise

New area of coral growth

2 Approximately 9,000 years ago, following the last Ice Age, the water level rose to submerge the hills. Coral began to grow in new places.

Coastal rainforest

Outer reef

Inner reef

3 Over succeeding millennia, coral formed "walls" on the continental shelf (the outer reef), while an array of fringing and platform reefs, coral cays and lagoons formed around the former hills (the inner reef).

Ribbon reefs are narrow strips that occur only in the north along the edge of the continental shelf. Exactly why they form here remains a mystery to marine biologists.

Life on the Great Barrier Reef

More than 2,000 species of fish and innumerable species of hard and soft coral are found in the waters of the Great Barrier Reef. The diversity of life forms is extraordinary, such as echinoderms (including sea urchins), crustaceans and sponges. There is also an array of invertebrates, such as the graceful sea slug, some 12 species of sea grasses and 500 types of algae. The reef islands and coral cays support a wonderfully colourful variety of tropical birdlife. This environment is protected by the Great Barrier Reef Marine Park Authority, established by an Act of Parliament in 1975.

Diving amid the dazzling colours and formations of soft coral.

Hard coral *(see p217)* is formed from the outer skeleton of polyps. The most common species is staghorn coral.

Soft coral has no outer skeleton and resembles the fronds of a plant, rippling in the waves.

Wobbegongs are members of the shark family. They sleep during the day under rocks and caves, camouflaged by their skin tones.

Manta rays are huge fish, measuring up to 6 m (20 ft) across. Despite their size, they are gentle creatures that are happy to swim close to divers.

Potato cod are known for their friendly demeanour and are often happy to swim alongside divers.

Great white sharks are occasional visitors to the reef, although they usually live in the open ocean and swim in schools.

Giant clams, which are large bivalves, are sadly a gourmet delicacy. Australian clams are now protected by law to save them from extinction.

Coral groupers inhabit the reef waters and grow up to 15 kg (33 lb). They are recognizable by their deep red skin.

The sea bed of the Barrier Reef is 60 m (195 ft) deep at its lowest point.

The Fragile Reef

Ecotourism is the only tourism that is encouraged on the Great Barrier Reef. The important thing to remember when on the reef is to look but not touch. Coral is easily broken; avoid standing on it and be aware that the taking of coral is strictly forbidden and carefully monitored. Camping on the reef's islands requires a permit from the Great Barrier Reef Marine Park Authority.

Beaked coralfish are abundant and some of the most attractive fish of the Barrier Reef. They often swim in pairs, in shallow waters and around coral heads.

Gobies feed on sand, ingesting the organic matter. They are found near the shoreline.

Blenny

Butterfly fish

The Reef as a Marine Habitat

Hard corals are the building blocks of the reef. Together with soft corals, they form the "forest" within which the fish and other sea creatures dwell.

Schultz pipefish

Goatfish

Clown anemonefish have an immunity to the stinging tentacles of sea anemones, among which they reside.

Batfish swim in large groups and colonize areas of the reef for long periods before moving on elsewhere. They mainly feed on algae and sea jellies.

Moray eels grow to 2 m (6 ft) in length, but are gentle enough to be hand-fed by divers.

Birds of the Great Barrier Reef

Gulls, gannets, frigate birds, shearwaters and terns all make use of the rich environment of the islands of the Great Barrier Reef to breed and rear their young, largely safe from mainland predators such as cats and foxes. The number of sea birds nesting on some of the coral cays is astounding – for example, on the tiny area of Michaelmas Cay, 42 km (26 miles) northeast of Cairns, there are more than 30,000 birds, including herons and boobies. **Red-footed booby**

The crown of thorns starfish feeds mainly on staghorn coral. In the 1960s, a sudden growth in the numbers of this starfish led to worries that it would soon destroy the whole reef. However, many now believe that such a population explosion is a natural and common phenomenon. It contributes to reef life by destroying old coral and allowing new coral to generate.

Activities on the Great Barrier Reef

Fewer than 20 of the Great Barrier Reef's 2,000 islands cater for tourists *(see map and table below)*. Accommodation on the islands ranges from luxury resorts to basic camp sites. To make the most of the coral, take a tourist boat trip to the outer reef; most operators provide glass-bottomed boats to view the coral. The best way of seeing the reef, however, is by diving or snorkelling. There are many day trips from the mainland to the reef and between the islands. Some resorts were devastated by a cyclone in 2011 and are still being rebuilt.

Reef walking involves walking over dead stretches of the reef at low tide. Wear strong shoes and be very careful to avoid standing on living coral under the water.

Snorkelling is one of the most popular activities in the Great Barrier Reef, offering the chance to see beautiful tropical fish at close range.

The Main Islands

Tropical fish are largely harmless – the majority will let you swim close, but may nip your fingers if you attempt to touch them.

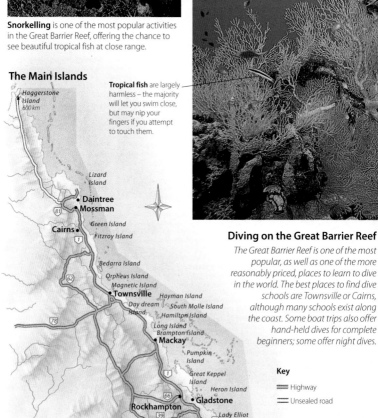

Haggerstone Island 600 km

Lizard Island

Daintree
Mossman
Cairns
Green Island
Fitzroy Island

Bedarra Island
Orpheus Island
Magnetic Island
Townsville   Hayman Island
Day dream   South Molle Island
Island   Hamilton Island
Long Island
Brampton Island
Mackay

Pumpkin Island

Great Keppel Island
Heron Island
Gladstone
Rockhampton
Lady Elliot Island
Bundaberg

Diving on the Great Barrier Reef

The Great Barrier Reef is one of the most popular, as well as one of the more reasonably priced, places to learn to dive in the world. The best places to find dive schools are Townsville or Cairns, although many schools exist along the coast. Some boat trips also offer hand-held dives for complete beginners; some offer night dives.

Key

▭▭ Highway
▭▭ Unsealed road

0 km   150
0 miles   150

Heron Island is one of the few coral cay resorts and is known for its excellent diving. From October to March, turtle-spotting is a popular activity as they make their way up the beach to lay their eggs. Bird-watching is also popular as the island's pisonia trees are home to thousands of birds, including Noddy terns. Guided nature walks around the cay are available.

Gorgonian fan coral grows in thickets in the deep waters of the Barrier Reef and is recognizable by its orange-yellow colour.

Getting to the Tourist Islands

Bedarra Island: from Mission Beach, helicopter from Cairns. Daydream Island: 🚤 from Port of Airlie, Airlie Beach. Fitzroy Island: 🚤 from Cairns. Great Keppell Island: ✈ from Rockhampton. Green Island: 🚤 from Cairns. Haggerstone Island: ✈ from Cairns. Hamilton Island: 🛬 from state capitals & Cairns. 🚤 from Port of Airlie, Airlie Beach. Hayman Island: 🚤 from Port aof Airlie, Airlie Beach. Heron Island: ✈ 🚤 from Gladstone. Lady Elliot Island: ✈ from Bundaberg, Hervey Bay. Brisbane & Gold Coast: ✈ from Cairns. Long Island: 🚤 from Shute Harbour, Airlie Beach or Hamilton Island. Magnetic Island: 🚤 from Townsville. Orpheus Island: ✈ from Cairns & Townsville. Pumpkin Island: 🚤 from Yeppon.

Scuba is an acronym for Self-contained Underwater Breathing Apparatus.

Hamilton Island is a popular resort island featuring a wide range of activities, including parasailing, skydiving, golf, tennis and children's entertainments.

The Low Isles, 25 km (15 miles) offshore from Port Douglas, are a perfect example of the reef's day-trip opportunities. This glass-bottomed boat offers sunbathing areas, snorkelling, views of reef life and lunch, before returning to the mainland.

Activities on the Tourist Islands

These islands are accessible by boat or air and offer a range of activities.

	DIVING	SNORKELLING	FISHING	DAY TRIPS	BUSHWALKING	WATERSPORTS	FOR CHILDREN
Bedarra Island	●	●	●	●	●	●	
Daydream Island	●	●	●	●	●	●	●
Fitzroy Island	●	●		●	●	●	
Gt Keppel Island		●	●	●	●	●	●
Green Island *(see p257)*	●	●		●	●		
Haggerstone Island		●	●	●	●	●	
Hamilton Island	●	●	●	●	●	●	●
Hayman Island	●	●	●	●	●	●	
Heron Island	●	●		●	●		●
Lady Elliot Island	●	●		●			●
Lizard Island	●	●	●	●	●	●	
Long Island		●	●		●	●	●
Magnetic Island *(see p251)*	●	●	●	●	●	●	●
Orpheus Island	●	●	●	●	●	●	
Pumpkin Island	●	●	●		●	●	●

BRISBANE

Brisbane is the capital of Queensland and, with a population of over 2.3 million, ranks third in size in Australia after Sydney and Melbourne. Situated on the Brisbane River and surrounded by misty blue hills, the city is known for its scenic beauty, balmy climate and friendly atmosphere. Its tropical vegetation is a great attraction, particularly the bougainvillea, poinciana and fragrant frangipani.

In 1823, the Governor of New South Wales, Sir Thomas Brisbane, decided that some of the more intractable convicts in the Sydney penal settlement needed more secure incarceration. The explorer John Oxley was dispatched to investigate Moreton Bay, noted by Captain Cook on his journey up the east coast 50 years earlier. Oxley landed at Redcliffe and thought he had stumbled across a tropical paradise. He was soon disappointed and it was decided to move the colony inland up the Brisbane River. This was mainly due to Brisbane's more reliable water supply and the fact that the river had a bend in it, which made escape more difficult for the convicts.

Free settlers began arriving in 1837, although they were not permitted to move closer than 80 km (50 miles) to the famously harsh penal settlement. This set a pattern of decentralization which is still evident today: Brisbane consists of several distinct communities as well as the central area. The city's growth was rapid and, in 1859, when Queensland became a self-governing colony, Brisbane was duly named as the state capital.

As Queensland's natural resources, including coal, silver, lead and zinc, were developed, so its major city flourished. Brisbane's status as a truly modern city, however, is relatively recent, beginning with a mining boom in the 1960s. Hosting the Commonwealth Games in 1982 and the 1988 World Expo were also milestones, bringing thousands of visitors to the city. Today, Brisbane is a cosmopolitan place boasting some superb restaurants, streetside cafés and a lively arts scene centred around its vibrant cultural precinct, as well as an impressive year-round schedule of festivals. Yet amid all the high-rises and modernity, pockets of traditional wooden cottages with verandas can still be found.

The Streets Beach swimming lagoon on Brisbane's South Bank with the city's high-rise skyline as a backdrop

◄ Brisbane's River Street Pier area by night

Exploring Central Brisbane

Brisbane's city centre fits neatly in a U-shaped loop of the Brisbane River, so one of the best ways to get acquainted with the city is by ferry. The city centre can also be easily explored on foot. The streets follow a grid and are named after British royalty: queens and princesses run north–south, kings and princes run east–west. Brisbane's suburbs also have their own distinct feel: to the east is chic Kangaroo Point; just west of the centre is trendy Paddington; while to the northwest Fortitude Valley has a diverse and multicultural population.

Cenotaph in Anzac Square

Mount Coot-tha Botanic Gardens

Key

— Highway
— Major road
═ Minor road

Sights at a Glance

Historic Streets and Buildings

- ❶ General Post Office
- ❸ Commissariat Store Museum
- ❹ Parliament House
- ❻ Old Government House
- ❼ City Hall & Museum of Brisbane
- ❽ Customs House
- ❾ Anzac Square
- ❿ Old Windmill
- ⑫ Fortitude Valley and Chinatown
- ⑯ Story Bridge
- ⑰ Newstead House

Churches and Cathedrals

- ❷ Cathedral of St Stephen
- ⑪ St John's Anglican Cathedral

Parks and Gardens

- ❺ Brisbane City Botanic Gardens
- ⑭ South Bank Precinct
- ⑱ Lone Pine Koala Sanctuary
- ⑲ Brisbane Botanic Gardens
- ⑳ South D'Aguilar National Park

Museums and Galleries

- ⑬ *Queensland Cultural Precinct pp232–3*
- ⑮ Queensland Maritime Museum

Getting Around

Tours of the city centre are readily available and public transport is cheap and efficient. City centre bus stops are colour-coded for easy route identification, and Free Loop buses do a loop around the main city area and Spring Hill. The best place for boarding the city's ferries is Riverside Centre.

Street-by-Street: Central Brisbane

Central Brisbane is a blend of glass and steel high-rises co-existing with graceful 19th-century constructions. The latter fortunately managed to survive the frenzy of demolishing old buildings that took place throughout the country during the 1970s. Queen Street, now a pedestrian mall, is the hub of the city. Reflecting the city's beginnings as a port, most of the historic buildings are found near the river. Near the city's first Botanical Gardens, which border Alice Street, many old pubs have been renovated to cater for a largely business-lunch clientele.

Central Brisbane's modern skyline, looming over the Brisbane River

Elizabeth Arcade is filled with New Age, alternative and bohemian style bookstores and retail shops.

❷ **Cathedral of St Stephen**
One of the landmarks of Brisbane's city centre is this Gothic-style cathedral. Particularly notable are its white twin spires.

❸ ★ **Commissariat Store Museum**
The original façade of these former 19th-century granary stores has been preserved, although the interior is now a museum detailing Queensland's history.

The former Coal Board building was erected in the mid-1880s and is an example of the elaborate warehouses that once dominated the city.

Smellie & Co. was a 19th-century hardware merchant housed in this attractive building. Note the Baroque doorway on the eastern side.

Queensland Club

This charming old building has housed the private, men-only Queensland Club since 1884. Panelled wood walls and elegant columns were intended to emulate British gentlemen's clubs.

Locator Map

The Mansions

The Mansions are a row of 1890s three-storey, red brick terrace houses. The arches of lighter coloured sandstone create a distinctive design. Stone cats sit atop the parapets at each end of the building.

Key

— Suggested route

0 metres	100
0 yards	100

❹ ★ Parliament House
This stained-glass window depicting Queen Victoria is one of the many beautiful features of this late 19th-century building. Unlike many early parliamentary buildings in Australia, it is still used for its original purpose.

The restored colonial Commissariat Store Museum

❶ General Post Office

261 Queen St. **Tel** 13 13 18. 🚉
Brisbane Central. 🚌 Free Loop. ⛴
Eagle St Pier, Riverside. **Open** 7am–
6pm Mon–Fri, 10am–1:30pm Sat. ♿

Built between 1871 and
1879, this attractive Neo-Classical
building was erected to house
the city's first official postal
service. It replaced the barracks
for female convicts previously on
the site. The building continues
to operate as central Brisbane's
main post office.

Post Office Square, opposite
the General Post Office, is a
pleasant place to relax, while
looking out over the landscaped
greenery and fountains of
Anzac Square.

❷ Cathedral of St Stephen

249 Elizabeth St. **Tel** (07) 3324 3030.
🚉 Brisbane Central. 🚌 Free Loop.
⛴ Eagle St Pier. **Open** 8am–6pm
Mon–Fri, 7am–6pm Sat–Sun.
♿ 🕙 10:30am Mon–Fri, by appt Sun.
🌐 **cathedralofststephen.org.au**

Early settlers provided the funds
for this lovely English Gothic-
style Catholic cathedral,
designed by noted colonial
architect Benjamin Backhouse
and completed in 1874. The
main façade features restored
twin spires on each side of the
elaborate stained-glass windows.

Next door is St Stephen's
Chapel, the original cathedral.
It was designed by A W Pugin,
an English architect who also
worked on London's Houses
of Parliament.

❸ Commissariat Store Museum

115 William St. **Tel** (07) 3221 4198.
🚉 South Brisbane, Central. 🚌 Free
Loop. ⛴ North Quay. **Open** 10am–
4pm Tue–Fri. **Closed** Good Fri,
Easter Sun, 25 & 26 Dec. 🎫 ♿
🌐 **commissariatstore.org.au**

The Commissariat Stores,
constructed by convict labour
in 1829, is the only surviving
building from Brisbane's penal
colony days open to the public.
Having been restored in 2000,
it is now open to visitors and
houses the Royal Historical
Society of Queensland.

❹ Parliament House

Cnr George and Alice sts. **Tel** (07) 3553
6000. 🚉 Brisbane Central. 🚌 40,
Free Loop. ⛴ Gardens Point.
Open 9am– 4:15pm Mon–Fri (on
sitting days); govt-issued ID required.
Closed public hols. ♿ 🕙 free; call
(07) 3553 6470 for times and details.
🌐 **parliament.qld.gov.au**

Queensland's Parliament
House was designed in French
Renaissance style by architect
Charles Tiffin, who won an
architectural competition.
Begun in 1865, it was completed
in 1868. Tiffin added features
more suited to Queensland's
tropical climate, such as shady
colonnades, shutters and an
arched roof which is made from
Mount Isa copper *(see p261)*.
Other notable features are the
cedar staircases and the intricate
gold leaf detailing on the
Council Chamber ceilings.

The building is still used for
its original purpose and the
public is permitted to watch
when parliament is sitting.
Unlike other state parliaments,
consisting of an Upper and
Lower House, Queensland has
only one parliamentary body.

Parliament House is also
notable as being the first
legislative building in the British
Empire to be lit by electricity.

Interior of the Assembly Chamber in
Parliament House

❺ Brisbane City Botanic Gardens

Alice St. **Tel** (07) 3403 8888. 🚉 Brisbane
Central. 🚌 Free Loop. ⛴ Edward St.
Open 24 hours. ♿ 🕙 Guided walks:
11am & 1pm Mon–Sat (free).
🌐 **brisbane.qld.gov.au**

Brisbane's first Botanic Gardens
on the Brisbane River are the
second oldest botanic gardens
in Australia. Their peaceful loca-

Mangrove boardwalk in the Botanic Gardens

Arcade and arches of the north façade of Old Government House

tion is a welcome haven from the city's high-rise buildings. In its earliest incarnation, the area was used as a vegetable garden by convicts. It was laid out in its present form in 1855 by the colonial botanist Walter Hill, who was also the first director of the gardens. An avenue of bunya pines dates back to the 1850s, while an avenue of weeping figs was planted in the 1870s.

Hundreds of water birds, such as herons and plovers, come to the lakes dotted throughout the gardens' 18 ha (44 acres). Brisbane River's renowned mangroves are now a protected species and can be admired from a specially built boardwalk.

❻ Old Government House

Queensland University of Technology Campus, Gardens Point, 2 George St. **Tel** (07) 3138 8005. 🚉 Brisbane Central. 🚌 Free Loop. 🚌 Gardens Point. **Open** 10am–4pm Sun–Fri. 🚻 🖪 🗎 **W** ogh.qut.edu.au

Home to the National Trust of Queensland since 1973, the state's first Government House was designed by colonial architect Charles Tiffin and completed in 1862. The graceful sandstone building served not only as the state governor's residence, but also as the administrative base and social centre of the state of Queensland until 1910. It was then occupied by the fledgling University of Queensland. Old Government House reopened

in 2009 after renovation. It now has an art gallery dedicated to the works of William Robinson, one of Australia's greatest living landscape artists.

❼ City Hall and Museum of Brisbane

King George Sq, Adelaide and Ann sts. **Tel** (07) 3403 8888; Museum: (07) 330 0800. 🚉 Brisbane Central, Roma St. 🚌 Free Loop. 🚌 North Quay. **Open** 8am–5pm daily (from 9am Sat & Sun). 🚻 🖪 Museum of Brisbane and clocktower: **Open** 10am–5pm daily. **Closed** public hols. Museum of Brisbane: **Open** 10am–5pm daily. **W** brisbane.qld.gov.au; **W** museumofbrisbane.com.au

Completed in 1930, the Neo-Classical City Hall is home to Brisbane City Council, the largest council in Australia, and the small Museum of Brisbane.

Brisbane's early settlement is depicted by a beautiful sculpted tympanum above the main entrance. In the King George Square foyer, some fine examples

of traditional craftsmanship are evident in the floor mosaics, ornate ceilings and woodwork carved from Queensland timbers. City Hall's 92-m (300-ft) Italian Renaissance- style tower gives a panoramic view of the city from a platform at its top. A display of contemporary art and Aboriginal art and ceramics is housed in the Museum of Brisbane on level 3. Free tickets to access the clock-tower are available from the museum, with small group departures every 15 minutes. The Shingle Inn, an iconic 1936 walnut-panelled café/bakery in City Hall, has been restored to its former glory.

The attractive King George Square, facing City Hall, has several interesting statues, including *Form del Mito* by Arnaldo Pomodoro. The work's geometric forms and polished surfaces, for which this Italian sculptor is noted, reflect the changing face of the city from morning to night. The bronze *Petrie Tableau*, by Tasmanian sculptor Stephen Walker, was designed for Australia's bicentenary.

City Hall, with its Italian Renaissance clocktower

8 Customs House

399 Queen St. **Tel** (07) 3365 8999.
🚉 Brisbane Central. 🚌 Free Loop.
⛴ Riverside. **Open** from 9am daily.
Closed public hols. ♿ 🚫 Sun. 🚫
🌐 **customshouse.com.au**

Restored by the University of
Queensland in 1994, Customs
House, with its landmark copper
dome and stately Corinthian
columns, is now open to the
public. Commissioned in 1886,
this is one of Brisbane's oldest
buildings, predating both City
Hall (see p229) and the Treasury.
Early renovations removed the
hall and staircase, but these
have now been carefully
reconstructed from the original
plans. Today, the building is
primarily a function centre and
restaurant. Limited public areas
are open to visitors.

9 Anzac Square

Ann & Adelaide sts. 🚉 Brisbane
Central. 🚌 Free Loop. ⛴ Waterfront
Place, Eagle St Pier.

All Australian cities commemorate those who have
given their life for their
country. Brisbane's war
memorial is centred on Anzac
Square, an attractive park
planted with, among other flora,
rare boab (baobab) trees. The
Eternal Flame burns in a Greek
Revival cenotaph at the Ann
Street entrance to the park.
Beneath the cenotaph is the
Shrine of Memories, containing
various tributes and wall
plaques to those who gave
their lives in war.

The distinctive Old Windmill

10 Old Windmill

Wickham Terrace. 🚉 Brisbane Central.
🚌 Free Loop, 30. **Closed** to public.

Built in 1828, the Old Windmill
is one of two buildings still
standing in Brisbane from convict
days, the old Commissariat
Stores being the other survivor
(see p228). Originally the
colony's first industrial building,
it proved unworkable without
the availability of trained
operators, so it was equipped
with treadmills to punish
recalcitrant convicts. It later
served as a time signal, with a
gun fired and a ball dropped
each day at exactly 1pm.
 The mill was chosen as the
first television image in Australia
in the 1920s. It is now a weather
observatory. The windmill is not
open to the public, but it makes
a striking photograph.

11 St John's Anglican Cathedral

373 Ann St. **Tel** (07) 3835 2231.
🚉 Brisbane Central. 🚌 Free Loop.
⛴ Riverside Centre. **Open** 9:30am–
4:30pm daily for visits (see website
for worship times). ♿ 🚫
🌐 **stjohnscathedral.com.au**

Designed along French Gothic
lines in 1888, with the foundation
stone laid in 1901, St John's
Anglican Cathedral is regarded
as one of the most splendid
churches in the southern
hemisphere. The interior is of
Helidon sandstone. On display
are numerous examples of local
needlework, wood, glass and
stone craft. Over 400 cushions
depicting Queensland's flora and
fauna attract a lot of interest.
 Queensland was made a
separate colony at the adjacent
Deanery in 1859. The Deanery
was the temporary residence of
Queenland's first governor.

Nave and altar of St John's
Anglican Cathedral

12 Fortitude Valley and Chinatown

Ann and Wickham sts, Fortitude Valley.
🚉 Brunswick St. 🚌 Buses to cnr
Wickham & Brunswick sts, Bribane
Explorer.

The ship Fortitude sailed from
England and up the Brisbane
River in 1859 with 250 settlers on
board, and the name stuck to the
valley where they disembarked.
For a time the area was the
trading centre of the city and
some impressive buildings were

Greek cenotaph in Anzac Square

Entrance to the Pedestrian Hall in Chinatown, Fortitude Valley

erected during the 1880s and 1890s. It then degenerated into one of Brisbane's seedier areas.

In the 1980s, the city council began to revive the district. It is now the bohemian centre of Brisbane, with some of the city's best restaurants (see pp512–14). McWhirter's Emporium, an Art Deco landmark, was originally a department store. Shops now occupy the lower levels with apartments above. On weekends, there is also a busy outdoor market in Brunswick Street.

Also within the valley is Brisbane's Chinatown, a bustling area of Asian restaurants, supermarkets, cinemas and martial arts centres. The lions at the entrance were turned around when a *feng shui* expert considered their original position to be bad for business.

⑬ Queensland Cultural Precinct

See pp232–3.

⑭ South Bank Precinct

Brisbane River foreshore, South Bank. 🚉 South Bank. 🚌 Cultural Centre bus station, South Bank Busway routes, George St nr Adelaide St routes. 🚢 South Bank 1, 2, 3. 🅿 Visitors' Centre: **Tel** (07) 3156 6366. **Open** 9am–5pm daily. 🆆 visitsouthbank.com.au

The South Bank of the Brisbane River was the site of Expo '88 and is now a 17 ha (42 acres) centre of culture, entertainment and recreation. The area known as the parklands includes the Queensland Performing Arts Centre, the State Library, the Queensland Museum & Science Centre, and Queensland Art Gallery and Gallery of Modern Art (see pp232–3), the Conservatorium, Opera Queensland, two colleges and an exhibition centre.

The South Bank area abounds with restaurants, cafés, weekend market stalls and street entertainers. Classical music and pop concerts are also regularly held here. There is even a man-made lagoon, Streets Beach,

Butterfly at South Bank Parklands

with a "real" sandy beach, with suntanned lifesavers. Brisbane Greeters run free parkland tours (visitbrisbane.com.au).

South Bank also features the Wheel of Brisbane, offering great views, and Goodwill Bridge, a 450-m (1,500-ft) pedestrian and cycle bridge, one of two linking the area with the Botanic Gardens and city centre.

⑮ Queensland Maritime Museum

End of Goodwill Bridge, South Bank. **Tel** (07) 3844 5361. 🚉 South Bank. 🚌 Southbank Busway & Cultural Centre routes to Mater Hill or South Bank. 🚢 Maritime Museum, South Bank. **Open** 9:30am–4:30pm daily. **Closed** Good Fri, 25 Apr (am), 24–26 Dec. 🈂 🅱 🅲 🆆 maritimemuseum.com.au

Queensland Maritime Museum lists among its exhibits shipbuilders' models, reconstructed cabins from early steamers and relics from early shipwrecks in the area. In the dry dock, as part of the National Estate, sits HMAS *Diamantina*, a frigate that served during World War II.

A coal-fired tug, *Forceful*, is kept in running order and cruises with passengers to Moreton Bay two seasons a year. Also on display is the pearling lugger *Penguin* and the bow of a Japanese pleasure boat, a *yakatabume*, donated to Brisbane by Japan after Expo '88.

HMAS *Diamantina* at the Queensland Maritime Museum

⑬ Queensland Cultural Precinct

The Queensland Cultural Precinct is the hub of Brisbane's arts scene, with a spectacular setting on the South Bank. It incorporates the Queensland Art Gallery (QAG), the Gallery of Modern Art (GOMA), the Queensland Museum & Science Centre, the State Library of Queensland and the Queensland Performing Arts Centre.

First established in 1895, QAG has a fine collection of Australian art, including works by Sidney Nolan and Margaret Preston, together with Indigenous Australian art. The international collection includes 15th-century European art and Asian art from the 12th century. QAG and GOMA together create QAGOMA, Australia's second-largest public art museum, offering distinct yet complementary experiences.

Bathers *(1906)*
One of Australia's most highly regarded artists, Rupert Bunny gained international fame with paintings of Victorian life.

Bushfire *(1944)*
Russell Drysdale is known for his depiction of harsh Outback life, such as this farm house destroyed by a fire. It is an abstract piece with slightly discordant colours.

Melbourne street entrance Level 1

Level 1

Asian and international art is represented by more than 3,000 European and American works.

★ **La Belle Hollandaise** *(1905)*
One of Picasso's transitional works between his blue and rose periods, this was painted during a visit to the Netherlands. The gallery paid a then world record price of £55,000 in 1959 for the work of a living artist.

Ground Level

Key

- ▦ Asian and international art
- ▢ Australian art
- ▦ Indigenous Australian art
- ▦ Watermall
- ▢ Sculpture Courtyard
- ▦ Temporary/Feature exhibition
- ▦ Non-exhibition space
- ▦ Queensland artists

For hotels and restaurants in this area see p486 and pp512–14

Queensland Art Gallery Guide

The collection is housed over three levels. Fine collections of Asian and International art from the 12th century are on Level 2. Indigenous Australian art begins on Level 2 and moves up to Level 4. Level 3 contains Australian art after 1970. The work in this gallery is complemented by the contemporary art housed in GOMA. QAGOMA's Children's Art Centre presents engaging exhibitions and events for all ages. Also of interest is the Watermall's indoor water feature.

★ **Under the Jacaranda**
R. Godfrey Rivers' work is part of a collection of Australian art.

Stanley Place entrance

The Sculpture Courtyard and surrounding fountains are a pleasant place to relax or enjoy a picnic.

The Watermall's indoor water feature is surrounded by various pieces of art from the gallery's collection.

🏛 Gallery of Modern Art (GOMA)

Australia's largest gallery of modern and contemporary art focuses on 20th- and 21st-century works from Australia, Asia and the Pacific. The cinemas here feature films by influential and popular directors and artists.

🏛 Queensland Museum & Sciencentre

Tel (07) 3840 7555. **Open** 9:30am–5pm daily. **Closed** Good Fri, 25 Apr (open 1:30pm), 25 & 26 Dec. 🎨 (Science Centre only). 🔲 ✎ 🏠

This natural history museum is filled with full-scale models, both prehistoric and current. A large-scale model of Queensland's unique dinosaur, the *Mutta-burrasaurus*, stands in the foyer. The Sciencentre offers hands-on, interactive exhibitions.

🏛 State Library of Queensland

Tel (07) 3840 7666. **Open** 10am–8pm Mon–Thu, 10am–5pm Fri–Sun daily. **Closed** 1 Jan, Good Fri, 25 Apr (am), 25 & 26 Dec. 🔲 🔲 🏠

The State Library houses collections from around the world. Its extensive resources cover all interests and most of its services are free. There are innovative exhibitions, an Indigenous Knowledge Centre and The Edge, a digital culture space.

Exterior of the Queensland Performing Arts Centre

🏛 Queensland Performing Arts Centre (QPAC)

Tel (07) 3840 7444. **Open** performances only. 🔲 advise when booking.

The Queensland Performing Arts Centre comprises a main concert hall and three theatres where internationally acclaimed opera, classical music and theatrical productions are staged.

River view from Brisbane's Story Bridge

⑯ Story Bridge

Level 1, 170 Main St, Kangaroo Point.
Tel 1300 254 627. **Open** daily.
W sbac.net.au

Brisbane's iconic Story Bridge was constructed during the Great Depression, taking five years to build and opening in July 1940. With a bridge already across the Brisbane River, this new bridge was more a means of creating jobs and boosting the city's morale.

The Story Bridge Adventure Climb is a spectacular way to discover Brisbane. Climbs take place several times a day as well as at night. Throughout the two-and-a-half hour experience, the climb leader reveals the history of the bridge and talks about the city's transition from a 19th-century penal settlement to a 21st-century metropolis. At the summit, climbers enjoy views of Brisbane, its river and the surrounding mountains.

⑰ Newstead House

Newstead Park, Breakfast Creek Rd, Newstead. **Tel** (07) 3216 1846.
Bowen Hills. 300, 306, 322.
Newstead Point. **Open** 9am–4pm daily (to 1pm Sat). **Closed** Good Fri, 25 Apr, 25–26 Dec. by arrangement. **W** newsteadhouse.com.au

Built in 1846 for Patrick Leslie, one of the first European settlers in the Darling Downs region, Newstead House is the oldest surviving home in Brisbane. This charming building was sold

in 1847 to government resident and magistrate, Captain John Wickham.

The centre of the new colony's social life, Newstead House was the scene of lavish parties. A huge fig tree, under which elegant carriages once waited, still graces the drive. In 1939, it became the first Australian house to be preserved by its very own act of parliament. Restored by the Newstead House Trust from 1976, the house is furnished with Victorian antiques.

Decorated Victorian music box in Newstead House

⑱ Lone Pine Koala Sanctuary

Jesmond Rd, Fig Tree Pocket. **Tel** (07) 3378 1366. 430, 445. North Quay. **Open** 9am–5pm daily. **Closed** until 1:30pm 25 April.
W koala.net

The oldest koala sanctuary in Australia (opened in 1927), Lone Pine is also the world's largest, home to more than 130 koalas, as well as kangaroos, emus, possums, dingoes, wombats,

reptiles and many Australian birds. Visitors can hand feed kangaroos and, for a small fee, have their photograph taken holding a koala.

A pleasant and scenic way to get to Lone Pine Sanctuary is on a 45-minute river cruise (including commentary) with Mirimar Cruises (mirimar.com). Tickets include return trip and Lone Pine entry (with three hours at the park before heading back). Depart from Cultural Centre pontoon.

⑲ Brisbane Botanic Gardens

Mt Coot-tha Rd, Toowong. **Tel** (07) 3403 2535. 471. **Open** 8am–4pm daily.
W brisbane.qld.gov.au

Brisbane Botanic Gardens, in the foothills of Mount Coot-tha Forest Park 8 km (5 miles) from the city centre, were founded in 1976 and feature more than 20,000 specimens, from 5,000 species, of exotic herbs, shrubs and trees laid out in themed beds. Highlights include eucalypt groves, a Japanese Garden, a Tropical Display Dome, which includes lotus lilies and vanilla orchids, a Lagoon and Bamboo Grove, Fern House, National Freedom Wall (celebrating 50 years of peace) and a large collection of Australian native plants. Many arid and tropical plants, usually seen in green-houses, thrive in the outdoor setting. There is also a Bonsai House, and exotic and Australian rainforest sections. Free guided walks are held at 11am and 1pm

Koala at Lone Pine Koala Sanctuary

Lush landscape of the Brisbane Botanic Gardens

Mon–Sat, excluding public holidays and late Dec–late Jan.

Mount Coot-tha Forest Park offers both spectacular views and attractive picnic areas. The Aboriginal name means "place of wild honey", a reference to the tiny bees found in the area. On a clear day, from the summit lookout you can admire a spectacular panorama that encompasses the skyscrapers of central Brisbane, encircled by the winding river, Moreton and Stradbroke islands, the Glasshouse Mountains and the Lamington Plateau backing onto the Gold Coast (see pp242–3). The park also offers easygoing walking trails through the woodland, including Aboriginal trails which detail traditional uses of native plants.

⑳ South D'Aguilar National Park

🚌 385. 🛈 The Gap (07) 3614 3600 or 13 74 68. Visitor Centre: **Open** 9am– 4:30pm daily. **Closed** 1–2 Jan, Good Fri, 25 April am, 25–26 & 31 Dec. 🅿
🌐 **nprsr.qld.gov.au/parks/daguilar**

South D'Aguilar National Park, within the D'Aguilar Mountain Range, stretches for more than 50 km (30 miles) northwest of Brisbane city centre. Covering more than 28,500 ha (70,250 acres) of natural bushland and eucalypt forests, the park offers driving routes with breathtaking views over the surrounding countryside. The most scenic driving route is along Mount Nebo Road, which winds its way through the lush mountains. Another scenic drive extends from Samford up to the charming mountain village of Mount Glorious and down the other side. It is worth stopping from time to time to hear the distinctive calls of bellbirds and whipbirds.

Six km (4 miles) past Mount Glorious is the Wivenhoe Outlook, with spectacular views down to Lake Wivenhoe, an artificial lake created to prevent the Brisbane River from flooding the city. One km (half a mile) north of Mount Glorious is the entrance to Maiala Recreation Area, where there are picnic areas, some wheelchair accessible, and several walking trails of varying lengths, from short walks to longer, 8-km (5-mile) treks. These pass through the rainforest, which abounds with animal life. Other excellent walks are at Manorina and at Jolly's Lookout, the oldest formal lookout in the park, which has a good picnic area. Also in the park is the Westridge Outlook, a boardwalk with sweeping views.

The engrossing **South East Queensland Wildlife Centre at Walkabout Creek** park's headquarters is a re-created large freshwater environment. Water dragons, pythons, water rats, catfish and tiny rainbow fish flourish within these natural surroundings. Visitors also have the chance to see the extraordinary lungfish, a unique species which is equipped with both gills and lungs. The on-site restaurant looks out over the beautiful bush landscape.

About 4 km (2 miles) from the park headquarters is Bellbird Grove, which includes an outdoor Aboriginal collection of bark huts. It has a picnic area and also grassed picnic areas at Ironbark Gully and Lomandra.

🏛 **South East Queensland Wildlife Centre at Walkabout Creek** 60 Mt Nebo Rd, The Gap. **Tel** (07) 3300 2558. **Open** 9am–4:30pm daily. **Closed** Good Fri, 25 Dec & 25 Apr (until 1:30pm). 🅿 ♿ limited.
🌐 **nprsr.qld.gov.au/parks/daguilar/walkabout-creek.html**

Spectacular waterfall in South D'Aguilar National Park

BRISBANE PRACTICAL INFORMATION

Brisbane, built around a serpentine river, takes full advantage of its idyllic subtropical weather. Trendy riverside cafés, heritage trails, miles of boardwalk and a floating walkway, ferries and fast catamaran-style CityCats make Brisbane a relaxed holiday destination. The city offers centrally located five-star hotels, budget inns and historic guesthouses (see pp486). There are dining choices in all price ranges, such as silver service at luxury hotels, riverfront cafés, ethnic cuisine and alfresco restaurants, most offering menus based on superb local produce and fresh seafood (see pp512–14). Public transport is reasonably priced and easily accessed. Taxi stands are well signposted, and tourist information centres, identified by the international "I" symbol, are situated throughout the city.

Shopping

Brisbane is a shopping heaven, with its hidden arcades, small boutiques, quaint tea shops, pedestrian malls and multi-storied shopping centres. Finding what you are looking for is not difficult as the city is divided into small precincts, each offering a unique shopping experience. The pedestrianized **Queen Street Mall** has more than 1,000 speciality stores and six shopping centres, including **QueensPlaza**. **Brisbane Arcade**, one of the city's most elegant shopping areas, runs off the Mall. With classic marbled interior and polished wood balustrades, it was opened in 1923 and offers quality jewellers and stylish fashion. The **Fireworks Gallery** exhibits aboriginal art and local

The South Bank, dominated by the Wheel of Brisbane

Restored interior of the 19th-century Brisbane Arcade

artists, and is nestled in the art and design hub of Doggett Street, in Newstead. The **James Street Precinct** in Fortitude Valley has developed around an urban inner-city lifestyle. It is a great place for coffee, small delicatessens, trendy fashion shops, designer boutiques and galleries. Brisbane's weather encourages outdoor markets. The **Riverside at the Gardens Markets** with over 250 stalls are open every Sunday afternoon, displaying a huge variety of local arts, crafts, clothes and jewellery. The **Collective Markets at South Bank** feature unique and eclectic artisan goods and are held every Friday night and on weekends. Its parklands, man-made beach, cafés and restaurants make the South Bank a great place for a shopping experience.

Entertainment

The **Queensland Performing Arts Centre** has an exciting calendar of events, including opera, classical and contemporary dance, and live stage shows. The **La Boite Theatre** in Kelvin Grove is a 200-seat theatre in the round, and home to one of the oldest production companies in Australia. Brisbane hosts a myriad of music festivals, including the Brisbane River Festival. For live music there are nightclubs in the Fortitude Valley and Caxton Street areas. **Treasury Casino** is open 24 hours. Entertainment listings can be found online at www. visitbrisbane.com.au and at themusic.com.au and scenestr. com.au, which offer great gig guides. Tickets for most events can be obtained from **Ticketek**.

CityCat ferry service on the Brisbane River

Getting Around

Brisbane is a compact city which can be explored on foot. Maps are available from most hotels and information centres. There are excellent self-guided heritage trails and riverside pathways on both sides of the river.

Public transport in Brisbane is operated by **TransLink** and includes buses, commuter trains and ferries. The river has become one of the main ways of moving about the city. **CityCat** ferries service popular locations including South Bank, Eagle Street, Riverside, Dockside, New Farm and Kangaroo Point. Free CityHopper ferry services operate in inner-city precincts.

The most economical way to travel is with a prepaid electronic Go card, which provides unlimited travel on TransLink public buses, trains and ferries. It can be used in Brisbane, the Gold Coast, Ipswich and Sunshine Coast. Three- and five-day SEEQ cards are useful if travelling extensively between Brisbane and the Gold Coast and their airports. Single-journey paper tickets are also available. Buses with routes beginning with a P are prepaid services and require a Go card or pre-purchased single ticket before boarding. Another flexible way to see the city is on a **Big Bus Brisbane Explorer Tour**. Buy a one- or two-day ticket and you can get on and off at any of the Explorer bus stops along two routes, which take in major sights and landmarks.

Brisbane's Free Loop bus service travels around the city centre, with a bus every ten minutes. A second Free Loop bus services Spring Hill. The Cityxpress buses service the suburbs with limited stops. All buses stop at the Queen Street Bus Station. Blue and Maroon CityGlider buses (routes 60 and 61) are frequent, prepaid services that take in the main city and tourist areas.

Commercially operated bus companies also offer tours of the city's highlights, as well as to the city and surrounding areas, including Stradbroke Island, Moreton Bay and Surfers Paradise *(see pp242–3)* and the mountainous hinterland *(see pp244–5)*.

All types of public transport run until midnight, some later, and taxis are plentiful in the city centre at night. Driving is increasingly difficult but there are many well-maintained bike tracks.

A Translink public bus – a popular form of transport in Brisbane

DIRECTORY

Shopping

Brisbane Arcade
160 Queen St Mall.
W brisbanearcade.com.au

The Collective Markets at South Bank
Stanley St, South Bank.
W collectivemarkets.com.au

Fireworks Gallery
52a Doggett St, Newstead.
W fireworksgallery.com.au

James Street Precinct
James Street, Fortitude Valley.
Tel (07) 3850 0111.
W jamesst.com.au

Queen Street Mall
Queen Street.
Tel (07) 3006 6290.

QueensPlaza
Queen Street.
Tel (07) 3234 3900.

Riverside at the Gardens Markets
City Botanic Gdns, 157 Alice St.
Tel (07) 3870 2807.

Entertainment

Treasury Casino & Hotel
159 William St. **Tel** (07) 3306 8888.
W treasurybrisbane.com.au

La Boite Theatre
6–8 Musk Ave, Kelvin Grove.
W laboite.com.au

Queensland Performing Arts Centre
Cnr Grey & Melbourne sts,
South Bank. W qpac.com.au

Ticketek
Tel 13 28 49. W ticketek.com.au

Public Transport

Administration Centre
George Street. **Tel** phone
TransLink (see below).

Big Bus Brisbane Explorer Bus Tour
W theaustralianexplorer.
com.au

TransLink
(for public transport information)
Tel 13 12 30 or (07) 3851 8700.
W translink.com.au

Tourist Information Centres

Brisbane Visitor Information
W visitbrisbane.com.au

SOUTH OF TOWNSVILLE

Southern Queensland is renowned for two distinct features: its fine coastal surfing beaches and, inland, some of the richest farming land in Australia. The area is the centre of the country's beef and sugar industries, and the Burdekin River Delta supports a fertile "salad basin" yielding tomatoes, beans and other small crops. Ports such as Mackay and Gladstone service some rich inland mines.

Recognizing the land's potential, pastoralists followed hard on the heels of the explorers who opened up this region in the 1840s. Sugar production had begun by 1869 in the Bundaberg area and by the 1880s it was a flourishing industry, leading to a shameful period in the country's history. As Europeans were considered inherently unsuited to work in the tropics, growers seized on South Sea Islanders for cheap labour. Called Kanakas, the labourers were paid a pittance, housed in substandard accommodation and given the most physically demanding jobs. Some Kanakas were kidnapped from their homeland (a practice called "blackbirding"), but this was outlawed in 1868 and government inspectors were placed on all Kanakas ships to check that their emigration was voluntary. It was not until Federation in 1901 that the use of island labour stopped but by then some 60,000 Kanakas had been brought to Queensland.

In tandem with this agricultural boom, southern Queensland thrived in the latter half of the 19th century when gold was found in the region. Towns such as Charters Towers have preserved much of their 19th-century architecture as reminders of the glory days of the gold rush. Although much of the gold has been extracted, the region is still rich in coal and has the world's largest sapphire fields. Amid this mineral landscape, there are also some beautiful national parks.

Today, the area is perhaps best known for its coastal features. Surfers from all over the world flock to the aptly named resort of Surfers Paradise, and the white sand beaches of the Gold Coast are crowded throughout the summer months. The region is also the gateway to the southern tip of the Great Barrier Reef and the Whitsunday Islands, and is popular with both locals and visitors.

Surfers trying to catch the best wave in Surfers Paradise

◄ Lake Wabby, the deepest lake on the largest sand island in the world

Exploring South of Townsville

With easy access from Brisbane *(see pp222–37)*, the southern coastline of Queensland is one of the most popular holiday locations in Australia, with its sunny climate, sandy beaches and good surf. Fraser Island is one of the region's undisputed highlights with its vast beaches, cool blue lakes and interior rainforests. Behind the fertile coastal plains are many of the 1850s gold rush "boom towns", while the Capricorn Hinterland, inland from Rockhampton, has the fascinating sapphire gem fields near Emerald and the dramatic sandstone escarpments of the Carnarvon and Blackdown Tableland national parks. To the north of the region is the busy city of Townsville, a major gateway to the Whitsundays and the islands of the Great Barrier Reef *(see pp216–21).*

Irrigating sugar cane fields in Mackay, near Eungella National Park

Sights at a Glance

1 Lamington National Park
2 Darling Downs
3 Sunshine Coast Hinterland
4 Maryborough
5 Hervey Bay
6 *Fraser Island p246*
7 Mon Repos Conservation Park
8 Gladstone
9 Rockhampton
10 Blackdown Tableland
    National Park
11 *Carnarvon National Park p249*
12 Eungella National Park
13 Whitsunday Islands
14 Ayr
15 Charters Towers
16 Townsville and Magnetic Island

Key

━━ Highway
━━ Major road
┅┅ Minor road
– – Track
━━ Scenic route
•━•━ Main railway
──── Minor railway
━━ State border
△ Summit

0 kilometres 100
0 miles 100

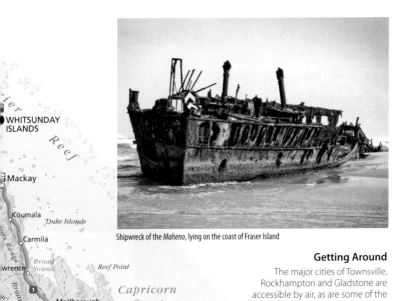
Shipwreck of the *Maheno*, lying on the coast of Fraser Island

Getting Around

The major cities of Townsville, Rockhampton and Gladstone are accessible by air, as are some of the smaller regional centres. There are frequent coach services along the Bruce Hwy and the main inland roads. The Brisbane-Cairns railway runs alongside the Bruce Hwy with stops at all the major centres (the trip from Brisbane to Townsville takes about 25 hours). However, the best way to see the area is by car. Some companies may insist on 4WD in remote areas.

Southern Queensland Coastline

An hour's drive either north or south of Brisbane, the southern Queensland coast is Australia's most popular beach playground. The famous Gold Coast extends 75 km (45 miles) south of Brisbane and is a flashy strip of holiday apartments, luxury hotels, shopping malls, nightclubs, a casino and, above all, 42 km (25 miles) of golden sandy beaches. To the north, the Sunshine Coast is more restrained and elegant. Inland, the Great Dividing Range provides a cool alternative to the hot coastal climate, with flourishing arts and crafts communities, superb bushwalking and wonderful panoramas.

Burleigh Heads National Park is a tiny park that preserves the dense eucalypt forests that once covered the entire region. The nutritious volcanic soil stemming from Mount Warning, 30 km (20 miles) southwest of the park, allows the rainforest to thrive.

The Gold Coast has three theme parks. Sea World has dolphin, sea lion and penguin displays; Warner Bros. Movie World features stunts and tours of replica film sets; Dreamworld fairground park has wildlife such as Bengal tigers. There are also two water parks: Wet 'n' Wild® and Whitewater World.

Australia Zoo began as a small, 1.6-ha (4-acre) park known as Beerwah Reptile Park. Its founder, the late Steve "the Croc Hunter" Irwin, became a household name. Today the zoo is a 28-ha (70-acre) wildlife haven with more than 1,000 animals.

② Tewantin 🔼
This well-known town is in the heart of the Sunshine Coast area, with spectacular sunsets and beautiful beaches. It is also the ferry access point to Cooloola National Park.

Maryboro

⑤ Maroochydore Beach 🚶🏖️🏄🎣♿🚻
An ocean beach and the Maroochy riverfront make the main commercial centre of the Sunshine Coast a popular holiday destination, with good hotels and restaurants.

⑥ Mooloolaba Wharf 🚶🏖️🏄🎣♿
The wharf at Mooloolaba is a popular tourist development. Underwater World, said to be the largest oceanarium in the southern hemisphere, contains crocodiles and barramundi.

⑦ Bulcock Beach, Caloundra 🏖️🏄🎣♿🚻
The central location of sandy Bulcock Beach means it is often crowded with tourists and families. Nearby Golden Beach and Shelly Beach are also beautiful, but quieter.

⑧ Moreton Bay 🏖️🏄🎣♿🚻
This is the access point to some 370 offshore islands, the most popular being Moreton, Bribie and South Stradbroke. Fishing, bird-watching and boating are the main activities.

⑫ Coolangatta 🚶🏖️🏄🎣♿🚻
On the Queensland–New South Wales border, Coolangatta has some of the best surfing waters in the area, but relatively uncrowded beaches. Surfing tuition and boards for hire are available here.

① ★ Cooloola National Park

Attractive lakes and sclerophyll woodland abound in this area. A 60-km (35-mile) 4WD to Rainbow Beach passes the Teewah Coloured Sands, produced by natural chemicals.

Locator Map

QUEENSLAND

③ ★ Noosa Heads, Main Beach

Extraordinary natural beauty, a north-facing beach and an extensive river system have combined to make Noosa a fashionable holiday resort.

④ ★ Noosa National Park

Consisting of 380 ha (940 acres) of headland surrounded by coastline containing secluded coves, this national park is inhabited with koalas.

⑨ ★ Sanctuary Cove

Situated on Hope Island, the glamorous resort of Sanctuary Cove is aimed particularly at golfers and includes two luxury golf courses.

⑩ ★ South Stradbroke Island Beach

This unspoiled sand island offers peaceful but relatively basic accommodation. Catching crabs and bird-watching are popular activities.

0 km   20

0 miles   20

⑪ ★ Surfers Paradise Beach

This is the focal point of the Gold Coast with block after block of high-rise developments and a range of entertainment options for visitors.

Key

- Highway
- Major road
- Minor road
- River
- Viewpoint

ympie

Caloundra

Australia Zoo

Caboolture

Redcliffe

BRISBANE

Moreton Island

North Stradbroke Island

Coomera

Burleigh Heads National Park

Byron Bay ↓

● Lamington National Park

🚌 Canungra. 🛈 Park Ranger Office (07) 5544 0634 or 13 74 68. **Open** daily. 🌐 **npsr.qld.gov.au/parks/lamington**

Lamington National Park, set within the McPherson Mountain Range, is one of Queensland's most popular parks. Declared in 1915, it contains 200 sq km (78 sq miles) of thick wooded country, with more than 160 km (100 miles) of walking tracks through subtropical rainforests of hoop pine, black booyongs and strangler figs. The highest ridges in the park reach more than 1,000 m (3,280 ft) and are lined with Antarctic beech trees – the most northerly in Australia. Some 150 species of birds, such as the Albert's lyrebird, make bird-watching a popular pastime. The global importance of the area was recognized in 1994, when Lamington was declared a World Heritage Area.

Nearby Macrozamia National Park has macrozamia palms (cycads) – one of the oldest forms of vegetation still growing in the world.

Stunning king parrot

❷ Darling Downs

🚌 Toowoomba. 🛈 Toowoomba (07) 4639 3797 or 1800 331 155.

Only 90 minutes' drive from Brisbane, stretching west of the Great Dividing Range, is the fertile country of the Darling Downs. The first area to be settled after Brisbane, the region encompasses some of the most productive agricultural land in Australia, as well as one of the most historic areas in Queensland.

Toowoomba is the main centre of the Downs and is also one of Queensland's biggest cities. Early settlers transformed this one-time swamp into the present "Garden City", famous for its jacarandas and Carnival of Flowers *(see p44).*

About 45 km (28 miles) north-west of Toowoomba along the Warrego Hwy is **The Woolshed at Jondaryan**. Built in 1859 to handle 200,000 sheep in one season, it has now been restored as a working memorial to the early pioneers of the district.

South of Toowoomba is Warwick, the oldest town in Queensland after Brisbane and known for its roses and its 19th-century sandstone buildings. It also claims one of the oldest rodeos in Australia, dating from 1857 when £50 (a year's pay) was wagered on the outcome of the riding contest. Today the rodeo follows the Rose and Rodeo Festival in October *(see p45).*

About 60 km (40 miles) south of Warwick and 915 m (3,000 ft) above sea level, Stanthorpe celebrates its freezing winters with Brass Monkey Season *(see p47)* and holds its Apple & Grape Harvest Festival in even-numbered years. The town is at the heart of the Granite Belt, one of Queensland's few wine regions *(see p41).*

Near Warwick, Queen Mary Falls National Park is a 78-ha (193-acre) rainforest park with picnic areas and a 40-m (130-ft) waterfall.

🏛 **The Woolshed at Jondaryan**
Evanslea Rd, Jondaryan. **Tel** (07) 4692 2229. **Open** 8:30am–4:30pm daily. **Closed** 24–26 Dec. 🅿 ♿ 🌐 **jondaryanwoolshed.com**

❸ Sunshine Coast Hinterland

🚌 Glasshouse Country Coaches (07) 5496 9249. 🛈 Cnr 6th Ave & Melrose Pde, Maroochydore (07) 5458 8842. 🌐 **glasshousecoaches.com.au**

To the west of the Sunshine Coast is the Blackall Range. The area has become a centre for artists and artisans, with numerous guesthouses and some fine

Waterfall in Queen Mary Falls National Park, Darling Downs

The Glasshouse Mountains, a Queensland landmark on the hinterland of the Sunshine Coast

restaurants. The most attractive centres are Montville and Maleny. The drive from Maleny to Mapleton is one of the most scenic in the region, with views across to Moreton Island, encompassing pineapple and sugar cane fields.

Consisting of ten volcanic cones, the Glasshouse Mountains were formed 20 million years ago. The craggy volcanic peaks were named by Captain Cook in 1770 because they reminded him of the glass furnaces in his native Yorkshire.

❹ Maryborough

🏙 21,300. ✈ 🚊 🚌
ℹ City Hall, Kent St, 1800 214 789.
🌐 visitmaryborough.info

Situated on the banks of the Mary River, Maryborough has a strong link with Australia's early history. Founded in 1843, the town provided housing for Kanakas' labour *(see p239)* and was the only port apart from Sydney where free settlers could enter. This resulted in a thriving town – the buildings reflecting the wealth of its citizens.

Many of these buildings survive, earning Maryborough the title of "Heritage City". A great many of the town's private residences also date from the 19th century, ranging from simple workers' cottages to beautiful old "Queenslanders". These houses are distinctive like cottages, set high off the ground to catch the cool air currents and with graceful verandas on all sides.

❺ Hervey Bay

🏙 41,000. ✈ 🚌 🚢 ℹ 227 Maryborough-Hervey Bay Rd, Torquay, Hervey Bay (07) 4197 4730 or 1800 811 728. 🌐 visitherveybay.info

As recently as the 1970s Hervey Bay was just a string of five fishing villages. However, the safe beaches and mild climate have quickly turned it into a metropolis of over 40,000 people and one of the fastest-growing holiday centres in Australia.

Hervey Bay is also the best place for whale-watching. Humpback whales migrate more than 11,000 km (7,000 miles) every year from the Antarctic to northern Australian waters to mate and calve. On their return, between August and October, they rest at Hervey Bay to give the calves time to develop a protective layer of blubber before they

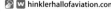
Bundaberg rum

begin their final run to Antarctica. Since whaling was stopped in the 1960s, numbers have quadrupled from 300 to approximately 5,000.

Environs
The sugar city of central Queensland, Bundaberg is 62 km (38 miles) north of Hervey Bay. It is the home of Bundaberg ("Bundy") rum, the biggest-selling spirit label in Australia. Bundaberg is an attractive town with many 19th-century buildings. The city's favourite son, Bert Hinkler (1892–1933), was the first man to fly solo from England to Australia in 1928. His original "Ibis" aircraft is displayed in the **Hinkler Hall of Aviation.**

🏛 Hinkler Hall of Aviation
Young St, Botanic Gardens. **Tel** (07) 4130 4400. **Open** 9am–4pm daily. **Closed** Good Fri, 25 Apr, 25 Dec. ♿ 📷 🌐 hinklerhallofaviation.com

Classic Queenslander-style house in Maryborough

❻ Fraser Island

Situated off the Queensland coast near Maryborough *(see p245)*, Fraser Island World Heritage area is the largest sand island in the world. Measuring 123 km (76 miles) in length and 25 km (16 miles) across, the island is a mix of hills and valleys, rainforest and clear lakes. Ferries to the island operate from Urangan, River Heads and Inskip Point. There is a range of resorts and numerous camp sites on the island. Vehicle (4WD only) and camping permits are required.

VISITORS' CHECKLIST

Practical Information
🛈 Hervey Bay Visitor Information Centre 1800 811 728.
♿ 🏕 🚾 ✏ 🚻

Transport
🚢 from Urangan, River Heads & Inskip Point.

Sandy Cape has treacherous waters; its lighthouse has saved many ships from potential danger.

Indian Head was named by Captain James Cook *(see pp54–5)* as a result of a number of Aborigines he saw assembled here on arrival.

HERVEY BAY

Watumba

Lake Allom, fringed by melaleuca trees and sedges, is surrounded by a towering rainforest. Freshwater turtles can be seen in the lake.

Lake McKenzie
The beautiful clear waters here are surrounded by white sands and blackbutt trees.

The Cathedrals
These striking, deep red sand formations stretch 18 km (11 miles) along the beach.

PACIFIC OCEAN

Seventy-Five Mile Beach is notable as the site of the *Maheno*, the only visible shipwreck on the island.

Kingfisher Bay

Central Station was once the hub of the island's logging industry and is a starting point for beautiful walks.

Lake Birabeen

Eurong

Lake Boomanjin

Eli Creek is large and spectacular, pouring gallons of water each hour into the surf.

0 km   5
0 miles   5

Key
▬ 4WD road
▬ Walking trail

James and Elizabeth Fraser

In 1836, survivors from the shipwreck *Stirling Castle*, including Captain James Fraser and his wife Elizabeth, known as Eliza, landed on Fraser Island and were captured by Aboriginals. Captain Fraser perished, but Eliza was rescued and returned to England, where she told her story widely. The story inspired Patrick White's novel *A Fringe of Leaves (see p39)*.

Survivor Elizabeth Fraser

Hook Point

Loggerhead turtle laying eggs on Mon Repos Beach

❼ Mon Repos Conservation Park

Tel (07) 4159 1652, tour bookings (07) 4153 8888. **Open** daily. 🐢 Turtle tours. ♿ 📷 obligatory Nov–Mar.
Ⓦ **npsr.qld.gov.au/parks/ mon-repos**

Mon Repos Beach, 15 km (9 miles) from Bundaberg (see p245), is one of the most significant and accessible turtle rookeries on the Australian mainland. Egg-laying of loggerhead and other turtles takes place from November to February. By January, the first young turtles begin to hatch and make their way down the sandy beach to the ocean.

An information centre within the environmental park has videos and other information about these fascinating reptiles. Supervised public viewing ensures that the turtles are not unduly disturbed.

Just behind Mon Repos Beach is an old stone wall built by Kanakas and now preserved as a memorial to these South Sea Island inhabitants (see p239).

❽ Gladstone

🏙 29,000. ✈ 🚉 🚌 🚍
ℹ Gladstone Marina, Bryan Jordan Drive (07) 4972 9000.
Ⓦ **gladstoneregion.info**

Gladstone is a town dominated by industry. However, industry is in harmony with tourism and the environment. Tours of the area are popular with visitors. The world's largest alumina refinery is located here, processing bauxite mined in Weipa on the west coast of Cape York Peninsula. Five per cent of the nation's wealth and 20 per cent of Queensland's wealth is generated by Gladstone's industries. Gladstone's port, handling more than 35 million tonnes of cargo a year, is one of the busiest in Australia.

There are, however, more attractive sights in and around the town. The town's main street has an eclectic variety of buildings, including the Grand Hotel, rebuilt to its 1897 form after fire destroyed the original in 1993. Gladstone's Botanic Gardens were first opened in 1988 as a bicentennial project and consist entirely of native Australian plants. South of Gladstone are the tiny coastal villages of Agnes Waters and the quaintly named "1770" in honour of Captain Cook's brief landing here during his journey up the coast (see p54). About 20 km (12 miles) out of town lies the popular holiday location of Boyne Island.

Gladstone is also the access point for Heron Island, considered by many to be one of the most desirable of all the Great Barrier Reef islands, with its wonderful coral and diving opportunities. Other islands in the southern half of the reef can also be accessed from Gladstone by boat or helicopter (see pp220–21).

Pretty coastal village of Agnes Waters, near Gladstone

❾ Rockhampton

🚹 61,000. 🚌 🚑 🚆 🚢 ℹ️ Capricorn Info. Centre, Gladstone Rd (07) 4927 2055 or 1800 676 701.

Rockhampton is situated 40 km (25 miles) inland, on the banks of the Fitzroy River. Often referred to as the "beef capital" of Australia, the town is also the administrative and commercial heart of central Queensland. A spire marks the fact that, geographically, the Tropic of Capricorn runs through the town.

Rockhampton was founded in 1854 and contains many restored 19th-century buildings. Quay Street flanks the tree-lined river and has been classified in its entirety by the National Trust. Particularly outstanding is the sandstone Customs House. The beautiful **Botanic Gardens** were established in 1869, and have a fine collection of tropical plants. There is also on-site accommodation.

Built on an ancient tribal meeting ground, the **Aboriginal Dreamtime Cultural Centre** is owned and operated by local Aboriginals. Imaginative displays give an insight into their life and culture.

🌿 **Botanic Gardens**
Spencer St. **Tel** (07) 4932 9000. **Open** 6am–6pm daily. ♿

🏛️ **Aboriginal Dreamtime Cultural Centre**
Bruce Hwy. **Tel** (07) 4936 1655. **Open** 9am–3:30pm Mon–Fri. **Closed** public hols. 📷 🎫 ⓦ dreamtimecentre.com.au

Plaque at base of the Tropic of Capricorn spire

Environs

The heritage township of Mount Morgan is 38 km (25 miles) southwest of Rockhampton. A 2 sq km (0.5 sq mile) open-cut mine of first gold, then copper, operated here for 100 years and was an important part of the state's economy until the minerals ran out in 1981.

Some 25 km (15 miles) north of Rockhampton is Mount Etna National Park, containing spectacular limestone caves, discovered in the 1880s. These are open to the public via Olsen's Capricorn Caverns and Camoo Caves. A major feature of the caves is "cave coral" – stone-encrusted tree roots that have forced their way through the rock. The endangered ghost bat, Australia's only carnivorous bat, nests in these caves.

The stunning sandy beaches of Yeppoon and Emu Park are only 40 km (25 miles) northeast of the city. Rockhampton is also the access point for Great Keppel Island *(see pp220–21)*.

Sandstone cliff looking out over Blackdown Tableland National Park

❿ Blackdown Tableland National Park

Off Capricorn Hwy, via Dingo. Park Ranger **Tel** (07) 4986 1964. ♿ ⓦ npsr.qld.gov.au/parks/blackdown-tableland

Between Rockhampton and Emerald, along a 20-km (12-mile) untarmacked detour off the Capricorn Highway, is Blackdown Tableland National Park. A dramatic sandstone plateau that rises 600 m (2,000 ft) above the flat surrounding countryside, the Tableland offers spectacular views, escarpments, open forest and tumbling waterfalls. Wildlife includes gliders, brushtail possums, rock wallabies and the occasional dingo.

Emerald is a coal mining centre and the hub of the central highland region, 75 km (45 miles) west of the park; the town provides a railhead for the surrounding agricultural areas. Its ornate 1900 railway station is one of the few survivors of a series of fires that occurred between 1936 and 1969, which destroyed much of the town's heritage. About 60 km (37 miles) southwest of Emerald is Cullin-la-ringo, where there are headstones marking the mass grave of 19 European settlers killed in 1861 by local Aboriginals. At Comet is a tree carved with the initials of explorer Ludwig Leichhardt during his 1844 expedition to Port Essington *(see p253)*.

More in tune with its name, Emerald is also the access point for the largest sapphire fields in the world. The lifestyle of the gem diggers is fascinating, making it a popular tourist area.

Façade of Customs House on Quay Street, Rockhampton

For hotels and restaurants in this area see pp486–8 and pp514–15

⑪ Carnarvon National Park

The main access to Carnarvon National Park lies 250 km (155 miles) south of Emerald, while the park itself covers some 298,000 ha (730,000 acres). There are several sections of the park, but the stunning Carnarvon Gorge is the most accessible area to visitors. A 32-km (20-mile) canyon carved by the waters of Carnarvon Creek, the gorge consists of white cliffs, crags and pillars of stone harbouring plants and animals which have survived through centuries of evolution. The area is also rich in Aboriginal culture, and three cultural sites are open to the public. Comfortable cabin accommodation is available or there are various camp sites, provided you have an advance booking and a camping permit *(see p481).*

Wards Canyon is home to the King Fern, a remnant rainforest species.

The Amphitheatre's sheer walls were carved into the rock by water.

Carnarvon Gorge
The gorge is filled with lush eucalypt forests, sandstone cliffs and streams.

Boolimba Bluff has spectacular sunrise views of the park.

Kooraminya Creek

• **Big Bend**

Parrabooya

Kongaboola Creek

Kamoo Creek

Kamoodangie Creek

Wagoonoo Creek

CASUARINA GORGE

Carnarvon Creek

Koolaroo Creek

VIOLET GORGE

WARRUMBAH BLUFF

Warrumbah Creek

Mickey Creek

Cathedral Cave is a massive rock shelter, more than 30 m (100 ft) high. It is one of the major Aboriginal cultural sites in the park.

The Art Gallery
This important Aboriginal art site features stencil art of boomerangs, stone implements and shell pendants.

0 kilometres 1
0 miles 1

Moss Garden
This lush greenery of ferns, creepers, hornworts and liverworts is sustained by seepage from the spring waters down the rock walls.

For keys to symbols *see back flap*

Stunning estuary at Whitehaven Beach, the highlight of the Whitsundays

⑫ Eungella National Park

🚉 Mackay. 🚌 Mackay. 🛈 Mackay
(07) 4944 5888. 🇼 npsr.qld.gov.au/
parks/eungella

Eungella National Park is
the main wilderness area on the
central Queensland coast and
encompasses some 50,000 ha
(125,000 acres) of the rugged
Clarke Ranges. Volcanic rock
covered with rainforest and
subtropical flora is cut by steep
gorges, crystal clear pools and
impressive waterfalls tumbling
down the mountainside.

Finch Hatton Gorge is the main
destination for tourists, where
indigenous wildlife includes
gliders, ring-tailed possums,
bandicoots and pademelons (a
kind of wallaby). Broken River is
one of the few places in Australia
where platypuses can be spotted
at dusk and dawn.

The main access point for
Eungella is the prosperous sugar
town of **Mackay**. Somewhat
low-key from a tourist point of
view, Mackay boasts a balmy
climate by way of the
surrounding mountains
trapping the warm coastal air
even in winter. Thirty beautiful
white sand beaches are lined
with casuarinas. All around the
town sugar cane can be seen
blowing in the wind in the
many sugar cane fields.

The town centre of Mackay
has a number of historic
buildings worth visiting,
including the Commonwealth
Bank and Customs House, both
classified by the National Trust.

The second-largest coal-loader
in the world is at Hay Point,
where trains more than 2 km
(1 mile) long haul coal from
the western mines for
shipping overseas.

⑬ Whitsunday Islands

🚉 Proserpine. 🚌 Airlie Beach.
✈ Hamilton Island; Proserpine.
🛳 Port of Airlie, Airlie Beach.
🛈 (07) 4945 3967.
🇼 tourismwhitsundays.com.au

The Whitsunday Islands
are an archipelago of 74 islands,
situated within the Great Barrier
Reef Marine Park, approximately
1,140 km (700 miles) north of
Brisbane and 640 km (400 miles)
south of Cairns. These beautiful
islands and sandy atolls are
among the most stunning
holiday destinations in Australia.
Whitehaven Beach on Whitsunday
Island is recognized as one
of the world's best beaches,
with 9 km (6 miles) of pure
white silica sand and
turquoise sea.

Only a few of the islands
offer accommodation, including
Hamilton, Daydream, Hayman,
South Molle and Long, while
some 66 islands remain
uninhabited. A wide range
of accommodation is available
including luxury hotels,
hostels, guesthouses and
self-catering apartments.

There are many activities on
offer including scuba diving,
whale watching, seaplane
flights and charter sailing.

Many companies at Airlie Beach
on the mainland offer sailing
packages, which include diving
or snorkelling and a night or two
moored on the Great Barrier Reef.

⑭ Ayr

🚉 8,000. 🚌 🛈 Plantation Park,
Bruce Hwy (07) 4783 5988.

The busy town of Ayr, at the
heart of the Burdekin River
Delta, is the major sugar cane-
growing area in Australia.

Within the town itself is the
modern Burdekin Cultural
Complex, which includes a 530-
seat theatre, a library and an art
gallery. Among its art collection
are the renowned "Living Lagoon"
sculptures by the contemporary
Australian sculptor Stephen
Walker. The Ayr Nature Display
consists of an impressive rock
wall made from 2,600 pieces
of North Queensland rock,
intricate pictures made from
preserved insects and a display
of Australian reptiles, shells,
fossils and Aboriginal artifacts.
In Plantation Park is the Juru
walking trail and Gubulla
Munda, a giant snake sculpture
15 m (50 ft) long.

Environs

Approximately 55 km (35 miles)
north of Ayr is Alligator Creek,
which is the access point for
Bowling Green Bay National
Park. Here you will find geckos
and chirping cicadas living
alongside each other in this lush
landscape. Within the park are
rock pools, perfect for swimming,
and plunging waterfalls.

"Living Lagoon" sculpture at the Burdekin
Complex, Ayr

For hotels and restaurants in this area see pp486–8 and pp514–15

Ornate 19th-century façade of City Hall in Charters Towers

⓯ Charters Towers

🏠 8,000. 🚍 🚌 🚎 ℹ️ 74 Mosman St (07) 4761 5533.

Charters Towers was once the second-largest town in Queensland with a population of 27,000, following the 1871 discovery of gold in the area by a 10-year-old Aboriginal boy. Gold is still mined in the area, as well as copper, lead and zinc.

The old Charters Towers Stock Exchange is a historic gem set amid a group of splendid 19th-century buildings in the city centre, including a small mining museum. This international centre of finance was the only such exchange in Australia outside a capital city and was built during the gold-mining days. Charters Towers fell into decline when the gold ran out in the 1920s. Its economy now depends on the beef industry and its status as the educational centre for Queensland's Outback and Papua New Guinea – school students make up one-fifth of the population.

⓰ Townsville and Magnetic Island

🏠 129,000. ✈️ 🚍 🚌 🚎
ℹ️ Bulletin Square (07) 4721 3660.

Townsville is the second-largest city in Queensland and a major port for the beef, sugar and mining industries. Boasting, on average, 300 sunny days a year, the beachfront is a source of local pride. The city was founded in the 1860s by Robert Towns, who began the practice of "blackbirding" – kidnapping Kanakas from their homeland and bringing them to Australia as cheap labour (see p239).

Among the city's tourist attractions is **Reef HQ**, a "living coral reef aquarium" and the **Museum of Tropical Queensland**, which displays artifacts from the shipwreck *Pandora*. Townsville is also an access point for the Barrier Reef and a major diving centre, largely because of the nearby wreck of the steamship *Yongala*, which sank in 1911.

Situated 8 km (5 miles) offshore and officially a suburb of Townsville, Magnetic Island has 2,500 inhabitants and is the only reef island with a significant permanent population. It was named by Captain Cook, who erroneously believed that magnetic fields generated by the huge granite boulders he could see were causing problems with his compass. Today, almost half of the island is a national park.

🛥️ **Reef HQ**
Flinders St East. **Tel** (07) 4750 0800.
Open 9:30am–5pm daily. **Closed** 25 Dec. 🅿️ ♿ 🖥️ 🌐 reefhq.com.au

🏛️ **Musuem of Tropical Qld**
Flinders St East. **Tel** (07) 4726 0600.
Open 9:30am–5pm daily. **Closed** Good Fri, 25 Apr, 25 & 26 Dec. 🅿️
🌐 mtq.qm.qld.gov.au

Idyllic blue waters of Rocky Bay on Magnetic Island

NORTHERN AND OUTBACK QUEENSLAND

European explorers who made epic journeys into the previously impenetrable area of Northern and Outback Queensland in the 1800s found a land rich in minerals and agricultural potential. They also discovered places of extreme natural beauty, such as the Great Barrier Reef and other unique regions now preserved as national parks.

Northern Queensland was first visited by Europeans when Captain Cook was forced to berth his damaged ship, the *Endeavour*, on the coast. The area remained a mystery for almost another 100 years, however, until other intrepid Europeans ventured north. These expeditions were perilous and explorers were faced with harsh conditions and hostile Aboriginal tribes. In 1844, Ludwig Leichhardt and his group set out from Brisbane to Port Essington, but most of the men were wounded or killed by Aboriginals. In 1848, Edmund Kennedy led an expedition from Cairns to the top of Cape York. All but two of this party perished, including Kennedy, who was killed by Aboriginals.

In the late 19th century, Northern Queensland found sudden prosperity when gold was discovered in the region. The population rose and towns grew up to service the mines, but by the beginning of the 20th century much of the gold had dried up. These once thriving "cities" are now little more than one-street towns, lined with 19th-century architecture as a reminder of their glory days. Today, much of the area's wealth stems from its booming tourist trade. Luxury resorts line the stunning coastline, and tourists flock to experience the spectacular natural wonders of the Great Barrier Reef.

Queensland's Outback region has a strong link with Australia's national heritage. The Tree of Knowledge at Barcaldine marks the meeting place of the first Australian Labor Party during the great shearer's strike of 1891. The town of Winton is where "Banjo" Paterson *(see p39)* wrote Australia's national song "Waltzing Matilda" in 1895. Today, the vast Outback area is known for agriculture and a wide range of mining operations.

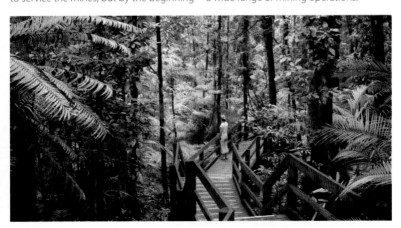

A treetop walkway through incredible rainforest surroundings in Daintree National Park, Northern Queensland

◀ A shoal of bigeye trevally swimming in a spiral pattern at the Great Barrier Reef

Exploring Northern Queensland

The area north of Townsville leading up to Cairns is Australia's sugar-producing country, the cane fields backed by the Great Dividing Range. Northern Queensland is sparsely populated: Cairns is the only city, while Port Douglas and Mossman are small towns. The only other villages of note in the region are Daintree and Cooktown. Cape York Peninsula is one of the last untouched wildernesses in the world, covering 200,000 sq km (77,220 sq miles) – roughly the same size as Great Britain. The landscape varies according to the time of year: in the green season (November–March) the rivers are swollen and the country is green; during the dry winter the riverbeds are waterless and the countryside is bare and arid.

Lush rainforest in Daintree National Park, near Cairns

Getting Around

Cairns is well served by public transport, with regular air, train and coach connections from southern Queensland and the other states. It also benefits from an international airport. The tropical terrain north of Cape Tribulation to Cooktown and the Outback requires approved 4WD hire cars unless you take an organized tour. Many car rental companies will insist on a 4WD all the way along the 326-km (202-mile) coast road from Cairns to Cooktown. During the wet season, Cape York is generally impassable.

View across the Marlin Marina in Cairns

Badu Is   Moa Is

TORRES STRAIT ISLANDS ②
Thursday Island
Prince of Wales   Cape York
Island
Bamaga
Injinoo Aboriginal
Community
Jardine
River
National
Park

C a p e

Mapoon
Aboriginal
Community

Wenlock

Duyfken
Point   Weipa

Y o r k

Boyd
Point
Aurukun
Aboriginal
Worbody   Community
Point
Archer

Archer Bend
National Park

P e n i n s u l a

Holroyd

Pormpuraaw
Aboriginal
Community

Kowanyama
Aboriginal   Mitchell and
Community   Alice Rivers
National Park

Mitchell

Gulf of
Carpentaria   Dunbar

Staate

Staaten R
Staaten Rn
National P

Red

Gilbert

Mount Isa

Carron

Croydon

Key

— Major road

⋯⋯ Minor road

- - Track

— Scenic route

▬▬ Main railway

— Minor railway

The lush greenery and idyllic beach of Dunk Island

Locator Map
■ Northern Queensland
□ Queensland's Outback
pp260–61

Sights at a Glance

❶ Rinyirru (Lakefield) National Park
❷ Torres Strait Islands
❸ Cooktown
❹ Daintree National Park
❺ Port Douglas
❻ Green Island
❼ *Cairns p258*
❽ Atherton Tablelands
❾ Wooroonooran National Park
❿ Babinda and the Boulders
⓫ Mission Beach
⓬ Hinchinbrook Island

Queensland's Outback

See pp260–61
⓭ Normanton & Gulf Savannah
⓮ Burketown
⓯ Mount Isa
⓰ Longreach

❶ Rinyirru (Lake-field) National Park

🚌 Cooktown. ℹ️ Cooktown (07) 4069 6004. Park Office (07) 4060 3271. Campsite bookings 13 74 68. **Open** Jun–Nov: Mon–Fri. 🌐 **npsr.qld.gov. au/parks/rinyirru-lakefield**

Covering approximately 540,000 ha (1,300,000 acres), Rinyirru (Lakefield) National Park is the second-largest national park in Queensland. It encompasses a wide variety of landscapes, including river forests, plains and coastal flats. The centre of the park abounds with birds. Camping is the only accommodation option and a permit must be obtained at the park's self-registration stations. The park is largely inaccessible during the wet season between December and April when the rivers flood the plains.

The nearby town of **Laura**, at the base of the Cape York Peninsula, is a typical Australian Outback town, with a sealed road flanked by a pub, a general store and a few houses. In the late 19th century, Laura was the rail terminus for the Palmer River gold fields and some 20,000 people passed through each year. Today, it is almost forgotten, but the discovery in 1959 of Aboriginal art sites of great antiquity is reviving interest in the area. One of the most notable sites is the "giant horse gallery", which contains huge horse paintings thought to record the first sightings of European explorers.

River forest landscape in Rinyirru (Lakefield) National Park

View from Thursday Island, in the Torres Strait island group

❷ Torres Strait Islands

🛫 from Cairns. 🚢 from Cairns. ℹ️ Cairns (07) 4069 6004. 🌐 **torres.qld.gov.au/tourism**

The Torres Strait divides the northern coastline of Australia from Papua New Guinea and is dotted with numerous islands. Approximately 19 of these islands are inhabited and have been governed by Queensland since 1879.

Thursday Island is the "capital" island and was once the centre of the local pearling industry. Many Japanese pearlers who lost their lives in this occupation are buried in the island's cemetery. In 1891, Green Hill Fort was built to prevent invasion by the Russians. Murray Island was the birthplace of Eddie Mabo, who, in 1992, won his claim to traditional land in the Australian High Court and changed Aboriginal-European relations *(see p62)*.

Chinese gravestone in Cooktown

❸ Cooktown

🏔️ 1,300. 🛫 🚌 🚢 ℹ️ Nature's Powerhouse, Botanic Gardens, Walker St (07) 4069 6004.

When the *Endeavour* was damaged by a coral reef in 1770, Captain Cook and his crew spent six weeks in this area while repairs to the ship were made *(see pp54–5)*. Cooktown's proud boast, therefore, is that it was the site of the first white settlement in Australia.

Like most towns in the area, Cooktown originally serviced the gold fields and its present-day population of less than 2,000 is half the 4,000 inhabitants who once sustained its 50 pubs. However, many of its historic buildings survive, including the Westpac Bank, originally the Old National Bank, with its stone columns supporting an iron-lace veranda. The **James Cook Museum**, which houses the old anchor from the *Endeavour*, started life in the 1880s as a convent. In the cemetery of the town, a memorial and numerous gravestones are testimony to the difficulties faced by the many Chinese who came to the gold fields in the 1870s *(see p59)*.

Between Cooktown and Bloomfield, Black Mountain National Park is named after the geological formation of huge black granite boulders. The boulders were formed around 260 million years ago below the earth's surface and were gradually exposed as surrounding land surfaces eroded away.

🏛️ **James Cook Museum**
Cnr Helen & Furneaux sts. **Tel** (07) 4069 5386. **Open** May–Sep: 9am–4pm daily; Oct–Apr: 9am–4pm Tue–Sat. 🅿️ ♿ limited. 🌐 **nationaltrust.org.au/places/james-cook-museum**

❹ Daintree National Park

from Port Douglas. ℹ️ Port Douglas (07) 4099 5599 or 13 74 68.
🌐 npsr.qld.gov.au/parks/daintree

Daintree National Park, north of Port Douglas, covers more than 76,000 ha (188,000 acres). The Cape Tribulation section of the park is a place of great beauty, and one of the few places where the rainforest meets the sea. Captain Cook named Cape Tribulation in rueful acknowledgment of the difficulties he was experiencing navigating the Great Barrier Reef. Today, it is a popular spot with backpackers.

The largest section of the park lies inland from Cape Tribulation. It is a mostly inaccessible, mountainous area, but 5 km (3 miles) from Mossman lies the Mossman Gorge, known for its easy and accessible 2.7-km (1-mile) track through the rainforest.

❺ Port Douglas

🏙️ 3,500. 🚌 🚐 ℹ️ 23 Macrossan St (07) 4099 5599.

Situated 75 km (47 miles) from Cairns, Port Douglas was once a tiny fishing village. Today it is a tourist centre, but it has managed to preserve some of its village atmosphere.

At the end of Macrossan Street is the beautiful Four-Mile Beach, which is a very popular walking spot. Many 19th-century buildings still line the street, such as the Courthouse Hotel, and the modern shopping centres have been designed to blend with the town's original architecture.

The original port was set up during the gold rush of the 1850s, but it was superseded by Cairns as the main port of the area. A disastrous cyclone in 1911 also forced people to move elsewhere, leaving the population at less than 500. The construction of the luxurious Sheraton Mirage Resort in the early 1980s heralded the beginning of a new boom, and now a range of accommodation and restaurants is on offer *(see p488 and p516)*.

Port Douglas is an alternative departure point to Cairns for Great Barrier Reef tours.

Tropical Myall Beach in Daintree National Park

❻ Green Island

from Cairns. ℹ️ (07) 4031 3300.
♿ 🌐 npsr.qld.gov.au/parks/green-island or
🌐 greenislandresort.com.au

Green Island is one of the few inhabited coral cays of the Great Barrier Reef *(see pp220–21)*. Despite its small size (a walk around the entire island takes about 15 minutes), it is home to a small scale eco-resort.

Green Island's proximity to the mainland means its coral is not as colourful as the outer reef, but it offers snorkelling from shore and visitors can spot sea turtles feeding on sea grass from the long jetty. Its accessibility by a ferry trip from Cairns makes it popular with day trippers.

The islands Marineland Melanesia complex has daily crocodile feeding shows and is home to Cassius, the world's largest crocodile in captivity.

Green Island, a coral cay at the heart of the Great Barrier Reef

❼ Cairns

Cairns is the main centre of Northern Queensland. Despite its coastal waterfront esplanade, it has a city atmosphere and instead of sandy beaches there are mudflats, abundant with native birdlife. Its main attraction is as a base for exploring the Great Barrier Reef *(see pp216–21)*, the Daintree Rainforest *(p257)* and the Atherton Tableland *(p259)*. However, Cairns itself does have several places of interest to visit.

🏵 Flecker Botanic Gardens
Collins Ave, Edge Hill. **Tel** (07) 4032 6650. **Open** daily. 🚻 ▢

Dating from 1886, the Flecker Botanic Gardens, one of five precincts that comprise the Cairns Botanic Gardens, has more than 100 species of palm trees, plus many other tropical plants. The gardens include an area of Queensland rainforest with native birdlife. The Centenary Lakes were created in 1976 to mark the city's first 100 years.

🏛 Cairns Historical Society Museum
City Place, cnr Lake & Shield sts. **Tel** (07) 4051 5582. **Open** 10am–3pm Mon–Fri. **Closed** Good Fri, 25 Apr, 25 Dec. 📷 ⓦ **cairnsmuseum.org.au**

Housed in the 1907 School of Arts building, this museum

Tropical orchid in the Flecker Botanic Gardens

is a fine example of the city's early architecture. Among the exhibits are the contents of an old Chinese joss house.

🚢 Reef Fleet Terminal
Pier Point Rd.

This is the departure point for most cruises to the Great Barrier Reef. Some 19th-century

façades nearby offer a glimpse of the city's early life.

Cairns is the game-fishing centre of Australia and, from August to December, tourists crowd Marlin Jetty to see the anglers return with their catch.

Adjacent Pier Marketplace has boutiques, restaurants, markets and accommodation.

Environs
On the eastern edge of the Atherton Tablelands is the tiny village of **Kuranda**. A hippie hang-out in the 1960s, it has since developed into an arts and crafts centre with markets held here daily. Nearby, at Smithfield, is the Tjapukai Cultural Centre, home to the renowned Aboriginal Tjapukai Dance Theatre.

Cairns City Centre
① Flecker Botanic Gardens
② Cairns Historical Society Museum
③ Reef Fleet Terminal

Mount Hypipamee Crater's green lake, Atherton Tablelands

❽ Atherton Tablelands

ℹ️ Cnr Silo & Main St, Atherton (07) 4091 4222. **Open** 9am–5pm daily. **Closed** 1 Jan, Good Fri, Easter Sun, 25 Dec, 26 Dec. 🆆 itablelands.com.au

Rising sharply from the coastal plains of Cairns, the northern landscape levels out into the lush Atherton Tablelands. At their highest point, the tablelands are 900 m (3,000 ft) above sea level. The cool temperature, heavy rainfall and rich volcanic soil make this one of the richest farming areas in Queensland. For many decades, tobacco was the main crop, but, with the worldwide decline in smoking, farmers have diversified into peanuts, macadamia nuts, sugar cane, bananas and avocados.

The town of **Yungaburra**, with its many historic buildings, is listed by the National Trust. Nearby is the famed "curtain fig tree". Strangler figs attach themselves to a host tree and eventually kill the original tree. In this case, the aerial roots, growing down from the tree tops, form a 15-m (50-ft) screen. Southwest of Yungaburra is the eerie, green crater lake at Mt Hypipamee. Stretching 60 m (200 ft) in diameter.

Millaa Millaa contains the most spectacular waterfalls of the region. A 15-km (9-mile) sealed circuit drive takes in the Zillie and Ellinjaa falls, while not far away are the picturesque Mungalli Falls. **Atherton** is the main town of the region, named after its first European settlers, John and Kate Atherton, who established a cattle station here in the mid-19th century. The wealthy agricultural centre of Mareeba now stands on the site of this former ranch.

❾ Wooroonooran National Park

🚌 Innisfail. 🚐 Innisfail. ℹ️ ANZAC Memorial Park, cnr Gladdy St & Bruce Highway 0428 228 962, or Cardwell Visitor Information (07) 4066 2412. 🆆 npsr.qld.gov.au/parks/ wooroonooran

Wooroonooran National Park contains the state's two highest mountains. Bartle Frere, reaching 1,611 m (5,285 ft) and Bellenden Ker, rising to 1,591 m (5,220 ft), are often swathed in cloud. Cassowaries (large flightless birds, under threat of extinction) can be spotted on the mountains.

Much of the park is wilderness, although tracks do exist. A popular area is Josephine Falls, south of the park, about 8 km (5 miles) from the Bruce Highway.

❿ Babinda and the Boulders

🏔️ 1,300. ℹ️ Cnr Munro St & Bruce Hwy, Babinda (07) 4067 1008.

The rural town of Babinda is a survivor of old-world Queensland, lined with veranda-fronted houses and a wooden pub.

The Babinda Boulders, 7 km (4 miles) inland, are water-worn rock shapes and a popular photographic subject.

⓫ Mission Beach

🚌 Tully. 🚐 Mission Beach. 🚤 Mission Beach. ℹ️ Mission Beach (07) 4068 7099. 🆆 **missionbeachtourism.com**

Located halfway between Cairns and Townsville, Mission Beach comprises four beach villages linked by 14 km (9 miles) of golden sand in an unspoilt, natural environment. Its boutiques, galleries and restaurants are set against a rainforest backdrop and views across to nearby Dunk Island, just 4 km (2.5 miles) off the coast. Dunk Island's rugged terrain is covered with a variety of vegetation. Day trips from Mission Beach are popular, offering snorkelling, diving and windsurfing.

⓬ Hinchinbrook Island

🚌 Ingham. 🚐 Cardwell. 🚤 Lucinda, Cardwell. ℹ️ Ingham (07) 4776 4792, or Cardwell (07) 4066 8601.

Hinchinbrook is the largest island national park in Australia, covering 635 sq km (245 sq miles). Dense rainforest, much of which remains unexplored, makes the island popular with bushwalkers. Hinchinbrook's highest point, Mount Bowen, rises 1,121 m (3,678 ft) above sea level and is often capped with cloud. The native wildlife includes wallabies, dugongs and the magnificent blue Ulysses butterfly. The island is separated from the mainland town of Cardwell by a narrow, mangrove-fringed channel.

Water-worn boulders near the town of Babinda

Queensland's Outback

In stark contrast to the lush green of the eastern rainforests, the northwest of Queensland is made up of dry plains, mining areas and Aboriginal settlements. The vast distances and high temperatures often dissuade tourists from venturing into this harsh landscape; yet those willing to make the effort will be rewarded with unique wildlife and an insight into Australia's harsh Outback life.

Locator Map

▢ Queensland's Outback

▢ Northern Queensland
pp252–59

Sights at a Glance

⑬ Normanton and
Gulf Savannah

⑭ Burketown

⑮ Mount Isa

⑯ Longreach

Key

━━━ Major road

┈┈┈ Minor road

╴╴╴ Track

─── Minor railway

▬▬▬ State border

0 km   150

0 miles   150

⑬ Normanton and Gulf Savannah

🚂 Normanton. 🛈 29–33 Haig St, Normanton (07) 4747 8422.

Normanton, situated 70 km (45 miles) inland on the Norman River, is the largest town in the region. It began life as a port, handling copper from Cloncurry and then gold from Croydon. The famous Gulflander train still commutes once a week between Normanton and Croydon.

En route from Normanton to the Gulf of Carpentaria, savannah grasses give way to glistening salt pans, barren of all vegetation. Once the rains come in November, however, this area becomes a wetland and a breeding ground for millions of birds, including jabirus, brolgas, herons and cranes, as well as crocodiles, prawns and barramundi. Karumba, at the mouth of the Norman River, is the access point for the Gulf of Carpentaria and the head-quarters of a multi-million-dollar prawn and fishing industry. It remains something of an untamed frontier town, especially when the prawn trawlers are in.

Covering approximately 350,000 sq km (135,000 sq miles), the most northwesterly region of Queensland is the Gulf Savannah. Largely flat and covered in savannah grasses, abundant with bird and animal life, this is the remotest landscape in Australia. The economic base of the area is fishing and cattle. Prawn trawlers go out to the Gulf of Carpentaria for months at a time and cattle stations cover areas of more than 1,000 sq km (400 sq miles). Given the distances, local pastoralists are more likely to travel via light aircraft than on horseback.

Gum trees and termite mounds on the grassland of Gulf Savannah

For additional map symbols *see back flap*

Mount Isa, dominated by Australia's largest mine

⓮ Burketown

🗺 170. ✈ ℹ 19 Musgrave St, cnr Burke St (07) 4745 5111, City Council, 65 Musgrave St (07) 4745 5111.

In the late 1950s, Burketown found fleeting fame as the setting for Neville Shute's famous novel about life in a small Outback town, *A Town Like Alice*. Situated 30 km (18 miles) from the Gulf of Carpentaria, on the Albert River, Burketown was once a major port servicing the hinterland. The spectacular propagating roll cloud known as a Morning Glory appears here in the early mornings from September to November. Burketown is rich in history and Aboriginal culture. It is also famous for the World Barramundi Fishing Championship.

About 150 km (90 miles) west of Burketown is Hell's Gate, an area so named at the beginning of the 20th century because it was the last outpost where the state's police guaranteed protection.

⓯ Mount Isa

🗺 19,000. ✈ 🚉 🚌
ℹ 19 Marian St (07) 4749 1555.

Mount Isa is the only major city in far western Queensland. Its existence is entirely based around the world's largest silver and lead mine, which dominates the town's industry and landscape. Ore was first discovered at Mount Isa in 1923 by a prospector called John Campbell Miles and the

first mine was set up in the 1930s. In those early days, "the Isa" was a shanty town, and Tent House, now owned by the National Trust, is an example of the half-house-half-tents that were home to most early settlers. Also in town is **Outback at Isa**, which incorporates mine tours, the Riversleigh Fossil Centre and Isa Experience Gallery *(see pp30–31)*.

One of the most popular events in town is the Mount Isa Rodeo in August *(see p47)*. With prize money totalling more than A\$100,000, riders come from all over the world to perform spectacular displays of horsemanship.

🏛 Outback at Isa
19 Marian St. **Tel** (07) 4749 1555. **Open** daily. **Closed** Good Fri, 25 Dec. 🅿 ♿ 🌐 mietv.com.au

Environs
Cloncurry, 120 km (75 miles) east of Mount Isa, was the departure point for the Queensland and Northern Territory Aerial Service's (QANTAS) first flight in 1921. Now Australia's national airline, Qantas is also the oldest airline in the English-speaking world.

⓰ Longreach

🗺 3,000. ✈ 🚉 🚌 ℹ Qantas Park, Eagle St (07) 4658 4150. 🌐 longreachtourism.com.au

Situated in the centre of Queensland, Longreach is the main town of the central west of the state.

From 1922 to 1934, Longreach was the operating base of Qantas and there is a Founders Museum at Longreach Airport. The **Australian Stockman's Hall of Fame** is a fascinating tribute to Outback men and women. Aboriginal artifacts, as well as documented tales of the early European explorers are included in the impressive displays.

There are daily flights or a 17-hour coach ride from Brisbane to Longreach. Other access points are Rockhampton and Townsville.

🏛 Australian Stockman's Hall of Fame
Landsborough Hwy. **Tel** (07) 4658 2166. **Open** 9am–4pm daily. **Closed** 25 & 26 Dec. 🅿 ♿ 🌐 outbackheritage.com.au

---

The Royal Flying Doctor Service

The Royal Flying Doctor Service was founded by John Flynn, a Presbyterian pastor who was sent as a missionary to the Australian Outback in 1912. The young cleric was disturbed to see that many of his flock died due to the lack of basic medical care and he founded the Australian Inland Mission together with Hudson Fysh (the founder of Qantas), self-made millionaire Hugh Victor McKay, Alfred Traeger (the inventor of the pedal wireless) and Dr Kenyon St Vincent Welch. Today, the Royal Flying Doctor Service deals with some 130,000 patients a year, and most Outback properties have an airstrip on which the Flying Doctor can land. Emergency medical help is rarely more than two hours away and advice is available over a special radio channel.

A Royal Flying Doctor plane flying over Australia's Outback

THE NORTHERN TERRITORY

The Northern Territory at a Glance

That most famous of Australian icons, the red monolith of Uluṟu (Ayers Rock) lies within the Northern Territory, but it is just one of the area's stunning natural features, which also include the tropical splendour of Kakadu National Park. The main centres are Darwin in the lush north and Alice Springs in the arid Red Centre. Much of the Outback land is Aboriginal-owned. The Northern Territory has yet to achieve full statehood owing to its low population and relatively small economy, but it has been self-governing since 1978.

Tiwi Islands *(see p278)* lie 80 km (50 miles) off the north coast. The islands are inhabited by Tiwi Aboriginals, who have preserved a culture distinct from the mainland which includes unique characteristics such as these burial poles.

```
0 kilometres    150
0 miles         150
```

Darwin *(see pp274–7)* is the Northern Territory's capital city with an immigrant population of more than 50 nationalities *(see pp268–9)*. The colonial Government House is one of the few 19th-century survivors in what is now a very modern city.

Uluṟu-Kata Tjuṯa National Park *(see pp290–93)* is dominated by the huge sandstone rock rising up out of the flat, arid desert and the nearby Olgas, a series of 36 mysterious rock domes.

◀ A "beware of kangaroos" road sign next to Uluṟu (Ayers Rock)

Darwin

Pine Creek

Katherine

Timber Creek

Kalkarindji

The Red Centre *(see pp282–93)*

Yuendumu

Yulara

Kakadu National Park (see pp280–81) is an ancient landscape of tropical rainforest and majestic rock formations. Covering 1.7 million ha (4.3 million acres), it is the largest national park in Australia. The Jim Jim Falls are the most impressive in the park, and the Aboriginal rock art sites are among the most important in the country.

Locator Map

Elsey Homestead Replica, 110 km (70 miles) southeast of Katherine (see pp278–9), was the setting for Jeannie Gunn's novel *We of the Never Never*, depicting 19th-century Outback life.

Roper Bar

Darwin and the Top End (see pp270–81)

Daly Waters

Borroloola

Karlu Karlu/Devil's Marbles (see p289) are a remarkable collection of granite boulders in the heart of the flat, sandy desert. Caused by millions of years of erosion, they are traditionally believed to be the eggs of the Rainbow Serpent.

Dunmarra

Cape Crawford Roadhouse

ee Ways adhouse

Tennant Creek

Alice Springs (see pp286–7) lies at the heart of Australia. Its Old Telegraph Station Historical Reserve was the site of the area's first settlement in 1871.

Ti-Tree

Utopia

Aileron

Harts Range

Alice Springs

Chambers Pillar Historical Reserve (see p288) is a strange, 50-m (165-ft) sandstone column which served as a landmark for explorers of the area in the 19th century.

dunda

Aboriginal Lands

Aboriginal people are thought to have lived in the Northern Territory for between 20,000 and 50,000 years. The comparatively short 200 years of European settlement have damaged their ancient culture immensely, but in the Northern Territory more traditional Aboriginal communities have survived intact than in other states – mainly due to their relatively greater numbers and determination to preserve their identity. Nearly one-third of the Northern Territory's people are Aboriginal and they own almost 50 per cent of the land through native title legislated enacted by the federal government *(see p63)*. For Aboriginals, the concept of land ownership is tied to a belief system that instructs them to care for their ancestral land.

This X-ray image *(see p37)* of the dreaming spirit Namarrgon at Nourlangie Rock is centuries old, but was continually repainted until the 1900s.

Nourlangie Rock in Kakadu National Park is significant to Aborigines as home of the Lightning Dreaming *(see pp280–81)*.

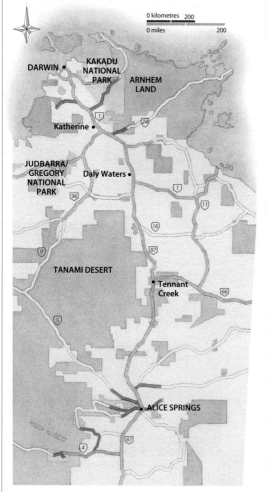

Key

- Aboriginal land
- National park
- Highway
- Major road
- Unsurfaced road

Access and Permits

Northern Land Council
Tel (08) 8920 5100.
For access to all Aboriginal land in the Top End, including Arnhem Land. **W** nlc.org.au

Parks and Wildlife Commission of the Northern Territory
Tel (08) 8999 4555.
For permits to Garig Gunak Barlu National Park.
W dtc.nt.gov.au

Tiwi Land Council
Tel (08) 8970 9373.
For access to Melville and Bathurst (Tiwi) islands.
W tiwilandcouncil.com

Central Land Council
Tel (08) 8951 6211. For access to all Central Australian Aboriginal lands. **W** clc.org.au

Aboriginal Tourism

Most visitors who come to the Northern Territory are keen to learn more about the region's unique Aboriginal culture. There are now many Aboriginal organizations which take tourists into Aboriginal areas that would otherwise be inaccessible, and explain the Aboriginal view of the land. Excursions available include boat trips in Kakadu National Park *(see pp280–81)* with a Guluyambi guide; bush camping with the Manyallaluk community near Katherine; or a safari camp in Arnhem Land with Umorrduk Safaris. Also well worth visiting are the information and cultural centres, such as those in Kakadu and Uluru-Kata Tjuta national parks, where native owners share their creation stories and culture, adding another layer to visitors' appreciation of these special places.

Ubirr in Kakadu National Park is one of the finest Aboriginal rock art sites in the Northern Territory. Many paintings in Ubirr's gallery depict the area's wildlife in an X-ray style *(see p37)*, such as this barramundi. They date from 20,000 years ago to the present day.

Visitors climbing to the lookout at Ubirr

Uluru *(see pp290–93)* has many sites sacred to the Anangu people around its base. Most are closed to the public, but it is possible to walk around the area, including a route around the entire perimeter of Uluru, and learn the associated stories.

Bush Tucker Dreaming, painted in 1991 by Gladys Napanangka of the Papunya community of the Central Western Desert, records the Dreaming or creation stories passed down to the artist through hundreds of generations *(see pp34–5)*.

Aboriginal Culture and Law

Every Aboriginal clan lives according to a set of laws linking the people with their land and their ancestors. These laws have been handed down through generations and are embedded in Aboriginal creation stories. The stories, which tell how the first spirits and ancestors shaped and named the land, also form a belief system which directs all aspects of Aboriginal life. All Aboriginals are born into two groups: their family clan and a "Dreaming" totem group such as the crocodile – determined by place and time of birth. These decide their links with the land and place in the community and the creation stories they inherit.

Aboriginals in body make-up for a traditional tribal dance

Multicultural Northern Territory

The Northern Territory, with its proximity to Indonesia and the Pacific Islands, has long served as Australia's "front door" to immigrants. Around 500 years ago, Portuguese and Dutch ships charted the waters of the northern coast and from the 1700s traders from the Indonesian archipelago visited the northern shores. From 1874, when Chinese gold prospectors arrived in Darwin, the tropical north has appealed to Southeast Asians and, being closer to Indonesia than to Sydney or Melbourne, the city markets itself as Australia's gateway to Asia. There are now more than 50 ethnic groups living in Darwin, including Greeks and Italians who arrived in the early 20th century, and East Timorese, Indonesians, Thais and Filipinos, together with the town's original mix of Aboriginals and those of Anglo-Celtic stock.

Harry Chan, elected in 1966, was the first Mayor of Darwin of Chinese descent.

Mindil Beach Sunset Market is among several Asian-style food markets in the Darwin area. More than 60 food stalls serve Thai, Indonesian, Indian, Chinese, Sri Lankan, Malaysian and Greek cuisine (*see p276*).

The Darwin Festival features indigenous and multicultural performances from local artists and acts from Asia and Australia.

The Chinese in the Top End

In 1879, a small carved figure dating from the Ming dynasty (1368–1644) was found in the roots of a tree on a Darwin beach, causing much speculation that a Chinese fleet may have visited this coast in the 15th century. If so, it was the start of an association between China and the Top End which endures today. Chinese came here in search of gold in the 1870s. By 1885, there were 3,500 Chinese in the Top End, and 40 years later Darwin had become a Chinese-run shanty town with Chinese families managing its market gardens and general stores. Today, many of the area's leading families are of Chinese origin; Darwin has had two Lord Mayors of Chinese descent, and fifth-generation Chinese are spread throughout the city's businesses.

Chinese man using buffalo to haul wood in early 19th-century Darwin

Aboriginal people are believed to have arrived in the Northern Territory 20,000 to 50,000 years ago, overland from Asia when the sea level was much lower. Here, young male initiates from an Arnhem Land tribe are carried to a ceremony to be "made men".

With a quarter of its present population born overseas and another quarter Aboriginal, Darwin's racial mix is best seen in the faces of its children.

Darwin Festival

The 18-day Darwin Festival held in August reflects the city's unique indigenous and multicultural population and proximity to Asia. This colourful arts-based celebration focuses on cultural performances, including concerts, workshops, theatre, dance, music, comedy, film and visual arts.

Darwin Festival began as a floral event in 1979 after the devastation of Cyclone Tracey. The focus shifted to cultural celebration in the 1990s.

The Filipino community in Darwin preserves its traditions, as seen by these two girls in national costume at the Darwin Festival.

Paspaley Pearls is Darwin's wealthiest local company. Founded by Greek settlers, it owns pearl farms across northern Australia.

The East Timorese community of Darwin performs traditional dancing at a city arts festival. Most of the East Timorese have arrived in the city since 1975, in the wake of Indonesia's invasion of East Timor.

DARWIN AND THE TOP END

The tropical tip of the Northern Territory is a lush, ancient landscape. For thousands of years it has been home to large numbers of Aboriginals and contains one of the oldest collections of rock art in the world. Its capital, Darwin, is small and colourful. The World Heritage-listed Kakadu National Park has a raw beauty combined with the fascinating creation stories of its Aboriginal tribes.

The Port of Darwin was first named in 1839, when British captain John Lort Stokes, commander of HMS *Beagle*, sailed into an azure harbour of sandy beaches and mangroves, and named it after his friend Charles Darwin. Although the biologist would not publish his theory of evolution in the *Origin of the Species* for another 20 years, it proved to be a wonderfully apt name for this tropical region, teeming with unique and ancient species of birds, plants, reptiles and mammals. The Aboriginal tribes that have lived for many thousands of years in the northern area known as the Top End are recognized by anthropologists as one of the world's oldest races.

Darwin itself is a city that has fought hard to survive. From 1869, when the first settlement was established at Port Darwin, it has endured isolation, bombing attacks by the Japanese in World War II *(see p274)* and devastation by the force of Cyclone Tracy on Christmas Eve in 1974 *(see p276)*. Despite having been twice rebuilt, it has grown into a multicultural modern city, with a relaxed atmosphere, great beauty and a distinctly Asian feel.

Beyond Darwin is a region of Aboriginal communities and ancient art sites, wide rivers and crocodiles, lotus-lily wetlands and deep gorges. For visitors, Kakadu National Park superbly blends sights of great scenic beauty with a cultural and spiritual insight into the complex Aboriginal culture. Also to be enjoyed are the plunging waterfalls and giant termite mounds of Litchfield National Park, the deep red-rock gorge of Nitmiluk (Katherine Gorge) National Park, and expeditions into the closed Aboriginal communities of Arnhem Land and Melville and Bathurst Islands.

An Aboriginal child gathering water lilies in the lush and tropical Top End

◀ Jim Jim Falls, in Kakadu National Park, at the end of the wet season

Exploring Darwin and the Top End

The Top End is a seductive, tropical region on the remote tip of the Northern Territory. On the turquoise coast there are palm trees; inland are winding rivers, grassy wetlands, gorge pools and sandstone escarpments. The Territory's capital, Darwin, has many attractions and is a good base for day trips to areas such as Berry Springs and Melville and Bathurst Islands. The climate is hot, but the dry season has low humidity, making it the best time to visit. The wet season makes up for its humidity and downpours with thundering rivers and waterfalls, and lush vegetation. Some seasonal businesses, like restaurants, close during the wet season, and many attractions limit opening times.

Pearl lugger-turned-cruise boat in Darwin Harbour

COBOURG PENINSULA
Croker Island
Pularumpi
Mur
MELVILLE ISLAND
BATHURST ISLAND
Van Diemen Gulf
Nguiu
Beagle Gulf
Oenpelli
DARWIN
Ubirr
Howard Springs Nature Park
Jabir
Territory Wildlife Park
Noonamah
ARNHEM HWY
KAKADU NATIONAL PARK
Batchelor
Cooinda
Mary
LITCHFIELD NATIONAL PARK
STUART HWY
Twin Falls
Gunlom Waterhole
Mary River Roadhouse
Daly River
Pine Creek
Katherine Gorge National Park
Palumpa
Daly
KATHERINE
Cutta Cutta Caves
Fitzmaurice
Mataranka
VICTORIA HIGHWAY
Yambarran Range
Victoria
Dry
Larrimah
Timber Creek
Victoria River
BUNTINE HWY
KEEP RIVER NATIONAL PARK
JUDBARRA/GREGORY NATIONAL PARK
96
Daly Wa
80
Top Springs Roadhouse
Dunm
Wickham
80
Stirling
Kalkarindji
Halls Creek

Getting Around

The Top End's reputation as an isolated region is long gone. Darwin is linked by the Stuart Highway to Alice Springs, Adelaide and Melbourne in the south, and along interstate highways to Mount Isa, Cairns and Brisbane in the east. The centre of Darwin can be explored on foot or using the open trolley Tour Tub which stops at all the main attractions in an hourly circuit. The Top End's major attractions, such as Kakadu National Park and Katherine Gorge, can be visited without driving on a dirt road. Bus connections to the main towns are regular, but a car is vital to make the most of the scenery. Distances are not great for Australia; Kakadu is 210 km (130 miles) from Darwin and Katherine 300 km (186 miles) away on the Stuart Hwy.

Spectacular Jim Jim Falls in Kakadu National Park

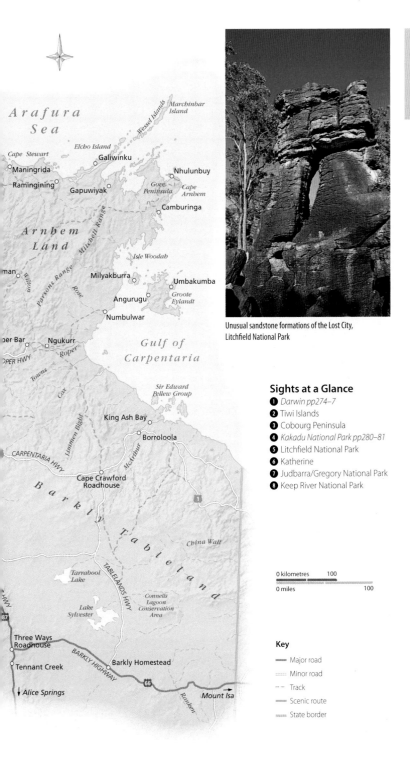

Arafura Sea

Cape Stewart

Maningrida

Ramingining

Elcho Island

Galiwinku

Wessel Islands

Marchinbar Island

Nhulunbuy

Gapuwiyak

Gove Peninsula

Cape Arnhem

Camburinga

Arnhem Land

Mitchell Range

Parsons Range

Rose

Wilton

man

Isle Woodah

Milyakburra

Umbakumba

Angurugu

Groote Eylandt

Numbulwar

Gulf of Carpentaria

er Bar

Ngukurr

Roper

PER HWY

Towns

Cox

Limmen Bight

Sir Edward Pellew Group

King Ash Bay

McArthur

Borroloola

CARPENTARIA HWY

Barkly Tableland

Cape Crawford Roadhouse

China Wall

Tarrabool Lake

TABLELANDS HWY

Connells Lagoon Conservation Area

HWY

Lake Sylvester

87

Three Ways Roadhouse

BARKLY HIGHWAY

Barkly Homestead

Tennant Creek

66

↓ *Alice Springs*

Ranken

Mount Isa

Unusual sandstone formations of the Lost City, Litchfield National Park

Sights at a Glance

❶ *Darwin pp274–7*
❷ Tiwi Islands
❸ Cobourg Peninsula
❹ *Kakadu National Park pp280–81*
❺ Litchfield National Park
❻ Katherine
❼ Judbarra/Gregory National Park
❽ Keep River National Park

0 kilometres   100

0 miles   100

Key

━━ Major road

┅┅ Minor road

--- Track

━━ Scenic route

▬▬ State border

❶ Darwin

Following European settlement in 1864, for the first century of its life Darwin was an outpost of the British Empire, with vast cattle farms established around it. In its short, colourful history it has experienced the gold rush of the 1890s, life as an Allied frontline during World War II and almost total destruction in 1974 by the fearful winds of Cyclone Tracy *(see p276)*. Darwin has now emerged as a modern but relaxed town where more than 50 ethnic groups mingle, including Asian-born Australians, Aboriginals, Europeans, particularly Greeks, and Chinese.

Shady palm trees in Bicentennial Park, seen from The Esplanade

🌳 Bicentennial Park

The Esplanade. ♿

This lush, green park, with its pleasant shady walks and panoramic lookouts, is home to many World War II memorials. One commemorates the attack by Japanese bombers which flew over Darwin Harbour on 19 February 1942, sinking 21 of the 46 US and Australian naval vessels in port and killing 243 people. It was the closest Australia came to war on its own soil.

🏛 Old Admiralty House

Cnr Knuckey St & The Esplanade.

Across the road from Lyons Cottage is Old Admiralty House, once the headquarters of the Australian navy and one of the oldest surviving buildings in Darwin. It was built in the 1930s by the territory's principal architect, Beni Carr Glynn Burnett, in an elevated tropical style using louvres, open eaves and three-quarter-high walls to aid ventilation.

🏬 Smith Street Mall

Bennett & Knuckey sts. ♿

The heart of Darwin's shopping area is Smith Street Mall, with its glass air-conditioned plazas shaded by tall tropical trees. Always full of buskers, tour operators offering trips, locals and visitors, the mall is a favourite meeting place. Noteworthy buildings include the 1890 Victoria Hotel, one of the few old structures in town to survive Cyclone Tracy. During the dry season, many outdoor events are held at Raintree Park, at the northern end of the mall.

🏛 Parliament House

Mitchell St, State Square. **Tel** (08) 8946 1512. **Open** 8am–4:30pm daily. May–Aug. ♿ **W** nt.gov.au/lant

Dominating the edge of Darwin's sea cliffs is the new Parliament House. With architecture that appears to borrow from both Middle Eastern and Russian styles, this imposing building is home to the Territory's 25 parliamentarians, who administer just 200,000 people. It has a granite and timber interior which is filled with Aboriginal art. Self-guided and free 90-minute guided tours are available; times and days vary by season, so check the website for full details.

🏛 Old Town Hall

Smith St. ♿

The limestone ruin of the Old Town Hall lies at the bottom of Smith Street. The original council chambers, built in 1883, became a naval workshop and store in World War II. Later it was a bank and then a museum, before being destroyed by Cyclone Tracy in 1974. Curved brick paving built against the remaining wall symbolizes the fury of the cyclone's winds.

🏛 Brown's Mart

12 Smith St. **Tel** (08) 8981 5522. ♿

Opposite the town hall ruins is Brown's Mart, built during the gold boom in 1885. A former mining exchange, it now houses an intimate theatre. The iconic space hosts bands, plays, workshops and other live shows.

Front entrance of Parliament House

🏛 Old Police Station and Courthouse

Cnr Smith St & The Esplanade. **Tel** (08) 8999 7103. ♿

The 1884 limestone Old Police Station and Courthouse have both been restored after being damaged by Cyclone Tracy and are now used as the Office of the Administrator.

Across the road, overlooking the harbour, is Survivors' Lookout, where photographs and written accounts tell of Darwin's wartime role as an Allied frontline. Thousands of US and Australian troops were based in the Top End, which endured 63 bombing raids by Japanese forces *(see p61)*.

Darwin's Old Police Station and Courthouse

🏛 Government House

The Esplanade. **Tel** (08) 8999 7103. ♿
🌐 **govhouse.nt.gov.au**

Above the harbour, the 1871-built Government House, or the House of Seven Gables, is Darwin's oldest surviving edifice. It has withstood bomb raids, cyclones, earthquakes and infestations of white ants. This gracious sandstone building with stunning tropical gardens is the residence of the Administrator of the Northern Territory.

🏛 Stokes Hill Wharf

McMinn St. ♿ 🖥

The long, wooden Stokes Hill Wharf, stretching out into Darwin Harbour, was once the town's main port area. Now a centre for tourist and local life, it has restaurants and shops. Boats leave on tours from the wharf.

At the wharf entrance is the excellent Indo-Pacific Marine exhibit, which has re-created local coral reef ecosystems, with bright tropical fish in its tanks. In the same building, the Australian Pearling Exhibition describes the history and science of local pearl farming.

VISITORS' CHECKLIST

Practical Information
🗺 100,000. ℹ Cnr Smith & Bennett sts, 1300 138 886/(08) 8980 6000. 🎭 Festival of Darwin (Aug).

Transport
✈ Darwin Airport, 15 km (9 miles) SE of the city. 🚌 Smith St Mall, Karama, Casuarina & Palmerston shopping centres. ⛴ Cullen Bay Marina.

Restaurant at the end of Stokes Hill Wharf overlooking the harbour

Darwin City Centre

① Bicentennial Park
② Old Admiralty House
③ Smith Street Mall
④ Parliament House
⑤ Old Town Hall
⑥ Brown's Mart
⑦ Old Police Station and Courthouse
⑧ Government House
⑨ Stokes Hill Wharf

0 metres 250
0 yards 250

For keys to symbols *see back flap*

Greater Darwin

Many of Darwin's best attractions are not in the city centre but located a short drive away. The Tour Tub, an open-sided trolley bus that picks up from major hotels, does an hourly circuit of tourist attractions, allowing visitors to hop on and off at will for a daily charge. Outside Darwin, alongside the mango farms and cattle stations, there are some fine bush and wetland areas which provide excellent opportunities for swimming, fishing and exploring.

Feeding the friendly fish at Aquascene in Doctor's Gully

🐠 Aquascene

28 Doctor's Gully Rd, cnr of Daly St & The Esplanade. **Tel** (08) 8981 7837. **Open** daily, with the tide. **Closed** 25 Dec. 🚻 W aquascene.com.au

Ever since the 1950s, the fish of Darwin Harbour have been coming in on the tides for a feed of stale bread in Doctor's Gully. At Aquascene's fish-feeding sanctuary, visitors can feed hundreds of catfish, mullet and milkfish. Feeding times vary depending on tides.

Crowds of food lovers at the ever-popular Mindil Beach Sunset Market

🏮 Mindil Beach Sunset Market

Mindil Beach. **Tel** (08) 8981 3454. **Open** late Apr–late Oct: 5–10pm Thu, 4–9pm Sun. 🚻

Thursday and Sunday nights during the dry season are when Darwinians flock to Mindil Beach at dusk to enjoy some 60 outdoor food stalls, street theatre, live music and over 200 craft stalls.

🌱 George Brown Darwin Botanic Gardens

Gardens Rd, Stuart Park. **Tel** (08) 8999 4418. **Open** daily. 🚻 limited.

Just north of town, the 42-ha (100-acre) Botanic Gardens, established in the 1870s, boast over 1,500 tropical species, including 400 palm varieties and wetland mangroves.

🏛 Darwin Military Museum and Fannie Bay Gaol

Alec Fong Lim Drive, East Point. **Tel** (08) 8981 9702. **Open** 9:30am–5pm daily. 🚻🚻

An attraction for all the family, this pleasant harbourside reserve contains an artificial lake that is ideal for swimming and the fascinating Darwin Military Museum. Nearby Fannie Bay Gaol now houses an interesting museum (free entry).

🏛 Australian Aviation Heritage Centre

557 Stuart Hwy, Winnellie. **Tel** (08) 8947 2145. 🚌 5, 8. **Open** 9am–5pm daily. **Closed** Good Fri, 25 Dec. 🚻🚻 W darwinsairwar.com.au

Along the Stuart Highway at Winnellie, 6 km (4 miles) from the city centre, Darwin's Aviation Centre displays a variety of historic and wartime aircraft. Its exhibits are dominated by a B-52 bomber, one of only two in the world on display outside the US.

🦎 Territory Wildlife Park

Cox Peninsula Rd, Berry Springs. **Tel** (08) 8988 7200. **Open** 9am–5pm daily. **Closed** 25 Dec. 🚻🚻🚻 W territorywildlife park.com.au

Only 60 km (37 miles) from Darwin is the town of Berry Springs and the Territory Wildlife Park with its hundreds of unique indigenous species, in natural surroundings. Nearby, Berry Springs Nature Reserve has a series of deep pools, fringed with vegetation, that make for great swimming.

🦌 Howard Springs Nature Park

Howard Springs Rd. **Tel** (08) 8983 1001. **Open** daily. 🚻 limited.

This nature park, 35 km (22 miles) south of Darwin, has clear, freshwater spring-fed pools, filled with barramundi and turtles. It's an ideal place to have a barbecue or a picnic in the shade after a hot day of exploring.

Cyclone Tracy

Late Christmas Eve, 1974, a weather warning was issued that Cyclone Tracy, gathering force off the coast, had turned landward and was heading for Darwin. Torrential rain pelted down and winds reached a record 280 km/h (175 mph) before the measuring machine broke. On Christmas morning, 66 people were dead, thousands injured and 95 per cent of the buildings flattened. More than 30,000 residents were airlifted south in the biggest evacuation in Australia's history. The city ruins were bulldozed and Darwin has been rebuilt, stronger and safer than before.

Cyclone Tracy's devastation

For hotels and restaurants in this area see p489 and pp517–18

Museum and Art Gallery of the Northern Territory

The Museum and Art Gallery of the Northern Territory has exhibitions on regional Aboriginal art and culture, maritime history, visual arts and natural history.

The museum's collection of Aboriginal art is considered to be the best in the world and has some particularly fine carvings and bark paintings, along with explanations of Aboriginal culture. Other displays include a chilling exhibition on Cyclone Tracy and displays that explain the evolution of some of the Top End's unique and curious wildlife, including the popular stuffed crocodile named "Sweetheart".

VISITORS' CHECKLIST

Practical Information
Conacher St.
Tel (08) 8999 8264.
W magnt.net.au
Open 9am–5pm Mon–Fri,
10am–5pm Sat & Sun.
Closed 1 Jan, Good Fri, 25 & 26
Dec. 🖼 ♿ 🎁 🖊 🖥

Transport
🚌 6.

Key

- Indigenous Art Gallery
- Natural Sciences Gallery
- Cyclone Tracy Gallery
- Visual Art Gallery
- Amphitheatre
- Maritime Galleries
- Temporary exhibitions
- Non-exhibition space
- Monsoon Forest Pathway
- Fish Pond

★ Indigenous Art Gallery
In this gallery, exhibits describe both the anthropology and creation stories of local Aboriginal groups as an introduction to the artworks on display that portray their lives and culture.

Upper floor

Ground floor

Discovery Centre

Theatrette

Entrance

Sweetheart
This large male crocodile, measuring 5 m (16 ft) in length, is called Sweetheart. It was caught in 1979 in the Finnis River, which is between Darwin and Kakadu. He drowned while being captured, after becoming entangled with a log.

Façade of the Museum and Art Gallery
Located 4 km (2 miles) north of Darwin's centre, the museum's stylish low-level building is in a tropical beachside setting overlooking Fannie Bay.

Tiwi islander making handicrafts from local fibres, Bathurst Island

❷ Tiwi Islands

🛬 ℹ️ Tiwi Tours, Mitchell St, Darwin (08) 8923 6523; SeaLink (08) 8981 2878 (tours and ferry run dry season only).

Just 80 km (50 miles) north of Darwin lie the Tiwi Islands, the collective name given to the small island of Bathurst and its larger neighbour, Melville. The latter is the second-largest island off the Australian coast after Tasmania and is rich in history and Aboriginal culture. The islands' inhabitants, the Tiwi people, had little contact with mainland Aboriginals until the 20th century.

With beautiful waters, sandy beaches and lush forest, the islands are a tropical paradise, but only Bathurst can be visited on tours from Darwin. Day trips (May–Oct) offer a glimpse of the unique blend of Aboriginal, Indonesian and Tiwi traditions. Tourists can visit Aboriginal art centres, Tiwi printworks for screen-printed fabrics and a *pukumani* burial site.

❸ Cobourg Peninsula

ℹ️ Venture North Australia, Darwin (08) 8927 5500. 🌐 **venturenorth.com.au**

The Cobourg Peninsula is one of the most remote parts of Australia. It is only accessible by vehicle during the dry season and with an access permit *(see p266)*, travelling through the closed Aboriginal Arnhem Land

to the wild coastal beaches of Garig Gunak Barlu National Park. The number of vehicles allowed to enter the region each week is restricted and there are permit fees, too, so going on a tour is sometimes a convenient option.

Garig is a large park, with sandy beaches and the calm waters of Port Essington. Two attempts by the British to settle this area in the early 1800s were abandoned, due to the inhospitable environment and malaria epidemics. The ruins of Victoria Settlement can be reached by boat from Smith Point. Luxury accommodation is available at Seven Spirit Bay Wilderness Lodge, reached by plane from Darwin; the Venture North company, which tours the region, has a safari-style camp overlooking Port Essington.

❹ Kakadu National Park

See pp280–81.

❺ Litchfield National Park

ℹ️ Parks and Wildlife Commission of the Northern Territory (08) 8976 0282. 🌐 **nt.gov.au**

The spectacular Litchfield National Park, only 129 km (80 miles) south of Darwin, is very popular with Darwinians. There are waterfalls, gorges and deep, crocodile-free pools for swimming at Florence Falls,

Giant magnetic termite mound in Litchfield National Park

Wangi, in the wet season, and Buley Rockhole. The park has some amazing giant magnetic termite mounds. They are so-called because they point north in an effort by the termites to control temperature by having only the mound's thinnest part exposed to the sun. Also popular are the sandstone block formations further south, known as the "Lost City" due to their resemblance to ruins.

❻ Katherine

🏞️ 11,000. ✈️ 🚌 🚌 ℹ️ Cnr Katherine Terrace & Lindsay St (08) 8972 2650. 🌐 **visitkatherine.com.au**

The town of Katherine, situated on the banks of the Katherine River, 320 km (200 miles) south of Darwin, is both a thriving regional centre and a major Top End tourist destination. Home for thousands of years to the Jawoyn people, Katherine River has long been a rich source of food for the Aboriginal people. The river was first crossed by white explorers in 1844, and the area was not settled by Europeans until 1872, with the completion of the Overland Telegraph Line. Springvale Homestead was built on the Katherine River in 1879. It is now the oldest homestead in the Territory and is open to the public. Tours are offered at 3pm daily during dry season.

Only 30 km (20 miles) from town lies the famous **Nitmiluk (Katherine Gorge) National Park**. Its string of 13 separate gorges along 50 km (30 miles) of the Katherine River has been carved out by torrential seasonal rains cutting through cliffs of red sandstone which are 1,650 million years old. The result is a place of deep pools, silence and grandeur.

The best way to explore the park is by boat or canoe. Canoe trips are guided or self-guided, with nine navigable gorges and overnight camping possible. There are also cruise trips operated by the Jawoyn people, who own the park and run it in conjunction with the Parks and Wildlife Commission of the Northern Territory. There are also

Upper waterfall and pools of Edith Falls, Nitmiluk (Katherine Gorge) National Park near Katherine

around 100 km (60 miles) of marked trails in the park, ranging from the spectacular lookout walk to the five-day 72-km (45-mile) Jatbula Trail to Edith Falls, which can also be reached by car from the Stuart Highway.

Environs
Just 27 km (17 miles) south of Katherine are the Cutta Cutta caves, limestone rock formations 15 m (50 ft) under the earth's surface and formed five million years ago. They are home to both the rare orange horseshoe bat and the brown tree snake.

Further southeast, 110 km (70 miles) from Katherine, lies the small town of Mataranka. This is "Never Never" country, celebrated by female pioneer Jeannie Gunn in her 1908 novel, *We of the Never Never*, about life at nearby Elsey Station at the turn of the century. The area is called Never Never country because those who live here find they never, never want to

leave it. About 8 km (5 miles) east of Mataranka is Elsey National Park. Visitors can swim in the hot waters of the Mataranka Thermal Pool which flow from Rainbow Springs to this idyllic spot. Built in 1916 **Mataranka Homestead** is now a tourist resort, which includes a motel, cabins and camp sites.

🏨 **Mataranka Homestead**
Tel (08) 8975 4544. **Open** daily.
🚐 ♿ 🏕 W mataranka
homestead.com.au

❼ Judbarra/Gregory National Park

ℹ️ Timber Creek (08) 8975 0888, Bullita (08) 8975 0833. **Open** 7am–4pm Mon–Fri. W nt.gov.au

This massive national park is 280 km (174 miles) by road southwest of Katherine. Broken into two sections, its eastern part contains a 50-km (31-mile) section of the Victoria River gorge accessible by a 2WD boat ramp for much of the year. In the north of the larger western section of the park are some crocodile-infested areas of the Victoria River. Here boat trips combine close-up views of the crocodiles.

Limestone Gorge in Judbarra/Gregory National Park

A "no swimming" policy covers the entire park. In the west of the park, the stunning Limestone Gorge has dolomite blocks, huge cliffs and good fishing opportunities.

Walking trail by a sandstone escarpment, Keep River National Park

❽ Keep River National Park

ℹ️ Victoria Hwy (08) 9167 8827. **Open** Apr–Sep: daily; Oct–Mar: Mon–Fri. Closed when inaccessible. W nt.gov.au

Located only 3 km (2 miles) from the Western Australian border, Keep River National Park includes the dramatic Keep River gorge and some of Australia's most ancient rock art sites. The park, once the location of an ancient Aboriginal settlement, today has some superb walking trails for all levels of trekkers.

● Kakadu National Park

The vast 19,757 sq km (7,628 sq miles) of Kakadu
National Park, with its stunning diversity of stony
plateaux, red escarpment cliffs, waterfalls, billabongs,
long twisting rivers, flood plains and coastal flats,
is one of Australia's most extraordinary places.
A UNESCO World Heritage Area *(see pp30–31)*, Kakadu
encompasses both scenic wonders and huge galleries
of Aboriginal rock art. The park is Aboriginal land
leased back to the government *(see p63)* and is
managed jointly. The entire catchment area of
the South Alligator River lies within the park,
and is home to thousands of plant and
animal species. Some areas in Kakadu are
not accessible during the wet season.

Yellow Water
A cruise on the wetlands of Yellow Water shows
Kakadu in all its glory. Lotus lilies, crocodiles,
kookaburras, magpie geese, jabirus and other
bird species can be seen.

Flora and Fauna in Kakadu National Park

More than one-third of all bird species
recorded in Australia live in Kakadu National
Park; as do more than 60 mammal species,
117 reptile species, 1,700 plant species
and at least 10,000 insect species.
Approximately 10 per cent of the
birds are estimated to be unique
to Kakadu. Magpie geese are
especially abundant; at times there
are three million in the park, which is
60 per cent of the world's population.

The stately jabiru, seen near shallow
water in the dry season

Gunlom Waterhole
The southern and drier end of Kakadu is less visited,
but holds some magical places such as the Gunlom
plunge pool and waterfall, home to the Rainbow
Serpent, Borlung, in Aboriginal legend.

Ubirr
This rock has many Aboriginal rock art galleries, some with paintings more than 20,000 years old *(see p37)*.

VISITORS' CHECKLIST

Practical Information
Hwy 36. **W kakadu.com.au**
Bowali Visitors' Centre, Kakadu Hwy, 2.5 km (1.5 miles) S of Jabiru (08) 8938 1120.
Kakadu Cultural Tours & Guluyambi Cultural Cruise, 1800 525 238.
W kakaduculturaltours.com.au

Ranger Uranium Mine
This mine is rigorously monitored to ensure that the natural and cultural values of the park are not endangered.

Bowali Visitors' Centre
This award-winning centre features excellent displays describing the animals, Aboriginal culture and geology of Kakadu.

Nourlangie Rock
Another fine Aboriginal rock art site, this includes paintings of Namarrgon, the Lightning Man *(see p266)*.

Key

═══ Highway

▬▬▬ Major road

▪ ▪ 4WD only

▬▬ National park boundary

KEY

① **Guluyambi Cultural Cruises** take visitors up the East Alligator River with Aboriginal guides who explain local Aboriginal traditions and culture.

② **Oenpelli** is a small Aboriginal town in Arnhem Land outside Kakadu. Some day tours take visitors to this restricted area.

③ **Jabiru** is a small town that provides accommodation for visitors to the park.

Twin Falls
This waterfall (accessible by 4WD and boat transfer) is most dramatic in the wet season, when it thunders over a high plateau into rock pools. Scenic flights go over the top of these falls.

0 km   20

0 miles   20

East Alligator River

Creek

Jim Jim Falls

For keys to symbols *see back flap*

THE RED CENTRE

The Red Centre stretches roughly from Tennant Creek to the South Australian border, and is made up almost entirely of huge desert areas. The region occupies the centre of the Australian continent, with its main town, Alice Springs, at the country's geographical heart. Its signature colour is red: red sand, soil, rocks and mountains are all pitched against a typically blue sky.

The Red Centre contains some of the finest natural scenery in the world, much of it dating back about 800 million years. At that time, central Australia was covered by an inland sea; here sediments were laid down which form the basis of some of the region's best-known topographical features today. These include the huge monolith Uluru (formerly Ayers Rock), the domes of Kata Tjuta (also known as the Olgas), the giant boulders of Karlu Karlu/Devil's Marbles and the majestic MacDonnell Ranges. Between these sights are vast open spaces where remnants of tropical plant species grow beside desert-hardy stock. Verdant plants fed by occasional rains flourish next to animal skeletons.

Aboriginal people have lived in the region for more than 30,000 years, and their ancient tradition of rock painting is one of many tribal rituals still practised. By comparison, the history of white settlement here is recent. Explorers first arrived in the area during the 1860s. Alice Springs, founded in 1888, was a tiny settlement until improved communications after World War II led to the town's growth. It is now a modern, bustling town with much to offer. Tennant Creek, the only other sizeable settlement in the area, lies on the main Stuart Highway that bisects the Red Centre.

Much of the Territory has now been returned to its Aboriginal owners (see pp266–7), and today many Aborigines are actively involved in tourism. Access to Aboriginal lands is restricted but visiting them is a rewarding encounter to add to the unforgettable experience of the Red Centre.

Trekking through the desert landscape on a camel safari near Alice Springs

◀ The red monolith Uluru (Ayers Rock), sacred to the Aborigines

Exploring the Red Centre

The Red Centre's biggest draw is its stunning array of natural features. Alice Springs is the main city, with other towns at Yulara (Ayers Rock Resort) and Tennant Creek. The best time to travel is from April to October, thus avoiding the intense summer heat. The MacDonnell Ranges run like a huge spine on either side of Alice Springs; elsewhere the land is largely flat, formed by millions of years of erosion, and covered by spinifex grasslands. The region's gorges have been carved out by rivers, many of which flow only once or twice a year, soaking the surrounding desert plains.

The striking Olga Gorge in Uluru-Kata Tjuta National Park

Getting Around

There is a wide range of transport options available in central Australia. Domestic airports serve Alice Springs and Yulara. Overland, coaches connect the region with all the state capital cities, and the famous Ghan railway *(see p287)* operates between Darwin, Alice Springs and Adelaide. The most popular way to explore the region, however, is by car, and there are many car rental companies in the area. Standard vehicles are adequate for most journeys, but 4WD is advisable for off-road travel. Alternatively, many guided tours are also available. The Stuart Hwy is the main road running through the area, linking Port Augusta in South Australia with Darwin in the north. Alice Springs itself has taxis, bike hire and a town bus service, but the relatively short distances within the city also make walking popular.

Sights at a Glance

The awe-inspiring MacDonnell Ranges, on the outskirts of Alice Springs

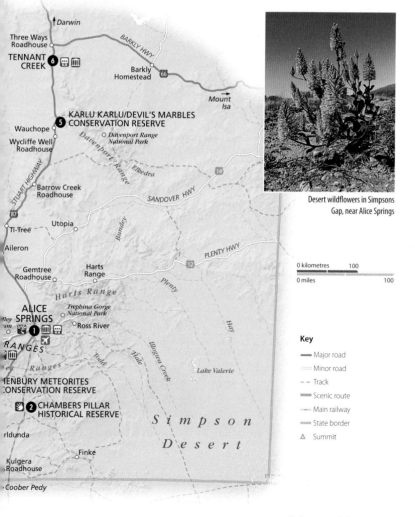

Desert wildflowers in Simpsons Gap, near Alice Springs

0 kilometres   100
0 miles   100

Key

— Major road

┄┄ Minor road

– – Track

— Scenic route

╍ Main railway

▬ State border

△ Summit

❶ Alice Springs

Alice Springs is named after the Alice Spring permanent waterhole, near which a staging post for the overland telegraph line was built in the 1870s. The waterhole was named after Alice Todd, wife of the line's construction manager. The town developed nearby in the 1880s, but, with no rail link until 1929 and no surfaced road link until the 1940s, it grew slowly. The huge increase in tourism since the 1970s, however, has brought rapid growth and Alice Springs is now a lively city with around 400,000 visitors a year, many of whom use it as a base from which to tour the surrounding spectacular natural sights.

Out-of-service plane exhibited at the Royal Flying Doctor Service Visitor Centre

Exploring Alice Springs

Although many of its sights are spread around the city, Alice Springs is small enough to tour on foot. Its compact centre, just five streets across running from Wills Terrace in the north to Stuart Terrace in the south, contains many of the town's hotels and restaurants and the pedestrianized Todd Mall. The city's eastern side is bordered by Todd River, dry and sandy most of the time and scene of the celebrated Henley-on-Todd Regatta (see p47).

🏕 Anzac Hill
Anzac Hill Rd. 🚹

At the northern end of Alice Springs, Anzac Hill overlooks the city and affords fine views of the MacDonnell Ranges (see p288). Named after the 1934 Anzac memorial at the site, the hill is a perfect vantage point for visitors to familiarize themselves with the city's layout, as well as for viewing the area at sunrise or sunset.

🏛 Old Courthouse
Cnr Parsons & Hartley sts. **Tel** (08) 8953 6073. **Open** on request. 🏞 🚹
Built in 1928 by Emil Martin, also responsible for The Residency, the Old Courthouse was in use until 1980, when new law courts were opened nearby.

🏛 Old Stuart Town Gaol
8 Parsons St. **Tel** (08) 8953 6073. **Open** Wed, Thu & Sat. **Closed** mid-Dec–1 Feb, public hols. 🏞 🚹
🌐 heritagealicesprings.com.au
The oldest building in central Alice Springs is the Old Stuart Town Gaol, which operated as a jail between 1909 and 1938, when a new prison was built on

Stuart Terrace. The gaol is now open to the public, but call ahead to be granted access.

Old Stuart Town Gaol, the oldest building in Alice Springs

🏛 The Residency
Cnr Parsons & Hartley sts. **Tel** (08) 8953 6073. **Open** 10am–3pm Mon–Fri. **Closed** Dec–Mar, public hols.
🏞 Donation. 🌐 heritagealice springs.com.au

The Residency, built in 1927 for the regional administrator of Central Australia, was the home of Alice Springs' senior public servant until 1973. It was opened to the public in 1996 and houses a local history display.

🏛 Adelaide House Museum
Todd Mall. **Tel** (08) 8952 1856. **Open** 10am–4pm Mon–Sat. **Closed** Good Fri. 🏞 🚹

Adelaide House Museum, Alice Springs' first hospital, opened in 1926. Designed by John Flynn, founder of the Royal Flying Doctor Service (see p261), it is preserved as a museum dedicated to his memory.

🏛 Royal Flying Doctor Service Visitor Centre
8–10 Stuart Terrace. **Tel** (08) 8958 8412. **Open** 9am–5pm Mon–Sat, 1–5pm Sun & public hols. **Closed** 25 Dec, 1 Jan. 🏞 🎧 obligatory. 🖥 📷
🚹 🌐 rfdsalicesprings.com.au

The centre can only be visited accompanied by a guide, and visitors are taken on a 45-minute tour of the base that includes the Radio Communications centre, where staff recount the history of the Service and explain the day-to-day operations. There is also a museum, containing old medical equipment, model aircraft and an original Traeger Pedal Radio. The Visitor Centre opened in the late 1970s but has been extended to include a café and a souvenir shop.

🏛 National Pioneer Women's Hall of Fame
Old Alice Springs Gaol, 2 Stuart Tce. **Tel** (08) 8952 9006. **Open** 10am–5pm daily. **Closed** late Dec–early Feb. 🏞
🚹 🌐 pioneerwomen.com.au

The displays in this museum document the achievements of Australia's pioneering women.

🏛 Museum of Central Australia
Alice Springs Cultural Precinct, Memorial Ave. **Tel** (08) 8951 1121. **Open** 10am–4pm Mon–Fri, 11am–4pm Sat & Sun. **Closed** Good Fri, two weeks over Christmas. 🏞 🚹
🌐 magnt.net. au/museum-of-central-australia

Meteorite fragment in the Museum of Central Australia

This museum, situated in the Cultural Precinct, focuses on

A scenic landscape view of the water's edge at Alice Springs

town and features three habitat
types: desert river, sand country
and woodlands. Visitors may
see many of the birds and
animals of Central Australia
here at close range.

local natural history with displays
of fossils, flora and fauna,
meteorite pieces and minerals.
It also houses fine pieces of
Aboriginal art and artifacts.

🚂 Alice Springs Telegraph Station Historical Reserve
Off Stuart Hwy. **Tel** (08) 8952 3993.
Open 9am–5pm daily. **Closed** 25 Dec.

This, the site of the first settlement in Alice Springs, features
the original buildings and

equipment of the telegraph
station built in 1871. A small
museum describes the task of
setting up the station and running the overland telegraph.

🏞 Alice Springs Desert Park
Off Larapinta Drive. **Tel** (08) 8951 8788.
Open 7:30am–6pm daily (last entry
4:30pm). **Closed** 25 Dec. 🅿 ♿
w alicespringsdesertpark.com.au

An excellent introduction to
Central Australia, this park lies
on the western edge of the

🏛 National Road Transport Hall of Fame
1 Norris Bell Ave. **Tel** (08) 8952
7161. **Open** 9am–5pm daily.
Closed 1 Jan, 25 Dec.
w roadtransporthall.com

This museum pays homage to
all the great trucks, buses and
other vehicles that have crossed
the Australian continent. The
Ghan, the first train to run from
Adelaide to Alice Springs in
1929, is commemorated with
a fascinating collection of
vintage memorabilia.

Alice Springs Town Centre

① Anzac Hill
② Old Courthouse
③ Old Stuart Town Gaol
④ The Residency
⑤ Adelaide House Museum
⑥ Royal Flying Doctor Service
 Visitor Centre
⑦ National Pioneer Women's
 Hall of Fame
⑧ Museum of Central
 Australia

❷ Chambers Pillar Historical Reserve

Tel (08) 8951 8250. 🚗 Alice Springs. 🚌 Alice Springs. 📷
🌐 **nt.gov.au**

Chambers Pillar, a 50-m (165-ft) high sandstone obelisk, was used by explorers as an important navigational landmark during early colonial exploration. The pillar is made of mixed red and yellow sandstone deposited more than 350 million years ago. Many of the explorers, such as John Ross who visited the area in 1870, carved their names and inscriptions into the rock.

Located 160 km (110 miles) south of Alice Springs, with the final section of the journey accessible only by 4WD vehicles, the pillar is also a sacred Aboriginal site.

❸ Henbury Meteorites Conservation Reserve

Tel (08) 8951 8250. 🚗 Alice Springs. 🚌 Alice Springs. 📷 🌐 **nt.gov.au**

This cluster of 12 craters, located 145 km (89 miles) southwest of Alice Springs, was formed by a meteorite which crashed to earth several thousand years ago. It is believed that local Aborigines witnessed the event, as one of the Aboriginal names for the area suggests a fiery rock falling to earth. The largest crater in the group is 180 m (590 ft) across and is 15 m (50 ft) deep. Signs on a trail mark significant features.

Lush Palm Valley in Finke Gorge National Park, MacDonnell Ranges

❹ MacDonnell Ranges

🚗 Alice Springs. 🚌 Alice Springs. ℹ️ Alice Springs (08) 8951 8250. Simpsons Gap: **Open** daily. ♿ Standley Chasm: **Open** daily. 📷 ♿ 🌐 **nt.gov.au**

The MacDonnell Ranges are the eroded remnants of an ancient mountain chain which was once as monumental as the Himalayas. Still impressive and filled with striking scenery, the East and West MacDonnells contain gorges, waterholes and walking tracks. Running east and west of Alice Springs and easily accessible, they are popular with day-trippers. Visitors will notice the layers of rock thrust up in the ranges, evidence of geological movements more than 300 million years ago. Culturally, they contain many areas sacred to the Aranda people.

In the West MacDonnells, 7 km (4 miles) from Alice Springs, is John Flynn's Memorial Grave, which honours Presbyterian minister, Rev John Flynn, who founded the Royal Flying Doctor Service *(see p261)*.

A further 10 km (6 miles) from town, **Simpsons Gap** is the first of a series of attractive gorges in the MacDonnells. A pretty spot, it is home to some rare local plant species. Nearby is **Standley Chasm**, a narrow, deep gorge whose sheer rock-faces glow a glorious red, particularly under the midday sun.

The large 18-m (60-ft) deep permanent waterhole within Ellery Gorge at Ellery Creek Big Hole is a good swimming spot. Serpentine Gorge, 20 km (12 miles) further west, is another narrow gorge created by an ancient river. A walking track leading to a lookout gives a fine view of its winding path.

Pushed up out of Ormiston Creek, the 300-m (985-ft) high walls of Ormiston Gorge are an awesome sight. The gorge consists of two layers of quartzite, literally doubled over each other, thus making it twice the height of others in the region.

Along Larapinta Drive is the small Aboriginal settlement of Hermannsburg, site of an 1870s Lutheran Mission which pre-dates Alice Springs. Famous as the home of the popular Aboriginal painter Albert Namatjira (1902–59), most of the town is contained within the **Hermannsburg Historic Precinct**, which includes a museum devoted to the mission and an art gallery. Twenty km (12 miles) south of here lies

Sacred site of Corroboree Rock in the East MacDonnell Ranges near Alice Springs

For hotels and restaurants in this area see pp489–90 and pp518–19

the popular **Finke Gorge National Park**, home to Palm Valley, an unusual tropical oasis in the dry heart of the country with rare, ancient palm species.

On the other side of Alice Springs, the East MacDonnell Ranges boast some beautiful sites accessible via the Ross Highway. Close to town is Emily Gap, one of the most significant Aranda sites in Australia. Further east, Corroboree Rock, a strangely shaped outcrop, has a crevice once used to store sacred Aranda objects. Trephina Gorge is the most spectacular of the East MacDonnell sights, with quartzite cliffs and red river gums.

🏛 **Hermannsburg Historic Precinct**
Larapinta Drive. **Tel** (08) 8956 7402. **Open** daily. **Closed** Good Fri, 25 Dec.
🅿 👤 **W** hermannsburg.com.au

🌳 **Finke Gorge National Park**
Tel (08) 8951 8250. 🅿 🚌 Alice Springs. **W** nt.gov.au

Spherical boulders of the Devil's Marbles

❺ Karlu Karlu/ Devil's Marbles Conservation Reserve

Tel (08) 8951 8250, Tennant Creek Office (08) 8962 4599. 🚌 from Tennant Creek Tourist Information. 👤 📷

Approximately 104 km (65 miles) south of Tennant Creek, this reserve features a series of huge, spherical, red-granite boulders, scattered across a shallow valley in the Davenport Ranges. The result of geological activity from 1,700 million years ago, the boulders were created when molten lava was compressed to create huge domes just below the earth's surface. Subsequent erosion of the overlying rock exposed the marbles.

Mining building at Battery Hill, Tennant Creek

❻ Tennant Creek

🏔 3,500. ✈ 🚌 **i** Battery Hill Mining Complex, Peko Rd (08) 8962 1281.

Tennant Creek was chosen as the site of a telegraph station on the Overland Telegraph Line in 1872. The town grew after gold was discovered in the area in 1932. The **Battery Hill Mining Centre** has two museums and an underground mine. The complex also houses the Tennant Creek Visitor Information Centre.

Tennant Creek today is the second-largest town in the Red Centre. Nearly 500 km (310 miles) north of Alice Springs, it is also a major stopover along the Stuart Highway, between Darwin and South Australia. Other local attractions include the recreational Lake Mary Ann, 5 km (3 miles) out of town and ideal for sailing and swimming. The remote **Tennant Creek Telegraph Station**, 12 km (8 miles) north of the town, built in 1874, is now a museum.

🏛 **Battery Hill Mining Centre**
Battery Hill, Peko Rd. **Tel** (08) 8962 1281. **Open** daily. **Closed** Good Fri; 7, 8 & 25 Dec. 📷 👤 📷

🏛 **Tennant Creek Telegraph Station**
Stuart Highway. **Tel** (08) 8962 4599.

❼ Kings Canyon

🚗 Alice Springs. 🚌 Alice Springs, Yulara. **i** Alice Springs (08) 8951 8250. **W** nt.gov.au

The spectacular sandstone gorge of Kings Canyon, set within Watarrka National Park, has walls more than 100 m (330 ft) high that have been formed by millions of years of erosion. They contain the fossilized tracks of ancient marine creatures, and even ripplemarks of an ancient sea are visible. Several walking tracks take visitors around the rim of the gorge where there are some stunning views of the valley below. Watarrka National Park has many waterholes and areas of lush vegetation that contain more than 600 plant species. The park also provides a habitat for more than 100 bird species and 60 species of reptiles.

Rich vegetation deep in the sandstone gorge of Kings Canyon

❽ Uluṟu-Kata Tjuṯa National Park

The most instantly recognizable of all Australian symbols is the huge, red monolith of Uluṟu (Ayers Rock). Rising high above the flat desert landscape, Uluṟu is one of the world's natural wonders, along with the 36 rock domes of Kata Tjuṯa (The Olgas) and their deep valleys and gorges. Both sights are in Uluṟu-Kata Tjuṯa National Park, 463 km (288 miles) southwest of Alice Springs, which was established in 1958 and was named as a World Heritage site in 1987 *(see pp30–31)*. The whole area is sacred to Aboriginal people and, in 1985, the park was handed back to its indigenous owners and its sights reassumed their traditional names. As Aboriginal land, it is leased back to the Australian government and jointly managed with the local Anangu people. Within the park is an excellent cultural centre which details the Aboriginal lives and traditions of the area. Yulara, 12 km (7 miles) from Uluṟu, is the park's growing tourist resort *(see p293)*.

The Maruku Gallery
This Aboriginal-owned gallery sells traditional and modern Aboriginal crafts.

Kata Tjuṯa (The Olgas)
This magnificent view of Kata Tjuṯa's domes is from the sunset viewing area. The site has drinking water and interpretive panels giving information on local flora and fauna.

KEY

① **Kata Tjuṯa's** domes rise in the distance behind Uluṟu.

② **Uluṟu** is famous for its colour changes, which range from deep red at sunrise and sunset to shiny black after rain.

③ **Vegetation** is sparse on this desert plain except for a few areas of greenery found in sheltered spots where rainwater collects.

Uluṟu-Kata Tjuṯa National Park

Guided walks *(see p292)* around Uluṟu teach visitors about the desert flora and fauna, and explain the awesome landscape and its deep cultural significance.

Sunset viewing area

Kata Tjuṯa

Yulara Resort

Sunset viewing area

AIRPORT

Key
▬▬ Major road
▭▭ Minor road
- - Walking track

0 km 5
0 miles 2

Kantju Gorge

Uluṟu

Cultural Centre

Olga Gorge
This scenic gorge runs between two of Kata Tjuta's huge domes. A walking track leads to a cliff face at the end where there is a rock pool and a trickling stream.

Hare Wallaby
This mammal is significant to the Anangu people, who call it *Mala*. According to tradition, Mala people lived at Uluru and created many of the rock formations that are seen today.

Dehydration in the Desert

Uluru-Kata Tjuta National Park is in the heart of Australia's vast desert region. It can experience summer daytime temperatures of more than 45°C (113°F). To avoid dehydration and heat exhaustion all visitors are advised to wear hats, long-sleeved shirts with collars and sunscreen, and to avoid any strenuous activity between 10am and 4pm. Most importantly, each person should drink one litre of water per hour while walking in hot weather.

Mala Walk
This free, ranger-guided walk leads visitors to places created and used by the ancestral Mala people. It ends at Kantju Gorge, sacred to the Anangu, which contains a waterhole beneath a waterfall.

Exploring Uluṟu-Kata Tjuṯa National Park

It is impossible to arrive at Uluṟu-Kata Tjuṯa National Park and not be filled with awe. The sheer size of the world's largest monolith, Uluṟu, rising from the flat desert plain, is a moving and impressive sight. Just as magical are the rounded humps of Kata Tjuṯa not far distant. All the rocks change colour from oranges and reds to purple during the day. Getting around the park, understanding some of its deep Aboriginal significance and learning about its geology, flora and fauna should not be rushed. There is much more to this fascinating area than can be seen or experienced in one day, and a two- or three-day stay is recommended.

Tourists enjoying the Mala walk around part of the base of Uluṟu

Blue-tongued lizard basking in the sun

🔆 Uluṟu (Ayers Rock)

Uluṟu, 3.6 km (2.25 miles) long and 2.4 km (1.5 miles) wide, stands 348 m (1,142 ft) above the plains. It is a single piece of sandstone extending 5 km (3 miles) beneath the desert surface. Besides its immense Aboriginal cultural significance, Uluṟu is an outstanding natural phenomenon, best observed by watching its changing colours at dusk and taking a guided walk at the rock's base.

There are a number of walking trails around Uluṟu. The three-hour, 9.5-km (6-mile) tour around the base gives the greatest sense of its size and majesty. Sacred sights en route are fenced off, and entering is an offence. The Mala (hare wallaby) walk takes in several caves, some with rock art. The Liru (snake) walk starts at the cultural centre, with Aboriginal tour guides explaining how they use bush materials in their daily lives. The Kuniya (python) walk visits the Mutijulu waterhole on the southern side of Uluṟu where local Anangu people tell creation stories and display art describing various

legends. Details of all walks can be found at the Uluṟu-Kata Tjuṯa Cultural Centre.

🔆 Kata Tjuṯa (The Olgas)

Kata Tjuṯa, meaning "many heads", is a collection of massive rounded rock domes, 42 km (25 miles) to the west of Uluṟu. Beyond lies a vast, remote desert; permits from the Central

Land Council *(see p266)*, 4WDs and full travel survival kits are needed in this inhospitable land.

Kata Tjuṯa is not one large rock; it is a system of gorges and valleys that you can walk around, making it a haunting, quiet and spiritual place. To the Anangu people, it is of equal significance to Uluṟu, but fewer stories about it can be told as they are restricted to initiated tribal men. The tallest rock, Mount Olga, is 546 m (1,790 ft) high, nearly 200 m (660 ft) higher than Uluṟu. There are two recommended walking trails. The Valley of the Winds walk takes about three hours and wanders through several deep gorges. This walk is partially closed when the temperature exceeds 36°C (97°F).

Climbing Uluṟu

The climbing of Uluṟu by the chain-rope path that has been in place since the 1960s is a contentious issue. Physically, it is a steep, 1.6-km (1-mile) climb in harsh conditions, and several tourists die each year from heart attacks or falls. Culturally, the route to the top follows the sacred path taken by the ancestral Mala (hare wallaby) men for important ceremonies. The Anangu ask that visitors respect their wishes and do not climb the rock; a push to ban all climbing on Uluṟu is now gathering pace.

If you do decide to climb, the ascent takes about two hours. Climbing the rock is banned for the remainder of the day if the temperature reaches 36°C (97°F) at any point of the climb. A dawn climb is most popular.

Sign warning tourists of the dangers of climbing Uluṟu

For hotels and restaurants in this area see pp489–90 and pp518–19

The Anangu of Uluru

Archaeological evidence suggests that Aboriginal people have lived at Uluru for at least 22,000 years and that both Uluru and Kata Tjuta have long been places of enormous ceremonial and cultural significance to a number of Aboriginal tribes.

The traditional owners of Uluru and Kata Tjuta are the Anangu people. They believe that both sites were formed during the creation period by ancestral spirits who also gave them the laws and rules of society that they live by today. The Anangu believe they are direct descendants of these ancestral beings and that, as such, they are responsible for the protection and management of these lands.

The Anangu Aborigines performing a traditional dance

The Olga Gorge (Walpa Gorge) walk leads up the pretty Olga Gorge to its dead-end cliff face and a rock pool. Walkers here may spot the small brown spinifex bird or the thorny devil spiked lizard.

🏛 Uluru-Kata Tjuta Cultural Centre

Tel (08) 8956 1128. **Open** 7am–6pm (last entry 5:30pm) daily. Information desk: 8am–5pm. 🅿 ♿
W parksaustralia.gov.au/uluru

Near to the base of Uluru is an award-winning cultural centre, with multilingual displays, videos and exhibitions. It is an excellent introduction to the park and well worth visiting before exploring the rock and its surrounding area. The Nintiringkupai display focuses on the history and management of Uluru-Kata Tjuta National Park and includes up-to-date brochures and information on walking trails, sights and tours. The Tjukurpa display, with its art, sounds and videos, is a good introduction to the complex system of Anangu beliefs and laws. Attached to the cultural centre is the Aboriginal-owned Maruku Arts and Craft

shop, where artists are at work and dancers and musicians give performances for tourists. The traditional art, on bark and canvas, tells the story of Uluru Tjukurpa legends.

Ayers Rock Resort

Yulara Drive. ℹ 1300 134 044.
W ayersrockresort.com.au
Yulara is an environmentally friendly, modern tourist village well equipped to cater for the 500,000 annual visitors. Nestling between the desert dunes 20 km (12 miles) north of Uluru and just outside the national park boundary, it serves as a comfortable, green and relaxing base for exploring Uluru and Kata Tjuta. The resort offers all standards of accommodation, from five-star luxury to backpacker accommodation and camping grounds, and is the only option for those who want to stay in the immediate vicinity (see pp489–90).

The visitors' centre at Yulara has information about the park and its geology, flora and fauna. It also sells souvenirs and helps to arrange tours with the licensed operators in the park. Every day at 7:30am there is a free guided walk through the wonderful native garden of the Desert Gardens Hotel (174 Yulara Drive; Tel: 08 8957 7714). Each evening at the Amphitheatre there is an hour-long concert of Aboriginal music featuring a variety of indigenous instruments, including the didgeridoo. A stargazing Astro Tour combining mythology and astronomy is also available – the low humidity and minimal unnatural light provide excellent viewing conditions.

Yulara also has a shopping centre, which includes a post office, bank and supermarket, and many different restaurants and outdoor eating options (see pp518–19). Other facilities include a childcare centre for children up to the age of eight.

Aerial view of Yulara Resort, with Uluru in the distance

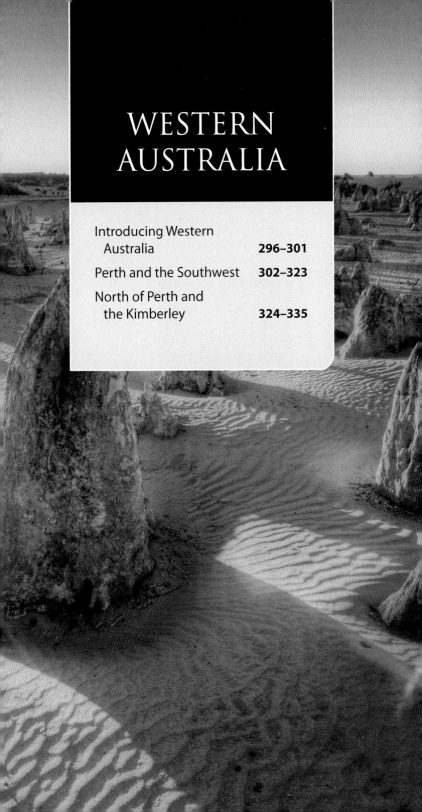

WESTERN AUSTRALIA

Western Australia at a Glance

The huge state of Western Australia encompasses a land mass of more than 2,500,000 sq km (1,000,000 sq miles). In recent years, the state's popularity as a tourist destination has increased, with large numbers of visitors drawn to its many areas of extreme natural beauty. The landscape ranges from giant karri forests, imposing mountains and meadows of wildflowers to vast expanses of untamed wilderness with ancient gorges and rock formations. The coastline has an abundance of beaches, ideal for surfing, and some stunning offshore reefs. In the east, great deserts stretch to the state border. The capital, Perth, is home to 80 per cent of the state's population, but there are many historic towns scattered around the southwest, such as the gold field settlements of Kalgoorlie and Coolgardie.

Locator Map

Karijini National Park is in the Pilbara region and is a spectacular landscape of gorges, pools and waterfalls. The area is particularly popular with experienced hikers; guided tours are also available for more novice bushwalkers *(see p333)*.

Shark Bay World Heritage and Marine Park is Australia's westernmost point. Visitors flock to this protected area to watch the dolphins swim in the waters close to the shore *(see pp330–31)*.

Port Hedland

Exmouth

Coral Bay

Carnarvon

Meekath

Mount Magr

Kalbarri

Geraldton

Perth is Australia's most isolated yet most modern state capital. Gleaming skyscrapers, an easy-going atmosphere and its coastal setting make it a popular destination *(see pp306–11)*.

Perth

Frer

Mandurah

Bunbury

Busselton

Fremantle's heyday as a major port was at the end of the 19th century. Many of its historic buildings remain. Today the town is renowned for its crafts markets *(see pp314–15)*.

◀ Dawn at the Pinnacles, in Nambung National Park

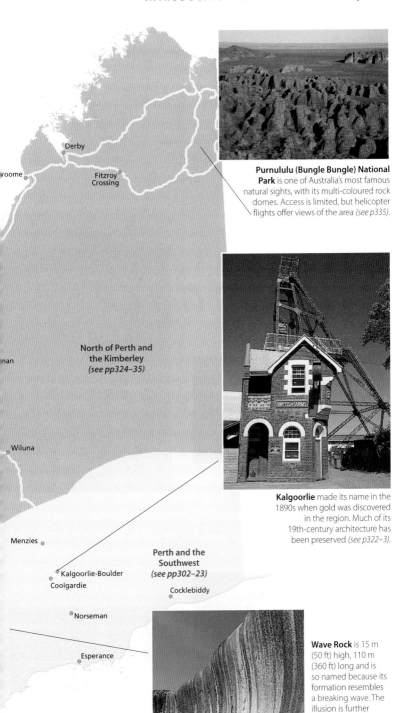

Purnululu (Bungle Bungle) National Park is one of Australia's most famous natural sights, with its multi-coloured rock domes. Access is limited, but helicopter flights offer views of the area (*see p335*).

Derby

roome

Fitzroy Crossing

North of Perth and the Kimberley
(*see pp324–35*)

nan

Wiluna

Kalgoorlie made its name in the 1890s when gold was discovered in the region. Much of its 19th-century architecture has been preserved (*see p322–3*).

Menzies

Perth and the Southwest
(*see pp302–23*)

Kalgoorlie-Boulder
Coolgardie

Cocklebiddy

Norseman

Esperance

Wave Rock is 15 m (50 ft) high, 110 m (360 ft) long and is so named because its formation resembles a breaking wave. The illusion is further enhanced by years' worth of water stains running down its face (*see p322*).

bany

0 kilometres   200
0 miles   200

Wildflowers of Western Australia

Western Australia is truly the nation's wildflower state. In the spring, from June to November, more than 12,000 species of flowers burst into brilliantly coloured blooms, carpeting deserts, plains, farmland and forests with blazing reds, yellows, pinks and blues.

A staggering 60 per cent of these flowers are unique to the state, giving it one of the world's richest floras. It is home to such remarkable plants as the kangaroo paw, the cowslip orchid and the carnivorous Albany pitcher plant, as well as giant jarrah and karri forests.

The elegant kangaroo paw looks exactly like its name suggests. The state's floral emblem, it has many different species and mostly grows in coastal heath and dry woodland areas.

When and Where to see the Wildflowers

Bushwalking or driving among the flower carpets of Western Australia is an experience not to be missed. Most of the wildflowers bloom in spring, but exactly when depends on their location in this vast state. The wildflower season begins in the northern Pilbara in July and culminates in the magnificent flowering around the Stirling Ranges and the south coast in late October and November.

The Albany pitcher plant grows near coastal estuaries around Albany in the southwest. One of the world's largest carnivorous plants, it traps and devours insects in its sticky hairs.

The magnificent royale hakea is one of many hakea species in Western Australia. It is found on the coast near Esperance and in Fitzgerald River National Park.

Red flowering gum trees in the Stirling Ranges burst into bright red flowers every November, attracting honey bees.

The cowslip orchid is a bright yellow orchid with red streaks and five main petals. It can usually be found in October, in the dramatic Stirling Ranges region.

Much of Western Australia is arid, dusty outback country where the only vegetation is dry bush shrubs and, after rainfall, wildflowers.

Many wild flowers possess an incredible ability to withstand even the driest, hottest ground.

Leschenaultia biloba is a brilliant blue, bell-shaped flower found in jarrah forests near Collie, or in drier bush and plain country where it flowers in carpets of blue.

The boab tree is a specimen related to the African baobab. Growing in the rocky plains of Kimberley *(see pp300–301),* it holds a great deal of water in its swollen trunk and can grow many metres in circumference.

The bright daisy flowers of the everlastings come in a host of creams, pinks, yellows, oranges and reds.

Giants of the Western Australian Forest

It is not only the native flowers that are special to Western Australia. So, too, are the trees – especially the towering jarrah and karri eucalypts of the southern forests. A major hardwood timber industry, harvesting the jarrah and karri, remains in the state's southwest near Manjimup and Pemberton. Today, however, thousands of trees are preserved in national parks such as Shannon and Walpole-Nornalup, which has a walkway high in the trees for visitors.

Giant karri trees grow to a height of 85 m. They live for up to 300 years, reaching their maximum height after 100 years.

Everlasting Flowers

Native to Australia, everlastings carpet vast areas in many parts of Western Australia. Especially prolific in the southeast, they can also be seen from the roadside in the north, stretching as far as the eye can see.

Everlastings are so called because the petals stay attached to the flower even after it has died.

The scarlet banksia, is one of 41 banksia species found in Western Australia. It is named after Sir Joseph Banks, the botanist who first noted this unusual tree and its flower in 1770.

Sturt's desert pea is actually South Australia's floral emblem, but is also prolific in the dry inland areas of Western Australia. Its bright flowers spring up after rain in the deserts, sometimes after lying dormant for years.

The Kimberley

One of the last truly remote regions in Australia, the Kimberley in northwestern Australia covers 423,000 sq km (164,000 sq miles), yet has a population of less than 40,000. Geologically it is one of the oldest regions on earth. Its rocks formed up to 2,000 million years ago, with little landscape disturbance since. Aboriginal people have lived here for thousands of years, but this unique land has been a tourist attraction only since the 1980s.

Key

⎯ Highway
▬ Major road
⎯ Unsealed road
— National park boundary

The Bungle Bungles

The tiger-striped beehive mountains that comprise the Bungle Bungle range were only discovered by tourists in the 1980s. These great geological and scenic wonders are now protected in Purnululu National Park *(see p335)*. The large, weathered sandstone domes are most easily viewed by air from Kununurra or Halls Creek, but visitors who make the effort to explore this 4WD-only park will also encounter some stunning narrow gorges and clear pools.

The black and orange moulded domes of the Bungle Bungles

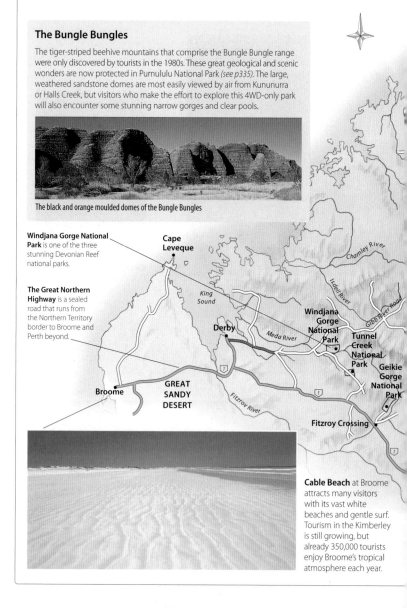

Windjana Gorge National Park is one of the three stunning Devonian Reef national parks.

The Great Northern Highway is a sealed road that runs from the Northern Territory border to Broome and Perth beyond.

Cape Leveque

King Sound

Derby

Broome

GREAT SANDY DESERT

Chamley River

Isdell River

Gibb River Road

Windjana Gorge National Park

Meda River

Tunnel Creek National Park

Geikie Gorge National Park

Fitzroy River

Fitzroy Crossing

Cable Beach at Broome attracts many visitors with its vast white beaches and gentle surf. Tourism in the Kimberley is still growing, but already 350,000 tourists enjoy Broome's tropical atmosphere each year.

The Cockburn Ranges have deep, inaccessible caves and sandstone cliffs separating the summit from the surrounding plains. The ranges tower above the crocodile-infested Pentecost River on the Gibb River Road. As with many sites in the region, they hold great Aboriginal significance.

The Aborigines of the Kimberley

Legend suggests that the first Aborigines arrived on the continent, near Broome, 200,000 years ago (see p51). While this is not confirmed by scientific evidence (which points more towards 55,000 years ago), the fact that many of the "songlines" (see p35) marked by landmarks and ceremonial sites end or start around the Kimberley suggests the area has long been inhabited by humans.

Around 44 per cent of the region's population remains Aboriginal, and Aboriginal culture here is one of the most traditional in Australia. Local Aboriginal communities equip their children with a strong identity to help them cope with the demands of living in a mixed-race society.

Aboriginal art in the Kimberley differs from most other parts of Australia. Instead of dot art, there are the outstanding Wandjina figures of the central Kimberley and the object paintings of the Purnululu community based near the Bungle Bungles.

The mysterious Wandjina figures can be seen throughout the Kimberley region.

Aboriginal rock art in the Kimberley has now been dated back to around 50,000 to 60,000 years ago.

Timor Sea

DRYSDALE RIVER NATIONAL PARK

Wyndham

Kununurra

Lake Argyle

Pentecost River

PURNULULU NATIONAL PARK

Halls Creek

Great Northern Highway

0 km   100

0 miles   100

Gibb River Road is a rough highway which is used by locals and adventurous travellers.

Emma Gorge is one of hundreds of deep, cool waterholes hidden across the Kimberley. Located near El Questro Station, it was made by waterfalls cascading off the red sandstone plateau into gorges and valleys below.

PERTH AND THE SOUTHWEST

Western Australia's pretty capital, Perth, is the most isolated city in the world, closer to Southeast Asia than it is to any other Australian city. The state's stunning southern region takes in magnificent forests and diverse coastal scenery. To the east, the vast Nullarbor Plain covers more than 250,000 sq km (100,000 sq miles), and rolling wheat fields lead to the arid interior and the gold fields.

Aborigines have lived in the southern region of Western Australia for at least 30,000 years. However, within 20 years of the settlement of the state's first European colony, in 1829, most Aboriginal groups had been either forcibly ejected from the region, imprisoned or stricken by European diseases.

Europeans visited the southern part of the state as early as 1696, but it was not until 1826 that British colonist Captain James Stirling arrived in the Swan River area, declaring the Swan River Colony, later Perth, in 1829. Convicts arrived in 1850 and helped to build public buildings and the colony's infrastructure, until transportation to Western Australia ceased in 1868.

In the 1890s, gold strikes in Coolgardie and Kalgoorlie led to a wave of prosperity in the region. Many ornate late Victorian-style buildings were erected, several of which are still standing.

The beginning of the 20th century saw huge changes: a telegraph cable was laid connecting Perth with South Africa and London, and, in 1917, the railway arrived to join Kalgoorlie with the eastern states. In the 1920s, immigrants and returning World War I servicemen were drafted to the area to clear and develop land under the Group Settlement Scheme. Much of the land, however, was intractable and many people abandoned it.

Today, Perth and the Southwest are fast becoming popular international tourist destinations. Blessed with superb beaches and a glorious climate, the region has everything to offer visitors from climbing the tallest fire-lookout tree in the country to whale-watching along the coast. World-class wineries abound in the Margaret River region and, in springtime, vast tracts of the south are covered with wildflowers.

Dramatic beauty of the Stirling Ranges rising from the plains in the southwest of the state

◀ Architectural contrast of Victorian and modern buildings in Perth

Exploring Perth and the Southwest

The city of Perth lies on the Swan River, just 20 km (12 miles) from where it flows into the Indian Ocean. The coastal plain on which it stands is bordered to the north and west by the Darling Range, beyond which lie the region's wheat fields. To the south is a diverse landscape: forests with some of the tallest trees on earth, mountains that dramatically change colour during the course of each day and a spectacular coastline. Inland are the gold fields that kept the colony alive in the 1890s; beyond lies the Nullarbor Plain, bordering the raging Southern Ocean.

Beach and raging surf in Leeuwin Naturaliste National Park, near the mouth of the Margaret River

Getting Around

Perth's public transport is fast and reliable, and travel by bus within the city centre is free. TransWa, Greyhound and Skywest (a state-based airline) offer rail, coach and air services to many of the region's towns. Distances are not overwhelming, so travelling by car allows visits to the many national parks in the area. The arterial routes are fast roads often used by gigantic road trains. However, there are many tourist routes which lead to places of interest and great natural beauty. Some national parks have unsealed roads, and a few are accessible only by 4WD.

Sights at a Glance

0 kilometres   50

0 miles   5

Mt Magne

Geraldton   New Norci

Ledge Point

Guilderton   Gingin

Yanchep   Muchea

Wanneroo

Sorrento

PERTH 1

ROTTNEST 2   3 FREM
ISLAND

Rockingham

Mandurah   Pinja

Harvey

Australind   Bruns
Junc

BUNBURY 4

Tuart Forest   Boyanup
National Park

Dunsborough   Donr

Yallingup   5 BUSSELTON

Ellensbrook
Homestead

MARGARET RIVER 6   BRIDGETOW

Nannup

Leeuwin-Naturaliste   MAN
National Park   Glenoran Falls

Hamelin Bay   Augusta

Cape   PEMBERTON
Leeuwin

D'Entr
Natio

Windy Harbo

Sweeping panoramic view of Perth, the capital of Western Australia

Locator Map

- Perth and the Southwest
- The Goldfields and Nullarbor Plain pp322–3

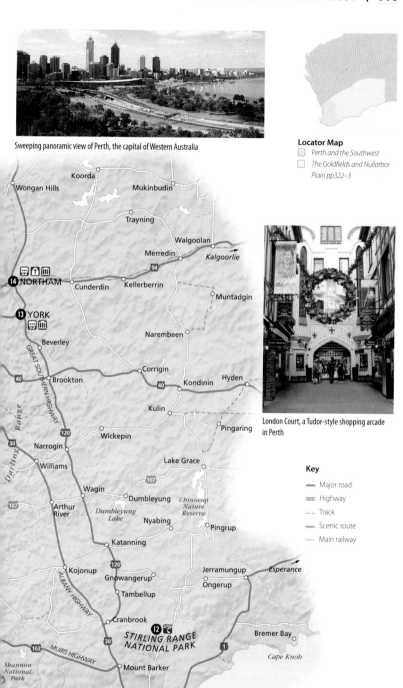

London Court, a Tudor-style shopping arcade in Perth

Koorda
Wongan Hills
Mukinbudin
Trayning
Walgoolan
Merredin
Kalgoorlie
94
14 NORTHAM
Cunderdin
Kellerberrin
Muntadgin
13 YORK
Beverley
Narembeen
GREAT SOUTHERN HIGHWAY
Corrigin
40
Brookton
40
Kondinin
Hyden
Kulin
Pingaring
120
Wickepin
Narrogin
Williams
Lake Grace
Wagin
107
Darling Range
30
Dumbleyung
Chinocup Nature Reserve
Arthur River
Dumbleyung Lake
Nyabing
107
Pingrup
Katanning
120
Kojonup
Jerramungup
Esperance
Gnowangerup
Ongerup
ALBANY HIGHWAY
Tambellup
Cranbrook
12 STIRLING RANGE NATIONAL PARK
Bremer Bay
Cape Knob
102
MUIRS HIGHWAY
30
Shannon National Park
Mount Barker
1
DENMARK 10
Cheyne Beach
Walpole
Cape Vancouver
Nornalup
11 ALBANY

Key

- — Major road
- — Highway
- -- Track
- — Scenic route
- — Main railway

❶ Street-by-Street: Perth

The history of Perth has been one of building and rebuilding. The makeshift houses of the first settlers were soon replaced with more permanent buildings, many erected by convicts in the latter half of the 1800s. The gold rush of the 1890s and the mining boom of the 1960s and 70s brought waves of prosperity, reflected in the replacement of older buildings. As a result, much of the early city has gone, but a few traces remain, hidden between skyscrapers or in the city's public parks.

The Bell Tower

Barrack Square

BARRA

RIVERSIDE DRIVE

TERRACE ROAD

Elizabeth Quay
Opened in January 2016, Elizabeth Quay is full of public art, and there is always something new to see and do. There are also plenty of food options nearby.

Supreme Court Gardens

Government House
Hidden behind walls and trees, the original residence of the state governor was built by convicts between 1859 and 1864. The building's patterned brickwork is typical of the period.

The Deanery
Built in 1859, the Deanery was originally the residence of the Dean of St George's. It now houses the Cathedral administration.

For hotels and restaurants in this area see p490 and pp519–21

★ St George's Anglican Cathedral
This Victorian Gothic Revival-style cathedral, built in the late 19th century, has a fine rose window (see p308).

0 metres 100

0 yards 100

Key

— Suggested route

St Mary's Cathedral
Built in 1865, this Roman Catholic cathedral has undergone an architecturally stunning restoration (see p309). Opposite St Mary's is the beautiful Convent of Mercy.

Perth Concert Hall

★ Perth Mint
Perth Mint is Australia's oldest working mint. Built in 1899 to utilize the finds of the gold rush, it is open for tours and demonstrations (see p309).

Central Perth

Perth is a relatively small and quiet city compared with those on the east coast. Its main commercial and shopping areas can be easily explored on foot. The city's atmosphere is brisk but not hurried. Redevelopment projects in the 1970s brought skyscrapers and more roads, but they also made space for city parks and courtyards lined with cafés and shady trees. The city centre is bordered to the south and east by a wide stretch of the Swan River known as Perth Water, and to the north lies Northbridge, Perth's restaurant and entertainment centre.

Exploring Central Perth

St Georges Terrace is Perth's main commercial street. At its western end stands Parliament House, and in front of this is Barracks Archway. Further east, the Cloisters, built in 1850 as a school, boast some fine decorative brickwork. Nearby is the Old Perth Boys' School, a tiny building that was Perth's first school for boys. Towards the river is Elizabeth Quay.

Perth's shopping centre lies between William and Barrack streets. It is a maze of arcades, plazas and elevated walkways. The main areas are Hay Street Mall and Murray Street Mall. On the corner of William Street and St Georges Terrace lies the Town Hall (1870), close to the site where Perth was founded.

Beyond the railway tracks is Northbridge, the focus of much of Perth's nightlife. James Street is lined with many restaurants, cafés and food halls offering a variety of ethnic cuisines. The ornate façade of the former Brass Monkey Hotel (now a pub), is a perfect example of colonial gold rush architecture.

🎦 Barracks Archway

Cnr St Georges Terrace & Elder St.
Barracks Archway is all that remains of the 1863 barracks that once housed the soldiers brought in to police convicts.

🏛 Perth Cultural Centre

James St. Art Gallery of Western Australia: **Tel** (08) 9492 6622. **Open** 10am–5pm Wed–Mon. **Closed** Good Fri, 25 Apr, 25 Dec. Donations. &
W mra.wa.gov.au/ projects-and-places

The Perth Cultural Centre is a pedestrianized complex on several levels. The centre is home to the Art Gallery of Western Australia, which has a collection of modern Aboriginal and Australian art, and some international pieces. The Perth Institute of Contemporary Art (PICA), State Library and State Theatre are also here.

🏛 Western Australian Museum – Perth

Perth Cultural Centre, James St. **Tel** (08) 9212 3700. **Open** 9:30am–5pm daily; 25 Apr: 1–5pm. **Closed** 1 Jan, Good Fri, 25–26 Dec. & limited.
W museum.wa.gov.au

Within the Perth Cultural Centre stands the Western Australian Museum complex. Among its buildings are the Old Perth Gaol (1856), with exhibitions on life in the original Swan River colony. The exhibition "Western Australia Land and People" tells the story of Western Australia from dinosaurs to indigenous beginnings and the environmental issues now facing the state. International and temporary exhibitions enhance the permanent displays.

🏛 DFES Education and Heritage Centre

25 Murray St. **Tel** (08) 9395 9862. **Open** 10am–3pm Tue–Thu. **Closed** public holidays. &
W dfes.wa.gov.au

Perth City Fire Brigade moved from this, its original home, to a much larger site in 1979. The old fire station became a fascinating museum charting the history of the fire service in Perth and Western Australia, and a fire safety centre. Exhibits here include some well-preserved old fire appliances and reconstructions of rooms.

Perth Fire Station's original fire bell

⛪ St Mary's Cathedral

Victoria Sq. **Tel** (08) 6104 3650. **Open** 7am–6pm daily. &
Following an extensive restoration project, St Mary's Cathedral is an architectural delight. The cathedral has retained its splendid stained-glass windows and rich heritage, while also providing a modern space, seating 1,400 people. St Mary's is renowned for its superb choir.

🏛 Perth Mint

310 Hay St. **Tel** (08) 9421 7222. **Open** 9am–5pm daily. **Closed** public holidays. 🎦 &
W perthmint.com.au

Perth Mint was opened in 1899, under British control, to refine gold from Western Australia's gold fields to make British sovereigns and half-sovereigns. Although it no longer produces coins for circulation, the mint produces proof coins

The elaborately decorated Brass Monkey Hotel on William Street

For hotels and restaurants in this area see p490 and pp519–21

and specialist pure precious-metal coins, making it Australia's oldest operating mint. The mint has an interesting exhibition with coins, precious metal exhibits and displays on gold mining and refining. In addition, every hour a "Gold Pour" takes place in the Melting House that has been in operation for over a century.

🏠 St George's Anglican Cathedral

38 St Georges Terrace.
Tel (08) 9325 5766. **Open** daily. ♿

St George's Cathedral, consecrated in 1888, was only the second permanent Anglican place of worship in Perth. The city's first Anglican church was built between 1841 and 1845 in Classical Revival style close to the site of the existing cathedral. In 1875 a more prestigious place of worship was required, and the old church was demolished. Some artifacts from the original

church remain, however, such as some of the jarrah pews and the carved eagle lectern. This Gothic Revival building has some notable features including the intricate English alabaster *reredos* at the base of the east window, the

Western façade of St George's Cathedral showing rose window

modernistic medallions cast for the Stations of the Cross and some original 19th-century Russian icons.

🔔 The Bell Tower: Home of the Swan Bells

Barrack Sq. **Tel** (08) 6210 0444.
Open 10am–4pm daily.
Closed Good Fri, 25 Dec. ♿
W thebelltower.com.au

One of Perth's main attractions, the Bell Tower contains 12 bells from St Martin-in-the-Fields in London, England. There are displays and exhibitions inside the tower, including the oldest bell in Australia – the Upon Grey Bell – cast in 1550, a restored late Victorian turret clock which is wound daily for visitors, and an observation deck. Expert bell ringers give a brief history of bell ringing, and the bells ring daily, except Wednesday and Friday, when there is a bell handling demonstration instead.

Perth City Centre

① Barracks Archway
② Perth Cultural Centre
③ Western Australian Museum – Perth
④ DFES Education and Heritage Centre
⑤ St Mary's Cathedral
⑥ Perth Mint
⑦ St George's Anglican Cathedral
⑧ The Bell Tower

Key

▨ Street-by-Street map, pages 306–7

0 metres 500
0 yards 500

Exploring Greater Perth

Beyond the city centre, Greater Perth covers the Darling Range in the northeast to the Indian Ocean in the west. It has several large parks, including Kings Park, overlooking the river. On the coast, beaches stretch from Hillarys Boat Harbour in the north to Fremantle in the south *(see pp314–15)*. Perth's suburbs are accessible by train, local bus or car.

Sights at a Glance

1. Kings Park
2. Sunset Coast
3. Hills Forest
4. Whiteman Park
5. Perth Zoo
6. AQWA
7. Swan Valley

Key

- Central Perth
- Highway
- Major road
- Minor road

Snorkellers and qualified divers can explore the reef at AQWA

AQWA, Aquarium of Western Australia

Hillarys Boat Harbour, 91 Southside Drive, Hillarys. **Tel** (08) 9447 7500. **Open** 10am–5pm daily. **Closed** 25 Dec. aqwa.com.au

At Hillarys Boat Harbour, to the north of Perth's Sunset Coast, is this magnificent aquarium complex. A transparent submerged tunnel allows visitors to observe native sea creatures, including sharks and stingrays. There is a Touch Pool, where rays and sharks can be stroked. The denizens of the outside seal pool never fail to delight.

Swan Valley

Swan Valley Visitor Centre, Guildford Courthouse, cnr Meadow & Swan Sts, Guildford. **Tel** (08) 9207 8899. **Open** 9am–4pm daily. **Closed** 25 Dec. swanvalley.com.au

Western Australia's oldest wine-growing region is only a 25-minute drive from Perth. The historic suburb of Guildford is the gateway to a mix of award-winning wineries, breweries and gourmet offerings. Contact the Visitor Centre for details of wine tours and tastings.

Sunset Coast

Via West Coast Hwy.

Perth's Sunset Coast is lined with 30 km (20 miles) of white sandy beaches, many of them virtually deserted during the week. There are beaches to suit all tastes. Cottesloe Beach, Perth's most popular coastal spot, offers safe swimming and good services, making it a big hit with families, as is Sorrento Beach in the north. Scarborough Beach is

Kings Park

Fraser Ave, Kings Park. **Tel** (08) 9480 3600. **Open** daily. bgpa.wa.gov.au

Established at the end of the 19th century, Kings Park is 400 ha (1,000 acres) of both wild and cultivated parkland. Situated on Mount Eliza, it offers views of the city and the Swan River. Most of the park is bushland, which can be seen from the DNA Tower.

A landscaped parkland area on the eastern side includes the 17 ha (42 acres) Western Australian Botanic Garden. Treetops Walkway, a 629-m- (689-yd-) long elevated walkway, gives another perspective of the garden. The State War Memorial on Anzac Bluff is dedicated to the Western Australians who died in the two world wars. The Minmara

Gun Gun and Pioneer Women's Memorial are monuments to the women who helped build the Swan River Colony and, later, the state.

Bronze statue of a mother and child in Kings Park Western Australian Botanic Garden

very popular with surfers, but it is for experienced swimmers only as strong currents can make it dangerous on windy days. Trigg Beach just above Scarborough is also a good surfing spot. Just north of Cottesloe, Swanbourne Beach is a naturist beach.

Many of the city's beaches have no shade whatsoever and Perth residents are constantly reminded that the sun's rays, unshielded due to the hole in the ozone layer, can burn within minutes. Beachgoers are strongly advised to take sunscreen, a hat, t-shirt and sun umbrella *(see p549)*.

Students admiring a magnificent tiger in Perth Zoo

international-standard zoo. Attractions include a Nocturnal House, a wildlife park, an African savannah exhibit, an Australian walkabout and an Asian rainforest zone.

🐾 Hills Forest
Via Great Eastern Hwy.
Only 30 minutes' drive from Central Perth, Hills Forest lies in the Darling Range and offers a wide range of bush-related activities. Conserved since 1919 as the catchment area for the Mundaring Reservoir, which provided water for the southern gold fields in the 19th century *(see p59)*, Hills Forest is now managed as a conservation and recreation area. It is well served with barbecue and picnic areas and camp sites. At Mundaring Weir landscaped gardens are a lovely backdrop for picnics. On

Surfing on Scarborough Beach

🏛 Perth Zoo
20 Labouchere Rd. **Tel** (08) 9474 0444.
Open 9am–5pm daily. 🅿 ♿ ✎
🌐 perthzoo.wa.gov.au
In South Perth, a ferry-ride away from the city centre, lies Perth Zoo. Dedicated to conservation, it has all the features of an

the northern edge of the forest is John Forrest National Park, Western Australia's first national park. It consists of woodland and heathland with trails leading to beautiful pools and waterfalls, including Hovea Falls.

🐾 Whiteman Park
Lot 99 Lord St, Whiteman. **Tel** (08) 9209 6000. **Open** 8:30am–6pm daily. 🖥 ♿
Northeast of the city centre lies popular Whiteman Park. Visitors can tour the park on a 1920s tram or by train. A craft village displays local craftsmanship and there is also a motor museum with a collection of vehicles from the last 100 years. Within Whiteman Park, Caversham Wildlife Park is home to 200 species of native Australian animals from koalas to Tasmanian devils.

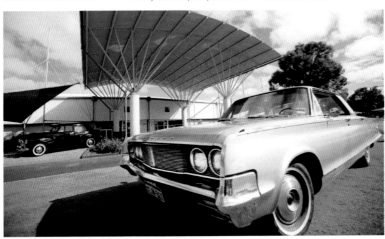

A Chrysler Newport on display by the entrance to the motor museum in Whiteman Park

❷ Rottnest Island

Less than 20 km (12 miles) west of Fremantle lies the idyllic island of Rottnest. Settled by Europeans in 1831, it was used as an Aboriginal prison between 1838 and 1902. In 1917, in recognition of its scenic beauty and rich bird life, the island became a protected area and today it is a popular tourist destination. Rottnest's oldest settlement, Thomson Bay, dates from the 1840s. The island's other settlements, all built in the 20th century, are found at Longreach Bay, Geordie Bay and Kingstown. Rottnest's rugged coastline comprises beaches, coves and reefs – ideal for many water-based activities – salt lakes and several visible shipwrecks. Private cars are not allowed on the island, so the only way to get around is by bicycle or bus, or on foot.

Aerial View of Rottnest
Rottnest is 11 km (7 miles) long, 4.5 km (3 miles) wide, and is governed by strict conservation regulations.

Wadjemup Lighthouse
The lighthouse on Wadjemup Hill was built in 1895. "Wadjemup" is the Aboriginal name for the island.

Rocky Bay
Overlooked by the sandy Lady Edeline beach, this popular, picturesque bay also contains the wreck of the barque *Mira Flores*, which sank in 1886.

Cape Vlamingh Lookout
Named after Dutch explorer Willem de Vlamingh, Rottnest's most famous early European visitor, this lookout stands at the furthest tip of the island, 10.5 km (6.5 miles) from Thomson Bay. The view is spectacular.

KEY

① **Strickland Bay** was named after Sir Gerald Strickland, governor of Rottnest from 1909 to 1912, and is a prime surfing spot.

② **City of York Bay** was named after Rottnest's most tragic shipwreck. In 1899, the captain of the *City of York* mistook a lighthouse flare for a pilot's signal and headed towards the rocks.

③ **Parakeet Bay** is popular with snorkellers. It is also an excellent spot to see the rock parrots after which it is named.

④ **The Basin** is the most popular beach on Rottnest

Island, particularly with families with children, as it is easily accessible on foot from Thomson Bay.

⑤ **The Rottnest Museum** is housed in the old granary, which dates from 1857. Exhibits cover the island's geology, its many shipwrecks, flora and fauna, and memorabilia of the early settlers and convicts.

⑥ **Henrietta Rocks** are a hazardous place for shipping. No less than three ships have been wrecked in the waters off this point.

⑦ **Mabel Cove**

For hotels and restaurants in this area see p490 and pp519–21

Hotel Rottnest

This hotel complex was built in 1864 as the state governor's summer residence and features turrets, crenellations and a courtyard garden *(see p490)*.

VISITORS' CHECKLIST

Practical Information
Visitors' Centre, Main Jetty, Rottnest. **Tel** (08) 9372 9732.
W rottnestisland.com

Transport
from Perth, Fremantle, Hillarys Boat Harbour.

Key

— Minor road

-- Paths and trails

0 metres 1000
0 yards 1000

Oliver Hill

At this lookout stand two 9.2-inch (23.5-cm) guns, brought here for coastal defence purposes in 1937, but obsolete since the end of World War II. A railway to the hill has been renovated by volunteers.

The Quokka

When de Vlamingh first visited Rottnest in 1696, he noted animals somewhat bigger than a cat, with dark fur. Thinking they were a species of rat, he called the island the "rats' nest". In fact the animals were a type of wallaby, called quokkas by the Aborigines. Although there is a small mainland population in Western Australia, this is the best place to see these timid creatures in areas of undergrowth. On Rottnest such habitat is scarce, and they are often visible at dusk. Quokkas are wild and should not be fed.

For keys to symbols *see back flap*

❶ Fremantle

Fremantle is one of Western Australia's most historic cities. A wealth of 19th-century buildings remains, including superb examples from the gold rush period. Founded on the Indian Ocean in 1829, at the mouth of the Swan River, Fremantle was intended to be a port for the new colony, but was only used as such when an artificial harbour was dredged at the end of the 19th century. The town still has thriving harbours and, in 1987, it hosted the America's Cup. Many sites were renovated for the event, and street cafés and restaurants sprang up.

Busy fruit and vegetable stall in the Fremantle Markets

Twelve-sided Round House

the site are clear views across Bathers Bay to Rottnest Island (see pp312–13).

🏛 Western Australian Museum – Shipwreck Galleries
Cliff St. **Tel** (08) 9431 8469.
Open 9:30am–5pm daily (25 Apr: 1–5pm). **Closed** 1 Jan, Good Fri, 25–26 Dec. Donation. ♿
W museum.wa.gov.au

Housed in the Commissariat building, an 1850s convict-built government storehouse, the Shipwreck Galleries is a renowned centre for maritime archaeology and exploration. The museum's prize possession is a reconstruction of part of the hull of the Dutch East Indiaman *Batavia* from timbers discovered at the wreck off the Abrolhos Islands in 1629 (see p328). The exhibit tells the story of the shipwreck and mutiny of the vessel and gives an insight into life on board.

🚪 The Round House
Below High St. **Tel** (08) 9336 6897.
Open 10:30am–3:30pm daily. Donation. ♿ limited.

Built in 1830, the Round House is Fremantle's oldest building. It was the town's first gaol and, in 1844, site of the colony's first hanging. Beneath is a tunnel, dug in 1837 to allow whalers to transfer cargo from the jetty to the High Street. To the left of

🛒 Fremantle Markets
Cnr South Terrace & Henderson St. **Tel** (08) 9335 2515. **Open** 9am–8pm Fri–Sun (to 6pm public hols). **Closed** 25 Dec. ♿

In 1897, a competition was held to design a suitable building to act as Fremantle's market hall. The winning design still stands today, having been renovated in 1975. There are more than 170 stalls offering everything from vegetables to opals. The market is open until 8pm on Fridays.

⛪ St John the Evangelist Anglican Church
Cnr Adelaide & Queen sts. **Tel** (08) 9335 2213. **Open** 9am–5pm daily. ♿

This charming church, completed in 1882, replaced a smaller church on the same site. Its Pioneer Window tells the story of a pioneer family across seven generations, from its departure from England in the 18th century, to a new life in Western Australia. The window next to it is from the old church. The ceiling and altars are of local jarrah wood.

🏛 Western Australian Museum – Maritime
Victoria Quay. **Tel** (08) 9431 8444.
Open 9:30am–5pm daily (25 Apr: 1–5pm). **Closed** 1 Jan, Good Fri, 25–26 Dec. ♿
W museum.wa.gov.au

This museum houses the *Australia II*, the racing yacht with the winged keel that won the America's Cup in 1983. Also popular is the submarine HMAS *Ovens*, which can be toured (pre-booking essential). Visitors can find out what life is like aboard a submarine and immerse themselves in Fremantle's wartime history.

The America's Cup Bonanza

The America's Cup yachting race has been run every four years since 1851. Not until 1983, however, did a country other than the United States win this coveted trophy. This was the year that *Australia II* carried it home. In 1987, the Americans were the challengers, and the races were run in *Australia II*'s home waters, off Fremantle. Investment poured into the town, refurbishing the docks, cafés, bars and hotels for the occasion.

The Americans regained the trophy, but Fremantle remains forever changed by being, for once, under the world's gaze.

The 1983 winner, *Australia II*

⊞ Fremantle Arts Centre

Cnr Ord & Finnerty Vale sts. **Tel** (08) 9432 9555. **Open** 10am–5pm daily. **Closed** public holidays. ♿ limited. Ⓦ **fac.org.au**

This beautiful Gothic Revival mansion with its shady gardens was first conceived as an insane asylum. The main wing was built between 1861 and 1865, and an extension was added between 1880 and 1902.

The building, which after its use as an asylum became the wartime headquarters for US forces, was slated for demolition in 1967. But, principally through the efforts of Fremantle's mayor, it was rescued and renovated to become the Fremantle Arts Centre.

The centre is one of Western Australia's most dynamic multi-arts organisations, offering a rich cultural program of exhibitions, residences, art courses, music and events. It also showcases local contemporary artists, with many of the works for sale.

During the summer months (October to March), the centre's Sunday Music series takes place from 2–4pm. The outdoor event is free and features an extensive line up of established local acts, touring artists and young up-and-coming musicians.

⊞ Fremantle Prison

1 The Terrace. **Tel** (08) 9336 9200. **Open** 9am–5pm daily. **Closed** Good Fri, 25 Dec. 🗎 📷 ♿ limited. Ⓦ **fremantleprison.com.au**

In the 1850s, when the first group of convicts arrived in the Swan River Colony, the need arose for a large-scale prison. Fremantle Prison, an imposing building with a sturdy gatehouse and cold, forbidding limestone cell blocks, was built by those first convicts in 1855. It was used as a maximum-security prison until 1991. Today, visitors tour the complex, visiting cells, punishment cells, the chapel and the chilling gallows

VISITORS' CHECKLIST

Practical Information
🗺 30,000.
ℹ️ Town Hall, Kings Square, 8 William St (08) 9431 7878.
📷 Fremantle Festival (Nov).

Transport
🚉 Elder Place. 🚌 Elder Place.

room, last used in 1964. The torchlight tours and tunnel tours are highly recommended.

Fremantle Prison's striking façade

Fremantle City Centre

① The Round House
② WA Museum – Shipwreck Galleries
③ Fremantle Markets
④ St John the Evangelist Anglican Church
⑤ WA Museum – Maritime
⑥ Fremantle Arts Centre
⑦ Fremantle Prison

The Southern Coastline

Western Australia's southwest corner has diverse coastal scenery. Two oceans meet here, the Indian and the Southern, resulting in discernible climate changes: the southern coastline is often windy and cooler than the western coast, and the oceans are much less gentle. Lined by national parks, the coast incorporates limestone, reefs, granite formations, beautiful sand dunes and crags topped by low vegetation. There are also world-class surfing spots in the region.

⑤ ★ Flinders Bay, Augusta

Augusta was founded in 1830 and is the third oldest settlement in the state. Only 5 km (3 miles) from Cape Leeuwin, the southwestern tip of the continent, today it is a popular holiday resort. The beautiful Flinders Bay is particularly favoured by windsurfers.

```
0 km              20
0 miles           20
```

④ ★ Hamelin Bay

This busy beach in the centre of Cape Leeuwin is particularly attractive to families, with its calm waters and fine swimming and fishing opportunities.

① Bunker Bay, Dunsborough

This excellent beach in the tourist resort of Dunsborough benefits from dolphin- and whale-watching in season and fine views of Cape Naturaliste.

② Smiths Beach, Yallingup

This popular honeymoon spot is also a haven for surfers. Nearby is the spectacular Yallingup Cave. Yallingup is the indigenous word for "place of love".

③ Boodjidup Beach, Margaret River

The coastline in this holiday town consists of long beaches, sheltered bays and cliff faces looking out on to the surf.

⑦ Peaceful Bay

Keen anglers and sailors can often be spotted within this aptly named inlet, which is also a popular picnic spot. Nearby Walpole is the gateway to Walpole-Nornalup National Park, with its impressive karri and eucalypt trees.

⑩ Middleton Beach, Albany

The waters of Middleton Beach are regularly filled with windsurfers and bodyboarders. A short drive around the point is Torndirrup National Park, with a multitude of natural coastal formations, including offshore islands and some excellent locations for whale-watching in season.

On the map: Busselton, BUNBURY, Leeuwin-Naturaliste National Park, Margaret River, Augusta, Pemberton, D'Entrecasteaux National Park, Sha... Nat... Park

Lake Cave, near Margaret River, is just one of an estimated 200 underground caves along the Leeuwin-Naturaliste Ridge that runs from Busselton to Augusta. It is one of the few caves open to the public and is a fairyland of limestone formations, reflected in dark underground waters.

WESTERN AUSTRALIA

Locator Map

D'Entrecasteaux National Park, 40 km (25 miles) southwest of Pemberton, is a wild and rugged park with spectacular coastal cliffs, pristine beaches and excellent coastal fishing. Much of the park, including some isolated beach camp sites, is only accessible by 4WD. Inland, heathland is home to a range of animal and plant habitats.

Leeuwin-Naturaliste National Park is a 15,500-ha (40,000-acre) protected area of scenic coastline, caves, heathlands and woodlands. Its rugged limestone coast with long beaches and sheltered bays faces the Indian Ocean. It has long been popular as a holiday destination and has excellent opportunities for swimming, surfing and fishing.

⑧ ★ Ocean Beach, Denmark

Denmark is a popular haunt for surfers from many countries. Ocean Beach, in particular, is the setting for international surfing competitions.

⑨ ★ Wilson Inlet

From Denmark's main street it is a relatively short walk through well-kept woodland to Wilson Inlet where there are spectacular views and great fishing spots.

↑ *ESPERANCE*

Walpole

Albany

Walpole Nornalup National Park

William Bay National Park

Southern Ocean

West Cape Howe National Park

Torndirrup National Park

⑥ ★ Conspicuous Beach

Impressive cliffs face on to the beautiful white sands of Conspicuous Beach. It is also the access point for the Valley of the Giants, with its massive red tingle trees.

Key

═══ Highway

─── Major road

┄┄┄ Minor road

～ River

Wide first-floor veranda and ornate ironwork of the Rose Hotel, Bunbury

❹ Bunbury

🏔 67,000. 🚃 🚌 🚐 🚢 ℹ Old Railway Station, Carmody Place (08) 9792 7205. 🌐 **visitbunbury.com.au**

The city of Bunbury lies about 180 km (110 miles) south of Perth at the southern end of the Leschenault Inlet. The state's second-largest city, it is the capital of the southwest region. Since the 19th century it has grown into a thriving port and a centre for local industry. It is also a popular holiday destination, with many water sports available.

Historic buildings in Bunbury include the Rose Hotel, built in 1865, with its first-floor veranda and intricate ironwork detail. The Anglican St Boniface Cathedral contains some pretty stained glass. Nearby are the Bunbury Art Galleries, housed in the former Sisters of Mercy convent built in the 1880s. Today they are the centre for community arts events.

On the beachfront stands the **Dolphin Discovery Centre**, which has fascinating audiovisual exhibits and a shallow pool where visitors can interact with dolphins. Wild dolphins regularly appear off the beach in front of the centre, and visitors come to see them and swim with them. The centre also runs cruises and swim-with-dolphin tours.

The **King Cottage Museum**, is run by the Bunbury Historical Society. It exhibits local artifacts dating from the 1880s to the 1920s and a wealth of photographs.

🐬 **Dolphin Discovery Centre**
Lot 830 Koombana Drive. **Tel** (08) 9791 3088. **Open** Jun–Sep: 9am–2pm; Oct–May: 8am–4pm. **Closed** 25 Dec. 🅿 ♿

🏛 **King Cottage Museum**
77 Forrest Ave. **Tel** (08) 9721 7546. **Open** 2–4pm daily. **Closed** public holidays. 🅿 ♿ limited.

❺ Busselton

🏔 32,000. 🛫 🚌
ℹ 38 Peel Terrace (08) 9752 5800.
🌐 **geographebay.com**

Standing on the shores of Geographe Bay, Busselton offers more than 30 km (19 miles) of beaches and an array of water-based activities, including fishing, whale-watching and scuba-diving. Busselton Jetty, 2 km (1 mile) long and once the longest in Australia, is a reminder of the town's origins as a timber port.

Some of Busselton's oldest surviving buildings are located at the Old Courthouse site, now

Entrance to Busselton's original courthouse building

used as an arts complex. Here, the jail cells, police offices, courthouse and bond store all date from 1856. Local crafts are sold in the old jail cells, and other outbuildings act as studio space for artists.

The 1871 *Ballarat*, the first steam locomotive used in the state, stands in Victoria Park.

Environs

About 10 km (6 miles) north of Busselton is **Wonnerup House**, a lovingly restored house built by pioneer George Layman in 1859 and now owned by the National Trust. Three other buildings share the site, the earliest being the first house Layman erected in the 1830s. Both buildings stand in pretty grounds within farmland and are furnished with Layman family memorabilia and artifacts. In 1874, Layman's son built a school and, in 1885, a teacher's house close by.

About 20 km (12 miles) north of Busselton is the beautiful Ludlow Tuart Forest National Park, probably the largest area of tuart trees left in the world.

🏚 **Wonnerup House**
935 Layman Rd. **Tel** (08) 9752 2039. **Open** 10am–4pm Thu–Mon. **Closed** Good Fri, 25 Dec. 🅿 ♿

❻ Margaret River

🏔 13,500. 🛫 🚌 🚌
ℹ 100 Bussell Hwy (08) 9780 5911.
🌐 **margaretriver.com**

The attractive town of Margaret River, close to the Indian Ocean, was first settled by Europeans in the 1850s. The town became the centre of an agricultural and timber region, but in the past few decades has gained fame for its wineries (see pp40–41), and for its splendid surfing beaches.

Within the town are many galleries, studios and gourmet food and beverage specialists. The **Margaret River Gallery** showcases works by Western Australian artists. Featuring painting, sculpture, jewellery and furniture, the gallery also hosts exhibition openings. Set in 12 ha (30 acres) of bush on the outskirts of town, the **Eagles**

Heritage Raptor Wildlife Centre has a collection of birds of prey and gives eagle-flying displays.

🏛 Margaret River Gallery
Shop 4 no. 1 Charles West Ave. **Tel** (08) 9757 2729. **Open** 10am–5pm Mon–Sat, 11am–3pm Sun. **Closed** 1 Jan, Good Fri, 25 Dec. ♿

✷ Eagles Heritage Raptor Wildlife Centre
341 Boodjidup Rd. **Tel** (08) 9757 2960. **Open** 10am–4:15pm (last adm). **Closed** Fri (except WA school hols), Good Fri, 25 Dec. ♿

Environs
Eight km (5 miles) north of Margaret River stands the region's first homestead, Ellensbrook, built by pioneer Alfred Bussell in the 1850s. The stone cottage is close to a forest trail which leads to the pretty Meekadarribee Falls.

Margaret River's outlying wineries are very popular. Many, from Vasse-Felix, the oldest, to the large Leeuwin Estates Winery, offer tastings.

Ellensbrook Pioneer Homestead, near the town of Margaret River

7 Bridgetown
🗺 4,500. 🚌 ℹ 154 Hampton St (08) 9761 1740. 🌐 **bridgetown.com.au**

Nestled amid rolling hills on the banks of Blackwood River, Bridgetown began as a single one-room homestead in the 1850s. It was built by settler John Blechynden and can still be seen standing next to the second home he built, Bridgedale House. Both are National Trust properties.

The town's visitors' centre is home to its municipal history museum and the unusual Brierly

Hilltop view of picturesque Bridgetown

Jigsaw Gallery, which has hundreds of puzzles.

Sutton's Lookout, off Philips Street, offers panoramic views of the town and surrounding countryside. The Blackwood River and local jarrah and marri forests afford opportunities for walks and drives, and several river-based activities, including canoeing and marron fishing.

8 Manjimup
🗺 5,000. 🚌 ℹ Giblett St (08) 9771 1831. 🌐 **manjimupwa.com**

If you are travelling south from Perth, Manjimup acts as the gateway to the great karri forests for which the southwest is so famous. The town was settled in the late 1850s, and has been associated with the timber industry ever since. **Manjimup Timber Park** has a Timber Museum, Historical Hamlet and Bunnings Age of Steam Museum. A sculpture of a woodsman at the entrance commemorates the region's timber industry pioneers.

🏛 Manjimup Timber & Heritage Park
Cnr Rose & Edwards sts. **Tel** (08) 9771 7777. **Open** 9am–8pm daily. **Closed** 25 Dec. ♿

Environs
About 25 km (16 miles) west of Manjimup on Graphite Road lies Glenoran Pool, a pretty swimming

hole on the Donnelly River. The adjacent One-Tree Bridge is the site where early settlers felled a huge karri and used it to carry a bridge across the river. Nearby are the Four Aces, four giant karri trees in a straight line, thought to be up to 300 years old.

9 Pemberton
🗺 1,400. 🚌 ℹ Brockman St (08) 9776 1133. 🌐 **pembertonvisitor.com.au**

At the heart of karri country, Pemberton has the look and feel of an old timber town. The Pemberton Tramway, originally built to bring the trees to mills in town, now takes visitors through the forests. The **Pemberton Pioneer Museum** is a fascinating tribute to the pioneers of the area.

🏛 Pemberton Pioneer Museum
Brockman St. **Tel** (08) 9776 1133. **Open** daily. **Closed** Good Fri, 25 & 26 Dec. Donations. ♿

Environs
Southeast of the town lies Gloucester National Park, home to karri country's giant karri, the Gloucester Tree. At 61 m (200 ft), it is one of the highest fire look-out trees in the world. Southwest of Pemberton is Warren National Park with its cascades, swimming holes and fishing spots. Attractive Beedelup National Park is northwest of Pemberton.

Sculpture of a woodsman at Manjimup Timber Park

Example of local artist Andy Ducker's stained glass in Denmark

⑩ Denmark

🏙 6,000. 🚌 ℹ️ 73 Southcoast Hwy (08) 9848 2055. 🌐 denmark.com.au

Lying on Western Australia's southern coastline, Denmark was founded as a timber company settlement in 1895, but by the 1920s it was a fully fledged town. The town now attracts a host of visitors, many of whom come seeking the good surf of the Southern Ocean. There is also a large population of artists and artisans, and the atmosphere is distinctly bohemian.

Denmark's oldest building is St Leonard's Anglican Church, built by volunteers in 1899. Its Scandinavian-style pitched roof and interior detail are reminders of the Norwegian timber workers in the town at that time.

Nearby are the Old Butter Factory Galleries and the Wildwood Gallery, just two of Denmark's galleries where visitors can admire and buy paintings and craftwork from the region.

Berridge Park is often the scene for open-air, riverfront concerts.

Environs

A popular surfing spot is Ocean Beach; more sheltered locations for swimmers include Cosy Corner and Peaceful Bay. The coastline and Wilsons Inlet are popular with boaters and anglers.

⑪ Albany

🏙 37,000. ✈️ 🚌 🚌 ℹ️ Old Railway Station, Proudlove Parade (08) 9841 9290. 🌐 albanytourist.com.au

Albany was first visited by Captain Vancouver in 1791, but it was not until 1826 that the British settled here. Until Fremantle harbour was constructed (see pp314–15), Albany acted as the colony's main port and the harbour is still the commercial heart of the city. Whale migrations bring them close to the city's shores, which made it a base for whalers in the last century.

The **National Anzac Centre** in Albany was opened in 2014 to celebrate the 100-year anniversary of the Anzac landing at Gallipoli. Artifacts, interactive multimedia and images tell the stories of those who fought in the war. Albany includes many old buildings. **St John the Evangelist Anglican Church**, built in 1848, was the first Anglican church consecrated in Western Australia and is the epitome of an English country church.

Ship's wheel in Discovery Bay

The Residency Museum, originally part of the convict hiring depot built in the 1850s, details the history of the town and its surrounding area. The convict hiring depot itself and the Old Gaol now house the collection of the Albany Historical Society. In Duke Street is Patrick Taylor Cottage, built before 1836 of wattle and daub,

and the oldest building in Albany. On Albany's foreshore is a fully-fitted replica of the brig *Amity*, which brought the first settlers here from Sydney in 1826.

🏛 National Anzac Centre

1347 Forts Rd. **Tel** (08) 9841 9369. **Open** 9am–5pm daily. **Closed** 25 Dec. 🅿️ ♿ 🌐 nationalanzaccentre.com.au

⛪ St John the Evangelist Anglican Church

York St. **Tel** (08) 9841 5015. **Open** daily. ♿ 🌐 anglicanchurchalbany.org.au

Environs

The world's largest whaling museum is **Discovery Bay**. Tour guides take visitors around the remains of the Cheyne Beach whaling station and explain the process of extracting whale oil. From July to October, breaching displays of migrating whales can sometimes be seen offshore.

🏛 Discovery Bay

81 Whaling Station Rd, Frenchman Bay. **Tel** (08) 9844 4021. **Open** 9am–5pm daily. **Closed** 25 Dec. 🅿️ 🖥 ♿

Replica of the brig *Amity*

⑫ Stirling Range National Park

🚌 Albany. ℹ️ 120 Albany Highway, Albany (08) 9842 4500. Park Ranger & information: 8:30am–4:30pm Mon–Fri.

Overlooking the rolling farmland to the north of Albany is the Stirling Range National Park. The mountain peaks, noted for their colour changes from purple to red to blue, rise to more than 1,000 m (3,300 ft) above sea level and stretch for more than 65 km (40 miles). The highest peak is Bluff Knoll, which reaches 1,099 m (3,605 ft). Because of its sudden rise from the surrounding plains,

Stirling Range National Park as seen from Chester Pass Road

the park has an unpredictable climate which encourages a wide range of unique flora and fauna, including ten species of mountain bell. No less than 60 species of flowering plants are endemic to the park. They are best seen from September to November, when they are likely to be in flower. The park offers visitors a number of graded and signposted walks in the mountains (all are steep) and there are several picturesque barbecue and picnic areas.

⑱ York

3,200. 📧 ℹ️ 81 Avon Terrace (08) 9641 1301. 🎏 York Jazz Festival (Nov). 🔳 **yorkwa.org**

The town of York was founded in 1831, in the new colony's drive to establish its self-sufficiency via agriculture. Now registered as a historic town, it retains many mid–19th-century buildings, the majority of which are on Avon Terrace, the main street. The cells of York's Old Gaol, in use from 1865 until 1981, provide a chilling insight into the treatment of 19th-century offenders. Other historic buildings include Settler's House (1860s), now a hotel and restaurant *(see p490)*, and Castle Hotel, built in stages between 1850 and 1932, with its unusual timber verandas. Nearby stands the **York Motor Museum**, with

one of the largest collections of veteran cars and vehicles in Australia. These include the 1886 Benz (the world's first car), the very rare 1946 Holden Sedan Prototype and the extraordinary Bisiluro II Italcorsa racing car.

Also of note is the York Residency Museum, housed in the former home of York magistrate Walkinshaw Cowan, father-in-law to Edith Cowan, the state's first female Member of Parliament *(see p60)*. This extensive collection of artifacts and photographs is justly said to be the finest small museum in the state.

York's 1892 flour mill has now been converted into the Jah-Roc Mill Gallery, which exhibits and sells furniture made from jarrah wood.

🏛️ York Motor Museum
116 Avon Terrace. **Tel** (08) 9641 1288. **Open** call 9:30am–2pm for opening days and times. ♿ ⛔

⑭ Northam

🏔️ 7,000. 🚉 🚌 ℹ️ 2 Grey St (08) 9622 2100. 🔳 **northam.wa.gov.au**

At the heart of the Avon Valley and the state's wheat belt, Northam is Western Australia's largest inland town. Settled as an agricultural centre early in the colony's history, the town became a gateway to the gold fields of Kalgoorlie-Boulder for prospectors in the 1890s *(see p322)*. It retains a number of historic buildings, including the Old Girls' School (1877), now the town's Art Centre, and the beautiful St John's Church (1890). The town's jewel is Morby Cottage, built in 1836 and a fine example of the architectural style adopted by the early colonists.

Spanning the Avon River is the longest pedestrian suspension bridge in the country, offering views of the river.

The Northam Suspension Bridge stretching across the Avon River

The Gold Fields and Nullarbor Plain

Western Australia's southeast is a sparsely populated, flat region of extreme aridity and little fresh water. Vast stretches of its red, dusty landscape are inhabited by small Aboriginal communities and mining companies. The gold rush around Kalgoorlie in the 1890s ensured the state's success, but many places waned and ghost towns now litter the plains. Traversing the Nullarbor Plain, the Eyre Highway runs from Norseman to South Australia, 730 km (455 miles) away, and beyond. To the south is the windswept coast of the Great Australian Bight.

Locator Map

☐ *The Gold Fields and Nullarbor Plain*

☐ *Perth and the Southwest pp302–21*

Sights at a Glance

⑮ Wave Rock
⑯ Kalgoorlie-Boulder
⑰ Norseman
⑱ Esperance
⑲ Nullarbor Plain

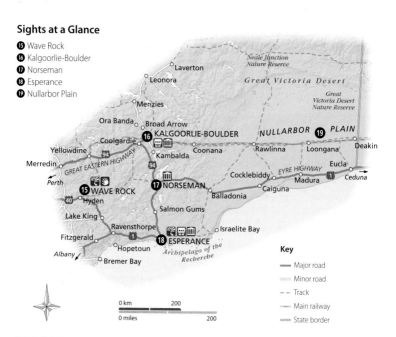

Key

— Major road

····· Minor road

– – Track

~~~ Main railway

▬▬ State border

Wave Rock, in the shape of a perfect wave about to break

⑮ Wave Rock

🚌 Hyden. Wave Rock Visitors' Centre: **Tel** (08) 9880 5182. **Open** 9am–5pm daily. 🏞 ♿ 🅿 by arrangement.

In Western Australia's wheat belt, 5 minutes' drive east of the small settlement of Hyden, stands one of the state's most surprising rock formations. A great granite wave has been created from a huge outcrop by thousands of years of chemical erosion, and reaction with rainwater has given it red and grey stripes. Other rock formations nearby include the Breakers and Hippo's Yawn. Facing Wave Rock, Lace Place is the unusual location for the largest collection of lacework in the southern hemisphere.

About 18 km (11 miles) northeast of Hyden lies Mulka's Cave, where several Aboriginal rock paintings can be seen.

⑯ Kalgoorlie-Boulder

🏚 35,000. ✈ 🚉 🚌 🚌 🛈 316 Hannan St (08) 9021 1966. **Open** daily. 🌐 **kalgoorlietourism.com**

Kalgoorlie and the nearby town of Boulder, with which it was amalgamated in 1989, constantly remind visitors of their gold-fever past. Gold was first discovered here by Irishman Paddy Hannan in 1893, and, within weeks, the area was besieged with prospectors. Gold fields in other areas soon dwindled, but this field has yielded rich pickings to this day, bolstered by nickel finds in the 1960s. Today, gold is mined in the world's largest open-cut mine and more than 150,000 visitors a year come to see historic Kalgoorlie.

A variety of heritage trails and tours are available, and details are at the tourist office. The **Museum of the Goldfields** has an impressive collection of gold nuggets and jewellery, as well as natural history displays and a history of the gold rush. Visitors can ride in a glass lift for magnificent views of the gold fields, or step back in time at a 1930s miner's cottage.

The ornate buildings hastily erected during the boom years are best seen on Hannan Street, in the York and Exchange hotels, classic examples of gold rush architecture, and Kalgoorlie Town Hall.

Around Kalgoorlie-Boulder are ghost towns, such as Ora Banda and Broad Arrow, deserted by prospectors in search of new mines.

Bronze statue of Paddy Hannan

🏛 **Museum of the Goldfields**
17 Hannan St. **Tel** 1300 134 081. **Open** 10am–3pm daily (25 Apr: 1–3pm). **Closed** 1 Jan, Good Fri, 25–26 Dec.
💲 $5 suggested donation. ♿

Baxters Cliff, east of Esperance, on the shores of the Southern Ocean

⑰ Norseman

🏠 1,600. 🚌 ℹ Lot 1781 Roberts St (08) 9039 1071.

At the start of the Eyre Highway, Norseman is the gateway to the Nullarbor Plain and the eastern states beyond. Like Kalgoorlie-Boulder, the town stands on a gold field, discovered when a horse pawed the ground, uncovering gold deposits. In gratitude, miners named the town after the horse, and its statue was erected in the main street. Many visitors try fossicking, or learn more about the history of gold mining in the area at the **The Norseman Historical Museum** housed in the old School of Mines. Nearby, Beacon Hill offers a panoramic view of the town and surrounding countryside.

🏛 **The Norseman Historical Museum**
Battery Rd. **Tel** (08) 9039 0367. **Open** 10am–1pm Mon–Sat. **Closed** Good Fri, Easter Mon, 25 Apr, 25 Dec. 💲

⑱ Esperance

🏠 10,000. ✈ 🚌 ℹ Historic Museum Village, Dempster St (08) 9083 1555. 🌐 visitesperance.com

Although this area was visited by Europeans as far back as 1627, it was not until 1863 that British colonists established a settlement here. Fronting the Southern Ocean, this part of the coast is said to have some of the most beautiful beaches in Australia. Offshore is the Recherche Archipelago, with its 110 islands, one of which, Woody Island, is a wildlife sanctuary and can be visited.

In Esperance itself, Historic Museum Village includes the town's art gallery, and Esperance Municipal Museum contains local artifacts.

⑲ Nullarbor Plain

🚃 Kalgoorlie. 🚌 Norseman. ℹ Norseman (08) 9039 1071.

The Nullarbor Plain stretches across the southeast of the state and into South Australia *(see p371)*. "Nullarbor" derives from the Latin meaning "no trees", and this is indeed a vast treeless plain. Only one road, the Eyre Highway, leads across the plain – one of the great Australian road journeys.

A few tiny settlements consisting only of roadhouses lie along the Eyre Hwy. Cockle-biddy, lying 438 km (270 miles) east of Norseman, has one of the world's longest caves and, at Eucla, 10 km (6 miles) from the state border, a telegraph station's remains can be seen. Nearby Eucla National Park has some fine views of the coastal cliffs.

The gold rush architecture of the York Hotel in Hannan Street, Kalgoorlie

NORTH OF PERTH AND THE KIMBERLEY

Western Australia covers one-third of Australia, and visitors to the area north of Perth start to get a feel for just how big the state really is. The region has many treasures: Ningaloo Reef and the Pinnacles rock formations; the Kimberley gorges; and a host of national parks, including the amazing Bungle Bungles.

The first people to set foot on the Australian land mass, the Aborigines, did so some 55,000 years ago in the north of Western Australia. This area is rich in Aboriginal petroglyphs, and some are thought to be more than 20,000 years old. The north of Western Australia was also the site of the first European landing in 1616 *(see p53)*. In 1688, English explorer William Dampier charted the area around the Dampier Peninsula and, on a later voyage, discovered Shark Bay and the area around Broome.

In the 1840s, the Benedictines set up a mission in New Norcia and, by the 1860s, settlements had sprung up along the coast, most significantly at Cossack, where a pearling industry attracted immigrants from Japan, China and Indonesia. In the 1880s, pastoralists set up cattle and sheep stations in a swathe from Derby to Wyndham. Gold was struck in 1885 at Halls Creek, and the northern part of the state was finally on the map. In the 1960s, mining came to prominence again with the discovery of such minerals as iron ore, nickel and oil, particularly in the Pilbara region.

Today, the region is popular with tourists who want to see and experience the natural beauty that Western Australia has to offer *(see p540)*. Its climate varies from Mediterranean-style just north of Perth to the tropical wet and dry pattern of the far north. Wildlife includes endangered species such as the dugongs of Shark Bay. Even isolated spots, such as the Kimberley and the resorts of Coral Bay and Broome, are receiving more visitors every year.

The daily ritual of feeding wild dolphins at Monkey Mia beach

◀ Stromatolites in Hamelin Pool, part of Shark Bay Marine Park

Exploring North of Perth

The north of Western Australia is a vast area of diverse landscapes and stunning scenery. North of Perth lies Nambung National Park, home to the bizarre Pinnacles Desert. Kalbarri National Park is a region of scenic gorges on the Murchison River. The Indian Ocean coastline offers uninhabited islands, coral reefs, breathtaking cliffs and sandy beaches, none more spectacular than in Shark Bay World Heritage and Marine Park. At the tip of the region is the Pilbara, the state's mining area and home to the fascinating national parks of Karijini and Millstream-Chichester.

St Francis Xavier Cathedral, Geraldton

The Pinnacles in Nambung National Park

Sights at a Glance

1. New Norcia
2. Nambung National Park
3. Geraldton
4. Houtman Abrolhos
5. Kalbarri National Park
6. *Shark Bay World Heritage and Marine Park pp330–31*
7. Carnarvon
8. Ningaloo Reef Marine Park
9. Exmouth
10. Dampier
11. Roebourne
12. Cossack Historical Town
13. Point Samson
14. Karijini National Park

The Kimberley and the Deserts
See pp334–5

15. Broome
16. Derby
17. Halls Creek
18. Purnululu (Bungle Bungle) National Park
19. Wyndham

0 kilometres   100

0 miles   100

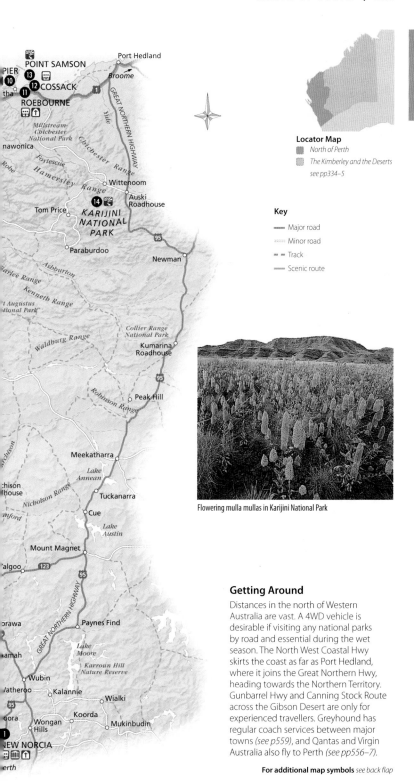

Locator Map

North of Perth

The Kimberley and the Deserts
see pp334–5

Key

━━━ Major road

╍╍╍ Minor road

━ ━ Track

━━━ Scenic route

Flowering mulla mullas in Karijini National Park

Getting Around

Distances in the north of Western
Australia are vast. A 4WD vehicle is
desirable if visiting any national parks
by road and essential during the wet
season. The North West Coastal Hwy
skirts the coast as far as Port Hedland,
where it joins the Great Northern Hwy,
heading towards the Northern Territory.
Gunbarrel Hwy and Canning Stock Route
across the Gibson Desert are only for
experienced travellers. Greyhound has
regular coach services between major
towns (see p559), and Qantas and Virgin
Australia also fly to Perth (see pp556–7).

For additional map symbols see back flap

● New Norcia

🏛 150. 💬 ℹ️ New Norcia Museum and Art Gallery, Great Northern Highway (08) 9654 8056.

One of Western Australia's most important heritage sites is New Norcia, 130 km (80 miles) northeast of Perth. A mission was established here by Spanish Benedictine monks in 1846, and it is still home to a small monastic community who own and run the historic buildings. There are daily tours of the monastery and visitors can stay at a guesthouse.

The town, known for its Spanish colonial architecture, has a pretty cathedral, built in 1860, at its centre. Also of note are two elegant colleges built early in the 20th century: St Gertrude's Residence for Girls and St Ildephonsus' Residence for Boys. The **New Norcia Museum and Art Gallery** has some fine art treasures and artifacts tracing the town's history.

🏛 **New Norcia Museum and Art Gallery**
Great Northern Hwy. **Tel** (08) 9654 8056. **Open** daily. **Closed** 25 & 26 Dec. 🐕 ♿ ground floor only.

Minarets adorning St Ildephonsus' Residence for Boys, New Norcia

❷ Nambung National Park

ℹ️ Pinnacles Visitors' Centre, Cadiz St (inside Post Office) (08) 9652 7700. **Open** 9am–5:30pm Mon–Sat (to 5pm Sun). 🌐 **visitpinnaclescountry. com.au**

This national park is composed of beach and sand dunes, with the dunes extending inland from the coast. It is best seen in spring when wildflowers bloom and the heat is not oppressive. The park is famous for the

The extraordinary Pinnacles, Nambung National Park

Pinnacles, a region of curious limestone pillars, the tallest of which stand 4 m (13 ft) high. Visitors can take a 3-km (2-mile) driving trail or a shorter walking trail which leads to lookouts with stunning views of the Pinnacles and the coastline. Most of the park animals are nocturnal, but some, including kangaroos, emus and many reptiles, may be seen in the cool of dawn or dusk.

❸ Geraldton

🏛 40,000. ✈️🚌🚌 ℹ️ 46 Marine Terrace (08) 9956 6670.
🌐 **visitgeraldton.com.au**

The city of Geraldton lies on Champion Bay, about 425 km (265 miles) north of Perth. It is known as "Sun City" because of its average eight hours of sunshine per day. The pleasant climate brings hordes of sun-seekers from all over Australia who take advantage of fine swimming and surfing beaches. It can also be very windy at times, a further enticement to windsurfers, for whom Geraldton (particularly Mahomets Beach) is a world centre.

The history of European settlement in the area extends back to the mutiny of the Dutch ship *Batavia*, after it was wrecked on the nearby Houtman Abrolhos in 1629. Two crew members were marooned here as a punishment. In 1721,

the Dutch ship *Zuytdorp* was wrecked, and it is thought that survivors settled here briefly. Champion Bay was first mapped in 1849, and a lead mine was established shortly afterwards. Geraldton grew up as a lead shipping point, and now is a port city with a large rock-lobster fleet.

The city retains many of its early historic buildings. The **Museum of Geraldton** includes the Shipwrecks Gallery, which contains relics of the area's early shipwrecks. The Old Railway Building has exhibits on local history, wildlife and geology. Geraldton has two cathedrals: the modern Cathedral of the Holy Cross, with its beautiful stained glass, and St Francis Xavier Cathedral, built from 1916 to 1938, in Byzantine style. Point Moore Lighthouse, with its distinctive red and white stripes, was shipped here from Britain and has been in continuous operation since 1878. The 1876 **Lighthouse Keeper's Cottage**, the town's first lighthouse, now houses Geraldton's Historical Society. Also in town, the **City of Greater Geraldton Regional Art Gallery** is one of the best galleries in the state, exhibiting the work of local artists and pieces from private and public collections.

A number of lookouts such as Separation Point Lookout and Mount Tarcoola Lookout give panoramic views of the city and ocean.

Geraldton's Point Moore Lighthouse

Museum of Geraldton

2 Museum Place, Batavia Coast Marina. **Tel** (08) 9921 5080.
Open 9:30am–3pm daily. **Closed** public holidays. Donation. ♿

Lighthouse Keeper's Cottage

355 Chapman Rd. **Tel** (08) 9923 1837.
Open Contact the Geraldton Visitor Centre for opening times: (08) 9956 6670. ♿

City of Greater Geraldton Regional Art Gallery

24 Chapman Rd. **Tel** (08) 9964 7170.
Open 10am–4pm Mon–Sat, 1–4pm public hols. **Closed** Sun, Good Fri, 25 & 26 Dec & 1 Jan. ♿

❹ Abrolhos Islands

Geraldton. from Geraldton.
Geraldton (08) 9956 6670.

About 60 km (37 miles) off Geraldton lie more than 100 coral islands called the Houtman Abrolhos – the world's southernmost coral island formation. While it is not possible to stay on the islands, tours enable visitors to fly over them or to dive among the coral.

❺ Kalbarri National Park

Kalbarri. Kalbarri (08) 9937 1140. **Open** sunrise–sunset daily. ♿
kalbarri.org.au

The magnificent landscape of Kalbarri National Park includes stunning coastal scenery and beautiful inland gorges lining the Murchison River. The park has a number of coastal and river walking trails which lead to breathtaking views and fascinating rock formations. The trails vary in length, from brief two-hour strolls to four-day hikes. Highlights of the park include Hawks Head, a picnic area with views of the gorge; Nature's Window, where a rock formation frames a view of the river; and Ross Graham Lookout, where visitors can bathe in the river pools. By the ocean, Pot Alley provides awesome views of the rugged coastal cliffs and Rainbow Valley is made up of layers of multi-coloured rocks.

The access town for the park, Kalbarri, is situated on the coast and provides good tourist facilities. The park's roads are accessible to most vehicles, but are unsuitable for caravans or trailers. The best time to visit is from July to October, when the weather is dry and the temperatures are not prohibitive. In summer, they can soar to 40°C (104°F).

❻ Shark Bay World Heritage and Marine Park

See pp330–31.

A bridge across the Gascoyne River in Carnarvon

❼ Carnarvon

5,000. 21 Robinson St, (08) 9941 1146. carnarvon.org.au

The town of Carnarvon, standing at the mouth of the Gascoyne River, acts as the commercial and administrative centre for the surrounding Gascoyne region, the gateway to Western Australia's north. Tropical fruit plantations line the river here, some offering tours and selling produce.

In Carnarvon itself, One Mile Jetty on Babbage Island is a popular place for fishing, and Jubilee Hall, built in 1887, houses a fine arts and crafts centre. Carnarvon is also home to a busy prawn and scallop processing industry.

Environs

About 70 km (43 miles) north of Carnarvon lie the Blowholes, a spectacular coastal rock formation where air and spray is forced through holes in the rocks in violent spurts up to 20 m (66 ft) high.

Stunning gorge views from Hawks Head Lookout, Kalbarri National Park

❻ Shark Bay World Heritage and Marine Park

Shark Bay Marine Park was designated a World Heritage Area in 1991 *(see pp30–31)*. The park is home to many endangered species of plants and animals, and various unusual natural processes have, over the millennia, given rise to some astounding natural features and spectacular coastal scenery. Because this is a World Heritage Area, visitors are asked to abide by conservation rules, particularly when fishing. The only way to travel around the park is by car, and large areas are only accessible by 4WD.

François Peron National Park

At the tip of Peron Peninsula, this national park, now accessible by 4WD, was a vast sheep station until 1990.

Bernier Island

Dorre Island

Dirk Hartog Island

④

Denham Sound

François Peron National Park

Useless Loop

Useless Loop Road

Peron Homestead

Originally the centre of the Peron sheep station, the homestead offers an insight into pastoral life. The station also has two artesian bores that carry hot water (44°C, 111°F) to tubs at the surface in which visitors may bathe.

KEY

① **The Zuytdorp Cliffs** are named after the Dutch ship *Zuytdorp*, wrecked in these waters in 1721.

② **Steep Point** faces the Indian Ocean and is the westernmost point of mainland Australia. From here it is possible to see the Zuytdorp Cliffs.

③ **Denham** was originally settled as a pearling community, but is now mainly a fishing and tourist centre.

④ **Cape Inscription** is the place where Dutchman Dirk Hartog became the first known European to set foot in Australia in 1616 *(see p53)*.

⑤ **Northwest Coastal Highway**

Eagle Bluff

The top of this bluff offers fine panoramic views across Freycinet Reach, with a chance of seeing the eagles that nest on the offshore islands and marine creatures in the clear ocean waters.

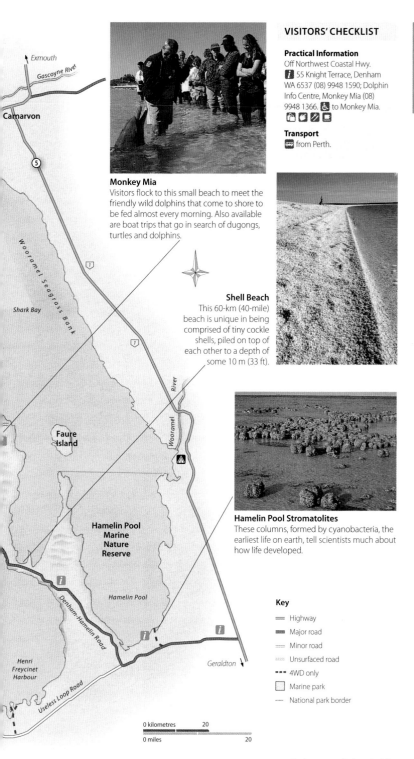

VISITORS' CHECKLIST

Practical Information
Off Northwest Coastal Hwy.
🅸 55 Knight Terrace, Denham
WA 6537 (08) 9948 1590; Dolphin
Info Centre, Monkey Mia (08)
9948 1366. ♿ to Monkey Mia.
🄯 🄯 🄯 🄯

Transport
🚌 from Perth.

Monkey Mia
Visitors flock to this small beach to meet the
friendly wild dolphins that come to shore to
be fed almost every morning. Also available
are boat trips that go in search of dugongs,
turtles and dolphins.

Shell Beach
This 60-km (40-mile)
beach is unique in being
comprised of tiny cockle
shells, piled on top of
each other to a depth of
some 10 m (33 ft).

Hamelin Pool Stromatolites
These columns, formed by cyanobacteria, the
earliest life on earth, tell scientists much about
how life developed.

Key

══ Highway
▬▬ Major road
═══ Minor road
╌╌╌ Unsurfaced road
▪▪▪ 4WD only
☐ Marine park
— National park border

0 kilometres   20
0 miles   20

Exmouth
Gascoyne River
Carnarvon
⑤
Wooramel Seagrass Bank
Shark Bay
Faure Island
Wooramel River
**Hamelin Pool
Marine
Nature
Reserve**
Hamelin Pool
*Henri
Freycinet
Harbour*
Denham–Hamelin Road
Useless Loop Road
Geraldton

For keys to symbols *see back flap*

❽ Ningaloo Reef Marine Park

🚌 Exmouth. **ℹ** Milyering Discovery Centre, Yardie Creek Rd, Cape Range National Park (08) 9949 2808. **Open** 9am–3:45pm daily. **Closed** 25 Dec.

This marine park runs for 260 km (162 miles) along the west coast of Exmouth Peninsula and around the tip into Exmouth Gulf. The Ningaloo Reef is the largest fringing barrier reef in the state and offers many of the attractions of the east coast's Great Barrier Reef *(see pp216–21)*. In many places, it lies very close to the shore, and its turquoise waters are popular with snorkellers. Apart from numerous types of coral and brightly coloured fish, the marine park also protects a number of species. Several beaches at the northern end of the park are used by sea turtles as mating and breeding areas. Further offshore, it is possible to see the gentle whale shark from late March to May. Capable of growing to up to 18 m (60 ft), this is the largest fish in the world.

The best areas for snorkelling are Turquoise Bay or the still waters of Coral Bay. A number of companies offer organized scuba diving outings. Visitors can camp on the park's coastline at several sites managed by the Department of Environment and Conservation (DEC). Fishing is another popular pursuit here, but catches are very strictly controlled.

Yardie Creek Gorge in Cape Range National Park, near Exmouth

❾ Exmouth

🏔 2,200. ✈ 🚌 **ℹ** Murat Rd (08) 9949 1176. **W** visitningaloo.com.au

Situated on the eastern side of the Exmouth Peninsula, this small town was originally built in 1967 to service the local airforce base. A military presence is still very much in evidence, but today the town is more important as a tourist destination, used as a base for exploring the Ningaloo Reef Marine Park and the Cape Range National Park. Giant turtles and whale sharks can frequently be seen from the nearby coastline.

Slightly outside of town, at Vlaming Head, lies the wreck of the SS *Mildura*, a cattle transporter which sank in 1907 and is still visible from the shore. Nearby stands the Vlaming

Lighthouse, on a high bluff offering striking, panoramic views across the entire peninsula.

Environs
Cape Range National Park contains a low mountain range with spectacular gorges and rocky outcrops. This area was originally under water and it is possible to discern the fossils of ancient coral in the limestone. Local wildlife includes kangaroos, emus and large lizards. There are two main wilderness walks, but visitors should not attempt these in summer as temperatures can reach as high as 50°C (120°F).

Yardie Creek is on the western side of the park, only 1 km (0.5 miles) from the ocean. A short walk along gorge cliffs leads to the spectacular canyon, where you may catch sight of rock wallabies on the far canyon wall. A cruise through the gorges is also available.

❿ Dampier

🏔 1,400. ✈ 🚌 **ℹ** Lot 4548 De Witt Road, Karratha (08) 9144 4600. **Open** 9am–4pm Mon–Sat (to 1pm Sat).

Dampier stands on King Bay on the Burrup Peninsula, facing the 40 or so islands of the Dampier Archipelago. It was established and still acts as a service centre and port for mining areas inland; natural gas from the nearby Northwest Shelf Project is processed here for domestic and export markets. The town also has the largest desalination plant in Australia. This can be viewed from the Dampier Solar Evaporated Salt Mine Lookout. Dampier is also a popular base for offshore and beach anglers. Every August, game-fishing enthusiasts converge on the town for the Dampier Classic and Game Fishing Classic.

The Burrup Peninsula is one of the most renowned ancient Aboriginal art sites in Australia, created by the Yapurrara Aborigines.

Environs
The Dampier Archipelago, within 45 km (28 miles) of the town, offers a range of activities

White sands of Turquoise Bay in Ningaloo Reef Marine Park

Honeymoon Cove, one of the most popular beaches in Point Samson

from game fishing to whale-watching. Sport fishing here is particularly good, with reef and game species such as tuna, trevally and queenfish on offer.

Almost half of the islands are nature reserves and are home to rare species, including the Pilbara olive python and the king brown snake. Access to the islands is by boat only.

Simple façade of the Holy Trinity Church in Roebourne

⑪ Roebourne

🏠 3,100. 🚌 ⓘ Queen St (08) 9182 1060. **Open** 9am–3pm daily.

About 14 km (9 miles) inland, Roebourne, established in 1866, is the oldest town in the Pilbara. The town retains several late 19th-century stone buildings, including the Old Gaol which now houses the tourist office and a craft gallery and the Holy Trinity Church (1894). Roebourne also marks the start of the 52-km (32-mile) Emma Withnell Heritage Trail, which takes a scenic route from here to Cossack and Point Samson. Trail guides are available at the tourist office.

Environs
Some 150 km (93 miles) inland lies the 200,000-ha (500,000-acre) Millstream-Chichester National Park with its lush freshwater pools.

⑫ Cossack Historical Town

🚌 ⓘ Queen St, Roebourne (08) 9182 1060. 🅦 **roebourne.org.au**

In 1863, the town of Tien Tsin Harbour was established and quickly became the home of a burgeoning pearling industry that attracted people from as far away as Japan and China. The settlement was renamed Cossack in 1872 after a visit by Governor Weld aboard HMS *Cossack*. However, the town's moment soon passed. The pearling industry moved on to Broome *(see p334)* and by 1910 Cossack's harbour had silted up. In the late 1970s, restoration work of this ghost town began and today, under the management of the Shire of Roebourne, it has become a curiosity that continues to fascinate many visitors.

Old courthouse in Cossack Historical Town

⑬ Point Samson

🏠 300. ⓘ Lot 4548 De Witt Rd, Karratha (08) 9144 4600. **Open** 9am–4pm Mon–Sat (1pm Sat).

This small settlement was founded in 1910 to take on the port duties formerly performed by Cossack. Today, there is a modest fishing industry and two harbours. The town's best beaches are found at Honeymoon Cove and Samson Reef, where visitors can snorkel or search for rock oysters at low tide.

⑭ Karijini National Park

ⓘ Banyjima Drive, Karijini National Park (08) 9189 8121. **Open** 9am–4pm daily. 🅦 **parks.dpaw.wa.gov.au**

Set in the Hamersley Range, in the heart of the Pilbara region, Karijini National Park covers some 600,000 ha (1,500,000 acres). It is the second-largest national park in the state after Purnululu National Park *(see p335)*.

The park has three types of landscape: rolling hills and ridges covered in eucalypt forests; arid, low-lying shrubland; and, in the north, spectacular gorges. The best times to visit the park are in winter, when the days are temperate, and in spring, when carpets of wildflowers are in spectacular bloom.

The Kimberley and the Deserts

Australia's last frontier, the Kimberley is a vast, remote upland region of dry, red landscape. Deep rivers cut through mountain ranges, and parts of the coastline have the highest tidal range in the southern hemisphere. Seasonal climatic extremes add to the area's sense of isolation as the harsh heat of the dry season and the torrential rains of the wet hamper access to the hostile terrain. April to September is the best time to visit, offering views of the country's best natural sights such as the Wolfe Creek Meteorite Crater and the Bungle Bungles. To the south lie the huge, inhospitable Great Sandy and Gibson deserts.

LOCATOR MAP

- The Kimberley and the Deserts
- North of Perth pp326–33

Sights at a Glance

- ⓯ Broome
- ⓰ Derby
- ⓱ Halls Creek
- ⓲ Purnululu (Bungle Bungle) National Park
- ⓳ Wyndham

Key

— Major road
=== Minor road
-- Track
— State border

⓯ Broome

▲ 14,500. ✈ 🚉 🚌
ℹ 1 Hamersley St (08) 9195 2200.
🌐 **visitbroome.com.au**

Broome, first settled by Europeans in the 1860s, soon became Western Australia's most profitable pearling region. Pearl divers from Asia swelled the town in the 1880s and helped give it the multicultural flavour that remains today. The tourist industry has now superseded pearling, but the town's past can still be seen in several original stores, as well as the Chinese and Japanese cemeteries that contain the graves of hundreds of pearl divers.

Just outside town is the popular Cable Beach. Nearby, the **Malcolm Douglas Crocodile Park** offers daily tours to see these animals (feeding tour is at 3pm).

🐊 **Malcolm Douglas Crocodile Park**
Broome Hwy. **Tel** (08) 9193 6580.
Open 2–5pm daily. **Closed** 25 Dec. ♿

Stunning natural rock formations at Broome

A freshwater crocodile basking in the sun, Windjana Gorge, near Derby

⓰ Derby

🏘 5,000. ✈ 🚌 ℹ 30 Loch St (08) 9191 1426. **Open** 9am–4pm Mon–Fri, 9am–noon Sat.

Derby is the gateway to a region of stunning gorges. Points of interest here include the 1920s Wharfingers House, Old Derby Gaol, and the Botanical Gardens.

South of town is the 1,000-year old Prison Boab (baobab) tree, 14 m (45 ft) in circumference. At the end of the 19th century, it was used to house prisoners overnight before their final journey to Derby Gaol.

Environs

Derby stands at the western end of the Gibb River Road, which leads towards the three national parks collectively known as the Devonian Reef National Parks. The parks of Windjana Gorge, Tunnel Creek and **Geikie Gorge** contain spectacular gorge scenery.

🏕 Geikie Gorge National Park

🚌 to Derby. ℹ Derby (08) 9191 5112. **Open** Apr–Nov: daily. **Closed** Dec–Mar.

⓱ Halls Creek

🏘 1,200. 🚌 ℹ 2 Hall St (08) 9168 6262.

Halls Creek was the site of Western Australia's first gold rush in 1885, and today is a centre for mineral mining. Close to the original town site is a vertical wall of quartz rock, known as China Wall. About 130 km (80 miles) to the south is the world's second-largest meteorite crater, in **Wolfe Creek Crater National Park**.

🏕 Wolfe Creek Crater National Park

🚌 Halls Creek. ℹ Lot 248 Ivanhoe Rd, Kununurra (08) 9168 6262. **Open** Apr–Sep: daily. **Closed** wet weather (roads impassable).

⓲ Purnululu (Bungle Bungle) National Park

🚌 Halls Creek. ℹ Purnululu National Park (08) 9168 7300. **Open** Apr–Nov: daily. 🏕 🚻

Covering some 320,000 ha (790,000 acres) of the most isolated landscape in Western Australia, Purnululu National Park was declared in 1987. It is home to the local Kija and Jaru

The intriguing domes of the Bungle Bungles, Purnululu National Park

people, who co-operate with national park authorities to develop cultural tourism.

The most famous part of the park is the Bungle Bungle Range, consisting of unique beehive-shaped domes of rock encased in a skin of silica and cyanobacterium.

⓳ Wyndham

🏘 700. ✈ 🚌 ℹ Kimberley Motors, 6 Great Northern Hwy (08) 9161 1281.

The port of Wyndham lies at the northern tip of the Great Northern Highway, on Cambridge Gulf. The town was established in 1888, partly to service the Halls Creek gold rush and partly as a centre for the local pastoral industry. It also provided supplies, which were carried by Afghan camel-trains, for cattle stations in the northern Kimberley. The town's Afghan cemetery is a reminder of those traders who were essential to the survival of pioneer home-steads in the interior.

The part of the town known as Old Wyndham Port was the original town site and still con-tains a number of 19th-century buildings, including the old post office, the old courthouse and Anthon's Landing, where the first jetty was erected. The Port Museum displays a vivid photo-graphic history of the port.

The area around Wyndham has a large crocodile population. Freshwater and saltwater crocodiles can be seen occasionally in the wild at Blood Drain Crocodile Lookout and Crocodile Hole. To complete the picture, a 4-m (13-ft) high concrete saltwater crocodile greets visitors at the entrance to the town. Saltwater crocodiles have a taste for people, so exercise caution.

About 25 km (15 miles) from Wyndham, Aboriginal petro-glyphs can be seen at the picnic spot of Moochalabra Dam. Also worth mentioning is the Five Rivers Lookout located at the highest point from which to view the landscape. It provides a spectacular view of the five rivers which enter the Cambridge Gulf and surrounding mangroves.

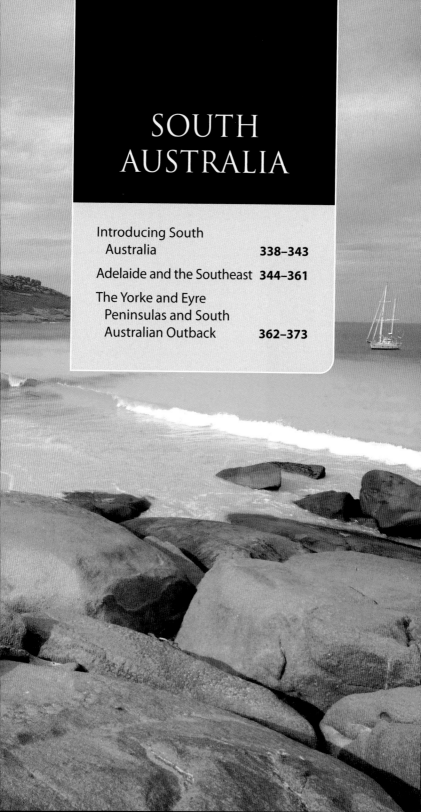

SOUTH AUSTRALIA

South Australia at a Glance

South Australia contains a wide range of landscapes. A striking coastline of sandy beaches and steep cliffs gives way to lush valleys, mountains and rolling plains of wheat and barley. Further inland, the terrain changes starkly as the climate becomes hotter and drier. The South Australian Outback encompasses huge areas and includes the Flinders Ranges and Coober Pedy, the opal-mining town with "dugout" homes. Most of the population lives in the capital, Adelaide, and the wine-making regions of Clare Valley and the Barossa.

Locator Map

The Yorke and Eyre Peninsulas and South Australian Outback
(see pp362–73)

William Creek

Coober Pedy

Coober Pedy's golf course is one of the few features above ground in this strange Outback mining town. Many of the town's houses are built underground to escape the area's harsh, dusty climate *(see p372)*.

Kingoonya

Nullarbor Roadhouse

Penong

Ceduna

Port Au

Kyancutta

Whya

Port Lincoln

Port Augusta *(see p369)* is a major road and rail hub that also serves as the gateway to the Far North of the state. It retains several early homesteads among its modern buildings.

Kangaroo Island *(see p358)* is an unspoilt haven for abundant native wildlife. At Kirkpatrick Point in the southwest lie the Remarkable Rocks, sculpted by the wind, rain and sea.

0 km	100
0 miles	100

◀ Coastline around Pearson Island, in the Eyre Peninsula

Quorn *(see p373)* was an important railway town at the end of the 19th century and has many reminders of its pioneering days. Today it marks the start of the Pichi Richi Railway, a restored track running vintage trains and locomotives for tourists.

The Flinders Ranges *(see p373)* stretch from north of St Vincent's Gulf far into the Outback. They include some of South Australia's most rugged scenery and offer fine bushwalking.

Moomba

The Barossa wine region encompasses the Barossa Valley and Eden Valley. Both are lush areas of rolling hills and home to dozens of famous wineries dating from the 19th century *(see pp360–61)*.

Adelaide *(see pp348–63)* is an elegant state capital on the River Torrens. Its cosmopolitan atmosphere is enhanced by a lively restaurant, arts and entertainment scene.

Adelaide

Adelaide and the Southeast *(see pp344–61)*

Mount Gambier *(see p358)* lies on the slopes of an extinct volcano of the same name. One of the volcano's crater lakes, Blue Lake, shows its intense hue in the summer months.

Mount Gambier

Birds of South Australia

The vast, varied habitats of South Australia are home to some 380 bird species. Gulls, sea eagles and penguins live along the coast, while waders, ducks and cormorants are found in the internal wetlands. Parrots are common in Adelaide's parkland. The mallee scrub, which once covered much of the state, is home to the mallee fowl and an array of honeyeaters. The Flinders Ranges and the South Australian Outback are the domain of birds of prey such as the peregrine falcon and the wedge-tailed eagle. Although much land has been cleared for farming, many habitats are protected in the national parks.

Fairy penguins are the smallest penguins found in Australia. The only species to breed on the mainland, they feed on fish and squid skilfully caught underwater.

The Flinders Ranges and Outback Habitat

The rugged mountains and deep gorges of the Flinders Ranges support a wide variety of bird species. Most spectacular are the birds of prey. Wedge-tailed eagles' nests can be found in large gum trees or on rock ledges, and the eagles are commonly seen feeding on dead animals in the arid Outback regions.

Mallee Scrub Habitat

Much of this low-level scrubland has been cleared for agriculture. Remaining areas such as Billiat National Park near Loxton provide an important habitat for several elusive species. Golden whistlers, red and brush wattlebirds and white-eared honeyeaters can be seen here by patient bird-watchers. The best seasons to visit are late winter, spring and early summer.

Wedge-tailed eagles, with their huge wingspan of up to 2.3 m (7 ft 6 in), typically perch on dead trees and telephone poles.

Peregrine falcons do not build nests; they lay their eggs on bare ledges or in tree hollows. Magnificent in flight, they descend on their prey at great speed with wings half or fully closed.

Mallee fowls, a wary species, stand 60 cm (24 in) tall. They spend most of the year building mounds, made of soil, leaves and twigs in which to lay their eggs.

Southern scrub robins hop along the ground to forage for food around mallee trees and shrubs. The female lays a single green-grey egg, the colour providing camouflage within the scrub.

The Emu

Emus are huge flightless birds unique to Australia. Second only to the ostrich in height, they stand 1.5–1.9 m (5–6 ft 3 in) tall. They have long powerful legs and can run at speeds of up to 50 km/h (30 mph) over short distances. The females have a distinctive voice like a thudding drum. They lay their eggs on the ground on a thin layer of grass and leaves. The male incubates them for seven weeks, then broods and accompanies the young for up to 18 months. Common all over Australia, emus are found mainly in open, pastoral areas. Moving alone or in flocks, they are highly mobile and have a large home range.

Alert gaze of the Australian emu

Soft, grey-black plumage of an emu

Wetland Habitat

Wetlands such as Coorong National Park *(see p355)* are vital feeding and breeding grounds for a wide range of water birds. They provide essential refuge in times of drought for many endangered birds. Migratory birds, such as sharp-tailed sandpipers from Siberia, use these areas to feed and rest before continuing on their annual journeys.

Brolgas stand up to 1.3 m (4 ft 3 in) tall, with a wingspan of up to 2.3 m (7 ft 6 in). They are renowned for their impressive dancing displays, leaping, bowing and flapping.

Freckled ducks are similar to primitive waterfowl, with swan-like characteristics. Dark, with no obvious markings, they are hard to spot. This is one of the world's rarest ducks.

Woodland Habitat

Habitats in woodland areas such as the Belair National Park near Adelaide support many species such as honeyeaters, rosellas and kookaburras. There is usually an abundance of food in such places and good opportunities to nest and roost. Despite increased human settlement in these areas, the birdlife is still rich. Dawn and dusk are the best times for seeing birds.

Adelaide rosellas are commonly found in the Mount Lofty Ranges and the parklands of Adelaide. Their plumage is in brilliant shades of red, orange and blue.

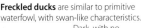

Laughing kookaburras are the world's largest kingfishers. They are renowned for their loud, manic laughing call, often begun by one bird and quickly taken up by others.

Wines of South Australia

South Australia produces more than half of Australia's wines, including many of its finest. From its numerous vineyards comes a dazzling diversity of wines – several are made from some of the oldest vines in the world. The state has a long history of wine-making and is home to some very famous producers, such as Hardys, Penfolds, Jacob's Creek and Banrock Station. Virtually all wineries welcome tourists for tastings.

Sevenhill Cellars is in the heart of the Clare Valley, one of South Australia's prime wine-producing regions.

Knappstein Winery is located in the Enterprise winery and brewery in Clare Valley and produces Riesling that is European in style.

Bridgewater Mill winery is renowned in the area for its excellent restaurant. Daily tastings of its own labels and Petaluma wines are offered at the cellar door.

Wine Regions

South Australia has eight designated wine zones and within these zones are many well-known regions. These include the Barossa (see pp360–61), which has been producing wine for 150 years; the Clare Valley, which is noted for its Riesling, Cabernet Sauvignon and Shiraz; and Coonawarra, which is Australia's best red wine region, due to its soil. McLaren Vale, the Murray Valley, the Adelaide Plains, the Riverland, the Limestone Coast, and the Adelaide Hills are the other major districts.

Cabernet Sauvignon grapes are very successful in the state, with a ripe, fruity flavour.

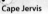

The Adelaide Hills are known for their excellent Pinot Noir, Chardonnay and Riesling grapes.

Kadina

Clare •

•**Bur**

Gawler •

ADELAIDE

• **Cape Jervis**

*La
Alexandrir*

Key

▦	Clare Valley	▦	Riverland
▦	Barossa Valley	▦	Langhorne Creek
▦	Eden Valley	▦	Padthaway
▦	Adelaide Hills	▦	Wrattonbully
▦	McLaren Vale	▦	Coonawarra

Wolf Blass' Barossa Black Label has a rich, oaky flavour, and is just one of this world-renowned vintner's individual wines. Blass has earned more than 2,000 international medals for his wine.

Olary Creek

...nda Creek

Murray River

Waikerie

Renmark

...ilem Bend

Key Facts

Location and Climate
The climate of Australia's central state ranges from Mediterranean-style in the Murray Valley to the cool Adelaide Hills and districts in the southeast. Vintage begins in high summer, when grapes are often picked and crushed at night to preserve maximum flavour.

Grape Varieties

The diverse climate ensures that a wide range of grape varieties is planted. These include the whites of Riesling, Semillon, Sauvignon Blanc, Chardonnay; and the reds of Shiraz, Grenache, Pinot Noir, Cabernet Sauvignon, Merlot.

Good Producers
Penfolds, Bethany, Grant Burge, St Hallett, Henschke, Seppelt, Charles Melton, Turkey Flat, Paracombe, Hardys, Orlando, Wolf Blass, Yalumba, Rockford, Willows, Petaluma, Grosset, Wendoree, Pauletts, Pikes, Wynns, Bowen, Chapel Hill, d'Arenberg, Peter Lehmann, Noons, Bridgewater Mill, Hollicks.

Barrel maturation at the Berri Renmano winery in the Murray Valley is one of the traditional techniques still used in the production of top-quality table wines.

• Keith

Kingston

Ready Creek

• Mount Gambier

0 km   50

0 miles   50

Wynns Winery at Coonawarra is known for fine Cabernet Sauvignon and other reds. The winery itself is equally distinctive – an image of its triple-gable architecture appears on the wine labels.

Yalumba 'Menzies' Vineyard, founded in 1849, is one of the oldest in the Coonawarra region. The grapes are grown here, but the wine is made at the winery in the Barossa Valley (*see p360–61*). The climate in the Coonawarra area is similar to that of Bordeaux in France.

ADELAIDE AND THE SOUTHEAST

The Southeast is a region rich with pine forests, wineries and a spectacular coastline. The state capital, Adelaide, is a vibrant city, whose surrounding hills abound with vineyards from the Barossa to McLaren Vale. To the east, the great Murray River meanders from the Victoria border down to the Southern Ocean. Just off the Fleurieu Peninsula lies Kangaroo Island, a haven for wildlife.

Home to Aborigines for more than 50,000 years, this region was settled by Europeans in 1836 when Governor John Hindmarsh proclaimed the area a British colony. William Light, the Surveyor General, chose the site of the city of Adelaide.

The settlement was based on a theory of free colonization funded solely by land sales, and no convicts were transported here. Elegant Adelaide was carefully planned by Colonel Light: its ordered grid pattern, centred on pretty squares and gardens, is surrounded by parkland. Wealth from agriculture and mining paid for many of Adelaide's fine Victorian buildings. In the mid-20th century, the city established a significant manufacturing industry, in particular of motor vehicles and household appliances. Adelaide still has a focus on high technology.

South Australia has always had a tradition of tolerance. Many of the first settlers were non-conformists from Great Britain seeking a more open society. Other early migrants included Lutherans escaping persecution in Germany. They settled in Hahndorf and the Barossa, where they established a wine industry.

With high rainfall and irrigated by the Murray River, the region is the most fertile in the state. The coastline includes the Fleurieu Peninsula and the beautiful Coorong National Park. Offshore, Kangaroo Island has stunning scenery and bountiful native wildlife.

Port and sherry casks at a winery in the Barossa

◀ Evening falls on the vineyards of the Barossa

Exploring Adelaide and the Southeast

Adelaide and the Southeast area encompass the most bountiful and productive regions of South Australia. Adelaide, the state's capital city and the most obvious base for exploring the region, lies on a flat plain between the Mount Lofty Ranges and the popular white sandy beaches of Gulf St Vincent, to the east of Cape Jervis. The city itself is green and elegant, with many historic sites to explore. To the northeast, beyond the Adelaide Hills, are quaint 19th-century villages and the many wineries of the Barossa. To the east and south lies Australia's largest river, the Murray River, and the rolling hills of the Fleurieu Peninsula. Further to the southeast the beauty of the coastal Coorong National Park and the Southern Ocean coastline contrasts with the flat, agricultural area inland. Offshore lies the natural splendour of Kangaroo Island, with its abundance of native wildlife and striking rock formations.

Riverton
Port Pirie
Kapunda
Tanunda
Angas
Gawler
THE
Gulf St Vincent
Springton
GORGE
WILDLIFE PARK
BIRDW
ADELAIDE
MOUNT LOFTY
Man
BELAIR NATIONAL PARK
HAHN
Port Noarlunga
Murray Bridg
McLaren Vale
STRATHAL
Lake Alexand
Cape Jervis
Victor Harbor
Port Elliot
Goolwa
Meni
Kingscote
Penneshaw
Limestone
Parndana
American River
KANGAROO ISLAND
Flinders Chase National Park
Cape du Couedic

Sights at a Glance

1. *Adelaide pp348–53*
2. Belair National Park
3. Gorge Wildlife Park
4. Hahndorf
5. Strathalbyn
6. Mount Lofty
7. Birdwood
8. Kangaroo Island
9. Mount Gambier
10. Penola
11. Naracoorte Caves National Park
12. Murray River

Tour

13. The Barossa

St Peter's Anglican Cathedral, seen across Adelaide's parkland

Murray River winding between Swan Reach and Walker Flat

Getting Around

The inner city of Adelaide is best explored on foot; it is compact, well laid out and flat. There is a public transport system of mostly buses, and some trains, throughout the metropolitan area, although services are often restricted at weekends. However, for those with a car, the city's roads are good and the traffic generally light. Outside Adelaide, public transport is very limited, although coach tours are available to most areas. A car provides the most efficient means of exploring the region, with a network of high-standard roads and highways. In addition, a domestic air service operates between Adelaide and Mount Gambier. Kangaroo Island is serviced by air from Adelaide and also by ferry from Cape Jervis. The predominantly flat landscape also makes this a popular area for cyclists and walkers.

Key

══	Highway
──	Major road
⋯⋯	Minor road
──	Scenic route
⊷⊶	Main railway
──	Minor railway
══	State border

0 kilometres   50

0 miles   50

For keys to symbols *see back flap*

● Street-by-Street: Adelaide

Adelaide's cultural centre lies between the grand, tree-lined North Terrace and the River Torrens. Along North Terrace is a succession of imposing 19th-century public buildings, including the state library, museum and art gallery and two university campuses. To the west, on the bank of the river, is the Festival Centre. This multipurpose complex of theatres, including an outdoor amphitheatre, is home to the renowned annual Adelaide Festival *(see p45)*. To the east, also by the river, lie the botanic and zoological gardens and the National Wine Centre of Australia.

River Torrens
Visitors can hire paddleboats to travel along this gentle river and see Adelaide from water level.

The Migration Museum tells the stories of the thousands of people from more than 100 nations who left everything behind to start a new life in South Australia.

Festival Centre
Completed in 1977, this arts complex enjoys a picturesque riverside setting and is a popular place for a walk.

Parliament House
Ten marble Corinthian columns grace the façade of Parliament House, which was completed in 1939, more than 50 years after construction first began.

★ **Adelaide Botanic Garden**
Begun in 1855, these peaceful gardens cover an area of 20 ha (50 acres). They include artificial lakes and the beautiful Bicentennial Conservatory, in which a tropical rainforest environment has been re-created.

VISITORS' CHECKLIST

Practical Information
1.2 million.
108 North Terrace
1300 655 276. Adelaide Fringe; Adelaide Festival; WOMADelaide (all in Feb/Mar).

Transport
West Beach, 10 km (6 miles) W of the city.
North Terrace (suburban); Richmond Rd, Keswick (interstate). Central Bus Station, Franklin St.

Art Gallery of South Australia
Contemporary works, such as Christopher Healey's *Drinking Fountains*, feature here alongside period painting and sculpture.

Key
— Suggested route

0 metres 100
0 yards 100

The State Library of South Australia houses an extensive collection of reference material and various exhibitions, such as *South Australiana*, a permanent exhibition that explores South Australia's history and culture.

★ **South Australian Museum**
Chiefly a natural history museum, the South Australian Museum has an excellent reputation for its fine Aboriginal collection, including this painting on bark, *Assembling the Totem*, by a Melville Island artist *(see p278)*.

Exploring Adelaide

Adelaide, a city of great charm with an unhurried way of life, is easily explored on foot. Well planned on a grid pattern, it is bordered by wide terraces and parkland. Within the city are a number of garden squares and gracious stone buildings. However, while Adelaide values its past, it is very much a modern city. The balmy climate and excellent local food and wine have given rise to an abundance of streetside restaurants and cafés. With its acclaimed Adelaide Festival *(see p45)*, the city prides itself on being an important bastion of traditional arts and culture.

Central Market
Gouger St. **Tel** (08) 8203 7494.
Open Tue–Sat (limited stalls on Wed).
Closed public hols.

Just west of Victoria Square, between Gouger and Grote streets, Adelaide Central Market has provided a profusion of tastes and aromas in the city for more than 140 years. The changing ethnic pattern of Adelaide society is reflected in the diversity of produce available today. Asian shops now sit beside older European-style butchers and delicatessens, and part of the area has become Adelaide's own little Chinatown. Around the market are dozens of restaurants and cafés.

Victoria Square
King William & Franklin sts.

Victoria Square lies at the geographic heart of the city. At the southern end of the square stands a fountain designed by sculptor John Dowie in 1968. Its theme is the three rivers from which Adelaide draws its water: the Torrens, the Murray and the Onkaparinga. Government buildings were erected around much of the square during colonial days and many of these buildings still stand as reminders of a bygone age.

On the north side of Victoria Square stands the General Post Office, an impressive building with an ornate main hall and a clock tower. Opened in 1872, it was hailed by English novelist Anthony Trollope as the "grandest edifice in the town".

On the corner of Wakefield Street, to the east of Victoria Square, stands St Francis Xavier Catholic Cathedral. The original cathedral, dedicated in 1858, was a simpler building and plans for expansion were hampered by the lack of rich Catholics in the state. The cathedral was only completed in 1996, when the spire was finally added.

To the south of the square is Adelaide's legal centre and the Magistrates Court. The Supreme Court, built in the 1860s, has a Palladian façade.

Adelaide Town Hall
128 King William St.
Tel (08) 8203 7515. **Open** Mon–Fri.
Closed public hols.
W adelaidetownhall.com.au

When Adelaide Town Hall, designed in Italianate style by Edmund Wright, was built in 1866, it became the most significant structure on King William Street. It was not long before it took over as the city's premier venue for concerts and civic receptions, and it is still used as such today. Notable features include its grand staircase and decorative ceiling.

Detail of the ornate front parapet of Edmund Wright House

Edmund Wright House
59 King William St.

Edmund Wright House, originally built for the Bank of South Australia in 1878, was set to be demolished in 1971. However, a general outcry led to its public purchase and subsequent restoration. The building was renamed after its main architect, Edmund Wright. The skill and workmanship displayed in the finely proportioned and detailed façade is also evident in the beautiful interior. Today the building is the Migrant Resource Centre, and it offers only limited access to the general public.

Further along King William Street, at the corner of North Terrace, stands one of Adelaide's finest statues, the South African War Memorial. It shows a "spirited horse and his stalwart rider" and stands in memory of those who lost their lives in the Boer War.

Victoria Square in the centre of Adelaide

For hotels and restaurants in this area see p491 and pp522–3

🏛 **Migration Museum**

82 Kintore Ave. **Tel** (08) 8207 7580.
Open 10am–5pm Mon–Fri, 1–5pm
Sat & Sun. **Closed** Good Fri, 25 Dec.
🚻 **w** migration.history.sa.gov.au

The Migration Museum is
located behind the State Library
in what was once Adelaide's
Destitute Asylum. It reflects the
cultural diversity of South
Australian society by telling the
stories of people from many
parts of the world who came
here to start a new life. Exhibits,
including re-creations of early
settlers' houses, explain the
immigrants' reasons for leaving
their homeland and their hopes
for a new life. The Memorial
Wall acknowledges that many
people were forced to leave
their homelands.

🏛 **South Australian Museum**

North Terrace. **Tel** (08) 8207 7500.
Open 10am–5pm daily.
Closed Good Fri, 25 Dec. 🚻
w samuseum.sa.gov.au

This museum, whose entrance
is framed by huge whale skeletons, has a number of interesting collections including an

Egyptian room and natural
history exhibits. Its most
important collection is its
internationally acclaimed
collection of Aboriginal artifacts
which boasts more than 37,000
individual items and 50,000
photographs, as well as many
sound and video recordings.

A street performer in Rundle Mall,
Adelaide's main shopping precinct

🖵 **Rundle Mall**

Rundle Mall. **Tel** (08) 8203 7200.
Open daily. **Closed** Good Fri, 25 Dec,
public hols. **w** rundlemall.com

Adelaide's main shopping area is
centred on Rundle Mall, with its

mixture of small shops, boutiques
and department stores. Several
arcades run off the mall, including
Adelaide Arcade. Built in the
1880s, it has Italianate elevations
at both ends and a central dome.
The interior was modernized in
the 1960s, but has since been
fully restored to its former glory.

🏛 **Tandanya**

253 Grenfell St. **Tel** (08) 8224 3200.
Open 10am–5pm Mon–Sat.
Closed most public holidays. 📷 🎭
🚻 **w** tandanya.com.au

Tandanya, the Kaurna Aboriginal
people's name for the Adelaide
area (it means "place of the red
kangaroo"), is an excellent
cultural institute celebrating
the Aboriginal and Torres Strait
Islander art and cultures. It was
established in 1989 and is the
first Aboriginal-owned and run
arts centre in Australia. The
institute features indigenous art
galleries, educational workshops
and performance areas. It is also
possible for visitors to meet
indigenous people. A great gift
shop sells authentic artifacts,
arts and crafts.

Adelaide City Centre

① Central Market
② Victoria Square
③ Adelaide Town Hall
④ Edmund Wright House
⑤ Migration Museum
⑥ South Australian
　 Museum
⑦ Rundle Mall
⑧ Ayers House
　 (see pp352–3)
⑨ Tandanya

0 metres　　　　500
0 yards　　　　　500

Ayers House

Ayers House is one of the best examples of Victorian architecture in Australia. It was the home of Sir Henry Ayers, a former Premier of South Australia and an influential businessman, from 1855 until his death in 1897. The original house was quite simple but was expanded over the years with the growing status and wealth of its owner. The final form of this elegant mansion is due largely to the noted colonial architect Sir George Strickland Kingston. The restored house is now run by the National Trust and also incorporates a function centre. The oldest section is open to the public and houses a fine collection of Victorian furniture, furnishings, memorabilia and art. Be sure to take the After Dark tour – if you dare!

Front of the house viewed from North Terrace

★ Bedroom
The main bedroom has been carefully restored to its late-Victorian style. Its authentic furnishings reflect the prosperity brought by South Australia's rich mining discoveries in the 1870s.

KEY

① **The Library**, furnished with a long dining table, can be hired for functions.

② **Slate roof**

③ **The Conservatory** is based around the original stables and coachhouse. Now a function centre, the whole area has been flooded with light by the addition of a glass roof.

④ **Local bluestone** was used in constructing the house, as with many 19th-century Adelaide houses. The north façade faces onto North Terrace, one of the city's main streets (see pp348–9).

⑤ **Veranda's original chequered tile flooring**

⑥ **The family drawing room** along with the adjacent family dining room, had test strips removed from its walls and ceiling to uncover some stunning original decoration. These rooms have now been fully restored.

Ballroom
This intricately decorated cornice dates from the 1870s. It is likely that it was painted by Charles Gow, an employee of the Scottish firm of Lyon and Cottier, who is believed to have undertaken extensive work at the house.

★ **State Dining Room**
Sir Henry loved to entertain, and lavish dinners were often held here. It boasts a hand-painted ceiling, grained woodwork and the original gas-lamp chandeliers.

VISITORS' CHECKLIST

Practical Information
288 North Terrace, Adelaide.
Tel (08) 8223 1234.
Open 10am–4pm Tue–Fri;
1–4pm Sat, Sun & public hols.
Closed Mon, Good Fri, 25 Dec.
🅿 📷 🎁 ♿ ground floor only.
ⓦ ayershousemuseum.org.au

Transport
🚌 99c (free).

③

④

Front entrance

⑥   ⑤

The story of Sir Henry Ayers

Sir Henry Ayers (1821–97) was born in Hampshire, England, the son of a dock worker. He married in 1840 and, a month later, emigrated with his bride to South Australia. After working briefly as a clerk, Ayers made his fortune in the state's new copper mines. Entering politics in 1857, he was appointed South Australia's Premier seven times between 1863 and 1873, and was President of the Legislative Council, 1881–93. Among many causes, he supported exploration of the interior (Ayers Rock, now Uluṟu, was named after him), but is chiefly remembered for his prominent role in the development of South Australia.

Statesman and businessman,
Sir Henry Ayers

Fleurieu Peninsula and Limestone Coast

The coastline south of Adelaide is rich and varied with beautiful beaches, magnificent coastal scenery and abundant birdlife. The southern coastline of the Fleurieu Peninsula is largely exposed to the mighty Southern Ocean. Here there are surfing beaches, long expanses of sand, sheltered bays and harbours and stark, weathered cliffs. The western side of the peninsula is more sheltered. There are very few commercial developments on the southeast's coastline and it is easy to find quiet, secluded beaches for swimming, surfing, fishing or walking. Just off South Australia's mainland, Kangaroo Island boasts both pristine swimming beaches and ruggedly beautiful windswept cliffs.

② ★ Cape Jervis

Visitors to the tiny hamlet of Cape Jervis can catch the ferry to Kangaroo Island across Backstairs Passage. The cape has good boating and fishing and is a hang-gliding centre.

McLaVale

Normanville

Fleurieu Peninsul

Flinders Chase National Park

Kangaroo Island

③ ★ Kingscote, Kangaroo Island

Kingscote, the island's largest town, has a small sandy beach with a tidal pool. There is rich birdlife in swampland south of the town.

① Port Noarlunga

Port Noarlunga boasts a fantastic beach and a protected reef with marine ecosystems that can be explored by snorkellers and scuba divers on a fully marked 800-m (2,600-ft) underwater trail.

④ Waitpinga Beach

Waitpinga Beach, on the southern coast of the Fleurieu Peninsula and part of Newland Head Conservation Park, is a spectacular surfing beach with waves rolling in off the Southern Ocean. Strong, unpredictable currents make the beach unsafe for swimming and suitable for experienced surfers only. The long stretch of clean white sand is a favourite for beach walkers.

⑥ Port Elliot

Port Elliot, together with nearby Victor Harbor, has long been a favourite place to escape the summer heat of Adelaide. Established in 1854 as a port for the Murray River trade, the town has a safe swimming beach and a fine cliff-top walk.

⑤ Victor Harbor

During the early 19th century, Victor Harbor gained notoriety as a whaling station. Today, the southern right whales frolicking offshore from June to October are a popular tourist attraction.

⑦ Hindmarsh Island

The quiet escapist destination of Hindmarsh Island can be reached by bridge from the town of Goolwa. On the island there are several good vantage points from which visitors can see the mouth of the Murray River.

Seal Bay, a windswept beach on the south coast, is a major Kangaroo Island tourist attraction, with visitors taking guided tours to see the endangered sea lions.

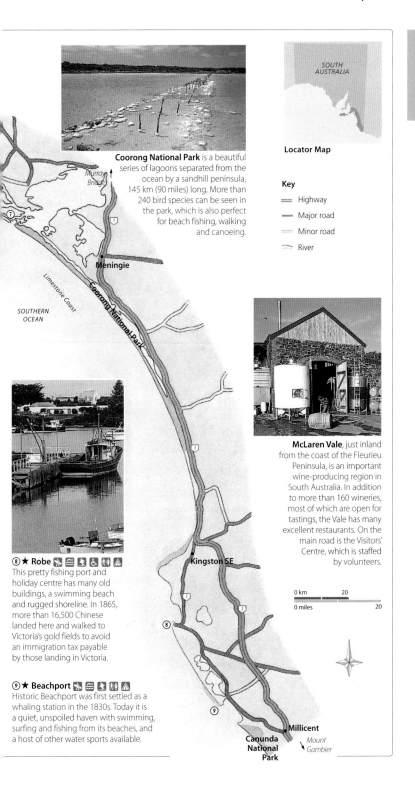

Coorong National Park is a beautiful series of lagoons separated from the ocean by a sandhill peninsula, 145 km (90 miles) long. More than 240 bird species can be seen in the park, which is also perfect for beach fishing, walking and canoeing.

Locator Map

Key

= Highway

— Major road

⋯ Minor road

~ River

McLaren Vale, just inland from the coast of the Fleurieu Peninsula, is an important wine-producing region in South Australia. In addition to more than 160 wineries, most of which are open for tastings, the Vale has many excellent restaurants. On the main road is the Visitors' Centre, which is staffed by volunteers.

⑧ ★ **Robe**
This pretty fishing port and holiday centre has many old buildings, a swimming beach and rugged shoreline. In 1865, more than 16,500 Chinese landed here and walked to Victoria's gold fields to avoid an immigration tax payable by those landing in Victoria.

⑨ ★ **Beachport**
Historic Beachport was first settled as a whaling station in the 1830s. Today it is a quiet, unspoiled haven with swimming, surfing and fishing from its beaches, and a host of other water sports available.

Old Government House in Belair National Park

❷ Belair National Park

Tel (08) 8278 5477. 🚊 from Adelaide. **Open** 8am–sunset daily. **Closed** 25 Dec. 🚗 for cars only. ♿ limited. 🌐 **environment.sa.gov.au**

Established in 1891, Belair is the eighth-oldest national park in the world. Only 9 km (5 miles) from Adelaide, it is one of the most popular parks in South Australia. Tennis courts and pavilions are available for hire and there are picnic facilities throughout the park. Visitors can meander through the tall eucalypt forests and cool valleys, and see kangaroos, emus, echidnas and other native wildlife.

In spring, many native plants bloom. The park is closed occasionally in summer on days of extreme fire danger. Within the park lies **Old Government House**. Built in 1859 as the governor's summer residence, it offers a glimpse of the lifestyle enjoyed by the colonial gentry.

🏛 **Old Government House**
Belair National Park. **Tel** (08) 8278 5477. **Open** 1–4pm Sun & public hols. **Closed** Good Fri, 25 Dec. 🚗

❸ Gorge Wildlife Park

30 Redden Drive, Cudlee Creek. **Tel** (08) 8389 2206. 🚌 Adelaide. **Open** 9am–5pm daily. **Closed** 25 Dec. 🚗 📷 🌐 **gorgewildlifepark.com.au**

Situated on 5.5 ha (14 acres) of land, Gorge Wildlife Park is home to an abundance of native Australian species, including kangaroos, dingos, wombats, wallabies and fruit bats. There are also birds – from ostriches to fairy wrens – and a colony of free-flying rainbow lorikeets. For those who prefer their animals crawling or swimming, there is a reptile house. The most popular residents of the park, however, are the koalas. Cuddling sessions with these friendly marsupials are held three times daily (11:30am, 1:30pm and 3:30pm, subject to weather conditions). The park also offers a kiosk, a souvenir shop, picnic areas and free gas BBQs.

A koala at Gorge Wildlife Park

❹ Hahndorf

🏠 2,500. 🚌 from Adelaide. 🛈 68 Mount Barker Rd 1800 353 323. 🌐 **hahndorfsa.org.au**

Hahndorf is the oldest surviving German settlement in Australia. The first settlers arrived in 1838 aboard the *Zebra* under the command of Captain Dirk Hahn. Escaping religious persecution in their homeland, they settled in the Adelaide Hills and established Hahndorf (Hahn's Village), a German-style town.

The tree-lined main street has many examples of classic German architecture, such as houses with *fachwerk* timber framing filled in with wattle and daub, or brick. Visitors can take a stroll around the town and enjoy its historic atmosphere.

Wallabies roaming through Gorge Wildlife Park

For hotels and restaurants in this area see pp491–2 and pp522–5

Nineteenth-century mill in the historic town of Hahndorf

Just outside Hahndorf is **The Cedars**, the former home of South Australia's best-known landscape artist, the late Sir Hans Heysen *(see p38)*. Both his home and his studio are open to the public. South of the town is Nixon's Mill, a stone mill built in 1842.

▦ The Cedars
Heysen Rd. **Tel** (08) 8388 7277. **Open** 10am–4:30pm Tue–Sun & public hols. **Closed** Good Fri, 25 & 26 Dec. ▨ ♿ **W** hansheysen.com.au

❺ Strathalbyn

🚆 6,000. 🚌 ℹ️ Railway Station, South Terrace 1300 007 842. **W** strathalbynsa.com.au

The designated heritage town of Strathalbyn was originally settled by Scottish immigrants in 1839. Links with its Scottish ancestry can still be seen today in much of the town's architecture, reminiscent of small highland towns in Scotland.

Situated on the banks of the Angas River, Strathalbyn is dominated by St Andrew's Church with its sturdy tower. A number of original buildings have been preserved. The police station, built in 1858, and the 1865 courthouse together house the National Trust Museum. The prominent two-storey London House, built as a general store in 1867, has, like a number of buildings in or near the High Street, found a new use as an antiques store. As in many country towns in Australia, the hotels and banks are also architectural reminders of the past. About 16 km (10 miles) southeast of Strathalbyn, on the banks of the Bremer River, is Langhorne Creek,

renowned as one of the earliest wine-growing regions in Australia; wine has been produced here since the 1850s.

St Andrew's Church, Strathalbyn

❻ Mount Lofty

🚌 Mount Lofty Summit Rd. ℹ️ Mount Lofty Summit Information Centre (08) 8370 1054. 🏧 🚻 The Summit **Open** 9am–5pm daily. ▨ **W** environment.sa.gov.au

The hills of the Mount Lofty Ranges form the backdrop to Adelaide. The highest point, Mount Lofty, reaches 727 m (2,385 ft) and offers a fine view

of the city from the modern lookout at the summit, where there is also an interpretive centre. The hills are dotted with grand summer houses to which Adelaide citizens retreat during the summer heat.

Just below the summit is the **Cleland Wildlife Park** where visitors can stroll among the kangaroos and emus, have a photograph taken with a koala or walk through the aviary to observe native birds at close quarters.

About 1.5 km (1 mile) south of here, Mount Lofty Botanic Gardens feature temperate-climate plants such as rhodo-dendrons and magnolias.

☒ Cleland Wildlife Park
365 Mount Lofty Summit Rd, Crafters. **Tel** (08) 8339 2444. **Open** 9:30am–5pm daily. **Closed** 25 Dec. ▨ 🅿️ ♿ 🏧 🖥 **W** environment.sa.gov.au

❼ Birdwood

🚆 1,300. ℹ️ FJ Café, Shannon St (08) 8388 1185.

Nestled in the Adelaide Hills is the quiet little town of Birdwood. In the 1850s, wheat was milled in the town and the old wheat mill now houses Birdwood's most famous asset: the country's largest collection of vintage, veteran and classic motor cars, trucks and motorbikes. The **National Motor Museum** has more than 400 on display and is considered to be one of the best collections of its kind in the world.

▥ National Motor Museum
Shannon St. **Tel** (08) 8568 4000. **Open** 10am–5pm daily. **Closed** 25 Dec. ▨ ♿ **W** motor.history.sa.gov.au

Hand-feeding kangaroos at Cleland Wildlife Park, Mount Lofty

❽ Kangaroo Island

🚢 Sea Link ferry connection from Cape Jervis. 🚐 ℹ️ Kangaroo Island Gateway Visitor Information Centre, Howard Drive, Penneshaw (08) 8553 1185. ♿
📷 ⓦ **tourkangarooisland.com.au**

Kangaroo Island, Australia's third-largest island, is 155 km (96 miles) long and 55 km (34 miles) wide. Located 16 km (10 miles) off the Fleurieu Peninsula, the island was the site of South Australia's first official free settlement, established at Reeves Point in 1836. The settlement was short-lived, and within just four years had been virtually abandoned. The island was then settled by degrees during the remainder of the 19th century as communications improved with the new mainland settlements.

There is no public transport on the island and visitors must travel on a tour or by car (available for hire at Kingscote Airport). It is also possible to bike or hike. Though the roads to the main sights are good, many roads are unsealed and extra care should

Remarkable Rocks at Kirkpatrick Point, Kangaroo Island

be taken. Sparsely populated and geographically isolated, the island has few introduced predators and is a haven for a wide variety of animals and birds, many protected in its 19 conservation and national parks.

At Kingscote and Penneshaw fairy penguins can often be seen in the evenings, and the south coast windswept beach of Seal Bay is home to a large colony of Australian sea lions.

In Flinders Chase National Park, kangaroos will sometimes approach visitors, but feeding them is discouraged.

The interior is dry, but does support tracts of mallee scrub, and eucalypts. The coastline, however, is varied. The north coast has sheltered beaches ideal for swimming. The south coast, battered by the Southern Ocean, has more than 85 shipwrecks. At Kirkpatrick Point to the southwest stands a group of large rocks. Aptly named Remarkable Rocks, they have been eroded into weird formations by the winds and sea.

❾ Mount Gambier

🏔️ 29,000. 🚐 🚌 🚍 ℹ️ The Lady Nelson Visitor Centre, 35 Jubilee Hwy East (08) 8724 9750. ⓦ **mount gambier.sa.gov.au**

Mount Gambier, a major regional city midway between Adelaide and Melbourne, is located on the slopes of an extinct volcano. Established in 1854, it is now surrounded by farming country and large pine plantations. The volcano has four crater lakes which are attractive recreation spots, with walking trails, picnic facilities and a wildlife park. The Blue Lake, up to 75 m (245 ft) deep, is a major draw between November and March when its water mysteriously turns an intense blue. From April to October, it remains a dull grey.

There are also a number of caves to explore within the city. Engelbrecht Cave is popular with cave divers.

Strange and vividly coloured water of Mount Gambier's Blue Lake

For hotels and restaurants in this area see pp491–2 and pp522–5

Sharam's Cottage, the first house built in Penola

⑩ Penola

🗺 1,700. 🚌 ℹ Penola Coonawarra Visitor Information Centre, 27 Arthur St 1300 045 373. 🌐 **penola.org**

One of the oldest towns in the Southeast, Penola is the commercial centre of the Coonawarra wine region *(see pp342–3)*. The region's first winery was built in 1893. There are now some 20 wineries, most of which are open for sales and tastings.

Penola itself is a quiet town which takes great pride in its history. A heritage walk takes visitors past most of its early buildings, including the restored Sharam's Cottage, which was built in 1850 as the first dwelling in Penola.

Environs
Situated 40 km (25 miles) north of Penola, Bool Lagoon Game Reserve (designated a wetland of international significance by UNESCO), is an important refuge for an assortment of native wildlife including more than 150 species of birds. The park provides an opportunity to observe at close quarters many of these local and migratory birds *(see p341)*.

⑪ Naracoorte Caves National Park

Tel (08) 8760 1210. 🚌 from Adelaide. **Open** 9am–5pm daily (last tour 3:30pm). **Closed** 25 Dec. 🐾 🎥 🖥 🌐 **naracoortecaves.sa.gov.au**

Located 19 km (12 miles) south of Naracoorte is the Naracoorte Caves National Park. Within this 600-ha (1,500-acre) park, there are 28 known caves (only four are open to the public), most notably Victoria Fossil Cave, which is on the World Heritage List as a

result of the fossil deposits discovered here in 1969 *(see pp30–31)*. The site offers self-guided, guided and adventure-caving tours year-round. From November to February thousands of bent-wing bats come to breed in the Bat Cave. They can be seen leaving the cave en masse at dusk to feed in summer. Entrance to this cave is forbidden, but visitors can view via infra-red cameras in the park.

Ancient stalactites inside one of the Naracoorte caves

⑫ Murray River

🚌 from Adelaide. ℹ Renmark 1300 661 704. 🌐 **murrayriver.com.au**

Australia's largest river is a vital source of water in this, the driest state in Australia. As well as supplying water for Adelaide it supports a vigorous local agricultural industry that produces 40 per cent of all Australian

wine *(see pp342–3)*. It is also a popular destination for houseboating, water-skiing and fishing.

The town of Renmark, close to the Victoria border, lies at the heart of the Murray River irrigation area and is home to the Riverlands' first winery. At the town's wharf is the restored paddlesteamer *Industry*, now a floating museum and a reminder of days gone by.

Just south of Renmark, Berri is the area's commercial centre and site of the largest combined distillery and winery in the southern hemisphere. The Murray River meanders through Berri and on to the small town of Loxton before winding up towards the citrus centre of Waikerie. Surrounded by more than 5,000 ha (12,000 acres) of orchards, Waikerie is a favourite gliding centre and has hosted world gliding championships.

Another 40 km (25 miles) downstream, the Murray River reaches the town of Morgan, its northernmost point in South Australia, before it turns south towards the ocean. The **Morgan Museum**, located in the old landseer warehouse, aims to recapture the river-trading days, telling the story of what was once the second-busiest port in the state. Local crafts are for sale in the original railway ticket office.

🏛 **Morgan Museum**
Railway Terrace, Morgan. **Tel** (08) 8540 2641 or 8540 2643. **Open** Call for opening times. **Closed** 25 Dec. 🐾

An old paddlesteamer cruising along the Murray River

⑬ Barossa Tour

The Barossa, which is comprised of the Barossa and Eden valleys, is one of Australia's most famous wine regions and has an international reputation. First settled in 1842 by German Lutheran immigrants, villages were established at Bethany, Langmeil (now Tanunda), Lyndoch and Light's Pass. Signs of German traditions can be seen in the 19th-century buildings, churches and in the region's food, music and festivals. The Barossa Vintage Festival takes place every April.

⑤ Seppeltsfield
Between Tanunda and Greenock, this winery was established in 1851 by the pioneering German family Seppelt. A historic complex of splendid stone buildings, it is reached via an avenue of palm trees planted in the 1920s.

① **Jacob's Creek Visitor Centre**
Established in 1847 by Bavarian-born Johann Gramp, Jacob's Creek winery is famous for its vast range of wines and its restaurant, and has won numerous awards for tourism.

② **Grant Burge**
Grant and Helen Burge founded this historic winery in 1988. Visitors have the option of stopping at Krondorf to enjoy the pretty views, sip on excellent wine and have a light meal. The Meshach Shiraz is one of the region's finest wines.

④ **Peter Lehmann**
A significant producer of quality Barossa wines, this winery was established by the late Peter Lehmann, a well-known character in the valley. The winery has won numerous domestic and international awards over the years.

③ **Rockford**
This winery uses 100-year-old equipment to make its famous traditional hand-crafted wines. In the summer months visitors can see the old equipment working. The winery itself is also more than a century old.

Key

▨ Tour route
═ Other road
▨ Vineyard

0 km   4
0 miles   4

⑥ Penfolds

Established in 1844, Penfolds moved to this site on the outskirts of Nuriootpa in 1974. This major winery (home of the famous Grange) matures its range of red and white table wines and ports in American oak barrels. Many wines are available for tasting and buying at the cellar door.

⑦ Wolf Blass

One of the younger wineries in the Barossa, established in 1966, Wolf Blass boasts elaborate tasting rooms and a wine-heritage museum. It specializes in premium red and white table wines, and sparkling and fortified wines.

⑧ Saltram

Established in 1859, this historic winery is set in beautiful gardens on a Barossa hillside outside Angaston. Popular with red- and fortified-wine enthusiasts, Saltram also has a restaurant, which is open for lunch daily (10am–3pm).

SALTRAM

⑨ Collingrove Homestead, Angaston

Now owned by the National Trust, Collingrove was built in 1856 as a home for a member of the influential pioneering Angas family. It has original furnishings and is set in an English-style garden. Accommodation is available.

⑩ Henschke

This winery is one of the world's greatest producers. Their wines are made from single vineyards. After visiting the cellar be sure to walk through the vineyards – the vines, some up to 100 years old, are among the oldest in the world.

Tips for Drivers

Although a tour of the Barossa can be made in a day from Adelaide, the region is best seen and enjoyed by taking advantage of the excellent local accommodation and restaurants. The roads are generally good, although drivers should take special care on those that are unsealed. Visitors planning to visit a number of wineries and sample the produce may prefer to take one of the many tours or hire a chauffeur-driven vehicle.

THE YORKE AND EYRE PENINSULAS AND SOUTH AUSTRALIAN OUTBACK

From the lush Clare Valley and the dunes of the Simpson Desert, to the saltbush of the Nullarbor Plain, the land to the north and west of Adelaide is an area of vast distances and dramatic changes of scenery. With activities ranging from surfing on the coast to bushwalking in the Flinders Ranges, one is never far from awesome natural beauty.

South Australia was first settled by Europeans in 1836, but suffered early financial problems partly due to economic mismanagement. These were largely remedied by the discovery of copper at Kapunda, north of Adelaide, in 1842, and at Burra, near Clare, in 1845. As these resources were depleted fresh discoveries were made in the north of the Yorke Peninsula, in the area known as Little Cornwall, at the town of Wallaroo and Kadina in 1859 and at Moonta in 1861. By the 1870s, South Australia was the British Empire's leading copper producer, and copper, silver and uranium mining still boosts the state's economy today.

The Yorke and Eyre peninsulas are major arable areas, producing more than 10 per cent of Australia's wheat and much of its barley. They also have several important fishing ports, most notably Port Lincoln, the tuna-fishing capital of the country. Both peninsulas have stunning coastal scenery. The Yorke Peninsula, only two hours' drive from Adelaide, is a popular holiday destination with excellent fishing, reef diving and surfing opportunities. The much larger Eyre Peninsula is also renowned for fishing and has many superb beaches. Despite extensive arable use, it still retains about half of its land area as parks, reserves and native bushland.

To the west, the vast Nullarbor Plain stretches far into Western Australia *(see p323)*, with the Great Victoria Desert extending above it. Much of this region is protected Aboriginal land and the RAAF Woomera Test Range.

North of the Yorke Peninsula lies the rugged majesty of the Flinders Ranges. Rich with sights of deep Aboriginal spiritual and cultural significance, the ranges are also home to abundant flora and fauna, and make for superb bush-walking. Further north, the immense, inhospitable but starkly beautiful desert regions of the South Australian Outback provide a challenging but rewarding destination for adventurous travellers.

Oyster beds in Coffin Bay at the southern tip of the Eyre Peninsula

◀ Red-sand dune in the Simpson Desert, in the South Australian Outback

Exploring the Yorke and Eyre Peninsulas

Just north of Adelaide *(see pp348–53)* lie the green hills of
the Clare Valley; then, further inland, as the rainfall diminishes,
the countryside changes dramatically. First comes the
grandeur of the Flinders Ranges with rugged mountains
and tranquil gorges. West of Adelaide are two peninsulas,
at the head of which is the industrial triangle of Port Pirie,
Port Augusta and Whyalla. The Yorke Peninsula is Australia's
richest barley growing district. Eyre Peninsula is also a
wheat- and barley-producing area. From here the Nullarbor
Plain runs beyond the Western Australian border.

Fishing boats moored in the harbour
of Port Lincoln

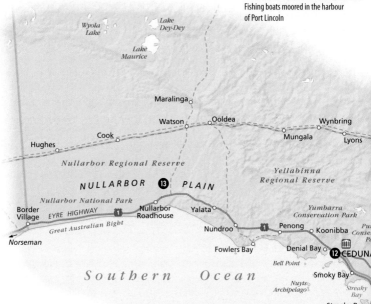

Getting Around

Despite the sparse population,
there is an extensive road network
throughout the region. The Stuart
Hwy runs up from Adelaide to
Coober Pedy and beyond into the
Northern Territory, and the Eyre
Hwy wends its way from Adelaide
along the tops of the Yorke and
Eyre peninsulas, across the
Nullarbor Plain and into Western
Australia. There is no state railway,
but interstate trains running from
Sydney to Perth, and Adelaide to
Alice Springs and Melbourne,
stop at major towns in the region.
Scheduled buses serve most
towns, and there are air services
from Adelaide to regional airports
in Port Lincoln, Ceduna, Coober
Pedy, Whyalla, and Port Augusta.

Saltbush landscape of the Eyre Peninsula

Sights at a Glance

1 Yorketown
2 Minlaton
3 Port Victoria
4 Maitland
5 Little Cornwall
6 Clare Valley
7 Port Pirie
8 Port Augusta
9 Whyalla
10 Port Lincoln
11 Coffin Bay National Park
12 Ceduna
13 Nullarbor Plain

South Australian Outback

See pp372–3

14 Coober Pedy
15 Witjira National Park
16 Simpson Desert
    Conservation Park
17 Lake Eyre National Park
18 Flinders Ranges

Locator Map

The Yorke and Eyre
Peninsulas

South Australian Outback
pp372–3

Key

— Major road
⋯⋯ Minor road
– – Track
━━ Scenic route
⋯•⋯ Main railway
— Minor railway
━━ State border
△ Summit

Raging waters of the Great Australian Bight

| 0 km | 100 |
| 0 miles | 100 |

❶ Yorketown

685. 🚌 🅸 29 Main St, Minlaton 1800 202 445.

Yorketown is the commercial centre of the earliest settled area on the southern Yorke Peninsula. It lies at the heart of a region scattered with nearly 200 salt lakes, many of which mysteriously turn pink at various times of the year, depending on climatic conditions. From the late 1890s until the 1930s, salt harvesting was a major industry in this part of South Australia.

Approximately 70 km (40 miles) southwest of Yorketown, at the tip of the Yorke Peninsula, is the spectacular Innes National Park. The park's geography changes from salt lakes and low mallee scrub inland to sandy beaches and steep, rugged cliffs along the coast. Kangaroos and emus have become accustomed to the presence of humans and are commonly seen, but other native inhabitants, such as the large mallee fowl, are more difficult to spot.

There is good surfing, reef diving and fishing in the park, especially at Browns Beach, the wild Pondalowie Bay, Chinamans Creek and Salmon Hole. Other beaches are considered unsafe for swimming. Also in the park are the rusting remains of the shipwrecked barque *Ethel*, which ran aground in 1904 and now lies with part of its hull protruding through the sand below the limestone cliffs of Ethel Beach.

"Red Devil" fighter plane in Minlaton

❷ Minlaton

770. 🚌 🚌 🅸 Yorke Pennisula Visitors Information Centre, 29 Main St 1800 202 445.

Centrally located, Minlaton is a service town to the surrounding farming community. Minlaton's claim to fame, however, is as the destination of the very first air mail flight across water in the southern hemisphere. Pilot Captain Harry Butler, a World War I fighter ace, set off on this record-breaking mission in August 1919 from Adelaide. Minlaton's Butler Memorial houses his 1916 Bristol fighter plane, "Red Devil", believed to be the only one left in the world, as well as displays detailing Butler's life.

❸ Port Victoria

345. 🅸 29 Main St, Minlaton (08) 8853 2600 or 1800 202 445.

Lying on the west coast of the Yorke Peninsula, Port Victoria is today a sleepy holiday destination, popular with anglers, swimmers and divers. In the early part of the 20th century, however, it was a busy sea port with large clippers and windjammers loading grain bound for the northern hemisphere. The last time a square rigger used the port was in 1949. The story of these ships and their epic voyages is told in the **Maritime Museum**, located adjacent to the jetty.

About 10 km (6 miles) off the coast lies Wardang Island, around which are eight known shipwrecks dating from 1871. Divers can follow the Wardang Island Maritime Heritage Trail to view the wrecks, each of which has an underwater plaque. Boats to the island can be chartered, but permission to land must be obtained from the Community Council in Point Pearce, the nearby Aboriginal settlement which administers the island.

🏛 **Maritime Museum**
Main St. **Tel** (08) 8834 2068. **Open** 2–4pm Sat, Sun, pub hols. 🅿 ♿

❹ Maitland

1,050. 🚌 🚌 🅸 CHATT Centre, 3 Robert St, Maitland (08) 8832 2174. 🆆 maitlandsa.com

Surrounded by some of the most productive farmland in Australia, Maitland lies in the centre of the Yorke Peninsula, on a ridge overlooking the Yorke Valley and Spencer Gulf.

Vast expanse of the salt lakes in the Yorketown region

Originally proclaimed in 1872, it is now the service centre for the surrounding community.

The pretty town, laid out on a classic grid pattern, retains many fine examples of colonial architecture, including the Maitland Hotel, built in 1874, and the 1875 St Bartholomew's Catholic Church.

The **CYP National Trust Museum** has an agricultural and folk collection housed in four buildings and focuses on the region's history and development.

🏛 **CYP National Trust Museum**
Cnr Gardiner & Kilkerran terraces. **Tel** (08) 8832 2220. **Open** 2–4pm Sun, public & school hols. **Closed** Good Fri, 25 Dec. 🖼 ♿

Miners' cottages at Moonta Mines, Little Cornwall

❺ Little Cornwall

🚂 Kadina. 🚌 Kadina. ℹ 50 Moonta Rd, Kadina 1800 654 991.

The three towns of Moonta, Kadina and Wallaroo were established after copper dis-coveries on Yorke Peninsula in 1859 and 1861. Collectively the towns are known as "The Copper Coast", and Moonta as "Australia's Little Cornwall". Many miners from Cornwall, England, came here in the 19th century seeking their fortunes. The biennial festival "Kernewek Lowender" (see p46) celebrates this Cornish heritage. The wealth created by the mines has left the towns with fine architecture.

Wallaroo, the site of the first copper ore smelting works, was also a shipping port for ore.

The original general cargo shed, which now houses the Maritime Museum, Port Victoria

When mining finished, the port was important for agricultural exports. The **Wallaroo Heritage and Nautical Museum** is in the old post office.

Moonta, once home to Australia's richest copper mine, contains a group of sites and buildings in the **Moonta Mines State Heritage Area**. The 1870 Miner's Cottage is a restored wattle and daub cottage. The history museum is in the old Moonta Mines Model School. Also of interest is the Moonta Mines Railway, a restored light-gauge locomotive.

Kadina, where copper was originally found, is the Yorke Peninsula's largest town.

The **Farm Shed Museum and Tourism Centre** has interesting displays on mining and folk history of the area.

🏛 **Wallaroo Heritage and Nautical Museum**
Jetty Rd. **Tel** (08) 8823 3015. **Open** 10am–4pm daily. **Closed** 25 Dec. 🖼 ♿

🏢 **Moonta Tourist Office**
Verran Terrace. **Tel** (08) 8825 1891. **Open** 9am–5pm daily. **Closed** 25 Dec. 🖼 ♿

🏛 **Farm Shed Museum and Tourism Centre**
50 Moonta Rd. **Tel** (08) 8821 2333. **Open** 9am–5pm Mon–Fri, 10am–4pm Sat & Sun. **Closed** Good Fri, 25 Dec. 🖼 ♿

Fishing and Diving on the Yorke Peninsula

There are fantastic opportunities for on- and offshore fishing and diving in the waters off the Yorke Peninsula. Many of the coastal towns have jetties used by keen amateur fishermen, and around Edithburgh anglers may catch tommy ruff, garfish and snook. Divers can enjoy the southern coast's stunning underwater scenery with brightly coloured corals and fish.

Offshore, the wreck of the *Clan Ranald* near Edithburgh is a popular dive and, off Wardang Island, eight wrecks can be explored on a unique diving trail. Angling from boats can be equally fruitful and local charter boats are available for hire.

A diver approaching a small shoal of fish in waters off the Yorke Peninsula

Restored 19th-century buildings at Burra Mine near the Clare Valley

❻ Clare Valley

🚍 Clare. 🛈 Clare Valley Wine, Food & Tourism Centre, 8 Spring Gully Rd, Clare. 1800 242 131. 🌐 **clarevalley.com.au**

Framed by the rolling hills of the northern Mount Lofty Ranges, Clare Valley is a picturesque and premium wine-producing region. At the head of the valley lies the town of Clare. This regional centre has many historic buildings, including the Old Police Station Museum, housed in the old Police Station, and Wolta Wolta, an early pastoralist's home, built in 1846, which has a fine collection of antiques. Visitors have the option of staying here.

Sevenhill Cellars, 7 km (4 miles) south of Clare, is the oldest vineyard in the valley. It was established by Austrian Jesuits in 1851, originally to produce altar wine for the colonies. The adjacent St Aloysius Church was completed in 1875. The winery is still owned by Jesuits and now produces both altar and table wines.

East of Sevenhill lies the heritage town of Mintaro, with many buildings making extensive use of the slate quarried in the area for more than 150 years. Also worth visiting is **Martindale Hall**, an elegant 1879 mansion situated just southeast of town.

Twelve km (7 miles) north of Clare lies **Bungaree Station**. This self-contained Merino sheep-farming complex was established in 1841 and is now maintained as a working 19th-century model. The historic exhibits here reveal the life and work at the station.

About 35 km (22 miles) northeast of Clare is the charming town of Burra. Five years after copper was discovered here in 1845, Burra was home to the largest mine in Australia. As such it was the economic saviour of the fledgling state, rescuing it from impending bankruptcy. Burra is now a State Heritage Area.

The **Burra Mine Site**, with its ruins and restored buildings around the huge open cut, is one of Australia's most exciting industrial archaeological sites. Morphett's Engine House Museum (open every morning) is a renovated three-storey Cornish engine house. An interpretive centre at the Bon Accord Mining Museum allows visitors access to the original mine shafts. The miners' dugouts, still seen on the banks of Burra Creek, were once home to more than 1,500 mainly Cornish miners. Paxton Square Cottages, built between 1849 and 1852, are unique in Australian mining history as the first decent accommodation provided for miners and their families. Many old buildings, including the police lockup and stables, the Redruth Gaol and the Unicorn Brewery Cellars, have been restored, as have a number of the 19th-century shops and houses. A museum chronicling the history is located in Burra market square.

🏛 Sevenhill Cellars
College Rd, Sevenhill 5453. **Tel** (08) 8843 4222. **Open** 10am–5pm daily. **Closed** 1 Jan, Good Fri, Easter Sun, 25 & 26 Dec. ♿

🏛 Martindale Hall
Manoora Rd, Mintaro 5415. **Tel** (08) 8843 9088. **Open** Wed–Mon. ⚐

🏛 Bungaree Station
431 Bungaree Rd, Clare. **Tel** (08) 8842 2677. **Open** accommodation available, check website. ⚐ ♿
🌐 bungareestation.com.au

🏛 Burra Visitor Information Centre
2 Market St, Burra. **Tel** (08) 8892 2154. **Open** 9am–5pm daily. **Closed** 25 Dec. ⚐ ♿ limited.

❼ Port Pirie

🏔 22,000. 🚍 🚍 🚍 🛈 3 Mary Elie St 1800 000 424. **Open** Mon–Fri.

Port Pirie was the state's first provincial city. An industrial hub, it is the site of the largest lead smelter in the southern hemisphere.

In the town centre, the National Trust Museum comprises three well-preserved buildings: the pavilion-style railway station built in 1902, the former customs house and the old police building. The Regional Tourism and Arts Centre, located in the former 1967 railway station, features artworks on lead, zinc and copper panels interpreting the city's historic wealth.

Port Pirie also boasts a miniature railway. Visitors can enjoy a ride on the 1st or 3rd Sunday of every month.

🏛 National Trust Museum
73–77 Ellen St. **Tel** (08) 8632 3435. **Open** daily. **Closed** 25 Dec. ♿ limited.

Victorian grandeur of Port Pirie's old railway station

For hotels and restaurants in this area see pp491–2 and pp522–5

Waterfront view of Port Augusta, with the jetty leading out into Spencer Gulf

❽ Port Augusta

🏘 14,000. 🛫 🚌 🚃 💬
ℹ️ 41 Flinders Terrace 1800 633 060.

Situated at the head of Spencer Gulf, Port Augusta is at the crossroads of Australia; here lies the intersection of the Sydney–Perth and Adelaide–Alice Springs railway lines, as well as the major Sydney–Perth and Adelaide–Darwin highways. Once an important port, its power stations now produce 40 per cent of the state's electricity. The coal-fired Northern Power Station, which dominates the city's skyline, offers free conducted tours.

Port Augusta is also the beginning of South Australia's Outback region. The School of the Air and the Royal Flying Doctor Service offices, both of which provide essential services to inhabitants of remote stations, are open to the public *(see p261)*. The **Wadlata Outback Centre** imaginatively tells the story of the Far North from 15 million years ago when rainforests covered the area, through Aboriginal and European history, up to the present day and into the future.

Australia's first **Arid Lands Botanic Garden** was opened nearby in 1996. This 200-ha (500-acre) site is an important research and education facility, as well as a recreational area.

It also commands panoramic views of the Flinders Ranges to the east *(see p373)*.

🏛 Wadlata Outback Centre
41 Flinders Terrace. **Tel** (08) 8641 9193.
Open 9am–5.30pm Mon–Fri, 10am–4pm Sat & Sun. **Closed** 25 Dec. 🅿️ ♿

🌿 Arid Lands Botanic Garden
144 Stuart Hwy. **Tel** (08) 8641 9116.
Open 7:30am–sunset daily. 🅿️
W **aalbg.sa.gov.au**

❾ Whyalla

🏘 22,000. 🛫 🚃 ℹ️ Lincoln Hwy 1800 088 589.

At the gateway to the Eyre Peninsula, Whyalla is the state's largest provincial city. Originally a shipping port for iron ore mined at nearby Iron Knob, the city was transformed in 1939 when a blast furnace was established, a harbour created and a shipyard constructed. The shipyard closed in 1978; however, the first ship built there, the HMAS *Whyalla* (1941), is now a major display of the **Whyalla Maritime Museum**.

Although an industrial centre, Whyalla has a number of fine beaches and good fishing. In recent years, Whyalla's fore-shore has been extensively redeveloped. Today, it is home to a bustling marina, lush gardens and cafés.

🏛 Whyalla Maritime Museum
Lincoln Hwy. **Tel** (08) 8645 8900.
Open 10am–4pm daily.
Closed Good Fri, 25 Dec. 🅿️ 📷
HMAS *Whyalla* can be accessed on guided tours only. ♿ museum only.
W **whyalla.sa.gov.au**

HMAS *Whyalla*, now part of the Whyalla Maritime Museum

Stunning coastline of Whalers Way at the southern end of the Eyre Peninsula near Port Lincoln

⑩ Port Lincoln

🏞 14,500. ✈ 🚌 ℹ 3 Adelaide Pl
1300 788 378.

At the southern end of the Eyre Peninsula, Port Lincoln sits on the shore of Boston Bay, one of the world's largest natural harbours. A fishing and seafood processing centre, it is home to Australia's largest tuna fleet.

Locals celebrate the start of the tuna season every January with the Tunarama Festival (see p45). This raucous event includes processions, concerts and a tuna-tossing competition.

Fishing and sailing are popular activities. Visitors can take a boat trip to Dangerous Reef, 31 km (20 miles) offshore, to view great white sharks from the relative safety of the boat or submerged cage. In the middle of the bay lies Boston Island, a working sheep station.

The Port Lincoln area has several buildings of note. South of Port Lincoln, **Mikkira Station**, established in 1842, is one of the country's oldest sheep stations. Today it is ideal for picnics or camping, with a restored pioneer cottage and a koala colony.

The **Koppio Smithy Museum**, located in the Koppio Hills 40 km (25 miles) north of Port Lincoln, is an agricultural museum with a furnished 1890 log cottage and a 1903 smithy that gives a glimpse into the lives of the pioneers.

Just 20 km (12 km) south of Port Lincoln is Lincoln National Park with its rocky hills, sheltered coves, sandy beaches and high cliffs. The park is also rich in birdlife. Emus and parrots are common and ospreys and sea eagles frequent the coast. Just west of the park, Whalers Way has some of Australia's most dramatic coastal scenery.

This land is private and entry is via a permit available from the visitors' centre.

🏠 **Mikkira Station**
621 Mikkira Lane. **Tel** (08) 8685 6020.
Closed when over 30°C (86°F). ⏻
Permit from Port Lincoln info centre.

🏛 **Koppio Smithy Museum**
RSD 1951 Koppio Rd. **Tel** (08) 8684 4243. **Open** 10am–5pm Tue–Sun.
Closed 25 Dec. ⏻ ♿

The prime surfing spot of Almonta Beach in Coffin Bay National Park

⑪ Coffin Bay National Park

🚌 Port Lincoln. ℹ (08) 8688 3111.
Open daily. **Closed** 25 Dec. ⏻ per vehicle. ♿ limited. 🌐 environment. sa.gov.au

To the west of the southern tip of the Eyre Peninsula is Coffin Bay Peninsula, which is part of the Coffin Bay National Park. This unspoilt area of coastal

---

Wedge-tailed eagle

Wildlife of the Eyre Peninsula

An enormous variety of wildlife inhabits the Eyre Peninsula. Emus and kangaroos are common, and the hairy-nosed wombat is found in large numbers on the west coast. Wedge-tailed eagles soar over the Gawler Ranges, while sea eagles, ospreys, albatrosses and petrels are all seen over the coast. In the water, dolphins, sea lions and occasional great white sharks feast on an abundance of marine life. The most spectacular sight, however, are the southern right whales which breed at the head of the Great Australian Bight every June to October. They can be seen from the cliffs at Head of the Bight, just east of the Nullarbor National Park.

For hotels and restaurants in this area see pp491–2 and pp522–5 wilderness has exposed cliffs, sheltered sandy beaches, rich birdlife and fantastic fishing. Wildflowers in the park can be quite spectacular from early spring to early summer.

There are several scenic drives through the park, but some roads are accessible to 4WD vehicles only. A favourite route for conventional vehicles is the Yangie Trail from the small town of Coffin Bay to Yangie and Avoid bays. To the east of Point Avoid is one of Australia's best surfing beaches, Almonta Beach.

Coffin Bay town has long been a popular centre for windsurfing, swimming, sailing and fishing. It now also produces oysters. The Oyster Walk is a pleasant walking trail along the foreshore through native bushland.

⓬ Ceduna

🏠 3,480. ✈ 🚌 ℹ 58 Poynton St (08) 8625 3343. 🎨 Oysterfest (end Sep/early Oct). 🖥 **ceduna.sa.gov.au**

At the top of the west side of the Eyre Peninsula, sitting on the shores of Murat Bay, Ceduna is the most westerly significant town in South Australia before the start of the Nullarbor Plain. The town's name comes from the Aboriginal word *cheedoona*, meaning "a place to rest".

Today, Ceduna is the commercial centre of the far west. Within the town is the **Old Schoolhouse National Trust Museum** with its collections of restored farm equipment from

An Indian-Pacific train crossing the vast Nullarbor Plain

early pioneer days. It also has a display on the British atomic weapons tests held at nearby Maralinga in the 1950s, and a selection of Aboriginal artifacts.

In the 1850s, there was a whaling station on St Peter Island, just off the coast of Ceduna, but now the town is a base for whale-watchers. Southern right whales can be seen close to the shore from June to October from the head of the Bight, 300 km (185 miles) from Ceduna.

The oyster-farming industry has established itself west and east of Ceduna at Denial and Smoky bays. Between Ceduna and Penong, a tiny hamlet 73 km (45 miles) to the west, there are detours to surfing beaches including the legendary Cactus Beach. Keen surfers are found here all year round trying to catch some of the best waves in Australia, rolling in from the great Southern Ocean.

🏛 **Old Schoolhouse National Trust Museum**
Park Terrace. **Tel** (08) 8625 2929. **Open** Mon–Sat. **Closed** 25 Dec. 📷 ♿

⓭ Nullarbor Plain

🚉 Port Augusta. 🚌 Ceduna. ℹ Ceduna (08) 8625 3343. **Open** 9am–5:30pm Mon–Fri, 9:30am–5pm Sat–Sun. **Closed** Good Fri, 25 Dec.

The huge expanse of the Nullarbor Plain stretches from Nundroo, about 160 km (100 miles) west of Ceduna, towards the distant Western Australia border 330 km (200 miles) away, and beyond into Western Australia (*see p323*).

This dry, dusty plain can be crossed by rail on the Trans-Australian Railway or by road on the Eyre Highway. The train travels further inland than the road, its route giving little relief from the flat landscape. The highway lies nearer the coast, passing a few isolated sights of interest on its way west. Visitors should plan ahead if they intend to drive as petrol stations are few and far between here.

Just south of the small town of Nundroo lies Fowlers Bay. Good for fishing, it is popular with anglers seeking solitude. West of here, the road passes through the Yalata Aboriginal Lands. Bordering Yalata to the west is Nullarbor National Park. This runs from the Nullarbor Roadhouse hamlet, 130 km (80 miles) west of Nundroo, to the border with Western Australia 200 km (125 miles) away. The Eyre Highway passes through the park, close to the coastal cliffs. This stretch of the plain has some spectacular views over the Great Australian Bight.

The world's longest cave system runs beneath the plain, and the border area has many underground caves and caverns. These should only be explored by experienced cavers, however, as many are flooded and dangerous.

Watching southern right whales from Head of the Bight, near Ceduna

South Australian Outback

South Australia's outback is an enormous area of harsh but often breathtaking scenery. Much of the region is untamed desert, broken in places by steep, ancient mountain ranges, huge salt lakes, gorges and occasional hot springs. Although very hot and dry for most of the year, many places burst into life after heavy winter rains and hundreds of species of wildflowers, animals and birds can be seen. The area's recent history is one of fabled stock routes, now Outback tracks for adventurous travellers. Isolated former mining and railway towns now cater for Outback tourists. Vast areas in the west form extensive Aboriginal lands, accessible by permit only.

Locator Map

   South Australian Outback

   The Yorke and Eyre Peninsulas see pp362–71

Key

— Major road

···· Minor road

--- Track

—·— Main railway

═══ State border

△ Summit

Sights at a Glance

⑭ Coober Pedy

⑮ Witjira National Park

⑯ Simpson Desert Conservation Park

⑰ Lake Eyre National Park

⑱ Flinders Ranges

0 km   200

0 miles   200

⑭ Coober Pedy

🏙 3,500. ✈ 🚌 ℹ Lot 773 Hutchison St (08) 8672 4600.

🌐 **cooberpedy.sa.gov.au**

One of Australia's most famous Outback towns, Coober Pedy, 850 km (530 miles) northwest of Adelaide, is an unusual settlement in the heart of an extremely hostile landscape. Frequent duststorms and a colourless plaster landscape littered with abandoned mines contribute to the town's desolate appearance, yet the small population has a cultural mix of over 42 nationalities.

Opal was discovered here in 1915, and today Coober Pedy produces a large percentage of the world's supply. Mining claims, limited to one per person, can measure no more than 100 m by 50 m (320 ft by 160 ft). For this reason opal mining is the preserve of individuals, not large companies, and this adds to the town's "frontier" quality. Coober Pedy's name comes

Underground "dugout" home in Coober Pedy

from the Aboriginal *kupa piti*, meaning "white man in a hole", and it is apt indeed. Not only the mines, but also houses, hotels and churches are built underground. This way, the residents escape the extreme temperatures of up to 50°C (122°F) during the day and 0°C (32°F) at night. Several such homes are open to the public.

The **Underground Art Gallery** displays Aboriginal art. It also has displays relating to opal mining, and visitors can dig for their own opals.

🏛 **Underground Art Gallery**

Hutchison St. **Tel** (08) 8672 5985. **Open** daily. **Closed** 25 Dec. 🚫 ♿

⓯ Witjira National Park

ℹ️ Desert Park Information (08) 8648 5328. **Open** daily.
Open 24 hours. Desert Parks pass required. 🅿️ 🆆 **environment. sa.gov.au**

About 200 km (125 miles) north of Coober Pedy lies the small town of Oodnadatta, where drivers can check the road and weather conditions before heading further north to Witjira National Park.

Witjira has dunes, saltpans, boulder plains and coolibah woodlands, but it is most famous for its hot artesian springs. Dalhousie Springs has more than 60 active springs with warm water rising from the Great Artesian Basin. These springs supply essential water for Aborigines, pastoralists and wildlife, including water snails, unique to the area.

⓰ Simpson Desert Conservation Park

ℹ️ Desert Parks Information (08) 8648 5328. **Open** daily. Desert Parks pass required. **Closed** Dec–15 Mar. 🅿️ 🆆 **environment.sa.gov.au**

The Simpson Desert Conservation Park is at the very top of South Australia, adjoining both Queensland and the Northern Territory. It is an almost endless series of sand dunes, lakes, spinifex grassland and gidgee woodland.

The landscape is home to some 180 bird, 92 reptile and 44 native mammal species, some of which have developed nocturnal habits as a response to the aridity of the region.

Dunes stretching to the horizon in Simpson Desert Conservation Park

⓱ Lake Eyre National Park

ℹ️ Natural Resource Centre, Port Augusta (08) 8648 5300. **Open** 24 hours. **Closed** Halligan Point Bay: Dec–15 Mar. 🅿️

Lake Eyre National Park encompasses all of Lake Eyre North and extends eastwards into the Tirari Desert. Lake Eyre is Australia's largest salt lake, 15 m (49 ft) below sea level at its lowest point, with a salt crust said to weigh 400 million tonnes. Vegetation is low, comprising mostly blue bush, samphire and saltbush. On the rare occasions when the lake floods, it alters dramatically: flowers bloom and birds such as pelicans and gulls appear, turning the lake into a breeding ground. In summer, the temperature can soar to more than 50° C (122° F).

⓲ Flinders Ranges

ℹ️ Quorn Railway Station, Railway Terrace (08) 8620 0510. **Open** daily. 🆆 **frc.sa.gov.au/tourism**

The Flinders Ranges extend for 400 km (250 miles) from Crystal Brook, just north of the Clare Valley, far into South Australia's Outback. A favourite with bushwalkers, the ranges offer a wide range of stunning scenery and wildlife, much of it protected in several national parks.

In the southern part of the Flinders Ranges is Mount Remarkable National Park, renowned for its fine landscape, abundant wildflowers and excellent walking trails.

About 50 km (30 miles) north of here is the town of Quorn, start of the restored Pichi Richi Railway. North of Quorn lie the dramatic Warren, Yarrah Vale and Buckaring gorges.

Much of the central Flinders Ranges are contained within the Flinders Ranges National Park. This beautiful park's best-known feature is Wilpena Pound, an elevated natural basin covering some 90 sq km (35 sq miles) with sheer outer walls 500 m (1,600 ft) high.

To the north is Gammon Ranges National Park, with mountain bushwalking for the experienced only. Just outside the park is **Arkaroola**, a tourist village with a wildlife sanctuary and a state-of-the-art observatory.

🏨 **Arkaroola**
Via Copley. **Tel** (08) 8648 4848. **Open** daily. 🅿️ for tours.

Shimmering expanse of Lake Eyre, the largest salt lake in Australia

VICTORIA

Victoria at a Glance

The state of Victoria can be easily divided into two distinct geographical halves, east and west. Western Victoria is known for its unusual landforms, including the Grampians and the Twelve Apostles. It was also the site of Australia's wealthiest gold rush during the 19th century, the legacy of which can be seen in the ornate buildings in the many surviving gold rush towns *(see pp58–9)*. Eastern Victoria's cooler climate benefits the vineyards that produce world-class wines, while the Alps are Victoria's winter playground. The rugged coastline is known for its lakes, forests and wildlife. Melbourne, the state's capital, is the second most populous city in Australia.

Mildura

Western Victoria
(see pp426–41)

Horsham

Ballarat

Portland

Warrnambool

Gee

Halls Gap is the main entrance to the Grampians National Park *(see p431)*. This beautiful area is filled with dramatic rock formations, spectacular ridges and wildflowers unique to the region.

Ballarat's Arch of Victory on the Avenue of Honour commemorates the soldiers of World War I. It is also the western entrance to this provincial city, which grew up during the 1850s gold rush *(see pp438–9)*.

The Twelve Apostles is the evocative name given to these eroded limestone rock formations in Port Campbell National Park, seen from the Great Ocean Road *(see pp432–33)*. Sunset is the best time to fully appreciate the view.

◀ Skiers at Mount Hotham, in the Victorian Alps

Tahbilk Wines is one of the best known of all the northeastern Victorian vineyards, not only for its excellent wines but also for the pagoda-style architecture of its winery. Eastern Victoria's cool climate has led to a range of successful wineries *(see pp454–5)*.

Locator Map

The Victorian Alps come into their own during the winter months as a ski area *(see p452–3)*.

Shepparton

Wangaratta

digo

Eastern Victoria
(see pp442–55)

| 0 kilometres | 100 |
| 0 miles | 100 |

Sunbury

hus Marsh

Melbourne

ribee

Dandenong

Parliament House in Melbourne, begun in 1856, is one of the city's finest surviving public buildings *(see pp396–7)*.

Melbourne
(see pp384–425)

ESSENDON

BRUNSWICK

MELBOURNE

CAMBERWELL

ST KILDA

Flinders Street Station is a main rail terminus, set in a fine 19th-century edifice *(see p406)*.

Rippon Lea's ornamental garden is an impressive feature of this 19th-century home *(see pp408–9)*.

| 0 kilometres | 4 |
| 0 miles | 4 |

Melbourne's Best: Parks and Gardens

Visitors to Melbourne should not miss the city's magnificent public and private gardens. A large proportion of the city's parks and gardens were created in the 19th century and have a gracious quality which has earned Victoria the nickname of Australia's "Garden State". Central Melbourne is ringed by public gardens, including the outstanding Royal Botanic Gardens, visited by more than 1.6 million people each year. Melbourne also has a network of public parks which offer a mix of native flora and fauna with recreational activities. The annual Open Gardens scheme allows visitors into some of the best private gardens in Victoria and Australia.

Statue of Queen Victoria in her eponymous gardens

Landscape Gardens

Melbourne abounds with carefully planned and formal 19th-century gardens, designed by prominent landscape gardeners.

A variety of trees from all over the world lines the formal avenues of **Carlton Gardens**, designed in 1857 by Edward La Trobe Bateman. The aim of the design was for every path and flowerbed to focus attention on the Exhibition Building, constructed in 1880 *(see p399)*. The main entrance path leads from Victoria Street to the Hochgurtel Fountain, in front of the Exhibition Building, decorated on its upper tier with stone birds and flowers which are indigenous to the state of Victoria.

The attractive **Fitzroy Gardens** in the heart of the city were also first designed by Bateman in 1856. His original plans were later revised by a Scotsman, James Sinclair, to make them more sympathetic to the area's uneven landscape. The avenues of elms that lead in to the centre of the gardens from the surrounding streets create the shape of the Union Jack flag and are one of the most distinctive features of the gardens *(see pp396–7)*. Fitzroy Gardens' Conservatory is renowned for its five popular annual plant shows. The **Queen Victoria Gardens** are considered one of the city's most attractive

Statue of Simpson and his donkey in Kings Domain

gardens. They were created as a setting for a new statue of the queen, four years after her death, in 1905. Roses now surround the statue. A floral clock near St Kilda Road was given to Melbourne by Swiss watchmakers in 1966. It is embedded with some 7,000 flowering plants.

Kings Domain *(see p402)*, established in 1854, was the dream of a German botanist, Baron von Mueller, who designed this impressive garden. The garden is dominated by elegant statues, including one of Simpson, a stretcher bearer during World War I, with his faithful donkey. The Shrine of Remembrance and Government House are located here.

Botanic Gardens

Begun in 1846, the **Royal Botanic Gardens** now cover 36 ha (90 acres). Botanist Baron von Mueller became the director of the gardens in 1857 and began to plant both indigenous and exotic shrubs on the site, intending the gardens to be a scientific aid to fellow biologists. Von Mueller's successor, William Guilfoyle, made his own mark on the design, by adding wide paths across the gardens and an ornamental lake.

Conservatory of flowers in Fitzroy Gardens

Ornamental lake in the Royal Botanic Gardens

Where to Find the Parks and Gardens

Alexandra Gardens **Map** 3 A2.
Carlton Gardens **Map** 2 D1.
Fawkner Park **Map** 3 C5.
Fitzroy Gardens **Map** 2 E2.
Flagstaff Gardens **Map** 1 A2.
Kings Domain *pp402–3.*
Princes Park, Royal Parade, Carlton.
Queen Victoria Gardens **Map** 2 D4.
Royal Botanic Gardens *pp402–3.*
Treasury Gardens **Map** 2 E3.
Yarra Park **Map** 2 F3.

Today, the gardens are home to more than 8,500 plant species *(see pp402–3).*

Recreational Gardens and Parks

Melburnians are avid sports participants as well as spectators, and many of the city's gardens offer a range of sporting facilities in attractive surroundings.

Flagstaff Gardens take their name from the site's role as a signalling station from 1840, warning of ships arriving in the Port of Melbourne. In the 1880s, with advances in communication, this role was no longer required and gardens were laid out on the land instead. Today the gardens are used for their recreational facilities, which include tennis courts, a children's playground and a barbecue area.

The **Alexandra Gardens** were designed in 1904 as a riverside walk along the Yarra River. Today, as well as the major thoroughfare of Alexandra Avenue, there is an equestrian path, a cycle path, boat sheds and barbecue facilities. The **Treasury Gardens** were designed in 1867 and are lined along its avenues with Moreton Bay Figs, which offer very welcome shade in the summer heat. The location in the centre of the city makes these gardens very popular with office workers during their lunch breaks. The gardens also host occasional community events.

Established in 1856, **Yarra Park** is today home to the city's most well-known sports ground, the impressive Melbourne Cricket Ground *(see p401)*, a mecca for cricket and football lovers. The wood and bark of the indigenous river red gums in the park were once used for canoes and shields by local Aborigines and many still bear the scars.

Fawkner Park, named after Melbourne's co-founder, John Pascoe Fawkner, was laid out in 1862 and became a large sports ground in the 1890s. Despite a temporary role as a camp site for the Armed Services during World War II, the 40 ha (100 acres) of the park are still used for cricket, football, hockey and softball games.

Another popular sporting area with Melburnians is **Princes Park**. Two sports pavilions were constructed in 1938, as were two playing fields. The park now contains a football oval and a large timber adventure playground, as well as a jogging track lined with exercise equipment at stages along its 3-km (1.8-mile) route. A gravel running track was also added in 1991.

Cricket match in progress in Fawkner Park

Melbourne's Best: Architecture

In 1835, Melbourne was a village of tents and impermanent dwellings. Fed by the wealth of the 1850s' gold rush and the economic boom of the 1880s, it rapidly acquired many graceful buildings. Today, the city's architecture is very eclectic, with a strong. Victorian element. The range of architectural styles is impressive, from beautiful restorations to outstanding contemporary novelties. The city's tallest building is the Eureka Tower, which is 300 m (985 ft) high.

Early colonial Cook's Cottage

Early Colonial

In colonial days, it was quite common for small edifices, such as La Trobe's Cottage, to be shipped from England as skilled builders were in short supply. Other imported structures included timber cottages and corrugated iron dwellings.

Wood structure Wooden shutters Chimney

La Trobe's Cottage is a prefabricated wooden cottage of 1839.

High Victorian

During the 19th century, Melbourne erected several grand state buildings equal to those in the USA and Europe. State Parliament House, begun in 1856, included a central dome in its original design which was omitted due to lack of funds (see p397). South of the city is the 1934 Shrine of Remembrance, which demonstrates the 20th century's yearning for classical roots (see p402).

Detail of Parliament House

Doric columns Balustrade Arched windows

State Parliament House has an impressive entrance with its grand Doric columns.

Cast-iron lacework at Tasma Terrace

Terrace Housing

Terrace houses with cast-iron lace balconies were popular during the Victorian era. Tasma Terrace (1878) was designed by Charles Webb and is unusual for its three-storey houses, double-storey being more typical.

Cast-iron filigree balconies Arched window

Tasma Terrace is now home to the National Trust.

Modernism and Post-modernism

The latter half of the 20th century has seen a range of post-modern buildings erected in Melbourne. The National Gallery of Victoria (*see p407*) was designed by Sir Roy Grounds and completed in 1968 (further modified in 2003 by Mario Bellini). It was the first time bluestone, widely used in the 19th century, was used in a modern structure. The magnificent stained-glass ceiling of the Great Hall was designed by Leonard French.

Melbourne's unique bluestone used in the walls of the National Gallery of Victoria

Flat roof

Blue-stone façade

Arched entrance

The National Gallery of Victoria has a monumental façade, impressive for its smooth simplicity and lack of ornamental details.

Multicoloured façade   Steel railings   Lighting

Royal Melbourne Institute of Technology's Building 8 façade is a complex blend of bright colours and diverse shapes.

Contemporary

Melbourne is known for its vibrant, experimental architecture scene. Some of the most radical Australian buildings of the 1990s can be found here. The Royal Melbourne Institute of Technology's Building 8 was designed by Peter Corrigan and completed in 1993. The building's interior and façade is both gaudy and Gaudían, with its bold use of primary colours. It is surrounded by a series of other equally avant-garde buildings belonging to the university.

Sports Architecture

Melbourne's modern architecture clearly reflects the importance of sport to its citizens. Rod Laver Arena at Melbourne Park, opened in 1988, has a retractable roof, a world first, and seats more than 15,000 people.

Aerial view of Melbourne Park, with Rod Laver Arena on the left

Where to Find the Buildings

Retractable roof   Glass exterior

Rod Laver Arena was designed by Philip Cox and Peddle Thorp and now hosts the annual Australian Open tennis championships.

Wines of Victoria

Victoria has approximately 850 wineries located in 21 distinct wine regions, some easily reached in less than an hour by car from the state capital, Melbourne. The northeast is famous for its unique fortified Muscats and Tokays (often described as liquid toffee), while from the cooler south come silky Chardonnays and subtle Pinot Noirs. There is no better way to enjoy Victorian wine than in one of the many restaurants and bistros in cosmopolitan Melbourne *(see pp526–9)*.

Best's is one of the oldest family-owned wineries in Australia. This producer makes excellent Shiraz, Merlot, Dolcetto and Riesling wines. Self-guided tours of its 150-year-old wooden cellar are free and available every day.

Warehouse lined with wine barrels at Seppelt Great Western

Key facts

Location and Climate
Warm in the north, cool in the south, Victoria's climate spectrum yields a diversity of wines. Many small, high-quality producers have been in the vanguard of the Australian wine revolution, which began in the 1970s.

Grape Varieties

Victoria's varied climate and soil means it is possible to grow a full range of grape varieties. Reds include Shiraz, Merlot, Cabernet Sauvignon and Pinot Noir. Whites include Semillon, Gewürztraminer, Riesling, Chardonnay, Marsanne, Frontignac and Pinot Gris. Victoria also produces excellent sparkling wine.

Good Producers
Morris, Campbells, Brown Brothers, De Bortoli, Trentham Estate, Seppelt, Best's, Mount Langi Ghiran, Jasper Hill, Yarra Yering, Coldstream Hills, Tahbilk Wines, Mitchelton.

Four Sisters was established by the pioneering winemaker Trevor Mast.

Wentworth

MILDURA

Ouyen

Sea Lake

Horsham

Glaneig River

BALL

Hamilton

Lc Coran

Colac

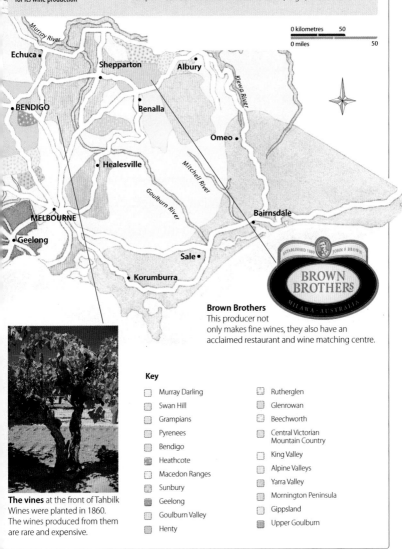

How Victoria's famous Muscats and Tokays are made

Brown Muscat and Muscadelle grapes are picked late, when they are at their sweetest, to produce fine Muscats and Tokays respectively. Once the grapes have been crushed, the resulting juice is often fermented in traditional open concrete tanks which have been in use for generations. The wine is then fortified with top-quality grape spirit, which will give it an ultimate alcohol strength of around 18.5 per cent. The solera system, in which young vintages are blended with older ones, gives more depth to the wines and also ensures that they retain a consistent quality. Some wineries, such as Morris, use a base wine combined with vintages going back more than a century. The flavour of wine in the oldest barrel is so intense that one teaspoon can add a new dimension to 200 l (45 gal) of base wine.

A sunbathed vineyard in Victoria, famed for its wine production

Brown Brothers
This producer not only makes fine wines, they also have an acclaimed restaurant and wine matching centre.

The vines at the front of Tahbilk Wines were planted in 1860. The wines produced from them are rare and expensive.

Key

- Murray Darling
- Swan Hill
- Grampians
- Pyrenees
- Bendigo
- Heathcote
- Macedon Ranges
- Sunbury
- Geelong
- Goulburn Valley
- Henty
- Rutherglen
- Glenrowan
- Beechworth
- Central Victorian Mountain Country
- King Valley
- Alpine Valleys
- Yarra Valley
- Mornington Peninsula
- Gippsland
- Upper Goulburn

MELBOURNE

John Batman, the son of a Sydney convict, arrived in what is now the Port Phillip district in 1835 and met with Aboriginal tribes of the Kulin, from whom he "purchased" the land. In just over two decades Melbourne grew from a small tent encampment to a sprawling metropolis. Today it is the second-largest city in Australia, with 4.6 million inhabitants.

Melbourne's rapid growth was precipitated in the 1850s by the huge influx of immigrants seeking their fortunes on the rich gold fields of Victoria. This caused a population explosion of unprecedented proportions as prospectors decided to stay in the city. The enormous wealth generated by the gold rush led to the construction of grand public buildings. This development continued throughout the land boom of the 1880s, earning the city the nickname "Marvellous Melbourne". By the end of the 19th century, the city was the industrial and financial capital of Australia. It was also the home of the national parliament until 1927, when it was moved to purpose-built Canberra (see p195).

Melbourne hosted the summer Olympics in 1956. Dubbed the "Friendly Games", the event generated great changes in the city's consciousness. The postwar period also witnessed a new wave of immigrants who sought better lives here. Driven by the will to succeed, they introduced Melburnians to a range of cultures, transforming the British traditions of the city. This transformation continues today with the arrival of immigrants from all parts of Asia and beyond.

Melbourne holds many surprises: it has the most elaborate Victorian architecture of all Australian cities; it has a celebrated range of restaurant cuisines and its calendar revolves around hugely popular spectator sports and arts events (see pp44–5). While the climate is renowned for its unpredictability, Melburnians still enjoy an outdoor lifestyle for much of the year, and the city possesses a unique, cosmopolitan charm that quietly bewitches many visitors.

The beautiful city of Melbourne across the Yarra River

◀ The Neo-Gothic interior of St Paul's Cathedral

Exploring Melbourne

Melbourne is organized informally into precincts.
Collins Street is a business centre and the site of the city's
smartest stores. To the east is the parliamentary precinct.
Swanston Street contains some fine Victorian architecture.
The south bank of the river is arts-orientated and includes
the Arts Centre Melbourne. The city also devotes much land
to parks and gardens.

Eureka Tower and Melbourne skyline

Getting Around

Despite the comprehensive Metro transport system of trams, trains and buses, many Melburnians use cars for commuting *(see pp416–17).* This has resulted in a network of major roads and highways that lead in all directions from Melbourne's central grid through inner and outer suburbs. CityLink is a tollway linking several of the major access routes; drivers must purchase a pass prior to travelling on or within three days of using CityLink roads. The city's flat landscape is also well suited to bicycles.

Sights at a Glance

Historic Streets and Buildings

③ Supreme Court
④ Melbourne Mint
⑧ Docklands
⑨ General Post Office
⑫ Melbourne Town Hall
⑭ Regent Theatre
⑯ No. 120 Collins Street
⑰ Chinatown
⑲ Old Magistrate's Court
⑳ Old Melbourne Gaol
㉑ Lygon Street
㉓ Brunswick Street & Fitzroy
㉛ Flinders Street Station
㉜ Federation Square
㉟ Fitzroy & Acland streets
㊲ Chapel Street
㊳ *Rippon Lea pp408–9*
㊴ Como Historic House
   and Garden

Shops and Markets

① Queen Victoria Market
⑩ Royal Arcade
⑪ Block Arcade

Churches and Cathedrals

② St Francis' Church
⑤ St James' Old Cathedral
⑬ St Paul's Cathedral
⑮ Scots' Church

Museums and Galleries

⑦ Immigration Museum
⑱ Museum of Chinese
   Australian History
㉒ Melbourne Museum
㉔ Old Treasury Building
㉕ National Sports Museum
㉙ Polly Woodside
㉚ Melbourne Aquarium
㉞ National Gallery of Victoria

Parks and Gardens

㉘ *Royal Botanic Gardens and*
   Kings Domain pp402–3

Modern Architecture

⑥ Rialto Towers
㉝ Eureka Tower

Sports Grounds

㉖ Melbourne Cricket Ground
㉗ Melbourne Park
㊱ Albert Park

Key

▨ Place of interest

Gothic turrets of the Old Magistrate's Court

Swanston Street Precinct

Swanston Street, home to Melbourne's town hall and other major civic buildings, has always been a hub of the city. It is an eclectic illustration of the city's Victorian and 20th-century public architecture and exemplary of one of the most interesting relics of Melbourne: an ordered grid of broad, evenly measured and rectilinear streets, lanes and arcades. This major thoroughfare was named after Captain Charles Swanston, a banker, politician and member of the Port Phillip Association.

Classically inspired Storey Hall, neighbour of the RMIT Building

The City Baths are set in a beautiful Edwardian building with twin cupolas as a distinctive feature. They have been carefully restored to their original 1903 condition.

① City Baths

② RMIT Building 8

⑬ St Paul's Cathedral
Architect William Butterfield designed St Paul's in a Gothic Revival style in the 1880s.

⑫ Melbourne Town Hall
The city's town hall was built in 1867, funded by proceeds of the gold rush (see pp58–9).

Neo-Classical columns

Sandstone façade

④ Melbourne Town Hall

⑤ St Paul's Cathedral

Building 8, RMIT
(Royal Melbourne Institute of Technology), is a gaudy, contemporary blend of bold, primary colours utilized within horizontal and vertical lines. It was met with very mixed reviews by Melburnians when it was completed.

Locator Map
See Melbourne Street Finder, map 1

The State Library was the first design by noted architect Joseph Reed in 1854. Inside is an attractive octagonal reading room, covered by the central dome which was added in 1913.

Neo-Classical
Corinthian columns line the façade.

③ State Library of Victoria

❸ **Flinders Street Station**
Melbourne's busiest rail terminus is one of the most recognizable sights in the city.

Young and Jackson's, a 19th-century hotel known for its nude portrait *Chloe*, is protected by the National Trust.

The Atrium in Federation Square is a remarkable building made of glass, steel and zinc. The Square itself has become the cultural centre of the city, with its restaurants, various attractions and outdoor events.

Station clock

⑥ Flinders Street Station

⑦ Young and Jackson's

⑧ Federation Square

Vegetable stall in Queen Victoria Market

❶ Queen Victoria Market

Elizabeth, Therry, Peel & Victoria sts.
Map 1 B2. **Tel** (03) 9320 5822.
🚉 Flagstaff & Melbourne Central
(Elizabeth St exit). 🚊 Elizabeth St
routes. **Open** 6am–2pm Tue & Thu;
6am–5pm Fri; 6am–3pm Sat; 9am–4pm
Sun. **Closed** public hols. ♿ 🏪
🌐 qvm.com.au

Melbourne's main fresh produce
and general goods market has
a strange history, occupying the
site of the original Melbourne
General Cemetery, which was
first used in 1837. In 1877, the
idea of converting part of the
original cemetery into a marketplace for fruit and vegetables
was considered a practical one.
At the time, it involved the
relocation of only three graves.
However, the choice created
controversy which did not
settle down for some time, as
the market's popularity made
it necessary to acquire further
portions of the cemetery.
In 1917, an act of Parliament
granted the removal of the
remains. However, only 900
were taken away. The rest still lie
there, mainly under the car park.
  Today the complex, occupying
7 ha (17 acres), attracts 130,000
visitors per week. Its decorative
high-vaulted ceilings and
open sides add to its ornate
atmosphere. About 1,000 stalls
sell fresh fruit and vegetables,
fish, meat, cheese, organic food
and souvenirs and clothing. The
impressive variety of produce
on offer reflects Melbourne's
multicultural makeup. The Deli
Hall is a highlight, with a

delicious range of local and
imported cheeses, cured meats
and continental pastries. Every
Wednesday from November
to February there is a Night
Market (5–10pm).

❷ St Francis' Church

326 Lonsdale St. **Map** 1 C2. **Tel** (03)
9663 2495. 🚉 Melbourne Central.
🚊 Elizabeth St routes. **Open** 7am–
6:30pm daily. ♿ 🏪 by arrangement.
🌐 stfrancismelbourne.org.au

St Francis' Church today is
Australia's busiest Roman
Catholic church, with 10,000
visitors each week. Built
between 1841 and 1845 on
the site of an earlier church,
it is also Victoria's oldest.
  Renowned for its beauty,
the church began as a simple
Neo-Gothic building and has
undergone many alterations.
It was the target of a $2.8 million
restoration appeal, and major
renovations were completed

in the early 1990s. During the
ceiling restoration, treasures
from the 1860s, such as a
painting of angels, stars and a
coat of arms, were discovered
and beautifully restored.
Vandalized statues have since
been replaced by faithful copies.
  The church holds regular
services, and has one of Australia's
most celebrated resident choirs.

Roof detail of St Francis' Church

❸ Supreme Court

210 William St. **Map** 1 B3. **Tel** (03) 9603
9300. 🚉 Flagstaff. 🚊 City Circle &
Bourke St routes. **Open** 9:30am–4pm
Mon–Fri (5pm Fri); courts sit
10am–4:15pm. ♿ 🚫

When the Port Phillip district
was still part of the New South
Wales colony, criminal and
important civil cases were
heard in Sydney. To ease the
inconvenience, Melbourne's
first resident judge arrived in
1841 to set up a Supreme Court
in the city. Following the

Domed library in the Supreme Court

For hotels and restaurants in this area see pp493–4 and pp526–9

Separation Act of 1851, which established the Colony of Victoria, the city set up its own Supreme Court in 1852. The court moved to the present building, with a design inspired by the Four Courts of Dublin in Ireland, in 1884.

The Supreme Court is an imposing building, with street façades on Lonsdale, William and Little Bourke streets. Its style is Classical, with a projecting portico and a double arcade with Doric and Ionic columns. Internally, a labyrinthine plan is centred on a beautiful domed library. The large bronze figure of Justice, defying tradition, is not blindfolded: rumour has it that an early Melbourne judge persuaded the authorities that Justice should be "wide-eyed if not innocently credulous". The Supreme Court Library is now classified by the National Trust.

❹ Melbourne Mint

280 William St. **Map** 1 B3. **Tel** (03) 8602 5188. 🚆 Flagstaff. 🚊 24, 30. 🚌 Lonsdale & Queen sts routes. **Closed** to the public. 🌐 melbournemint.com.au

This former Mint, built between 1871 and 1872, contains two courts which were formerly used to cope with the overflow from the Supreme Court.

The building replaced Melbourne's first Exhibition Building, erected in 1854 and subsequently destroyed by fire. When the mint opened in 1872 it processed finds from the Victoria gold fields and was a branch of the Royal Mint of London. The actual coining processes took place in an area now occupied by the car park. After the Common-wealth of Australia was founded in 1901 *(see p60)*, new silver coinage was designed, which the mint produced from 1916 to the mid-1960s. The Melbourne site ceased production in 1967

Melbourne Mint crest

when the Mint was relocated to Canberra. Although the Melbourne Mint building is now closed to the general public, visitors can still take in its imposing structure from the outside.

St James' Old Cathedral tower

❺ St James' Old Cathedral

Cnr King & Batman sts. **Map** 1 A2. **Tel** (03) 9329 0903. 🚆 Flagstaff. 🚊 30, 75. 🚌 220. **Open** 9am–3pm Mon–Fri; 10am service Sun. **Closed** public hols. ♿ 🅿 by appointment.

St James' was the first Anglican cathedral in the city, used until St Paul's opened in 1891 *(see p393)*. It was first built near the corner of Little Collins and William streets to replace a wooden hut, known as the "Pioneers' Church". It was relocated to its present site between 1913 and 1914. The stones were numbered to ensure that the original design was replicated. However, a few changes were made, such as a lower ceiling, a shortening of the sanctuary and a reshaping of the bell tower.

St James' was designed in a colonial Georgian style. The foundations are made of bluestone and the main walls were constructed with local sandstone. The cathedral was opened for worship on 2 October 1842, but was not consecrated until 1853.

Charles Perry, the city's first bishop, was enthroned here in 1848. The cathedral is still used for regular services. A small museum contains photographs, historic documents and cathedral mementos.

❻ Rialto Towers

525 Collins St (between King and William sts). **Map** 1 B4. 🚆 Southern Cross Station. 🚊 Collins St routes. **Open** 7am–7pm daily. ♿ 🅿 🌐 rialto.com.au

Rialto Towers is a member of the World Federation of Great Towers. It has 58 floors above street level and 8 below. From street level up, it measures 253 m (830 ft).

The structure was built in 1986 by Australian developer Bruno Grollo, who was also responsible for the Eureka Tower *(see p407)*. The former observation deck, on the 55th floor, is now the setting for the Vue de Monde restaurant including the sophisticated Lui Bar. This fine establishment is one of the city's most spectacular places to dine, with panoramic views over Melbourne. The bar area is also open to non-diners.

The lift travels from the ground floor to the 55th floor in 38 seconds and is one of the fastest in the world.

The mighty Rialto Towers

❼ Immigration Museum

400 Flinders St. **Map** 1 B4.
Tel 13 11 02. 🚇 Southern Cross
Station. 🚊 Collins St routes. **Open**
10am–5pm daily. **Closed** Good Fri,
25 Dec. ♿ ⬚ 🔲 museumvictoria.
com.au/immigrationmuseum

The Immigration Museum
explores the stories – some sad,
some funny, but all engaging –
of real people from all over the
world who have migrated to
Victoria. Located in the Old
Customs House, it uses moving
images, personal and community
memories, and memorabilia to
recreate the journey and arrival
of immigrants and to explore
the impact of immigration on
indigenous people.

❽ Docklands

Map 1 A4. 🚇 Southern Cross
Station. 🚊 City Circle 11, 35, 48, 70,
75. 🚢 Yarra River Shuttle.

The spectacular redevelopment
of Melbourne Docklands makes
it worth visiting for the modern
architecture alone. The total
redevelopment area is 200 ha
(490 acres), with 3 km (2 miles)
of Yarra River frontage. The final
stage of the project is to be
completed in 2020. Docklands
is also home to the 120-m-
(394-ft) tall Melbourne Star
Ferris wheel, with its panoramic
views of the skyline and bay.

The area has a beautiful
harbour and marina, magnificent public spaces, such as
Harbour Esplanade, Grand Plaza
and Docklands Park, historic
wharves, shops and restaurants.
There is also urban art (by
Australian artists such as Bruce
Armstrong) and a bronze statue

General Post Office's magnificent exterior, completed in 1907

of local pop icon Kylie Minogue.
Events such as the Summer
Boat Show are held here, and
it is home to Etihad Stadium
where sports events are held
and a weekly Sunday market.

❾ General Post Office

Cnr Little Bourke St Mall & Elizabeth St.
Map 1 C3. **Tel** (03) 9290 0200.
🚇 Flinders St & Melbourne Central.
🚊 Bourke & Elizabeth sts routes.
Open 10am–6pm Mon–Thu & Sat,
10am–8pm Fri, 11am–5pm Sun.
Closed Good Fri, 25 Dec, 1 Jan.
♿ via Little Bourke St.

Melbourne's postal service
moved to this site in 1841.
The present structure was
begun in 1859 and completed
in 1907. The first and second
floors were built between
1859 and 1867, with the third
floor and clocktower added
between 1885 and 1890. This
has resulted in an unusual
combination of styles, with
Doric columns on the ground
floor, Ionic on the second and
Corinthian on the top level.

The building had a post-
World War I redesign under

the direction of architect
Walter Burley Griffin *(see p201)*.
It closed as a post office in 1993
and is now an H&M megastore
containing some of the biggest
names in international and
Australian fashion.

Royal Arcade entrance

❿ Royal Arcade

Elizabeth, Bourke & Little Collins sts.
Map 1 C3. **Tel** (03) 9670 7777.
🚇 Flinders St. 🚊 Bourke, Elizabeth &
Collins sts routes. **Open** 9am–6pm
Mon–Thu, 10am–8pm Fri, 9am–5pm
Sat, 10am–5pm Sun.

Royal Arcade is Melbourne's
oldest surviving arcade, with
boutiques selling everything
from antique jewellery to fine
chocolates. It is part of a
network of lanes and arcades
which sprang up to divide the
big blocks of the city grid into
smaller segments.

The original arcade, built in
1869 and designed by Charles
Webb, runs between Bourke
Street Mall and Little Collins
Street. An annexe, with an
entrance on Elizabeth Street,

Docklands with the Etihad Stadium and the city's CBD in the background

For hotels and restaurants in this area see pp493–4 and pp526–9

was added in 1902. A statue of Father Time, originally on the Bourke Street façade, is now located inside the arcade at the northern end.

The arcade's most famous inhabitants are statues of Gog and Magog, mythical representations of the conflict between the ancient Britons and the Trojans. They are modelled on identical figures in the Guildhall in the City of London. Between them is Gaunt's Clock, crafted by an original tenant of the arcade, Thomas Gaunt.

Chapel of Ascension in St Paul's Cathedral

⑪ Block Arcade

282 Collins St. **Map** 1 C3. **Tel** (03) 9654 5244. 🚉 Flinders St. v Swanston & Collins sts routes. **Open** 7:30am–5:30pm daily. **Closed** Good Fri, 25 Dec. ♿ 📷 Tue & Thu, booking essential.

Built between 1891 and 1893, with period details including a mosaic floor and a central dome, Melbourne's most opulent arcade was named after the promenade taken by fashionable society in the 1890s. Known as "doing the block", the walk involved strolling down Collins Street between Elizabeth and Swanston streets.

The arcade was restored in 1988. It still includes the Hopetoun Tea-rooms, which have been in place since the structure was opened. Guided tours of the arcade are available.

Block Arcade façade

⑫ Melbourne Town Hall

Swanston St. **Map** 1 C3. **Tel** (03) 9658 9658. 🚉 Flinders St. 🚋 Swanston & Collins sts routes. **Open** 9am–6pm Mon–Fri, 9am–5pm Sat–Sun (ground level foyer only). **Closed** public hols. ♿ 📷 11am & 1pm daily, obligatory for areas other than ground level foyer.

Melbourne Town Hall was completed in 1870, designed by Joseph Reed's company, Reed & Barnes. The portico was added in 1887.

An adjacent administration block and the council's second chamber were added in 1908. This chamber combines a Renaissance-style interior with uniquely Australian motifs, such as a ceiling plasterwork of gum nuts.

Stained glass in Melbourne Town Hall

A fire in 1925 destroyed much of the building's interior, including the main hall which had to be rebuilt. The entrance to the building shows four motifs on the young city's coat of arms: a whale, a ship, a bull and a sheep, signifying the main colonial industries. In 1942, the College of Arms ordered an inversion of the motifs according to heraldic convention. This explains the discrepancy between earlier and later coats of arms.

The main hall frequently hosts public events and features an impressive three-storey-high pipe organ.

⑬ St Paul's Cathedral

Cnr Swanston & Flinders sts. **Map** 2 D3. **Tel** (03) 9653 4333. 🚉 Flinders St. 🚋 Swanston, Flinders & Collins sts routes. **Open** 8am–6pm Mon–Fri, 9am–4pm Sat, 7:30am–7:30pm Sun. ♿ 📷

St Paul's Cathedral was built by the Anglican Church in 1866 to replace a far smaller church of the same name on the site.

Construction, however, was plagued by difficulties, with dissension between the English architect, William Butterfield, and the Cathedral Erection Board. Building began in 1880, but Butterfield tendered his resignation in 1884. The final stages of construction were supervised by the architect Joseph Reed, who also designed many of the fittings. The cathedral was eventually consecrated in 1891.

There are many outstanding internal features, including the *reredos* (altar screen) made in Italy from marble and alabaster inset with glass mosaics. The organ, made by T C Lewis & Co. of London, is the best surviving work of this great organ-builder. The cathedral also has a peal of 13 bells – a rarity outside the British Isles.

The cathedral underwent a five-year restoration, completed in 2009, including the cleaning and upgrading of the spectacular stained-glass windows.

⑭ Regent Theatre

191 Collins St. **Map** 2 D3. **Tel** (03) 9299 9800. 🚆 Flinders St. 🚋 Swanston & Collins sts routes. ♿ ✏

When the Regent Theatre's auditorium was destroyed by fire in April 1945, the Lord Mayor of Melbourne promised the public that it would be rebuilt, despite the scarcity of building materials due to World War II, such was the popularity and local importance of the theatre.

Known as "Melbourne's Palace of Dreams", it was first constructed and opened in 1929. Its lavish interiors emulated both the glamour of Hollywood and New York's impressive Capitol Theater.

The building had two main venues. The auditorium upstairs, for live stage and musical entertainment, was known as the Regent Theatre. Downstairs, the Plaza Theatre was originally a ballroom, but, following the success of the "talkies", it was converted into a cinema.

Fortunately, the magnificent decor of the Plaza Theatre was not damaged in the fire of 1945 and the renovated auditorium re-opened in 1947.

The advent of television led to dwindling cinema audiences, and the Regent Theatre closed

Assembly hall adjacent to Scots' Church

for almost 30 years. The complex was restored in 1996 and is now listed by the National Trust. Today, the venue mostly hosts musical theatre. Ticket-holders can admire the beautiful interiors before seeing the latest big-name show.

⑮ Scots' Church

99 Russell St (cnr Collins St). **Map** 2 D3. **Tel** (03) 9650 9903. 🚆 Flinders St & Parliament. 🚋 Swanston & Collins sts routes. **Open** 11am–2:30pm Mon–Fri. 🕐 1pm, Wed; 11am & 7pm, Sun. ♿ ✏ on request.

Scots' Church, completed in 1874, was intended at the time to be "the most beautiful building in Australia". It was

designed by Joseph Reed in a "decorated Gothic" style, with bluestone used in the foundations and local Barrabool stone making up the superstructure.

There is also an assembly hall which was completed in 1913.

⑯ No. 120 Collins Street

120 Collins St. **Map** 2 D3. 🚆 Flinders St & Parliament. 🚋 Collins St routes. **Open** 7am–7pm Mon–Fri. ♿

Built in 1991, No. 120 Collins Street was designed by Daryl Jackson and Hassell Architects and houses the offices of many blue-chip corporations. In the heart of Melbourne's central business district, the office

Grandiose foyer of the Regent Theatre, restored to its original glory

For hotels and restaurants in this area see pp493–4 and pp526–9

block is now a city landmark. Its communications tower was for many years the highest point in the city, at 265 m (869 ft). Original 1908 Federation-style professional chambers, built on the grounds of the 1867 St Michael's Uniting Church, are incorporated into the building.

Chambers at No. 120 Collins Street

⓱ Chinatown

Little Bourke St. **Map** 2 D2.
🚇 Parliament. 🚊 Swanston & Bourke sts routes.

When Chinese immigrants began arriving in Melbourne to seek gold during the 1850s, many European residents were decidedly hostile. Only recent arrivals in the area themselves, they were still insecure about how strongly their own society had been established. This led to racial tension and violence.

The very first Chinese immigrants landed in Australia as early as 1818, but it was during the late 1840s that larger contingents arrived. These newcomers replaced the pool of cheap labour which had dried up with the winding down of convict settlements in the new colonies. This wave of immigration was harmonious until the vast influx of Chinese visitors who came not for labour, but to seek their fortune in the Victorian gold fields in the 1850s. The large numbers of immigrants and a decline in gold finds made the Chinese targets of vicious and organized riots.

This attitude was sanctioned by government policy. The Chinese were charged a poll tax in most states of £10 each – a huge sum, particularly as many were peasants. Even harsher was a restriction on the number of passengers that boat-owners could carry. This acted as a disincentive for them to bring Chinese immigrants to Australia. What resulted were "Chinese marathons", as new arrivals dodged the tax by landing in "free" South Australia and walking to the gold fields, covering distances of up to 800 km (500 miles) *(see pp58–9)*.

As an immigrant society in Melbourne, the Chinese were highly organized and self-sufficient. A city base was established during the 1850s, utilizing the cheap rental district of the city centre. As with other Chinatowns around the world, traders could live and work in the same premises and act as a support network for other Chinese immigrants. The community largely avoided prejudice by starting up traditional Asian businesses which included market gardening, laundering, green grocers and furniture-making (but work had to be stamped "Made by Chinese labour").

Stone lion in the Museum of Chinese Australian History

Traditional gateway in Little Bourke Street, Chinatown

Today, Chinatown is known for its restaurants and Chinese produce shops, with the community's calendar culminating in its New Year celebrations in January or February *(see p45)*. Ironically, in view of the early prejudices, this community is now one of Australia's oldest and most successful.

⓲ Museum of Chinese Australian History

22 Cohen Place (off Little Bourke St).
Map 2 D2. **Tel** (03) 9662 2888.
🚇 Parliament. 🚊 Swanston & Bourke sts routes. **Open** 10am–4pm daily. **Closed** 1 Jan, Good Fri, 25 Dec. ♿ 🛗 📷 🌐 **chinesemuseum.com.au**

Opened in 1985 to preserve the heritage of Australians of Chinese descent, this museum is in the heart of Chinatown. The subjects of its displays range from the influx of Chinese gold-seekers in the 1850s to exhibitions of contemporary Chinese art, thus offering a comprehensive history of the Chinese in Victoria and their cultural background. The second floor holds regular touring exhibitions from China and displays of Chinese art. On the third floor is a permanent exhibition covering many aspects of Chinese-Australian history, including elaborate costumes, furniture and temple regalia.

In the basement, another permanent exhibition traces the experiences of Chinese gold miners – visitors step into a booth which creaks and moves like a transport ship, then view dioramas of gold field life, a Chinese temple and a tent theatre used by Chinese performers to entertain miners. A guided heritage walk through Chinatown is also available.

The museum also houses the beautiful Melbourne Chinese dragon, the head of which is the largest of its kind anywhere in the world.

Street-by-Street: Parliament Area

The Parliament precinct on Eastern Hill is a gracious area of great historic interest. Early founders of the city noted the favourable aspect of the hill and set it aside for Melbourne's official and ecclesiastical buildings. The streets still retain the elegance of the Victorian era; the buildings, constructed with revenue from the gold rush *(see pp58–9)*, are among the most impressive in the city. The Fitzroy Gardens, on the lower slopes of the hill, date back to the 1850s *(see pp378–9)* and provide a peaceful retreat complete with woodlands, glades, seasonal plantings and magnificent elm tree avenues.

The Hotel Windsor, with its long and ornate façade, was built in 1883 and is the grandest surviving hotel of its era in Australia *(see p493)*.

Stanford Fountain
The beautiful centrepiece of the elegant Gordon Reserve was sculpted by the prisoner William Stanford while he was serving his sentence.

★ Old Treasury Building
This Renaissance Revival-style building was designed by draughtsman John James Clark in 1857. Built as government offices, with vaults to house the treasury's gold, it now holds permanent and temporary exhibitions.

Cook's Cottage
This cottage was the English home of the parents of Captain James Cook *(see p54)*. It was shipped to Australia in 1934 piece by piece and now houses displays about Cook and 18th-century life.

For hotels and restaurants in this area see pp493–4 and pp526–9

★ Parliament House
The Legislative Council in this 1850s building sits in a lavish, Corinthian chamber. The crimson colour scheme is based on that of the UK's House of Lords.

Locator Map
See Melbourne Street Finder, map 2

Tasma Terrace is a superb example of Melbourne's distinctive terrace houses with ornate cast-iron decoration *(see p380)*. It is now the headquarters of the National Trust.

St Patrick's Cathedral
This is one of the best examples of Gothic Revival church architecture in the world. It was constructed between 1858 and 1897, with its impressive spires completed in 1939.

★ Fitzroy Gardens
James Sinclair was head gardener when the superb formal gardens were first laid out, featuring follies, winding paths, a fern gulley and avenues of elms.

CATHEDRAL PLACE

ALBERT STREET

| 0 metres | 100 |
| 0 yards | 100 |

Key
— Suggested route

⑲ Old Magistrate's Court

Cnr La Trobe & Russell sts. **Map** 1 C2. **Tel** (03) 8663 7228. 🚇 Melbourne Central. 🚋 La Trobe & Swanston sts routes. **Open** during school hols.

The Melbourne Magistrate's Court, also called City Court, occupied this building until 1995. The area was formerly known as the police precinct – this is because the court lies opposite the former police headquarters, a very striking Art Deco skyscraper that was completed in the early 1940s, and next door to the Old Melbourne Gaol.

Built in 1911, the court's façades are made of native Moorabool sandstone. The building's intricate, Romanesque design features gables, turrets and arches. It originally contained three courtrooms. Court One is open to the public during school holidays as part of the Old Melbourne Gaol Crime and Justice Experience.

Ornate Romanesque tower of the Old Magistrate's Court

⑳ Old Melbourne Gaol

Russell St. **Map** 1 C2. **Tel** (03) 8663 7228. 🚇 Melbourne Central. 🚋 La Trobe & Swanston sts routes. **Open** 9:30am–5pm daily; also for night tours (check website for details). **Closed** Good Fri, 25 Dec. 🚻 ♿ limited. 🌐 oldmelbournegaol.com.au

Visiting the Old Melbourne Gaol, Victoria's first extensive gaol complex, is a chilling

Corridor of cells in Old Melbourne Gaol

experience, especially on a night tour. Between 1845 and 1929, it was the site of 133 executions. While much of the original complex has been demolished, the imposing Second Cell Block still stands and is home to a fascinating museum.

Ghosts are often reported at the gaol, which is hardly surprising given the tragic and grisly accounts of prisoners' lives and deaths. Conditions, based on London's Pentonville Model Prison, were grim, regulated and silent. When first incarcerated, prisoners were held in solitary confinement and were not permitted to mix with other prisoners until a later date, set according to their sentence. Exhibits showing these conditions include prisoners' chains and a frame used for flogging. But perhaps the most compelling exhibits are the many accounts of prisoners who were condemned to die at the gaol, accompanied by their death masks. Ned Kelly's death mask is the most famous of those on display. Visitors can also see the original gallows where executions took place.

Included with a ticket to the Old Melbourne Gaol, visitors can now tour the former city Watch House, which served as a central "lock up" for police from 1908 to 1994. With a Charge Sergeant as a guide, visitors are "arrested" and processed through the lock up, experiencing first hand an environment that has not changed since the police and inmates left it. The Watch House has a long and fascinating history, with characters such as

Ned Kelly

The most well-known execution at the Melbourne Gaol was that of Ned Kelly, Australia's most famous bushranger, on 11 November 1880. Edward "Ned" Kelly was the son of Ellen and ex-convict "Red" Kelly. At the time of Ned's final imprisonment and execution, Ellen was serving a sentence in the gaol's Female Ward after hitting a policeman over the head at her house when he came to arrest her son, Dan. She was therefore able to visit Ned, who had been captured at Glenrowan on 28 June 1880 (see p455). A crowd of 5,000 waited outside the gaol when Kelly was executed, most of them to lend their support to a man perceived to be rightfully rebelling against the English-based law and police authorities. In one instance, the Kelly Gang burned a bank's records of outstanding loans so they no longer had to be repaid. The controversy over whether Kelly was hero or villain continues to this day.

Ned Kelly's death mask

the 1920s gangster Squizzy Taylor, last man hanged Ronald Ryan and infamous Chopper Read all having been locked up here. The experience is enhanced by informative multimedia displays that illustrate the stories of former inmates.

㉑ Lygon Street

Lygon St, Carlton. **Map** 1 C1. 🚆 1, 8.
🚌 200, 207, 955, 966.

This Italian-influenced street is one of the main café, restaurant and delicatessen areas in central Melbourne *(see pp526)*.

The strong Italian tradition of Lygon Street began at the time of mass post-World War II immigration. With a general exodus to the suburbs in the 1940s, Carlton became unfashionable and new immigrants were able to buy its 19th-century houses and shops cheaply. More importantly, the immigrants were central in protecting these Victorian and Edwardian houses, which were built with post-gold rush wealth, from government plans to fill the area with low-income Housing Commission homes.

A distinctive architectural trait of Lygon Street's two-storey shops is their street verandas, built to protect both customers and merchandise from the sun. In the mid-1960s, the area became fashionable with university students, many of whom moved in to take advantage of its cheap accommodation, then stayed on after graduating to become the base of the suburb's contemporary middle-class and professional community. The street is only one block from the main University of Melbourne campus and can be reached from the city centre by foot, bus or tram. Its wide street resembles a French boulevard and is well suited to the Carlton Italian Festa held here every year *(see p44)*.

Coffee grinder in a Lygon Street coffee house

㉒ Melbourne Museum

Carlton Gardens, Melbourne.
Map 2 D1. **Tel** (03) 8341 7777.
🚆 86, 96. **Open** 10am–5pm daily.
Closed Good Fri, 25 Dec.
🅿 📷 🏠 ♿
Ⓦ **museumvictoria.com.au/ melbournemuseum**

Housed in an ultra-modern facility in verdant Carlton Gardens, it has exhibits over six levels, half of which are below ground level. Diverse displays offer insights into science, technology, the environment, the human mind and body, Australian society and indigenous cultures. One of the highlights is Bunjilaka, the Aboriginal Centre. It combines exhibition galleries with a performance space and meeting rooms. *Wurreka*, the 50-m- (150-ft-) long zinc wall etching at the entrance is by Aboriginal artist Judy Watson. On the Milarri Garden trail, you can learn about traditional uses of indigenous plants and explore a cave decorated with Aboriginal paintings.

The Forest Gallery is a living, breathing exhibit, featuring 8,000 plants from 120 different species. It is also home to around 20 different vertebrate species, including snakes, birds, fish and hundreds of insects. This gallery explores the complex ecosystem of Australia's temperate forests, using plants and animals, art and multimedia installations, soundscapes and other activities.

There is also a dedicated gallery for children, featuring a dinosaur dig to excavate fossils, a discovery garden and museum objects, as well as Aboriginal storytelling and sculptures.

One of the most popular exhibits is in the Australia Gallery. It displays the life of Phar Lap, the champion Australian racehorse of the early 1930s. Exhibits include race memorabilia of the period. Phar Lap himself is seen in an Art-Deco inspired showcase. Other curiosities on show in the museum include the skeleton of a blue whale, a car from Melbourne's first tram, a windmill and the Hertel, the first car to be imported.

Adjacent to the Melbourne Museum is the **Royal Exhibition Building**, offering an interesting 19th-century counterpart to the Museum's modern architecture. The Exhibition Building was built for the 1880 International Exhibition and is one of the few remaining structures from the 19th-century world fairs. It was designed by Joseph Reed, whose work can be found throughout Melbourne.

Elegant Royal Exhibition Building, near the Melbourne Museum

Cyclists passing a clothing store on Brunswick Street

㉓ Brunswick Street and Fitzroy

Brunswick St. **Map** 2 E1. 🚋 11.

Next to the university suburb of Carlton, Fitzroy was the natural choice for a post-1960s populace of students and other bohemian characters, who took advantage of the area's cheap postwar Housing Commission properties, unwanted by wealthier Melburnians. Despite becoming gentrified, Fitzroy's main strip, Brunswick Street, maintains an alternative air and a cosmopolitan street life.

Today, Brunswick Street is a vibrant mix of cafés, restaurants and trendy shops, especially popular are the numerous vintage stores where anyone can hunt for an undiscovered treasure. Vegie Bar (*p528*), a restaurant on the Brunswick street strip, is something of an institution among vegetarians. A little to the south is Gertrude Street, which has an eclectic mix of record stores, bars and galleries.

Nearby Johnston Street has a Hispanic flavour, with a few tapas bars and a Spanish grocery. In November, it hosts The Fiesta, an outdoor festival celebrating Hispanic-Latin American culture. Also nearby lies Smith Street, which has outgrown its formerly seedy reputation to become a hotspot for some of the trendier restaurants and bars in the city. All the streets in this area are most lively on Friday and Saturday nights and easily accessible on a tram.

㉔ Old Treasury Building

Old Treasury Building, Spring Street (top of Collins Street). **Map** 2 E2. **Tel** (03) 9651 2233. 🚋 11, 109. **Open** 10am–4pm Sun–Fri (other times group bookings only). **Closed** Good Fri, 25 & 26 Dec. 🅿 🎥 group tours by request. 🅰 🅿 **w** oldtreasurybuilding.org.au

Melbourne's beautiful, 19th-century Old Treasury Building (*see p396*) was designed in 1857 by John James Clark, a nineteen-year-old architectural prodigy. It provided secure storage for gold that flooded into Melbourne from the wealthy Victorian gold fields. It also served as office accommodation for the Governor of Victoria (a role it still fulfils to this day).

As well as an opportunity to see the building itself, a visit to the museum includes a look at the gold vaults that lie beneath the building. The vaults contain a dynamic multi-media exhibition *Built on Gold*, which tells the story of how Melbourne developed into a city of enormous wealth in a remarkably short period of ten years. In this time it went from a small colonial outpost to a vibrant city with magnificent buildings and grand boulevards, a dynamic theatre culture, a passion for sport and political activism.

㉕ National Sports Museum

Melbourne Cricket Ground, Yarra Park, Jolimont. **Map** 2 F3. **Tel** (03) 9657 8879. 🚈 Richmond. 🚌 48, 70, 75. **Open** 10am–5pm daily. **Closed** Good Fri, 25 Dec. 🅿 🅰 🎥

Following the redevelopment of the Melbourne Cricket Ground (MCG) for the 2006 Commonwealth Games, the MCG has become the home of the National Sports Museum. The museum honours all things sporting, including Aussie Rules football, cricket and the Olympic Games among others.

Located across two levels of the refurbished Olympic Stand, visitors can view some of the finest sports-related memorabilia using state-of-the-art technology. The Olympic Museum has displays of the history of all summer Olympic meets.

The Australian Cricket Hall of Fame, which opened with ten Australian players as initial members, includes Sir Donald Bradman. Each player is presented through a comprehensive historical display.

After you have wandered through the museum, you can take a tour which includes the Arena, the Ponsford Stand, the football and cricket changing rooms, heritage artworks and the corporate suites. Tours leave from Gate No.3 every half hour between 10am and 3pm, but only on non-event days. Booking is not essential.

Olympic Cauldron on display in the Olympic Museum

World-famous Melbourne Cricket Ground backed by the city skyline

❷❻ Melbourne Cricket Ground

Yarra Park, Jolimont. **Map** 2 F3. **Tel** (03) 9657 8888. 🚆 Jolimont. 🚋 48, 70, 75 (special trams run on sports event days). **Open** for tours (10am–3pm daily, except event days) or sports events. 🅿 ♿ 📷 obligatory. 🆆 **mcg.org.au**

Melbourne Cricket Ground (MCG) is Australia's premier sports stadium and a cultural icon. The land was granted in 1853 to the Melbourne Cricket Club (MCC), itself conceived in 1838.

The MCG predominantly hosts cricket and Australian Rules football, being the site for test matches and the first one-day international match and for the Australian Football League Grand Final, held on the last Saturday of September (see p44). Non-sporting events, such as pop concerts, are also held here.

There have been numerous stands and pavilions over the years, each superseded at different times by reconstructions of the ground. An 1876 stand, now demolished, was reversible, with spectators able to watch cricket on the ground and football in the park in winter. Following massive redevelopment of the ground ahead of the 2006 Commonwealth Games, the MCG can now seat crowds of more than 100,000. Guided tours usually take visitors to the members' pavilion, which includes the Melbourne Cricket Club (MCC) Museum. It traces the history of the MCG with an exhibition of information and artifacts. The Mythical Ashes is a fascinating display of Ashes mementoes.

❷❼ Melbourne Park

Batman Ave. **Map** 2 E4. **Tel** (03) 9286 1600. 🚆 Flinders St & Richmond. 🚋 70. **Open** for events. Tours of Rod Laver Arena at 11:30am, 1pm, 2:30pm Mon–Fri, 11:30am, 1pm Sat & Sun (call 1300 836 647 to book). 🆆 **mopt.com.au**

Melbourne Park (formerly the National Tennis Centre) on the northern bank of the Yarra River, is Melbourne's sports and large-scale concerts venue. Events include the Australian Open (see p45), one of the four Grand Slam competitions of tennis, played under Rod Laver Arena's unique retractable roof (see p381). There are also 22 outdoor and seven indoor tennis courts for public use.

Next to Melbourne Park is the Hisense Arena, which is home to Melbourne Vixens netball team. It also hosts a stadium for cycling, dance performances, family shows, concerts and other entertainment. Opposite the park is the Westpac Centre, which was originally built for the 1956 Olympics but has been redeveloped.

Nearby Olympic Park, formerly the location for international and national athletics, is the training ground for Collingwood Football Club. The AAMI Park is also a venue for soccer events. Its exterior is covered in thousands of LEDs that come to life at night.

Australian Open tennis match on one of the outdoor courts at Melbourne Park

㉘ Royal Botanic Gardens and Kings Domain

These adjoining gardens, established in 1852, form the green heart of Melbourne on what was originally a swamp on the edge of the city. The Botanic Gardens house one of the finest collections of botanic species in the world, as well as being highly regarded for their landscape design. William Guilfoyle, curator of the Gardens between 1873 and 1909, used his knowledge of English garden design to create a horticultural paradise. Kings Domain, once an inner-city wilderness, became instead a gracious parkland. Its civic function grew over the years, with the establishment of its monuments, statues, cultural venues and the hilltop residence of the Governor of Victoria.

Pioneer Women's Garden
This sunken, formal garden was built in 1934 to honour the memory of Victoria's founding women. A still, central pool is adorned by a bronze, female statue.

KEY

① **Observatory Gate Precinct**

② **Sidney Myer Music Bowl** is an architecturally acclaimed music "shell" which can accommodate up to 15,000 people for open-air concerts and ballets.

③ **The Temple of the Winds**

④ **The Perennial Border**, based on designer Gertrude Jekyll's traditional colour scheme, is planted with pastels, contrasting with grey and silver foliage.

⑤ **The Ian Potter Foundation Children's Garden**

⑥ **La Trobe's Cottage** was shipped from England in 1839 and was home to Victoria's first governor, Charles La Trobe. The building is now preserved by the National Trust.

★ **Shrine of Remembrance**
Based on the description of the Mausoleum of Halicarnassus in Asia Minor, now Turkey, this imposing monument honours Australian soldiers who gave their lives in war.

★ Government House
This elaborate Italianate building is a landmark of the gardens. Tours of the state rooms are held each week.

VISITORS' CHECKLIST

Practical Information
St Kilda Rd. **Map** 2 F5.
🛈 Birdwood Ave (03) 9252 2300.
🅆 rbg.vic.gov.au
Open 7:30am to sunset daily.
Closed varies seasonally.
♿ 🍽 times vary. 🏠 🌿 🖥

Transport
🚊 3, 5, 6, 8, 16, 64, 67, 72.

Algerian Oak
This magnificent mature oak in the centre of the Oak Lawn is particularly spectacular when it flowers in September.

★ Ornamental Lake
William Guilfoyle's lake forms the centrepiece of the Gardens. It reflects his adherence to 18th-century English garden design, which used water as a feature.

0 metres 200
0 yards 200

Arid Garden
Desert region plants from Australia and around the world thrive in this special garden, watered by a small stream which acts as a natural oasis.

The Yarra River

The Yarra River winds for 240 km (150 miles) from its source in Baw Baw National Park to the coast, emptying in Port Phillip Bay. The river has always been vital to the city, not just as its major natural feature, but also in early settlement days as its gateway to the rest of the world. Today, the Yarra is a symbol of the boundary between north and south Melbourne and many citizens live their whole lives on one side or the other. Since the 1980s, the rejuvenation of the central section of the river has given the south bank an important focus. The river is also used for sport: rowers in training are a daily sight and cycle trails run along much of the river.

Locator Map
See Melbourne Street Finder, maps 1, 2

Arts Centre Melbourne holds performances by the Australian Ballet and the Melbourne Theatre Company. Its 162-m (531-ft) spire is a local landmark. There is also a spiegeltent at some points in the year.

㉞ ★ National Gallery of Victoria
The gallery houses one of the largest collections of international art in Australia.

Victorian College of the Arts

Hamer Hall

㉛ Flinders Street Station
Melbourne's main railway terminus backs on to the Yarra River. A pedestrian walkway links the north and south of the city.

Eureka Tower *(see p407)*

Sandridge Bridge

Federation Square

Ian Potter Centre

Australian Centre for the Moving Image

Melbourne Exhibition Centre is home to various exhibitions and conventions, covering subjects as diverse as motor cars, DIY and alternative medicine.

㉙ ★ Polly Woodside
This 1885 barque now houses a fascinating and highly respected maritime museum.

The Melbourne Convention Centre is the largest conference centre in the southern hemisphere.

CLARENDON STREET

KINGS WAY

FLINDERS STREET

Melbourne Aquarium *(see p406)*

The Crown Entertainment Centre cost A\$1 billion to construct and includes the country's largest casino. Three luxury hotels are part of the complex *(see p494)*.

Key

— Suggested route

| 0 metres | 50 |
| 0 yards | 50 |

Yarra River
Rowing boats can be hired at various points along the banks of the Yarra River. Professional and amateur rowing teams are a regular sight on the iver, and regattas are frequently held.

Polly Woodside barque moored on the Yarra River

ⓩ Polly Woodside

21 S Wharf Promenade, Southbank. **Map** 1 A5. **Tel** (03) 9656 9800. 🚇 Southern Cross. 🚌 12, 96, 109. 🚶 Grimes Street Bridge. **Open** 10am–4pm Sat & Sun (daily during school holidays). 🐾 ♿ except for ship. 📷 book in advance. 🌐 pollywoodside.com.au

The *Polly Woodside* is an 1885 barque built in Belfast. When she was retired from service in the 1960s, she was the only deep-water commercial ship still afloat in Australia. Even in 1885, she was rare, as only one in four ships were then built with sails. Most of the last 40 years of her working life were spent as a coal hulk. Donated to the National Trust in 1968, she has since been restored. Interactive displays explore life at sea and working on Melbourne's docks.

Polly Woodside exhibit

⓪ Melbourne Aquarium

Cnr Flinders & King sts. **Map** 1 B4. **Tel** (03) 9923 5925. 🚇 Southern Cross, Flinders St. 🚌 70. **Open** 9:30am–6pm daily. 🐾 ♿ 🍴 📷 🌐 melbourne aquarium.com.au

Featuring species from the Australian, southern and tropical oceans, the Melbourne Aquarium puts humans close to some of the exotic inhabitants of the deep. Among the exhibits is the Oceanarium, approached through a viewing cylinder and housing sharks and rays as well as vibrantly coloured fish. Melbourne Aquarium is the only place in Victoria where you can see King and Gentoo penguins.

⓵ Flinders Street Station

Cnr Flinders & Swanston sts. **Map** 1 C4. **Tel** 13 16 38. 🚌 Swanston St and Flinders St routes. ♿

Flinders Street Station is the central metropolitan train terminus of Melbourne and one of the city's favourite meeting places. Generations of Melburnians have met each other on the corner steps of the station "under the Clocks". Although the original clocks are now operated by computer rather than by hand, they remain in working order. The Flinders Street site has been part of the public transport network since the city's early days. The first steam train in Australia left Flinders Street Station, then a small wooden building at the end of Elizabeth Street, in 1854. The present station building, completed in 1910, is one of the grandest in the city. Built in French Renaissance style, it features bright-yellow brickwork and an impressive bronze dome.

⓶ Federation Square

Cnr Flinders & Swanston sts. **Map** 2 D3/4. **Tel** (03) 9655 1900. 🚌 Swanston St and Flinders St routes. ♿ 🌐 fedsquare.com.au
The Ian Potter Centre – NGV: **Tel** (03) 8662 1555. ACMI: **Tel** (03) 8663 2200.

One of Melbourne's most visited public spaces, Federation Square opened in October 2002 to commemorate the centenary of the federation of the Australian states.

The square hosts up to 2,000 events each year. Its architectural highlight is the geometric design of the Atrium building, a covered public space that is a hotspot for exhibitions, festivals, book markets, wine showcases and public art installations. There are many outstanding attractions. **The Ian Potter Centre – NGV:** Australia, an offshoot of the National Gallery of Victoria *(see p407)*, is the world's first major gallery dedicated exclusively to the display of Australian art, and well worth a visit. Nearby, the **Australian Centre for the Moving Image (ACMI)** celebrates images on multimedia and film. Across four floors of the Alfred Deakin Building, the ACMI has two multi-format cinemas and the world's largest screen gallery. The square has two information points: the Melbourne Visitor Centre *(see p415)* and the Melbourne Mobility Centre at the bottom of the Federation Square car park.

Modern architecture of the Atrium building at Federation Square

View of Albert Park Lake and its wetlands

㉝ Eureka Tower

7 Riverside Quay. **Map** 1 C4.
Tel (03) 9693 8888. **Open** 10am–
10pm daily. 🅿 for Skydeck. ♿
🅦 eurekaskydeck.com.au

This 300-m (985-ft) tower
was named after the Eureka
Stockade, a rebellion that took
place during the Victoria gold
rush *(see p438)*. The skyscraper's
gold crown and gold-plated
windows refer back to this era.
The Skydeck on the 88th floor
has numerous viewfinders and
a glass cube called "The Edge",
which slides out 3 m (10 ft)
from the side of the building
with visitors inside.

㉞ National Gallery of Victoria

180 St Kilda Rd and Federation
Square. **Map** 2 D4. **Tel** (03) 8620
2222. **Open** 10am–5pm daily.
Closed Good Fri, 25 Apr, 25 Dec.
♿ 🎁 ♿
🅦 ngv.vic.gov.au

The first public art gallery in
Australia, the National Gallery
of Victoria opened in 1861
and housed the original State
Museum. The gallery moved to
St Kilda Rd in 1968 and contains
the largest and widest-ranging
art collection in the country.
Its most significant bequest
was from Melbourne
entrepreneur Alfred Felton
in 1904. Its collections of Old
Masters and contemporary
Australian art are outstanding.
   The international collection is
at 180 St Kilda Road *(see p404)*;
the Australian collection is
at the Ian Potter Centre in
Federation Square *(see p406)*.

㉟ Fitzroy and Acland Streets

St Kilda. **Map** 5 B5. 🚋 12, 16, 96.
🚌 246, 600, 623, 606. ⛴ St Kilda Pier.

Situated 6 km (4 miles) south
of the city centre, St Kilda
has long been the most
popular seaside suburb of
Melbourne. During the
boom-time era of the 1850s
(see pp58–9), the suburb was
inhabited by many wealthy
families. Other well-off
Victorians would holiday in
St Kilda during the summer.
St Kilda Pier, still a magnet for
visitors, was erected in 1859.
   Today St Kilda is densely
populated, with many Art
Deco apartment blocks. The
neighbourhood's main streets
are Fitzroy and Acland. The
latter, renowned as a district
of Jewish delicatessens and
cake shops, is packed with
visitors on Sundays. Fitzroy
Street is filled with upmarket
restaurants and shops.
Rejuvenated in the 1980s, the
beachside esplanade attracts
crowds to its busy arts and
crafts market each Sunday.

Melbourne tram running along the St Kilda
Beach route No.16

㊱ Albert Park

Canterbury Rd, Albert St & Lakeside
Drive. **Map** 5 B3. 🚋 1, 12, 96.

Encompassing the remains of
a former natural swampland,
Albert Park Lake is the attractive
centrepiece of a 225-ha (555-
acre) parkland which includes
sporting fields, a public golf
course and many other
recreational facilities. However,
it is now predominantly known
as the site of the annual
Australian Formula One Grand
Prix, which covers a 5,260-m
(5,754-yd) circuit around the
lake *(see p46)*. Apart from the
Grand Prix, the park is used for a
variety of purposes. The popular
Melbourne Sports and Aquatic
Centre is located here. Wetlands
have also been developed to
promote a diverse wildlife.
Sailing here is another popular
activity, whether by small yacht,
rowing boat or model boat.
   A large, ancient river red
gum tree standing in the centre
of the park is also reputed to
have been the site of many
Aboriginal *corroborees* (festive
night dances).

㊲ Chapel Street

South Yarra, Prahran and Windsor.
Map 6 E3. 🚉 South Yarra, Prahran.
🚋 6, 8, 78.

Chapel Street, Melbourne's
most fashionable street, is lined
with shops selling local and
international fashion designs.
A youthful clientele swarms
the street at weekends.
Up-market restaurants and
cafés abound and the nearby
Prahran Market sells the best
in fresh, delicatessen produce.
Founded in 1891, the market
also contains excellent Greek
and Italian delicatessens that
arrived in Melbourne during
the post-WWII migrant boom.
   Crossing Chapel Street is
Toorak Road, whose "village"
is patronized by Melbourne's
wealthiest community. More
akin to the bohemian area of
Brunswick Street *(see p400)* is
Greville Street to the west,
with its cafés, bars and chic
second-hand shops.

⑱ Rippon Lea

Rippon Lea Mansion, designed by Joseph Reed and built in 1868, is now part of the National Trust's portfolio. The house is a much loved fixture of the city's heritage. The first family of Rippon Lea were the Sargoods, who held many balls and parties during the 1880s and 1890s. The next owner, Premier Sir Thomas Bent, sold off parts of the estate in the early 1900s. The Nathans bought Rippon Lea in 1910 and restored its reputation as a family home. Benjamin Nathan's daughter Louisa added a ballroom and swimming pool to the house, which were the venue for parties in the 1930s and 1940s. The formal gardens are a highlight.

Façade of the elegant mansion, Rippon Lea

Victorian Bathroom
The decor of the bathroom remains in its original Victorian style as installed by the Sargoods. The earth closets were ingeniously processed into liquid manure and recycled for use in the garden.

Main entrance

KEY

① **The conservatory** housed ferns and orchids, beloved flowers of both Frederick Sargood and Benjamin Nathan. Horticultural experts were regularly invited to Rippon Lea.

② **The main staircase** is oak and mahogany like much of the rest of the house. Mirrors, another recurring theme in the house, are fitted into an archway at the foot of the stairs, courtesy of Louisa Jones.

③ **Arched windows** are a recurring decorative theme here, bordered by polychrome bricks.

④ **The Tower** was an unusual feature in the design of a domestic house. In this case, it may have been inspired by Sargood, who wanted his home to have the ornateness of a church.

⑤ **The brickwork** was inspired by a trip by Joseph Reed to Lombardy in Italy, where he came across this polychrome design.

For hotels and restaurants in this area see pp493–4 and pp526–9

★ **Dining Room**
American walnut blends with an Italian Renaissance style for the dining furniture of Louisa Jones.

Como House and its driveway

❸❾ Como Historic House and Garden

Cnr Williams Rd & Lechlade Ave, South Yarra. **Map** 4 F4. **Tel** (03) 9827 2500. 🅡 South Yarra. 🚋 8. Gardens: **Open** 9am–5pm daily (from 10am Sun). **Closed** Good Fri, 25 Dec. 🅐
🅖 ground floor and grounds only. 🅒 obligatory; 11am, 12:30pm, 2pm Sat & Sun (buy tickets online).
🅦 **comohouse.com.au**

Begun in 1847 by Edward Eyre Williams, Como House was occupied by the Armytage family for almost a century (1865–1959).

One of Como's highlights is its vast collection of original furnishings. These include pieces collected by the Armytage matriarch, Caroline, while on a Grand Tour of Europe during the 1870s, and include marble and bronze statues. The tour was undertaken as an educational experience for her nine children after the death of her husband, Charles Henry. It was important to this prominent Melbourne family to be seen as well educated. On their return, they held a series of sophisticated parties here.

Set in the picturesque remnants of its once extensive gardens, the house overlooks Como Park and the Yarra River. The original facets of the magnificent grounds, designed by William Sangster (who also had an input at Rippon Lea), remain: the fountain terrace, croquet lawn and hard standing area at the front of the house.

Como was managed by the Armytage women from 1876 until it was purchased by the National Trust in 1959. The house has undergone major restoration work over the years since then.

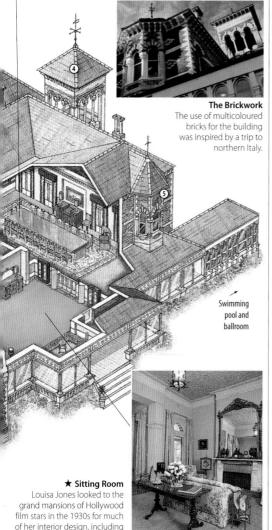

The Brickwork
The use of multicoloured bricks for the building was inspired by a trip to northern Italy.

Swimming pool and ballroom

★ **Sitting Room**
Louisa Jones looked to the grand mansions of Hollywood film stars in the 1930s for much of her interior design, including the plush sitting room.

SHOPPING IN MELBOURNE

The Central Business District (CBD) is a magnet for the city's shoppers. Major department stores are supplemented by a network of boutiques and specialist shops, many of which are tucked away in arcades and lanes. There is also a network of inner-city and suburban shopping streets: fashionable clothing and retail stores abound in urban areas, while large one-stop shopping towns are a feature of Greater Melbourne.

There are areas known for particular products, such as High Street, which runs through Armadale and Malvern, with its antiques stores. The city's multicultural society is also reflected in its shopping districts: Victoria Street, Richmond, has a stretch of Vietnamese stores; Sydney Road, Brunswick, is renowned for its shops selling Middle Eastern goods; and Carlisle Street, St Kilda, has many Jewish delicatessens.

Ornate and elegant Royal Arcade, which was built in 1869

Shopping Hours

In Victoria, most traders are open every day. Some small businesses close on Sundays but, increasingly, many stay open, competing with the long hours of chain stores and supermarkets (some of which are open 24 hours a day). Standard hours are 9am to 5:30pm (10am to 6pm in the CBD), although some retailers have extended hours on Thursdays or Fridays. Hours can vary at weekends. Most shops close on Christmas Day and Good Friday.

Department Stores

There are two major department stores in central Melbourne: **Myer** and **David Jones**, both are open for business seven days a week.

Australia's largest department store, Myer, encompasses a full two blocks of the city centre, with seven floors in Lonsdale Street and six in Bourke Street. Its main entrance is in Bourke Street Mall. Myer have nine other stores throughout Melbourne. David Jones, known to locals as DJs, has more up-market stock and high-quality service. The store has three sites within the city, with a main entrance adjacent to Myer in Bourke Street Mall; opposite is its menswear department. A third section is accessed in Little Bourke Street, again adjacent to Myer.

Two other popular stores are **Target** and K-mart. Both offer discounted prices on a range of goods. There are many branches of K-mart but they are located outside the CBD.

Arcades, Malls and Shopping Centres

Melbourne's best arcades and malls are located in the heart of the CBD. Chief among these are Bourke Street Mall, with shopfronts for the Myer and David Jones department stores. Occupied mostly by speciality stores and boutiques, other arcades and malls include the Galleria Shopping Plaza, with an emphasis on Australiana and Australian-owned stores. The ABC Shop sells merchandise associated with the national television and radio network, such as books, videos and DVDs. Australian Geographic is an excellent shop for information on Australian landscape and geology.

Located on Collins Street, renowned for its up-market shops, clothing and shoes, are St Collins Lane, Block Arcade (see p393) and Collins234. St Collins Lane comprises 60 shops over many levels, with an emphasis on luxury fashion and design from Australia and abroad. Collins234 contains a smaller selection of men's and women's fashion alongside other stores across four floors. Block Arcade, itself of historic interest, sells more classic clothing amid a beautifully restored 1890s interior; there is an entrance on Elizabeth Street. Also on

Up-market window display in Melbourne Central shopping centre

Locally grown fruit on sale at Queen Victoria Market

Elizabeth Street is the GPO *(see p392)*, which is now a popular H&M megastore.

Further up on Collins Street, past Russell Street, there are stores located in Collins Place, and in the Royal Arcade *(see p392)* nearby, which is also of historic and architectural interest. Running between Bourke Street Mall and Little Collins Street, further east, you will find **The Walk Arcade**, containing a small selection of smart and exclusive boutiques.

Little Bourke Street, above Elizabeth Street, and the intersecting Hardware Lane, are well known for a range of stores specializing in travel and adventure products.

Melbourne Central and **QV** are two outstanding shopping centres located on Lonsdale and Swanston streets. Between them, there are literally hundreds of shops to visit. Adjoining Melbourne Central is the more recently opened **Emporium Melbourne**, which is architecturally stunning and contains a mix of food icons, designer brands and flagship stores. Away from the city centre, the **Southgate Complex**, with its 40 shops on three levels, should not be missed by the avid shopper.

Markets

Melbourne has a number of fresh food markets. The most notable is the Queen Victoria Market *(see p390)*.

Other kinds of market are also popular. There is a huge range of second-hand goods for sale each Sunday at the **Camberwell Market**. For arts and crafts, **The Esplanade Market** is held on Sundays on Upper Esplanade. Other Sunday markets include the food market in **Prahran** and the arts and crafts market at the Arts Centre *(see p415)*. One of the oldest markets is the **South Melbourne Market**, which has been in continuous operation since 1867. It is open every Friday to Sunday, and also Wednesdays.

Brunswick Street has vintage clothing stores and retro boutiques

Shopping Strips

Village-style shopping centres abound in the many suburbs of Melbourne. Popular spots include High Street in Armadale; Sydney Road in Brunswick; Brunswick and Gertrude streets in Fitzroy; Bridge Road in Richmond; Chapel Street in South Yarra; and Maling Road in Canterbury.

Another major shopping centre in South Yarra is the **Como Centre**, which has stores selling furniture, homewares and fashion.

DIRECTORY

Department Stores

David Jones
310 Bourke St Mall. **Map** 1 C3.
Tel (03) 9643 2222.
w davidjones.com.au

Myer
314 Bourke St Mall. **Map** 1 C3.
Tel (03) 9661 1111.
w myer.com.au

Target
236 Bourke St. **Map** 1 C3. **Tel** (03) 9653 4000. w target.com.au

Arcades, Malls and Shopping Centres

Como Centre
650 Chapel St, South Yarra.
Map 4 E5. **Tel** (03) 9826 1248.
w comocentre.com.au

Emporium Melbourne
287 Lonsdale St, Melbourne.
Map 1 C2. **Tel** (03) 8609 8221.

Galleria Shopping Plaza
Cnr Bourke & Elizabeth sts.
Map 1 C3. **Tel** (03) 9604 5800.

Melbourne Central
300 Lonsdale St. **Map** 1 C2.
w melbournecentral.com.au

QV
Cnr Swanston and Lonsdale sts.
Map 1 C2. **Tel** (03) 9207 9200.
w qv.com.au

St Collins Lane
260 Collins St. **Map** 1 C3.
w stcollinslane.com

Southgate Complex
3 Southgate Ave, Southbank.
Map 2 C4. **Tel** (03) 9686 1000.

The Walk Arcade
309–325 Bourke St Mall. **Map** 1 C3.
w thewalkarcade.com.au

Markets

Camberwell Market
Station St, Camberwell.
w camberwellsunday
market.org

The Esplanade Market
Upper Esplanade, St Kilda.
w stkildaesplanademarket.
com.au

Prahran Market
Commercial Rd (near Chapel St).
Map 6 D1. **Tel** (03) 8290 8220.
w prahranmarket.com.au

South Melbourne Market
Cnr Cecil and Coventry sts.
Tel (03) 9209 6295. w south
melbournemarket.com.au

Specialist Shops and Souvenirs

Melbourne is Australia's most fashion-conscious capital and hosts major fashion weeks. The Melbourne Fashion Festival in March sees young designers launch their autumn/winter collections, while established labels showcase their spring/summer collections during Spring Fashion Week in September. New boutiques have opened in the Flinders Lane and Little Collins Streets precincts, either side of Swanston Street, and in the Central Business District's (CBD) revitalized arcades and laneways. This area rivals Fitzroy's Brunswick Street for trendy shopping. Melbourne is also a great place to buy outdoor gear, with several retailers located around Hardware Lane and Little Bourke Street. The city has a reputation for excellent bookshops and record stores, most of which are found in the city centre and inner suburbs of Carlton, Fitzroy, St Kilda and South Yarra.

Men's Clothing

The **Marcs** range is characterized by lightweight and colourful sweaters, shirts, t-shirts and trousers. They have a store in Melbourne Central (see pp411), among other locations. For sharp designer suits, head for **Calibre**, who also stock imported designer accessories. Both Little Collins Street and Collins Street proper have a selection of menswear stores, including **Déclic**, which specialises in business shirts and designer ties with names such as Duchamp, Vivienne Westwood and Zegna. Down the hill, **H&M** has a good range of smart casual gear. **Out of the Closet**, opposite Flinders Street Station, stocks groovy vintage wear. They also have a store in Brunswick Street, Fitzroy. Nearby is **Dangerfield**, a Melbourne label, which promotes edgy rock 'n' roll style. Everything from 50s, 60s and 70s fashion to the latest trends are available here. Brunswick Street is a good place to browse for vintage clothing, and Chapel Street, South Yarra is great for jeanswear and designer labels.

Women's Clothing

The CBD is the centre for haute couture in Melbourne. **Alannah Hill**'s fashions are feminine and sophisticated.

Scanlan & Theodore have made a name for themselves with elegant outfits, earthy tones and breezy designs. **Sass & Bide** sell glamorously cool outfits in stores throughout Melbourne, including in the Emporium (see p411). **Issey Miyake** is one of several international design houses represented in Melbourne. The appointment-only **Le Louvre**, in South Yarra, has been Melbourne society's couturier for decades. **Gorman** has bright, offbeat designs in stores across the city, including Fitzroy. **Kinki Gerlinki** stocks a appealing range of retro clothing. H&M and Marcs stock a good range of casual gear for women.

Peter Alexander has several branches throughout the city centre and is well regarded for a range of sleepwear, while **Smitten Kitten** offers imported lingerie, jewellery and exotic accessories. Bridge Road, Richmond has numerous discount fashion outlets. Another favourite label for fashion accessories – from handbags to jewellery and shoes – is **Mimco**.

Children's Clothing

In their Collins Street store, the popular Australian brand **Seed Heritage** offer high-quality clothing for newborns, children and teens in a range of playful and stylish designs. American label **OshKosh B'Gosh** sell colourful, affordable apparel for young children at their Melbourne outlet in the Emporium shopping complex.

Jewellery

Kozminsky's on Bourke Street has been a Melbourne institution for decades. It specialises in fine art and antique jewellery.

Collins Street has a profusion of jewellery stores and international fashion labels, including **Bulgari**.

Dinosaur Designs fashion distinctive and contemporary jewellery, and homewares from lustrous resins. They have several stores, including one in Chapel Street. **Studio Ingot** sells contemporary pieces made by more than 60 artisans. Local jeweller **Lucy Folk** stocks creative and playful designs in her flagship store in the city centre.

Shoes and Bags

The Westin hotel building in Collins Street is home to **Miss Louise**, a favourite with Melbourne's well-heeled women. A collection of finely crafted, handpicked men's and women's footwear can be found at **124**.

Crumpler bags are the brainchild of a former bicycle courier who saw a market for comfortable, durable and funky shoulder bags. They come in a variety of styles and types to suit everything from laptops, to videos to homework: a Melbourne design icon.

Outdoor Gear

To stock up on ski equipment and apparel, rock-climbing gear, tents, sleeping bags, maps and designer outdoor clothing, head for the Hardware Lane and Little Bourke Street precinct. There are numerous shops with good quality gear. Both **Paddy Pallin**, an established name in outdoor equipment, and **Snowgum**, which has shops across Melbourne, are recommended outlets. Smith Street, Collingwood has several factory shops for outdoor retailers selling discount clothing.

Books and Music

Collins Booksellers, an Australian chain, has several outlets including the **Hill of Content Bookshop**, which stocks an interesting range of titles. **Readings** is another home-grown favourite, which regularly hosts literary events. Its flagship store is in Carlton and it has a

branch in Acland Street, St Kilda. The **Brunswick Street Bookstore** is a quiet and relaxed venue for browsing books and magazines. **Thomas' Music** in the CBD caters to lovers of classical music and opera, while **Polyester Records** in Fitzroy stocks everything from Coltrane to the latest local indie bands.

DIRECTORY

Men's Clothing

Calibre
483 Chapel St, Sth Yarra 3141. **Map** 6 E1.
Tel (03) 9826 4394.
w calibre.com.au

Dangerfield
224 Flinders St, Melbourne 3000. **Map** 1 C3.
w shop.dangerfield.com.au

Déclic
Shop 105, Level 1, 260 Collins St, Melbourne 3000.
Map 1 C3.
Tel (03) 9650 2202.
w declic.com.au

H&M
323 Little Bourke St, Melbourne.
w hm.com/au

Marcs
576-584 Chapel St, Sth Yarra 3141. **Map** 6 E1.
Tel (03) 9826 4906.
w marcs.com.au

Out of the Closet
238B Flinders St, Melbourne 3000. **Map** 1 C3. **Tel** (03) 9639 0980.

Women's Clothing

Alannah Hill
533 Chapel St, Sth Yarra 3141. **Map** 4 E5.
Tel (03) 9826 2755.
w alannahhill.com.au

Gorman
235 Brunswick St, Fitzroy 3065. **Tel** (03) 9419 5999.
w gormanshop.com.au

Issey Miyake
Shop 2, 177 Toorak Rd, Sth Yarra 3141. **Map** 4 E5.
Tel (03) 9826 4900.
w isseymiyake.com

Kinki Gerlinki
22 Centre Place, Melbourne 3000. **Map** 1 C3. **Tel** (03) 9650 0465.

Le Louvre
2 Daly St, Sth Yarra 3141. **Map** 4 E5.
Tel (03) 9823 5300.
w lelouvre.com.au

Mimco
4/567 Chapel St, Sth Yarra 3141. **Map** 4 E5.
Tel (03) 9824 2678.
w mimco.com.au

Peter Alexander
Level 2, Shop 228 Melbourne Central, 300 Lonsdale St, Melbourne 3000. **Map** 1 C2. **Tel** (03) 9639 1299. w peteralexander.com.au

Sass & Bide
Shop 2-016, 269–321 Lonsdale St, Melbourne 3000. **Map** 1 C3.
Tel (03) 9650 2707.
w sassandbide.com

Scanlan & Theodore
566 Chapel St, Sth Yarra 3141. **Map** 4 E5. **Tel** (03) 9824 1800. w scanlanandtheodore.com.au

Smitten Kitten
1/217 Queen St, Melbourne 3000. **Map** 1 C3. **Tel** (03) 9654 2073.
w smittenkitten.com.au

Children's Clothing

OshKosh B'Gosh
Emporium Melbourne, Shop 316, 287 Lonsdale St, Melbourne 3000. **Map** 1 C3. **Tel** (03) 8609 8209.

Seed Heritage
Collins Pl, 45 Collins St, Melbourne 3000. **Map** 2 D3. **Tel** (03) 9654 1870.

Jewellery

Bulgari
123 Collins St, Melbourne 3000.
Map 2 D3.
Tel (03) 9663 8100.
w bulgari.com/en-au

Dinosaur Designs
562 Chapel St, Sth Yarra 3141. **Map** 4 E5.
Tel (03) 9827 2600.
w dinosaurdesigns.com.au

Kozminsky
421 Bourke St, Melbourne 3000.
Map 1 C3.
Tel (03) 9670 1277.
w kozminsky.com

Lucy Folk
1 Crossley St, Melbourne 3000.
Map 2 D2.
Tel (03) 9663 6829.
w lucyfolk.com

Studio Ingot
Shop 2, 234 Brunswick St, Fitzroy 3065.
Tel (03) 9415 6000.
w studioingot.com.au

Shoes and Bags

124
Shop 221, Level 2, 287 Lonsdale St, Melbourne 3000.
Map 1 C3.
Tel (03) 8609 8286.
w 124shoes.com.au

Crumpler
355 Little Bourke St, Melbourne 3000.
Map 1 C3.
Tel (03) 9600 3799.
w crumpler.com.au

Miss Louise
The Westin, 205 Collins St, Melbourne 3000. **Map** 2 D3. **Tel** (03) 9654 7730.

Outdoor Gear

Paddy Pallin
360 Little Bourke St, Melbourne 3000.
Map 1 C3.
Tel (03) 9670 4845.
w paddypallin.com.au

Snowgum
370 Little Bourke St, Melbourne 3000.
Map 1 C3
Tel (03) 9642 4340.
w snowgum.com.au

Books and Music

Brunswick Street Bookstore
305 Brunswick Street, Fitzroy 3065.
Tel (03) 9416 1030.
w brunswickstreetbookstore.com

Hill of Content Bookshop
86 Bourke St, Melbourne 3000.
Map 2 D2.
Tel (03) 9662 9472.

Polyester Records
387 Brunswick St, Fitzroy 3065.
Tel (03) 9419 5137.
w polyesterrecords.com

Readings
309 Lygon St, Carlton 3053.
Tel (03) 9347 6633.
112 Acland St, St Kilda, 3182.
Tel (03) 9525 3852.
w readings.com.au

Thomas' Music
31 Bourke St, Melbourne 3000.
Map 2 D2.
Tel (03) 9650 9111.
w thomasmusic.net.au

ENTERTAINMENT IN MELBOURNE

Melbourne could be defined as Australia's city of the arts. All year round there is a wealth of cultural events and entertainment on offer. The city's major festivals include the Melbourne Food and Wine Festival and Moomba *(see pp45–8)*. There are also fringe festivals and many other independent events. Arts Centre Melbourne, which includes

Hamer Hall *(see p404)*, stages productions by the state's theatrical companies and hosts both national and international groups. Large concerts are held at Rod Laver Arena in Melbourne Park Entertainment Centre or the Melbourne Cricket Ground *(see p401)*. Cinema chains are supplemented by smaller, arthouse cinemas.

Evening concert at the Sidney Myer Music Bowl *(see p402)*

Information

The *Age* newspaper publishes a comprehensive entertainment guide in its Saturday edition and on its website. This has listings, along with more information on all the up-coming highlights. The tabloid newspaper *Herald Sun*'s Saturday edition and website are also good sources of information and reviews. There is an array of free publications covering arts, entertainment and the nightclub scene. Visitors can obtain these from retailers and cafés in main inner-city precincts such as Fitzroy *(see p407)* and St Kilda. The **Melbourne Visitor Information**

Centre has a range of publications listing events.

There are also a number of websites that provide good events coverage, as well as other information helpful to visitors: www.theurbanlist.com/melbourne, www.visitvictoria.com and www.thatsmelbourne.com.au are worth a look. To find out what's showing and coming up at the **Arts Centre Melbourne** *(see p404)*, visit the venue's website (www.artscentremelbourne.com.au). Most ticket agencies and some venues also provide information on events taking place in the city.

Ticket Booking Agencies

Buying tickets in Melbourne is reasonably straightforward. There are two major ticket booking agencies in Victoria, **Ticketmaster** (with more than 50 outlets) and **Ticketek** (with more than 30 outlets). Both agencies offer ticketing for all major sporting events, concerts, theatre performances and festivals, as well as for theme parks and other attractions. There are some

Grand 1930s foyer of the Regent Theatre *(see p394)*

venues which handle their own bookings independently, but these are rare and tickets for most major events are more easily purchased at these agencies.

Bookings can either be made in person at the various outlets, or with a credit card by phone. Alternatively, bookings can be made online. The agencies also accept bookings from overseas. If not bought directly over the counter, tickets can be mailed out to customers for a small handling fee. If the event is impending, tickets can usually be picked up at the venue half-an-hour before the booked performance starts.

The hours for outlets vary according to their location, but almost all are open Monday through to Saturday, and some are open on Sundays. Neither Ticketmaster nor Ticketek offer refunds or exchanges, unless a show is cancelled. Remember that a nominal booking fee will be added to all ticket prices bought via a ticket agency.

Façade of the Princess Theatre, opposite the Parliamentary Precinct *(see p396)*

Street entertainers, a regular sight throughout Melbourne

Ticket Deals

Some major companies, especially those playing at the Arts Centre Melbourne, offer special "rush hour" ticket deals. These are available for tickets purchased in person after 6pm. The **Half Tix** booth at the Melbourne Town Hall on Swanston Street offers half-price deals for many events or try www.lasttix.com. au. Tickets must be bought in person and paid for in cash. They are also generally available only on the day of performance. Shows with tickets available are displayed at the booth.

Half Tix ticket booth sign on Swanston Street

Securing the Best Seats

If booking in person or online, you can usually consult a floor-plan showing the location of available seats. Over the telephone, both Ticketmaster and Ticketek have a "best available" system, with remaining seats arranged in a best-to-last order by individual venues. It is also possible to request particular seats and the booking agency will check their availability. Some seats are

retained for sale at the venue itself and this can be a way of getting good seats at the last minute.

Disabled Visitors

The vast majority of venues have access and facilities for disabled visitors. Booking agencies will take this into account. You should also enquire at individual venues.

Outdoor and Street Entertainment

Melbourne has a strong tradition of outdoor and street entertainment. Every summer there is a broad programme of theatre and music for adults and children in most major parks and gardens. During February, the Melbourne Symphony Orchestra (MSO) presents a series of free concerts at the Sidney Myer music bowl. The venue provides an atmospheric outdoor setting to enjoy the world-class orchestra.

Street buskers, many travelling on an international circuit, also frequent a number of areas, the most popular being Fitzroy (*see p407*) and St Kilda, and appear at festivals. The main spot for regular street performances is the Bourke Street Mall, outside Myer and David Jones department stores and at the Southgate Complex (*see p411*). The Arts Centre Melbourne also has regular programmes featuring free weekend street entertainment.

DIRECTORY

Information Centre

Melbourne Visitor Information Centre
Federation Square, cnr Swanston & Flinders sts. **Map** 2 D3. **Tel** (03) 9658 9658. W visitvictoria.com

Major Venues

Arts Centre Melbourne
100 St Kilda Rd. **Map** 2 D4.
Tel 1300 182 183.
W artscentremelbourne.com.au

Athenaeum Theatre
188 Collins St. **Map** 2 D3.
Tel (03) 9650 1500.
W athenaeumtheatre.com.au

Comedy Theatre
240 Exhibition St. **Map** 2 D2.
Tel (03) 9299 4950.

CUB Malthouse
113 Sturt St. **Map** 2 D4.
Tel (03) 9685 5111.
W malthousetheatre.com.au

Forum Theatre
154 Flinders St. **Map** 2 D3.
Tel (03) 9299 9700.
W forummelbourne.com.au

Her Majesty's
219 Exhibition St. **Map** 2 D2.
Tel (03) 8643 3300.
W hmt.com.au

Melbourne Town Hall
Cnr Swanston & Collins sts.
Map 1 C3. **Tel** (03) 9658 9658.
W melbourne.vic.gov.au

Palais Theatre
3182 Lower Esplanade, St Kilda.
Map 5 B5. **Tel** (03) 9525 3240.
W palaistheatre.net.au

Princess Theatre
163 Spring St. **Map** 2 D2.
Tel (03) 9299 9800.

Regent Theatre
191 Collins St. **Map** 2 D3.
Tel (03) 9299 9800.

Ticket Agencies

Half Tix
Melbourne Town Hall, cnr Swanston and Collins sts.
Map 1 C3. **Tel** (03) 9650 9420.
W halftixmelbourne.com

Ticketek
Tel 132 849. W ticketek.com

Ticketmaster
Tel 136 100.
W ticketmaster.com.au

MELBOURNE PRACTICAL INFORMATION

Melbourne is well served by public transport and is easy to negotiate, given the grid structure of the city centre and the flat layout of its suburbs. Many of the public facilities have been upgraded, with the aim of attracting both business and tourists.

Driving in the city is also easy and taxis are plentiful. Bureaux de change and automatic cash dispensers are located throughout the city. Melbourne is safe compared with many major cities, but common sense will also keep you out of trouble.

Driving and Cycling

Driving in Melbourne is easy. However, at particular intersections in the CBD marked by "Safety Zone" signs, a "hook turn" is required; cars must queue on the left to turn right in order to give way to trams. Cars left in No Standing zones will be towed away. The city has a tollway system known as **CityLink**, which uses electronic tolling: drivers must purchase a pass before travelling. Melbourne's flat landscape is well suited to cyclists and there are many

cycle tracks. Helmets are compulsory. Information on bicycle hire and good cycle routes can be found at **Bicycle Network**. The **Melbourne Bike Share** scheme is also popular.

Travelling by Public Transport

Melbourne has a comprehensive system of trains, buses and trams, known as Metro or Yarra Trams. This system also provides access to country and interstate travel, operated by the **V/Line** network.

The main railway station for suburban services is Flinders Street Station (see p406). Southern Cross Station is the main terminus for country and interstate trains.

The City Circle Tram circuits the city every 12 minutes, while the Melbourne Visitor Shuttle hop-on/hop-off tourist bus departs at half-hour intervals. Details are available from the **Melbourne Visitor Information Centre**. Another way to get around the city is via water taxis and cruises along the Yarra River.

Tram Routes

Melbourne's famous electric tram network covers 240 km (150 miles), reaching many of the city's attractions. Stops are located on central islands within the CBD area, and by the roadside in suburban areas. You must have a Myki card with sufficient fare to use the trams, unless you are within the Free Tram Zone in the city centre (see p417). Most routes operate at regular intervals (10 to 20 minutes) from 5am until midnight daily.

Flinders Street Station, the city's main suburban rail terminus

Tickets

The **iVenture** card allows you free and discounted entry to more than 30 popular attractions. The **Myki** system operates with a card that can be purchased from all 7Eleven stores ($6) then topped up online, at 7Eleven stores, train stations, and some tram stops. Tap the card before boarding trams, buses and trains. Fines apply for fare evading. A Free Tram Zone operates within the

Central Business District. Look for the signage at tram stops to identify the boundary.

Tourist Information

The main Tourist Information stop is the Melbourne Visitor Information Centre, which has free maps and guides to all attractions and activities.

Free travel publications available from information centres, covering attractions in Melbourne and Victoria.

Disabled Travellers

The useful "CBD Mobility Map" is available from the Melbourne Visitor Information Centre and shows the smoothest path of travel along the city's streets. The majority of public facilities in the city have disabled access and toilets. Parking zones are allocated in the city and suburbs for disabled drivers; disabled driver permits are available from Melbourne Town Hall *(see p393)*.

Central Melbourne area

Key

- ◼ Swanston Street
- ▢ Elizabeth Street
- ▨ William Street
- ▨ Latrobe Street
- ◼ Bourke Street
- ◼ Collins Street
- ▨ Flinders Street
- ◼ Batman Avenue
- ▢ City Circle
- ▨ Suburban trams

River cruise boats providing a leisurely way to see the city

DIRECTORY

Driving and Cycling

Bicycle Network
Tel (03) 8376 8888.
W bicyclenetwork.com.au

CityLink
Tel 13 26 29.
W citylink.com.au

Melbourne Bike Share
W melbournebikeshare.com.au

**Royal Automobile
Club of Victoria**
Tel 13 11 11.
W racv.com.au

Public Transport

Myki
W ptv.vic.gov.au

Public Transport Victoria
Tel 1800 800 007.
W ptv.vic.gov.au

Skybus Information Service
Tel 1300 759 287.
W skybus.com.au

V/Line
Spencer Street Station.
Tel 1800 800 007.
W vline.com.au

River Cruises

Melbourne Water Taxis
No 4 Southgate (outside Langham Hotel). **Tel** 0416 068 655.
W melbournewatertaxis.com.au

**Williamstown Ferries:
Bay and River Cruises**
Gem Pier Williamstown/No. 1 Southgate/Vault 12 Federation Square City. **Tel** (03) 9517 9444 (info), (03) 9682 9555 (booking).
W williamstownferries.com.au

Tourist Information

iVenture Card
W iventurecard.com/au/melbourne

**Melbourne Visitor
Information Centre**
Federation Sq, Cnr Swanston & Flinders sts. **Tel** (03) 9658 9658.

**Victorian Tourism
Information Service**
Tel 13 28 42. W visitvictoria.com

MELBOURNE STREET FINDER

The key map below shows the areas of Melbourne covered in the *Street Finder*. All places of interest in these areas are marked on the maps in addition to useful information, such as railway stations, bus termini and emergency services. The map references given for sights described in the Melbourne chapter refer to the maps on the following pages. Map references are also given for the city's shops and markets *(see pp410–13)*, entertainment venues *(see pp414–15)*, as well as hotels *(see pp493–4)* and restaurants *(see pp526–9)*. The different symbols used for sights and other major features on the *Street Finder* maps are listed in the key below.

Key

▦	Major sight
▦	Place of interest
▢	Other building
🚢	Ferry boarding point
🚇	Railway station
🚌	Bus station
i	Tourist information
✚	Hospital with casualty unit
🚓	Police station
⛳	Golf course
✚	Church
☪	Mosque
✡	Synagogue
=	Highway
—	Railway line
	Pedestrian street

Scale of Map Pages

0 metres	250
0 yards	250

0 km	1
0 mile	1

Deborah Halpern sculpture at the city's Southgate Plaza *(see pp404–5)*

Red brick façade of the City Baths on Swanston Street *(see pp388–9)*

Ornamental lake at Rippon Lea *(see pp408–9)*

The Collins Street area as seen from Princes Bridge on the Yarra River

WESTERN VICTORIA

The theme of Western Victoria is diversity. For nature lovers, there is the bare beauty of the mallee deserts of the north or the forested hills and coastal scenery of the south. For a sense of the region's history, 19th-century gold-mining towns lie in the centre, surrounded by beautiful spa towns which have attracted visitors for more than a century. The area's sights are all within easy reach of one another.

Just as the Aboriginal tribes of Western Victoria had their lives and culture shaped by the region's diverse landscape, so the lives of the early European settlers were inevitably determined by the region's geographical features and immense natural resources.

The discovery of gold was the single most important event in Victoria's economic history, drawing prospectors from all over the world and providing the state with unprecedented wealth. Part of the legacy of this period is seen in the grand 19th-century buildings still standing in a number of central western towns. Also of interest are the spa towns clustered nearby, which draw their therapeutic waters from the same mineral-rich earth.

To the northwest, Victoria's major agricultural region, the Murray River, supports several large townships. The area is blessed with a Mediterranean-type climate, resulting in wineries and fruit-growing areas.

In the south, the spectacular Grampian mountain ranges have long been of significance to the Aborigines. Fortunately, the steep cliffs and heavily forested slopes offered little prospect for development by early settlers and this beautiful area is today preserved as a wilderness. Wheat and sheep farmers have settled in parts of the Mallee region in the north of Western Victoria but, as in the Grampians, other settlers have been discouraged by its semi-arid conditions, and large areas of this stunning desert vegetation and its native wildlife have been left intact.

The southwestern coast was the site of the first settlement in Victoria. Its towns were developed as ports for the rich farmland beyond and as whaling stations for the now outlawed industry. Besides its history, this coastline is known for its extraordinary natural scenery of sandstone monoliths, sweeping beaches, forests and rugged cliffs.

Pioneer Settlement, a re-created 19th-century port town on the Murray River at Swan Hill

◀ The jagged edge of the Great Ocean Road coastline, with some of the Twelve Apostles

Exploring Western Victoria

Western Victoria abounds with holiday possibilities. The spa towns close to Melbourne make perfect weekend retreats, with excellent facilities set amid gentle rural scenery. By contrast, the large number of historic sites and architectural splendours of the Goldfields region requires an investigative spirit and sightseeing stamina. The Grampians National Park contains trekking opportunities and rugged views, while the Mallee region offers wide open spaces and undulating sandhills. The Murray River towns have their fair share of historic sites, as well as many recreational facilities, restaurants and accommodation. The Great Ocean Road is a popular touring destination – set aside several days to explore the historic towns and scenic beauty of the coastline.

Rupertswood mansion in the Macedon Ranges

Getting Around

The roads in Western Victoria are well signed and offer good roadside facilities. The Western Hwy is the route to Ballarat, the Grampians and the Mallee region. The Calder Hwy leads to the spa country and beyond to Bendigo, where it connects with highways to Mildura, Swan Hill and Echuca. Take the Princes Hwy to reach Geelong and the Great Ocean Road. All these places can also be reached by rail or a combination of rail and connecting coaches. However, in remoter areas, public transport may be a problem. In these areas, it may be best to use a tour company or to hire your own car.

0 kilometres 50

0 miles 50

Sandstone arch at Loch Ard Gorge along the Great Ocean Road

Sights at a Glance

1. Werribee Park
2. Bellarine Peninsula
3. Geelong
4. Grampians National Park
5. Big Desert Wilderness
6. Hattah-Kulkyne National Park
7. Mildura
8. Swan Hill
9. Echuca
10. Bendigo
11. Maldon
12. Castlemaine
13. *Ballarat pp438–9*
14. Sovereign Hill

Tour

15. Daylesford and the Macedon Ranges

Piangil

Nyah

8 SWAN HILL

Kerang

Cohuna

Quambatook

Wycheproof

Pyramid Hill

Barmah
State Park

Barmah

ECHUCA 9

Charlton

Wedderburn

Rochester

Kyabram

St Arnaud

Inglewood

Rushworth

10 BENDIGO

Heathcote

Wangaratta

MALDON 11

Avoca

12 CASTLEMAINE

Seymour

Daylesford Woodend Kyneton

Broadford

Hanging Rock

15 MACEDON RANGES

Trentham Falls

BALLARAT 13

Sunbury

14

Beaufort

SOVEREIGN HILL

Bacchus
Marsh

Melton

Brisbane Ranges
National Park

Lismore

WERRIBEE PARK 1

Port
Phillip Bay

Moe

GEELONG 3

2 BELLARINE
PENINSULA

Camperdown

Barwon Heads

Queenscliff

Colac

Torquay

Anglesea

Morningon
Peninsula

Lorne

Bass
Strait

ye Apostles

Apollo Bay

Otway National Park

Melbourne

Lake
gamite

Striking rock formations at the Grampians
National Park

Key

— Highway

— Major road

··· Minor road

-- Track

— Scenic route

⌁ Major railway

---- Minor railway

⌁ State border

For keys to symbols *see back flap*

Flamboyant Italianate façade of Werribee Park Mansion

❶ Werribee Park

K Rd, Werribee. **Tel** 13 1963.
🚉 Werribee. **Open** daily. 🅿️ ♿ ✅
📷 ✏️ 🌐 parkweb.vic.edu.au

From 1860 until 1890, the wool boom made millionaires of Australia's sheep farmers, with the Chirnside family of Werribee Park and later of Victoria's Western District among the richest and most powerful. Their former mansion is a striking Italianate house, built between 1873 and 1878. It has now been restored to reflect the lifestyle of wealthy pastoral families. Visitors can stroll through the sandstone mansion and see the room where renowned opera singer Dame Nellie Melba once slept. A wing added in the 1930s has been converted into a luxury hotel.

Next to Werribee Park Mansion and its formal gardens with popular picnic areas is the Victoria State Rose Garden, laid out in a symbolic Tudor Rose-shaped design. It contains more than 5,000 beautiful rose bushes of different varieties and colours that are in flower from November to April. Also attached to Werribee Park is **Werribee Open Range Zoo**, containing a range of exotic animals, including giraffes and hippopotami. The National Equestrian Centre is also part of the estate. This is home to some of Australia's premier

Chaise longue in Werribee Park

show-jumping and polo events. For bird-watchers, the nearby Western Treatment Plant and Point Cook Coastal Park provide magnificent views of some rare species from specially designated hides. Migratory birds such as the eastern curlew and tiny red-necked stint spend the whole summer in these protected wetlands before flying north to Japan and Siberia.

❌ **Werribee Open Range Zoo**
Tel 1300 966 784. **Open** 9am–5pm daily. 🅿️ ♿ ✅ 🌐 zoo.org.au

❷ Bellarine Peninsula

🚌 Geelong. ℹ️ 1251–1269 Bellarine Highway, Wallington 1800 755 611.
🌐 visitgeelongbellarine.com.au

The Bellarine Peninsula, at the western entrance to Port Phillip Bay, is one of Melbourne's many summer resorts. The white sand beaches of Barwon Heads, Point Lonsdale and Ocean Grove mark the start of the Great Ocean Road and its famous surf beaches (see pp432–3). The little village of **Point Lonsdale** lies at the entrance to the treacherous Heads – the most dangerous entry to any bay in the world due to its churning seas and whirlpools. It is only 3 km (2 miles) from Point Lonsdale, across the

swirling water (known as the Rip) with its hidden rocks, to Point Nepean on the Mornington Peninsula in Eastern Victoria (see p446).

The graceful old town of **Queenscliff** faces Port Phillip Bay so its beaches are calm. Its fort was the largest British defence post in the southern hemisphere during the 1880s, when a Russian invasion was feared. At the time Queenscliff was also a fashionable resort for Melburnians – its elegant hotels, such as the Vue Grand, are reminders of that opulent era. St Leonards and Portarlington are also popular holiday villages.

The peninsula has around 20 wineries, most offering cellar door sales and tastings.

Graceful wrought-iron detail on a Queenscliff façade

❸ Geelong

🏙️ 190,000. ✈️ 🚉 🚌 🚢
ℹ️ 26–32 Moorabool St 1800 755 611.
🌐 visitgeelongbellarine.com.au

Geelong is the second largest city in the state and has a rural and industrial past. Positioned on the north-facing and sheltered Corio Bay, the city has started to look once again on its port as a recreational front door, so popular in the first years of the 20th century. The wooden 1930s bathing complex at Eastern Beach, with its lawns, sandy beach and shady trees, was restored to its former Art Deco glory in 1994. Steampacket Place and Pier were part of an extensive redevelopment project that saw the gradual renovation of the old warehouses into a thriving waterfront quarter filled with excellent seafood restaurants, cafés, shops and hotels. Opposite Steampacket Place are the historic wool stores. Wool was auctioned, sold and stored here prior to its being shipped around the globe from the 1880s until the 1970s. This generated Geelong's wealth. These buildings have been transformed; the largest houses the award-winning **National Wool Museum**, tracing Australia's wool heritage from the shearing shed to the fashion catwalks.

A short drive from Geelong is the Brisbane Ranges National Park, near Anakie, with lovely walks and native wildflowers, such as grevilleas, wattles and wild orchids, in bloom between August and November. Nearby is Steiglitz, a ghost town from the 1850s gold rush. Few buildings remain of this once thriving town, among them the elegant 1870s courthouse, which is closed to the public.

🏛 **National Wool Museum**
26–32 Moorabool St. **Tel** (03) 5272 4701. **Open** daily. **Closed** Good Fri, 25 & 26 Dec. 🅿 ♿ 🖥 🚻 🔲 **geelong australia.com.au/nwm**

❹ Grampians National Park

🚉 Stawell. 🚌 Halls Gap. 🛈 Stawell 1800 065 599; Brambuk National Park and Cultural Centre (03) 5361 4000. **Open** daily. 🔲 **parkweb.vic.gov. au/explore/parks/grampians-national-park**

The mountains, cliffs and sheer rock faces of the Grampians rise

Flora and Fauna of the Grampians

The Grampians are a haven for a wide range of birds, animals, native wildflowers and plants. The park is home to almost one-third of all Victorian plant species, with many, such as the Grampians guinea flower and boronia, found only within its rocky walls. Koalas grunt at night around Halls Gap and the kangaroos at Zumsteins are unusually tame and friendly. The air, trees and scrub teem with beautiful blue wrens, rainbow lorikeets, gang gang cockatoos, scarlet robins and emus. In spring, various wildflowers, orchids and pink heath burst from every valley, and the creeks and

Rainbow lorikeet

rivers are full of rare brown-tree frogs. Just south of the Grampians in the town of Hamilton, a few surviving eastern barred bandicoots, once thought to be extinct, were discovered on the town rubbish tip. They were quickly rescued and have now become part of an active breeding and protection programme.

like a series of waves above the flat western plains. Within this awesome national park, the third largest in Victoria, is a diversity of natural features and wildlife.

There are craggy slopes, cascading waterfalls and sand-stone mountain tops, all formed 400 million years ago by an upthrust of the earth's crust. It has been known as *gariwerd* for thousands of years to local Aboriginal tribes, for whom it is a sacred place, and 80 per cent of Victoria's indigenous rock art is here. The Brambuk National Park and Cultural Centre displays the region's indigenous cultures through multimedia and artifact exhibits and is partly run by local Aboriginal com-

munities who conduct tours to the many sites. The Grampians offer many different experiences for tourists. Day trips take in the spectacular MacKenzie Falls and the Balconies rock formation. Longer stays offer bush camping, wildflower studies, exploration of the Victoria Valley over the mountains from Halls Gap and overnight hiking trips in the south of the park. Experienced rock climbers come from around the world to tackle the challenging rock forms in the park and also at the nearby Mount Arapiles.

Excellent maps of the area and guides to the best walks are all available from the park's visitors' centre.

Panoramic view from the rugged crags of the Grampians

The Great Ocean Road Coastline

The Great Ocean Road is one of the world's great scenic drives. Close to Melbourne, pretty holiday towns are linked by curving roads with striking views at every turn. Inland, the road cuts through the Otways, a forested landscape, ecologically rich and visually splendid. Between Port Campbell and Port Fairy is a landscape of rugged cliffs and swirling seas. The giant eroded monoliths, the Twelve Apostles, in Port Campbell National Park, are an awesome spectacle. To the far west, old whaling ports provide an insight into one of Australia's early industries; at Warrnambool, Southern Right Whales can still be seen.

Portland, a deep-water port at the end of the Princes Highway, was the site of the first European settlement in Victoria in 1834. Stunning scenery of craggy cliffs, blowholes and rough waters can be found near the town at Cape Bridgewater.

Tower Hill
Game Reserve

CAMPERDOWN

MOUNT GAMBIER Portland

Lady Julia Percy Island

Southern Ocean

A100

① ★ Port Fairy

The tiny cottages of Port Fairy are reminders of the days when the town thrived as a centre for whaling in the 1830s and 1840s. Although the whaling industry has come to an end, the town is now a popular tourist destination.

0 kilometres 25
0 miles 25

Key

═══ Highway
━━━ Major road
═══ Minor road
~~~ River

② ★ Warrnambool

This coastal town is best known for the Southern Right Whales that can often be spotted off Logans Beach between May and October. The town itself has many fine art galleries, museums and old churches.

Tower Hill Game Reserve, 13 km (8 miles) west of Warrnambool, is set in an extinct volcano crater. Dusk is the best time to visit and spot emus, koalas and kangaroos roaming the forests.

For keys to symbols *see back flap*

Locator Map

Otway National Park provides an introduction to some of the species of the southern temperate rainforest, including a famed 400-year-old myrtle beech tree.

⑤ ★ Loch Ard Gorge
This treacherous area claimed the clipper *Loch Ard* in 1878. Local walks focus on the shipwreck, geology and Aboriginal history of the site.

⑦ ★ Johanna Beach
Another of Victoria's renowned surf beaches is backed by rolling green hills. The area is quite remote, but popular with campers in summer.

⑨ ★ Lorne
Very popular in summer, this charming seaside village boasts excellent cafés, restaurants and accommodation. Nearby forests provide a paradise for walkers.

GEELONG

Colac

Anglesea

Port Campbell National Park

Twelve Apostles

Otway National Park

③ Peterborough
Victoria's dairy industry is based on this stretch of coastline. A popular rock pool beneath the cliff is known as the Grotto.

④ Port Campbell
Port Campbell beach is a sandy bay, safe for swimming. The town, set on a hill, has great views of the ocean.

⑥ Moonlight Head
Massive cliffs give way to rock platforms here in the heart of Otway National Park. Embedded anchors are reminders of the many ships lost along this perilous coastline.

⑧ ★ Apollo Bay
Fishing is the main activity here, and fishing trips can be taken from the town's wharf. The town itself has a relaxed village atmosphere and excellent restaurants.

⑪ Point Addis
The Great Ocean Road leads right to the headland with spectacular views from the car park of waves beating the rocks. There are also steps leading down the cliff for a more exhilarating experience of the rolling surf.

⑫ Bells Beach
A natural underwater rock platform contributes to the excellent surfing conditions at Bells. An international surfing competition is held here at Easter, bringing thousands of tourists to the area *(see p46)*.

⑩ Aireys Inlet
The red and white lighthouse is a landmark of this tiny coastal town with its beautiful ocean views.

Murrayville track in the Big Desert Wilderness Park

❺ Big Desert Wilderness

🚌 Hopetoun. 🛈 75 Lascelles St, Hopetoun (03) 5083 3001; Parks Victoria Information Line 131963.
🌐 **parkweb.vic.gov.au**

Victoria is so often seen as the state of mountains, green hills, river valleys and beaches that many visitors don't realize that a large part of the west of the state consists of arid desert and mallee scrubland.

These are areas of beauty and solitude, with sand hills, dwarf she-oaks, lizards, snakes and dry creek systems. Big Desert Wilderness Park and Murray-Sunset National Park are true deserts, with hot days and freezing nights. Murray-Sunset National Park is also home to Australia's rarest bird, the black-eared miner.

To the south, Wyperfeld and Little Desert national parks are not true deserts, as they contain lake systems that support diverse flora and fauna, including a wide range of reptiles.

❻ Hattah-Kulkyne National Park

🚉 Mildura. 🚌 Mildura.
🛈 Mildura (03) 5018 8380; Parks Victoria Information Line 13 19 63.
🌐 **parkweb.vic.gov.au**

Unlike its drier Mallee region counterparts, Hattah-Kulkyne National Park is a haven of creeks and lakes that are linked to the mighty Murray River through a complex billabong (natural waterhole) overflow system.

Its perimeters are typical dry Mallee country of low scrub, mallee trees and native pine woodland, but the large lakes, including Lake Hattah, Mournpoul and Lockie, are alive with bird and animal life. Ringed by massive red gums, the surrounding habitat is home to an abundance of emus, goanna lizards and kangaroos. The freshwater lakes teem with fish, while pelicans, ibis, black swans and other water birds flock on the surface.

The lakes are ideal for canoeing, and the twisting wetlands and billabongs along the Murray River and in the Murray-Kulkyne section of the park make for fine fishing, picnics, camping and bird-watching. Murray-Sunset National Park is also home to Victoria's largest flower, the Murray lily.

❼ Mildura

🏔 50,000. ✈ 🚉 🚌 🛈 180–190 Deakin Ave (03) 5018 8380.
🌐 **visitmildura.com.au**

In 1887, Mildura was little more than a village on the banks of the Murray River, situated in the middle of a red sandy desert. That year, two Canadian brothers, William and George Chaffey, came to town direct from their successful irrigation project in California and began Australia's first large-scale irrigation scheme. Since then, the red soil, fed by the Murray and Darling rivers, has become a vast plain of farms stretching for nearly 100 km (60 miles).

Today, Mildura is a modern city with a thriving tourist trade. The former home of William Chaffey, the **Rio Vista** is worth a visit. Built in 1890, it has been restored with its original furnishings and is now an Arts Centre. Grapes, olives, avocados and citrus fruit are grown successfully in the region and the area is rapidly expanding its vineyards

The Murray River Paddlesteamers

Old paddlesteamer on the Murray River

Between the 1860s and 1880s, Australia's economy "rode on the sheep's back" – from the Western District of Victoria to the Diamantina Plains in central Queensland, wool was king. But the only way to transport it from the remote sheep stations to coastal ports and then on to its thriving English market was by river. There were no roads other than a few dirt tracks, so the paddlesteamers that plied the Murray, Murrumbidgee and Darling river systems were the long-distance lorries of the day. Towing barges loaded with wool, they reached the Port of Echuca after sailing for days from inland Australia. Then, stocked up with supplies for the sheep stations and distant river settlements, they returned upriver. However, by the 1890s railway lines had crept into the interior and the era of the paddlesteamer was gone. Now the Port of Echuca is once again home to beautifully restored, working paddlesteamers, such as the PS *Adelaide* and PS *Success* (www.portofechuca.org.au).

Rio Vista, the elaborate home of irrigation expert William Chaffey, in Mildura

and wineries *(see pp382–3)*. The stark desert of Mungo National Park is only 100 km (60 miles) to the northeast of town.

🏠 Rio Vista
199 Cureton Ave. **Tel** (03) 5018 8330. **Open** 10am–5pm daily. **Closed** Good Fri, 25 Dec. 🅿 ♿ ⓦ **milduraartscentre.com.au**

8 Swan Hill

🔼 10,000. 🚂 🚌 🛈 cnr McCrae & Curlewis sts (03) 5032 3033.

Black Swans are noisy birds, as the early explorer Major Thomas Mitchell discovered in 1836 when his sleep was disturbed by their early morning calls on the banks of the Murray River. That's how the vibrant river town of Swan Hill got its name, and the black swans are still a prominent feature.

One of the most popular attractions of Swan Hill is the **Pioneer Settlement Museum**, a 3-ha (7-acre) living and working re-creation of a river town in the Murray-Mallee area during the period from 1830 to 1930. The settlement buzzes with the sound of printing presses, the blacksmith's hammer, the smell of the bakery and general daily life. "Residents" dress in period clothes and produce old-fashioned goods to sell to

tourists. Some of the log buildings are made of Murray pine, a hardwood tree impenetrable to termites. The sound and light show at night (bookings essential) is particularly evocative, providing a 45-minute journey through the town with accompanying sound effects, such as pounding hooves and a thundering steam locomotive.

🏠 Pioneer Settlement Museum
Monash Drive, Swan Hill. **Tel** (03) 5036 2410. **Open** 9:30am–4:30pm daily. **Closed** 25–26 Dec. 🅿 🎞 ♿ ⓦ **pioneersettlement.com.au**

9 Echuca

🔼 14,000. 🚂 🚌 🛈 2 Heygarth St (03) 5480 7555. ⓦ **echucamoama.com**

Ex-convict and entrepreneur Henry Hopwood travelled to the Murray River region in 1853, at the end of his prison sentence. He seized upon the need for a river punt at the Echuca crossing by setting up a ferry service, as well as the Bridge Hotel. However, Echuca really came into its own in 1864 when the railway from Melbourne reached the port. Suddenly the town, with its paddlesteamers on the Murray River, became the largest inland port in Australia. Today the port area features horse-drawn

carriages, working steam engines and old-fashioned timber mills. Tours of the area are available, along with regular river trips on a paddlesteamer. Visit the Star Hotel and discover the secret tunnel that let patrons leave after hours. There is also a paddlesteamer display opposite the hotel.

Approximately 30 km (19 miles) upstream from Echuca is Barmah Forest, the largest red gum forest in the world. A drive in the forest, with its 300-year-old river red gums and important Aboriginal sites, is highly recommended, as is the wetlands ecocruise that operates out of Barmah.

Gum trees on the road to Barmah Forest, outside Echuca

⑩ Bendigo

🏙 85,000. ✈ 🚊 🚌 🚌
ℹ 51–67 Pall Mall (03) 5434 6060.
Open daily. **Closed** 25 Dec.
🌐 bendigotourism.com

Bendigo celebrated the gold rush like no other city, and with good reason – the finds here were legendary. In 1851, the first year of gold mining, 23 kg (50 lbs) of gold were extracted from only one bucketful of dirt. When the surface gold began to disappear, the discovery of a gold-rich quartz reef in the 1870s reignited the boom.

Reflecting the city's wealth, Bendigo's buildings are vast and extravagant, often combining several architectural styles within one construction. Government architect G W Watson completed two buildings, the Law Courts and Post Office, in the French and Italian Renaissance styles. The tree-lined boulevard Pall Mall is reminiscent of a French provincial city. The elegant Hotel Shamrock opened to great fanfare in 1897 and is still in operation (*see p494*). The European-style building is given a distinctly Australian feel with its front veranda. Self-guided heritage walk brochures are available from Bendigo's information centre, and the Vintage Talking Tram provides an excellent commentary on the town's history.

A major part of Bendigo's gold rush history was made by its Chinese population. The **Joss House**, dating from the 1860s, is a restored Chinese temple.

Entrance to the Chinese Joss House in Bendigo

Typical 19th-century building in Maldon

The **Golden Dragon Museum** also has displays that chart the history of the Chinese in the city. A ceremonial archway links the museum with the **Garden of Joy**, built in 1996. Based on a traditional Asian design, the garden resembles the Chinese landscape in miniature, with mountains, trees and streams.

The **Bendigo Art Gallery** has a splendid collection of Australian painting, including works depicting life on the gold fields. Nearby are shops selling pieces from Australia's oldest working pottery, Bendigo Pottery, established in 1858.

Bendigo's
local pottery

The **Central Deborah Goldmine** offers visitors tours 86 m (260 ft) down to the last deep reef mine in town.

🏯 **Joss House**
Emu Point, Finn St, North Bendigo.
Tel (03) 5442 1685. **Open** 11am–4pm daily. **Closed** 25 Dec. 🈹
🌐 bendigojosshouse.com

🏛 **Golden Dragon Museum and Garden of Joy**
1–11 Bridge St. **Tel** (03) 5441 5044.
Open 9:30am–5pm daily.
Closed 25 Dec. 🈹 ♿ 🈹
🌐 goldendragonmuseum.org

🏛 **Bendigo Art Gallery**
42 View St. **Tel** (03) 5434 6088. **Open** 10am–5pm Tue–Sun. **Closed** 25 Dec. 🈹 ♿ by arrangement.
🌐 bendigoartgallery.com.au

🏯 **Central Deborah Goldmine**
76 Violet St. **Tel** (03) 5443 8322.
Open 9am–5pm daily.
Closed 25 Dec. 🈹 ♿

⑪ Maldon

🏙 1,200. 🚌 🚌 ℹ 93 High St (03) 5475 2569.

The perfectly preserved town of Maldon offers an outstanding experience of an early gold-mining settlement. This tiny town is set within one of the loveliest landscapes of the region. The hills, forests and exotic trees are an attractive setting for the narrow streets and 19th-century buildings. Maldon was declared Australia's "First Notable Town" by the National Trust in 1966. Cafés, galleries and museums cater to the town's stream of tourists.

Other attractions include Carmen's Tunnel, an old gold mine, and a 70-minute round-trip ride aboard a steam train to Muckleford. Visit at Easter to see the glorious golden leaves of the plane, oak and elm trees. There is also an Easter Fair, including an Easter parade and a street carnival (*see p46*).

⑫ Castlemaine

🏙 7,000. 🚊 🚌 🚌 ℹ Market Building, 44 Mostyn St (03) 5471 1795.

Castlemaine's elegance reflects the fact that gold finds here were brief but extremely prosperous. The finest attraction is the Market Hall, built in 1862. Architect William Benyon Downe designed this building in the Palladian style, with a portico and a large arched entrance leading into the building's restrained interior. The building is now the Visitors' Information Centre. **Buda Historic Home and Garden** was occupied from 1863 to 1981 by two generations of Hungarian silversmith, Ernest Leviny and his family. The house displays an extensive collection of arts and crafts works. The property is also noted for its largely intact 19th-century garden, a unique survivor of its period.

Castlemaine is also home to many writers and artists from Melbourne and has a lively collection of museums, cafés and restaurants.

🏠 Buda Historic Home and Garden
42 Hunter St. **Tel** (03) 5472 1032. **Open** noon–5pm Wed–Sat, 10am–5pm Sun & public hols. **Closed** Good Fri, 25 Dec. 🐾 ♿ teahouse and upper garden area. **W** budacastlemaine.org.au

⑬ Ballarat

See pp438–9.

⑭ Sovereign Hill

Bradshaw St, Ballarat. **Tel** (03) 5337 1100. **Open** 10am–5pm daily. **Closed** 25 Dec. 🐾 📷 ♿ **W** sovereignhill.com.au

Sovereign Hill is the gold fields' living museum. Located on the outskirts of Ballarat *(see pp438–9)*, it offers visitors the chance to explore a unique period of Australia's history. Blacksmiths, hoteliers, bakers and grocers in full period dress ply their trades on the main streets, amid the diggers' huts, tents, old meeting places and the Chinese Village. Among the most absorbing displays are those that reproduce gold-mining methods. The town's fields produced an estimated 640,000 kg (630 tonnes) of gold before being exhausted in the 1920s.

The nearby Gold Museum is part of the Sovereign Hill complex. Its changing exhibits focus on the uses of gold throughout history.

Sovereign Hill opens in the evenings for an impressive sound and light show, which re-enacts the events of the Eureka Stockade *(see p438)*.

The Chinese on the Gold Fields

The first Chinese gold-seekers landed in Melbourne in 1853. Their numbers peaked at around 40,000 in 1859. They worked hard in large groups to recover the tiniest particles of gold, but the Europeans became hostile, claiming that the new arrivals were draining the colony's wealth. In 1857, several Chinese were murdered. The state government tried to quell hostility by introducing an entry tax on Chinese who arrived by boat – the Chinese then landed in neighbouring states and walked overland to Victoria. At the end of the gold rush many stayed on to work as gardeners, cooks and factory hands. There is still a large Chinese community in the state.

Chinese workers on the gold fields

Actors in period costume walking along the main street in Sovereign Hill

⑲ Ballarat

In 1851, the cry of "Gold!" shattered the tranquillity of this pleasant, pastoral district. Within months, tent cities covered the hills and thousands of people were pouring in from around the world, eager to make their fortune. While there were spectacular finds, the sustainable prosperity was accrued to traders, farmers and other modest industries, and Ballarat grew in proportion to their growing wealth. The gold rush petered out in the late 1870s. However, the two decades of wealth can still be seen in the lavish buildings, broad streets, ornate statuary and grand gardens. Today, Ballarat is Victoria's largest inland city.

Ornate façades of historic buildings along Lydiard Street

🏛 Lydiard Street

The wealth of the gold fields attracted a range of people, among them the educated and well travelled. Lydiard Street reflects their influence as a well-proportioned streetscape, boasting buildings of exemplary quality and design.

At the northern end lies the railway station. Built in 1862, it features an arched train entrance and Tuscan pilasters. A neat row of four banks was designed by prominent architect Leonard Terry, whose concern for a balanced streetscape is clearly expressed in their elegant façades. Her Majesty's Theatre is an elaborate 19th-century structure and Australia's oldest surviving purpose-built theatre.

Opposite the theatre is Craig's Royal Hotel, begun in 1852. The hotel was extensively renovated in 1867 for a visit by Prince Alfred, Duke of Edinburgh, including the construction of a special Prince's Room. In 1881,

royal lanterns were constructed outside to honour a visit by the Duke of Clarence and the Duke of York (later King George V). This historic hotel is still in operation.

🏛 Art Gallery of Ballarat

40 Lydiard St North. **Tel** (03) 5320 5858. **Open** 10am–5pm daily. **Closed** Good Fri, 25 Dec. 🅿 ♿ 🅦 artgalleryof ballarat.com.au

Ballarat has always enjoyed the spirit of benefaction. Huge fortunes were made overnight and much of these found their way into the town's institutions. The Art Gallery of Ballarat has been a major recipient of such goodwill, enabling it to establish an impressive reputation as Australia's largest and arguably best provincial art institution.

More than 6,000 works chart the course of Australian art from colonial to contemporary times. Gold field artists include Eugene von Guerard, whose work *Old Ballarat as it was in the summer of 1853–54* is an extraordinary evocation of the town's early tent cities. The gallery's star exhibit is the original Eureka Flag, which has since come to symbolize the basic democratic ideals which are so much a part of modern Australian society.

🏛 Museum of Australian Democracy at Eureka (M.A.D.E)

Cnr Stawell Sth and Eureka streets. **Tel** 1800 287 113. **Open** 10am–5pm daily. 🅿 ♿ 🅦 made.org

The Museum of Australian Democracy at Eureka is located in East Ballarat, at what was the site of the Eureka Stockade. The

The Eureka Stockade

An insurrection at Eureka in 1854, which arose as a result of gold diggers' dissatisfaction with high licensing fees on the gold fields, heralded the move towards egalitarianism in Australia. When hotel-owner James Bentley was acquitted of murdering a young digger, James Scobie, after a row about his entry into the Eureka Hotel, it incited anger among the miners. Led by the charismatic Peter Lalor, the diggers built a stockade, burned their licences and raised the blue flag of the Southern Cross, which became known as the Eureka Flag. On Sunday, 3 December 1854, 282 soldiers and police made a surprise attack on the stockade, killing around 30 diggers. After a public outcry over the brutality, however, the diggers were acquitted of treason and the licence system was abolished.

Rebel leader Peter Lalor

For hotels and restaurants in this area see pp494–5 and pp529–31

Lily pond in Ballarat's beautiful Ballarat Botanical Gardens

centre celebrates the concept of democracy (from the Greek *demos* and *kratos*, meaning "people" and "power") through a series of interactive displays. The main gallery is surrounded by a cyclorama timeline that highlights the main events in the history of democracy, from its origins in Athens until the present day. The centre also hosts film screenings, photographic exhibitions and workshops, all focused on the struggle for democracy.

🟦 Ballarat Botanical Gardens

Wendouree Drive. **Tel** (03) 5320 5135. **Open** daily. **Closed** 25 Dec. ♿ 🅿

These gardens, in the northwest of the city, are a telling symbol of Ballarat's desire for Victorian gentility. The rough and ready atmosphere of the gold fields could be easily overlooked here among the statues, lush green lawns and exotic plants. The focus of the gardens has always been aesthetic rather than botanical, although four different displays are exhibited each year in the Robert Clark Conservatory. The most famous of these is the lovely begonia display, part of the Begonia Festival held here each March *(see p46)*.

There is a Statuary Pavilion featuring female biblical figures in provocative poses, as well as a splendid centrepiece, *Flight from Pompeii*. The Avenue of Prime Ministers is a double row of staggered busts of every Australian prime minister to date, stretching off into the distance. The gardens run along the shores of the expansive Lake Wendouree.

Ballarat Town Centre

① Ballarat Botanical Gardens
② Lydiard Street
③ Art Gallery of Ballarat
④ Museum of Australian Democracy at Eureka (M.A.D.E)

0 metres 500
0 yards 500

⓯ Tour of Daylesford and the Macedon Ranges

Daylesford and the Macedon Ranges lie to the northwest of Melbourne. The landscape is dotted with vineyards, small townships, craft markets and bed-and-breakfasts. The tour follows the Calder Highway, once taken by gold prospectors to the alluvial fields of Castlemaine and Bendigo *(see pp436–7)* before heading west into the spa country around Daylesford. The region's wealthy past is reflected in the 19th-century bluestone buildings, including wool stores and stately homes.

⑧ Malmsbury
During the gold rush, this peaceful hamlet was a busy stop for prospectors on their way to the gold fields.

⑨ Hepburn Springs
The Mineral Springs Reserve is a large area of native bushland. It is an idyllic place for walkers and those who want to "take the waters" from the old-fashioned pumps.

Daylesford

Wombat
State Forest

⑩ Trentham Falls
Victoria's largest single-drop falls, 33 m (108 ft) high, are a few minutes' walk from Falls Road.

Rupertswood and the Ashes

During the Christmas of 1882, eight members of the touring English cricket team were house guests of Sir William John Clarke at Rupertswood. The English won a social game between them and their hosts. Lady Clarke burnt a bail, placed the ashes in an urn and presented them to the English captain, Ivo Bligh. The urn was later presented to Marylebone Cricket Club by Bligh's widow, and thus the cricketing tradition of contesting for The Ashes began.

The original 1882 Ashes urn

0 kilometres 5

0 miles 5

Key
▨ Tour route
═ Other roads

⑦ Kyneton
Historic Kyneton was once a supply town for diggers during the gold rush. It still has part of its 19th-century streetscape intact. The town has some good cafés and antique shops.

⑥ Woodend
Named for its location at the edge of the Black Forest, Woodend has long been a haven for travellers. It has many restaurants, hotels and speciality shops.

⑤ Hanging Rock
This rock was formed 6 million years ago when lava rose up from the earth's surface and solidified. Erosion has caused the fissures through which you can now walk. Scene of the film *Picnic at Hanging Rock*, the area is steeped in Aboriginal history.

④ Mount Macedon
A short walk from the summit car park leads to the memorial cross reserve and spectacular views over the Keilor Plains to Melbourne, Port Phillip Bay, the You Yangs and the Dandenong Ranges *(see p447)*.

③ Rupertswood
This Italianate mansion was built in 1874. The estate includes the cricket field on which The Ashes were created. The once magnificent grounds are now used by a boys' school.

② Goona Warra
The original vineyards of this 1863 bluestone winery were replanted during the 1980s. They now produce highly respected wines, available for tasting and sales by appointment from the cellar door.

Gisborne

M79

derderg te Park

③ ② Sunbury

①

Melton

Melbourne

① Organ Pipes
These 20-m (65-ft) basalt columns were formed by lava flows a million years ago. The Pipes can be seen from a viewing area near the car park or via a trail down to the creek bed.

Tips for Drivers

Tour length: 215 km (133 miles).
Stopping off points: There are numerous places to stay and eat along the route, particularly at Woodend and Daylesford. Daylesford is also ideal for a romantic dinner or weekend lunch *(see p530)*.

EASTERN VICTORIA

Eastern Victoria is a region of immense natural beauty with snow-topped mountains, eucalyptus forests, fertile inland valleys, wild national parks and long sandy beaches. Some of the state's finest wine-growing areas are here, set around historic towns of golden sandstone. Fast rivers popular with rafters flow through the region and ski resorts resembling Swiss villages are found in the Victoria Alps.

Eastern Victoria has a range of attractions for the visitor. The fertile plains of the northeast, crossed by the Goulburn, Ovens, King and Murray rivers, offer a feast for the tastebuds: Rutherglen red wines; Milawa mustards; local cheeses; and luscious peaches, pears and apricots from Shepparton. Historic 19th-century towns such as Beechworth and Chiltern are beautifully preserved from their gold-mining days. Glenrowan is the site where Australia's most famous bushranger, Ned Kelly, was captured. An old-fashioned paddlesteamer rides regularly on the broad Murray River near Wodonga.

But towards the Victorian Alps and the towns of Bright and Mansfield another landscape emerges. This one is wild and very beautiful. In winter, there is exciting downhill skiing among the snow gums and peaks at village resorts such as Mount Buller and Falls Creek *(see pp452–3)*. In summer, walk among the wildflowers in Alpine National Park, hike to the summit of Mount Feathertop, or try a rafting expedition down rivers such as the mighty Snowy.

To the east of Melbourne are the magnificent beaches of the Gippsland region. Favourite attractions here include Phillip Island with its fairy penguins, and Wilsons Promontory National Park with its wildlife, granite outcrops and pristine waters. Near the regional centres of Sale and Bairnsdale lie the Gippsland Lakes, Australia's largest inland waterway and an angler's paradise. Beyond, stretching to the New South Wales border, is Croajingolong National Park and 200 km (125 miles) of deserted coastline.

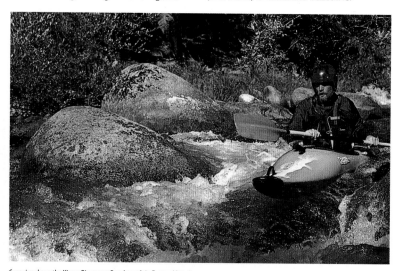

Canoeing down the Kiewa River near Beechworth in Eastern Victoria

◄ Snow daisies on Mount Hotham, in the Alpine National Park

Exploring Eastern Victoria

Excellent highways give access to the most popular tourist attractions and towns of Eastern Victoria. The Dandenong Ranges, Yarra Valley and Phillip Island are within an easy day trip from Melbourne; the region's coastline, which includes Gippsland Lakes, around Lakes Entrance, Wilsons Promontory and Croajingolong National Park, is further to the south and east. The mountains, ski resorts and inland farm valleys are better accessed from the northeast of the state. While most of the major sights can be reached by road, some areas of the Gippsland forests and the Victorian Alps must be explored in 4WD vehicles.

The 19th-century post office in Beechworth town centre

0 km   25
0 miles   25

Key

- ═══ Highway
- ▬▬▬ Major road
- ═══ Minor road
- - - Track
- ── Scenic route
- ▬▬▬ Main railway
- ── Minor railway
- ═══ State border
- △ Summit

For additional map symbols *see back flap*

Finley
Cobram
Barmah
Yarrawonga
Ruthergl
16
Echuca
NORTHEASTERN
WINERIES 14
CHILTER
BEECHWO
13
12
Kyabram
Wangaratta
Rochester
SHEPPARTON 17
GLENROWAN 15
Milawa
Myrtleford
Waranga
Basin
39
BENALLA 16
Goulburn
Euroa
Whitfield
Lake
Buffalo
Bendigo
HUME HIGHWAY
MANSFIELD 9
Mt Buller
Seymour
Mount Buller
1805m
Alp
Broadford
Alexandra
Natio
Yea
Eildon 8
Jamieson
Pa
Cathedral Range
State Park
LAKE
EILDON
Aus
31
Marysville
6 LIC
YARRA
Yarra Glen
VALLEY 5
Healesville
Lilydale
Thomson
Reservoir
Melbourne
Warburton
Ballarat
DANDENONG RANGES 4
Mount Gwinear
1509m
Belgrave
Gembrook
Mount Baw Baw
1565m
Heyfie
Dandenong
Geelong
Pakenham
Port Phillip Bay
3 CRANBOURNE
Warragul
Moe
Frankston
Trara
MORNINGTON
Morwell
PENINSULA
Hastings
Portsea
2
French
Island
Korumburra
Gippsland
Sorrento
Leongatha
Yarram
Flinders
Cowes
1
Foster
PHILLIP
Inverloch
Port Albert
ISLAND
Wonthaggi
Cape Liptrap
Wilsons
Promontory
South East Po

Sights at a Glance

1 Phillip Island
2 Mornington Peninsula
3 Royal Botanical Gardens, Cranbourne
4 Dandenong Ranges
5 Yarra Valley
6 Licola
7 Buchan Caves

8 Lake Eildon
9 Mansfield
10 Mount Beauty
11 Bright
12 Beechworth
13 Chiltern
14 Northeastern Wineries
15 Glenrowan
16 Benalla
17 Shepparton

Upper Murray Valley in the heart of northeastern Victoria

Getting Around

There are regular train services to the Dandenongs and the Gippsland Lakes. Bus tours can be arranged to Phillip Island and the Yarra Valley, while regular buses run in winter to the ski resorts. However, the best way of exploring is by car. The Hume Hwy provides access to the northeast, the Princes Hwy to the Gippsland Lakes and the South Gippsland Hwy to Phillip Island and Wilsons Promontory.

Lake Eildon at the gateway to the Victorian Alps

❶ Phillip Island

🚌 Cowes. 🚢 Cowes. ℹ️ Newhaven
1300 854 334. **Open** 9am–5pm daily;
summer hols: 9am–6pm daily.
W visitphillipisland.com

The penguin parade on Phillip
Island is an extraordinary
natural spectacle. Every evening
at sunset at all times of the year,
hundreds of little penguins
come ashore at Summerland
Beach and waddle across the
sand to their burrows in the
spinifex tussocks (spiky clumps
of grass), just as their ancestors
have been doing for generations. Once ashore, the small
penguins spend their time in
the dunes preening themselves
and, in summer, feeding their
hungry chicks.

At Seal Rocks, off the rugged
cliffs at the western end of the
island, is Australia's largest
colony of fur seals. Approximately 16,000 of these seals
can be seen playing in the surf,
resting in the sun or feeding
their pups on the rocks. Tourists
can watch them from the cliff
top or on an organized boat
trip. There is also a large koala
colony on Phillip Island.

Cape Woolamai, with its red
cliffs and wild ocean seas, has
good walking trails, excellent
bird-watching opportunities
and some great surfing. The
peaceful town of Cowes is
ideal for swimming, relaxing
and dining.

The island gets very crowded
during car and motorcycle race
events so you need to reserve
accommodation
at these times.

Fairy penguins making their way up the sand dunes
of Phillip Island

Rock pools at Sorrento on the Mornington Peninsula

❷ Mornington Peninsula

🚆 Frankston. 🚌 to most peninsula
towns. 🚢 Stony Point, Sorrento.
ℹ️ Dromana (03) 5987 3078
W visitmorningtonpeninsula.org

Only an hour's drive from
Melbourne, on the east side of
Port Phillip Bay, the Mornington
Peninsula is the city's summer
and weekend getaway. From
Frankston down to Portsea
near its tip, the area is ideal
for relaxing beach holidays.
The sandy beaches facing the
bay are sheltered and calm,
perfect for windsurfing, sailing
or paddling, while the rugged
coast fronting the Bass Strait
has rocky reefs, rock pools
and surf beaches.

Arthur's Seat, a high, bush
ridge offers views of the
peninsula. The surrounding
Red Hill wineries are fast
gaining a reputation for their
fine Chardonnays and Pinot
Noirs. Sip a glass of one of
these wines in the historic
village of Sorrento or take
a ferry trip across the
narrow and
treacherous Rip
to the beautiful
19th-century town
of Queenscliff
(see p430).
Running the length
of the peninsula,
the Mornington
Peninsula National
Park has lovely
walking tracks.
Point Nepean,
formerly a

quarantine station and defence
post, is now part of the national
park. The beach at the tip of The
Heads and Cheviot Beach, where
Prime Minister Harold Holt
disappeared while surfing in
1967, are both beautiful spots.

Environs

The village of Flinders is a
peaceful, chic seaside resort,
while Portsea is the summer
playground of Melbourne's rich
and famous. The atmosphere
at the remote French Island, a
short ferry trip from Crib Point,
is unique, with no electricity or
telephones. The island also
teems with wildlife, including
rare potoroo.

❸ Royal Botanic Gardens, Cranbourne

Off South Gippsland Hwy, 1000
Ballarto Rd. **Tel** (03) 5990 2200.
🚆 Cranbourne. 🚌 Cranbourne.
Open 9am–5pm daily. **Closed** 25
Dec, days of total fire ban. ♿ 📷
W rbg.vic.gov.au/visit-cranbourne

The Royal Botanic Gardens
in Melbourne are the city's
pride and joy *(see pp402–3)*, but
they have not concentrated
exclusively on native flora. The
Cranbourne Botanic Gardens
fill that niche. Amid the lakes,
hills and dunes of this bushland
park, banksias, wattles, grevilleas,
casuarinas, eucalypts and pink
heath bloom, while wrens,
honeyeaters, galahs, rosellas,
cockatoos and parrots nestle
among the gardens' trees.

❹ Dandenong Ranges

🚉 Ferntree Gully & Belgrave.
🚌 to most towns. 🛈 Ferntree
Gully (03) 9758 7522. **Open** 9am–5pm
daily. 🌐 **visitdandenongranges.
com.au**

Since the mid-19th century, the Dandenong Ranges, to the east of Melbourne, have been a popular weekend retreat for city residents. The cool of the mountain ash forests, lush fern gullies and bubbling creeks provide a welcome relief from the bayside heat.

The great gardens of the Dandenongs, many of which once belonged to the mansions of wealthy families, are magnificent for walks and picnics. Particularly popular is the Alfred Nicholas Memorial Garden at Sherbrooke with its oaks, elms, silver birches and Japanese maples around a boating lake. Flowers are the obvious attraction of the National Rhododendron Gardens at Olinda and Tesselaar's Tulip Farm at Silvan. A steam train, Puffing Billy, runs several times daily from Belgrave through 24 km (15 miles) of gullies and forests to Emerald Lake and on to Gembrook.

The superb lyrebird makes its home in the Dandenongs, particularly in Sherbrooke Forest. The 7-km (4-mile) Eastern Sherbrooke Lyrebird Circuit Walk through mountain ash offers a chance to glimpse these beautiful but shy birds.

Domaine Chandon vineyard in the Yarra Valley

Another tranquil walk is the 15-km (9-mile) path from Sassafras to Emerald.

Healesville Sanctuary, with its 30 ha (75 acres) of natural bushland, remains the best place to see indigenous Australian animals in relatively relaxed captivity. Highlights of any visit are the sightings of rare species such as platypuses, marsupials and birds of prey. This is a popular place to bring children who want to learn about Australian wildlife.

Further east are the Steavenson Falls and also nearby are the mountains of the Cathedral Ranges and the snow fields and trails of Lake Mountain (see pp452–3).

🦘 **Healesville Sanctuary**
Badger Creek Rd, Healesville.
Tel (03) 5957 2800. **Open** 9am–5pm
daily. 🏞 ♿ 🌐 **zoo.org.au**

❺ Yarra Valley

🚉 Lilydale. 🚌 Healesville service.
🛈 Healesville (03) 5962 2600.

The beautiful Yarra Valley, located at the foot of the Dandenong Ranges, is home to some of Australia's best cool-climate wineries (see pp382–3). They are known for their *Méthode Champenoise* sparkling wines, Chardonnays and Pinot Noirs. Most of the wineries are open daily for wine tastings. Several also have restaurants, serving food to accompany their fine wines.

Just past the bush town of Yarra Glen is the historic Gulf Station. Owned by the National Trust, it provides an authentic glimpse of farming life at the end of the 19th century.

Sparkling wine of the Yarra Valley

The famous Puffing Billy steam train, making its way through the Dandenong Ranges

The Gippsland Coastline

The beautiful coastline of Gippsland is equal to any natural wonder of the world. Approximately 400 km (250 miles) of deserted beaches, inlets and coves are largely protected by national park status. There is the largest inland lake system in Australia, Gippsland Lakes, the pristine sands of Ninety Mile Beach and rare natural features such as the Mitchell River silt jetties. Birds, fish, seals and penguins abound in the area. With little commercial development, the coastline is a popular location with anglers, sailors, divers, swimmers and campers.

③ **Woodside Beach**
This easily accessible white sandy beach is popular with families, sunbathers and surfers. The area behind the beach benefits from many well-signposted bushwalks.

⑥ **Gippsland Lakes**
The lagoons, backwaters, islands and lakes of this region make up Australia's biggest inland waterway. Lakeside settlements are home to large sailing and fishing fleets.

Port Albert, the oldest port in Gippsland, was used by thousands of gold diggers heading for the Omeo and Walhalla gold fields in the 1850s. Quaint buildings with shady verandas line its streets. The Maritime Museum displays the area's naval history.

⑤ ★ **Letts Beach**
This sandy beach benefits from the ocean on one side and beautiful lakes on the other. Part of the Lakes National Park, the beach is home to the endangered fairy tern.

② **Corner Inlet**
This small inlet protects some of the world's most southerly mangroves and seagrass beds, as well as rare birds such as the red-necked stint.

① ★ **Squeaky Beach, Wilsons Promontory National Park**
The white sand beach of this former land bridge to Tasmania is framed by granite boulders, spectacular mountain views, fern gullies and open heathlands which are a sanctuary for plants and wildlife.

④ ★ **Golden Beach**
The calm waters of this stretch of ocean make it a popular destination for water sports enthusiasts. Fishing and sailing are two of the regular activities available in the area.

Map labels: B500, Bairnsdale, Paynesville, GIPPSLAND, The Lakes National Park, Sale, A1, Bass Strait, C482, B440, Seaspray, MELBOURNE, Yarram, Port Albert, B440, Wilsons Promontory National Park, Tidal River

Bairnsdale is one of the major towns of the Gippsland region, together with its neighbour, Sale. St Mary's Church, in the centre of the town, has distinctive Italianate-style painted walls and ceilings, as well as beautiful carved statuary set in its exterior walls.

⑫ ★ **Gipsy Point, Mallacoota Inlet**
This idyllic spot within a pleasant holiday region is ideal for summer picnics. Bird-watching and bushwalking are popular local activities.

Locator Map

Croajingolong National Park

⑨ ★ **Lakes Entrance**
Lakes Entrance is the only entrance from the Gippsland Lakes to the sea, through the treacherous Bar. This major fishing port is also well equipped with motels, museums and theme parks for children.

⑦ **Eagle Point**
Silt banks from the Mitchell River stretch 8 km out into Lake King from Eagle Point. The silt banks are second only in length to those of the Mississippi River.

⑧ **Metung**
This pretty boating and holiday region, popular with campers, benefits from hot mineral pools.

⑩ **Marlo**
Located at the mouth of the great Snowy River, Marlo is a popular holiday destination, particularly with avid local anglers. Nearby is the large town of Orbost, the centre of East Gippsland's extensive timber industry.

⑪ **Mallacoota**
This remote fishing village is extremely popular with both Victorian and overseas tourists. It is set on an inland estuary of the Bass Strait, ideal for canoeing, fishing and sailing.

Croajingolong National Park is a magnificent stretch of rugged and coastal wilderness, classified as a World Biosphere Reserve. Captain Cook caught his first sight of Australia in 1770 at Point Hicks.

| 0 kilometres | 25 |
| 0 miles | 25 |

Key

~~~~ Freeway
— Major road
=== Minor road
〜 River

❻ Licola

🗺 20. 🚌 Heyfield. ℹ️ Licola Wilderness Village, Jamieson Rd (03) 5148 8791. 🔲 **licola.org.au**

Licola is a tiny village perched on the edge of Victoria's mountain wilderness. North of Heyfield and Glenmaggie, follow the Macalister River Valley north to Licola. The 147-km (90-mile) journey from Licola to Jamieson, along unsealed roads, takes in the magnificent scenery of Victoria's highest peaks. Only 20 km (12 miles) from Licola is Mount Tamboritha and the start of the popular Lake Tarli Karng bushwalk in the Alpine National Park, also a good base for those keen to explore the surrounding country. The village store has information.

Licola is entirely owned by the Lions Club of Victoria (the only privately owned town in the state). The club has developed the Lions Wilderness Village, which provides camp sites and a range of activities for young people.

Farmland near the tiny mountain village of Licola

❼ Buchan Caves

Buchan Caves Reserve, Buchan. **Tel** 13 19 63. **Open** daily except 25 Dec. 📅 daily 🔲 **parkweb.vic. gov.au**

Some of the most spectacular limestone formations in Australia can be found at Buchan Caves. Two of the finest are Fairy Cave and Royal Cave, within Buchan Caves Reserve. Both caves are lit and have walkways; guided tours are conducted throughout the day, alternating between the two caves. Dating back 300–400 million years, the caves and

their awe-inspiring stalactites and stalagmites were made by ancient rivers coursing and seeping through the limestone rock. Royal Cave also has colourful calcite-rimmed pools. Entry to the reserve, where there are picnic facilities and a spring-fed pool suitable for swimming, is free. There are also camp sites and walking trails, while the nearby township of Buchan offers other accommodation. The reserve is a wildlife refuge to native animals such as kangaroos, possums, bellbirds and lyrebirds.

Limestone formations at Buchan Caves

❽ Lake Eildon

🚌 Eildon. ℹ️ Eildon Visitors' Information Centre, Main St, Eildon. 🔲 **lakeeildon.com**

Lake Eildon, the catchment for five major rivers, including the Goulburn River, is a vast irrigation reserve that turns into a recreational haven in summer. Surrounded by the Great Dividing Range and Fraser and Eildon national parks, the lake is a good location for water-skiing, houseboat holidays, horse-riding, fishing and hiking. Kangaroos, koalas and rosellas abound around the lake, and trout and Murray cod are common in the Upper Goulburn River and in the lake. Canoeing on the Goulburn River is also a popular activity.

A variety of accommodation is available, from rustic cabins and camp sites in Fraser National Park to luxurious five-star lodges and guesthouses.

❾ Mansfield

🗺 2,500. 🚌 ℹ️ Visitors' Information Centre, 175 High St, Mansfield 1800 039 049. 🔲 **mansfieldmtbuller. com.au**

Mansfield, a country town surrounded by mountains, is the southwest entry point to Victoria's alpine country. A memorial in the main street of Mansfield, just near to the 1920s cinema, commemorates the death of three troopers shot by the infamous Ned Kelly and his gang at nearby Stringybark Creek in 1878 – the crime for which he was

Blue waters of Lake Eildon, backed by the Howqua Mountain Ranges

For hotels and restaurants in this area see pp495–6 and pp531–3

Classic 19th-century architecture in the rural town of Mansfield

hung in Melbourne in 1880 *(see p398)*.

The scenery of Mansfield became well known as the location for the 1981 film *The Man from Snowy River*, which was based on the poet "Banjo" Paterson's legendary ballad of the same name *(see p39)*. Today, visitors can ride a horse or bike on one of the many trails, or visit the Mansfield Zoo, which is home to more than 100 animals, including lions and kangaroos.

Environs

The excellent downhill slopes of the Mount Buller ski resort *(see pp452–3)* are less than one hour's drive from Mansfield. Mount Stirling *(see pp452–3)* offers year-round activities, such as mountain bike riding *(see p538)*.

⑩ Mount Beauty

🏔 2,300. 🚌 ℹ 31 Bogong High Plains Rd, Mt Beauty (03) 5755 0596. 🌐 **mtbeauty.com**

The town of Mount Beauty was first built to house workers on the Kiewa hydro-electricity scheme in the 1940s. It has since developed into a good base for exploring the beauty of the Kiewa Valley, with its tumbling river and dairy farms. Also nearby is the wilderness of the Bogong High Plains and the Alpine National Park *(see pp452–3)*, with their walks, wildflowers and snow gums.

Within the national park, Mount Bogong, Victoria's highest mountain, rises an impressive 1,986 m (6,516 ft)

above the town. The sealed mountain road to Falls Creek *(see pp452–3)* is one of the main access routes to the region's ski slopes in winter. In summer, Rocky Valley Dam is popular for boating, kayaking and swimming. There are beautiful bushwalks, and at the top of the High Plains, there are opportunities for fishing, mountain biking, horse-riding and hang-gliding.

⑪ Bright

🏔 2,500. 🚌 ℹ 5/6 Anderson St (03) 5755 2275. 🌐 **brightvictoria. com.au**

Bright is a picturesque mountain town near the head of the Ovens River Valley, with the towering rocky cliffs of Mount Buffalo *(see pp452–3)*

to the west and the peak of the state's second highest mountain, Mount Feathertop, to its south. The trees along Bright's main street flame into spectacular colours of red, gold, copper and brown for its Autumn Festival in April and May *(see p46)*. In winter, the town turns into a gateway to the snow fields, with the resorts of Mount Hotham and Falls Creek in the Victorian Alps close by *(see pp452–3)*. In summer, swimming and fly-fishing for trout in the Ovens River are popular activities.

The spectacular **Mount Buffalo National Park** is also popular all year round; visitors can camp amid the snow gums by Lake Catani and walk its flower-flecked mountain pastures and peaks, fish for trout, hang-glide off the granite tors over the Ovens Valley or rock-climb the imposing sheer cliffs. During the winter, Mount Buffalo is a great place for cross-country skiing and snow play. A range of walking trails are available with wonderful views of Buckland Valley. Other activities on offer include canoeing, caving, horse-riding and paragliding.

🏕 **Mount Buffalo National Park**
Mount Buffalo Rd. **Tel** 13 19 63. 🅿 ♿ some areas.

Buffalo River meandering through Mount Buffalo National Park

Skiing in the Victorian Alps

Australia offers fantastic skiing opportunities that rival the best in the world. Most of the resorts fall within Alpine National Park *(see pp444–5)*, and are open for business from June to late September. Given that the season is so short, conditions can be variable. Mount Buller, Falls Creek and Mount Hotham are the main resort villages, and the whole region is very fashionable. There are chic lounge bars, top-end lodges and fine dining prepared by some of Melbourne's best chefs.

Pistes are not as long as those in Europe and the USA, but the views of the High Plains are an unmissable experience.

Mount Buffalo 🎿 🎿
These less-crowded slopes are popular with beginners, intermediate and cross-country skiers.

Mount Buller 🎿 🎿 🎿
This is the most accessible of the major resorts, and hence the busiest and trendiest. Slopes suit beginners through to advanced skiers, with 80 km (48 miles) of groomed trails and a 405-m (1,300 ft)-vertical drop. The entrance car park at Mirimbah is 16 km (10 miles) from the village; there is a free shuttle bus for daytrippers.

Mount Stirling Entry to Mount Buller includes free cross-country skiing on Mount Stirling's groomed trails.

Lake Mountain This resort is ideal for cross-country skiing. Most runs are for beginners to intermediates. There is no on-mountain accommodation. Nearby Mount Donna Buang is fine for snowmen and toboggan runs.

Mount Baw Baw 🎿 🎿
The closest downhill ski resort to Melbourne is an excellent option for beginners, families and skiers on a budget. Nearby Mount St Gwinear offers superb cross-country skiing but no on-mountain accommodation.

Australian Alps Walking Track
The 655-km (393-mile) Australian Alps Walking Track runs from historic Walhalla north-east to the Brindabella Ranges outside Canberra.

Mount Buffalo
(5558 ft/1695m)

Lake
Buffalo

MT BUFFALO
NATIONAL
PARK

Mansfield

Mount Stirling
Alpine Resort
🎿

**Mount Buller
Alpine Village**
🎿

Lake
Eildon

Mount Buller
(5922 ft/1805m)

Eildon

Jamieson

**ALPINE
NATIONAL
PARK**

AUSTRALIAN

Lake
Mountain
🎿

Licola

**YARRA RANGES
NATIONAL PARK**

Dartmouth
Reservoir

Mount St Gwinear
(4915 ft/1509m)

Mount Baw Baw
(5134ft/1565m)

🎿

Thomson
Reservoir

**Mount
Baw Baw
Alpine Village**

Walhalla

Falls Creek Australia's only real ski-in ski-out resort village is popular with cross-country and advanced skiers. It also offers the country's longest green run and plenty of options for freestylers. The vibrant nightlife suits an extended stay.

Dartmouth Reservoir

Mount Bogong (6516 ft/1986 m)

Bright

Mount Beauty

Falls Creek Alpine Village

Falls Creek (6043 ft/1842 m)

Mount Hotham Alpine village

Mount Hotham (6106 ft/1861 m)

Dinner Plain

Omeo

ALPS

0 km   50

0 miles   50

Mount Hotham
Featuring mostly challenging terrain, this area best suits intermediate to more advanced skiers. The resort has definitely gone more up-market in recent years. There is an airstrip 20 km (12 miles) from the village. Nearby Dinner Plain is popular with cross-country skiers.

Advice for Skiers

Costs
Entry fees are about A$30 per car per day. Lifts cost about A$100 per day per adult.

Transport and Equipment Hire
Roads are sealed to all resorts except Dinner Plain, Mount Baw Baw and Mount Stirling. By law, vehicles must carry chains. Equipment can be hired from the resorts listed here. Coaches run from Melbourne to every resort except Mount Baw Baw. Aircraft and helicopters from Melbourne and Sydney fly to Mount Hotham and Mount Buller. A helicopter shuttle flies between Mount Hotham and Falls Creek.

Ski Resorts

Dinner Plain
w dinnerplain.com
Tel (03) 5159 6451 or 1800 670 019 (toll free).

Falls Creek
w fallscreek.com.au
Tel (03) 5758 1202.

Lake Mountain
w lakemountainresort.com.au
Tel (03) 5957 7222.

Mount Baw Baw
w mountbawbaw.com au
Tel (03) 5165 1136.

Mount Buller
w mtbuller.com.au
Tel (03) 5777 6077.

Mount Hotham
w mthotham.com.au
Tel (03) 5759 4444.

Mount Stirling
w mtstirling.com.au
Tel (03) 5777 6077.

For hotels in the area, see pp495–6.

Key

△ Peak

Resort

▬ Major road

═ Minor road

-- Walking track

Beginner

Intermediate

Advanced

Typical 19th-century honey granite building in Beechworth

⑫ Beechworth

🏠 3,500. 🚍 ℹ️ Town Hall, Ford St (03) 5728 8064.
🌐 **beechworth.com**

Beautifully sited in the foothills of the Victorian Alps, Beechworth was the centre of the great Ovens gold fields during the 1850s and 1860s *(see pp58–9)*. At the height of its boom, the town had a population of 42,000 and 61 hotels.

Today, visiting Beechworth is like stepping back in time. One of the state's best-preserved gold rush towns, it contains more than 30 19th-century buildings now classified by the National Trust. Its tree-lined streets feature granite banks and a courthouse, hotels with wide verandas and dignified brick buildings on either side. The majority of these are still in daily use, modern life continuing within edifices of

a bygone era. Many of the old buildings are now restaurants, and bed-and-breakfasts. Dine in the stately old bank which is now the Provenance restaurant *(see p532)*, stand in the dock of the courthouse where Ned Kelly was finally committed for his trial in Melbourne *(see p398)* and marvel at the old channel blasted through the granite to create a flow of water in which miners panned for gold.

The evocative Chinese cemetery is also worth a visit as a poignant reminder of the hundreds of Chinese who worked and died on the gold fields *(see pp58–9)*.

⑬ Chiltern

🏠 1,500. 🚍 ℹ️ 30 Main St (03) 5726 1611. 🌐 **chilternvic.com**

This sleepy village was once a booming gold-mining town with 14 suburbs. Only 1 km (half a mile) off the Hume Highway, halfway between the major towns of Wangaratta and Wodonga, today its colonial architecture and quiet atmosphere, as yet unspoiled by large numbers of tourists, make a visit to this pleasant town a worthwhile experience.

Chiltern has three National Trust properties: Dow's Pharmacy; the Federal Standard newspaper office; and Lakeview House. The last is the former

home of Henry Handel Richardson, the pen name of Ethel Richardson *(see p39)*, who wrote *The Getting of Wisdom*. Chiltern was her childhood home. The house, on Lake Alexander, has been restored with period furniture, and gives an insight into the life of the wealthy at the turn of the 20th century.

An unusual sight is the Grapevine museum. This shows the oldest and largest grapevine in the southern hemisphere – it once covered Chiltern's Star Hotel in its entirety.

For opening hours and other information on these attractions, check with the tourist information office in the town.

Lakeview House in Chiltern

⑭ Northeastern Wineries

🚍 Wangaratta & Rutherglen.
🚌 Wangaratta & Rutherglen.
ℹ️ Rutherglen (02) 6033 6300;
Wangaratta (03) 5721 5711.
Campbells Winery: **Tel** (03) 6033 6000.
Open 9am–5pm Mon–Sat, 10am–5pm Sun. **Closed** Good Fri, 25 Dec.
Chambers Rosewood Winery:
Tel (02) 6032 8641. **Open** 9am–5pm Mon–Sat, 10am–5pm Sun & public hols. **Closed** Good Fri, 25 Dec.
Brown Brothers: **Tel** (03) 5720 5500.
Open 9am–5pm daily.
Closed Good Fri, 25 Dec.
🌐 **brownbrothers.com.au**

The Northeastern area of Victoria is famous throughout the world for its vineyards and wineries *(see pp382–3)*. In a region that now spreads south to encompass the King and Ovens valleys around Glenrowan, Milawa, Everton, Rutherglen and Whitfield, the wines produced can vary in style enormously, depending on the elevation and microclimate of each vineyard.

Rutherglen is best known for its full-bodied "Rutherglen Reds",

Rows of grapevines in one of northeastern Victoria's many vineyards

For hotels and restaurants in this area see pp495–6 and pp531–3

Elegant Benalla Art Gallery on the shores of Lake Benalla

such as Cabernet Sauvignons from 100-year-old wineries including Campbells and Chambers. The Muscats, Tokays and ports from both Rutherglen and Glenrowan are even more internationally renowned, with Bullers, Morris and Bailey's among the best. Rutherglen itself is a graceful town lined with antiques shops, and a selection of hotels and restaurants.

The grapes grown in the cool-climate region around Whitfield and Milawa make for crisp whites and lighter, softer reds. One of the more popular wineries in Northeastern Victoria is Brown Brothers at Milawa. The winery is open daily for both wine tasting and sales at the cellar door, and its excellent restaurant specializes in local delicacies from the region, including particularly good trout, cheese, honey and lamb. While at Milawa, visits to the Milawa Cheese Factory and Milawa Mustards are recommended.

⑮ Glenrowan

🏛 1,000. 🚌 🚍 Wangaratta. ℹ️ Glenrowan Tourist Centre, 41 Gladstone St (03) 5766 2367. 🌐 glenrowantouristcentre.com.au

Glenrowan was the site of the last stand by Australia's most notorious bushranger, Ned Kelly, and his gang (see p398). In

a shoot-out with police in 1880, on Siege Street near the town's railway station, Kelly was finally captured after more than two years on the run. During this time he had earned almost hero status among Victoria's bush poor, particularly its many Irish Catholic farming families, as a Robin Hood-type character. Kelly knew the country around Glenrowan, especially the lovely Warby Ranges, in great detail and often used Mount Glenrowan, west of town, as a lookout. Kelly was later hanged at Melbourne Gaol.

Today Glenrowan thrives on its Kelly history as a tourist attraction. A giant iron effigy of the bushranger greets visitors at the entrance to the town and there are various displays, museums and re-enactments depicting the full Kelly story, including his last defeat.

Iron effigy of
Ned Kelly

⑯ Benalla

🏛 8,500. 🚆 🚌 🚍 ℹ️ The Creators' Gallery, 14 Mair St (03) 5762 1749. 🌐 benalla.vic.gov.au

The rural town of Benalla is where Ned Kelly grew up and first appeared in court at the age of 15. Today it is most famous for its art gallery, built over Lake Benalla, housing a fine collection of contemporary and Australian art. The Benalla Festival in November features food, art and family entertainment.

The town is also known as the Australian "capital" of gliding, with excellent air thermals rising from both the hot plains and nearby mountains.

⑰ Shepparton

🏛 50,000. 🚆 🚆 🚌 🚍 ℹ️ Greater Shepparton Visitors' Centre, 33 Nixon St 1800 808 839. 🌐 visitshepparton.com.au

The modern city of Shepparton, at the heart of the fertile Goulburn River Valley, is often called the "fruit bowl of Australia". The vast irrigation plains around the town support Victoria's most productive pear, peach, apricot, apple, plum, cherry and kiwi fruit farms. A summer visit of the town's biggest fruit cannery, SPC, when fruit is being harvested, reveals a hive of activity.

The area's sunny climate is also ideal for grapes. The two well-known wineries of Mitchelton and Tahbilk Wines, 50 km (30 miles) south of town, are both open for tours and tastings (see pp382–3).

Harvesting fruit in Shepparton's orchards

TASMANIA

Tasmania's Wildlife and Wilderness

Tasmania's landscape varies dramatically within its small area. Parts of Tasmania are often compared to the green pastures of England; however, the west of the state is wild and untamed. Inland there are glacial mountains and wild rivers, the habitat of flora and fauna unique to the island. More than 20 per cent of the island is now designated as a World Heritage Area *(see pp30–31).*

Russell Falls at Mount Field National Park

Mountain Wilderness

Inland southwest Tasmania is dominated by its glacial mountain landscape, including the beautiful Cradle Mountain – the natural symbol of the state. To the east of Cradle Mountain is the Walls of Jerusalem National Park, an isolated area of five rocky mountains. To the south is Mount Field National Park, a beautiful alpine area of glacial tarns and eucalypt forests, popular with skiers in the winter months.

Deciduous beech *(Nothofagus gunnii)* is the only such native beech in Australia. The spectacular golden colours of its leaves fill the mountain areas during the autumn.

The Bennett's wallaby *(Macropus rufogriseus)* is native to Tasmania's mountain regions. A shy animal, it is most likely to be spotted at either dawn or dusk.

Cradle Mountain, looking down over a glacial lake

Coastal Wilderness

The climate of Tasmania's eastern coastline is often balmy and sustains a strong fishing industry. The western coast, however, bears the full brunt of the Roaring Forties winds, whipped up across the vast expanses of ocean between the island state and the nearest land in South America. As a result, the landscape is lined with rocky beaches and raging waters, the scene of many shipwrecks during Tasmania's history.

The Tasmanian devil *(Sarcophilus harrisii)* is noisy, potentially vicious and one of only three marsupial carnivores that inhabit the island.

Banksia comes in many varieties in Tasmania, including *Banksia serrata* and *Banksia marginata*. It is distinctive for its seed pods.

Rugged coastline of the Tasman Peninsula

◀ Wild coastline at Rupert Point, in the Tarkine Wilderness

Calm area of Franklin Lower Gordon Wild River

River Wilderness

The southwest of Tasmania is well known for its wild rivers, particularly among avid whitewater rafters. The greatest wild river is the 120-km (75-mile) Franklin River, protected within Franklin-Gordon Wild Rivers National Park by its World Heritage status. This is the only undammed wild river left in Australia, and despite its sometimes calm moments it often rages fiercely through gorges, rainforests and heathland.

Huon pine (*Lagarostrobus franklinii*) is found in the southwest and in the south along the Franklin-Gordon River. It is prized for its ability to withstand rot. Some examples are more than 2,000 years old.

Brown trout (*Salmo trutta*), an introduced species, is abundant in the wild rivers and lakes of Tasmania, and a popular catch with fly-fishers.

The eastern quoll (*Dasyurus viverrinus*) once thrived in Tasmania but is now an endangered species.

Preserving Tasmania's Wilderness

An inhospitable climate, rugged landforms and the impenetrable scrub are among the factors that have preserved such a large proportion of Tasmania as wilderness. Although there is a long history of human habitation in what is now the World Heritage Area (Aboriginal sites date back 35,000 years), the population has always been small. The first real human threat occurred in the late 1960s when the Tasmanian government's hydroelectricity programme drowned Lake Pedder despite conservationists' protests. A proposal two decades later to dam a section of the Franklin River was defeated when the federal government intervened. The latest threat to the landscape is tourism. While many places of beauty are able to withstand visitors, others are not and people are discouraged from visiting these areas.

Dam protests were common occurrences in Tasmania during the 1980s, when conservationists protested against the damming of the Franklin River. The *No Dams* sticker became a national symbol of protest.

Protest badges

TASMANIA

Human habitation of Tasmania dates back 35,000 years, when Aborigines first reached the area. At this time it was linked to continental Australia, but waters rose to form the Bass Strait at the end of the Ice Age, 12,000 years ago. Dutch explorer Abel Tasman set foot on the island in 1642 and inspired its modern name. He originally called it Van Diemen's Land, after the governor of the Dutch East Indies.

Belying its small size, Tasmania has a remarkably diverse landscape that contains glacial mountains, dense forests and rolling green hills. Its wilderness is one of only three large temperate forests in the southern hemisphere; it is also home to many plants and animals unique to the island, including a ferocious marsupial, the Tasmanian devil. Tasmanians are fiercely proud of their landscape and the island saw the rise of the world's first Green political party, the "Tasmanian Greens". One-fifth of Tasmania is protected as a World Heritage Area (see pp30–31).

The Tasmanian Aboriginal population was severely depleted with the arrival of Europeans in the 19th century; however, around 20,000 people claim Aboriginality in Tasmania today. Evidence of their link with the landscape has survived in numerous cave paintings. Many Aboriginal sites remain sacred and closed to visitors, but a few, such as the cliffs around Woolnorth, display this indigenous art for all to see.

The island's early European history has also been well preserved in its many 19th-century buildings. The first real settlement was at the waterfront site of Hobart in 1804, now Tasmania's capital and Australia's second-oldest city. From here, European settlement spread throughout the state, with the development of farms and villages, built and worked by convict labour.

Today, Tasmania is a haven for wildlife lovers, hikers and fly-fishers, who come to experience the island's many national parks and forests. The towns scattered throughout the state, such as Richmond and Launceston, with their rich colonial histories, are well worth a visit, and make excellent bases from which to explore the surrounding wilderness.

The historic port area of Battery Point in Hobart

◄ Coastline at Boulder Point, part of Mount William National Park

Exploring Tasmania

Part, and yet not a part, of Australia, Tasmania's distinctive landscape, climate and culture are largely due to its 300-km (185-mile) distance from the mainland. The isolation has left a legacy of unique flora and fauna, fresh air, an abundance of water and a relaxed lifestyle. More than 27 per cent of Tasmania's land surface is given over to agriculture, with the emphasis on wine and fine foods. The state also benefits from vast expanses of open space, since approximately 40 per cent of Tasmanians live in the capital, Hobart. Tasmania, therefore, offers the perfect opportunity for a relaxing holiday in tranquil surroundings.

Nelson Falls in Franklin-Gordon Wild Rivers National Park

Yachts in Constitution Dock, Hobart

King Island

0 km   15

0 miles   15

Cape Wickham

Egg Lagoon

Yambacoona

16 KING ISLAND

Naracoopa

Currie

Grassy

Stokes Point

Key

— Major road

═══ Minor road

— Scenic route

For keys to symbols *see back flap*

Getting Around

Within this small, compact island, traffic is rarely a problem, and any visitor can journey across the diverse landscape with little difficulty. While all major cities and towns are linked by fast highways and major roads, some of the most splendid mountain, lake, coastal and rural scenery lies off the key routes, along the many alternative and easily accessible country roads. A car is recommended, but coach services run between most towns and to some of the state's natural attractions.

Sights at a Glance

1. Hobart pp464–5
2. Richmond
3. New Norfolk
4. Bothwell
5. Oatlands
6. Freycinet National Park
7. Bicheno
8. Ross
9. Ben Lomond National Park
10. Launceston
11. Flinders Island
12. Hadspen
13. Devonport
14. Burnie
15. Stanley
16. King Island
17. Woolnorth
18. Cradle Mountain Lake St Clair National Park
19. Macquarie Harbour
20. Franklin-Gordon Wild Rivers National Park
21. Mount Field National Park
22. Bruny Island
23. Port Arthur pp474–5

Wineglass Bay in Freycinet National Park

❶ Hobart

Spread over seven hills between the banks of the Derwent River and the summit of Mount Wellington, Australia's second oldest city has an incredible waterfront location, similar to that of her "big sister", Sydney. Hobart began life on the waterfront and the maritime atmosphere is still an important aspect of the city. From Old Wharf, where the first arrivals settled, round to the fishing village of Battery Point, the area known as Sullivans Cove is still the hub of this cosmopolitan city. It is the centre of attention in late December every year as the finish line of the famous Sydney to Hobart yacht race.

Hobart and its docks nestled on the Derwent River

🏛 Narryna Heritage Museum
103 Hampden Rd, Battery Point. **Tel** (03) 6234 2791. **Open** 10am–4:30pm Tue–Sun (from noon Sun). **Closed** 1 Jan, Good Fri, 25 & 26 Dec. 🅿 ♿ **w** tmag.tas.gov.au

Inside an elegant 1834 Georgian house called Narryna, in Battery Point, this is the oldest folk museum in Australia. Beautiful grounds make a fine backdrop for an impressive collection of early Tasmanian pioneering relics.

🏛 Battery Point
This maritime village grew up on the hilly promontory adjacent to the early settlement and wharves. The site was originally home to a gun battery, positioned to ward off potential enemy invasions. The old guardhouse, built in 1818, now lies within a leafy park, just a few minutes' walk from Hampden Road with its antiques shops, art galleries, tea-rooms and restaurants.

Battery Point retains a strong sense of history, with its narrow gas-lit streets lined with tiny fishermen's and workers' houses, cottage gardens and colonial mansions and pubs.

Book online for the Hobart Historic Walk (2pm Wed–Sun), which departs from the Travel & Information Centre on Davey and Elizabeth streets.

🏛 Salamanca Place
Once the site of early colonial industries, from jam-making to metal foundry and flour milling, this graceful row of sandstone warehouses at Salamanca Place is now the heart of Hobart's lively atmosphere and creative spirit.

Mount Wellington towers above the buildings lining the waterfront, which have been converted into art galleries, antique stores and antiquarian book shops. The Salamanca Arts Centre houses artists' studios, theatres and galleries. The area also has some of the city's best pubs, cafés and restaurants (see pp534–5). The Salamanca Market is held every Saturday morning.

🏛 Castray Esplanade
Castray Esplanade was originally planned in the 19th century as a riverside walking track and it still provides the most pleasurable short stroll within the city. En route are the old colonial Commissariat Stores. These have been beautifully renovated for inner-city living, architects' offices and art galleries, focussing on Tasmanian arts and crafts.

🏛 Parliament House
Salamanca Place. **Tel** (03) 6212 2200. **Open** Mon–Fri. **Closed** public hols. ♿ 🅿 10am & 2pm non-sitting days.

One of the oldest civic buildings in Hobart, designed by John Lee Archer and built by convicts between 1835 and 1841. Partly open to the public.

🏛 Maritime Museum of Tasmania
Cnr Davey & Argyle sts. **Tel** (03) 6234 1427. **Open** 9am–5pm daily. **Closed** Good Fri, 25 Dec. 🅿 ♿ **w** maritimetas.org

Steeped in seafaring history, the museum is housed in the Carnegie Building, the former Hobart Public Library. It contains a fascinating collection of old relics, manuscripts, and voyage documents, as well as an important photographic collection which records Tasmania's maritime history.

The famous Saturday market in Salamanca Place

For hotels and restaurants in this area see pp496–7 and pp533–5

⬚ Constitution Dock
Davey St.
The main anchorage for fishing boats and yachts also serves as the finish line of the annual Sydney to Hobart Yacht Race. This famous race attracts an international field of competitors (see p45).

Constitution Dock borders the city and the old slum district of Wapping, which has now been redeveloped. Many of the old warehouses have been restored to include restaurants and cafés. One houses the idiosyncratic restaurant, the Drunken Admiral.

▥ Tasmanian Museum and Art Gallery
40 Macquarie St. Tel (03) 6211 4134. Open 10am–4pm Tue–Sun. Closed Good Fri, 25 Apr, 25 Dec. & ▣ ▣
W tmag.tas.gov.au

This 1863 building, designed by the city's best-known colonial architect, Henry Hunter, is now home to a fine collection of prints and paintings of Tasmania, Aboriginal artifacts, and botanical displays.

⬚ Hunter Street
Once joined to Hobart Town by a sandbar and known as Hunter Island, this historic harbour-side locale is an art and culture precinct. It is lined with colonial warehouses and was once the site of the Jones & Co. IXL jam factory. The heart of this redevelopment is the award-winning Henry Jones Art Hotel (see p497).

⬚ Theatre Royal
29 Campbell St. Tel (03) 6233 2299. ▣ for shows only. & ▣ tours 11am Mon, Wed, Fri; book ahead by phone. W theatreroyal.com.au

Built in 1837, this is the oldest theatre in Australia. Almost gutted by fire in the 1960s, the ornate decor has since been restored and can be admired during a guided tour.

⬚ The Tench Penitentiary Chapel Historic Site
Cnr Brisbane & Campbell sts. Tel (03) 6231 0911. Open 10am–2:30pm daily. Closed Good Fri, 25 Dec. ▣ ▣ obligatory, by appt 10am, 11:30am, 1pm, 2:30pm Mon, Tue, Thu & Fri; 1pm, 2:30pm Sat & Sun.

Once a barracks for convicts sent to Australia from the UK, this building was later the Hobart Gaol for more than 100 years. A guided tour takes in the former chapel, cells and gallows.

▥ Museum of Old and New Art (MONA)
655 Main Rd, Berriedale. Tel (03) 6277 9900. Open 10am–6pm Wed–Mon. & ▣ W mona.net.au

One of Hobart's main attractions, this musem carved out of a sandstone cliff houses a collection that ranges from ancient Egyptian mummies to some of the world's most unusual contemporary art.

Hobart City Centre

① Narryna Heritage Museum
② Battery Point
③ Salamanca Place
④ Castray Esplanade
⑤ Parliament House
⑥ Maritime Museum of Tasmania
⑦ Constitution Dock
⑧ Tasmanian Museum and Art Gallery
⑨ Hunter Street
⑩ Theatre Royal
⑪ The Tench Penitentiary Chapel Historic Site

For keys to symbols see back flap

Hop farm on the Derwent River in New Norfolk

❷ Richmond

🗺 1,600. 🚌 ℹ️ Old Hobart Town, Bridge St (03) 6260 2502.
🆆 richmondvillage.com.au

In the heart of the countryside, 26 km (16 miles) from Hobart, lies the quaint village of Richmond. This was the first area granted to free settlers from England for farming, and at its centre they established a township reminiscent of their homeland. Richmond now includes some of Australia's oldest colonial architecture. Most of the buildings were constructed by convicts, including the sandstone bridge built in 1823, the gaol of 1825 and the Roman Catholic Church of 1834.

Today, Richmond is a lively centre for rural artists and artisans. On the main street, between the old general store and post office, they occupy many of the historic homes.

❸ New Norfolk

🗺 5,500. 🚌 ℹ️ Circle St (03) 6261 3700. 🆆 newnorfolk.org

From Hobart, the Derwent River heads north, then veers west through the Derwent River Valley. The hop farms and oast houses along the willow-lined river are testimony to the area's history of brewing.

At the centre of the valley, 38 km (24 miles) from Hobart, is the town of New Norfolk. Many of the first settlers in the region abandoned the colonial settlement of Norfolk Island to come here, hence the name. One of Tasmania's classified historic towns, it contains many interesting buildings, such as the Bush Inn of 1815, which claims to be one of Australia's oldest licensed pubs.

Typical 19th-century building in Bothwell

❹ Bothwell

🗺 400. 🚌 ℹ️ Australasian Golf Museum, Market Place (03) 6259 4033.
🆆 ausgolfmuseum.com

Nestled in the Clyde River Valley, Bothwell's wide streets are set along a river of the same name, formerly known as the "Fat Doe" river after a town in Scotland. The area's names were assigned by early Scottish settlers, who arrived from Hobart Town in 1817 with their families and 18-l (5-gal) kegs of rum loaded on bullock wagons.

The town's heritage is now preserved with some 50 National Trust buildings dating from the 1820s, including the Castle Hotel, the Masonic Hall (now

Richmond Bridge, constructed with local sandstone

an art gallery), Bothwell Grange Guest House and the Old Schoolhouse, now home to the Australasian Golf Museum. The stone heads above the door of the Presbyterian St Luke's Church depict a Celtic god and goddess. Even the town's golf course has a claim on history as the oldest in Australia.

The town lies at the centre of the historic sheep-farming district of Bothwell, stretching along Lakes Hwy from the southern midlands to the famous trout fishing area of the Great Lakes. There are several cheese-makers and a renowned whisky distillery in the area, too. It is also the gateway to the ruggedly beautiful Central Plateau Conservation Area – a tableland that rises abruptly from the flat countryside to an average height of 600 m (nearly 2,000 ft).

❺ Oatlands

🗺 550. 🚌 ℹ️ Heritage Highway Visitor Centre, 1 Mill Lane (03) 6254 1212.

Oatlands was one of a string of military stations established in 1813 during the construction of the old Midlands Hwy by convict chain gangs. Colonial Governor Lachlan Macquarie ordered the building of the road in 1811, to connect the southern settlement of Hobart *(see pp464–5)* with the northern settlement of Launceston *(see p468)*. During a later trip, he chose locations for the townships en route, naming them after places in the British Isles. The road ran through the area

Distinctive façade of the 1837 Callington Flour Mill, in Oatlands

Coles Bay, backed by the Hazards Mountains, Freycinet Peninsula

of Tasmania corresponding in name and geography to that of the British Midlands region, giving it its original name, but since the 1990s it has been dubbed the Heritage Hwy.

Oatlands soon became one of the colonial coaching stops for early travellers. Today, it has the richest endowment of Georgian buildings in the country, mostly made of local sandstone, including the 1829 courthouse and St Peter's Church (1838). As a result, the township is classified by the National Trust. Its most distinctive building, the Callington Flour Mill, still operates, with tours on the hour between 10am and 3pm daily.

❻ Freycinet National Park

🚌 from Bicheno. ℹ️ Visitors' Centre (03) 6256 7000. **Open** Nov–Apr: 8am–5pm daily; May–Oct: 9am–4pm daily. **Closed** 25 Dec.
🅦 parks.tas.gov.au

The Freycinet Peninsula on the east coast of Tasmania is a long, narrow neck of land jutting south, dominated by the granite peaks of the Hazards Mountain Range. Named after an early French maritime explorer, the peninsula consists of ocean beaches on its eastern rim and secluded coves and inlets to the west. The fishing village of Coles Bay lies in the largest cove, backed by the Hazards.

Freycinet National Park on the tip of the peninsula is criss-crossed with walking tracks along beaches, over mountains,

around headlands and across lagoons. The most popular walk is Wineglass Bay – a short, steep trip up and over the saddle of the mountains. The blue waters of the bay are cupped against a crescent of golden sand, which inspired the name.

The drive up the east coast is a highlight of Tasmania. There are superb ocean views and marshlands inhabited by black swans. Small towns such as Orford and Swansea are good for overnight stays.

❼ Bicheno

🗺 850. 🚌 ℹ️ 41B Foster St (03) 6375 1500. 🅦 bicheno.com.au

Together with Coles Bay, Bicheno is the holiday centre of Tasmania's east coast. In summer, the bay is very popular due to its sheltered location, which means temperatures are always a few degrees warmer than elsewhere in the state.

The area also includes Tasmania's smallest national park, the 16,080-ha (39,700-acre) Douglas Apsley National Park. It contains the state's largest dry sclerophyll forest, patches of rainforest, river gorges, waterfalls and spectacular views along the coast. This varied landscape can be taken in along a three-day north to south walking track through the park. The north of the park is only accessible by 4WD. Other attractions in the area include the Apsley Gorge Winery and a 3-km long penguin breeding colony.

Man-O-Ross Hotel at the Four Corners of Ross crossroads

❽ Ross

🏠 425. 🚌 ℹ️ Tasmanian Wool Centre, Church St (03) 6381 5466.
w taswoolcentre.com.au

Set on the banks of the Macquarie River, Ross, like Oatlands (see p467), was once a military station and coaching stop along the Midlands Hwy. It lies at the heart of the richest sheep farming district in Tasmania, internationally recognized for its fine merino wool. Some of the large rural homesteads in the area have remained within the same families since the 1820s when the village was settled.

The town's most famous sight is Ross Bridge, built by convict labour and opened in 1836. It features 186 unique carvings by convict sculptor Daniel Herbert, who was given a Queen's Pardon for his intricate work. The town centres on its historic crossroads, the Four Corners of Ross: "Temptation, Damnation, Salvation and Recreation". These are represented respectively on each corner by the Man-O-Ross Hotel, the jail, the church and the town hall.

Man O'Ross hotel sign

❾ Ben Lomond National Park

🎿 when ski slopes are open.
ℹ️ National Parks & Wildlife Service, 167 Westbury Rd Prospect, Launceston (03) 6777 2179. 🐾

In the hinterlands between the Midlands and the east coast, 50 km (30 miles) southeast of Launceston, Ben Lomond is the highest mountain in northern Tasmania and home to one of the state's two main ski slopes. The 16,000-ha (40,000-acre) national park surrounding the mountain covers an alpine plateau of barren and dramatic scenery, with views stretching over the northeast of the state. The vegetation includes alpine daisies and carnivorous sundew plants. The park is also home to wallabies, wombats and possums. From Conara Junction on the Heritage Hwy, take the Esk Main Road east before turning off towards Ben Lomond National Park.

The mountain's foothills have been devastated by decades of mining and forestry, and many of the townships, such as Rossarden and Avoca, have since suffered an economic decline. The road through the South Esk Valley along the Esk River loops back to the valley's main centre of Fingal. From here, you can continue through the small township of St Marys before joining the Tasman Hwy and travelling up the east coast.

❿ Launceston

🏠 71,400. ✈️ 🚌 ℹ️ Visitor Information Centre, 68–72 Cameron St 1800 651 827.

In colonial days, the coach ride between Tasmania's capital, Hobart, and the township of Launceston took a full day, but today the 200-km (125-mile) route is flat and direct. Nestling in the Tamar River Valley, Launceston was settled in 1804 and is Australia's third-oldest city. It has a charming ambience of old buildings, parks, gardens, riverside walks, craft galleries and hilly streets lined with weatherboard houses. The

Alpine plateau in Ben Lomond National Park, backed by Ben Lomond Mountain

For hotels and restaurants in this area see pp496–7 and pp533–5

Heritage buildings in central Launceston

Queen Victoria Museum and Art Gallery has the country's largest provincial display of colonial art, along with an impressive modern collection. It also shows Aboriginal and convict relics, and has displays on minerals, flora and fauna of the region.

Cataract Gorge Reserve is alive with birds, wallabies, pademelons, potoroos and bandicoots, only a 15-minute walk from the city centre. A chairlift, believed to have the longest central span in the world, provides a striking aerial overview.

In nearby Underwood is the award-winning **Treetops Adventure**, which combines the tranquillity of the forest with adrenalin-fueled canopy tours. These take place in all weathers, and there is also a night-time ride. Visitors enjoy a unique view of the beautiful forest environment from above.

Queen Victoria Museum and Art Gallery
Museum: 2 Wellington St, Royal Pk, Launceston; Gallery: 2 Invermay Rd, Inveresk. **Tel** (03) 6323 3777. **Open** 10am–4pm daily. **Closed** Good Fri, 25 Dec. **qvmag.tas.gov.au**

Treetops Adventure
66 Hollybank Road, off the Launceston–Lilydale Rd, Underwood. **Tel** (03) 6395 1390. **Open** 9am–5pm daily. **treetopsadventure. com.au**

Environs
In the 1830s, the Norfolk Plains was a farmland district owned mainly by wealthy settlers who had been enticed to the area by land grants. The small town of **Longford**, with its historic inns and churches, is still the centre of a rich agricultural district. It also has the greatest concentration of colonial mansions in the state. Many, such as Woolmers and Brickendon, are open for public tours.

Cape Barren geese in the Patriarch Sanctuary on Cape Barren Island

⓫ Flinders Island

from Launceston, Melbourne. from Bridport. Flinders Island Tourism (03) 6359 5002.

On the northeastern tip of Tasmania, in the waters of the Bass Strait, Flinders Island is the largest within the Furneaux Island Group. These 50 or so dots in the ocean are all that remains of the land bridge which once spanned the strait to the continental mainland (see pp26–7).

Flinders Island was also the destination for 133 Tasmanian Aborigines. With the consent of the British administration, the Reverend George Augustus Robinson brought them here in the 1830s. His aim was to "save" Tasmania's Aboriginal population from extinction by civilizing them according to European traditions and converting them to Christianity. In 1847, however, greatly diminished by disease and despair, the 47 survivors were transferred to Oyster Cove, a sacred Aboriginal site south of Hobart, and the plan was deemed a failure. Within a few decades, all full-blooded Tasmanian Aborigines had died.

Much of Flinders is now preserved as a natural reserve, including Strezelecki National Park, which is a particularly popular area with hikers. Off the island's south coast is Cape Barren Island, home to the Patriarch Sanctuary, a protected geese reserve.

Flinders Island can be reached by air from Launceston and Melbourne. Alternatively, there is also a leisurely ferry trip aboard the *Matthew Flinders*, which sets sail from the small coastal town of Bridport.

Entally House in Hadspen

⑫ Hadspen

🏠 2,100. 🚌 ℹ️ Visitor Information Centre, 68–72 Cameron St, Launceston 1800 651 827.

Heading west along the Bass Highway, a string of historic towns pepper the countryside from Longford through to Deloraine, surrounded by the Great Western Tiers Mountains. The tiny town of Hadspen is a picturesque strip of Georgian cottages and buildings which include an old 1845 coaching house.

The town is also home to one of Tasmania's most famous historic homes open to the public. Built in 1819 on the bank of the South Esk River, the **Entally House**, with its gracious veranda, has its own chapel, stables, horse-drawn carriages and 19th-century furnishings.

Period furniture in Entally House

🏛️ **Entally House**
782 Meander Valley Rd, via Hadspen. **Tel** (03) 6393 3200. **Open** 10am–4pm Thu–Mon. **Closed** 1 Jan, May–Aug, 25–28 Dec. 🅿️ ♿ 🌐 entally.com.au

⑬ Devonport

🏠 30,500. ✈️ 🚌 🛳️
ℹ️ Devonport Visitor Centre, 92 Formby Rd (03) 6424 4466.

Named after the county of Devon in England, the state's third-largest city is strategically sited as a river and sea port. It lies at the junction of the Mersey River and the Bass Strait, on the north coast. The dramatic rocky headland of Mersey Bluff is 1 km (half a mile) from the city centre, linked by a coastal reserve and parklands. Here, Aboriginal rock paintings and carvings can be seen on a short, self-guided walk from near the lighthouse. The walk route circles around the former Tiagarra Aboriginal Cultural Centre and Museum, which is closed to the public but in negotiations to reopen in the future.

From Devonport, the overnight car and passenger ferry *Spirit of Tasmania* sails to the Port of Melbourne on the mainland several times each week. With a local airport, Devonport is also an excellent starting point for touring northern Tasmania. Heading northwest, the old coast road offers unsurpassed views of the Bass Strait.

⑭ Burnie

🏠 20,000. ✈️ 🚌 ℹ️ 2 Bass Highway (03) 6430 5831.

Further along the northern coast from Devonport is Tasmania's fourth-largest city, founded in 1829. Along its main streets are many attractive 19th-century buildings decorated with wrought ironwork. Previously, Burnie's prosperity centred on a thriving wood-pulping industry. The area's history throughout the 19th and 20th centuries is showcased at the Burnie Regional Museum. Displays depict the lives of European settlers and include a replica shoe-marker's shop and blacksmith's forge. To enjoy some of the region's food, you can visit the Cheese Shop, which makes a variety of award-winning wares, from creamy Camemberts to sharp blue cheeses. Burnie also has a number of gardens, including Fern Glade, where platypuses are often seen feeding at dusk and dawn. Situated on Emu Bay, the area's natural attractions include forest reserves, fossil cliffs, waterfalls and canyons and panoramic ocean views from nearby Round Hill.

"The Nut" chairlift in Stanley

⑮ Stanley

🏠 470. 🚌 ℹ️ Stanley Visitors Centre, 45 Main Rd (03) 6458 1330.

The rocky promontory of Circular Head, known locally as "the Nut", rises 152 m (500 ft) above sea level and looms over the fishing village of Stanley. A chairlift up the rock face offers striking views of the area.

Stanley's quiet main street runs towards the wharf, lined with fishermen's cottages and many bluestone buildings dating from the 1840s. Stanley also contains numerous top-quality bed-and-breakfasts and eateries serving fresh, local seafood *(see p535)*.

Nearby, **Highfield House** was the original headquarters of the Van Diemen's Land Company, a London-based agricultural holding set up in 1825.

The home and grounds of its colonial overseer are now open for public tours.

🏠 **Highfield House**
Green Hills Rd, via Stanley. **Tel** (03) 6458 1100. **Open** 9:30am–4:30pm daily. **Closed** 25 Dec. 🅿 Ⓦ historic-highfield.com.au

⓰ King Island

🛫 ℹ Tasmanian Travel and Information Centre, cnr Davey & Elizabeth sts, Hobart (03) 6238 4222.

Lying off the northwestern coast of Tasmania in the Bass Strait, King Island is a popular location for wildlife lovers. Muttonbirds and elephant seals are among the unusual attractions.

Divers also frequent the island, fascinated by the ship-wrecks that lie nearby. The island is also noted for its cheese, beef and seafood.

⓱ Woolnorth

Via Smithton. ℹ Tasmanian Travel and Information Centre, cnr Davey & Elizabeth sts, Hobart (03) 6238 4222. 📷 obligatory.

The huge sheep, cattle and dairy farming property on the outskirts of Smithton is the only remaining land holding of the Van Diemen's Land Company. The last four Tasmanian tigers held in captivity were caught in the bush backing on to Wool-north in 1908. Day-long tours

Elephant seal bull on King Island – males can weigh up to 3 tonnes

of the property, booked in advance, include a lunch of local beef fillet and a trip to Cape Grim, known for the cleanest air in the world.

⓲ Cradle Mountain Lake St Clair National Park

🏠 Cradle Mountain, Lake St Clair. ℹ Cradle Mountain (03) 6492 1110 (shuttle from gate is every 20 mins in summer, infrequent at other times). Lake St Clair (03) 6289 1172. 🅿 ♿

The distinctive jagged peaks of Cradle Mountain are now recognized as an international symbol of the state's natural environment. The second-highest mountain in Tasmania reaches 1,560 m (5,100 ft) at the northern end of the 161,000-ha (400,000-acre) national park. The park then stretches 80 km (50 miles) south to the shores

of Lake St Clair, the deepest freshwater lake in Australia.

In 1922, the area became a national park, founded by Austrian nature enthusiast Gustav Weindorfer. His memory lives on in his forest home Waldheim Chalet, now a heritage lodge in Weindorfer's Forest. Nearby at Ronny Creek is the registration point for the celebrated Overland Track, which traverses the park through scenery ranging from rainforest, alpine moors, buttongrass plains and waterfall valleys. Walking the track takes an average of six days, stopping overnight in tents or huts. At the halfway mark is Mount Ossa, the state's highest peak at 1,617 m (5,300 ft). In May, the park is ablaze with the autumn colours of Tasmania's deciduous beech *Nothofagus gunnii*, commonly known as "Fagus" *(see p458)*.

Dove Lake backed by the jagged peaks of Cradle Mountain

Boats sailing on the deceptively calm waters of Macquarie Harbour

⑲ Macquarie Harbour

🚌 Strahan. 🛈 The Esplanade, Strahan (03) 6472 6800 or 1800 352 200.

Off the wild, western coast of Tasmania there is nothing but vast stretches of ocean until the southern tip of Argentina, on the other side of the globe. The region bears the full brunt of the "Roaring Forties" – the name given to the tremendous winds that whip southwesterly off the Southern Ocean.

In this hostile environment, Tasmania's Aborigines survived for thousands of years before European convicts were sent here in the 1820s and took over the land. Their harsh and isolated settlement was a penal station on Sarah Island, situated in the middle of Macquarie Harbour.

The name of the harbour's mouth, "Hell's Gates", reflects conditions endured by both seamen and convicts – ship-wrecks, drownings, suicides and murders all occurred here. Abandoned in 1833 for the "model prison" of Port Arthur (see pp474–5), Sarah Island and its penal settlement ruins can be viewed on a guided boat tour available from the fishing port of Strahan.

Strahan grew up around an early timber industry supported by convict labour. It became well-known in the early 1980s when protesters from across Australia came to Strahan to fight government plans to flood the wild and beautiful Franklin River for a hydroelectric scheme. A fascinating exhibition at the visitor centre in Strahan charts the drama of Australia's most famous environmental protest.

Strahan today is one of Tasmania's loveliest towns, with its old timber buildings, scenic port and natural backdrop of fretted mountains and dense bushland. One of its main attractions is a restored 1896 railway, which travels 35 km (22 miles) across rivers and mountains to the old mining settlement at Queenstown.

⑳ Franklin-Gordon Wild Rivers National Park

🚌 Strahan. 🛈 The Esplanade, Strahan (03) 6472 6800.
🌐 parks.tas.gov.au

One of Australia's great wild river systems flows through southwest Tasmania. This spectacular region consists of high ranges and deep gorges. The Franklin-Gordon Wild Rivers National Park extends southeast from Macquarie Harbour and is one of four national parks in the western part of Tasmania that make up the Tasmanian Wilderness World Heritage Area (see pp30–31). The park takes its name from the Franklin and Gordon rivers, both of which were saved by conservationists in 1983.

Within the park's 442,000 ha (1,090,000 acres) are vast tracts of cool temperate rainforest, as well as waterfalls and dolerite- and quartzite-capped mountains. The flora within the park is as varied as the landscape, with impenetrable horizontal scrub, lichen-coated trees, pandani plants and the endemic conifers, King William, celery top and Huon pines. The easiest way into this largely trackless wilderness is via a boat cruise from Strahan. Visitors can disembark and take a short walk to see a 2,000-year-old Huon pine. The park also contains the rugged peak of

The Tasmanian wilderness at the Franklin-Gordon Wild Rivers National Park

Idyllic, deserted beach on the rugged Bruny Island

Frenchmans Cap, accessible to experienced bushwalkers. The Franklin River is also renowned for its rapids.

The Wild Way, linking Hobart with the west coast, runs through the park. Sections of the river and forest can be reached from the main road along short tracks. Longer walks into the heart of the park require a higher level of survival skills and equipment.

Russell Falls in Mount Field National Park

㉑ Mount Field National Park

🛈 Lake Dobson Rd, at entrance to the Park, (03) 6288 1149.

Little more than 70 km (45 miles) from Hobart along the Maydena Road, Mount Field National Park's proximity and beauty make it a popular location with nature-loving tourists. As a day trip from Hobart, it offers easy access to a diversity of Tasmanian vegetation and wildlife along well-maintained walking tracks.

The most popular walk is also the shortest: the 10-minute trail to Russell Falls starts out from just within the park's entrance through a temperate rainforest environment. Lake Dobson car park is 15 km (9 miles) from the park's entrance up a steep gravel path. This is the beginning of several other walks.

The 10-km (6-mile) walk to Tarn Shelf is a bushwalker's paradise, especially in autumn, when the glacial lakes, mountains and valleys are spectacularly highlighted by the red-orange hues of the deciduous beech trees. Longer trails lead up to the higher peaks of Mount Field West and Mount Mawson, southern Tasmania's premier ski slope.

㉒ Bruny Island

Travel by car only – no public transport or taxis on Bruny Island.
🛈 Bruny D'Entrecasteaux Visitors' Centre, Ferry Road (inside Mermaid Café), Kettering (03) 6267 4494.

On Hobart's back doorstep, yet a world away in landscape and atmosphere, the Huon Valley and D'Entrecasteaux Channel can be enjoyed over several hours or days. In total, the trip south from Hobart, through the town of Huonville, the Hartz Mountains and Southport, the southernmost town in the country, is only 100 km (60 miles). On the other side of the channel are the orchards, craft outlets and vineyards around Cygnet.

Truganini, the Bruny Island Aborigine

The attractive marina of Kettering, just 40 minutes' drive from Hobart, is the departure point for a regular ferry service to Bruny Island.

The name Bruny Island actually applies to two islands joined by a narrow neck. The south island townships of Adventure Bay and Alonnah are only a half-hour drive from the ferry terminal in the north. Once home to a thriving colonial whaling industry, Bruny Island is now a haven for bird-watchers, boaters, swimmers and camel riders along its sheltered bays, beaches and lagoons.

Unfortunately, Bruny Island also has a sadder side to its history. Truganini, of the Wuenonne people of Bruny Island, is said to have been one of Tasmania's last full-blooded Aborigines. It was also from the aptly named Missionary Bay on the island that Reverend Robinson began his ill-fated campaign to round up the indigenous inhabitants of Tasmania for incarceration (see p469).

㉓ Port Arthur

Port Arthur was established in 1830 as a timber station and a prison settlement for repeat offenders. While transportation to the island colony from the mainland ceased in 1853, the prison remained in operation until 1877, by which time some 12,000 men had passed through what was commonly regarded as the harshest institution of its kind in the British Empire. Punishments included incarceration in the Separate Prison, a building set apart from the main penitentiary, where inmates were subjected to sensory deprivation and extreme isolation in the belief that such methods promoted "moral reform". Between 1979 and 1986, a conservation project was undertaken to restore the prison ruins. The 40-ha (100-acre) site is now Tasmania's most popular tourist attraction.

Commandant's House
One of the first houses at Port Arthur, this cottage has now been restored and furnished in early 19th-century style.

KEY

① **The Guard Tower** was constructed in 1835 in order to prevent escapes from the settlement and pilfering from the Commissariat Store, which the tower overlooked.

② **The Semaphore** was a series of flat, mounted planks that could be arranged in different configurations, in order to send messages to Hobart and across the peninsula.

③ **The Paupers' Mess** was the dining area for poor ex-convicts.

④ **Museum and café**

⑤ **The Separate Prison** was influenced by Pentonville Prison in London. Completed in 1854, the prison was thought to provide "humane" punishment. Convicts lived in 50 separate cells in silence and anonymity, referred to by number not by name.

⑥ **Trentham Cottage** was owned by the Trentham family who lived in Port Arthur after the site closed. The refurbished interior is decorated with early 20th-century furnishings.

⑦ **Government Cottage** was built in 1853 and was used by visiting dignitaries and government officials.

MASON COVE

To Jetty, Dock Yard and Isle of the Dead Cemetery

JETTY ROAD

★ **Penitentiary**
This building was thought to be the largest in Australia at the time of its construction in 1844. Originally a flour mill, it was converted into a penitentiary in the 1850s and housed almost 500 prisoners in dormitories and cells.

For hotels and restaurants in this area see pp496–7 and pp533–5

VISITORS' CHECKLIST

Practical Information
Hwy A9.
Tel 1800 659 101 or (03) 6251 2310.
 portarthur.org.au
Open 9am–dusk daily.

Hospital

This sandstone building was completed in 1842 with four wards of 18 beds each. The basement housed the kitchen with its own oven, and a morgue, known as the "dead room".

Asylum

By 1872, Port Arthur's asylum housed more than 100 mentally ill or senile convicts. When the settlement closed, it became the town hall, but now serves as a museum and café.

0 metres	50
0 yards	50

HAMP STREET

LETON STREET

CHURCH STREET

Church

Completed in 1836, Port Arthur's church was never consecrated because it was used by all denominations. The building was gutted by fire in 1884, but the ruins are now fully preserved.

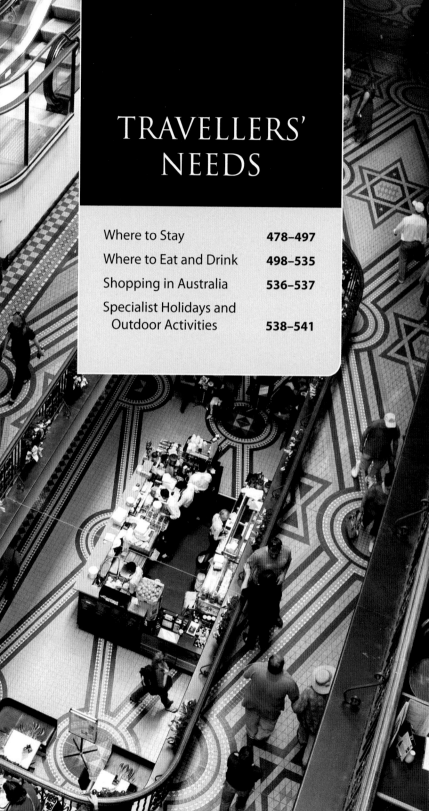

TRAVELLERS' NEEDS

WHERE TO STAY

The wide range of places to stay in Australia is a reflection of the country's size and diversity, as well as its position as a major tourist destination. There are tropical island resorts, luxury and boutique city hotels, ski lodges, converted shearers' quarters on vast sheep stations, colonial cottage bed and breakfasts, self-catering apartments, youth hostels, houseboats and, of course, all the usual international chains. Visitors will find accommodation options to suit every need and budget – from simple beds for the night to glitzy all-inclusive holiday resorts.

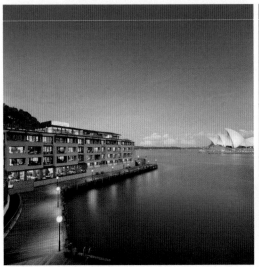

The superb harbour-front location of the Park Hyatt Sydney hotel *(see p482)*

Gradings and Facilities

State motoring organizations, some state and regional tourism bodies, and the **STAR Ratings** scheme rank hotels with one to five stars as a useful indicator of standards and facilities. **Ecotourism Australia** runs a certification scheme for environmentally friendly properties.

In city hotels, resorts and motels, air-conditioning in the summer and heating in the winter are almost always provided. Other standard features include tea- and coffee-making facilities, televisions, radios, bar fridges and ensuite shower rooms; bathtubs are less common. A room for two may have either a double or queen bed or twin beds. Luxury accommodation often features on-site swimming pools, exercise facilities, and a bar or restaurant.

Prices

Prices for accommodation vary according to the location and the facilities on offer. The presidential suite in a luxury city or resort hotel may have a four-figure daily rate, while a night in a backpacker hostel will generally cost less than A$35 for a bed in a shared room or A$90 for a private room. Budget motels and the majority of B&Bs operate within the A$120–A$220 range. Prices may increase slightly during peak seasons and come down during the low season. Tipping is not expected and is discretionary.

Bookings

Pressure on room availability can be high, especially in the capital cities and the coastal destinations in Queensland. For school holidays and major cultural and sporting events *(see pp44–7)*, it is advisable to book well in advance.

Local and state tourist offices can help with or even make bookings. Major airlines, agents and operators also often have discounted packages on offer *(see pp554–7)*.

Children

Travelling with children is relatively easy throughout the country. Most forms of accommodation will provide a rollaway or sofa bed or cot in family rooms, often at no extra charge; enquire about any special rates in advance. However, be aware

Impressive manicured gardens of Canberra's Hyatt Hotel *(see p485)*

The pool terrace at the Coral Sea Resort in Airlie Beach *(see p486)*

that some of the country house hotels and exclusive accommodation and island resorts are strictly child-free zones.

Disabled Travellers

Australian building codes stipulate that any new buildings or renovations must provide facilities and accessibility for the disabled. It is always advisable, however, to check in advance.

Luxury Hotels and Resorts

In the state capitals, well-known international names – **Hyatt**, **Hilton**, **InterContinental**, **Four Seasons**, **Sheraton** and **Westin** – stand side by side with local institutions such as The Hotel Windsor in Melbourne *(see p493)*. Major beach destinations abound with luxury resorts.

Chain Hotels

Australia's chain hotels and motels offer reliable and comfortable, if occasionally bland, accommodation. Some of the best-known chains are **Choice Hotels**, **Metro Hotels**, **Best Western**, **Travelodge**, **Silver Needle** (formerly Country Comfort) and **Accor**.

Country House Hotels

Ranging from elegant mansions to simple cottages, country house hotels can be found throughout the country. They offer the comforts of home and a more rustic experience than chain hotels.

Among the best country houses are those found in the wine regions *(see pp40–41)*, around the old gold fields *(see pp58–9)* and in Tasmania *(see pp456–75)*. Eco-lodges offering

a close-to-nature experience can be found in beautiful wilderness areas, including islands and coastal forests.

Leather armchairs in the Globe bar at the Langham Sydney hotel *(see p482)*

Backpacker Hotels and Youth Hostels

Despite their budget prices and basic facilities, most accommodation options for young backpackers are clean and comfortable, though standards can vary widely in different areas. The internationally renowned **Youth Hostel Association (YHA)** caters for all ages and covers all the major cities, ski resorts and many of the national parks. There are also numerous independent hostels. The backpacker scene changes quickly, so ask other travellers for recommendations.

While it is necessary to book at some hostels, others offer beds on a first-come-first-served basis. Apartments, rooms and dormitories are all available. Note that dormitories may sometimes be mixed sex, so check in advance, if needed.

Funky, contemporary suite at the Tolarno Hotel in St Kilda, Melbourne *(see p494)*

"The Grand" ballroom in the Hotel Windsor, Melbourne *(see p493)*

offering a unique perspective on rural Australian life. Some are near major cities, while others are in the vast Outback *(see pp32–3)*. Accommodation may be in traditional shearers' or cattle herders' quarters, or within the home. Ask state tourist offices for details.

Another interesting and more relaxing holiday option is to rent a houseboat on the vast Murray River, which crosses from New South Wales and Victoria to South Australia. An international driving licence is the only requirement to be your own riverboat captain.

Boutique Hotels and B&Bs

In Australia, the term "boutique" is used rather loosely to describe a small hotel or motel. The best offer luxury accommodation and an intimate atmosphere.

Australian bed and breakfasts (B&Bs), many in heritage-listed premises, tend to be of a high standard. They offer personalized accommodation and the best way to experience Australian life. Many have only one or two guestrooms and offer all the comforts of home. Some, instead of serving breakfast, offer guests provisions to prepare their own.

Self-Catering Apartments

Self-catering apartments usually come with full kitchen and laundry facilities. Within cities, some apartments also cater for business travellers. Prices are generally on a par with the major chain motels.

Pub Accommodation

In Australia, "hotel" is the historic term for a pub (originally known as public houses). Many pubs offer accommodation. The quality can vary and they can be noisy, especially if the pub has live music, but they are usually good value for money.

Farm Stays and Houseboats

Many farms and sheep and cattle stations welcome visitors to stay,

Camping and Caravan Parks

Camping and caravan sites are found throughout the country, most of them dotted along the vast coastline and in the inland national parks. They offer a cheap and idyllic way of enjoying the natural beauty and wildlife of Australia. Many camp sites don't insist on advance bookings, but some require a permit. Holiday parks often have on-site vans and cabins for rent at relatively low prices, although there are increasingly high end offerings too. Facilities usually include laundry and shower blocks and a small general store for provisions.

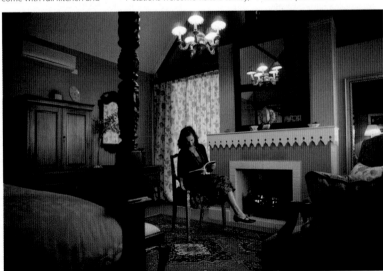

Comfortable room at Glen Isla House on Phillip Island *(see p496)*

A permanent tent in Wilpena Pound Resort, Wilpena *(see p492)*

Recommended Hotels

The hotel listings in this book offer a selection of recommended places to stay throughout the country across a range of budgets. Divided into 17 geographical areas corresponding to the chapters in this guide, the entries are then organized by town and price. Hotels listed as Value for Money are places that offer more than would usually be expected for the price – whether that's luxury toiletries, free airport transfers, Wi-Fi access or a convenient central location. Places listed as "Rural" are hotels, lodges, cottages and camps that are found in farmland, wilderness or the Outback. "Beach and Coast" accommodation have an enviable position near the sea. "Character" hotels are usually smaller guesthouses with additional charm and a friendly welcome; some are housed in a heritage building. Entries highlighted as "DK Choice" offer something extra special, whether that's a stunning location, notable history, excellent facilities and service, or a combination of factors. Whatever the reason, each one offers a memorable stay.

DIRECTORY

Grading and Facilities

Ecotourism Australia
w ecotourism.org.au

STAR Ratings
w starratings.com.au

Luxury Hotels and Resorts

Four Seasons
Tel 1800 222 200
or (02) 9250 3100 (Sydney).
w fourseasons.com

Hilton
Tel 1800 024 766.
w hilton.com

Hyatt
Tel 131 234.
w hyatt.com

InterContinental
Tel 138 388.
w ihg.com

Sheraton
Tel 1800 073 535.
w starwoodhotels.com

Westin
Tel 1800 656 535.
w starwoodhotels.com

Chain Hotels

Accor Hotels
Tel 1300 656 565.
w accorhotels.com.au

Best Western
Tel 131 779.
w bestwestern.com.au

Choice Hotels
Tel 132 400 or 1800 116 004. w choicehotels.com

Metro Hotels
Tel 1800 004 321.
w metrohotels.com.au

Silver Needle Hotels
Tel 1300 272 132. w silver needlehotels.com

Travelodge
Tel 1300 886 886.
w tfehotels.com

Backpacker Hotels and Youth Hostels

Youth Hostel Association (YHA)
Tel (02) 9261 1111
or 9218 9090.
w yha.com.au

Tourist Offices

Australian Capital Tourism
Regatta Point, Barrine Drive, Parkes, Canberra, ACT. **Tel** (02) 6205 0044.
w visitcanberra.com.au

South Australian Tourism Commission
9 James Place (off Rundle Mall), Adelaide, SA.
Tel 1300 764 227 or (08) 8463 4500.
w southaustralia.com

Tourism Australia
Sydney: **Tel** (02) 9360 1111. w australia.com
UK: Australia House, 6th Floor, Melbourne Place, Strand, London WC2B 4LA. **Tel** (020) 7379 4334 or +61 2 9360 1111.
USA: 6100 Center Dr, Los Angeles, CA 90045.
Tel (310) 695 3200.

Tourism NSW
55 Harrington St, Sydney, NSW.
Tel (02) 8273 0000.
w visitnsw.com

Tourism Queensland
Level 10, 30 Makerston St, Brisbane, QLD 4000.
Tel (07) 3535 3535.
w queensland.com

Tourism Tasmania
Level 3, 15 Murray St, Hobart, Tasmania.
Tel (03) 6115 5334.
w discovertasmania.com.au

Tourism Top End
Cnr Smith and Bennett sts, Darwin, NT.
Tel 1300 138 886 or (08) 8980 6000.
w tourismtopend.com.au

Tourism Victoria
2 Swanston St, Melbourne, VIC.
Tel (03) 9653 9777.
w visitvictoria.com

Tourism Western Australia
2 Mill St, Perth, WA 6000.
Tel 1300 361 351
or (08) 9483 1111.
w westernaustralia.com

Places to Stay

Sydney

The Rocks and Circular Quay

Lord Nelson Brewery Hotel $$
Character
19 Kent St, NSW 2000
Tel *(02) 9251 4044* **Map** 1 A2
W lordnelsonbrewery.com
The top floor of this convivial pub offers simple but cosy bedrooms with stone walls.

Sydney Harbour YHA $$
Hostel
110 Cumberland St, NSW 2000
Tel *(02) 8272 0900* **Map** 1 B2
W yha.com.au
Modern and comfortable hostel. The multishare or double rooms all have ensuites. A roof terrace provides top-dollar harbour views.

Holiday Inn $$$
Luxury
55 George St, NSW 2000
Tel *(02) 9252 0524* **Map** 1 B2
W ihg.com
Small enough to provide personal attention. Good amenities and a spectacular view from the rooftop.

The Langham Sydney $$$
Luxury
89–113 Kent St, NSW 2000
Tel *(02) 9256 2222* **Map** 1 A2
W sydney.langhamhotels.com.au
This celebrated top-of-the-range hotel is tastefully furnished with antiques and fine artworks.

Park Hyatt Sydney $$$
Luxury
7 Hickson Rd, NSW 2000
Tel *(02) 9256 1234* **Map** 1 B1
W sydney.park.hyatt.com
Top class hotel decorated with contemporary Australian art. Boasts Opera House views from many rooms.

Pier One Sydney Harbour $$$
Luxury
11 Hickson Rd, Walsh Bay, NSW 2000
Tel *(02) 8298 9999* **Map** 1 B1
W pieronesydneyharbour.com.au
Housed in a heritage building on a 1912 finger wharf, this hotel has crisp, sleek decor in neutral shades.

Shangri-La Sydney $$$
Luxury
176 Cumberland St, NSW 2000
Tel *(02) 9250 6000* **Map** 1 A3
W shangri-la.com
All the luxury and style one can expect from this brand, with great harbour views from higher floors.

City Centre and Darling Harbour

Railway Square YHA $$
Character
8–10 Lee St, NSW 2000
Tel *(02) 9281 9666* **Map** 4 E5
W yha.com.au
Unique hostel adjoining Central Station. Guests can sleep in a converted railway carriage and chill in the great spa pool.

Song Hotel Hyde Park $$
Value for Money
5–11 Wentworth Ave, NSW 2000
Tel *(02) 9264 2451* **Map** 4 F3
W songhotels.com.au
Modest but stylishly decorated hotel. Shared kitchen and laundry. Breakfast is included in the price.

The Darling $$$
Luxury
80 Pyrmont St, NSW 2009
Tel *(02) 9777 9000* **Map** 3 B1
W star.com.au
Located within the Star Casino complex. The upscale rooms all have floor-to-ceiling windows.

DK Choice

Establishment Hotel $$$
Boutique
5 Bridge Ln, NSW 2000
Tel *(02) 9240 3100* **Map** 1 B3
W merivale.com.au
Historic character meets contemporary style and elegance at this hip celebrity favourite. Rooms and suites boast marble or stone bathrooms, and either a lively or a tranquil colour scheme. Some of the city's best places to eat and drink can be found downstairs. Soundproofing ensures a peaceful stay.

Hilton Sydney $$$
Luxury
488 George St, NSW 2000
Tel *(02) 9266 2000* **Map** 1 B5
W hiltonsydney.com.au
A reliable choice with high standards. Quality furnishings and a fantastic health club.

Meriton World Tower $$$
Self-catering
91–95 Liverpool St, NSW 2000
Tel *(02) 8263 7500* **Map** 4 E3
W meritonapartments.com.au
Smart, serviced two- or three-bed apartments in Sydney's tallest residential building. Dazzling views.

Novotel Sydney on Darling Harbour $$$
Luxury
100 Murray St, NSW 2009
Tel *(02) 9934 0000* **Map** 3 C2
W noveldarlingharbour.com.au
This towering modern structure is a family-friendly luxury hotel. Outdoor tennis court and pool.

Sheraton on the Park $$$
Luxury
161 Elizabeth St, NSW 2000
Tel *(02) 9286 6000* **Map** 1 B5
W sheratonontheparksydney.com
From the entrance to the plush rooms, this hotel offers a deluxe stay. Helpful, 24-hour service.

Sofitel Sydney Wentworth $$$
Luxury
61–101 Phillip St, NSW 2000
Tel *(02) 9228 9188* **Map** 1 B4
W sofitelsydney.com.au
This hotel brilliantly blends 21st-century design with heritage-listed features. A true five-star experience.

The Westin $$$
Luxury
1 Martin Place, NSW 2000
Tel *(02) 8223 1111* **Map** 1 B4
W westinsydney.com
A marble-floored lobby sets the scene for this luxurious retreat. Many rooms have superb views.

Breathtaking views over Sydney harbour from the restaurant at Shangri-La Sydney

The York by Swiss-Belhotel $$$
Self-catering
5 York St, NSW 2000
Tel *(02) 9210 5000*   **Map** 1 A3
W theyorkapartments.com.au
Smart, fully equipped apartments, varying in size from studios to two-bedroom penthouses. Babysitting available.

Botanic Gardens and The Domain

Sir Stamford at Circular Quay $$$
Luxury
93 Macquarie St, NSW 2000
Tel *(02) 9252 4600*   **Map** 1 C3
W stamford.com.au/sscq
Elegant place opposite the Botanic Gardens decorated with beautiful antiques and fine art.

Kings Cross, Darlinghurst and Paddington

Arts Hotel $$
Value for Money
21 Oxford St, NSW 2021
Tel *(02) 9361 0211*   **Map** 5 B3
W artshotel.com.au
Basic but convenient. Pay a little extra for a room overlooking the courtyard garden.

Hughenden Boutique Hotel $$
Boutique
14 Queen St, Woollahra, NSW 2025
Tel *(02) 9363 4863*   **Map** 6 E4
W thehughendenhotel.com.au
Rambling 19th-century building comfortably furnished to retain a Victorian feel. Dogs welcome.

Medusa $$$
Boutique
267 Darlinghurst Rd, NSW 2010
Tel *(02) 9331 1000*   **Map** 5 B1
W medusa.com.au
A brightly coloured Modernist hotel with great amenities and artistic touches in each room.

Ovolo Woolloomooloo $$$
Luxury
6 Cowper Wharf Rd, Woolloomooloo, NSW 2011
Tel *(02) 9331 9000*   **Map** 2 E4
W ovolohotels.com
A glamorous place, with luxurious loft rooms, a fabulous cocktail bar and urban-industrial decor.

Regent's Court Apartments $$$
Self-catering
18 Springfield Ave, Potts Point, NSW 2011
Tel *(02) 9331 2099*   **Map** 2 E5
W regentscourtsydney.com.au
A charming Art Deco building with a lovely rooftop garden in a pretty tree-lined street.

The beautiful pool area at The Byron at Byron, Byron Bay

Further Afield

BONDI BEACH: Hotel Ravesi's $$$
Boutique
118 Campbell Parade, NSW 2026
Tel *(02) 9365 4422*
W hotelravesis.com.au
A beach-watching spot with show-stopping views of Bondi and a popular restaurant.

BONDI JUNCTION: Meriton Bondi Junction $$$
Self-catering
97 Grafton St, NSW 2022
Tel *(02) 8305 7600*
W meritonapartments.com.au
Tower-block complex of spacious apartments with one to three bedrooms. Fine views.

CHIPPENDALE: Old Clare Hotel $$$
Boutique
1 Kensington St, NSW 2025
Tel *(02) 8277 8277*
W theoldclarehotel.com.au
This hip gem retains the historic features of the pub and brewery that once occupied this site.

COOGEE: Dive Hotel $$$
Boutique
234 Arden St, NSW 2034
Tel *(02) 9665 5538*
W divehotel.com.au
A great alternative to Coogee's hostels, with designer bathrooms and a sleek colour scheme.

DOUBLE BAY: The Savoy Hotel Double Bay $$
Value for Money
41–45 Knox St, NSW 2028
Tel *(02) 9326 1411*
W savoyhotel.com.au
This well-established hotel is perfectly situated in tranquil surroundings.

MANLY: Novotel Sydney Manly Pacific $$$
Beach
55 North Steyne, NSW 2095
Tel *(02) 9977 7666*
W novotelmanlypacific.com.au
Right on the beach, and boasting unbeatable views. Light, spacious rooms with balconies.

SURRY HILLS: Adina Apartment Hotel Sydney, Crown Street $$$
Self-catering
359 Crown St, NSW 2010
Tel *(02) 8302 1000*
W tfehotels.com
Spacious one- and two-bedroom apartments with full-size kitchens and splashes of colour.

The Blue Mountains and Beyond

BALLINA: Ballina Heritage Inn $$
Motel
229 River St, NSW 2478
Tel *(02) 6686 0505*
W ballinaheritageinn.com.au
Comfortable motel with a pool and an outdoor seating area overlooking lovely gardens.

DK Choice

BYRON BAY: The Byron at Byron $$$
Luxury
77–97 Broken Head Rd, NSW 2481
Tel *(02) 6639 2000 or 1300 554 362*
W thebyronatbyron.com.au
Beautiful resort set within a rainforest including a fragrant grove of eucalyptus and palm trees. Contemporary suites are filled with luxury touches. Start the day with yoga by the pool, enjoy a spa treatment or wander through the trees to the beach.

BYRON BAY: The Oasis Resort $$$
Self-catering
24 Scott St, NSW 2481
Tel *(02) 6685 7390 or 1800 336 129*
W byronoasis.com.au
Spacious two-bedroom apartments and "treetop houses". A short walk from Tallow Beach, with a pool fringed by greenery.

COFFS HARBOUR: BreakFree Aanuka Beach Resort $$
Beach
11 Firman Dr, NSW 2450
Tel *(02) 6652 7555 or 1800 783 552*
W breakfreeaanukabeachresort.com.au
Beachfront resort with rooms and self-catering apartments. The café and restaurant have ocean views and live entertainment.

For more information on types of hotels *see page 481*

Safari-style tent at Paperbark Camp, Jervis Bay

GOSFORD: Terrigal Pacific Coast Retreat $$
Self-catering
224 Terrigal Dr, NSW 2260
Tel *(02) 4385 1555*
W terrigalpacific.net.au
Large apartments near the beach with kitchenettes and balconies overlooking lush gardens.

HUNTER VALLEY: Hunter Valley YHA $
Hostel
100 Wine Country Dr, Nulkaba, NSW 2325
Tel *(02) 4991 3278*
W yha.com.au
Low-key hostel in a timber cabin. Offers Wine Country tours and bike hire. Great service.

HUNTER VALLEY: Hunter Valley Resort $$
Luxury
Cnr Hermitage Rd & Mistletoe Ln, Pokolbin, NSW 2320
Tel *(02) 4998 7777*
W hunterresort.com.au
Pleasant rooms and cottages located in a Shiraz vineyard. Plenty of on-site activities.

KATOOMBA: Lilianfels Resort and Spa $$$
Luxury
Lilianfels Ave, NSW 2780
Tel *(02) 4780 1200*
W lilianfels.com.au
Historic country house amid English-style gardens. Idyllic spa, great food and stunning scenery.

KATOOMBA: The Mountain Heritage Hotel & Spa Retreat $$$
Character
Cnr Apex & Lovel sts, NSW 2780
Tel *(02) 4782 2155*
W mountainheritage.com.au
Classic country house hotel. Relax in the gardens or curl up by a log fire in the snug lounge.

LITHGOW: Eagle View Escape $$$
Luxury
271 Sandalls Dr, Rydal via Lake Lyell, NSW 2790
Tel *(02) 6355 6311 or 1300 851 829*
W eagleview.com.au
Perfect for a romantic getaway. Stay in either a suite or cabin at this lush 100-acre property west of the Blue Mountains.

MUDGEE: Cobb & Co Court Boutique Hotel $$
Boutique
97 Market St, NSW 2850
Tel *(02) 6372 7245*
W cobbandcocourt.com.au
This charming small hotel is located in the centre of town, a short stroll to bars, cafés and shops, and close to many wineries. The good on-site restaurant features regional food and wine.

NEWCASTLE: Crowne Plaza $$$
Luxury
Cnr Merewether St & Wharf Rd, NSW 2300
Tel *(02) 4907 5000*
W crowneplazanewcastle.com.au
The Crowne Plaza is an excellent harbourfront hotel right on the foreshore promenade. Modern facilities and a large pool.

PORT STEPHENS: Wanderers Retreat $$$
Rural
7 Koala Place, One Mile Beach, NSW 2316
Tel *(02) 4982 1702*
W wanderersretreat.com
Stay in eco-friendly cabins and tree houses in quiet bushland, home to koalas. Short stroll to the beach.

TAMWORTH: Plumes on the Green $$
Guesthouse
25 The Ringers Rd, NSW 2340
Tel *(02) 6762 1140*
W plumesonthegreen.com.au
Popular with birdwatchers and golfers, Plumes prides itself on its sophisticated atmosphere.

The South Coast and Snowy Mountains

BATEMANS BAY: Lincoln Downs Resort & Spa $$
Value for Money
Princes Hwy, NSW 2536
Tel *(02) 4478 9200*
W lincolndowns.com.au
A peaceful coastal resort set in an English country-style garden. Ornamental lake and tennis court.

BOWRAL: Milton Park Country House Hotel $$$
Luxury
Horderns Rd, NSW 2576
Tel *(02) 4861 8100*
W milton-park.com.au
A fine example of Federation Arts and Crafts architecture. Great day spa and parkland views.

BUNDANOON: The Bundanoon $$
Boutique
101 Railway Ave, NSW 2578
Tel *(02) 4883 6372*
W thebundanoonguesthouse.com.au
Quiet Edwardian house with log fires and four-poster beds, as well as a games room. Evening meals are available in the pretty dining room.

COOMA: Kinross Inn $$
Motel
15 Sharp St, NSW 2630
Tel *(02) 6452 3577*
W kinrossinn.com.au
Popular motel within walking distance of shops, restaurants and pubs. It is a 90-minute drive from the ski resorts of Perisher, Thredbo and Selwyn.

GOULBURN: Pelican Sheep Station $$
Rural
Braidwood Rd, NSW 2580
Tel *(02) 4821 4668*
W pelicansheepstation.com.au
Experience rural life at this family-owned sheep station. Camps, bunkhouses and cabins.

DK Choice

JERVIS BAY: Paperbark Camp $$$
Rural
571 Woollamia Rd, Woollamia, NSW 2540
Tel *(02) 4441 6066*
W paperbarkcamp.com.au
Stay in luxurious, safari-style tents tucked in a grove of gum trees at this peaceful, eco-friendly bush lodge. The treetop dining room serves imaginative cuisine based on local produce. Watch possums, sugar gliders and birds from the veranda.

MERIMBULA: Albacore Apartments $$$
Self-catering
Market St, NSW 2548
Tel *(02) 6495 3187*
W albacore.com.au
Five-storey block of large, smartly furnished apartments with heated pool, private balconies and sweeping lake views.

NAROOMA: Mystery Bay Cottages $$$
Self-catering
121 Mystery Bay Rd, NSW 2546
Tel *(02) 4473 7431*
W mysterybaycottages.com.au
Two-bedroom cottages in a peaceful location. Light and airy, with log fires.

PERISHER VALLEY: Marritz Hotel & Salzburg Apartments $$$
Ski Lodge
Kosciuszko Rd, NSW 2624
Tel *1800 767 756 or (02) 6457 5220*
W marritzsalzburg.com.au
Self-catering accommodation and hotel rooms by the Perisher ski fields, with access to a pool.

TATHRA: Tathra Beach House $$
Self-catering
57 Andy Poole Dr, NSW 2550
Tel *(02) 6499 9900*
W tathrabeachhouse.com.au
Apartments at this unpretentious complex sleep up to seven. In a great location near the surf beach.

THREDBO: Thredbo Alpine Hotel $$$
Ski Resort
Friday Dr, NSW 2625
Tel *(02) 6459 4100 or (02) 6459 4294*
W thredbo.com.au
Close to the ski lift, this hotel is cheaper and quieter in summer. Facilities include tennis and golf.

TILBA: The Two Story B&B $$
Character
Bate St, NSW 2546
Tel *(02) 4473 7290*
W tilbatwostory.com
Pleasantly chintzy, this B&B in a former post office is close to craft shops and bushwalks.

WOLLONGONG: Novotel Wollongong Northbeach $$$
Coast
2–14 Cliff Rd, NSW 2500
Tel *(02) 4224 3111*
W novotelnorthbeach.com.au
Right on the beachfront, this is the area's biggest hotel, close to restaurants, shops and parkland.

Canberra and ACT

CANBERRA: The Brassey of Canberra $$
Value for Money
Belmore Gardens & Macquarie St, Barton, ACT 2600
Tel *(02) 6273 3766*
W brassey.net.au
A good choice for business travellers, this comfortable hotel in a tree-lined suburb offers a car-sharing service.

CANBERRA: Canberra City YHA $$
Hostel
7 Akuna St, ACT 2601
Tel *(02) 6248 9155*
W yha.com.au
Facilities at this friendly hostel in the heart of the city, close to the bus terminal, include a café, indoor pool, games area and bar. Good terrace views.

CANBERRA: Hotel Kurrajong $$
Character
8 National Circuit, Barton, ACT 2604
Tel *(02) 6234 4444*
W hotelkurrajong.com.au
Facilities at this unpretentious hotel in a heritage Art Deco building include a conference centre, bar and restaurant.

DK Choice

CANBERRA: Hotel Realm $$
Luxury
18 National Circuit, Barton, ACT 2600
Tel *(02) 6163 1800*
W hotelrealm.com.au
Relaxed for a five-star, this beautifully designed hotel has striking decor. Apple gadgets, coffee machines and luxury bathroom goodies easily make this the coolest high-end hotel in the capital. The business centre is open round the clock.

CANBERRA: Novotel Canberra $$
Value for Money
65 Northbourne Ave, ACT 2600
Tel *(02) 6245 5000*
W novotelcanberra.com.au
Central hotel with contemporary finishings, indoor heated pool, gym and spa facilities.

CANBERRA: QT Canberra $$
Value for Money
1 London Circuit, ACT 2600
Tel *(02) 6247 6244*
W qthotelsandresorts.com/canberra
Designer guest rooms boasting wonderful views over Lake Burley Griffin.

CANBERRA: University House $$
Value for Money
Cnr Balmain & Liversidge sts, ACT 2601
Tel *(02) 6125 5275*
W anu.edu.au/unihouse
Peaceful place in the gardens of the Australian National University. Spacious rooms and apartments.

CANBERRA: Hyatt Hotel Canberra $$$
Luxury
Commonwealth Ave, Yarralumla, ACT 2600
Tel *(02) 6270 1234*
W canberra.park.hyatt.com
This sophisticated Art Deco hotel has Italian marble bathrooms and an impressive fitness centre.

CANBERRA: Peppers Gallery Hotel $$$
Boutique
15 Edinburgh Ave, ACT 2601
Tel *(02) 6175 2222 or 1300 737 444*
W peppers.com.au/gallery
A stylish hotel in a historic building with contemporary furniture and a sculpture garden.

MACGREGOR: Ginninderry Park $$
Rural
468 Parkwood Road, ACT 2615
Tel *(02) 0400 546 464*
W ginninderry.com.au
Beautiful guesthouse on a working farm, with gardens and mountain-framed views.

Brisbane

CITY CENTRE: Brisbane City YHA $
Hostel
392 Upper Roma St, QLD 4000
Tel *(07) 3236 1004*
W yha.com.au
Award-winning hostel with bright rooms. Good kitchen facilities and a rooftop pool.

Spacious, premier room at Peppers Gallery Hotel, Canberra

For more information on types of hotels *see page 481*

**CITY CENTRE: Brisbane
Marriott Hotel** $$
Luxury
515 Queen St, QLD 4000
Tel *(07) 3303 8000*
W marriott.com.au
This hotel, a short walk from the
city centre, has elegant decor, a
luxury spa and panoramic views.

CITY CENTRE: Hotel Ibis $$
Value for Money
27 Turbot St, QLD 4000
Tel *(07) 3237 2333*
W ibis.com
Surprisingly stylish for the price,
with useful extras such as laundry
and babysitting on request.

**CITY CENTRE: The New
Inchcolm Hotel** $$
Boutique
73 Wickham Terrace, QLD 4000
Tel *(07) 3226 8888*
W inchcolm.com.au
A heritage hotel with modern
furnishings amid original features
such as shutters and oak panelling.

**CITY CENTRE: George
Williams Hotel** $$$
Value for Money
317 George St, QLD 4000
Tel *(07) 3308 0700*
W hgw.com.au
Simple, contemporary, but decent
accommodation in the heart of
the city. Restaurant on site.

**CITY CENTRE:
Hilton Brisbane Hotel** $$$
Luxury
190 Elizabeth St, QLD 4000
Tel *(07) 3234 2000*
W brisbane.hilton.com
Dramatic atrium, pool, quality
fittings and excellent views at
this beautiful 20th-century hotel .

Contemporary conference room at Spicers
Balfour Hotel, Brisbane

DK Choice

**CITY CENTRE: Spicers
Balfour Hotel** $$$
Luxury
37 Balfour St, QLD 4005
Tel *(07) 3358 8888 or 1300 597 540*
W spicersretreats.com
Housed in a traditional
Queenslander building, Spicers
Balfour has contemporary decor
in rich jewel tones. Gorgeous
bed linen, Bose stereos and a
good library. Enjoy views of the
Story Bridge over fabulous
cocktails and pre-dinner
canapés in the rooftop bar.

**FORTITUDE VALLEY:
TRYP Fortitude Valley Hotel** $$
Boutique
14–20 Constance St, QLD 4006
Tel *(07) 3319 7888*
W trypbrisbane.com
This artfully restored historic
building in the city's cultural
precinct offers edgily stylish
rooms with playful artwork and
ultra-modern furnishings.

**FORTITUDE VALLEY:
Emporium Hotel** $$$
Boutique
1000 Ann St, QLD 4006
Tel *(07) 3253 6999*
W emporiumhotel.com.au
This design-driven, luxury
boutique hotel with a rooftop
pool is elegant and sophisticated.
It also has a fantastic cocktail bar
and on-site patisserie.

KANGAROO POINT: The Point $$
Value for Money
21 Lambert St, QLD 4169
Tel *(07) 3240 0888*
W thepointbrisbane.com.au
Spacious rooms with good
facilities and stunning views of
the city from the upper floors.

NEW FARM: Bowen Terrace $$
Value for Money
365 Bowen Terrace, QLD 4005
Tel *(07) 3254 0458*
W bowenterrace.com.au
Friendly and welcoming place
in a quiet residential area. Simple
shared and private rooms.

**PADDINGTON: Lucerne
on Fernberg** $$
Value for Money
23 Fernberg Rd, QLD 4064
Tel *(07) 3369 6686*
W lucerne.net.au
Two well-appointed heritage-
listed cottages nestled in lovely
gardens, close to cafés,
restaurants, theatres and
transport. One of Brisbane's
oldest residences.

**SPRING HILL: Metro Hotel
Tower Mill** $$
Value for Money
239 Wickham Terrace, QLD 4000
Tel *(07) 3832 1421*
W metrohotels.com.au
Located in a cylindrical tower
block, this hotel has great views
from the upper floors. Rooms are
simple; some have balconies.

**SPRING HILL:
Hotel Watermark** $$$
Luxury
551 Wickham Terrace, QLD 4000
Tel *(07) 3058 9333*
W watermarkhotelbrisbane.com.au
Spacious, comfortable rooms
overlooking Spring Hill or the
Roma Street Parkland.

**SPRING HILL: Punthill
Brisbane** $$$
Luxury
40 Astor Terrace, QLD 4000
Tel *(07) 3055 5777*
W punthill.com.au
Smart studio and one-bedroom
apartments. Great contemporary
decor. Laundry facilities and bike
hire available.

WEST END: Franklin Villa $$$
Boutique
35 Brighton Rd, QLD 4101
Tel *(07) 3255 0889*
W franklinvilla.com.au
Splendid rooms in a beautifully
restored mansion. The verandas
afford sweeping views of the
city skyline.

South of Townsville

**AGNES WATERS: Mango Tree
Motel** $$
Beach
7 Agnes St, QLD 4677
Tel *(07) 4974 9132*
W mangotreemotel.com.au
Budget motel close to the main
surf beach. Popular shops, cafés
and restaurants are all nearby.

**AIRLIE BEACH: Coral
Sea Resort** $$$
Coast
25 Oceanview Ave, QLD 4802
Tel *(07) 4964 1300*
W coralsearesort.com
Relaxed resort with nautically
themed decor. Spectacular ocean
views from the pool terrace.

**CARNARVON NATIONAL PARK:
Carnarvon Gorge Wilderness
Lodge** $$
Rural
4043 O'Briens Rd, QLD 4702
Tel *(07) 4984 4503 or 1800 644 150*
W carnarvon-gorge.com

Guests relaxing in one of the pool bars,
Kingfisher Bay Resort, Fraser Island

Stay in an airy safari-style cabin
nestled in woodland. Good spot
for walks and birdwatching.

**FRASER ISLAND: Eurong
Beach Resort** $$
Rural
Fraser Island, QLD 4655
Tel *(07) 4120 1600*
W eurong.com
Simple, comfortable resort in the
World Heritage wilderness, near
the rainforest. Access by 4WD only.

DK Choice

**FRASER ISLAND:
Kingfisher Bay Resort** $$$
Rural
Fraser Island, QLD 4655
Tel *(07) 4120 3313 or 4194 9300*
W kingfisherbay.com
An award-winning eco-lodge
with lovely grounds, a good
restaurant and lots of activities.
Surrounded by unspoilt coastal
dunes and forest, it is remote
but easy to reach. Rooms and
villas available.

**GLADSTONE: Auckland Hill
Bed and Breakfast** $$
Boutique
15 Yarroon St, QLD 4680
Tel *(07) 4972 4907*
W ahbb.com.au
Delightful guesthouse. There is a
large deck for relaxing at the end
of a day's exploring.

**GOLD COAST:
Palazzo Versace** $$$
Luxury
*94 Sea World Dr, Main Beach,
QLD 4217*
Tel *(07) 5509 8000*
W palazzoversace.com.au

Sensual and opulent hotel with
spectacularly decorated interiors,
rich fabrics and grand vistas. Features a lavish pool, gym and spa.

**GOLD COAST: Q1 Resort
and Spa** $$$
Luxury
*9 Hamilton Ave, Surfers Paradise,
QLD 4217*
Tel *(07) 5630 4500*
W q1.com.au
Gleaming luxury suites and
apartments in a striking skyscraper
that is the tallest building in the
southern hemisphere.

**GOLD COAST: Sheraton Grand
Mirage Resort & Spa** $$$
Luxury
*71 Sea World Dr, Main Beach,
QLD 4217*
Tel *(07) 5577 0000*
W sheratongrandmiragegoldcoast.
com
Sleek yet tasteful, this oceanfront
resort is set amid scenic lagoons
and tropical gardens.

**HERVEY BAY: Mantra
Hervey Bay** $$
Value for Money
Buccaneer Dr, Urangan, QLD 4655
Tel *(07) 4197 8200*
W mantraherveybay.com.au
Pleasant resort on the marina
with impressive views from the
balconies. Handy for whale-
watching trips.

**LADY ELLIOT ISLAND:
Lady Elliot Island Resort** $$
Rural
QLD 4216
Tel *(07) 5536 3644*
W ladyelliot.com.au
Unique, eco-friendly island
retreat located in an important
marine wildlife habitat.

**LAMINGTON NATIONAL PARK:
O'Reilly's Rainforest Retreat** $$
Rural
*3582 Lamington National Park Rd,
QLD 4275*
Tel *(07) 5544 0644*
W oreillys.com.au
Escape to this beautiful setting
in the peaceful Gold Coast
hinterland with modern comforts
in the heart of the park.

**LAMINGTON NATIONAL PARK:
Binna Burra Mountain
Lodge** $$$
Rural
Binna Burra Rd, Beechmont, QLD 4211
Tel *(07) 5533 3622*
W binnaburralodge.com.au
This rustic, heritage-listed
mountain lodge offers simple
rooms in a rainforest for an
authentic nature experience.

**MACKAY: Cape Hillsborough
Nature Tourist Park** $$
Rural
*51 Risley Parade, Cape Hillsborough,
QLD 4740*
Tel *(07) 4959 0152*
W capehillsboroughresort.com.au
Camp or stay in a room or cabin
surrounded by a coastal reserve.
Ideal for relaxing, hiking and
kangaroo-watching.

**MAGNETIC ISLAND:
Sails on Horseshoe** $$
Self-catering
*13–15 Pacific Dr, Horseshoe Bay,
QLD 4819*
Tel *(07) 4778 5117*
W sailsonhorseshoe.com.au
Modern two-bed and studio
apartments close to the beach.
Free use of kayaks and bikes.

NOOSA: Halse Lodge YHA $
Hostel
2 Halse Ln, Noosa Heads, QLD 4567
Tel *(07) 5447 3377*
W halselodge.com.au
This 1880s guesthouse is one of
Australia's most atmospheric
hostels. Relaxed café-restaurant.

**NOOSA: Sheraton
Noosa Resort & Spa** $$$
Luxury
*14–16 Hastings St, Noosa Heads,
QLD 4567*
Tel *(07) 5449 4888*
W sheraton.com/noosa
In a fashionable location, with
spacious rooms, superb beds
and the best breakfast in town.

**ROCKHAMPTON:
Myella Farm Stay** $$
Rural
*1591 Baralaba-Rannes Rd, Myella
Kokotungo, Baralaba, QLD 4702*
Tel *(07) 4998 1290*
W myella.com
Authentic Queensland holiday
experience on a cattle station.
Learn to milk cows and horse-ride.

**SUNSHINE COAST:
The Arabella Guesthouse** $$
B&B
297 Mooloolaba Rd, QLD 4556
Tel *(07) 5478 1339*
W arabellaguesthouse.com.au
Welcoming guesthouse located in
a quaint village. Enjoy breakfast on
the deck overlooking the ocean.

**SUNSHINE COAST:
Spicers Clovelly Estate** $$$
Luxury
68 Balmoral Rd, Montville, QLD 4560
Tel *(07) 5452 1111 or 1300 252 380*
W spicersretreats.com
This elegant country house hotel
offers guests fine dining and
sweeping gardens.

For more information on types of hotels *see page 481*

Spacious lounge of an Estate Suite at the Spicers Clovelly Estate, Sunshine Coast

TOOWOOMBA: Vacy Hall $$
Guesthouse
135 Russell St, QLD 4350
Tel *(07) 4639 2055*
W vacyhall.com.au
Heritage luxury in a boutique setting with exquisite gardens in the heart of Toowoomba. Gourmet breakfasts.

TOWNSVILLE: Seagulls Resort $$
Value for Money
74 The Esplanade, Belgian Gardens, QLD 4810
Tel *(07) 4721 3111*
W seagulls.com.au
This budget resort set in tropical landscaped gardens offers a range of recreational facilities.

WHITSUNDAY ISLANDS: Qualia $$$
Luxury
Hamilton Island, QLD 4803
Tel *1300 780 959*
W qualia.com.au
Plush resort on the northernmost tip of Hamilton Island. Splendid views of the Coral Sea. Offers a pool, gym and spa facilities.

Northern Queensland and the Outback

CAIRNS: Ellis Beach Oceanfront Bungalows $$
Beach
Captain Cook Hwy, Ellis Beach, QLD 4879
Tel *(07) 4055 3538 or 1800 637 036*
W ellisbeach.com
Bungalows and cabins that sleep up to four people in an idyllic and unspoilt setting. Gorgeous sea views. You may hear some traffic noise, depending on the cabin.

CAIRNS: Novotel Cairns Oasis Resort $$
Design
122 Lake St, QLD 4870
Tel *(07) 4080 1888*
W novotelcairnsresort.com.au

Good-value suites with Jacuzzis. Balconies overlook the tropical gardens, mountains or the pool.

CAIRNS: Pullman Reef Hotel Casino $$$
Character
35–41 Wharf St, QLD 4870
Tel *(07) 4030 8888*
W reefcasino.com.au
Smart, stylish rooms with plantation shutters. See lots of animals, including a crocodile, in the rainforest dome on the roof.

COOKTOWN: The Sovereign Resort Hotel $$
Character
128 Charlotte St, QLD 4895
Tel *(07) 4043 0500*
W sovereign-resort.com.au
This hotel is a unique combination of traditional Queensland pub and modern resort, with beautiful rooms.

DAINTREE: Daintree Riverview $$
Rural
2 Stewart St, QLD 4873
Tel *(07) 0409 627 434*
W daintreeriverview.com
Cabins and a camping ground can be found here, on the banks of the Daintree River. There are sweeping views of the rainforest-covered mountains, too.

KARUMBA: The End of the Road Motel $$
Self-catering
26 Palmer St, QLD 4891
Tel *(07) 4745 9599*
W endoftheroadmotel.com.au
Comfortable and spacious self-contained apartments on the beach. Watch the sun set over the Gulf of Carpentaria.

LONGREACH: Albert Park Motor Inn $$
Motel
Sir Hudson Fysh Dr, QLD 4730
Tel *(07) 4658 2411*
W longreachaccommodation.com

In an idyllic bush environment, this standard motel is close to all major attractions and the airport.

MOSSMAN: Marae B&B $$
Rural
Lot 1, Chook's Ridge, off Ponzo Rd, Shannonvale, QLD
Tel *(07) 4098 4900*
W marae.com.au
A glamorous secluded retreat in the bush, with only two rooms. Wallabies graze in the garden.

MOSSMAN: Silky Oaks Lodge and Healing Waters Spa $$$
Luxury
Finlayvale Rd, QLD 4873
Tel *(07) 4098 1666*
W silkyoakslodge.com.au
Luxury treehouses situated in the rainforest, all with private hammocks. Great spa.

MOUNT ISA: Isa Hotel $$
Boutique
Cnr Rodeo Drive & West St, QLD 4825
Tel *(07) 4749 8888*
W redearth-hotel.com.au
Modern, clean and comfortable choice in the heart of town.

PALM COVE: Pullman Palm Cove Sea Temple Resort & Spa $$$
Luxury
5 Triton St, QLD 4879
Tel *(07) 4059 8600 or 1800 010 241*
W pullmanhotels.com
Here you have the choice of studios, apartments and penthouses. Private plunge pools, rooftop terraces and a spa.

DK Choice

UNDARA VOLCANIC NATIONAL PARK: Undara Experience Lava Lodge $$
Rural
Savannah Way, QLD 4871
Tel *(07) 4097 1900 or 1800 990 992*
W undara.com.au
Set in the national park's amazing surroundings, with its ancient lava tubes and wildlife. Accommodation ranges from restored railway carriages to a luxury tent village, cabins and a camping ground. Start the day with a bush breakfast.

WINTON: Boulder Opal Motor Inn $$
Motel
16 Elderslie St, QLD 4735
Tel *(07) 4657 1211*
W boulderopalmotorinn.com.au
Comfortable motel with queen, single and two-bedroom choices. Good Outback-themed bistro food is also offered.

Darwin and the Top End

DARWIN: Palms City Resort $$
Value for Money
64 Esplanade, NT 0800
Tel *(08) 8982 9200*
W palmscityresort.com
Surrounded by tropical gardens, this charming resort offers simple, self-contained rooms and villas.

DARWIN: Vibe Hotel Darwin Waterfront $$
Design
7 Kitchener Dr, NT 0800
Tel *(08) 8982 9998*
W vibehotels.com.au
Casual, bright and fun, with spacious rooms, this hotel overlooks the swimming lagoon at Stokes Wharf.

DARWIN: SKYCITY Darwin $$$
Luxury
Gilruth Ave, NT 0801
Tel *(08) 8943 8888*
W skycitydarwin.com.au
Darwin's only five-star beachfront resort offers everything from standard rooms to luxury villas.

JABIRU: Mercure Kakadu Crocodile Hotel $$
Luxury
1 Flinders St, NT 0886
Tel *(08) 8979 9000*
W kakadutourism.com/accommodation/kakadu-crocodile-hotel
This 110-room hotel is built in the shape of a crocodile. While it is a little dated, it is still a comfortable choice near Kakadu.

JIM JIM: Kakadu Cooinda Lodge $$
Rural
Kakadu Hwy, NT 0886
Tel *(08) 8979 1500*
W kakadutourism.com/accommodation/cooinda-lodge

Safari bungalow interior, Bamurru Plains, Mary River

This comfortable lodge is equipped with spacious rooms and also offers convenient access to Kakadu National Park.

DK Choice

MARY RIVER: Bamurru Plains $$$
Rural
Harold Knowles Rd, Humpty Doo, NT 0836
Tel *1300 790 561 or (02) 9571 6399*
W bamurruplains.com
Bamurru offers luxury bungalows set on stilts overlooking the Mary River floodplain – an area frequented by bird and animal life. Packages can include safaris and meals. River cruises, fishing and helicopter trips are available. Air-conditioning on request. A truly memorable eco-adventure.

The Red Centre

ALICE SPRINGS: Alice Springs YHA $
Hostel
Cnr Parsons St & Leichhardt Terrace, NT 0870
Tel *(08) 8952 8855*
W yha.com.au
Award-winning hostel set around a historic outdoor movie theatre. Free nightly shows.

ALICE SPRINGS: Aurora Alice Springs $$
Value for Money
Leichhardt Terrace, NT 0870
Tel *(08) 8950 6666*
W alicespringsaurora.com.au
The town's most centrally located hotel has a riverside entrance. It also offers one hour of free Wi-Fi for guests.

ALICE SPRINGS: DoubleTree by Hilton $$
Luxury
82 Barrett Dr, NT 0870
Tel *(08) 8950 8000*
W doubletree3.hilton.com
This high-end resort offers mountain views from every room but is still within walking distance of town.

ALICE SPRINGS: Quest Alice Springs $$
Self-catering
9–10 South Terrace, NT 0870
Tel *(08) 8959 0000*
W questapartments.com.au
Stylish, spacious apartments perfectly suited to both business and leisure travellers.

ERLDUNDA: Erldunda Roadhouse $$
Value for Money
Cnr Stuart & Lasseters hwys, NT 0872
Tel *(08) 8956 0984*
W erldundaroadhouse.com
This no-frills roadhouse 250 km (155 miles) from Uluru National Park is a good base for exploring the sights of the Red Centre.

KINGS CANYON: Kings Canyon Resort Hotel $$$
Rural
Luritja Rd, Watarrka National Park, NT 872
Tel *(08) 8956 7442 or 1800 837 168*
W kingscanyonresort.com.au
Comfortable retreat after a day of hiking, with a swimming pool and a viewing platform for taking in the sunset.

YULARA: Outback Pioneer Hotel & Lodge $$
Hostel
Yulara Dr, NT 872
Tel *(02) 8296 8010*
W ayersrockresort.com.au/outback
Clean and basic. Some rooms have shared bathrooms. The communal barbecue area lends the place a friendly vibe.

YULARA: Desert Gardens Hotel $$$
Value for Money
Yulara Dr, NT 872
Tel *(02) 8296 8010*
W ayersrockresort.com.au/desert
Stroll in the gardens, sip cocktails by the pool and join in the free daily activities with the local Anangu people.

YULARA: Emu Walk Apartments $$$
Self-catering
Yulara Dr, NT 872
Tel *(02) 8296 8010*
W ayersrockresort.com.au/emu
Spacious apartments can be found here, with well-equipped kitchens, making it ideal for families and groups.

DK Choice

YULARA: Longitude 131 $$$
Luxury
Yulara Dr, NT 872
Tel *(02) 9918 4355*
W longitude131.com.au
The 15 secluded, elevated tents at Longitude 131 have magical views of Uluru, comfortable beds and ensuite bathrooms. Luxury in the wilderness in the truest sense of the word. Price includes airport transfers, and all meals and drinks.

For more information on types of hotels *see page 481*

Perth and the Southwest

ALBANY: The Beach House at Bayside $$$
Boutique
33 Barry Ct, Albany, WA 6330
Tel *(08) 9844 8844*
W thebeachhouseatbayside.com.au
Offering five-star accommodation, this hotel is just 100 m (110 yd) from the popular Middleton Bay. Rooms have a elegant country feel and plush furnishings.

BUNBURY: Bunbury Backpackers $
Hostel
16 Clifton St, WA 6230
Tel *1800 039 032*
W bunburybackpackers.com.au
Friendly hostel a short walk from the city and beach. Dorm-style rooms, plus singles and doubles.

BUSSELTON: The Sebel Busselton $$
Self-catering
553 Bussell Hwy, WA 6280
Tel *(08) 9754 9800*
W thesebel.com
Good leisure facilities. Margaret River's wineries, beaches and restaurants are a short drive away.

DK Choice

FREMANTLE: Be Fremantle $$$
Self-catering
43 Mews Rd, WA 6160
Tel *(08) 9430 3888*
W befremantle.com.au
In a prime spot overlooking Fremantle harbour, these modern, tasteful apartments offer views of the ocean. Choose from one-, two- and three-bedroom apartments.

Outdoor pool amid lush green lawns at Windmills Break, Yallingup

HYDEN: Wave Rock Motel $$
Motel
2 Lynch St, WA 6359
Tel *(08) 9880 5052*
W waverockhotel.com.au
Comfortable motel with a spa, solar-heated pool, two restaurants and two bar areas.

KALGOORLIE: Rydges Kalgoorlie Resort and Spa $$$
Luxury
21 Davidson St, WA 6430
Tel *(08) 9080 0800*
W rydges.com/kalgoorlie
An oasis in the desert offering a day spa and spacious rooms with dream beds. Easy connections to the airport.

MARGARET RIVER: Pullman Resort Bunker Bay $$$
Luxury
Bunker Bay Rd, off Cape Naturaliste Rd, WA 6281
Tel *(08) 9756 9100*
W pullmanhotels.com
Villa-style bungalows nestled on the beachfront. Close to the wineries.

PEMBERTON: Old Picture Theatre Holiday Apartments $$
Character
Cnr Ellis & Guppy sts, WA 6260
Tel *(08) 9776 1513*
W oldpicturetheatre.com.au
Unique accommodation in a converted 1929 movie theatre. Period fittings, modern amenities.

PERTH: Como The Treasury $$
Luxury
1 Cathedral Ave, WA 6000
Tel *(08) 6168 7888*
W comohotels.com/thetreasury
One of the newest and most luxurious hotels to open in Perth, located in the center of the CBD, this accommodation occupies a state building dating from the mid-19th century. Offers exceptional service. Award winning restaurants nearby.

PERTH: Travelodge $$
Value for Money
417 Hay St, WA 6000
Tel *(08) 9238 1888*
W tfehotels.com
Fabulously located in heart of Perth's CBD, this hotel is close to many popular tourist attractions including the Elizabeth Quay and Perth Concert Hall and is a short bus ride away from Kings Park. Rooms have a modern feel.

PERTH: Fraser Suites $$$
Self-catering
10 Adelaide Terrace, WA 6004
Tel *(08) 9261 0000*
W frasershospitality.com

Executive accommodation in a 19-storey tower overlooking the Swan River. Elegant open living areas and chic bathrooms.

ROTTNEST ISLAND: Hotel Rottnest $$$
Beach
Bedford Ave, WA 6161
Tel *(08) 9292 5011*
W hotelrottnest.com.au
This hotel is the island's only resort on the beach. Guests can choose between bayside and garden courtyard rooms.

YALLINGUP: Cape Lodge $$$
Luxury
3341 Caves Rd, WA 6282
Tel *(08) 9755 6311*
W capelodge.com.au
Secluded lodge in distinctive Cape Dutch style. Excellent restaurant offering fine local food and wine.

YALLINGUP: Seashells Yallingup $$$
Self-catering
Yallingup Beach Rd, WA 6282
Tel *(08) 9750 1500*
W seashells.com.au
Luxuriously furnished Art-Deco style apartments set in pretty gardens. Restaurant and bar next door.

YALLINGUP: Windmills Break $$$
Boutique
2024 Caves Rd, WA 6282
Tel *(08) 9755 2341*
W windmillsbreak.com.au
The beautiful rooms here are complete with leather seats. Surrounded by lush grounds, this makes the ideal spot for a romantic retreat.

YORK: Settlers House $$
Character
125 Avon Terrace, WA 6302
Tel *(08) 9641 1884*
W settlershouseyork.com.au
This modern motel with a colonial façade is located in the middle of the historic town of York. Close to nearby attractions.

North of Perth and the Kimberley

BROOME: Cable Beach Club Resort & Spa $$$
Luxury
Cable Beach Rd, WA 6725
Tel *(08) 9192 0400*
W cablebeachclub.com
Asian serenity and Colonial indulgence meet in this tropical haven overlooking Cable Beach.

BROOME: Oaks Cable Beach Sanctuary $$$
Beach
1 Lullfitz Dr, WA 6726
Tel *(08) 9192 8088*
w minorhotels.com/en/oaks-cable-beach-sanctuary
Range of self-contained options, including three-bedroom villas with private plunge pools.

BROOME: Pinctada McAlpine House $$$
Boutique
55 Herbert St, WA 6725
Tel *(08) 9192 0588*
w pinctada.com.au
Renovated 1910 pearler's home set in tropical gardens with exotic birds. Tranquil and private.

CAPE RANGE NATIONAL PARK: Sal Salis Ningaloo Reef $$$
Rural
Yardie Creek Rd, WA 6707
Tel *(08) 9949 1776*
w salsalis.com.au
Barefoot luxury abounds at this safari camp hidden in sand dunes, just metres from a pristine beach.

DAMPIER: Cygnet Bay Pearl Farm $$$
Rural
Cape Leveque Rd, WA 6725
Tel *(08) 9192 4283*
w cygnetbaypearls.com.au
This operational pearl farm offers stays in safari tents, historic pearlers' cottages and divers' quarters. Ideal for groups.

KUNUNURRA: Kununurra Country Club Resort $$
Value for Money
47 Coolibah Dr, WA 6743
Tel *(08) 9168 1024*
w kununurracountryclub.com.au
A sanctuary to return to after exploring Kimberley. Modern rooms and beautiful grounds.

DK Choice

NEW NORCIA: Monastery Guesthouse $
Character
Great Northern Hwy, WA 6509
Tel *(08) 9654 8002*
w newnorcia.wa.edu.au
A special and unusual experience, where guests can seek quiet contemplation, learn about the workings of the monastery and use it as a base to explore the town. Home-style meals and simply furnished rooms, most with ensuites. Guests are invited to dine with the monks. Payment is by donation only – A$80 recommended.

Stylish lounge room in a guest suite at The Louise in the Barossa

SHARK BAY: Monkey Mia Dolphin Resort $$$
Beach
1 Monkey Mia Rd, Denham, WA 6537
Tel *(08) 9948 1320*
w monkeymia.com.au
Offers a range of accommodation. Good facilities include an artesian spring hot tub. Dolphins visit the beach daily.

Adelaide and the Southeast

ADELAIDE: Adelaide Central YHA $
Hostel
135 Waymouth St, SA 5000
Tel *(08) 8414 3010*
w yha.com.au/adelaide
Big, friendly place close to the city's nightlife. Rooms for couples, families and solo travellers.

ADELAIDE: Majestic Roof Garden Hotel $$
Luxury
55 Frome St, SA 5000
Tel *(08) 8100 4400*
w roofgardenhotel.com.au
Comfortable, quiet and airy rooms in a prime location near Rundle Mall. Rooftop views.

ADELAIDE: Adina Apartment Hotel Adelaide Treasury $$$
Character
2 Flinders St, SA 5000
Tel *(08) 8112 0000*
w adinahotels.com.au
Old-world elegance in the old State Treasury building, converted into spacious and convenient self-contained apartments.

ADELAIDE: Stamford Grand Adelaide $$$
Luxury
2 Jetty Rd, Glenelg, SA 5045
Tel *(08) 8376 1222*
w stamford.com.au/sga
Up-market hotel in the popular beachside suburb of Glenelg. Good dining and resort facilities.

THE BAROSSA: Abbotsford Country House $$$
Luxury
219 Yaldara Dr, Lyndoch, SA 5351
Tel *(08) 8524 4662*
w barossa-accommodation.com
This rural retreat in the heart of the Barossa Valley offers the best views in the region.

THE BAROSSA: Collingrove Homestead $$$
Character
Angaston Rd, Angaston, SA 5353
Tel *(08) 8564 2061*
w collingrovehomestead.com.au
The former servants' quarters in this grand old home are now elegant guest rooms.

THE BAROSSA: The Kirche @ Charles Melton Wines $$$
Luxury
Krondorf Rd, Tanunda, SA 5253
Tel *(08) 8563 3606*
w meltons.com.au
Two rooms, a living area and a stunning kitchen in a renovated church. Great vineyard setting.

DK Choice

THE BAROSSA: The Louise & Appellation $$$
Luxury
375 Seppeltsfield Rd, Marananga, SA 5355
Tel *(08) 8562 2722*
w thelouise.com.au
This boutique hotel features stylish suites, spa tubs and outdoor rain showers. The kitchen garden grows produce for the award-winning restaurant.

KANGAROO ISLAND: Southern Ocean Lodge $$$
Luxury
Hanson Bay, SA 5223
Tel *(02) 9918 4355*
w southernoceanlodge.com.au
Exclusive cliff-top lodge with dramatic ocean views. Rates include breakfast, light lunch, dinner and beverages.

For more information on types of hotels *see page 481*

McLAREN VALE: Serafino $$
Value for Money
39 Kangarilla St, SA 5171
Tel *(08) 8323 8911*
W serafinowines.com.au
Serafino offers spacious rooms overlooking the gardens, 200-year-old gum trees and pool.

McLAREN VALE: McLaren Vale Studio Apartments $$$
Self-catering
222 Main St, SA 5171
Tel *(08) 8323 9536*
W mvsa.com.au
Bright, modern apartments, each themed around a different wine. Great beds and a spa bath.

MOUNT GAMBIER: Lakes Resort $$$
Value for Money
17 Lakes Terrace W, SA 5290
Tel *(08) 8725 5755*
W lakesresort.com.au
On the edge of the Valley Lake Crater, with spectacular views from most rooms, this is ideal for a romantic getaway.

PENOLA: Must @ Coonawarra $$
Self-catering
126 Church St, SA 5277
Tel *(08) 8737 3444*
W mustatcoonawarra.com.au
These self-contained luxury apartments are a great option for couples or groups. Bikes for hire.

PORT ELLIOT: Port Elliot Beach House YHA $
Hostel
13 The Strand, SA 5212
Tel *(08) 8554 1885*
W yha.com.au
Affordable and comfortable dorms, double and family rooms in a stunning historic building.

ROBE: Robe House $$
Character
1 Hagen St, SA 5276
Tel *(08) 8768 2770*
W robehouse.com.au

Five apartments with high-vaulted ceilings are available here, inside a charming 1847 sandstone building.

STIRLING: Thorngrove Manor Hotel $$$
Luxury
2 Glenside Ln, SA 5152
Tel *(08) 8339 6748*
W thorngrove.com.au
The flamboyant, castle-inspired suites at Thorngrove Manor offer outstanding amenities and absolute privacy.

VICTOR HARBOR: The Bluff Resort Apartments $$$
Luxury
123 Franklin Parade, Encounter Bay, SA 5211
Tel *(08) 8552 1200*
W bluffresort.com.au
These self-contained apartments offer guests many homely comforts, as well as breathtaking views across Encounter Bay.

The Yorke and Eyre Peninsulas and South Australian Outback

DK Choice

ARKAROOLA: Arkaroola Wilderness Sanctuary $$
Rural
Arkaroola Rd, SA 5701
Tel *(08) 8648 4848*
W arkaroola.com.au
The family-run Arkaroola is a good base for exploring the spectacular Flinders Ranges. The resort has accommodation to suit all budgets, from camping to motel and self-contained apartments. Do not miss the Ridgetop tour's breathtaking 360-degree panoramic views.

The distinctive turrets and towers of Thorngrove Manor, Stirling

CLARE VALLEY: Burra Heritage Cottages $$
B&B
8–18 Truro St, Burra, SA 5417
Tel *0408 922 625*
W burraheritagecottages.com.au
Built in 1856, these self-contained cottages comfortably sleep up to four adults. Breakfast is included.

CLARE VALLEY: Clare Valley Motel $$
Character
74A Main North Rd, Clare, SA 5453
Tel *(08) 8842 2799*
W clarevalleymotel.com.au
This family run motel is close to the wine region and two minutes' drive from the centre of Clare. Outdoor dining options available.

COOBER PEDY: Desert Cave Hotel $$
Character
1 Hutchison St, SA 5723
Tel *(08) 8672 5688*
W desertcave.com.au
Experience dugout-style living with underground sleeping options, shops, bar and opal display areas. Above-ground rooms also available.

PORT HUGHES: The Lighthouse Port Hughes $$$
Character
42B Dowling Dr, SA 5554
Tel *0415 056 611*
W lighthouseporthughes.com.au
Well-appointed holiday home that can accommodate up to 12 guests. Ideal for families.

PORT LINCOLN: Port Lincoln YHA $
Hostel
24–26 London St, SA 5606
Tel *(08) 8682 3605*
W yha.com.au
Spacious multishares and twin/double and family accommodation. Guests can enjoy the bar/café and outdoor barbecue.

PORT LINCOLN: Port Lincoln Hotel $$
Beach
1 Lincoln Hwy, SA 5606
Tel *1300 766 100*
W portlincolnhotel.com.au
Deluxe spa suites and rooms with balconies overlooking beautiful Boston Bay.

WILPENA: Wilpena Pound Resort $$
Rural
Wilpena Rd (via Hawker), SA 5434
Tel *(08) 8648 0004*
W wilpenapound.com.au
Guests can stay in safari tents, resort-style rooms or camp on site. Area tours can be booked.

Façade of Hotel Windsor, one of Melbourne's grandest hotels

Melbourne

ALBERT PARK: Pullman Melbourne Albert Park $$
Luxury
65 Queens Rd, VIC 3004
Tel *(03) 9529 4300* **Map** 3 B5
W pullmanalbertpark.com.au
Smart business and leisure hotel with views of the city's Formula 1 Grand Prix track and golf course.

CARLTON: Carlton Terrace $$
Boutique
196 Drummond St, VIC 3053
Tel *(03) 9662 2735* **Map** 1 C1
W carltonterrace.com.au
Elegant mini apartments in a restored 19th-century house on a quiet tree-lined street.

CARLTON: Downtowner on Lygon $$
Value for Money
66 Lygon St, VIC 3053
Tel *(03) 9663 5555* **Map** 1 C1
W downtowner.com.au
Simple, good-quality rooms and serviced apartments aimed at sports fans and business travellers.

CITY CENTRE: Greenhouse Backpacker $
Hostel
228 Flinders Ln, VIC 3000
Tel *(03) 9639 6400* **Map** 1 C4
W greenhousebackpacker.com.au
Appealing budget choice with well-sized rooms and dormitories. Rooftop with barbecue.

CITY CENTRE: Quest Gordon Place $$
Self-catering
24 Little Bourke St, VIC 3000
Tel *(03) 9663 2888* **Map** 1 D2
W questgordonplace.com.au
Compact but appealing serviced apartments in an attractive brick building with a gym and pool.

CITY CENTRE: Victoria Hotel $$
Value for Money
215 Little Collins St, VIC 3000
Tel *(03) 9669 0000* **Map** 1 C3
W victoriahotel.com.au
Trusted landmark hotel with no-fuss hospitality. Close to theatres, restaurants and boutiques.

CITY CENTRE: The Crossley Hotel $$$
Boutique
51 Little Bourke St, VIC 3000
Tel *(03) 9639 1639* **Map** 2 D2
W crossleyhotel.com.au
Crisp, clean rooms in a great location. Friendly service.

CITY CENTRE: The Grand Hotel Melbourne $$$
Self-catering
33 Spencer St, VIC 3000
Tel *(03) 9611 4567* **Map** 1 B4
W grandhotelmelbourne.com.au
On offer here are elegantly styled serviced apartments inside a heritage building.

CITY CENTRE: Grand Hyatt $$$
Luxury
123 Collins St, VIC 3000
Tel *(03) 9657 1234* **Map** 2 D3
W melbourne.grand.hyatt.com
Five-star hotel designed to impress. Marble bathrooms and a large fitness centre.

CITY CENTRE: Hotel Causeway $$$
Boutique
275 Little Collins St, VIC 3000
Tel *(03) 9660 8888* **Map** 1 C3
W causeway.com.au
Basic rooms in a 1920s Art Deco building. Rooftop terrace, gym and steam room.

CITY CENTRE: Hotel Lindrum $$$
Boutique
26 Flinders St, VIC 3000
Tel *(03) 9668 1111* **Map** 2 D3
W hotellindrum.com.au
This chic place, in a heritage building, has striking photography on the walls.

CITY CENTRE: The Hotel Windsor $$$
Character
111 Spring St, VIC 3000
Tel *(03) 9633 6000* **Map** 2 D2
W thehotelwindsor.com.au
Grand Victorian hotel, built in the Gold Rush era. Five-star luxury.

CITY CENTRE: Jasper Hotel $$$
Boutique
489 Elizabeth St, VIC 3000
Tel *(03) 8327 2777* **Map** 1 B2
W jasperhotel.com.au
Sleek hotel with funky lighting and first-rate service. Rooms and suites available.

CITY CENTRE: Mantra on the Park $$$
Self-catering
333 Exhibition St, VIC 3000
Tel *(03) 9668 2500* **Map** 2 D2
W mantra.com.au
The spacious apartments at Mantra sleep up to six people. The styling is contemporary.

CITY CENTRE: Rydges Melbourne $$$
Luxury
186 Exhibition St, VIC 3000
Tel *(03) 9662 0511* **Map** 2 D2
W rydges.com/melbourne
Rydges is a stylish hotel in a large block opposite Her Majesty's Theatre. The beds and finishes are all top quality.

CITY CENTRE: Sofitel Melbourne on Collins $$$
Luxury
25 Collins St, VIC 3000
Tel *(03) 9653 0000* **Map** 2 D3
W sofitel-melbourne.com.au
Great comfort, facilities and service are offered here, and the huge windows provide guests with panoramic views.

CITY CENTRE: Stamford Plaza Melbourne $$$
Luxury
111 Little Collins St, VIC 3000
Tel *(03) 9659 1000* **Map** 2 D3
W stamford.com.au/spm
The plush one- and two-bedroom suites here are beautifully finished with stylish touches.

CITY CENTRE: The Westin Melbourne $$$
Luxury
205 Collins St, VIC 3000
Tel *(03) 9635 2222* **Map** 1 C3
W westinmelbourne.com
The rooms here are large and chic. Some even have balconies and offer guests magnificent views of the city.

FITZROY: Metropole Hotel Apartments $$
Self-catering
44 Brunswick St, VIC 3065
Tel *(03) 9411 8100* **Map** 2 E1
W metropolecentral.co.au
Peaceful accommodation can be found at the Metropole, which is conveniently situated within easy reach of the city.

FITZROY: The Nunnery $$
Character
116 Nicholson St, VIC 3065
Tel *(03) 9419 8637* **Map** 2 D1
W nunnery.com.au
A former convent with elegant Georgian features. Guesthouse rooms or dorms with bunk beds.

For more information on types of hotels *see page 481*

FITZROY: Quest Royal Gardens Apartments $$
Self-catering
8 Royal Ln, VIC 3065
Tel *(03) 9419 9888*   **Map** 2 D1
W questapartments.com.au
The apartments here are modern, and there is a pool and barbecue in the shared garden.

RICHMOND: Amora Hotel Riverwalk $$
Value for Money
649 Bridge Rd, VIC 3121
Tel *(03) 9246 1200*
W melbourne.amorahotels.com
Pleasant apartments or clean, modern rooms with lovely views.

RICHMOND: Richmond Hill Hotel $$
Character
353 Church St, VIC 3121
Tel *(03) 9428 6501*   **Map** 4 E2
W richmondhillhotel.com.au
Housed in a beautiful heritage-listed Victorian terrace. Choice of basic or more elegant rooms.

SOUTH YARRA: Hotel Claremont $
Character
189 Toorak Rd, VIC 3141
Tel *(03) 9826 8000*
W hotelclaremont.com
Friendly and popular budget hotel with comfortable double or family rooms and dorm bunks.

SOUTH YARRA: The Como Melbourne $$$
Luxury
630 Chapel St, VIC 3141
Tel *(03) 9825 2222*   **Map** 4 E5
W comomelbourne.com.au
Stylish pad with a bar favoured by celebrities. Cool, minimal design with colourful accents.

SOUTHBANK: Crown Promenade Hotel $$$
Luxury
8 Whiteman St, VIC 3006
Tel *(03) 9292 6688*   **Map** 1 C5
W crownhotels.com.au
Contemporary hotel with first-class leisure facilities, such as a sauna, steam rooms and a pool.

SOUTHBANK: Langham Hotel $$$
Luxury
1 Southgate Ave, VIC 3006
Tel *(03) 8696 8888*   **Map** 1 C4
W melbourne.langhamhotels.com.au
At the Langham you will find luxury at its best, with chandeliers, sweeping staircases and marble bathrooms. Superb facilities.

ST KILDA: Base Backpackers $
Hostel
17 Carlisle St, VIC 3182
Tel *(03) 8598 6200*   **Map** 5 C5
W stayatbase.com
This is a budget hostel with a modern vibe. One special feature is its women-only level, ideal for safety-conscious lone females.

DK Choice

ST KILDA: The Prince $$
Boutique
2 Acland St, VIC 3182
Tel *(03) 9536 1111*   **Map** 5 B5
W theprince.com.au
Slick minimalist design and understated luxury hide behind the Art Deco façade of this boutique hotel. The rooms are all tastefully decorated and good value. Spend a relaxing day at the spa before enjoying dinner at the celebrated restaurant, Circa.

ST KILDA: Tolarno Hotel $$
Boutique
42 Fitzroy St, VIC 3182
Tel *(03) 9537 0200*   **Map** 5 B4
W hoteltolarno.com.au
The Tolarno is a style-driven boutique hotel that features bold contemporary design through-out the property.

ST KILDA ROAD PRECINCT: Royce Hotel $$$
Boutique
379 St Kilda Rd, VIC 3004
Tel *(03) 9677 9900*   **Map** 3 B4
W roycehotels.com.au
This chic, designer hotel goes the extra mile with its ballroom and glamorous bar.

Western Victoria

AIREYS INLET: Airey's Inlet Getaway Resort $$$
Character
2 Barton Court, VIC 3221
Tel *(03) 5289 7021*
W aireysinletgetaway.com.au
Fantastic leisure facilities, gardens and proximity to the ocean make this a popular resort.

APOLLO BAY: Chris's Beacon Point Restaurant & Villas $$$
Luxury
280 Skenes Creek Rd, VIC 3233
Tel *(03) 5237 6411*
W chriss.com.au
These well-equipped villas are situated high above the town. Floor-to-ceiling windows offer stunning views.

BALLARAT: Comfort Inn Sovereign Hill $$
Character
41 Magpie St, VIC 3350
Tel *(03) 5337 1199*
W sovereignhill.com.au
Accommodations here range from up-market suites to bunk room units. Close to Sovereign Hill.

BENDIGO: Hotel Shamrock $$
Character
Cnr Pall Mall & Williamson St, VIC 3550
Tel *(03) 5443 0333*
W hotelshamrock.com.au
Elegant, affordable rooms in one of Bendigo's best hotels. A fixture on the social scene since 1854.

CASTLEMAINE: Castlemaine Colonial Motel $$
Character
252 Barker St, VIC 3450
Tel *(03) 5472 4000*
W castlemainemotel.com.au
Stay in your choice of luxury rooms or apartments housed in a renovated 19th-century building.

CASTLEMAINE: The Empyre $$$
Boutique
68 Mostyn St, VIC 3450
Tel *(03) 5472 5166*
W empyre.com.au
Painstakingly restored beautiful suites with antique furnishings, stately beds, chandeliers and leadlight windows.

DAYLESFORD: Lake House $$$
Luxury
King St, VIC 3460
Tel *(03) 5348 3329*
W lakehouse.com.au
Lake House is an all-round experience that includes an award-winning restaurant, a spa, deluxe suites and country gardens.

Deluxe courtyard room, Amora Hotel, Richmond

Key to Price Guide *see page 482*

ECHUCA: Cock 'n' Bull $$
Character
17–21 Warren St, VIC 3564
Tel *(03) 5480 6988*
W cocknbullechuca.com
This is a tastefully restored
heritage home that has luxury
suites and a courtyard.

GEELONG:
Hotel Novotel Geelong $$$
Value for Money
10–14 Eastern Beach Rd, VIC 3220
Tel *(03) 5223 1377*
W novotelgeelong.com.au
Situated on the waterfront, this
hotel has great views of the bay.
It is also close to the central
business district.

GELLIBRAND:
Otways Tourist Park $$
Value for Money
25 Main Rd, VIC 3239
Tel *(03) 5235 8357*
W otwaystouristpark.com
This well-run park is ideally located
close to the beaches. There are
self-contained apartments and
camping facilities on offer.

HALLS GAP:
Grampians YHA Eco-Hostel $
Hostel
Grampians Rd, VIC 3381
Tel *(03) 5356 4544*
W yha.com.au
This eco-hostel incorporates solar
electricity, reverse cycle fans, and
waste-water and rainwater
management to minimize its
impact on the environment.

HALLS GAP: Aurora Cottages $$$
Rural
300 Tunnel Rd, Pomonal, VIC 3381
Tel *0433 131 054*
W auroracottages.com.au
A private sanctuary in the bush,
Aurora offers lovely cottages,
while the resident wildlife keep
the guests company.

DK Choice

HEPBURN SPRINGS:
Peppers Mineral
Springs Hotel $$
Luxury
124 Main Rd, VIC 3461
Tel *(03) 5348 2202*
W mineralspringshotel.com.au
Relaxing and romantic, this
1930s guesthouse has been
transformed into a deluxe
retreat but still retains its
Art Deco character. It fits
in wonderfully with the
surrounding landscape. Guests
here can enjoy a roaring fire, an
outstanding restaurant and a
rejuvenating day spa.

LORNE: Mantra $$$
Luxury
Mountjoy Parade, VIC 3232
Tel *(03) 5228 9777*
W mantralorne.com.au
The only hotel in Lorne directly
on the beachfront. Excellent
leisure facilities and beautiful
landscaped gardens.

MALDON: Miners Cottages $$$
Character
41 Main Street, VIC 3463
Tel *(04) 1354 1941*
W heritagecottages.com.au
Comfortable, self-contained
private cottages with quality
linen and full kitchens.

MILDURA: Quality Mildura
Grand Hotel $$
Value for Money
Seventh St, VIC 3500
Tel *(03) 5023 0511*
W milduragrand.com.au
Variety of accommodation
choices. Home to the award-
winning Stefano's restaurant.

PORT FAIRY: Oscars
Waterfront Boutique Hotel $$$
Boutique
41B Gipps St, VIC 3284
Tel *(03) 5568 3022*
W oscarswaterfront.com
Overlooking the marina, the
stylish riverfront rooms have
comfortable king-sized beds. Just
a short stroll to the beach.

TORQUAY:
Peppers The Sands Resort $$$
Luxury
2 Sands Blvd, VIC 3228
Tel *(03) 5264 3333*
W peppers.com.au
Perched on a headland with
spectacular views. Excellent golf
course and heated indoor pool.

Eastern Victoria

BAIRNSDALE:
The Riversleigh $$
Rural
1 Nicholson St, VIC 3875
Tel *(03) 5152 6966*
W riversleigh.com.au
Victorian property with ornate
balconies, comfortable rooms and
fine views of the Mitchell River.

BEECHWORTH:
Barwood House $$$
Character
15B Loch St, VIC 3747
Tel *0409 284 110*
W barwoodhouse.com.au
Elegant Victorian country house
offering well-appointed rooms
with modern furnishings.

Entrance to Peppers Mineral Springs
Retreat, Hepburn Springs

BRIGHT: Ashwood Cottages $$
Self-catering
22A Ashwood Ave, VIC 3741
Tel *(03) 5755 1081*
W ashwoodcottages.com.au
The charming one-bedroom
cottages here are equipped with
wood-burning stoves. Peaceful
green surroundings.

FALLS CREEK:
The Falls Creek Hotel $$$
Ski Lodge
23 Falls Creek Rd, VIC 3699
Tel *(03) 5758 3282*
W fallscreekhotel.com.au
Ski-in, ski-out chalet-style hotel
open from June until the end of
the skiing season. All rooms have
slope views.

GIPPSLAND LAKES:
The Moorings at Metung $$
Self-catering
44 Metung Rd, VIC 3904
Tel *(03) 5156 2750*
W themoorings.com.au
Spacious waterfront apartments
with one to three bedrooms and
good facilities.

KING VALLEY: Casa Luna $$$
Rural
1569 Boggy Creek Rd, Myrrhee,
VIC 3732
Tel *(03) 5729 7650*
W casaluna.com.au
Stylish and tranquil retreat. King
suites have private balconies
and queen suites have walk-in
showers. Gourmet getaway
featuring Italian-style cuisine.

LAKES ENTRANCE: Comfort Inn
& Suites Emmanuel $$
Value for Money
151 Esplanade, VIC 3909
Tel *(03) 5155 1444*
W comfortinnemmanuel.com.au
With rooms, apartments, a
barbecue area and a playground,
this is a good option for families.

For more information on types of hotels *see page 481*

MANSFIELD:
Mansfield Valley Motor Inn $$
Value for Money
Cnr Elvins St & Maroondah Hwy,
VIC 3722
Tel *(03) 5775 1300*
W mansfieldmtbuller.com.au
Simple rooms and apartments
are available here, with views of
Mount Buller. Big gardens with a
barbecue area.

MANSFIELD: The Riverhouse at
Howqua Dale $$
Luxury
85 Howqua River Rd, VIC 3722
Tel *(03) 5777 3503*
W theinspiredtraveller.com.au
This country house set among
beautiful riverside gardens offers
privacy and comfort. Guests can
go self-catering or B&B. There is
also a tennis court on site.

MORNINGTON PENINSULA:
Bayplay Adventure Lodge $$$
Hostel
46 Canterbury Jetty Rd, Blairgowrie,
VIC 3942
Tel *(03) 5984 0888*
W bayplay.com.au
Simple rooms and good facilities.
Accommodating up to 30
people, it is perfect for group
getaways. The property features a
pool and a large garden with
barbecue facilities, and is walking
distance from the beach.

MORNINGTON PENINSULA:
Mount Martha B&B
By the Sea $$$
B&B
539 The Esplanade, Mount
Martha, VIC 3934
Tel *(03) 5974 1019*
W mountmarthabandb
bythesea.com.au
Peaceful accommodation with
spacious rooms, elegant decor
and furnishings, and splendid
ocean or garden views.

Glen Isla House surrounded by heritage
gardens, Phillip Island

MOUNT BAW BAW:
Kelly's Lodge $$$
Rural
11 Frosti Ln, VIC 3068
Tel *(03) 5165 1129*
W kellyslodge.com.au
Intimate alpine lodge very close
to the ski lift and toboggan run.
Big summer discounts.

MOUNT BULLER:
Mount Buller Chalet $$$
Rural
207 Summit Rd, VIC 3723
Tel *(03) 5777 6566*
W bullerholidays.com.au
A winter-only luxury retreat with
first-class fitness facilities, including
sauna, gym and squash court.

MOUNT HOTHAM:
Snowbird Inn $$
Rural
Great Alpine Rd, VIC 3741
Tel *(03) 5759 3503*
W snowbirdinn.com.au
This central, no-frills lodge near
the ski lift offers backpacker-style
rooms. There is a bistro and café.

DK Choice

NARBETHONG: Woodlands
Rainforest Retreat $$$
Rural
137 Manby Rd, VIC 3778
Tel *(03) 5963 7150*
W woodlandscottages.com.au
Built using local beech and
mountain ash, each of the four
cottages in this beautiful
woodland property is perfectly
secluded for a romantic escape.
Watch or hear cockatoos, parrots,
wallabies and wombats from the
balcony. Savour the chef-
prepared dinners for two.

PHILLIP ISLAND: Phillip Island
Apartments $$
Self-catering
9–11 Bass Avenue, Cowes, VIC 3922
Tel *(03) 5952 2644*
W phillipislandapartments.net.au
A five-minute walk from the
beach, these sleek, modern
apartments have spacious living
areas and balconies. The property
boasts an outdoor pool and hot
tub, as well as a barbecue area.

PHILLIP ISLAND:
Glen Isla House $$$
Luxury
230–232 Church St, Cowes, VIC 3923
Tel *(03) 5952 1882*
W glenisla.com
Award-winning hotel in a heritage
property with a homely atmos-
phere. Set amid lush gardens
with 100-year-old oak trees.
Close to the beach.

POREPUNKAH: Buffalo Motel
& Country Retreat $$
Value for Money
6774 Great Alpine Rd, VIC 3740
Tel *(03) 5756 2242*
W buffalomotelretreat.com.au
Modest and relaxed family retreat
with comfortable, warm rooms.
Close to the Rail Trail bike track.

WALHALLA:
Windsor House B&B $$
Character
12 Right Hand Branch Rd, VIC 3825
Tel *(03) 5165 6237*
W windsorhouse.com.au
This beautiful heritage property
is one of the only original brick
buildings surviving in Walhalla.
The boutique B&B includes
period features dating back to
the 1890s.

WILSONS PROMONTORY:
Tidal River Cabins $$
Rural
National Parks Service,
Tidal River, VIC 3690
Tel *(03) 5680 9555*
W parkweb.vic.gov.au
National Park camps, eco-friendly
cabins and luxury safari-style
tents. Open from February
to November. Book well ahead.

YARRA VALLEY: Sanctuary
House Resort Motel $$
Value for Money
326 Badger Creek Rd, Healesville,
VIC 3777
Tel *(03) 5962 5148*
W sanctuaryhouse.com.au
Surrounded by native bush,
this is a resort-style motel
offering good family facilities.

Tasmania

BURNIE: Glen Osborne House $$
Character
9 Aileen Crescent, TAS 7320
Tel *(03) 6431 9866*
W glenosbornehouse.com.au
This ornate two-storey mansion
houses an elegant B&B furnished
with antiques and fireplaces.

COLES BAY: Freycinet Lodge $$$
Rural
Freycinet National Park, TAS 7215
Tel *(03) 6256 7222*
W freycinetlodge.com.au
Eco-friendly lodge with one- and
two-room cabins set in bushland.
Some balconies have sea views.

COLES BAY: Saffire Freycinet $$$
Luxury
2532 Coles Bay Rd, TAS 7215
Tel *(03) 6256 7888*
W saffire-freycinet.com.au

The award-winning contemporary luxury suites that complement the natural coastal bush setting. Views of Great Oyster Bay.

CRADLE MOUNTAIN: Cradle Mountain Lodge $$$
Rural
4038 Cradle Mountain Rd, TAS 7306
Tel *(03) 6492 2100*
W cradlemountainlodge.com.au
Award-winning lodge in a rainforest setting. Don't miss the fantastic Waldheim Alpine Spa.

HOBART: The Shipwright's Arms $
Value for Money
29 Trumpeter St, Battery Pt, TAS 7004
Tel *(03) 6223 1846*
W shipwrightsarms.com.au
This is a traditional English-style pub in the quaint village setting of Battery Point. The available rooms are comfortable.

**HOBART:
Customs House Hotel** $$
Character
1 Murray St, TAS 7000
Tel *(03) 6234 6645*
W customshousehotel.com
Large Colonial-style rooms and a historic sandstone pub situated right on Hobart's historic waterfront.

DK Choice

HOBART: The Henry Jones Art Hotel $$$
Luxury
25 Hunter St, TAS 7000
Tel *(03) 6210 7700*
W thehenryjones.com
This hotel is located in a former jam factory on the harbourfront. The individually designed guest rooms, erected around a magnificent glass atrium, reflect Australia's early trade with China and India. The walls display art by emerging local artists.

HOBART: The Islington $$$
Luxury
321 Davey St, TAS 7000
Tel *(03) 6220 2123*
W islingtonhotel.com
Lavish and tasteful historic home looking out on to Mt Wellington. King-sized beds, large bathtubs and a choice of sitting rooms.

HOBART: Macquarie Manor $$$
Character
172 Macquarie St, TAS 7000
Tel *(03) 6224 4999*
W macmanor.com.au
Classic 19th-century Colonial-style manor house. Quiet and centrally located, with elegant furnishings. Modern facilities.

Elegant furnishings of a garden room at the Islington hotel, Hobart

**HOBART:
The MONA Pavilions** $$$
Luxury
655 Main Rd, Berriedale, TAS 7011
Tel *(03) 6277 9900*
W mona.net.au
These state-of-the-art pavilions are located on the banks of the Derwent River. Part of the MONA complex *(see p465)*.

HOBART: Wrest Point $$$
Luxury
410 Sandy Bay Rd, TAS 7005
Tel *(03) 6221 1888*
W wrestpoint.com.au
Wrest Point is a casino-hotel complex that offers plush, spacious rooms and features an iconic revolving restaurant.

LAUNCESTON: Country Club Resort & Villas $$
Rural
Country Club Ave, TAS 7250
Tel *(03) 6335 5777*
W countryclubtasmania.com.au
Spacious rooms and villas are offered here, in a sprawling setting. Lots of activities, from golf to horse riding. Wallabies graze in the grounds.

**LAUNCESTON:
Peppers Seaport Hotel** $$$
Character
28 Seaport Blvd, TAS 7250
Tel *(03) 6345 3333*
W peppers.com.au
Built in the shape of a ship and located in a former dock, this smart hotel has contemporary rooms, each with a kitchenette.

**LAUNCESTON:
York Mansions** $$$
Character
9–11 York St, TAS 7250
Tel *(03) 6334 2933*
W yorkmansions.com.au
Airy two-room apartments built within a National Trust classified mansion house. Some are furnished with antiques.

**PORT ARTHUR:
Stewarts Bay Lodge** $$
Rural
6955 Arthur Hwy,TAS 7182
Tel *(03) 6250 2888*
W stewartsbaylodge.com.au
One-, two- or three-bedroom log cabins in the bush, all with decks overlooking the water. Close to the Port Arthur Historic Site.

ROSS: Man-o-Ross Hotel $
Character
35 Church St, TAS
Tel *(03) 6381 5445*
W rosshotel.com.au
Sandstone pub with Colonial-style rooms, in the heart of a picturesque village.

STANLEY: Old Cable Station $$
Character
435 Green Hills Rd, TAS 7331
Tel *(03) 6458 1312*
W cablestationstanley.com.au
This 1930s telecommunications station on the remote northwest coast is now a stylish B&B with self-contained suites.

STRAHAN: Risby Cove $$
Rural
The Esplanade, TAS 7468
Tel *(03) 6471 7572*
W risbycove.com.au
Luxury waterfront motel overlooking a private marina. Studio, one- and two-room suites Superb restaurant and art gallery.

One of the impressive hi-tech MONA pavilions, Hobart

For more information on types of hotels *see page 481*

WHERE TO EAT AND DRINK

Australia has developed a strong culinary identity. Modern Australian (or Mod Oz, as it is more commonly known) cuisine is a fresh, inventive style that gives local ingredients, particularly seafood and beef, a French, Mediterranean or Asian twist. Australia also has a wealth of ethnic restaurants, reflecting the country's multicultural population. Native Australian food is increasingly popular, as some chefs begin to embrace meats such as kangaroo and native fruits and vegetables. The best restaurants offer a superb selection of local wines or beers *(see pp502–3)*.

Picturesque outside terrace at Lavandula La Trattoria *(see p531)*

Types of Restaurants

All major Australian cities have a wide variety of formal and informal restaurants, bistros, cafés and pubs offering everything from haute cuisine to quick snacks. Many have outdoor tables for alfresco dining. Outside the main cities, some restaurants, particularly at wineries and high-end resorts, are destinations in themselves.

Prices vary widely, but there is generally a quality offering to suit every budget, though drinks add significantly to the bill in restaurants. As a general guideline, the bill at a showcase restaurant in Melbourne or Sydney featuring a celebrity chef will be at least A$150 per head, including a shared bottle of wine. At a BYO (Bring Your Own) or an unpretentious Asian or Italian restaurant, it may be A$30–50 per head. A meal at a pub, café or snack bar should generally cost no more than A$20–30 per head, if you include the price of a drink.

Eating Hours and Reservations

Most restaurants serve lunch between noon and 3pm. Dinner tends to be served from 6:30 to 10:30pm, but budget and ethnic eateries often close earlier. Some bistros and cafés stay open from breakfast time until late at night. Restaurants in hotels are usually open daily, but other eateries may close one day a week, usually Mondays. For fashionable, high-end restaurants, booking in advance by phone or online is highly recommended.

Paying and Tipping

Most Australian restaurants accept major credit cards, but in cafés and pubs a minimum spend (usually $10–20) may be required. A 10 per cent Goods and Services Tax (GST) is included in all restaurant bills in Australia. Tipping is discretionary and not compulsory. In a restaurant, adding 10 per cent of the total bill to the credit card transaction, or leaving the same in cash on the table following very good service, is appreciated.

Children

Most restaurateurs will allow admission to children as long as they are well behaved. Many restaurants also provide high chairs and a children's menu. The best budget options for families are local sports club bistros, pub bistros, hamburger chains or one of the many no-fuss Italian or Asian eateries.

Wheelchair Access

Spurred by legislation in the various states, most restaurants now provide special wheelchair access and toilet facilities for the disabled. However, it is still advisable to check the facilities available in advance.

Vegetarians

Most restaurants offer dishes for vegetarians; a variety of choices is the norm, particularly in regions where there is an abundance of home-grown produce. There are also specialist vegetarian and even vegan restaurants and cafés in the major cities. Many

Alfresco dining at Skillogalee Wines in the Clare Valley *(see p525)*

Doyles on the Beach in Watsons Bay, Sydney *(see p507)*

restaurants also identify gluten-free items on the menu. In the event of special dietary requirements, it is best to call the restaurant in advance, especially in rural areas.

Ravesi's on Bondi Beach, one of many great eateries at the famous beach *(see p507)*

Alcohol and Other Drinks

If a restaurant is described as licensed, it refers to its licence to sell alcohol on its premises. Australian wine lists are outstanding and generally highlight the wines of the particular state or district *(see pp40–41)*. Wine is sold by the bottle, carafe or glass. There is usually a good choice of beers, ales, ciders and spirits as well.

BYO restaurants, which are not licensed to sell alcohol, are extremely popular. These offer diners the opportunity to bring the wines they wish to drink with their meal. Beer, however, may not be permitted. A corkage fee is usually charged.

Tap water is safe, though many restaurants offer relatively expensive still and sparking bottled water. It is illegal for restaurants to charge for tap water, but feel free to request it. Fresh fruit juices and Italian-style coffee are also very popular *(see pp502–3)*.

Dress

The phrase "smart casual" sums up the Australian approach to eating out. Dress codes are virtually non-existent, although a handful of the more up-market restaurants may ask men to wear a tie in the evenings.

Most places, including beachside cafés, are relaxed and informal, but it is best to cover up swimwear.

Smoking

Smoking is banned inside all restaurants, cafés and pubs, but it is permitted in limited designated outside areas.

Recommended Restaurants

The restaurants recommended on the following pages are among the best in their categories, whether serving haute cuisine or pub meals.

The list includes a range of eateries that offer everything from Modern Australian dishes, such as fresh fish with Oriental spices, to pub classics, such as pies and burgers (more popularly known as counter meals), as well as excellent

options for coffee and cake. In international cuisine, there are Italian classics such as pizza and pasta, Chinese banquets of meat or seafood with rice or noodles, and Japanese-style sushi to choose from. Some top-end restaurants offer degustation or tasting menus – a succession of tiny, delicious courses. Other culinary trends are afternoon tea – a selection of savouries and cakes or scones, served with speciality tea or coffee and "share plates" designed for diners to share a variety of dishes.

Restaurants which are labelled as "DK Choice" are distinctive and highly acclaimed options. Many of these are award-winning, special-occasion restaurants that offer something truly unique.

Stunning views of the Opera House from the Dining Room, Sydney *(see p504)*

The Flavours of Australia

Modern Australian cuisine has been evolving from traditional British since World War II. An influx of people from Italy, Greece, Turkey, Lebanon, Thailand, China, Malaysia, Indonesia and Vietnam (to name but a few) have contributed influences to what is now known as Mod-Oz cuisine. However, a lot of Aussies will still swelter over a hot roast lunch on a midsummer Christmas day. Dramatically varying climates over such a large country mean an abundance and diversity of local produce, so it's no surprise that some of the world's best chefs hail from this rich and exciting culinary playground.

Wattleseed, pepperberry and lemon myrtle

Chef filleting snapper, one of Australia's finest fish

Native Ingredients

There are many native foods in Australia that have been used by Aborigines for thousands of years, and which are becoming more widely recognized. Quandong, munthari, bush tomato, wild limes and rosellas are native fruits with distinctive colours, flavours and textures, while warrigal greens are a spinach-like herb. All of them are still primarily wild-harvested by Aboriginal communities. Although native Australians never used seasonings in their campfire cooking, modern Australians have discovered the exciting flavours of such indigenous herbs and spices as lemon myrtle, wattleseed, mountain pepperleaf, pepperberry, forest berry and akudjura. Native meats like kangaroo and, to a lesser extent, emu are also being used more frequently, although don't expect to see witchity grubs on many menus. These meats sit alongside a vast and impressive array of beef, lamb, chicken and seafood. Fish native to Australia include barramundi, trevally and blue-eye trevalla. The popular native shellfish, yabbies and Moreton Bay bugs, are similar to, but smaller than, lobster. Also worth a mention is the lovely honey produced out of native Australian forests.

Samphire   Snapper   Lobster   Oysters
Scallops   Red mullet
Selection of seafood to be found in the oceans around Australia

Australian Dishes and Specialities

Anzac biscuits

Vegemite on toast is the most unique Australian taste a visitor can try. It's salty, though, so spread a thin amount. Australians love a barbecue, as a social and culinary hub, and throw a wide variety of meats and seafood on the grill. Major cities offer a huge variety of foods. Melbourne, in particular, has a strong Greek and Italian influence and prides itself on a vibrant café culture, serving unbeatable coffee. Meat pies are a traditionally popular food that has been given a sophisticated twist with innovative fillings, and you will see pies inspired by different cuisines such as Thai, Indian and Moroccan.

For those with a sweet tooth, pumpkin scones are a traditional Queensland favourite, alongside vanilla slices from bakeries, lamingtons, pavlova, and oat and coconut-based Anzac biscuits.

Kangaroo pizza The Italian classic is given a modern Australian spin with the addition of seared lean fillet of kangaroo.

Fruit and vegetables on a stall at Queen Victoria Market, Melbourne *(see p390)*

The World on a Plate

Having one of the most eclectic populations on earth means great things for food (or "tucker"). Australians are as happy exporting their wealth of homegrown produce as they are embracing international cuisine.

Farming plays a very important role in Australia, the world's largest producer of beef. The lush pastures on the coast are particularly good for farming, and the milk-fed lamb from New South Wales is as wonderful as the brie produced in South Australia. King Island, between Victoria and Tasmania in Bass Strait, is dedicated to dairy produce; farmers sell their amazing cheese and creams all around the country. Alongside the vast wine industry is olive oil and balsamic vinegar production, examples of which are found at the cellar door of many vineyards.

Australia has one of the most diverse marine faunas in the world, due to its range of

Wooden crate of sweet, juicy apples from Tasmania

habitats, from the warm tropical northern waters to the sub-Antarctic Tasman sea, as well as its geographical isolation. A total of 600 marine and freshwater species are caught in Australian waters, providing chefs with plenty of inspiration.

Every kind of fruit and vegetable is produced in Australia. Pineapples and mangoes are widely grown in Queensland, apples in Victoria, strawberries in New South Wales and rambutans in the Northern Territory. Exotic and notoriously hard to farm, truffles have been cultivated in several states, highlighting just how versatile Australia's land is.

Food on the Run

Sushi Major cities are dotted with tiny counters offering fresh sushi to grab on the go.

Juice bars This healthy, delicious fruit option can be found on most city streets.

Vietnamese rolls Many Vietnamese-run eateries serve delicious, cheap *banh mi* – pork (or chicken or tuna) and salad rolls on French-style bread.

Coffee & cake Many cafés sell Italian-style cakes and pastries.

Pubs Most pubs serve a decent steak sandwich.

Pies An Aussie institution, pies are readily available. Look out for gourmet versions.

Grilled barramundi Served on ginger and bok choy risotto, this is a great mix of local seafood and Asian flavours.

Prawn laksa This spicy coconut noodle soup can be found all over the country in noodle bars, cafés and pubs.

Lamingtons These little Victoria sponge cakes are coated in chocolate icing and shredded coconut.

What to Drink in Australia

Australia has one of the world's finest cuisines and part of its enjoyment is the marriage of the country's wine with great food. Australians have a very relaxed attitude to food and wine mixes, so red wine with fish and a cold, dry Riesling as an aperitif can easily be the order of the day. Also, many of the restaurants in the wine regions offer exclusive brands or offer small-run wines, so these are worth seeking out. It is estimated that there are 10,000 different Australian wines on the market at any one time. Australians enjoy some of the best-value wine in the world *(see pp40–41)* and love their beer, with a wide range of choices available, including locally made craft beers. While the health-conscious can choose from a variety of bottled waters and select-your-own, freshly-squeezed fruit juices. Imported wines, beers and spirits are also readily available.

Domaine Chandon in the Yarra Valley *(see p447)* in Eastern Victoria

Sparkling Wine

Australia is justly famous for its sparkling wines, from Yalumba's Angas Brut to Seppelts Salinger. Most recently, Tasmania has showed considerable promise in producing some high quality sparkling wines, particularly Pirie from Pipers Brook. However, the real hidden gems are the sparkling red wines – the best are made using the French *Méthode Champenois*, matured over a number of years and helped by a small drop of vintage port. The best producers of red sparkling wines are Rockford and Seppelts. These sparkling wines are available throughout the country from "bottle shops".

Angus Brut premium

White Wine

The revolution in wine making in the 1970s firmly established dry wines made from international grape varieties on the Australian table. Chardonnay, Sauvignon Blanc, and more recently Viognier and Pinot Gris are all popular. However, there has also been a renaissance and growing appreciation for Riesling, Marsanne and Semillon, which age very gracefully. Australia's other great wines are their fortified and desert wines. Australian winemakers use *botrytis cinera*, or noble rot, to make luscious dessert wines such as De Bortoli's "Noble One".

Rhine Riesling

Botrytis Semillon

Some of the vines in Australia are the oldest in the world

Grape Type	Best Regions	Best Producers
Chardonnay	Geelong, Beechworth (VIC)	Bannockburn, Giaconda, Stonier
	Hunter Valley (NSW)	Lakes Folly, Rosemount, Tyrrell's
	Margaret River (WA)	Leeuwin Estate, Pierro, Cullen
	The Barossa (SA)	Penfolds, Mountadam
Semillon	Hunter Valley (NSW)	Brokenwood, McWilliams, Tyrrell
	The Barossa (SA)	Peter Lehmann, Willows, Penfolds
	Margaret River (WA)	Moss Wood, Voyager, Evans & Tate
Riesling	Clare Valley and Adelaide Hills (SA)	Grosset, Pikes, Petaluma, Mitchells
	The Barossa (SA)	Richmond Grove, Leo Buring, Yalumba
	Tasmania (TAS)	Piper's Brook
Marsanne	Goulburn Valley (VIC)	Chateau Tahbilk, Mitchelton

Red Wine

Vineyards of Leeuwin Estate, Margaret River

Australia's benchmark red is Penfold's Grange, the creation of the late vintner Max Schubert in the 1950s and 1960s. Due to his work, Shiraz has established itself as Australia's premium red variety. However, there is also plenty of diversity with the acknowledged quality of Cabernet Sauvignon produced in the Coonawarra. Recently, there has also been a re-appraisal of traditional "old vine" Grenache and Mourvedre varieties in the Barossa and McLaren Vale.

Shiraz   Pinot Noir

Grape Type	Best Regions	Best Producers
Shiraz	Hunter Valley (NSW)	Brokenwood, Lindmans, Tyrrells
	Great Western, Sunbury (VIC)	Bests, Seppelts, Craiglee
	The Barossa (SA)	Henschke, Penfolds, Rockford, Torbreck
	McLaren Vale (SA)	Hardys, Coriole, Chapel Hill
	Margaret River, Great Southern (WA)	Cape Mentelle, Plantagenet
Cabernet Sauvignon	Margaret River (WA)	Cape Mentelle, Cullen, Moss Wood
	Coonawarra (SA)	Wynns, Lindemans, Bowen Estate
	The Barossa, Adelaide Hills (SA)	Penfolds, Henschke, Petaluma
	Yarra Valley, Great Western (VIC)	Yarra Yering, Yerinberg, Bests
Merlot	Yarra Valley, Great Western (VIC)	Bests, Yara Yering
	Adelaide Hills, Clare Valley (SA)	Petaluma, Pikes
Pinot Noir	Yarra Valley (VIC)	Coldstream Hills, Tarrawarra
	Gippsland, Geelong (VIC)	Bass Philip, Bannockburn, Shadowfax

Beer

Young Henrys   Cascade
Newtowner   Premium Lager

Most Australian beer is vat fermented real ale or lager, both consumed chilled. Full-strength beer has an alcohol content of around 4.8 per cent, mid-strength beers have around 3.5 per cent, while "light" beers have less than 3 per cent. Traditionally heat sterilized, cold filtration is also popular. Craft beers are booming, with locally produced, often quirkily named boutique beers taking on the big-name breweries. Young Henrys from Newtown in Sydney offers a particularly good range. Aficionados of real ale should seek out a pub brewery. Beer is ordered by glass size: a schooner is a 426 ml (15 fl oz) glass and a middy is 284 ml (10 fl oz) in NSW, though glass sizes can vary.

Spirits

Australian distillers produce fine dark and white rums from Queensland's sugar cane plantations (see p250). Notable labels include Bundaberg, from the town of that name, and Beenleigh. Australia's grape vintage is also the basis of good-value domestic brandies. Popular labels are St Agnes and McWilliams.

Bundaberg
rum

Other Drinks

With a climate ranging from tropical to alpine, Australia has year-round fresh fruit for juicing. Its apples are also used to make cider. Scores of still and sparkling mineral and other bottled waters now supply an annual market of nearly 200 million litres. Juice bars using healthy ingredients do a booming trade in shopping areas. A thriving coffee culture and niche organic-tea market mean a wide range of hot beverages are readily available.

White coffee

Caffe latte

Pear and kiwi
frappé

Banana
smoothie

Strawberry
juice

Where to Eat and Drink

Sydney

The Rocks and Circular Quay

Vintage Café on the Rocks $
Mediterranean **Map** 1 B2
Shop R2, 3 Nurses Walk,
NSW 2000
Tel *(02) 9252 2055*
In a cobbled courtyard, this is a
great little place for a breakfast
omelette, tapas or a plate of
paella and a glass of sangria.

Glenmore Hotel $$
Pub **Map** 1 B2
96 Cumberland St, The Rocks,
NSW 2000
Tel *(02) 9247 4794*
Rooftop dining with harbour
views at this casual spot popular
with young city workers.

Heritage Belgian Beer Café $$
Belgian **Map** 1 B3
135 Harrington St, NSW 2000
Tel *(02) 8488 2460*
Lively bar and restaurant with a
selection of Belgian beers on tap.
Try the mussels, cooked one of
eight ways and served in a pot.

MCA Café $$
Modern Australian **Map** 1 B2
Museum of Contemporary Art,
140 George St, NSW 2000
Tel *(02) 9250 8443*
Sydney favourites such as
pan-fried kingfish and twice-
baked cheese soufflé. Fabulous
harbour views from the terrace.

Pei Modern $$
Modern Australian **Map** 1 B3
199 George St, NSW 2000
Tel *(02) 9250 3160*

Fine dining in a relaxed, bistro
setting in the Four Seasons
Hotel. Pre-theatre and bar
menus are also available.

Aria $$$
Modern Australian **Map** 1 C2
1 Macquarie Street, East Circular
Quay, NSW 2000
Tel *(02) 9240 2255*
Striking harbour views and
imaginative fine dining in this
elegant space close to the Opera
House. Extensive international
wine list.

Café Sydney $$$
Modern Australian **Map** 1 B3
Level 5, Customs House, 31 Alfred St,
NSW 2000
Tel *(02) 9251 8683* **Closed** *Sat lunch*
Buzzing restaurant in the historic
Customs House. A tandoor oven,
wood-fired grill, rotisserie and
wok turn out a variety of food.

The Dining Room $$$
Modern Australian **Map** 1 B1
Park Hyatt Sydney, 7 Hickson Rd,
NSW 2000
Tel *(02) 9256 1661* **Closed** *Mon–Fri*
lunch
This is a stylish spot that offers
incredible views of the Sydney
Opera House. Guests can enjoy
elegant food while watching the
ferries pass by.

Eleven Bridge $$$
Modern Australian **Map** 1 B3
11 Bridge St, NSW 2000
Tel *(02) 9252 1888* **Closed** *Sun; Sat*
lunch
A grand dining room inside a
sandstone heritage building,
serving the finest sustainable
produce from celebrated chef
Neil Perry.

Price Guide
Prices are based on a three-course meal
per person, with half a bottle of house
wine and service charges.
$ up to A$50
$$ A$50 to A$90
$$$ over A$90

DK Choice

Est $$$
Modern Australian **Map** 1 B3
Level 1, Establishment,
252 George St, NSW 2000
Tel *(02) 9240 3000* **Closed** *Sun;*
Sat lunch
With highly imaginative food,
a superb wine list and top-
notch service, this fine-dining
restaurant keeps hauling in the
awards. Head chef Peter Doyle
is considered one of the
founding fathers of Modern
Australian cuisine. His tasting
menus offer diners a series of
key dishes, matched with wines.

Quay $$$
Modern Australian **Map** 1 B2
Upper Level, Overseas Passenger
Terminal, NSW 2000
Tel *(02) 9251 5600* **Closed** *Mon–*
Thu lunch
Great views and food to match.
Star chef Peter Gilmore combines
ingredients in surprising ways.

City Centre and Darling Harbour

Bodhi in the Park $
Chinese **Map** 1 C5
Cook & Phillip Park, 2–4 College St,
NSW 2000
Tel *(02) 9360 2523* **Closed** *Mon*
A wonderful place for lunch or
dinner in warm weather, when
seating is under the fig trees.
Superb organic vegan *yum cha*.

Chat Thai $
Thai **Map** 4 E4
20 Campbell St, Haymarket, NSW 2000
Tel *(02) 9211 1808*
Trendy Thai eatery serving tangy
and authentic dishes. Groovy
decor and youthful staff. Often
busy, so be prepared to wait.

Din Tai Fung $
Chinese **Map** 4 E3
Level 1, World Square, 644 George St,
NSW 2000
Tel *(02) 9264 6010*
Delicious Chinese food, including
gorgeous dumplings, wonton
soup and steamed buns. Be sure
to try the mango ice cream.

Impressive view of Sydney Opera House from The Dining Room, Sydney

Madame Nhu $
Vietnamese **Map** 4 E2
Shop 5, The Galeries, 500 George St, NSW 2000
Tel *(02) 9283 3355*
Great place to sample fresh, flavourful Vietnamese street food. Choose from the traditional *pho* (noodle soup), or stir fries.

Mamak $
Malaysian **Map** 4 D4
15 Goulburn St, NSW 2000
Tel *(02) 9211 1668*
Popular restaurant offering tasty, traditional fare served on low tables with wooden stools. Fans queue round the block.

Mother Chu's Vegetarian Kitchen $
Vegetarian **Map** 4 E3
367 Pitt St, NSW 2000
Tel *(02) 9283 2828*   **Closed** *Sun*
Cheerful canteen-style restaurant serving hearty stir-fries and curries that blend the flavours of Taiwan, China and Japan.

Diethnes $$
Greek **Map** 1 B5
336 Pitt St, NSW 2000
Tel *(02) 9267 8956*   **Closed** *Sun*
Diethnes is a Sydney institution, with its kitsch decor and hearty meals. Come here for traditional Greek dishes such as *tzaziki* and *spanakopita*.

Marigold $$
Chinese **Map** 4 E3
683 George St, NSW 2000
Tel *(02) 9281 3388*
Classic *yum cha* restaurant, with waiters pushing laden trolleys. Go for the Cantonese seafood or the roast suckling pig. Diners pick their fish from a tank.

Zaaffran $$
Indian **Map** 3 C2
Level 2, 10 Darling Drive, 345 Harbourside Shopping Centre, NSW 2000
Tel *(02) 9211 8900*
This restaurant is a haven for vegetarians, but the lamb shank stew and chicken biryani are superb too. Outdoor seating.

Café del Mar $$$
Seafood **Map** 4 D2
The Roof Terrace, Cockle Bay Wharf, 201 Sussex St, NSW 2000
Tel *(02) 9267 6700*
Eat fresh, local seafood right by the water. The graphic dining room decor and harbour views are spectacular.

Golden Century $$$
Seafood/Chinese **Map** 4 E4
393–399 Sussex St, NSW 2000
Tel *(02) 9212 3901*

A selection of tasty Chinese dishes at Bodhi in the Park, Sydney

Huge menu of Cantonese seafood dishes. Specialities include deep-fried mud crab and steamed baby abalone.

DK Choice

Momofuku Seiobo $$$
Modern Asian **Map** 3 B1
The Star, Level G, 80 Pyrmont St, NSW 2009
Tel *(02) 9777 9000*   **Closed** *Sun; Mon–Fri lunch*
The open kitchen here makes a night out at this much-lauded restaurant a theatrical experience. The chefs are a cool crowd with fast fingers. The food is imaginative and innovative. Do not miss the stuffed steamed buns, which chef David Chang has turned into an art form. Book in advance.

Pendolino $$$
Italian **Map** 4 E2
Shop 100, Level 2, The Strand Arcade, 412–414 George St, NSW 2000
Tel *(02) 9231 6117*   **Closed** *Sun*
Elegant and romantic restaurant with an award-winning menu and attentive service. The artfully presented dishes burst with flavour.

An intimate dining area at the Spice Temple restuarant, Sydney

Spice Temple $$$
Chinese **Map** 4 F1
10 Bligh St, NSW 2000
Tel *(02) 8078 1888*
Modern Chinese restaurant, softly lit by lanterns. Chillies feature in many forms – dried, fresh, salted, pickled, brined and fermented.

Tetsuya's $$$
Japanese **Map** 4 E3
529 Kent St, NSW 2000
Tel *(02) 9267 2900*   **Closed** *Sun & Mon*
Tetsuya's is revered as one of Australia's best restaurants. The set tasting menu fuses Japanese flavours with French technique. Book well in advance.

Botanic Garden and The Domain

Botanic Gardens Restaurant $$
Modern Australian **Map** 2 D4
Royal Botanic Gardens, Mrs Macquaries Rd, NSW 2000
Tel *(02) 9241 2419*   **Closed** *dinner*
Set among lush greenery, this excellent-value lunch venue opens on to a terrace, letting in the sounds of the gardens.

Chiswick at the Gallery $$
Modern Australian **Map** 2 D4
The Art Gallery of New South Wales, Art Gallery Rd, NSW 2000
Tel *(02) 9225 1819*   **Closed** *dinner*
Discuss the latest exhibition over lunch in the gallery's contemporary dining room. The menu at the more casual café is great for children.

The Pavilion $$
Modern Australian **Map** 2 D4
1 Art Gallery Rd, NSW 2000
Tel *(02) 9232 1322*   **Closed** *Mon*
This is the ideal spot for a decadent breakfast, casual lunch or afternoon treat. Serene and enchanting ambience.

For more information on types of restaurants *see page 498*

The elegant dining room at the Buon Ricordo, Paddington

Kings Cross, Darlinghurst and Paddington

Bill and Toni's
Italian   **Map** 5 A1
74 Stanley St, NSW 2010
Tel *(02) 9360 4702*
A Sydney stalwart offering home-style Italian cooking, Bill and Toni's is much loved for its old-fashioned feel.

Gelato Messina
Ice Cream   **Map** 5 B2
Shop 1, 241 Victoria St, NSW 2010
Tel *(02) 9331 1588*
Rightly popular, this *gelateria* produces scrumptious ice cream in imaginative flavours such as tiramisu, salted caramel with white chocolate, or pear and rhubarb. Choice of sorbets also available.

Govinda's
Vegetarian   **Map** 5 B1
112 Darlinghurst Rd, NSW 2010
Tel *(02) 9380 5155*   **Closed** *Mon & Tue; lunch*
Much-loved restaurant where locals pile up a plate of delicious curries from the all-you-can-eat buffet. Movie room upstairs.

Buzo
Modern Australian   **Map** 6 D4
3 Jersey Rd, NSW 2025
Tel *(02) 9328 1600*   **Closed** *Mon*
A lighter take on traditional European styles. You'll be spoiled for choice, with a seasonal menu, bar menu and extensive wine list.

The Fish Shop
Seafood   **Map** 2 E4
22 Challis Ave, Potts Point, NSW 2011
Tel *(02) 9326 9000*
Enjoy locally caught and freshly prepared seafood at this casual, nautical-themed restaurant. Try the fisherman's basket or the fish burger. The whitewashed interior is decked up with fishing gear.

Fu Manchu
Chinese   **Map** 5 B2
229 Darlinghurst Rd, NSW 2010
Tel *(02) 9360 9424*   **Closed** *Mon–Sat lunch*
This sleek spot is always crowded with *yum cha* enthusiasts on Saturdays and Sundays. Sample the gorgeous dumplings and prawn sesame rye toast.

Mahjong Room
Chinese   **Map** 5 A2
312 Crown St, NSW 2010
Tel *(02) 9361 3985*
Delicious Cantonese food served on *mah jong* tables. Drop in at lunchtime on Friday or Saturday to learn this Chinese game.

Paddington Inn
International   **Map** 6 D4
338 Oxford St, NSW 2021
Tel *(02) 9380 5913*
Handmade burgers are served at the front bar at the Paddington Inn, but step into the stylish contemporary dining room to enjoy a meal from an artistically presented modern menu.

Saint Peter
Seafood   **Map** 6 D4
362 Oxford St, NSW 2021
Tel *(02) 8937 2530*
The menu changes daily with no land-raised meat here; it's all about the best from the ocean, impeccably prepared by husband-and-wife team Josh and Julie Niland. There is also a dedicated pastry chef.

Buon Ricordo
Italian   **Map** 5 C2
108 Boundary St, NSW 2021
Tel *(02) 9360 6729*   **Closed** *Sun & Mon*
Off-duty chefs love this restaurant with a Neapolitan and Roman menu. The signature dish is fettuccine with Parmesan cheese, cream and truffled egg.

Lucio's
Italian $$$
     Map 6 D3
47 Windsor St, NSW 2021
Tel *(02) 9380 5996*   **Closed** *Sun & Mon*
This art-lovers' eatery is adorned with works by contemporary Australian artists, such as John Olsen, John Coburn and Tim Storrier. On the menu is expertly cooked, seasonal food.

Otto
Italian $$$
     Map 2 D4
Area 8, 6 Cowper Wharf Rd, NSW 2011
Tel *(02) 9368 7488*
Otto is an upbeat, modern Italian restaurant offering fabulously colourful dishes in relaxed and attractive surroundings. Sample from its impressive list of wines from Australia, New Zealand, Italy and France.

Further Afield

BONDI BEACH:
Bondi Trattoria
Modern Australian $$
34 Campbell Parade, NSW 2026
Tel *(02) 9365 4303*
A café by day and a restaurant at night. Join the locals for superb views of the beach from every table. Try the buttermilk pancakes with blueberry compote for breakfast, or angel hair pasta with raw tuna for dinner.

BONDI BEACH: Hotel Ravesis $$
International
118 Campbell Parade, NSW 2026
Tel *(02) 9365 4422*
Exciting dishes with multicultural influences are offered at Hotel Ravesis. Dine inside or out on the terrace, and take in the buzz of the beach.

The trendy bar area at Hurricane's Grill, Bondi beach

BONDI BEACH:
Hurricane's Grill $$
Grill
130 Roscoe St, NSW 2026
Tel *(02) 9130 7101*
Juicy steaks, burgers, chicken, ribs and vegetarian dishes are basted in South African sauces before being grilled to perfection at this upbeat restaurant and bar.

BONDI BEACH:
Icebergs Dining Room $$$
Italian
1 Notts Ave, NSW 2026
Tel *(02) 9365 9000*
One of Bondi's swishest restaurants. A palette of ocean blues, giant chandeliers and silk cushions create a glamorous beach feel.

BONDI BEACH: Sean's
Panorama $$$
Modern Australian
270 Campbell Parade, NSW 2026
Tel *(02) 9365 4924* **Closed** *Mon & Tue*
Intimate restaurant serving rustic seasonal dishes. Menu changes daily. Attentive, friendly staff and a pleasant beachside location.

MANLY: The Manly Wharf
Hotel $$
Seafood
Manly Wharf, 21 East Esplanade, NSW 2095
Tel *(02) 9977 1266*
Zoom across from Sydney's central business district by boat to soak up Manly's relaxed vibe and tuck into fresh calamari. Locals come here to enjoy drinks on sunny afternoons.

ROSE BAY: Catalina $$$
Modern Australian
1 Sunderland Ave, Lyne Park, NSW 2029
Tel *(02) 9371 0555* **Closed** *Sun dinner*
A lovely spot for an alfresco lunch, this award-winning eatery resembles a docked ship. Fresh food with Mediterranean and Asian influences.

SURRY HILLS:
Bourke St Bakery $
Café
633 Bourke St, NSW 2010
Tel *(02) 9699 1011*
Tremendously popular for its artisan bread and handmade pies, tarts and pastries. Be prepared to wait for a table.

SURRY HILLS: Café Mint $
Middle Eastern
579 Crown St, NSW 2010
Tel *(02) 9319 0848* **Closed** *Mon*
This tiny café serves excellent coffee and fabulous-value food. Sample the *mezze* plate for a rainbow of dips and pickles. It can be crowded.

SURRY HILLS: Longrain
Restaurant & Bar $$$
Thai **Map** 4 F4
85 Commonwealth St, NSW 2010
Tel *(02) 9280 2888* **Closed** *Sat–Thu lunch*
Modern Asian dining serving great hot, sour, salty and sweet dishes to combine and share, in an industrial-chic setting.

SURRY HILLS: Porteño $$$
Argentinian
358 Cleveland St, NSW 2010
Tel *(02) 8399 1440* **Closed** *Sun & Mon*
One of the coolest places to eat in town, Porteño pays homage to South American cuisine by grilling succulent meats over a fire pit. The 8-hour slow-roasted pork with crisp crackling is superb.

SURRY HILLS: Toko
Restaurant & Bar $$$
Japanese
490 Crown St, NSW 2010
Tel *(02) 9357 6100* **Closed** *Sun; Sat & Mon lunch*
Informal *izakaya*-style dining inspired by Japanese sake bars. Toko serves a large range of tasty little courses.

SURRY HILLS: The Winery $$$
Modern Australian
285A Crown St, NSW 2010
Tel *(02) 8322 2007*
Fun wine bar and restaurant that can often get rowdy. Posh bar snacks and juicy steaks served on a board with chips.

WATSONS BAY:
Doyles on the Beach $$$
Seafood **Map** 1 C2
11 Marine Parade, NSW 2030
Tel *(02) 9337 2007*
Head out to Doyles for tasty fish and chips by the harbour. The barramundi and lobster are pricey but worth every cent.

The Blue Mountains and Beyond

BELLINGEN: Oak Street
Food & Wine $$
Modern Australian
2 Oak St, NSW 2454
Tel *(02) 6655 9000* **Closed** *Sun–Tue*
Award-winning restaurant with an understated feel. Treats from chef Ray Urquhart include flowerpot bread with roast garlic oil.

BROKEN HILL: The Silly Goat $
Modern Australian
360 Argent St, NSW 2080
Tel *(08) 8088 4774* **Closed** *dinner*
A bustling café as well as a breakfast and lunch spot serving a good range of freshly prepared dishes. Great coffee, organic juices and shakes.

BYRON BAY:
Fishmonger's Byron $
Seafood
Bay Lane, NSW 2010
Tel *0412 059 771*
Sample fresh seafood, hand-cut chips and vegetable tempura at this cult café and takeaway.

BYRON BAY: St. Elmo $$
Mediterranean
22 Fletcher St, NSW 2481
Tel *(02) 6680 7426* **Closed** *lunch*
Urban eating space that is both chic and relaxed. Serves Spanish-style tapas to share.

BYRON BAY:
Byron Beach Restaurant $$$
Modern Australian
Clarke's Beach, Lawson St, NSW 2481
Tel *(02) 6685 8400*
Quality casual fine dining in a busy, bright setting with great ocean views. Also offers takeaways to enjoy on the beach.

Excellent view of Bondi Beach from the outdoor terrace of Hotel Ravesis

For more information on types of restaurants *see page 498*

Delicious honey-glazed duck with fennel, mandarin and chestnuts at Subo, Newcastle

COFFS HARBOUR: Shearwater $$
Modern Australian
321 Harbour Drive, NSW 2450
Tel *(02) 6651 6053*   **Closed** *Sun–Tue dinner*
Dine right beside the water at this pleasant restaurant on Coffs Creek. Local seafood gets top billing, followed by meat dishes.

COFFS HARBOUR: Y-Knot Bistro $$
International
30 Marina Drive, NSW 2450
Tel *(02) 6651 1741*
An airy, easy-going coastal eatery. The brunch is especially popular with local yacht owners, beach fans and families.

GOSFORD: Point Café $$
Café
36 Webb St, NSW 2250
Tel *(02) 4324 8099*   **Closed** *dinner*
Set in Japanese-style gardens with a picturesque lake and waterfall, as well as a regional gallery. Crowd-pleasing menu of light and more filling meals.

HUNTER VALLEY: The Servants Quarters Tea Rooms $
Café
175 Swan St, Morpeth, NSW 2321
Tel *(02) 4934 1857*   **Closed** *Mon–Wed; dinner*
Enjoy breakfast, morning tea or lunch inside this quaint café or out in the garden. Home-made scones with jam and fresh cream are irresistible.

HUNTER VALLEY: Matilda Bay Brewhouse & Dining $$
Italian
Hunter Resort, 917 Hermitage Rd, Pokolbin, NSW 2320
Tel *(02) 4998 7777*
Relax over pizza, pasta and a glass of great wine; or a selection of 12 craft brews including tasting notes for each.

HUNTER VALLEY: Esca Bimbadgen $$$
Winery Restaurant
Bimbadgen Estate, 790 McDonald's Rd, Pokolbin, NSW 2320
Tel *(02) 4998 4666*   **Closed** *Sun–Thu dinner*
The menu suggests a wine to match every dish. Finish with a scrumptious dessert tasting plate paired with Botrytis Semillon.

HUNTER VALLEY: EXP. Restaurant $$$
Modern Australian
1596 Broke Rd, Pokolbin, NSW 2320
Tel *(02) 4998 7264*   **Closed** *Mon & Tue; dinner Sun*
At this chic gem, guests can sit at the bar and interact with the chef. Some ingredients come from the restaurant garden.

HUNTER VALLEY: Leaves and Fishes $$$
Modern Australian
737 Lovedale Rd, Lovedale, Pokolbin, NSW 2320
Tel *(02) 4930 7400*   **Closed** *Sun–Tue; dinner Sun–Thu*
Sample sublime, healthy dishes out of first-class ingredients, particularly seafood.

DK Choice

HUNTER VALLEY: Muse Restaurant & Café $$$
Winery Restaurant
Hungerford Hill Wines, 1 Broke Rd, Pokolbin, NSW 2320
Tel *(02) 4998 6777*   **Closed** *Mon–Fri lunch; Sun–Tue dinner*
With dramatic architecture and impeccable food and wine, Muse sets the bar for Australian winery restaurants. The emphasis here is on craftsmanship, with everything – from bread and pasta, to pastries and ice cream – lovingly handmade.

KATOOMBA: The Yellow Deli $
Café
214 Katoomba St, NSW 2780
Tel *(02) 4782 9744*   **Closed** *Fri dinner; Sat*
Unique café run by a Messianic Christian community. Quirky, rustic interior and wonderfully wholesome fare, such as soup and healthy treats.

KATOOMBA: Darley's $$$
Modern Australian
Lilianfels, Lilianfels Ave, NSW 2780
Tel *(02) 4780 1200*   **Closed** *Sun & Mon; lunch*
Polished restaurant in a beautiful 19th-century retreat house with open fireplaces. Well known for venison. It also has an enviable wine list.

KATOOMBA: The Rooster $$$
French
48 Merriwa St, NSW 2780
Tel *(02) 4782 1206*
Sit near the fireplace in this gorgeous Federation-style guesthouse and enjoy delicious food paired with the perfect wine.

KINGSCLIFF: Fins $$$
Seafood
5–6 Bells Blvd, Salt Village, NSW 2487
Tel *(02) 6674 4833*   **Closed** *Mon–Thu lunch, Sun dinner*
At Fins, only the freshest produce is used, often from the chef's own garden. The fish is line-caught wherever possible, sometimes only hours before the meal is prepared.

LAKE MACQUARIE: Lakehouse Café $$
Café
11 Shoreside Row, Murrays Beach, NSW 2281
Tel *(02) 4971 1745*   **Closed** *dinner*
A wide range of good if slightly pricey treats is served here, from breakfast treats and sweets to more substantial lunches.

LENNOX HEAD: Mi Thai $
Thai
2/76 Ballina St, NSW 2478
Tel *(02) 6687 5820*
Local surfers love the food at this intimate restaurant. Modern and classic Asian cuisine, including mouth-watering *choo chee* curry, made with coconut milk.

LEURA: Silk's Brasserie $$$
International
128 The Mall, NSW 2780
Tel *(02) 4784 2534*
Silk's is a family-friendly fine-dining place that even gives colouring pencils to any accompanying children to keep them busy. Book ahead.

Key to Price Guide *see page 504*

MEGALONG VALLEY:
Megalong Valley Tea Rooms $
Café
Megalong Rd, NSW 2785
Tel *(02) 4787 9181*
Watch kangaroos graze nearby
while tucking into apple pie
or scones with cream at this
long-established family-run
tearoom.

NEWCASTLE:
Customs House Hotel $$
International
1 Bond St, NSW 2300
Tel *(02) 4925 2585* **Closed** *Sun dinner*
Good, flavoursome food and
reasonably priced drinks in
unfussy surroundings. The
menu is inspired by French
brasserie fare.

**NEWCASTLE: Scratchleys on
The Wharf** $$
Modern Australian
200 Wharf Rd, NSW 2300
Tel *(02) 4929 1111*
An eco-friendly restaurant
housed in an energy-efficient
pavilion that perches over
the harbour. Particularly good
for fish.

NEWCASTLE: Subo $$$
Modern Australian
551D Hunter St, NSW 2300
Tel *(02) 4023 4048* **Closed** *Mon &
Tue; lunch*
A husband-and-wife team
produce imaginative, aromatic
and textured dishes. The five-
course degustation menu is
highly recommended. Warm and
knowledgeable staff.

PORT MACQUARIE:
The Stunned Mullet $$$
Modern Australian
12 William St, NSW 2444
Tel *(02) 6584 7757*
Easy-going restaurant. Inventive
combinations include prawns
with shiitake mushrooms and
oat flakes, and baby squid with
green papaya.

PORT STEPHENS:
Evviva Café & Bar $$
Modern Australian
14a Stockton St, Nelson Bay, NSW 2315
Tel *(02) 4984 2211* **Closed** *dinner
Sun–Wed*
Enjoy a tasty breakfast or lunch,
or indulge in tapas and drinks, at
this cool little spot where service
is friendly and efficient.

PORT STEPHENS: The Point $$$
International
*Soldiers Point Marina, Sunset
Boulevard, Soldiers Point, NSW 2317*
Tel *(02) 4984 7111*
Waterfront restaurant offering the
freshest catch such as Tasmanian
salmon and Red Emperor, along
with meat dishes and salads.

WAGGA WAGGA:
Indian Tavern Tandoori $
Indian
81 Peter St, NSW 2650
Tel *(02) 6921 3121*
Cuisine from across India, ranging
in spiciness from super hot to
mild. The butter chicken with
cashew nut butter is a favourite.

The South Coast and
Snowy Mountains

BATEMANS BAY: On the Pier $$
Seafood
Old Punt Rd, NSW 2536
Tel *(02) 4472 6405* **Closed** *Mon–
Thu lunch, Tue & Wed dinner*
Seafood with great bay views.
Four seasonal menus, plus daily
specials served in a heritage
former punt house on the river.

BERMAGUI: Il Passaggio $$
Italian
*Shop 5, Level 1, Fishermen's Wharf,
NSW 2546*
Tel *(02) 6493 5753* **Closed** *Mon &
Tue; Wed lunch*
Highly rated Italian food. Enjoy
the fabulous *antipasti*, thin-crust
pizzas and succulent pasta dishes.

BERRIMA: Eschalot $$$
Modern Australian
24 Old Hume Hwy, NSW 2577
Tel *(02) 4877 1977* **Closed** *Mon &
Tue; Wed lunch & Sun dinner*
Eschalot presents a contemporary
take on regional European
cuisine in an elegant heritage
building from the 1840s.
Enjoy pre-dinner drinks by
the open fire.

BERRY:
Berry Sourdough Café $$
Café
23 Prince Alfred St, NSW 2535
Tel *(02) 4464 1617* **Closed** *Mon &
Tue; dinner*
Sample organic sourdough
bread, cakes and savouries from
the owners' own bakery. Light
meals and good coffee as well.

BERRY: Silos Estate $$$
Winery Restaurant
*Silos Estate, B640 Princes Hwy,
NSW 2535*
Tel *(02) 4448 6160* **Closed** *Sun dinner*
Taking its name from the estate's
old grain stores, Silos Estate
serves a select menu of superb
Middle Eastern, Asian and
Modern Australian fare. The wine
list contains fine local wines,
including some of Silos' own.

DK Choice

BOWRAL: Biota Dining $$$
Modern Australian
Kangaloon Rd, NSW 2576
Tel *(02) 4862 2005* **Closed** *Tue–
Wed; Thu lunch*
This excellent restaurant loves
to experiment. The interesting
menu may feature blackened
forest mushrooms with
chlorophyll, pine seeds and
yogurt made with goat's
milk, or mulloway with sweet
carrid shrimps and sea lettuce.
Top-quality ingredients, many
coming straight from the
kitchen garden.

Relaxing outdoor seating area at Customs House Hotel, Newcastle

For more information on types of restaurants *see page 498*

BOWRAL:
Hordern's Restaurant $$$
Modern Australian
Milton Park Country House Hotel, Hordern's Rd, NSW 2576
Tel *(02) 4861 8100*
Elegant country hotel with two dining rooms, high-backed chairs, sumptuous fabrics and garden views. Contemporary menu with European and Asian influences.

EDEN: Sprout $
Café
134 Imlay St, NSW 2551
Tel *(02) 6496 1511*
Appealing, community-focused, eco-friendly produce store and café. Breakfast includes BLT (bacon, lettuce, tomato) sandwich with organic avocado on toasted panini. Tasty lunch specials, too.

GOULBURN: Fireside Inn $$
Modern Australian
23 Market St, NSW 2580
Tel *(02) 4821 2727* **Closed** *Sun & Mon*
True to its name, this landmark mock-Tudor restaurant has a large, open fire to welcome guests in the winter months. Serves hearty seasonal fare.

JERVIS BAY: Supply $
Café
Shop 1, 54 Owen St, Huskisson, NSW 2540
Tel *(02) 4441 5815* **Closed** *dinner*
Airy café, deli and fresh-produce market in a sunny location with sparkling bay views. Good coffee, tasty breakfasts and fresh, flavoursome lunches.

JERVIS BAY: The Gunyah at Paperbark Camp $$$
Modern Australian
571 Woollamia Rd, Woollamia, NSW 2540
Tel *(02) 4441 7299* **Closed** *early Jun–end Aug*
Architect-designed treetop dining room in serene bushland. Dishes based on local produce include kangaroo fillet, local fish and seasonal berries.

Duck confit dish at The Gunyah at Paperbark Camp, Jervis Bay

KIAMA: Hanoi on Manning $$
Vietnamese
10 Manning St, NSW 2533
Tel *(02) 4232 3315* **Closed** *Tue*
Welcoming restaurant with good vegetarian and vegan options. Popular with Sydneysiders who visit the coast at weekends.

MERIMBULA:
Waterfront Café $
Café
2 Waterfront Drive, NSW 2548
Tel *(02) 6495 2211* **Closed** *Mon & Tue*
Stunning waterfront location with a solid selection of typical café fare, from sweet treats to heartier offerings, including burgers and fish and chips.

MITTAGONG:
Esco Pazzo $$
Italian
84 Main St, NSW 2575
Tel *(02) 4872 2400* **Closed** *Mon*
Italian-born chef Emilio Picchio serves up stone-fired pizzas, fresh pastas and authentic seafood and meat dishes.

MOLLYMOOK: Bannister's Pool and Cocktail Bar $$
Italian
191 Michell Parade, NSW 2539
Tel *(02) 4455 3044* **Closed** *lunch*
Delicious and affordable light fare, pizzas and desserts served

nightly (from 6pm) in a casual, airy and stylish poolside-bar setting with ocean views.

NAROOMA: Quarterdeck $
Seafood
Riverside Drive, NSW 2546
Tel *(02) 4476 2723* **Closed** *Mon–Wed*
Popular, child-friendly café overlooking Wagonga Inlet. Seafood favourites include fish 'n' chips, salt-and-chilli squid, bouillabaisse, tapas and local Narooma oysters.

THREDBO:
Cascades Restaurant $$$
Modern Australian
Thredbo Alpine Resort, Friday Drive, NSW 2625
Tel *(02) 6459 4200* **Closed** *Sun & Mon*
Mountain dining at its best in summer and winter, with fresh, modern cuisine, friendly service and sweeping views.

THREDBO: Cuisine Restaurant & Bar $$$
Modern Australian
Lake Crackenback Resort, 1650 Alpine Way, NSW 2627
Tel *(02) 6451 3000*
This restaurant with inspiring views of Lake Crackenback focuses on local produce such as smoked mountain trout and poached rabbit. Book ahead.

WOLLONGONG:
Diggies $
Modern Australian
1 Cliff Rd, North Beach, NSW 2500
Tel *(02) 4226 2688* **Closed** *dinner*
Housed in a small, hip beach shack this place serves scrumptious breakfasts and brunches with awesome views.

WOLLONGONG:
Caveau $$$
French
122–124 Keira St, NSW 2500
Tel *(02) 4226 4855* **Closed** *Sun & Mon*
Modern French restaurant and cookery school led by master chef Peter Sheppard. The seasonal menu changes monthly.

Canberra and ACT

CANBERRA:
Porkbarrel $
International
King George Terrace, Parkes, ACT 2600
Tel *(02) 6273 1455* **Closed** *Sat & Sun; dinner*
This lovely café in the National Rose Gardens serves a selection of casual dining options from big breakfasts to pizzas.

Light and airy dinning area at Cuisine Restaurant & Bar, Thredbo

Key to Price Guide *see page 504*

CANBERRA: Portrait Café　$
Café
National Portrait Gallery,
King Edward St, ACT 2600
Tel *(02) 6102 7162*　**Closed** *dinner*
For a break during a visit to the
National Portrait Gallery, head
to the back of the building and
enjoy delicious tea or a seasonal
lunch with a glass of wine.

CANBERRA: Timmy's Kitchen　$
Chinese/Malaysian
Manuka Village, Furneaux St,
Manuka, ACT 2603
Tel *(02) 6295 6537*　**Closed** *Mon*
This popular restaurant offers
cheap, speedy and good food.
The Malaysian items, including the
curry *laksas*, are recommended.

CANBERRA:
Benchmark Wine Bar　$$
European
65 Northbourne Ave, ACT 2600
Tel *(02) 6262 6522*　**Closed** *Sat*
lunch; Sun & Mon
Over 100 wines by the glass and
another 600 bottles to choose
from. Great food and friendly
service in a lively atmosphere.

CANBERRA: La Cantina　$$
Italian
4 Iluka St, Narrabundah, ACT 2604
Tel *(02) 6239 5556*
Authentic, classic Italian food is
served in a bustling setting with
Roman-style brick walls and
Italian oil paintings.

CANBERRA: The Chairman
and Yip　$$
Chinese
Burbury Hotel, 1 Burbury Close,
Barton, ACT 2600
Tel *(02) 6162 1220*　**Closed** *Sun &*
Mon; Sat lunch
Creative Asian restaurant that
combines Cantonese and Western
flavours to produce contemporary
dishes. Has been popular ever
since it opened in the early 1990s.

CANBERRA:
Ethiopia Down Under　$$
Ethiopian
Shop 1, 70 Hodgson Crescent,
Pearce, ACT 2607
Tel *(02) 6286 1659* **Closed** *Mon; lunch*
An unpretentious place to try
Ethiopia's staple, *injera* (pancake),
with dollops of spicy sauces.
Finish off with the ice cream
made with Ethiopian coffee.

CANBERRA: Italian and Sons　$$
Italian
7 Lonsdale St, Braddon, ACT 2612
Tel *(02) 6162 4888*　**Closed** *Sun; Sat*
& Mon lunch
Styled after a traditional Roman
trattoria. Good renditions

Outdoor seating in a peaceful lakeside setting at The Boat House by the Lake, Canberra

of regional classics such as
charcuterie, pasta dishes and
pizzas, as well as daily specials.

CANBERRA: Morks　$$
Thai
Unit 3, 37 Kesteven St, Florey, ACT 2615
Tel *(02) 6259 0112*　**Closed** *Sun*
dinner; Mon
One of Canberra's best
contemporary Thai restaurants
offers traditional banquets and
a tasting menu in a simple,
uncluttered space with plain
wooden furniture.

CANBERRA: Pistachio Dining
at Torrens　$$
Modern Australian
3A Torrens Place, Torrens, ACT 2607
Tel *(02) 6286 2966*　**Closed** *Sun &*
Mon; lunch
The menu at this Woden Valley
restaurant features flavour-
packed dishes such as roast pork
tenderloin with baby beetroot,
and Tasmanian salmon pie with
garlic potato purée.

CANBERRA: Aubergine　$$$
European
18 Barker St, Griffith, ACT 2603
Tel *(02) 6260 8666* **Closed** *Sun; lunch*
The inventive menu at Aubergine
may feature veal tartare with
bitter cocoa and quail egg, or
ribeye with smoked potato
and bone-marrow vinaigrette.

CANBERRA: The Boat House
by the Lake　$$$
Modern Australian
Grevillea Park, Menindee Drive,
Barton, ACT 2600
Tel *(02) 6273 5500* **Closed** *Sun; lunch*
Quality creative fare in a serene
location with views over Lake
Burley Griffin. Try the blue
cheesecake for dessert. In good
weather, ask for a table on the
deck. Bookings are essential.

DK Choice

CANBERRA: Courgette　$$$
European
54 Marcus Clarke St, ACT 2601
Tel *(02) 6247 4042*　**Closed** *Sun*
Courgette has been showered
with praise by critics, locals
and visitors alike. Owner James
Mussillon trained under chef
Marco Pierre White. His culinary
creations are elegant but
uncomplicated, and the decor
reflects this. Exceptionally
good-value three-course lunch
and four-course dinner menus.

CANBERRA: Rubicon　$$$
European
6A Barker St, Griffith, ACT 2603
Tel *(02) 6295 9919*　**Closed** *Sat*
lunch; Sun
White tablecloths and candlelight
in understated surroundings set
the scene for one of Canberra's
most pleasant dining experiences.
Excellent vegetarian options.

CANBERRA:
Sage Dining Rooms　$$$
International
Gorman House Arts Centre,
Batman St, Braddon, ACT 2612
Tel *(02) 6249 6050* **Closed** *Sun & Mon*
Sage is a fine-dining venue with
a buzzing yet discreet atmo-
sphere. Every plate served is a
delicate and delicious work of art.
Be sure to book ahead.

CANBERRA: Water's Edge　$$$
European
40 Parkes Place, Parkes, ACT 2600
Tel *(02) 6273 5066*　**Closed** *Mon & Tue*
Sweeping views across Lake Burley
Griffin, fine cuisine and excellent
service guarantee a memorable
meal at this stylish restaurant.
Treat yourself to the delightful
passion fruit soufflé for dessert.

For more information on types of restaurants *see page 498*

Wonderful view of the Story Bridge from the atmospheric terrace at Customs House, Brisbane

Brisbane

ALBION:
Breakfast Creek Hotel $$
Grill
2 Kingsford Smith Drive, QLD 4010
Tel *(07) 3262 5988*
An iconic pub that has been a Queensland favourite since 1889. Noted for its steaks – guests can choose theirs before it is cooked.

CAMP HILL:
Restaurant Rapide $$$
Modern Australian
4 Martha St, QLD 4152
Tel *(07) 3843 5755* **Closed** *Sun & Mon*
Fine-dining bistro with a changing contemporary menu that takes advantage of seasonal produce.

CITY CENTRE: Esq $$
Modern Australian/Korean
145 Eagle St, QLD 4000
Tel *(07) 3220 2123* **Closed** *Sun & Mon; Sat lunch*
The little brother of Esquire, Brisbane's much-lauded fine-dining restaurant, Esq is a superb charcoal grill in fashionably simple and casual surroundings.

CITY CENTRE:
Aria Brisbane $$$
Modern Australian
1 Eagle St, QLD 4000
Tel *(07) 3233 2555* **Closed** *lunch Sat & Sun*
Attention to every detail is the hallmark of celebrity chef-owner Matt Moran's team. Fine dining at its best, with sweeping views across the city and river a bonus.

CITY CENTRE: Cha Cha Char $$$
Grill
Shop 3, 1 Eagle St, Eagle St Pier, QLD 4000
Tel *(07) 3211 9944* **Closed** *Sat; Sun lunch*
A favourite of local and visiting businessmen, this wood-fired steak restaurant specializes in grain-fed wagyu and mayura beef.

CITY CENTRE:
Customs House $$$
Modern Australian
399 Queen St, QLD 4001
Tel *(07) 3365 8921* **Closed** *Sun & Mon dinner*
Heritage icon standing grandly on the riverbank. Dine inside or on the terrace with views of the Story Bridge. Quality fare and friendly, professional service.

CITY CENTRE: E'cco Bistro $$$
Modern Australian
100 Boundary & Adelaide sts, QLD 4000
Tel *(07) 3831 8344* **Closed** *Sun & Mon; Sat lunch*
Philip Johnson's award-winning bistro is simple and welcoming. The menu is based on fresh seasonal ingredients. Vegetarian and vegan options available.

DK Choice

CITY CENTRE: Esquire $$$
Modern Australian
145 Eagle St, QLD 4000
Tel *(07) 3220 2123* **Closed** *Sun & Mon; Sat lunch*
Brisbane's most imaginative and highly awarded restaurant has turned many heads with its cool, cutting-edge cuisine and stripped-down decor. The degustation menu changes every day and features hand-picked seasonal ingredients. Guests are served either seven or 15 delicious little courses that are expertly prepared and elegantly presented.

CITY CENTRE:
Fix Restaurant $$$
Modern Australian
40 Edward St, Port Office Hotel, QLD 4000
Tel *(07) 3210 6016* **Closed** *Sat lunch; Sun*
In an 1880s heritage building, Fix has many classic options, from bar snacks and wood-fired pizza to Moreton Bay bugs (local lobster).

CITY CENTRE: Il Centro
Restaurant and Bar $$$
Italian
Eagle St Pier, 1 Eagle St, QLD 4000
Tel *(07) 3221 6090* **Closed** *Sat lunch*
Modern Italian fare, but with flavours unique to Queensland: fresh seafood, prime cuts of meat, tropical fruit, seasonal vegetables and delicate garden herbs.

CITY CENTRE: Moda $$$
Mediterranean
12 Edward St, QLD 4000
Tel *(07) 3221 7655* **Closed** *Sun; lunch (except Thu & Fri)*
Enjoy fine cuisine in an elegant setting. The house special is the Pica Pica lunch: five small Spanish-inspired dishes with coffee and sweet treats.

CITY CENTRE: Saké $$$
Japanese
Level 1, 45 Eagle St Pier, QLD 4000
Tel *(07) 3015 0557*
Lively, colourful little sushi joint with a fantastic reputation. Grab a table, or sit at the bar to watch the chefs in action.

CITY CENTRE: Urbane $$$
Modern Australian
181 Mary St, QLD 4000
Tel *(07) 3229 2271* **Closed** *Sun–Wed; lunch*
A critics' favourite, Urbane offers five- and nine-course menus in a relaxed and hip contemporary setting. Impressive wine list. Vegetarians catered for.

FORTITUDE VALLEY:
Campos Coffee $
Café
11 Wandoo St, QLD 4006
Tel *(07) 3252 3612*
The flagship branch of this speciality coffee chain. Also offers "cupping" (coffee tasting) sessions on weekends.

Chic interior of Il Centro Restaurant and Bar, Brisbane

Sweet dessert pizza with berries and mascarpone, Beccofino, Teneriffe

FORTITUDE VALLEY:
Chouquette $
Café/French
19 Barker St, QLD 4005
Tel *(07) 3358 6336* **Closed** *Mon & Tue*
Friendly, French-speaking staff
are on hand to serve café crème
and scrumptious gâteau in this
authentic *boulangerie* (bakery).

FORTITUDE VALLEY:
Gerard's Bar Charcuterie $$
Tapas
13a, 22 St James St, QLD 4006
Tel *(07) 3252 2606* **Closed** *Mon–Thu
lunch*
Tucked down a lane, away from
the hustle and bustle, Gerard's
serves Spanish-inspired morsels
and a wide selection of drinks.

FORTITUDE VALLEY:
Pig 'n' Whistle $$
Pub
446 Brunswick St, QLD 4006
Tel *(07) 3852 6420*
Steak, seafood and British pub
classics such as beef and
Guinness pie and Lincolnshire
sausage to be washed down
with craft beers. Dozens of TVs
to watch live sports while dining.

FORTITUDE VALLEY: Tartufo $$
Italian
1000 Ann St, QLD 4006
Tel *(07) 3852 1500*
This stylish place serves classic
Italian dishes inspired by the
chef's home town of Naples. It
also has a pizzeria and a wine bar
with a good menu of bar snacks.

FORTITUDE VALLEY: Wagaya $$
Japanese
*Level 1, TCB Centre, 315 Brusnwick St,
QLD 4006*
Tel *(07) 3252 8888*
Fun bistro with accessible
izakaya-style dining, the Japanese
answer to tapas. A menu highlight
is the pork *gyoza* with hints of
ginger and herbs.

NEW FARM: Majo's $$
Italian
695 Brunswick St, QLD 4005
Tel *(07) 3254 0275*
Family-friendly restaurant serving
some of the best pizzas in
Brisbane, plus an assortment of
delicious home-style Italian
dishes to choose from. Good list
of Italian wines and beers.

NEW FARM:
New Farm Deli & Café $$
Italian
900 Brunswick St, QLD 4005
Tel *(07) 3358 2634*
A Brisbane institution for four
decades, this busy Italian deli
serves great coffee, gourmet
treats and a wonderful selection
of meats, cheeses and pasta.

NEW FARM:
The Purple Olive $$
Modern Australian
79 James St, QLD 4005
Tel *(07) 3254 0097* **Closed** *Mon*
This popular spot is styled like
a classic European restaurant.
Authentic Mediterranean
flavours are adapted to
modern Australian tastes.

PADDINGTON:
Montrachet $$$
French
224 Given Terrace, QLD 4064
Tel *(07) 3367 0030* **Closed** *Sat & Sun*
Waving the flag for traditional
French cuisine, this delightful,
intimate restaurant is the
creation of French-Australian
chef Thierry Galichet.

SOUTH BRISBANE:
Bamboo Basket $
Chinese
Shop 1003-4, 199 Grey St, QLD 4101
Tel *(07) 3844 0088*
Succulent noodles and fresh *xiao
long baos* (steamed dumplings,
literally "little dragon buns") are
the best things at this busy eatery.

SOUTH BRISBANE: GOMA
Restaurant $$
Modern Australian
Stanley St, QLD 4101
Tel *(07) 3842 9916* **Closed** *Mon &
Tue; dinner (except Fri)*
Sophisticated alfresco seating
makes this an elegant spot for
lunch before, after or during a
visit to Brisbane's world-class
GOMA complex.

TENERIFFE: Beccofino $$
Italian
10 Vernon Terrace, QLD 4005
Tel *(07) 3666 0207* **Closed** *Mon;
Tue & Wed lunch*
Enjoy excellent food in a
contemporary café-restaurant.
The scarlet signage and seating
make it impossible to miss.
Pizzas are the speciality here.

TOOWONG: 85 Miskin St $$$
Modern Australian
85 Miskin St, QLD 4066
Tel *(07) 3371 4558* **Closed** *Mon;
Tue lunch*
Housed in an old cottage with
minimalist interiors. Serves
innovative contemporary cuisine
in a relaxed atmosphere.

WEST END: The Gunshop Café $
Café/Modern Australian
53 Mollison St, QLD 4101
Tel *(07) 3844 2241* **Closed** *Sun–
Thu dinner*
This delightful, award-winning
spot, dotted with quirky artworks,
is always buzzing. They also
serve superbly flavoursome
main meals.

WEST END: Little Greek Taverna $
Greek
Shop 5, 1 Browning St, QLD 4101
Tel *(07) 3255 2215* **Closed** *Mon*
Family-run restaurant with a
bright, airy feel. Offers scrump-
tious Greek salads with fat olives
and tasty dips, plus classics such
as *souvlaki* skewers.

For more information on types of restaurants *see page 498*

WEST END: Trang $
Chinese/Vietnamese
2/59 Hardgrave Rd, QLD 4101
Tel *(07) 3255 1610*
Fast, friendly service makes this a good place before a show in the nearby theatre precinct. It is famed for its large, tasty portions.

WEST END: Mondo Organics $$$
Modern Australian
166 Hardgrave Rd, QLD 4101
Tel *(07) 3844 1132* **Closed** *Mon & Tue; Wed & Thu lunch; Sun dinner*
This inspiring modern eatery only uses the finest natural, organic ingredients. A firm favourite with Brisbane's health conscious and environmentally aware.

WOOLLOONGABBA: Pawpaw $$
Malaysian/Thai
898 Stanley St East (cnr Potts St), QLD 4169
Tel *(07) 3891 5100* **Closed** *Mon & Tue dinner*
Unpretentious restaurant. Sample delicately flavoured soups, curries and seafood dishes garnished with fresh vegetables and spicy sauces. Cooking lessons available.

South of Townsville

AIRLIE BEACH: Mr Bones $
Pizzeria
263 Shute Harbour Rd, QLD 4802
Tel *(04) 1301 7331* **Closed** *Sun & Mon*
Breezy café-restaurant famous for its pizzas. It also serves breakfast, light bites and daily specials.

BUNDABERG: Indulge $
Café/Modern Australian
80 Bourbong St, QLD 4670
Tel *(07) 4154 2344* **Closed** *Sun*
Burgers, salads and sandwiches on sourdough or Turkish bread, plus luscious breakfasts. The focus is on local, seasonal produce.

Freshly made gourmet burgers – an ever-popular choice in many restaurants

Vanitas restaurant overlooking the lagoon pool at Palazzo Versace hotel *(see p487)*, Gold Coast

GLADSTONE: Rocksalt Bar & Restaurant $$
Modern Australian
24–26 Roseberry St, QLD 4680
Tel *(07) 4972 9884*
At this warm, friendly place, tasty sharing plates and local seafood are popular choices. There is a good range of desserts, too.

GOLD COAST: Burleigh Bluff Café $
Café
The Old Burleigh Theatre Arcade, 66 Goodwin Terrace, Burleigh Heads, QLD 4220
Tel *(07) 5576 6333*
Lively at breakfast time, sunny for lunch and beautiful at sundown, this café is a favourite for its reasonably priced food and friendly service. Close to the beach.

GOLD COAST: Elk Espresso $
Café
16 Chelsea Ave, Broadbeach, QLD 4218
Tel *(07) 5592 2888* **Closed** *dinner*
Simple, well-priced café fare at breakfast and lunch. Burgers, salads and good coffee served in a rustic, relaxed, no-fuss space.

GOLD COAST: Stingray $$
American
7 Staghorn Ave, Surfers Paradise, QLD 4217
Tel *(07) 5584 1200*
Lively, sophisticated and fun, with super-cool retro decor, Stingray is the perfect place for sharing cocktails or cold beers and mini-bites.

GOLD COAST: Bazaar $$$
International
7 Staghorn Ave, Surfers Paradise, QLD 4217
Tel *(07) 5584 1200*
Buffet dining with a global twist: for a set price, guests can sample a dizzying array of dishes inspired by global culinary specialities.

GOLD COAST: Seaduction $$$
Seafood
Level 2, 8 The Esplanade, Surfers Paradise, QLD 4217
Tel *(07) 5635 5728* **Closed** *Mon; Sun dinner*
A contemporary, sophisticated space with ocean views from every table. Excellent food on an menu that brings a fusion of sea and earth tastes to the table.

GOLD COAST: Vanitas $$$
Modern Australian
94 Seaworld Drive, Main Beach, QLD 4217
Tel *(07) 5509 8000* **Closed** *Sun & Mon*
Elegant and tasteful hotel-restaurant with original art and fine-quality furnishings. The food and wine list are equally superb.

MOUNT MEE: Birches $$
Modern Australian
1350 Mount Mee Rd, QLD 4521
Tel *(07) 5498 2244* **Closed** *Mon & Tue*
Birches offers a range of fare, including gluten-free and vegetarian options. Welcoming country atmosphere.

NOOSA: Organika $
Café
Shop 2, 3 Gibson Rd, Noosaville, QLD 4566
Tel *(07) 5442 4973* **Closed** *dinner*
Purveyor of all things fresh and fragrant, this organic produce store has a deck for guests to bite into something savoury and sip a first-class coffee.

NOOSA: Thomas Corner Eatery $$
Modern Australian
1/201 Gympie Terrace, Noosaville, QLD 4566
Tel *(07) 5470 2224* **Closed** *Sun dinner*
This superb casual eatery has a chic urban-beach vibe. It is owned by David Rayner, one of the chefs to seal Noosa's reputation as a food lovers' paradise.

**NOOSA: Berardo's Bistro
on the Beach** $$$
Modern Australian
*Noosa Beachfront on the Beach
Resort, 49 Hastings St,
Noosa Heads, QLD 4567*
Tel *(07) 5448 0888*
Healthy or decadent breakfasts
and fresh, flavourful lunches and
dinners are accompanied by the
relaxing sound of the ocean
waves. Good coffee and tasty
sweet and savoury muffins as well.

NOOSA: Wasabi $$$
Japanese
*2 Quamby Place, Noosa Sound,
QLD 4567*
Tel *(07) 5449 2443* **Closed** *Mon &
Tue; Fri & Sun lunch*
Situated on the waterfront, with
lovely sunset views over the
Noosa River. Come here to indulge
in excellent flavoursome food.
There is a fashionable dining
room, plus a *tatami* room that
seats 20 diners in traditional style.

DK Choice

**NORTH TAMBORINE:
Songbirds Rainforest
Retreat** $$$
Modern Australian
*Lot 10, Tamborine Mountain Rd,
QLD 4272*
Tel *(07) 5545 2563* **Closed** *dinner
Mon–Thu*
This multiple award-winning
hinterland hotel-restaurant
offers organic fine dining in a
beautiful, tranquil rainforest
setting. The ambience is smart
yet relaxed. The well-presented,
delicious food is carefully
matched with local and
imported wines. Parrots, whip
birds, lorikeets and lyrebirds all
make their presence heard in
the leafy surroundings.

**ROCKHAMPTON:
The Coffee House** $$
Café/Bistro
51 William St, QLD 4700
Tel *(07) 4927 5722* **Closed** *Sun dinner*
Tidy and compact café-restaurant
with a bistro-style menu featuring
beef from the local area. Gluten-
free meals for the health-minded.

**SUNSHINE COAST:
The Curry Bowl** $
Indian
*7/115 Point Cartwright Drive,
Buddina, QLD 4575*
Tel *(07) 5478 0800* **Closed** *Mon; lunch*
Sunshine Coast curry house with
a reputation for friendly service
and tasty, fresh ingredients. Great
samosas (stuffed fried pastry)
and *naan* bread.

**TOOWOOMBA:
Sofra** $$
Turkish
164 Margaret St, QLD 4350
Tel *(07) 4638 0044*
At this vibrant place, authentic,
tasty, generous dishes combine
Mediterranean and Eastern
flavours. Ideal for sharing, they
are served with characteristic
Ottoman charm. There is an
impressive drinks list too.

**TOWNSVILLE:
Watermark** $$
Modern Australian
72–74 The Strand, QLD 4810
Tel *(07) 4724 4281*
Waterfront restaurant with a
sleek, stylish vibe and modern
Queensland cuisine. The terrace,
under a striking glass canopy, is
great for cocktails or dinner on a
warm evening.

**YANDINA:
Spirit House** $$
Asian
20 Ninderry Rd, QLD 4561
Tel *(07) 5446 8994* **Closed** *Sun–
Tue dinner*
Tropical garden restaurant and
cooking school. Sample Asian-
style stir-fries and curries to the
sound of birds, wind chimes and
water features. Book in advance.

Northern Queensland and the Outback

CAIRNS: Cruze $
Café
105 Grafton St, QLD 4870
Tel *(07) 4051 1444* **Closed** *Sun*
Relish fresh coffee prepared by
a team that know their coffee
beans perfectly. Choose from
a wide variety of beans and
brewing styles, plus tasty treats
to accompany the drinks.

Bright and colourful building of Ochre
Restaurant, Cairns

**CAIRNS: Barnacle Bill's
Seafood Inn** $$
Seafood
103 The Esplanade, QLD 4870
Tel *(07) 4051 2241*
An established local favourite,
with a menu offering fresh
oysters, mussels, scallops,
calamari, prawns, lobster and
fish. The house speciality is a hot
and spicy seafood jambalaya.

CAIRNS: L'Unico Trattoria $$
Italian
*75 Vasey Esplanade, Trinity Beach,
QLD 4879*
Tel *(07) 4057 8855*
Smart, relaxed place making use
of local ingredients. Pizzas have
unusual toppings. Buzzing vibe,
with a deck and beach views.

**CAIRNS:
Mondo Café Bar & Grill** $$
Café
34 The Esplanade, QLD 4870
Tel *(07) 4052 6780*
Outdoor café under the shade
of a giant poinciana tree. Light
meals, burgers, salads and snacks
with an international flavour.
Great for a casual drink, too.

CAIRNS: Ochre Restaurant $$
Native Australian
6/1 Marlin Parade, QLD 4870
Tel *(07) 4051 0100*
Interesting food, with an
emphasis on Australian bush fare.
The menu features game (emu,
crocodile and kangaroo), seafood
and native fruits like quandong.

**CAIRNS:
Perrotta's at the Gallery** $$
International
Abbott & Shields sts, QLD 4870
Tel *(07) 4031 5899*
Popular local haunt, crowded
at breakfast and particularly
busy at weekends. Casual café
food with a tropical twist and
good coffee.

**CAIRNS: Simple Italian Bar &
Grill** $$
Italian
*Hilton Cairns, 34 The Esplanade,
QLD 4870*
Tel *(07) 4050 2020*
Savour traditional Italian delights
such as handmade pastas, pizzas
and salads, all made from fresh,
local produce. Friendly staff.

CHARLEVILLE: Heinemann's $
Café
84 Alfred St, QLD 4470
Tel *(07) 4654 3991*
This small bakery and café is a
great place to fuel up for the day
with fresh, tasty pies and sweet
baked goods.

For more information on types of restaurants *see page 498*

CLONCURRY: The Gidgee Inn Bar & Grill $$
Modern Australian
Matilda Hwy, QLD 4824
Tel *(07) 4742 1599*   **Closed** *Sun*
The menu at this à la carte restaurant features seafood from the Gulf of Carpentaria and beef from the surrounding region. Choose from oysters, prawns and barramundi, or succulent steaks.

DAINTREE:
Tea House Restaurant $
Native Australian
3225 Mossman Daintree Rd, QLD 4873
Tel *(07) 4098 6161*   **Closed** *dinner*
Lovely spot in a breathtaking rainforest setting. Serves delectable food featuring local produce and tropical fruits.

KARUMBA: Sunset Tavern $$
Modern Australian
The Esplanade, QLD
Tel *(07) 4745 9183*
The signature seafood platter is piled with local fish and mud crabs. Excellent Gulf prawn. Good steaks, pizzas and pastas, too.

LONGREACH: Oasis Restaurant $$
Modern Australian
Albert Park Motor Inn, Sir Hudson Fysh Drive, QLD 4730
Tel *(07) 4658 2411*   **Closed** *lunch; Sun dinner*
Steak, grilled chicken and pork, as well as seafood dishes feature on the menu here. Generous servings at reasonable prices.

MAREEBA: Skybury Coffee $
Café
136 Ivicevic Rd, QLD 4880
Tel *(07) 4093 2190*   **Closed** *dinner; Sat & Sun*
Set in a coffee plantation, this casual restaurant spills on to an elevated deck. It offers a range of light meals, cakes and coffee.

MOSSMAN: Mojos Bar & Grill $$
International
41 Front St, QLD 4873
Tel *(07) 4098 1202*   **Closed** *Sat lunch; Sun*
Casual but classy restaurant. The signature Surf & Turf dish is char-grilled sirloin with salt-and-pepper squid and garlic aïoli. Try one of the seafood *antipasti* platters.

PALM COVE:
Vivo Bar & Grill $
International
49 Williams Esplanade, QLD 4879
Tel *(07) 4059 0944*
Colonial-style restaurant with a wide veranda. Choose from a tapas menu or a range of dishes featuring seafood and local produce with a tropical twist.

PALM COVE: Beach Almond $$$
Modern Asian/Seafood
145 Williams Esplanade, QLD 4879
Tel *(07) 4059 1908*
Relax in the huge veranda that overlooks the sea at this former beach shack, while enjoying fresh seafood prepared with vibrant Asian colours and flavours.

DK Choice

PALM COVE: NuNu $$$
International
123 Williams Esplanade, 1 Veivers Rd, QLD 4879
Tel *(07) 4059 1880*
The award-winning NuNu features an interesting and innovative menu with Asian and Mediterranean influences. It offers simply prepared dishes alongside more elaborate specialities. The Queensland mud crab will have guests talking about it long after their meal is over. The beachfront atmosphere is casual, and the staff friendly.

PORT DOUGLAS:
The Yachty $
Bistro
1 Spinnaker Close, QLD 4877
Tel *(07) 4099 4386*
Set within the Port Douglas Yacht Club, this eatery offers a wide selection of excellent food at very reasonable prices. It's a great location on the water, too, with a family-friendly atmosphere.

PORT DOUGLAS:
On the Inlet $$
Seafood
3 Inlet St, QLD 4877
Tel *(07) 4099 5255*
Built out over the water, this is a great spot at sunset. Choose the mud crab or lobster from the live seafood tank.

PORT DOUGLAS:
Salsa Bar & Grill $$
Modern Australian
26 Wharf St, QLD 4877
Tel *(07) 4099 4922*
Trendy place, visited by everyone from presidents to pop stars. Terrific food, great prices and lively service. Leave room for the delectable desserts.

PORT DOUGLAS: Zinc $$
Modern Australian
Shop 3, 53–61 Macrossan St, QLD 4877
Tel *(07) 4099 6260*
Delicious creative food, service with a smile and a children's menu keep patrons coming back. Check out the cutting-edge restrooms, with floor-to-ceiling aquariums.

PORT DOUGLAS: Bistro H
by Harrisons $$$
International
22 Wharf St, QLD 4877
Tel *(07) 4099 4011*
Northern Queensland's sole Michelin-starred chef, Spencer Patrick creates sensational dishes with a small selection that is big on quality and flavour.

PORT DOUGLAS: Nautilus $$$
International
17 Murphy St, QLD 4877
Tel *(07) 4099 5330*
A Port Douglas institution since the 1950s. Dine within a romantic rainforest oasis, right in the heart of town. Expensive, but a great experience. No children under 8 years.

WINTON: North Gregory Hotel $
Modern Australian
67 Elderslie St, QLD 4735
Tel *(07) 4657 0647*
A refurbished historic pub famed for hosting the first performance of "Waltzing Matilda" in 1895. Good pub fare.

Tables situated in a beautiful rainforest setting at Nautilus restaurant, Port Douglas

YUNGABURRA: Obi's $$
Modern Australian
20 Gillies Hwy, QLD 4884
Tel *(07) 4095 2022*   **Closed** *Mon–Wed*
Fine dining in elegant, tropical surrounds at the heritage building in Eden House Retreat. This family-friendly restaurant's menu features local produce.

Darwin and the Top End

DALY WATERS:
Daly Waters Historic Pub $$
Steaks/Seafood
Stuart St, NT 0852
Tel *(08) 8975 9927*
Iconic pub serving burgers, kangaroo, crocodile and wild-caught barramundi with hot crusty damper bread (traditional Australian soda bread).

DARWIN: The Deck Bar $
Bistro
22 Mitchell St, NT 0800
Tel *(08) 8942 3001*
A cut above the usual corner pub, with a modern menu and creative food. Grand view of the impressive Colonial-style Parliament House.

DARWIN: Jetty & The Fish $
Seafood
260 Casaurina Drive, Nightcliff, NT 0810
Tel *(04) 2449 4057*   **Closed** *Mon–Wed; Jan*
Fish is the focus at this food truck that offers everything from fish and chips to fish tacos, calamari and fish nuggets to take away.

DARWIN: Shenannigans Restaurant & Bar $
Native Australian
69 Mitchell St, NT 0800
Tel *(08) 8981 2100*
A large menu of pub favourites, including some inspired by the Northern Territory, such as the platter of crocodile sausage, buffalo sausage and barramundi.

DARWIN:
Crustaceans on the Wharf $$
Seafood
Stokes Hill Wharf, NT 0800
Tel *(08) 8981 8658* **Closed** *lunch; last 3 wks Jan*
Set on a pier where dolphins can sometimes be seen playing in the water. The menu showcases Australian seafood at its best.

DARWIN:
Ducks Nuts Bar & Grill $$
Bistro
76 Mitchell St, NT 0800
Tel *(08) 8942 2122*

An assortment of delectable dishes on offer at Moorish Café, Darwin

Something to suit all tastes – salads, burgers, steaks, seafood, curries and lamb shanks, as well as excellent coffee. Try the popular slow roasted beef cheeks.

DK Choice

DARWIN: Hanuman $$
Asian
Holiday Inn Esplanade, 93 Mitchell St, NT 0800
Tel *(08) 8941 3500*
Offering some of the Territory's best Asian food, Hanuman draws on Thai, Malaysian and Indian cuisines for its innovative menu. The skillfully prepared dishes are served against a stylish back-drop, but prices are reasonable and the atmosphere relaxed. Try the signature dish: oysters with lemongrass, sweet basil, chilli and coriander.

DARWIN: Il Lido $$
Italian
Building 3, 19 Kitchener Drive, NT 0800
Tel *(08) 8941 0900*
Linger over a drink, pizza or Italian specials at this polished restaurant with terraces overlooking the waterfront and wave pool.

DARWIN: Moorish Café $$
International
37 Knuckey St, NT 0800
Tel *(08) 8981 0010*   **Closed** *Sun & Mon; Jan*
A Darwin favourite, with dishes inspired by the flavours of Spain, the Mediterranean and Northern Africa. Tropical cocktails and great coffee, too.

DARWIN: Thailicious $$
Thai
Shop 26/69 Mitchell St, NT 0800
Tel *(08) 8941 9966*
Delicious flavours of Thailand in the heart of Darwin city, with

relaxed rooftop dining, under-cover seating and traditional floor cushions.

DARWIN: Viva la Vida $$
Tapas
48–50 Smith St Mall, NT 0800
Tel *(08) 8942 0544*   **Closed** *Sun*
Funky bar with a vast menu of tapas. Great drinks list, too, with around 50 wines by the glass.

DARWIN: Cove $$$
Seafood
Skycity Darwin, Gilruth Ave, The Gardens, NT 0800
Tel *(08) 8943 8940*
Heaven for seafood lovers. The selection of modern and classic dishes highlight fresh Australian seafood and local produce.

DARWIN: Evoo $$$
Fine Dining
Skycity Darwin, Gilruth Ave, The Gardens, NT 0800
Tel *(08) 8943 8940*   **Closed** *Sun & Mon; Jan*
For an extravagant night out, enjoy first-class dining at Evoo and watch the sun set over Mindil Beach.

DARWIN: Pee Wee's at the Point $$$
Modern Australian
Alec Fong Lim Drive, East Point Reserve, Fanny Bay, NT 0801
Tel *(08) 8981 6868*   **Closed** *lunch; Nov–Apr: Sun & Mon*
Most tables here have views over the water. The menu reflects the Top End's multicultural flavour. Specialities include banana prawns and buffalo cheese.

JABIRU: Escarpment $$
Modern Australian
Mercure Kakadu Crocodile Hotel, Flinders St, NT 0886
Tel *(08) 8979 9013*
Local meats, seafood and bush-tucker in a bistro setting, open for breakfast, lunch and dinner.

KATHERINE: Big Fig $
Bistro
20 Shadforth Rd, NT 0850
Tel *(08) 9872 3311* **Closed** *Oct–Apr*
Nestled amid the trees in a caravan park, Big Fig dishes up good-value, home-style meals and sweet treats. Friendly service.

KATHERINE: The Finch Cafe $
Café
Katherine Terrace, NT 0850
Tel *(08) 8972 1990* **Closed** *Mon*
Fresh food, good coffee and a lively atmosphere makes this eatery a good choice, particularly for healthy breakfasts.

KATHERINE: Savannah Bar & Restaurant $$
Bistro
Knott's Crossing Resort, cnr Giles & Cameron sts, NT 0850
Tel *(08) 8972 2511* **Closed** *lunch*
Serving a colourful menu that highlights the tastes and produce of the Top End. Go for the roast pork, steaks, or salads.

MATARANKA: Katherine Country Club $
Bistro
40 Pearce St (off Victoria Hwy), NT 0850
Tel *(08) 8972 1276*
Basic bistro fare with limited choice served in a casual setting. Welcoming atmosphere.

The Red Centre

ALICE SPRINGS: Epilogue Lounge $
Tapas
1/58 Todd St, NT 0870
Tel *0429 003 874* **Closed** *Tue; Jan*
Popular casual spot with alfresco seating on the rooftop and occasional live music. Good coffee and tapas menu.

ALICE SPRINGS: Loco Burrito $
Mexican
Shop 10, 74 Todd St, NT 0870
Tel *(08) 8953 0518* **Closed** *Sun; 24 Dec–2 Jan*
A go-to place for a quick, hearty lunch. Choose from a wide range of burrito fillings on the menu, or build your own. The pulled pork is a favourite.

ALICE SPRINGS: Monte's Lounge $
International
95 Todd St, cnr Stott Terrace, NT 0870
Tel *(08) 8952 4336* **Closed** *Mon & Tue*
Part restaurant, part cabaret venue. A fun place to have dinner while

Stunning scenery surrounds the dining area at Under a Desert Moon, Kings Canyon

enjoying music and dance performances. Extensive menu: pizzas, steaks, curries and seafood.

ALICE SPRINGS: Page 27 $
Café
3 Fan Arcade, NT 0870
Tel *(08) 8952 0191* **Closed** *dinner*
Great café and an ideal pit stop for breakfast or lunch. Enjoy freshly prepared juices, coffees and tasty, filling food.

ALICE SPRINGS: Hanuman $$
Asian
DoubleTree by Hilton Hotel, 82 Barrett Drive, NT 0870
Tel *(08) 8950 8000* **Closed** *24 Dec–2 Jan*
Elaborate Thai artifacts greet diners at this stylish restaurant. The menu is an innovative fusion of Thai, Malaysian and Indian.

ALICE SPRINGS: Red Ochre Grill $$
Native Australian
11 Leichhardt Terrace, NT 0870
Tel *(08) 8952 9614*
Seafood and native game take on the flavours of the Australian bush. Panoramic photographs by Ken Duncan adorn the walls.

ALICE SPRINGS: Sporties $$
Bistro
36 Todd St Mall, NT 0870
Tel *(08) 8953 0935* **Closed** *Sun lunch*
A favourite with locals, this restaurant-style pub boasts a wide menu and friendly service. Light meals, pasta, meat and vegetarian dishes in big portions.

ALICE SPRINGS: Overlanders Steakhouse $$$
Steak
72 Hartley St, NT 0870
Tel *(08) 8952 2159* **Closed** *lunch*
Serious meat, including huge steaks, camel and kangaroo. World-class wine cellar. Cricket memorabilia on the walls.

KINGS CANYON: Desert Oaks Bistro $$
Bistro
Kings Canyon Resort, Luritja Rd, Watarrka National Park
Tel *(08) 8956 7442* **Closed** *dinner*
Basic light meals and snacks during the day including the staple burgers, pizza and pasta, all served in an Outback setting.

KINGS CANYON: Outback BBQ & Grill $$
Bistro
Kings Canyon Resort, Luritja Rd, Watarrka National Park
Tel *(08) 8956 7442* **Closed** *Nov–Mar*
Enjoy a true Aussie experience on an Outback veranda. This casual bar and grill offers barbecued fare, salads and vegetables.

KINGS CANYON: Under a Desert Moon $$$
Modern Australian
Kings Canyon Resort, Luritja Rd, Watarrka National Park
Tel *(08) 8956 7442* **Closed** *Nov–Mar; Tue, Thu & Sun*
Dine under the stars in this intimate venue with space for 16 people. Begin with bubbly by the campfire before indulging in a four-course menu of fine food.

TENNANT CREEK: Sporties Steak & Grill $
Bistro
387 Ambrose St, NT 0860
Tel *(08) 8962 3338* **Closed** *Sun*
Generous portions of hearty fare, with meats a speciality. Relaxed setting popular with locals.

YULARA: Bough House Restaurant $$
Native Australian
Outback Pioneer Hotel, Yulara Drive, NT 0870
Tel *(02) 8296 8010*
This family-friendly restaurant brings the spirit of the Outback to the table. A good selection,

including meats and sushi, all feature in the buffet and set-menu offerings.

YULARA: Ilkari Restaurant $$
International
Sails in the Desert Hotel,
Yulara Drive, NT 0870
Tel *(02) 8296 8010* **Closed** *lunch*
Indigenous flavours add a local touch to an eclectic international menu of roasts, grills, pasta dishes and Asian specialities.

YULARA: Arnguli Grill $$$
Brasserie
Desert Gardens Hotel, Yulara Drive,
NT 0870
Tel *(02) 8296 8010*
Delectable food – the highlight being steaks cooked to perfection – along with lovely decor and good service make this pleasant restaurant a go-to place in Yulara.

YULARA:
Sounds of Silence $$$
Modern Australian
Ayers Rock Resort, Yulara Drive,
NT 0870
Tel *(02) 8296 8010*
Listen to the sound of the didgeridoo as the sun sets, enjoy a buffet of bush tucker-inspired dishes, and finish the evening with a round of storytelling and star-gazing.

DK Choice

YULARA: Tali Wiru $$$
Modern Australian
Ayers Rock Resort, Yulara Drive,
NT 0870
Tel *(02) 8296 8010* **Closed** *Nov–Mar*
Much more than just a dining experience, Tali Wiru offers a memorable night under the stars, limited to just 20 people. As the sun sets on Uluṟu, guests enjoy a four-course dinner with premium wines and soak up the spirituality of the indigenous people and their connection to the land.

Perth and the Southwest

ALBANY: Due South $$
Pub
6 Toll Place, WA 6330
Tel *(08) 9841 8526*
This waterfront restaurant offers fantastic views of Albany and King George Sound. The menu includes regular pub favourites and a choice of drinks.

COWARAMUP: Vasse Felix $$$
Winery Restaurant
Cnr Tom Cullity Dr & Caves Rd,
WA 6284
Tel *(08) 9756 5050* **Closed** *dinner;*
public hols
The beautiful setting of vineyards and bush is surpassed only by the food, which incorporates local produce in a superb array of flavourful contemporary dishes.

DARLINGTON:
Darlington Estate Winery $$$
Winery Restaurant
1495 Nelson Rd, WA 6070
Tel *(08) 9299 6268* **Closed** *Mon–Wed*
Just 25 minutes from Perth's CBD, this place has picturesque views over the bush land. The seasonal menu has low-fat, gluten-free and vegetarian options. Book ahead.

FREMANTLE: Gino's Cafe
& Trattoria $$
Italian
1–5 South Terrace, WA 6160
Tel *(08) 9336 1464*
Located at Fremantle's famous Cappuccino Strip, this café is a great place to unwind while enjoying coffee or chilli mussels – the house favourite.

FREMANTLE: Little Creatures
Brewery $$
Tapas
40 Mews Rd, WA 6160
Tel *(08) 6215 1000*
Order some tapas dishes and a glass of Little Creatures Pale Ale, then kick back and relax in this busy brewery-café. Try the signature kangaroo skewers.

GRACETOWN: Sunsets Café
Gracetown $$
Café/Pub
4 Bayview Drive, WA 6284
Tel *(08) 9755 9271* **Closed** *Jun–Aug*
This cosy café and restaurant has an Austrian-influenced menu and serves a range of breakfasts, burgers, soups and muffins.

JARRAHDALE:
Millbrook Winery $$$
Winery Restaurant
Old Chestnut Lane, WA 6124
Tel *(08) 9525 5796* **Closed** *Tue &*
Wed; dinner
Spectacular forest setting with sweeping views. Seasonal menu prepared using local produce and vegetables picked daily from the restaurant's kitchen garden.

MANDURAH: The Bridge Garden
Bar & Restaurant $$
Bistro
Cnr Mandurah Terrace & Pinjarra Rd,
WA 6210
Tel *(08) 9535 1004*
Located in one of the city's most historic buildings. Guests enjoy fresh local ingredients in a lovely waterside setting.

MANDURAH:
M on the Point $$
Modern Australian
1 Marco Polo Drive, WA 6210
Tel *(08) 9534 9899*
Modern gastropub with an easy-going vibe and water views. Extensive menu with burgers and pizzas, as well as hearty dishes.

MANJIMUP:
The Truffle & Wine Co $$
Modern Australian
490 Seven Day Rd, WA 6258
Tel *(08) 9777 2474* **Closed** *dinner*
The menu and chalkboard specials highlight seasonal local produce. Excellent truffles in season. Local wines to match.

MARGARET RIVER: Cullen
Restaurant $$
Winery Restaurant
4323 Caves Rd, WA 6280
Tel *(08) 9755 5656* **Closed** *dinner*
Sophisticated dishes made with fresh, organic ingredients, many of them sourced from the winery's own garden.

Spectacular setting looking out to Uluṟu at Tali Wiru, Yulara

For more information on types of restaurants *see page 498*

MARGARET RIVER:
Elkamo $$
Tapas
107 Bussell Hwy, WA 6285
Tel *(08) 9758 8877*   **Closed** *lunch*
The regularly changing menu
here offers guests a wonderful
selection of tapas. All food is
made on site from scratch.

MARGARET RIVER:
Leeuwin Estate Winery $$$
Modern Australian
Stevens Rd, WA 6285
Tel *(08) 9759 0000*   **Closed** *dinner*
(except Sat)
One of Margaret River's finest
restaurants, serving outstanding
food and wine in a peaceful,
picturesque setting.

MARGARET RIVER: Xanadu $$$
Modern Australian
Boodjidup Rd, WA 6285
Tel *(08) 9758 9500*   **Closed** *Tue &*
Wed; dinner
A lovely place to linger over a
sophisticated lunch of Middle
Eastern-inspired dishes, including
some great vegetarian options.

MUNDARING:
Little Caesars Pizza $
Pizzeria
7125 Great Eastern Hwy, WA 6073
Tel *(08) 9295 6611*   **Closed** *Tue; lunch*
Creativity and the use of top-
quality ingredients have won this
pizza company a string of awards.
Don't miss the dessert pizzas.

PEMBERTON:
Foragers Field Kitchen $$
Modern Australian
1 Roberts Rd, Pemberton, WA 6260
Tel *(08) 9776 1580*   **Closed** *call ahead*
to check times
Cooking school offering a
unique dining experience at
long tables. The seasonal menu
relies on ingredients grown
locally and on site.

PERTH:
Peninsula Tea Gardens $
Tearoom
Peninsula Farm, 2A Johnson Rd,
Maylands, WA 6051
Tel *(08) 9272 8894*   **Closed** *dinner*

The picturesque Leeuwin Estate Winery, home to an excellent restaurant

On the site of one of Perth's first
farms, Peninsula is a lovely spot
to enjoy afternoon tea with
tranquil views of the river.

PERTH: Varsity Bar $
American
88 Broadway Fair, Nedlands, WA 6009
Tel *(08) 9386 5147*
This American college-themed
bar is a favourite with local
students. Exciting venue offering
great service, American-style
food and sport on TV.

PERTH:
The Bird Cage Restaurant $$
Asian
Level 1, 140 William St, WA 6000
Tel *(08) 9226 0259*   **Closed** *Sun & Mon*
Cool restaurant and bar in The
Aviary, which offers an Asian-
inspired menu and bird's-eye
views. Dishes are designed to be
shared to encourage guests to
explore different flavours.

PERTH: The Garden $$
Modern Australian
742 Newcastle St, Leederville, WA 6007
Tel *(08) 9202 8282*
Beer, wine, cider and cocktails are
served here alongside seasonal
shared plates and hearty main
meals. The laid-back atmosphere,
and industrial design make it a
Perth favourite.

PERTH: The George $$
Modern Australian
216 St Georges Terrace, WA 6000
Tel *(08) 6161 6662*   **Closed** *Mon;*
Sun breakfast

A sophisticated venue open
for breakfasts, leisurely lunches,
dinners and drinks. Afternoon
teas on offer at weekends.

DK Choice

PERTH: Greenhouse $$
Australian
100 St Georges Terrace, WA 6000
Tel *(08) 9481 8333* **Closed** *Mon–*
Wed dinner
The menus at this eco-friendly
venue are always interesting.
There is a thoughtful and
sometimes playful use of
seasonal, local ingredients,
served in quirky surrounds.
Here recycling is chic; chairs
are made from road signs
and water poured from old
milk bottles.

PERTH: La Vie Champagne
Lounge $$
Canapés & Cocktails
Crown Perth, Great Eastern Hwy,
Burswood, WA 6100
Tel *1800 556 688*   **Closed** *Sun & Mon;*
lunch
Enjoy a stunning array of delicate
canapés, including oysters and
caviar. There is an opulent lounge
serving the finest champagne,
cocktails and spirits.

PERTH: Meeka Restaurant $$
International
361 Rokeby Rd, Subiaco, WA 6008
Tel *(08) 9381 1800*   **Closed** *Sun &*
Mon; lunch
Head chef Leah Clarke dishes up
a wonderful menu of contemporary Australian delights infused
with a Middle Eastern twist. Don't
miss their delicious desserts.

PERTH: St Michael 6003 $$
Modern Australian
483 Beaufort St, Highgate, WA 6003
Tel *(08) 9328 1177*   **Closed** *Sun &*
Mon; Sat–Thu lunch
Inventive small plates prepared
using local ingredients. Degus-
tation menu on offer for dinner.
Exceptional service.

Foragers Field Kitchen nestled in the forest, Pemberton

Key to Price Guide *see page 504*

PERTH: Balthazar $$$
Modern Australian
6 The Esplanade, WA 6000
Tel *(08) 9421 1206* **Closed** *Sat lunch; Sun*
Busy spot inside a heritage building. Creative and seasonal menu offering oysters, snapper, emu and duck, all cooked to perfection. The wine list includes 400 to choose from.

PERTH: C Restaurant $$$
Fine Dining
Level 33, 44 St Georges Terrace, WA 6000
Tel *(08) 9220 8333*
Enjoy stunning city and river views from this revolving restaurant. The sophisticated menu matches the prime location. Elegant afternoon tea, too.

PERTH: Divido $$$
Modern Italian
170 Scarborough Beach Rd, Mt Hawthorn, WA 6050
Tel *(08) 9443 7373* **Closed** *Sun*
A casual Italian eating and drinking experience in an intimate, cosy venue. Highly experienced chef.

**PERTH:
Fraser's Restaurant** $$$
Modern Australian
Fraser's Ave, King's Park, West Perth, WA 6005
Tel *(08) 9481 7100*
Informal yet refined, with views of the city and Swan River. The menu changes regularly and draws on European and Asian flavours and quality local fare.

PERTH: Must Wine Bar $$$
Modern Australian/Wine Bar
519 Beaufort St, Highgate, WA 6003
Tel *(08) 9328 8255*
Food and wine aficionados flock to this little slice of France. Great bistro fare, cool ambience and more than 500 wines.

PERTH: Restaurant Amuse $$$
Modern Australian
64 Bronte St, East Perth, WA 6004
Tel *(08) 9325 4900* **Closed** *Sun & Mon; lunch*
A special-occasion restaurant whose degustation menu is a delight. The food is pure artistry.

SWAN VALLEY: Elmars in the Valley $$$
German
8731 West Swan Rd, Henley Brook, WA 6055
Tel *(08) 9296 6354* **Closed** *Mon & Tue*
Great dining venue in the valley offering German-flavoured dishes. Don't forget to sample their locally brewed beers.

Expertly prepared dish from the "Trust the chef" menu at Knee Deep in Margaret River

WALPOLE: Slow Food Café $$
Winery Restaurant
Old Kent River Winery, South Coast Hwy, Kentdale, WA 6397
Tel *(08) 9840 8136* **Closed** *Mon; dinner*
A pleasant stop after the treetop walk. Home-grown menu based around marron, a local crustacean, and lamb reared on the property.

WILYABRUP: Flutes $$
Winery Restaurant
Brookland Valley Wines, 4070 Caves Rd, WA 6280
Tel *(08) 9755 6250* **Closed** *dinner*
Sample the chef's fine cooking in a magical setting overlooking the Wilyabrup Brook. Great local wines, too.

**WILYABRUP:
Knee Deep Wines in Margaret River** $$$
Winery Restaurant
160 Johnson Rd, WA 6280
Tel *(08) 9755 6776* **Closed** *dinner*
Fine seasonal food befitting the beautiful vineyard setting. The "Trust the chef" degustation menus add a fun element.

YALLINGUP: Cape Lodge $$$
Fine Dining
3341 Caves Rd, WA 6282
Tel *(08) 9755 6311* **Closed** *lunch*
Boutique hotel offering cooking classes, a superb cellar and fine food featuring local ingredients. The menu changes daily. Reservations essential.

North of Perth and the Kimberley

**BROOME:
1861 Restaurant & Bar** $$
Modern Australian
Oaks Broome, 99 Robinson St, WA 6725
Tel *(08) 9192 9500* **Closed** *lunch*
Indulge in gourmet pizzas, barramundi, Kimberley ribeye and porterhouse steak.

BROOME: The Aarli $$
Modern Australian
Cnr Frederick & Hamersley sts, WA 6725
Tel *(08) 9192 5529*
Situated right in the heart of Chinatown, The Aarli is open for breakfast, lunch and dinner. The twice-cooked pork belly is an absolute must.

BROOME: The Mango Place $$
Modern Australian
Lot 4, 120 Kanagae Drive, 12 Mile, Kanagae Estate, WA 6725
Tel *(08) 9192 5462* **Closed** *dinner*
Sample mango wine and relax in the shade with beef and mango pie or a slice of mango liqueur cake. Wood-fired pizzas on Friday and Sunday (Apr–Jan).

BROOME: Matso's Broome Brewery $$
Modern Australian
60 Hamersley St, WA 6725
Tel *(08) 9193 5811*
Try the mango-flavoured beer at this microbrewery. The menu changes seasonally.

BROOME: Zanders at Cable Beach $$
Modern Australian
Cable Beach Rd, WA 6726
Tel *(08) 9193 5090*
This relaxed, child-friendly beachfront haven offers a contemporary menu with culinary influences from all over the world. Lively atmosphere and friendly service.

DK Choice

**BROOME:
Club Restaurant** $$$
Italian
Cable Beach Club Resort, 1 Cable Beach Rd, WA 6725
Tel *(08) 9192 0411* **Closed** *Sun & Mon; lunch*
This award-winning restaurant serves local dishes such as Harvey grain-fed beef, pearl meat and barramundi with a tropical twist. Enjoy exquisite food and wine under the stars or inside, among extraordinary artworks by the likes of Elizabeth Durack and Sir Sydney Nolan.

BROOME: Sunset Bar & Grill at Cable Beach Club $$$
Modern Australian
1 Cable Beach Rd W, WA 6725
Tel *(08) 9192 0470*
Relax with a cocktail as the sun sets over the Indian Ocean. For food, choose from the casual bar menu or à la carte dinner menu. A truly memorable experience.

For more information on types of restaurants *see page 498*

CARNARVON:
The Carnarvon Hotel $$
Modern Australian
121 Olivia Terrace, WA 6701
Tel *(08) 9941 1181*   **Closed** *breakfast*
Watch the glorious sunset while
enjoying your favourite pub meal.
Good selection of wines and
beer. Kids' meals also available.

CARNARVON: The Good
Paddock Restaurant $$$
International
The Gascoyne Hotel,
57 Olivia Terrace, WA 6701
Tel *(08) 9941 1412*
This delightfully relaxing spot
offers various specials according
to the night of the week, with an
emphasis on local seafood and
produce. There are also eight
beers on tap.

CORAL BAY: Fins Café $$
International
Peoples Park Shopping Village,
Robinson St, WA 6701
Tel *(08) 9942 5900*
The eclectic menu highlights
local seafood; the seafood
platter is a must here! Good
selection of breakfast options
to start the day.

DENHAM:
The Old Pearler Restaurant $$
Modern Australian
71 Knight Terrace, WA 6537
Tel *(08) 9948 1373*   **Closed** *lunch*
Full of character, the Old Pearler
is the world's only restaurant
built entirely of coquina shells.
Seafood is a speciality here.

ECO BEACH:
Jack's Bar & Restaurant $$$
Modern Australian
Lot323 Great Northern Hwy, WA 6725
Tel *(08) 9193 8015*
Situated on Aboriginal land, this
eco-friendly place offers great
ocean views. The focus is on natu-
ral flavours, and much of the food
is home-grown. The menu is
seasonal and changes regularly.

Bistro Dom, a popular restaurant
in Adelaide

EXMOUTH:
Mantaray's Restaurant $$$
Brasserie
Mantarays Ningaloo Beach Resort,
Madaffari Drive, WA 6707
Tel *(08) 9949 0000*   **Closed** *lunch*
A relaxed ambience with great
views of Exmouth Gulf. The
seasonal menu emphasizes meat
and local seafood.

KALBARRI:
Finlay's Fresh Fish BBQ $$
Seafood
24 Magee Crescent, WA 6536
Tel *(08) 9937 1260*   **Closed** *Mon;*
lunch
No-frills BYO eatery in a tin shed
where guests can actually sing
for their supper and gain a free
meal. Wonderfully fresh seafood,
as well as barbecued steaks
and chicken, burgers.

KARRATHA:
Blanche Bar $$$
Modern Australian
Pelago Centre, cnr Warambie Rd &
Sharpe Ave, WA 6714
Tel *(08) 9185 6667*
Great wine and cocktail list,
boutique beers and ciders,
tapas and mains. Go for the Surf
& Turf – barramundi with seared
lamb cutlets and cider jus.

Devilled lamb cutlets with crushed potato and mustard seed salad, Blanche Bar, Karratha

ONSLOW: Onslow Beach Club $$
Modern Australian
Second Ave & Third St, WA 6710
Tel *(08) 9184 6586*
With a vibe to match the beach
clubs of Europe, this is the place
to be as the sun goes down.
Great selection of drinks and
cocktails on offer. The menu
offers daily specials.

POINT SAMSON:
Tata's Restaurant $$$
Modern Australian
56 Samson Rd, WA 6720
Tel *(08) 9187 1052*
Premium fresh seafood, prime
beef and free-range chicken
feature in an internationally
inspired menu. Tata's offers
one of the region's finest food
and wine experiences.

PORT HEDLAND:
Silver Star Café $$
Café
12a Edgar St, WA 6721
Tel *(04) 1114 3663*   **Closed** *dinner;*
Mon
The Sundowner, a 1930s railway
dining car, gets a new lease
of life as a quirky BYO café. Silver
Star offers arguably the best
breakfasts in town.

SHARK BAY:
Boughshed Restaurant $$
Modern Australian
Monkey Mia Dolphin Resort,
Monkey Mia, WA 6537
Tel *(08) 9948 1171*
At Boughshod, you can dine
within metres of the ocean.
Dinner includes fresh local
seafood, beef and vegetarian
fare. Coffee and snacks all day.

Adelaide and the South East

ADELAIDE: Bar 9 $
Australian
96 Glen Osmond Rd, Parkside,
SA 5063
Tel *none*   **Closed** *dinner*
A local favourite, Bar 9 is a
popular go-to place for good-
value, healthy breakfasts (which
are served till 2pm). Don't forget
to try their famous coffee.

ADELAIDE: Ying Chow $
Asian
114 Gouger St, SA 5000
Tel *(08) 8221 7998*   **Closed** *Fri lunch*
Although loud and with little
atmosphere, this popular eatery
has a loyal following. Try the
salt-and-pepper flounder and
shallot pancakes.

ADELAIDE: Andre's Cucina & Polenta Bar $$
Italian
94 Frome St, SA 5000
Tel *(08) 8224 0004* **Closed** *Sun; Mon lunch*
This light-filled Italian restaurant with an organic garden offers set menus and quick lunches.

ADELAIDE: Bistro Dom on Waymouth $$
French
24 Waymouth St, SA 5000
Tel *(08) 8231 7000* **Closed** *Sun & Mon; Tue & Sat lunch*
This French-inspired bistro offers a changing seasonal menu, with imaginative desserts and an extensive wine list.

ADELAIDE: Chianti $$
Italian
160 Hutt St, SA 5000
Tel *(08) 8232 7955*
This long-established and highly regarded Italian diner delivers the classics with precision. The menu changes seasonally.

ADELAIDE: Jolleys Boathouse $$
Modern Australian
1 Jolleys Lane, SA 5000
Tel *(08) 8223 2891* **Closed** *Sat lunch, Sun dinner*
An elegant space by the river with alfresco dining in summer and a fire in winter. The menu is changed seasonally.

ADELAIDE: Kenji Modern Japanese $$
Japanese
Shop 5, 242 Hutt St, SA 5000
Tel *(08) 8232 0944* **Closed** *Sun; lunch*
Behind an unassuming shopfront, this compact restaurant delivers creative East-meets-West dishes with a Japanese touch. Try the signature slow-cooked pork belly.

ADELAIDE: The Pot Food & Wine $$
Bistro
160 King William Rd, Hyde Park, SA 5061
Tel *(08) 8373 2044* **Closed** *Mon*
Enjoy food inspired by Southeast Asian and French cuisine. The menu offers a mix of grazing, vegetable, meat and poultry dishes. Breakfasts on weekends.

ADELAIDE: Press Food and Wine $$
Modern Australian
40 Waymouth St, SA 5000
Tel *(08) 8211 8048* **Closed** *Sun*
A popular and trendy downstairs area, plus a more formal section upstairs. Good food and an extensive wine list. The tasting menu is a highlight.

Casual outdoor seating at the Appellation at The Louise, The Barossa

ADELAIDE: The Unley $$
Modern Australian
27 Unley Rd, Parkside, SA 5063
Tel *(08) 8271 5544*
Sophisticated bar and restaurant with modern interiors. It has an outdoor rooftop and lounge areas. Daily specials.

ADELAIDE: Peel St $$$
Modern Australian
9 Peel St, SA 5000
Tel *(08) 8231 8887* **Closed** *Sun, Tue; Sat lunch*
Fresh, simple produce is used to create unique, robust dishes at Peel St, drawing on a variety of culinary influences.

ADELAIDE: Restaurant Orana $$$
Modern Australian
285 Rundle St, SA 5000
Tel *(08) 8232 3444* **Closed** *Sun*
This place offers an innovative touch to contemporary Australian cuisine. The fixed tasting menu makes good use of indigenous produce. Impressive selection of wines.

THE BAROSSA: Jacob's Restaurant $$
Winery Restaurant
Barossa Valley Way, Tanunda, SA 5352
Tel *(08) 8521 3000* **Closed** *dinner*
The contemporary menu is designed by one of the state's leading chefs. A great spot to dine while experiencing some of Australia's wine-making history.

THE BAROSSA: The Lord Lyndoch $$
Bistro
23 Barossa Valley Way, Lyndoch, SA 5351
Tel *(08) 8524 5440*
Quaint, old-world eatery with a somewhat retro menu that delivers highly praised food. Cape Grim steak is a favourite. Generous portions.

THE BAROSSA: Taste Eden Valley $$
Winery
6–8 Washington St, Angaston, SA 5353
Tel *(08) 8564 2435* **Closed** *dinner*
Housed in a historic building. Great opportunity to taste award-winning, boutique wines made in the valley. Helpful and knowledgeable staff.

THE BAROSSA: 1918 Bistro & Grill $$$
Modern Australian
94 Murray St, Tanunda, SA 5352
Tel *(08) 8563 0405*
A gorgeous 1918 stone villa is the setting for an Australian menu with a touch of the Middle East and Asia. Beautiful garden.

THE BAROSSA: Appellation at The Louise $$$
Modern Australian
Cnr Seppeltsfield & Stonewall rds, Maranga, SA 5355
Tel *(08) 8562 4144* **Closed** *lunch*
This boutique hotel offers five-star set menu with ingredients from its kitchen garden and bespoke producers. Helicopter transfer can be arranged from Adelaide.

THE BAROSSA: FermentAsian $$$
Asian
90 Murray St, Tanunda, SA 5352
Tel *(08) 8563 0765* **Closed** *Mon & Tue; Wed lunch & Sun dinner*
This award-winning restaurant brings a fresh Asian touch to the European-focused Barossa wine region. The seasonally changing menu makes use of local ingredients, many from the restaurant's own garden.

For more information on types of restaurants *see page 498*

THE BAROSSA:
Hentley Farm $$$
Winery Restaurant
Cnr Gerald Roberts & Jenke rds,
Seppeltsfield, SA 5355
Tel *(08) 8562 8427* **Closed** *Mon–*
Wed; Thu, Fri & Sun dinner
Great food served in the restored
stables of an 1840s homestead,
now a boutique cellar door.

BRIDGEWATER: Petaluma's
Bridgewater Mill $$
Modern Australian
386 Mount Barker Rd, SA 5155
Tel *(08) 8339 9200* **Closed** *Sun;*
Mon–Thu dinner
Housed in a historic 1860s flour
mill. Sample elegant food with a
distinctive European edge, such as
seared venison with soy-braised
daikon, wakame and mustard.

COONAWARRA: Fodder $
Café
5 Memorial Drive, SA 5263
Tel *(08) 8736 3170* **Closed** *Tue &*
Wed; dinner
Organic produce – mainly from
the Fodder garden – is used
here. There is a great selection
of wood-fired pizzas. Book ahead.

COONAWARRA:
Upstairs at Hollick $$
Winery Restaurant
Cnr Riddoch Hwy & Ravenswood Ln,
SA 5263
Tel *(08) 8737 2752* **Closed** *Mon &*
Tue; dinner (except Sat)
Sublime food and wine served in
quiet and relaxing surroundings.
The full-length windows afford
great views of the vineyard.

GUMERACHA:
Talunga Estate $$
Modern Australian
198D Torrens Valley Rd, SA 5233
Tel *(08) 8389 1222* **Closed** *Mon–*
Thu; dinner
Come here for tasting platters
and matching wines. There is also
a good selection of pizza.

HAHNDORF:
Chocolate @ No 5 $
Café
5 Main St, SA 5245
Tel *(08) 8388 1835* **Closed** *Mon &*
Tue; dinner
Popular café to indulge in
scrumptious sweet treats,
including waffles, chocolate
brownies and caramel slices.

HAHNDORF: The German Cake
Shop Family Restaurant $
Dessert
2 Pine Ave, SA 5245
Tel *(08) 8388 7086* **Closed** *dinner*
This family-run business offers a
great selection of traditional
German meals and cakes. Be sure
to try the Bavarian mixed grill.

HAHNDORF:
The Lane Vineyard $$$
Winery Restaurant
5 Ravenswood Lane, SA 5245
Tel *(08) 8388 1250* **Closed** *dinner*
Exquisite food served in a
beautiful setting overlooking the
vineyard and hills beyond. There
is a wood fire in winter and alfresco
dining in the summer months.

KINGSTON-ON-MURRAY:
Banrock Station $$
Modern Australian
Holmes Rd, SA 5331
Tel *(08) 8583 0299* **Closed** *dinner*
Native Australian ingredients –
wattleseed, pepperleaf, lemon
myrtle – take centre stage here.
Sit on the deck and enjoy grazing
platters, pizzas or hearty mains.

McLAREN VALE:
The Barn Bistro $$
Modern Australian
252 Main Rd, SA 5171
Tel *(08) 8323 8618* **Closed** *Mon–Thu*
lunch
The Barn Bistro is renowned for
its high-quality food, ambience
and good service. Guests can
choose from the à la carte-
styled menu.

Pleasant outdoor terrace at Chocolate @
No 5, Hahndorf

McLAREN VALE:
The Kitchen Door $$
Modern Australian
Penny's Hill Winery, 281 Main Rd,
SA 5171
Tel (08) 8557 0840 Closed Tue & Wed
Diners look out to vineyards and
grazing sheep at The Kitchen
Door, the restaurant of the
renowned Penny's Hill Winery.
Tasting menu of four courses
matched or unmatched with
wine, as well as an à la carte selec-
tion of more substantial seasonal
dishes. Book in advance.

McLAREN VALE:
Serafino $$
Winery Restaurant
Kangarilla Rd, SA 5171
Tel *(08) 8323 8911* **Closed** *Sun*
dinner
Located near a tranquil lake,
Serafino is surrounded by 200-
year-old gum trees. It is a great
place to relax and enjoy dishes
such as the superb slow-cooked
lamb shanks.

DK Choice

McLAREN VALE:
d'Arry's Verandah $$$
Winery Restaurant
d'Arenberg Winery, Osborn Rd,
SA 5171
Tel *(08) 8329 4848* **Closed** *dinner*
There are few better ways
to spend an afternoon than
dining on the veranda
looking out over undulating
vineyards and the distant
hills. The postcard view at
d'Arry's Verandah provides
a perfect backdrop for the
signature dish of succulent
lamb or locally sourced
Willunga olives and desserts
such as passion fruit soufflé
or the wonderfully soft-centred
chocolate pudding.

A beautifully presented entrée platter at Coterie Restaurant, McLaren Vale

McLAREN VALE:
Coterie Restaurant $$$
Winery Restaurant
*Woodstock Wine Estate, Douglas
Gully Rd, McLaren Flat, SA 5171*
Tel *(08) 8383 0156* **Closed** *Sat–Thu
dinner*
Sample the regional platter or
choose from the à la carte menu
at this lovely restaurant in the
bush. There is an impressive list
of wines from the family winery.

NORTON SUMMIT:
The Scenic Hotel $$
Modern Australian
Old Norton Summit Rd, SA 5136
Tel *(08) 8390 1705* **Closed** *Mon
dinner*
Dine on the deck in summer and
by open fires in winter. Blackboard
specials change nearly every day.
The wine list focuses on the
Adelaide Hills. Breathtaking views.

OVERLAND CORNER:
Overland Corner Hotel $$
Modern Australian
Old Coach Rd, SA 5345
Tel *(08) 8588 7021* **Closed** *Mon*
Built in 1859, this National Trust-
owned hotel takes guests back
in time. The restaurant serves
hearty, wholesome seasonal fare.

PENOLA: Pipers of Penola $$
Modern Australian
58 Riddoch St, SA 5277
Tel *(08) 8737 3999* **Closed** *Sun & Mon*
In a lovely old building that once
served as a church. Stylish yet
casual restaurant showcasing
top-quality regional produce.

PORT WILLUNGA:
Star of Greece $$
Modern Australian
1 Esplanade, SA 5173
Tel *(08) 8557 7420* **Closed** *Mon &
Tue; Sun & Wed dinner*
Beach-house vibe, with amazing
ocean views. Fresh seafood and
local produce are presented with
flair. Excellent wine list.

STIRLING: Locavore $
Modern Australian
49 Mount Barker Rd, SA 5152
Tel *(08) 8339 4416* **Closed** *Mon;
Sun dinner*
The food, wherever possible, is
sourced from within a 160-km
(100-mile) radius of this Adelaide
Hills eatery. The wine list is from
the region as well. Great for
sharing, the tapas platter includes
regional favourites and gnocchi.

STIRLING:
Organic Market & Café $
Café
5 Druid Ave, SA 5152
Tel *(08) 8339 4835* **Closed** *dinner*

The pretty patio area at Reilly's Cellar Door and Restaurant, Clare Valley

This organic grocer-cum-café
serves simple, wholesome food
including *antipasti*, soups, salads,
focaccias, bruschetta, curries and
cakes. Good coffee, too.

WILLUNGA: Le Mistral $
French
8 Hill St, SA 5712
Tel *(08) 8556 4488* **Closed** *Mon & Tue*
Guests here can enjoy French-
inspired food made with local
produce while also enjoying a
spectacular view of Wilunga Hill.

WILLUNGA: Russell's Pizza $$
Pizzeria
13 High St, SA 5712
Tel *(08) 8556 2571* **Closed** *Sun–Wed*
The decor at Russell's Pizza is
rustic, with old wooden tables
and stone floors. The thin-crust
pizzas have toppings such as
slow-cooked lamb, fresh seafood
and roasted vegetables.

The Yorke and Eyre Peninsulas and South Australian Outback

CLARE VALLEY: Mr. Mick $
Tapas
7 Dominic St, SA 5453
Tel *(08) 8842 2555* **Closed** *dinner
(except Fri)*
Enjoy tapas-style dining in a
casual atmosphere at this award-
winning restaurant. The wine cellar
offers tasting notes for a range of
wines crafted in-house.

CLARE VALLEY: Artisans Table $$
Modern Australian
Wendouree Rd, SA 5453
Tel *(08) 8842 1796* **Closed** *Mon &
Tue; Wed–Fri lunch, Sat & Sun dinner*
In a picturesque country setting,
the chef offers a diverse menu
of meticulously crafted food
inspired by and featuring
Mediterranean and North
African flavours.

**CLARE VALLEY: Reilly's Cellar
Door and Restaurant** $$
Australian
*Cnr Hill St & Leasingham Rd,
Mintaro, SA 5415*
Tel *(08) 8843 9013* **Closed** *dinner*
Dine in a heritage-listed stone
cottage. Daily specials feature
fresh local produce. Leave some
room for the home-made cakes
and desserts.

CLARE VALLEY:
Skillogalee Wines $$
Winery Restaurant
*Trevarrick Rd, via Clare, Sevenhill,
SA 5453*
Tel *(08) 8843 4311* **Closed** *dinner*
This charming 1850s cottage
serves a contemporary Australian
menu to match the wines on
offer. Dine on the veranda or
under the olive tree.

**COFFIN BAY: 1802 Oyster
Bar + Bistro** $$
Seafood
61 Esplanade, SA 5607
Tel *(08) 8685 4626* **Closed** *Mon;
Sun–Wed dinner*
Relish local oysters caught
straight from the bay, cooked
and served at your table.
Outdoor seating available.

**COOBER PEDY: Barbecue Inn
Underground** $$
Mediterranean
335 Trow St, SA 5723
Tel *(08) 8672 3100*
Top-quality fresh meat and
seafood cooked over charcoal.
Enjoy the unique experience of
dining underground.

**COOBER PEDY: Umberto's
Restaurant** $$
International
*Desert Cave Hotel, 20 Hutchison St,
SA 5723*
Tel *(08) 8672 5688* **Closed** *lunch*
Perched atop the underground
Desert Cave Hotel, the modern
menu here focuses on produce
from the Outback to the sea.

For more information on types of restaurants *see page 498*

Simple interior of Marion Bay Tavern, Marion Bay

HAWKER: The Woolshed Restaurant $$
Modern Australian
Flinders Ranges Way, SA 5434
Tel *(08) 8648 0700*
Sit inside a renovated authentic woolshed or dine on the outdoor deck with views across Rawnsley Bluff. The seasonal menu makes the best of local produce, including Rawnsley's own lamb.

MARION BAY: Marion Bay Tavern $$
Bistro
Section 90/Stenhouse Bay Rd, SA 5575
Tel *(08) 8854 4141*
Corrugated iron and old jetty pylons lend this bistro a rustic beachside vibe. Wood-fired pizzas and innovative seafood dishes.

MOONTA BAY: Coffee Barn Gelateria $
Dessert
Warren St, SA 5558
Tel *(08) 8825 2315* **Closed** *Mon–Thu*
Unpretentious café set on 11 ha (27 acres) of historical mining country. Try the tasty pancakes and home-made gelato. Relaxed atmosphere and friendly service.

PARACHILNA: Prairie Hotel $$
Native Australian
Cnr of High St & West Terr , SA 5730
Tel *1800 331 473*
Outback pub renowned for its creative use of native and feral (wild plant) ingredients. There are plenty of choices for the less adventurous, too.

PORT LINCOLN: The Rogue & Rascal $
Café
62 Tasman Terrace, SA 5606
Tel *(04) 6741 1086* **Closed** *dinner (except Fri)*
A perfect spot to enjoy a light lunch followed by great coffee, or sip on a glass of whiskey or wine after dinner.

Key to Price Guide *see page 504*

DK Choice

PORT LINCOLN: Del Giorno's Café Restaurant $$
Seafood
80 Tasman Terrace, SA 5606
Tel *(08) 8683 0577*
Port Lincoln offers some of South Australia's finest seafood. For the best of the catch, visit Del Giorno's, where Kinkawooka mussels, King George whiting, Arno Bay kingfish and southern bluefin tuna feature regularly. The extensive menu draws on local produce, including beef and lamb, served in friendly, comfortable surroundings.

WALLAROO: Prince Edward Hotel $
Modern Australian
32 Hughes St, SA 5556
Tel *(08) 8823 2579*
Value-for-money pub food at this local favourite. Salad bar, veggie options and great seafood platters. The fish 'n' chips features the prized King George whiting.

WAROOKA: Inland Sea $$
Seafood
12918 Yorke Hwy, SA 5577
Tel *(08) 8854 5499* **Closed** *Mon & Tue; Sun dinner*
The perfect setting for a casual dinner. Dine inside or alfresco in the courtyard. Signature dishes may include a seafood platter or the classic reef and beef. Bookings essential.

WHYALLA: Watersedge Restaurant $
Modern Australian
12 Watson Terrace, SA 5600
Tel *(08) 8645 8877* **Closed** *Sun; lunch (except Fri)*
Local ingredients star in dishes such as panko crumbed King George whiting and the signature dessert Eton Mess.

Melbourne

CARLTON: Abla's $$
Lebanese
109 Elgin St, VIC 3053
Tel *(03) 9347 0006* **Closed** *Sun; lunch (except Thu & Fri)*
Melbourne's love affair with Lebanese and Middle Eastern cuisine was kindled by Abla Amad's hearty, tangy classics. Try the chicken rice pilaf with almonds and pine nuts.

CARLTON: Brunetti $$
Italian
380 Lygon St, VIC 3053
Tel *(03) 9347 9281*
Classy café and restaurant with outdoor seating. Wonderful cakes, pastries and ice cream. Fill up on delicious regional Italian cuisine.

CARLTON: Hotel Lincoln $$
Modern Australian **Map** 1 C1
91 Cardigan St, VIC 3053
Tel *(03) 9347 4666*
This revamped pub aims high, with quality fare such as egg-plant and lentils, coffee-cured salmon and whole baby snapper.

CARLTON: Shakahari $$
Vegetarian
201–203 Faraday St, VIC 3053
Tel *(03) 9347 3848* **Closed** *Sun lunch*
Fresh, light, inventive food at reasonable prices. Start with the house speciality – avocado wedges and red capsicums served with a coriandar purée.

CENTRAL MELBOURNE: Grill'd $
Modern Australian **Map** 1 C2
222 Lonsdale St, QV Centre, VIC 3000
Tel *(03) 9663 0399*
This growing burger chain uses quality ingredients and a flame grill for healthy scrumptiousness. Vegetarian options available too. Friendly service.

DK Choice

CENTRAL MELBOURNE:
Hardware Société $
Café   **Map** 1 B3
120 Hardware St, VIC 3000
Tel *(03) 9078 5992*
I the heart of Melbourne, this
popular café is an ideal place
to enjoy a hearty breakfast
or lunch. Try the baked eggs
with chorizo sausage, piquillo
peppers and *queso de cabra*
(goat cheese), or some of
their delicious sweet treats
along with a cup of coffee.
The contemporary dining area
has a large communal table.

CENTRAL MELBOURNE:
Pellegrini's Espresso Bar $
Café   **Map** 2 D2
66 Bourke St, VIC 3000
Tel *(03) 9662 1885*
Lively eatery that has been a
Melbourne icon for decades.
Simple pasta dishes. Quick service.

CENTRAL MELBOURNE:
Becco $$
Italian   **Map** 2 D2
11–25 Crossley St, VIC 3000
Tel *(03) 9663 3000*   **Closed** *Sun*
An inspiring and innovative
Italian bistro. Dishes include
barramundi with *caponata*
fregola (an aubergine dish), crispy
saltbush and *verjuice* (sour juice).

CENTRAL MELBOURNE:
Chin Chin $$
Southeast Asian   **Map** 2 D3
125 Flinders Lane, VIC 3004
Tel *(03) 8663 2000*
A place based on the concept
of shared eating. If deciding on
any particular dish proves tricky,
simply tell the waiter "feed me",
and you will receive up to six
of their most popular dishes of
the day. All-Australian wine list.
No bookings.

CENTRAL MELBOURNE:
Cookie $$
Thai   **Map** 1 C2
252 Swanston St, VIC 3000
Tel *(03) 9663 7660*
An unusual combination of beer
hall and Thai restaurant. The
kitsch decor and lively atmo-
sphere attract a large, arty crowd.

CENTRAL MELBOURNE:
Cumulus Inc $$
International   **Map** 2 D3
45 Flinders Lane, VIC 3000
Tel *(03) 9650 1445*
Good design, fine wine and
great, unpretentious food at this
popular restaurant.

CENTRAL MELBOURNE:
Grossi Florentino $$
Italian   **Map** 2 D2
80 Bourke St, VIC 3000
Tel *(03) 9662 1811*   **Closed** *Sun*
Three eateries on three levels: a
casual Tuscan grill, sumptuous
fine dining in the *fin-de-siècle*
Mural Room, and light bites in
the cellar bar.

CENTRAL MELBOURNE:
Il Solito Posto $$
Italian   **Map** 2 D3
Basement, 113 Collins St, VIC 3000
Tel *(03) 9654 4466*   **Closed** *Sun*
A welcoming basement *trattoria*
with well-stocked shelves of
both local and Italian wines and
a delectable menu of regional
Italian specialities, such as squid
ink linguini and leek risotto.

CENTRAL MELBOURNE:
Mamasita $$
Mexican   **Map** 2 D3
Level 1, 11 Collins St, VIC 3000
Tel *(03) 9650 3821*
This popular upbeat restaurant
champions authentic Mexican
food with its flavoursome dishes
including chicken *tostaditas* and
corn with chipotle mayo.

CENTRAL MELBOURNE:
MoVida $$
Spanish   **Map** 2 D3
1 Hosier Lane, VIC 3000
Tel *(03) 9663 3038*
Australia's finest proponent of
modern Spanish tapas. Daily
specials, along with a list of
small dishes. Book ahead.

CENTRAL MELBOURNE:
The European $$$
European   **Map** 2 D2
161 Spring St, VIC 3000
Tel *(03) 9654 0811*
Smart place attracting politicians
and the pre-theatre crowd.
Styled like an old-school bistro,
with superb wines from France,
Italy, Germany and Spain.

CENTRAL MELBOURNE:
Ezard $$$
Modern Australian   **Map** 2 D3
187 Flinders Lane, VIC 3000
Tel *(03) 9639 6811*   **Closed** *Sat*
lunch & Sun
Renowned chef Teage Ezard
explores the complexities of
contemporary Australian fare in
an ultra-modern, lively setting.

CENTRAL MELBOURNE:
Flower Drum $$$
Chinese   **Map** 2 D2
17 Market Lane, VIC 3000
Tel *(03) 9662 3655* **Closed** *Sun lunch*
Considered by many the best
Cantonese restaurant in the
whole of Australia. Flower Drum
attracts celebrities but remains
accommodating and relaxed.

CENTRAL MELBOURNE:
Hanabishi $$$
Japanese   **Map** 1 B3
187 King St, VIC 3000
Tel *(03) 9670 1167* **Closed** *Sat & Sun*
Often voted Melbourne's best
Japanese restaurant, this is an
excellent place for sashimi,
steaming hotpots and melt-in-
your-mouth tempura.

CENTRAL MELBOURNE:
Kappo $$$
Japanese   **Map** 2 D3
1 Flinders Lane, VIC 3000
Tel *(03) 9639 9500*   **Closed** *lunch*
(except Fri); Sun dinner
This highly regarded *omakase*
(chef's selection) restaurant
allows you to choose from five,
seven or nine courses. Ingredients
include yam, candy beetroot,
abalone and sea urchin.

CENTRAL MELBOURNE:
Pei Modern $$$
Modern Australian   **Map** 2 D3
Collins Place, 45 Collins St, VIC 3000
Tel *(03) 9654 8545* **Closed** *Sat & Sun*
Celebrated chef Mark Best's
eatery serves natural-flavoured
dishes. Sleek café decor.

The sleek interior of the popular Cumulus Inc restaurant in Melbourne

For more information on types of restaurants *see page 498*

DK Choice
CENTRAL MELBOURNE:
Vue de Monde **$$$**
Modern Australian **Map** 1 B4
Level 55, Rialto, 525 Collins St,
VIC 3000
Tel *(03) 9691 3888* **Closed** *Mon–*
Wed lunch
Eating at Vue de Monde is a
beautiful, delicious experience.
Exciting, award-winning fine
cuisine is served in a striking,
modern interior. The wagyu
beef, the beef cheek and the
kangaroo with native fruits
are sensational. The owner,
acclaimed Australian chef
Shannon Bennett, aims to make
this Australia's most sustainable
restaurant and uses organic,
small-farm produce and cutting-
edge eco-technology.

COLLINGWOOD:
Huxtaburger **$**
American **Map** 2 F1
106 Smith St, VIC 3066
Tel *(03) 9417 6328*
Superb beef or tofu burgers
with crinkle-cut chips. Delicious
extras include bacon, beetroot,
jalapeños and sesame soy mayo.

COLLINGWOOD:
Jim's Greek Tavern **$$**
Greek
32 Johnston St, VIC 3066
Tel *(03) 9419 3827* **Closed** *lunch*
One of the best tavernas in
the city, Jim's Greek is a favourite
among Melbourne's large Greek
community. Generous and
flavourful seafood platters.

FITZROY:
Babka Bakery Café **$**
Eastern European
358 Brunswick St, VIC 3000
Tel *(03) 9416 0091* **Closed** *Mon*
Small, casual café. Light meals,
many with a Russian flavour,
include meat pies and salads.
Guests can dine outdoors in
fine weather.

FITZROY: Moroccan Soup Bar **$**
Moroccan
183 St Georges Rd, VIC 3068
Tel *(03) 9482 4240* **Closed** *Mon; lunch*
This bohemian café does great
things with chickpeas, lentils,
couscous and yogurt. Vegetarian
food, enticingly presented.

FITZROY: Charcoal Lane **$$**
Native Australian **Map** 2 E1
136 Gertrude St, VIC 3065
Tel *(03) 9418 3400* **Closed** *Sun & Mon*
This imaginative restaurant serving
food based on Aboriginal ingre-
dients and recipes provides work
experience to disadvantaged
young people. Minimalist decor.

FITZROY:
Fitzroy Social **$$**
Bistro
222 Brunswick St, VIC 3065
Tel *(03) 9825 8950*
This buzzing bar and restaurant is
in a large dining hall and has a
trendy clientele. Popular for beer,
cocktails, and no-fuss meals such
as pizzas and burgers.

FITZROY: Ladro **$$**
Italian
224 Gertrude St, VIC 3065
Tel *(03) 9415 7575* **Closed** *lunch*
weekdays
Award-winning restaurant with
roasts, the best crispy wood-
fired pizzas in town and a
reasonably priced wine list.
Hugely popular.

FITZROY: Mario's **$$**
Italian
303 Brunswick St, VIC 3065
Tel *(03) 9417 3343*
A cool retro vibe and classic café
food – *antipasti* and pasta dishes –
make this bustling joint a favourite
with the local arty crowd.

FITZROY:
RST Seafood Restaurant **$$**
Seafood
5 Rae St, VIC 3065
Tel *(03) 9489 1974* **Closed** *Sun &*
Mon; Sat lunch

Snug but light and airy seafood
restaurant. The fish is delivered
daily and filleted on the premises.
Superb mixed platters. Casual
interiors and attentive staff.

FITZROY: Vegie Bar **$$**
Vegetarian
380 Brunswick St, VIC 3065
Tel *(03) 9417 6935*
Fun, community-spirited place.
Generous portions of healthy
vegetarian fare ensure an
enthusiastic following. Vegan and
gluten-free dishes available.

FITZROY: Cutler & Co **$$$**
Modern Australian **Map** 2 E1
55–57 Gertrude St, VIC 3065
Tel *(03) 9419 4888* **Closed** *Mon–*
Thu dinner
Converted metalworks with a
gritty, urban feel. In an interesting
contrast, the food is deliciously
delicate, scattered with tiny
flowers and leaves.

RICHMOND: Richmond Hill
Café and Larder **$$**
Café **Map** 4 D2
48–50 Bridge Rd, VIC 3121
Tel *(03) 9421 2808* **Closed** *dinner*
This light and airy venue serves
great coffee and light meals in
a characterful 1860s building.
The cheeses are to die for.

RIPPON LEA: Attica **$$$**
Modern Australian
74 Glen Eira Rd, VIC 3185
Tel *(03) 9530 0111* **Closed** *Sun &*
Mon; lunch
The chef at this upscale restaurant
experiments with unusual ingre-
dients and techniques. Five- or
eight-course menus only.

SOUTHBANK: Persimmon **$$**
Modern Australian **Map** 2 D4
Ground Level, NGV International,
180 St Kilda Rd, VIC 3004
Tel *(03) 8620 2434* **Closed** *Tue*
Lunch at Melbourne's finest
gallery restaurant is a real treat.
The garden views add to the
serene experience.

Chefs working to create exquisite dishes at the stylish Vue de Monde, Melbourne

The cheerful, wood-furnished interiors of Donovans, St Kilda

SOUTHBANK: Saké $$

Japanese   **Map** 2 D4
Hammer Hall, Arts Centre Melbourne,
100 St Kilda Rd, VIC 3004
Tel *(03) 8687 0775*
Perfect choice for a pre- or post-theatre meal. New-style and classic Japanese cuisine served at the sushi bar or at the intimate booths.

SOUTHBANK:
Rockpool Bar & Grill $$$
Grill   **Map** 1 B5
Crown Complex, 8 Whiteman St,
VIC 3006
Tel *(03) 8648 1900*   **Closed** *Sat lunch*
Rockpool Bar & Grill has an uncompromising eye for the very best cuts of meat. Succulent wagyu burgers and steaks. Crisp, business-like decor.

SOUTH MELBOURNE:
Hercules Morse $$
Modern Australian
283 Clarendon St, VIC 3205
Tel *(03) 9690 9402*   **Closed** *Mon*
Centrally located, this modern restaurant serves an array of delectable and hearty meals and creative cocktails. Relaxed and comfortable ambience.

SOUTH MELBOURNE:
O'Connell's $$
Modern Australian
407 Coventry St, VIC 3205
Tel *(03) 9810 0086*
Convivial, gentrified corner pub featuring an extensive international wine list and plenty of craft beers on tap. The menu has a broad range of gastropub classics.

SOUTH MELBOURNE:
Pony Fish Island $$
Pub   **Map** 1 C4
Southgate Pedestrian Bridge,
VIC 3006
Located at the heart of Yarra river, this bar-restaurant is accessible only via stairs on the pedestrian bridge. Take in a spectacular view of Melbourne while enjoying a light lunch or cocktails.

SOUTH YARRA:
Caffé Sienna Ristorante $$
Italian   **Map** 6 E1
Shop 2, 402 Chapel St, VIC 3142
Tel *(03) 9827 1353*
Contemporary, yet relaxed spot that serves Italian classics. Come for coffee and cocktails, or for light meals, cakes and tasty desserts.

SOUTH YARRA:
Caffé e Cucina $$$
Italian   **Map** 4 E5
581 Chapel St, VIC 3141
Tel *(03) 9827 4139*
Bustling café-restaurant, with style and attitude aplenty, serves excellent traditional Italian fare. A perennial favourite with Melbourne's people-watchers and younger celebrities. Intimate atmosphere and attentive service.

SOUTH YARRA:
France-Soir $$$
French   **Map** 4 D5
11 Toorak Rd, VIC 3141
Tel *(03) 9866 8569*
Energetic bistro serving *plats de résistance* such as *filet de boeuf béarnaise* (beef steak with Béarnaise sauce) and *poisson du jour* (catch of the day). It is also said to make Melbourne's best crème brûlée.

ST KILDA: Cicciolina $$$
Italian
130 Acland St, VIC 3182
Tel *(03) 9525 3333*
Earthy, full-bodied comfort food is the order of the day at this simple restaurant. Jammed with small tables and often full. Extensive wine list.

ST KILDA: Circa $$$
Modern Asian   **Map** 5 B5
The Prince, 2 Acland St, VIC 3182
Tel *(03) 9536 1122*
Subtle yet unexpected combinations define this modern eatery. The setting is low-key but highly stylish. Service is unobtrusive.

ST KILDA: Donovans $$$
Modern Australian
40 Jacka Boulevard, VIC 3182
Tel *(03) 9534 8221*
Set in a former foreshore bathing house, this unique restaurant has the feel of a large family beach house. Finely rendered seafood and meat dishes.

WINDSOR: Journeyman $$
Café   **Map** 6 E2
169 Chapel St, VIC 3181
Tel *(03) 9521 4884*
This local favourite is perfect for breakfasts. Serves world-class coffee. Don't miss the signature avocado hummus toast. Excellent service.

Western Victoria

AIREYS INLET:
A La Grecque $$$
Greek
60 Great Ocean Rd, VIC 3231
Tel *(03) 5289 6922*   **Closed** *Mon & Tue*
Run by a family who have produced a cookbook, this place is known worldwide for its Greek-inspired cuisine. Good selection of *mezze* and beautifully cooked seafood.

APOLLO BAY: La Bimba $$
Moroccan
125 Great Ocean Rd, VIC 3233
Tel *(03) 5237 7411*
Service can vary, but the food always hits the spot with Middle Eastern and Asian influences. Tiled balcony tables and wall hangings add an exotic touch. Go for the seafood platter for two.

APOLLO BAY: Chris's Beacon
Point Restaurant $$$
European
280 Skenes Creek Rd, VIC 3233
Tel *(03) 5237 6411*   **Closed** *Mon–Fri lunch*
This much-lauded clifftop restaurant offers a modern Mediterranean-inspired menu. Seafood is a speciality here, as are the chef's popular Greek-style dishes. While dining, guests can also enjoy jaw-dropping views of the coastline.

For more information on types of restaurants *see page 498*

BALLARAT: Kambei Japanese Restaurant $$$
Japanese
501 Main Rd, VIC 3350
Tel *(03) 5331 1468* **Closed** *Mon & Tue; Wed & Thu lunch*
Relax and enjoy some of the best Japanese food Ballarat has to offer. The dishes are prepared from freshest ingredients.

BENDIGO: Bouchon $$
French
61 High St, VIC 3550
Tel *(03) 5444 5272* **Closed** *Sun & Mon*
A little slice of France. Well-priced, beautifully cooked food includes snails, charcuterie, confit duck and other classics with a local twist.

BENDIGO: Mr. Beebe's $$
Modern Australian
17 View Point, VIC 3550
Tel *(03) 5441 5557*
Delicious food with an extensive drinks menu. Order from the chef's tasting menu for a multi-course delight.

**BIRREGURRA:
The Meating Place Café** $$
Modern Australian
43 Main St, VIC 5422
Tel *(03) 5236 2611* **Closed** *lunch Mon–Fri; dinner*
Boutique chic meets old-world charm at this butcher's shop, provedore, wine merchant and café. Weekend brunch and lunch; only drinks and cakes Tue–Sun.

BIRREGURRA: Brae $$$
Modern Australian
4285 Cape Otway Rd, VIC 5422
Tel *(03) 5236 2226* **Closed** *Tue & Wed; Thu–Sat lunch; Fri–Mon dinner*
This modern restaurant offers a seasonally changing menu that uses the highest quality local produce, most of it grown in the restaurant's organic, on-site garden.

Sophisticated interior of the Royal Mail Hotel restaurant, Dunkeld

The red-brick exterior of the mid-19th-century Farmers Arms in Daylesford

DAYLESFORD: Cliffy's $
Café
30 Raglan St, VIC 3460
Tel *(03) 5348 3279* **Closed** *dinner*
Part café, part general store, this quirky place is like stepping into the past. The menu changes daily based on what farmers bring in.

DAYLESFORD: Farmers Arms $$
Modern Australian
1 East St, VIC 3460
Tel *(03) 5348 2091*
This charming pub dating back to 1857 serves fresh food from a great menu. No bookings.

DAYLESFORD: Sault $$
International
2349 Ballan-Daylesford Rd, VIC 3460
Tel *(03) 5348 6555* **Closed** *Mon & Tue; Wed & Thu lunch*
French-style country house restaurant overlooking lavender fields. Blending contemporary Australian and Spanish cuisine, the menu offers a selection of tapas and other savoury items.

DAYLESFORD: Kazuki's $$$
International
1 Camp St, VIC 3460
Tel *(03) 5348 1218* **Closed** *Tue & Wed; Mon, Thu & Fri lunch*
The owner-chef Kazuki Tsuya efficiently blends Japanese and modern Australian flavours to create an unforgettable experience for patrons. The dishes use only the best local produce.

DAYLESFORD: Lake House $$$
Modern Australian
4 King St, VIC 3460
Tel *(03) 5348 3329*
Fine country dining with a seasonal, cutting-edge slant is available here. The chef works tirelessly to support small local suppliers.

DK Choice

**DUNKELD:
Royal Mail Hotel** $$$
Modern Australian
Royal Mail Hotel, 98 Parker St (Glenelg Hwy), VIC 3294
Tel *(03) 5577 2241*
A gastronomic destination, this country hotel in the shadow of the Grampians has won every award under the sun for its world-class food. The chef prepares two menus every day based on produce from his garden, local artisan producers and the wild.

GEELONG: Tulip $$
Modern Australian
9–11 Pakington St, VIC 3218
Tel *(03) 5229 6953*
Helmed by esteemed chefs, this restaurant boasts minimalist decor and high-quality ingredients including grass-fed ribeye and whole lamb shoulder. The atmosphere is relaxed and dishes are made to be shared.

**HEPBURN SPRINGS:
The Argus Dining Room** $$$
Australian
Peppers Mineral Springs Retreat, 124 Main Rd, VIC 3461
Tel *(03) 5348 4199*
This elegant restaurant in an Art Deco dining room focuses on fresh, seasonal, locally grown food. Indulge in the five- or seven-course tasting menu.

KYNETON: La Bonta $$$
Italian
12–14 Piper St, VIC 3444
Tel *(03) 5422 3683* **Closed** *Sun & Mon*
Tim Austin, the owner-chef, draws on traditional Italian recipes and adds his modern spin. Wonderful service.

LORNE: Cuda Bar $$
Modern Australian
84 Mountjoy Pde, VIC 3232
Tel *(03) 5289 5006*
Enjoy picturesque views of Louttit
Bay while savouring contemporary
delights. Friendly ambience.

MACEDON: Ida Red $$
Italian
14–16 Victoria St, VIC 3440
Tel *(03) 5426 4888* **Closed** *Mon &*
Tue; lunch (except Sun)
Wood-fired-oven pizzas are the
speciality here, with toppings
ranging from pork and fennel, to
Serrano ham and leek. Dessert
pizzas are available too.

MILDURA: Mildura Brewery $$
Modern Australian
20 Langtree Ave, VIC 3500
Tel *(03) 5022 2988*
This lively brewery and restaurant
produces a range of its own natural
beers. The food menu lists gastro-
pub dishes such as Scotch fillet
steak and slow-cooked duck confit.
Creative vegetarian options, too.

MILDURA:
Spanish Grill $$$
Steakhouse
Quality Mildura Grand Hotel, cnr
Seventh St & Langtree Ave, VIC 3502
Tel *(03) 5021 2377*
Exceptionally good steaks, local
ingredients and superb cooking.
There is nothing Spanish about
this place – the name is simply a
tribute to its forerunner.

MOONAMBEL: Warrenmang
Vineyard Resort $$$
Modern Australian
188 Mountain Creek Rd, VIC 3478
Tel *(03) 5467 2233* **Closed** *Mon;*
Sun dinner
European-style hospitality and
fine food. Local yabbies, berries,
cheese, rabbit and trout can often
be found on the menu. Lodging
options in cottages as well.

PORT FAIRY: Merrijig Inn $$$
Modern Australian
1 Campbell St, VIC 3284
Tel *(03) 5568 2324* **Closed** *Tue &*
Wed; lunch
Lots of charm in the dining room
of Victoria's oldest inn. The menu
(written daily) features the area's
best produce. Excellent wine list.

QUEENSCLIFF: Vue Grand $$$
Modern Australian
46 Hesse St, VIC 3225
Tel *(03) 5258 1544* **Closed** *lunch;*
Sun–Tue dinner
Step back into a bygone era
at this hotel, where you can
dine in a chandelier-lit room
as a grand piano plays in the
background. Light, modern
food on the menu. Open for
breakfast every day.

SHEPHERDS FLAT: Lavandula
La Trattoria $$
Italian
350 Hepburn–Newstead Rd, VIC 3461
Tel *(03) 5476 4393* **Closed** *Wed & Thu*
(Mon–Thu in winter); dinner
Indulge in lavender scones and
tea or enjoy a Mediterranean-
style lunch. Dine inside the warm
café or alfresco, overlooking the
lavender fields.

TIMBOON: Timboon Railway
Shed Distillery $$
Modern Australian
Bailey St, VIC 3268
Tel *(03) 5598 3555* **Closed** *dinner*
This old railway shed-cum-
micro-distillery demonstrates
a deep commitment to locally
grown produce. The eclectic
offerings include Asian dishes,
pub favourites and kids' meals.

TRENTHAM: Du Fermier $$
French
42 High St, VIC 3458
Tel *(03) 5424 1634* **Closed** *Tue–Thu*
lunch; dinner
Annie Smithers' delightful
restaurant serves rustic French
fare. The menu changes weekly
featuring ingredients from the
restaurant's garden and the best
poultry and meat from the region.

WOODEND: Colenso $$
Modern European
Cnr Old Bakery Ln & Anslow St,
VIC 3442
Tel *(03) 5427 2007* **Closed** *Sun;*
Mon–Thu dinner
Enjoy good coffee and casual
food by day, and choose from a
more sophisticated set menu on
Friday and Saturday nights. Works
by local artists add to the vibe.

Eastern Victoria

AVENEL: Bank Street Woodfired
Pizzas and Gardens $$
Pizzeria
5 Bank St, VIC 3664
Tel *(03) 5796 2522* **Closed** *Mon–Thu*
Laid-back weekend eatery in a
former bank with dark-wood fit-
tings. Creates imaginative pizzas in
a wood-fired oven. The "Smooshed
Potato" pizza won't disappoint.
Eat inside or in the garden.

AVENEL: Fowles $$
Winery Restaurant
1175 Lambing Gully Rd (cnr Hume
Freeway & Lambing Gully Rd), VIC 3664
Tel *(03) 5796 2150* **Closed** *dinner*
(except Fri)
Fowles is a welcome pit stop
while exploring the wineries
of the region. Offers *antipasti*,
charcuterie and other European
dishes, especially game.

BEECHWORTH:
Bridge Road Brewers $$
Brewery/Pizzeria
Old Coach House, Brewers Lane,
Ford St, VIC 3747
Tel *(03) 5728 2703* **Closed** *Mon–*
Wed dinner
Gourmet pizzas made by
an Austrian chef who adds
Bavarian wheat beer to the
dough mix. The food is perfectly
matched with Bridge Road's
hand-crafted ales.

BEECHWORTH: The Press
Room Wine Bar $$
Spanish
37 Camp St, VIC 3747
Tel *(03) 5728 2360* **Closed** *Mon,*
Tues; lunch
Offers a range of tapas, local wines,
craft beer and cocktails. Don't
miss the delectable churros (fried
dough pastry). Book ahead.

The restored historic stone building at Lavandula La Trattoria, Shepherds Flat

For more information on types of restaurants *see page 498*

Spacious, modern interior of Ten Minutes by Tractor, Mornington Peninsula

BEECHWORTH:
Provenance $$$
Modern Australian
86 Ford St, VIC 3747
Tel *(03) 5728 1786*
Highly acclaimed restaurant in a stately 1856 bank building with a shady courtyard. The old gold vault is now a cellar, stocked with fine Australian wines.

BRIGHT: Coral Lee $
Café
8 Barnard St, VIC 3741
Tel *(03) 5755 5113*
This friendly little café is a great lunch spot. House specialities include a twice-baked cheese soufflé, spicy sausages and beetroot tart. Great retro feel.

BRIGHT: Simone's $$$
Italian
98 Gavan St, VIC 3741
Tel *(03) 5755 2266*
Located in a renovated heritage building. Signature dishes include Umbrian-style home-made pasta, rabbit, duck and Welsh black beef, enhanced by local produce such as wild spinach.

BRUTHEN: Bullant Brewery $$
Brewery/International
46 Main St, VIC 3885
Tel *(03) 5157 5307*
Cheerful contemporary café decked out in timber and corrugated iron. Serves tasty bites such as cheese, rustic chips and pizza to accompany the beers brewed on site.

DINNER PLAIN: Graze $$$
Bistro
Rundells Alpine Lodge,
Big Muster Dr, VIC 3898
Tel *(03) 5159 6422*
Appealing à la carte and tasting menus. After dinner, relax by the fire with a warming glass of schnapps from the Wildbrumby distillery in the Snowy Mountains.

DANDENONG RANGES:
Café de Beaumarchais $
Café/French
Shop 1, 372 Mt Dandenong Tourist Rd, Sassafras, VIC 3787
Tel *(03) 9755 1100*
The dark, elegant decor lends a Baroque edge to this inviting café. Fresh salads, filled baguettes and a wonderful selection of cakes on offer. Try the pistachio and orange cake or indulge in a rich chocolate brownie served with cream. Wonderful coffee.

DANDENONG RANGES:
The General Food Store $
Café
377 Belgrave Gembrook Rd, Emerald, VIC 3782
Tel *(03) 5968 3580*
One of the best places in the area for coffee or a cooked breakfast. Good lunches and cakes, too. The menu is updated monthly according to available seasonal produce. Friendly staff.

FALLS CREEK:
Astra Lodge $$$
Modern Australian
5 Sitzmark St, VIC 3699
Tel *(03) 5758 3496*
Beautifully designed ski lodge with a restaurant that uses locally grown ingredients, such as bush tomatoes and wild berries, to create delicious dishes.

LAKES ENTRANCE:
Ferrymans Seafood Café $$
Café
Middle Boat Harbour, Princes Hwy, VIC 3909
Tel *(03) 5155 3000*
This floating café and restaurant is set among the fishing fleet of Lakes Entrance and offers the freshest seafood from the local area. Sit outside and admire the view while eating creative dishes with prawns, calamari and fish.

MILAWA: Milawa
Cheese Factory Restaurant $$
Winery Restaurant
17 Milawa–Bobinawarrah Rd, VIC 3678
Tel *(03) 5727 3589*
Amazing bread and handmade cheese are just two of the highlights served in this bright, simple café. Pizzas and simple bistro fare are also available. Cheese tastings on request.

MILAWA: Patricia's Table
Restaurant $$$
Modern Australian/French
Brown Brothers Winery, 239 Bobinawarrah Rd, VIC 3678
Tel *(03) 5720 5540*
Every dish at this family-owned restaurant is designed to complement Brown Brothers' own wine. First-rate local barramundi and lamb on the menu. Booking is essential.

MORNINGTON:
The Rocks $$
Seafood
1 Schnapper Point Drive, VIC 3931
Tel *(03) 5973 5599*
This award-winning restaurant offers pleasant waterfront dining and contemporary dishes, with an emphasis on fresh seafood and Asian flavours.

MORNINGTON PENINSULA:
Montalto Vineyard and Grove $$
Winery Restaurant
33 Shoreham Rd, Red Hill, VIC 3937
Tel *(03) 5989 8412*
Contemporary architecture with French-inspired cuisine and views over the olive grove, vineyard and gardens. This is a picturesque spot for a picnic, too.

MORNINGTON PENINSULA:
Ten Minutes by Tractor $$$
Winery Restaurant
1333 Mornington Flinders Rd, Main Ridge, Red Hill, VIC 3928
Tel *(03) 5989 6080*
Remarkable wine list with around 400 options from all over the world. The food is accomplished Modern Australian.

NOOJEE:
The Toolshed $$
Bistro
The Outpost Retreat, 38 Loch Valley Rd, VIC 3833
Tel *(03) 5628 9669*
Noojee's landmark watering hole has an appealingly rustic feel and fare to match. The lamb pot roast and hand-crumbed chicken parmigiana are always popular.

Elegant dining area looking out over the gardens at Eleonore's, Yarra Valley

OXLEY: King River Café $$
Modern Australian
1143 Snow Rd, VIC 3678
Tel *(03) 5727 3461*
Housed in the town's charming 1860s post office and general store. The menu favours King Valley wines and produce, and delivers ever-changing flavours. Make sure you save room for the tangy lemon tart.

PHILLIP ISLAND:
Rusty Water Brewery $$
Brewery
1821 Phillip Island Rd, Cowes, VIC 3922
Tel *(03) 5952 1666*
Down-to-earth place with delicious hand-crafted ales and good local food such as pies and fish 'n' chips. Gluten-free and vegetarian options are available. Live jazz or folk music every Friday evening.

WARRAGUL:
Wild Dog $$
Winery Restaurant
Warragul–Korumburra Rd, VIC 3820
Tel *(03) 5623 2211*
Housed in a striking building with a large open deck surrounded by lawns. Offers pizza, charcuterie, sliders and multi-course set meals. A good place for an enjoyable lunch.

YARRA VALLEY:
Innocent Bystander $$
Winery Restaurant
336 Maroondah Hwy, Healesville, VIC 3777
Tel *(03) 5962 6111*
Winery restaurant in an urban setting. The in-house staff create wood-fired pizzas, bake artisan bread and brew great coffee.

YARRA VALLEY: Quince Dining $$
Modern Australian
Healesville Hotel, 256 Maroondah Hwy, Healesville, VIC 3777
Tel *(03) 5962 4002*
Laid-back eatery in a smart country pub offering quality local produce. Slow-cooked lamb, Yarra Valley cheeses and home-grown herbs and salad greens.

DK Choice

YARRA VALLEY:
Eleonore's $$$
Modern Australian
Chateau Yering, 42 Melba Hwy, Yering, VIC 3770
Tel *(03) 9237 3333*
Superb dining in a 19th-century house. The dining room has white linen, upholstered chairs and large sash windows with views of lawns and trees. The renowned head chef creates delicious contemporary menus inspired by the changing seasons. Impeccable service.

YARRA VALLEY: Locale $$$
Winery Restaurant
De Bortoli, Pinnacle Lane, Dixons Creek, VIC 3775
Tel *(03) 5965 2271*
The De Bortoli family are wine-making legends. The North Italian menu boasts a scrumptious rabbit and pork pithivier served with broad beans and beetroot.

Tasmania

BARRINGTON:
Glencoe Rural Retreat $$
French
1468 Sheffield Rd, TAS 7306
Tel *(03) 6492 3267*   **Closed** *Mon & Tue lunch*
A little slice of rural France in Tasmania, with a café open to the public by day.

CAMBRIDGE: Barilla Bay $$
Seafood
1388 Tasman Hwy, TAS 7170
Tel *(03) 6248 5454*   **Closed** *Sun–Thu dinner*
Located near Hobart Airport, this restaurant overlooks an oyster farm. Select the "Shucking Awesome" platter – 30 cooked, natural oysters with a variety of toppings.

CAMPBELL TOWN: Zeps Café $
Café
92–94 High St, TAS 7210
Tel *(03) 6381 1344*
Convenient stop on the highway. All-day breakfasts, pizzas, panini and pasta dishes, along with good coffee, pastries and cakes.

CRADLE MOUNTAIN:
Highland Restaurant $$$
Modern Australian
Peppers Cradle Mountain Lodge, 4038 Cradle Mountain Rd, TAS 7306
Tel *(03) 6492 1303*   **Closed** *lunch*
Be pampered with fine Tasmanian food and wine at this spot in one of Australia's most scenic locations. The salmon fillet with squid and prawn ravioli is a winner.

CYGNET: Lotus Eaters Café $
Café
10 Mary St, TAS 7112
Tel *(03) 6295 2147*   **Closed** *Tue & Wed; dinner*
Rustic and informal café. Pies, curries, gourmet pizzas, soups and vegetarian dishes, all made from scratch using local produce.

CYGNET: School House
Coffee Shop $
Café
23 Mary St, TAS 7112
Tel *(03) 6295 1206*   **Closed** *Sat; dinner*
Good coffee and delectable home-made pies served in a cosy little space. The curried scallop pie is a crowd favourite. Welcoming service.

Homely dining room at Glencoe Rural Retreat, Barrington

For more information on types of restaurants *see page 498*

**ELIZABETH TOWN: Christmas
Hills Raspberry Farm** $
Café
9 Christmas Hills Rd, TAS 7304
Tel *(03) 6362 2186* **Closed** *dinner*
Savour fresh raspberries by the
bowlful (in season, Dec–May) or
enjoy the berries in cakes, ice
creams, muffins, desserts, jams and
wine at this busy farm restaurant.

**GEORGE TOWN:
Cove Restaurant and Bar** $$
Modern Australian
*Peppers York Cove, 2 Ferry Blvd,
TAS 7253*
Tel *(03) 6382 9990* **Closed** *Mon
lunch & Sun dinner*
Bright, contemporary interior
with stunning river views.
The menu plays homage to
the finest local ingredients.Try
the salmon or the confit duck
terrine. Sample the region's
award-winning wines.

HOBART: Fish Frenzy $
Seafood
Shop 1, Elizabeth St Pier, TAS 7000
Tel *(03) 6231 2134*
There is a great vibe at this
waterfront eatery where the fish
is served simply in big paper
cones. Grilled seafood, oysters,
scallops and seafood chowder
also tempt. No bookings.

**HOBART: Maldini's Café
Restaurant** $$
Italian
47 Salamanca Place, TAS 7000
Tel *(03) 6223 4460*
Relaxed dining, either in a historic
warehouse or on the esplanade.
Watch the passing parade over a
light lunch or delicious Italian
meal, or simply a coffee or drink.

**HOBART:
Prossers on the Beach** $$
Seafood
*19 Beach Rd, Long Point,
Sandy Bay, TAS 7005*
Tel *(03) 6225 2276* **Closed** *Mon &
Tue lunch, Sun dinner*
A relaxed seaside vibe and an
international menu. The owners
source fresh food directly from
local fishermen. Tanks with
live crayfish.

**HOBART:
Ristorante Da Angelo** $$
Italian
*47 Hampden Rd, Battery Point,
TAS 7004*
Tel *(03) 6223 7011* **Closed** *lunch
(except Fri)*
A Hobart institution, this popular
Italian restaurant has a cheerful
feel and a loyal following.
Traditional pizzas and desserts
feature on the menu, as well as
fresh home-made pasta.

**HOBART:
Tavern 42 Degress South** $$
Modern Australian
*Elizabeth St Pier, Elizabeth St,
TAS 7000*
Tel *(03) 6224 7742*
Kick back and watch the boats
sail by this cool, casual venue
offering reasonably priced bistro
fare and an extensive list of more
than 200 wines.

HOBART: Franklin $$$
Modern Australian
28 Argyle St, TAS 7000
Tel *(03) 6234 3375* **Closed** *Sun*
Housed in a renovated Ford
showroom, Franklin features
a minimalist concrete interior
with an open kitchen. The

ever-changing seasonal menu
includes Tasmanian produce,
particularly seafood.

HOBART: Islington $$$
Fine Dining
321 Davey St, TAS 7000
Tel *(03) 6220 2123*
The small, stylish menu befits this
sophisticated boutique hotel in a
Regency-style building. Mountain
views and fine wine cellar. Dining
only for in-house guests.

HOBART: Lebrina $$$
European
*155 New Town Rd, New Town,
TAS 7008*
Tel *(03) 6228 7775* **Closed** *Sun &
Monday; lunch*
Set in an elegant and charming
1840s cottage decorated with
antiques and modern art.
Sublime dishes created with
European techniques are served
with carefully chosen wines.

HOBART: Me Wah $$$
Chinese
16 Magnet Ct, Sandy Bay, TAS 7005
Tel *(03) 6223 3688*
Locals rave about the refined
Cantonese food here. The menu
features traditional dishes such as
Peking duck, alongside offerings
with local seafood including
oysters, abalone and crayfish.

**HOBART: The Point Revolving
Restaurant** $$$
International
410 Sandy Bay Rd, Sandy Bay, TAS 7005
Tel *1800 030 611* **Closed** *Sun & Mon;
lunch (except Fri)*
Revolving 17th-floor restaurant
with spectacular views. Dine on
French-inspired cuisine with a

Modern, trendy decor at the Islington, Hobart

The contemporary exterior of The Source, Hobart

local twist. Braised beef short rib and the orange crème brûlée are both superb. Book in advance.

HOBART: Smolt $$$
Tapas
2 Salamanca Square, TAS 7000
Tel *(03) 6224 2554*
A cool, modern, light-filled space serving good, simple food. Gourmet pizzas, pastas, tapas, seafood and meat dishes. The salmon tasting plate is a good choice.

HOBART: The Source $$$
Fine Dining
655 Main Rd, Berriedale, TAS 7011
Tel *(03) 6277 9904*   **Closed** *Tue; Sun & Mon dinner*
Part of MONA, the island's art museum. There is a modern, edgy feel to both the food and the surroundings at this light-filled dining room. The three-course degustation menu won't disappoint.

LATROBE: House of Anvers $
Chocolate Café
9025 Bass Hwy, TAS 7307
Tel *(03) 6426 2958*   **Closed** *dinner*
All chocolate dreams come true at this café and chocolate-making facility. Indulge in chocolates, hot cocoa and chocolate desserts. Light meals as well.

DK Choice

LAUNCESTON:
Black Cow Bistro $$$
Steakhouse
70 George St, TAS 7250
Tel *(03) 6331 9333*   **Closed** *lunch*
This up-market offshoot of Launceston's acclaimed Stillwater is located in a lovely Art Deco building that was once a butcher's shop, now smartly attired with white tablecloths and a warm ambience. An ode to beef, this steakhouse sources the best dry-aged, grass-fed, free-range steak from around Tasmania. The menu also includes grilled calamari with fennel. The service is excellent.

LAUNCESTON: Josef Chromy $$$
Modern Australian
370 Relbia Rd, Relbia, TAS 7258
Tel *(03) 6335 8700*   **Closed** *dinner (except Fri & Sat)*
Pretty gardens and manicured vineyards provide a seductive backdrop for fine food made with top-quality local produce such as Flinders Island lamb and East Coast oysters.

LAUNCESTON:
Stillwater River Café $$$
Modern Australian
Ritchies Mill, 2 Bridge Rd, TAS 7250
Tel *(03) 6331 4153*   **Closed** *Sun & Mon dinner*
In a charming old wooden building overlooking the Tamar River, Stillwater celebrates Tasmanian produce in beautifully executed dishes. The six-course degustation menu is a triumph.

RANELAGH: Home Hill Winery Restaurant $$
Modern Australian
38 Nairn Rd, TAS 7109
Tel *(03) 6264 1200*   **Closed** *dinner*
This attractive restaurant serves classy regional food. Southern rock lobster, Tasmanian salmon

---

and a game pie of wallaby, venison and hare all appear on the menu.

SHEFFIELD:
T's Chinese Restaurant $$
Chinese
83 Main St, TAS 7306
Tel *(03) 6491 2244*
Owned by the Zhao family, who grow their produce and rear their own cows and lamb for meat. The food is a cut above the rest.

STANLEY:
Stanley Hotel Bistro $$
Modern Australian
19–21 Church St, TAS 7331
Tel *1800 222 397*
This relaxed pub offers fresh local seafood, including shark, scallops and lobster, alongside a variety of dishes that include vegetables from nearby farms and succulent beef from grass-fed cattle.

STRAHAN: Risby Cove $$
Bistro
The Esplanade, TAS 7468
Tel *(03) 6471 7572*   **Closed** *lunch*
Waterfront eco-tourism centre highly regarded for its food and wine. Take in the west coast sunset and bask in the peaceful setting while enjoying scrumptious dishes.

WOODBRIDGE: Peppermint Bay Bar Dining & Terrace Bistro $$
Modern Australian
3435 Channel Hwy, TAS 7162
Tel *(03) 6267 4088*
Cruise from Hobart or drive the scenic route to this relaxed establishment in a striking building with breathtaking water views. Choose from a range of light meals featuring local produce, freshly baked goods and Tasmanian wines.

The shop at House of Anvers in Latrobe where guests can buy chocolate treats to take home

For more information on types of restaurants *see page 498*

SHOPPING IN AUSTRALIA

Australia has much to offer the visiting shopper beyond the standard tourist fare of koala bear purses and plastic boomerangs. The tourist shops can be worth exploring, because stock can be of a high standard and include goods not available in other countries. In each state capital, especially Sydney (see pp136–9) and Melbourne (see pp410–13), there are precincts and open-air markets with a range of shops, stalls and cafés to explore. Wine and gourmet food products are a major attraction, and a wide range of reasonably priced world-class goods is available. Australian contemporary design has a refreshing irreverence for convention – look out for homewares and fashion in the inner-city precincts. In country areas, items made by local craftspeople make good buys. Australia has a 10 per cent goods and services tax (GST) on the cost of most manufactured items (included in displayed prices).

Browsers at a stall in Mindil Beach Sunset Markets, Darwin (see p276)

Shopping Hours

Standard weekday opening times are 10am–5:30pm, Monday to Friday. Late night shopping is usually available on Thursdays or Fridays, when stores stay open until 9pm. Weekend hours vary greatly. Almost all stores are open Saturday and Sunday in city areas, while some in country areas may close early on Saturday and remain closed on Sunday, although it varies widely. A few supermarkets in city and suburban areas operate 24 hours. Bookshops and other specialist shops stay open late – until around 10pm – in downtown areas.

How to Pay

Major credit cards are accepted by most stores, sometimes with a minimum purchase limit and or a credit card surcharge, between 1.5 and 3 per cent in smaller retailers. Payment by cash is the preferred method for smaller traders keen to avoid credit-card fees and may help to negotiate a lower price for your goods. Asking for a discount is not uncommon, particularly on big-ticket items in larger department and chain stores.

Rights and Refunds

The laws on consumer rights in Australia vary slightly from state to state. You are entitled to a refund or replacement if the goods are faulty, do not meet the description or are not "fit for purpose", even if the item was discounted. If you decide you don't like an item, try to get a refund, but you will may have to settle for a credit note or exchange. As a general rule, the larger stores are more lenient – you can always ask to speak to a manager or customer relations officer if you are unhappy with the service you receive.

Essentially Australian

Aboriginal or indigenous art is available for purchase from community-owned or managed galleries in the Northern Territory and good specialist galleries in the cities. Take the time to discuss the work with the painter or gallery staff: spiritual and cultural meanings are inextricably linked with aesthetic properties, and the painting or artifact that you choose will be all the more valuable with a little knowledge. These artworks are by their nature expensive, so do not be beguiled by cheaper imitations.

Australia produces 95 per cent of the world's opals. Their quality varies greatly, so when considering a purchase a little research will go a long way.

Shoppers in London Court, Perth's Tudor-style street (see p309).

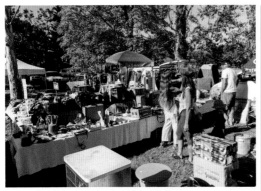
A garage sale at the Channon Craft Market in Northern Rivers

of the best and most interesting shopping in the country. Young designer outlets, specialist book stores, craft studios and galleries sit next to food stores, cafés, restaurants and bars. Some of these precincts are decidedly up-market, while others relish their bohemian roots. There is nearly always a strong mix of cultural influences – Jewish, Italian, Lebanese, Vietnamese, for example – depending on the area and the city. Ask at tourist information centres for the best precincts in each city.

Opals are widely available at duty-free stores. Many other places will deduct the luxury excise tax from the price if you produce your passport.

Outback clothing is a specialist industry in Australia. Look for Akubra hats, boots by RM Williams and Driza-bone over-coats in camping and army stores. Surf clothing has become highly desirable among tourists, as it can be cheaper to buy in Australia than abroad. Board shorts and bikinis are popular purchases.

The impressive food court at Springvale Market, Melbourne

Markets

Most Australian cities have a large central produce market and a range of small community markets that operate at the weekend. The bustling city food markets are as sensational for their vibrant multicultural atmosphere as they are for the extraordinary range of fresh, cheap produce available. Look out for local specialities such as cheeses, olives and unusual fruits. Melbourne's Queen Victoria Market *(see p390)* and the Adelaide Central Market *(see*

p350) are particularly good and well worth visiting. Community markets, such as those in Paddington, Sydney *(see p128)*, and Salamanca Place, Hobart *(see p464)*, offer an interesting and eclectic range of locally designed clothing and crafts. In a class of their own, the Mindil Beach Sunset Markets in Darwin combine eating, shopping and entertainment in a spectacular tropical setting *(see p276)*.

Department Stores

Department stores occupy the up-market end of the chain-store scale and sell quality merchandise. They include names such as Myer and David Jones *(see p410)* and some of the top stores are sumptuously decorated. Local and overseas designer fashions, top-brand cosmetics and all manner of household goods and furnishings can be purchased. These stores are competitive and will often match prices on identical items found at more down-market stores. Their shopper facilities and standards for customer service are excellent.

Shopping Precincts

Because the city centres have been colonized by the retail giants in Australia, many small and interesting shops have moved out to the lively precincts that lie somewhere between the city centre and suburbia. These precincts represent some

A colourful traditional gateway entrance into Melbourne's Chinatown *(see p395)*

Out of Town

Shopping in Australian country areas can be a mixed experience. In some areas the range of standard items is limited and prices can be much higher than you would expect to pay in the city. However, there are always unexpected surprises such as dusty second-hand shops with rare knick-knacks at absurdly low prices and small craft out-lets and galleries with unusual items that make great gifts.

The attractive tiled interior of a shopping arcade in Adelaide

SPECIALIST HOLIDAYS AND OUTDOOR ACTIVITIES

To make the most of a trip to a country as vast and geographically diverse as Australia, a specialist holiday is an excellent idea. Whether you're pursuing an interest, acquiring a new skill or learning about the environment, such holidays can be very rewarding experiences. There is a wide range of specialist operators to choose from. If travelling to Australia from abroad, the best starting points are the local Tourism Australia offices or website, or your local travel agent. Once in the country, the state tourism bodies *(see p547)* offer expert advice and can help you make bookings with reputable companies and contact local activity associations for information.

Bushwalking in Namadgi National Park in the ACT *(see p211)*

Bushwalking

National Parks are without doubt the best places for bushwalking in Australia. Not only do they preserve the best of the country's natural heritage, but they also offer expert advice and well-marked trails for bushwalkers. These parks are state-managed and each state has a central information service. Each state's national parks authority maintains a website with information on each national park within its jurisdiction.

Equipment, including backpacks, boots and tents, is available from camping stores in city and country areas. Joining up with a tour is a good alternative for those planning long bushwalking trips, as tour members will benefit from a guide's expertise on local flora and fauna, and access to remote wilderness areas. Exceptional bushwalking regions in Australia include Cradle Mountain in Tasmania *(see p471)*, the MacDonnell Ranges in the Northern Territory *(see p288)* and the Blue Mountains in New South Wales *(see pp172–5)*.

Cycling

With its vast stretches of near-empty roads, many of them without a hill in sight, it is no wonder that Australia is popular as a long-distance cycling destination. Visitors can bring their own bicycles, but are advised to check first whether this is acceptable with the airlines and what charges may apply. Trains and buses will usually carry bikes for a small extra charge. There is limited space allocated, so book a bike space when buying your ticket. To hire a bike in Australia, look under "Bicycles" at yellowpages.com.au. Bike helmets are a legal requirement throughout Australia and can be bought cheaply or hired.

Many cyclists spend several days on the road camping along the way, while others will arrange an itinerary that allows them to stop for the comfort of a bed and meal in a town. The wine-growing areas of South Australia *(see pp342–3)*, the Great Ocean Road in Victoria *(see pp432–3)* and almost anywhere in Tasmania *(see pp460–75)* are terrific cycling destinations.

Bicycling associations in Australia also arrange regular cycling tours that anyone can join. These include accommo-dation, food and vehicle back-up; most of the organizations are non-profit-making, so the costs are generally low. Contact **Bicycle New South Wales** for a catalogue specializing in Australian cycling publica-tions. They will also provide information on their sister associations in other states.

Cycling around Canberra's lake *(see pp198–9)*

Adventure Sports

Appropriate training is a component of adventure sports in Australia, so novices are always welcome alongside more expert adventurers. Contact specialist tour operators or national associations *(see p541)* for information about anything from a one-day class to a two-week tour.

Abseiling, canyoning, rock climbing and caving are all popular in Australia, which has some fantastic natural landscapes ideally suited to these pursuits. The Blue Mountains are something of a mecca for enthusiasts of all the above. Naracoorte in South Australia *(see p359)* is a great location for caving, while the Grampians National Park in Victoria *(see p431)* attracts a large share of abseilers and climbers.

Climbing on Wilsons Promontory in Victoria *(see p448)*

Golf

There are more than 1,500 golf courses in Australia and 1,580 golf clubs. Many clubs have affiliations with clubs overseas and offer reciprocal membership rights, so check with your own club. There are also public municipal golf courses in many towns.

Australian courses are of a high standard, and Melbourne is home to two of the top 30 courses in the world, the Royal Melbourne and Kingston Heath. A round of golf will cost anything from A$20–$250. The **Australian Golf Union** has a handbook that lists all of the golf courses in Australia.

Camel trekking along Cable Beach, Broome *(see p334)*

Aboriginal Heritage Tours

Aboriginal heritage tours can range from a visit to an Aboriginal art gallery to days spent with an Aboriginal guide touring Arnhem Land or Kakadu National Park in the Northern Territory *(see pp280–81)*. With the highest percentage of Aboriginal land and people in the country, the Northern Territory has the greatest number of activities, but there are sights and operators all over Australia. The focus of activities varies and may encompass a number of themes, including traditional bush food, hunting, rock art and Aboriginal culture.

Perhaps the best aspect of many of these tours is the chance to see the remarkable Australian landscape from a different perspective; Aboriginal spirituality is closely linked with the land. In addition, some tours will journey to Australia's most remote areas and travel through Aboriginal lands that are usually closed to all but members of the local Aboriginal communities.

Camel Trekking

Camels have been an invaluable form of transport in Australia's Outback since Afghan-run camel trains were used to carry goods across the Australian desert from the 1840s until the coming of the railway. Joining a camel trek today is still an adventure, and activities range from a one-hour jaunt to a two-week trek. Food and accommodation (usually camping) are provided by tour operators. Alice Springs *(see pp286–7)* is the most popular starting point, but tours are available country-wide.

Aerial Tours

Aerial Tours can provide an exhilarating overview of an area and are a good option for time-restricted travellers who want to see some of the more far-flung attractions. Aerial safaris, stopping at major sights, are popular in the Outback. For charter flights to Australia's furthest flung territory, a section of Antarctica, contact **Croydon Travel**.

Seaplane moored at Rose Bay in Sydney, ready for a scenic flight

Fishing

Australia has around four million fishing enthusiasts and, given the country's natural advantages, it's not difficult to see why. Vast oceans, a 12,000-km (7,500-mile) shoreline and a large inland river system, all combined with a terrific climate, make Australia a haven for local and visiting anglers alike.

Fishing for barramundi in the remote inland waters of the Northern Territory and game fishing off Australia's tropical coastline for species such as black marlin and yellowfin tuna are among the world's best fishing experiences. You will need to join a charter as these activities require a great deal of local expertise.

The inland waters of Tasmania are famed for their excellent trout fishing prospects. The estuaries and beaches in the southern states, such as the Fleurieu Peninsula in South Australia (see pp354–5), are full of species such as bream, salmon and flathead. Small boats are readily available for hire and fishing tackle can be bought and occasionally hired at most popular fishing destinations. Each state has a government department with a fisheries section. Staff provide excellent information on locations, restrictions, safety issues and obtaining licences. Check the weather forecast and heed warnings about danger areas, particularly rock platforms. Several people die each year rock fishing in dangerous conditions.

Fishing for yellowfin tuna is a popular pursuit

Canoeing on the Roper River in the Northern Territory (see pp272–3)

Ecotourism

This tourism concept has its roots in activities as old as bird watching and wildflower identification. It incorporates many of the activities mentioned in this section, but is generally distinguished by its emphasis on issues concerning the appreciation and conservation of natural heritage. Given Australia's enormous natural bounty, it is hardly surprising that the market is now flooded with operators offering an astonishing range of nature-based activities. These encompass wildlife watching (including whales, birds and dolphins), nature walks, and trekking and rafting expeditions to remote wilderness areas. Visitors can also stay at resorts that are operated along strictly "green" guidelines. These are eco-friendly and are usually located within some of the most environmentally valuable and vulnerable regions in the country. The **Ecotourism Association of Australia** can provide information on tour operators and publications.

Water Sports

Australia is one of the world's great diving destinations, and the Great Barrier Reef is the centre of most of the diving activity (see pp216–21). Visitors can combine a holiday on the reef with a few days of diving instruction from one of the many excellent schools in the area. There are opportunities for diving all around Australia, however, and other popular locations include Rottnest Island (see pp312–13) and Esperance (see p323) in Western Australia and the beautiful World Heritage Area of Lord Howe Island off the coast of New South Wales.

Canoeing in Australia can mean a quiet paddle in a hire-boat on a city lake, or an exciting adventure in a kayak on the high seas. It is a reasonably priced sport and is widely available throughout the country. Popular spots include the Murray River (see p359), Sydney Harbour (see pp148–9) and the rivers of national parks nationwide.

Whitewater rafting is another favourite sport in this land of outdoor enthusiasts and there are many opportunities for people of all abilities to have a go. The inexperienced can try a day with an instructor on an easy run; the confident can tackle a two-week tour on the rafter's mecca, the Franklin-Gordon River system in Tasmania (see p472).

Sailing in Gippsland Lakes Coastal Park, Eastern Victoria (see p448)

Long stretches of unspoilt coastline, remote bays and harbours, tropical reefs and uninhabited islands make Australia an excellent destination for sailing enthusiasts. Skippered cruises are the most usual kind of holiday, but some visitors will want to hire a vessel and set off for themselves – a practice known as bareboating. To do this you will need to prove to the operator that you are an experienced sailor. It is difficult to beat the tropical splendours of the Whitsunday Islands in Queensland *(see p250)* as a location. Other popular sailing areas include Pittwater in New South Wales and Queensland's Gold Coast *(see pp242–3)*.

Australia is also world-renowned for its abundance of outstanding surfing beaches. For more information about the country's best places to surf, *see pages 42–3*.

Skiing

The Ski season in Australia extends from June to September. Downhill skiing is restricted to the Victorian Alps *(see p450–53)*, the New South Wales mountains and two small resorts in Tasmania *(see p473)*. The ski villages have excellent facilities, but the fields can get crowded during school holidays and long weekends, and prices for ski-lifts and equipment hire can be high.

Upland areas around these resorts are superb for cross-country skiing. Traversing gentle slopes and rounded peaks,

Skiing Eagle Ridge on Mount Hotham in the Victoria Alps

skiers will be treated to glimpses of Australia's rare alpine flora and fauna, and spectacular sweeping scenery.

Spectator Sports

Most sports enthusiasts will enjoy taking in a fixture during their trip, while a few visitors come to Australia especially for a sporting event, such as yacht races, cricket or tennis events. Early booking is advisable as competition for tickets can be fierce. Regular highlights include the Australian Tennis Open, Melbourne Cup and the Formula 1 Grand Prix, all Melbourne events, and international Test cricket and the Australian Open golf that moves each year *(see pp44–7)*. Rugby League and Australian Rules football are the most popular spectator sports. The finals are the main event, but excitement is high at almost any match.

DIRECTORY

Clubs and Associations

Australian Golf Union
Level 2, 111 Coventry St, South Melbourne, VIC 3205. **Tel** (03) 9626 5050. W golf.org.au

Australian Parachute Federation
Unit 3, 2994 Logan Road, Underwood, QLD 4119. **Tel** (07) 3457 0100. W apf.asn.au

Australian Yachting Federation
22 Atchison St, St Leonards, NSW 2065. **Tel** (02) 8424 7400. W yachting.org.au

Bicycle New South Wales
1st Floor, Heritage Building A, 1 Herb Elliott Ave, Sydney Olympic Park, Homebush Bay, NSW 2127. **Tel** (02) 9704 0800. W bicyclensw.org.au

Ecotourism Association of Australia
Tel (07) 3252 1530. W ecotourism.org.au

Gliding Federation of Australia
C4/1–13 The Gateway, Broadmeadows, VIC, 3047. **Tel** (03) 9359 1613. W gfa.org.au

New South Wales Snow Sports Association
PO Box 934, Jindabyne, NSW 2627. **Tel** 0408 006 415. W nswsnowsports.com.au

Skiing Australia
1 Cobden St, South Melbourne, VIC 3205. **Tel** (04) 2863 6516. W ski.com.au

Tour Operators

Adventure Associates
Level 8, 309 Pitt St, Sydney. **Tel** (02) 6355 2022. W adventureassociates.com

Croydon Travel
34 Main St, Croydon, VIC 3136. **Tel** (03) 9725 8555. W croydontravel.com.au

STA Travel
Tel 134 782. W statravel.com.au

World Expeditions
Level 5, 71 York St, Sydney, NSW 2000. **Tel** 1300 720 000. W worldexpeditions.com.au

An AFL Australian Rules football match in full swing

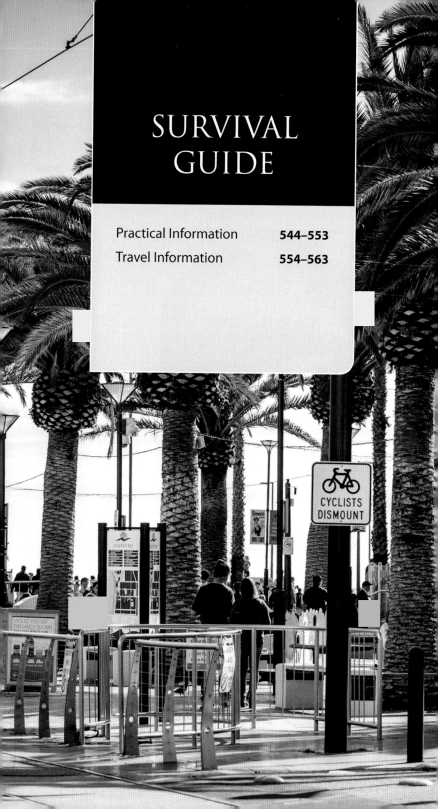

SURVIVAL GUIDE

PRACTICAL INFORMATION

Australia is a massive country of modern, global cities, booming regional centres and vast wide-open spaces in between. Tourism is one of the biggest contributors to the national economy, and the country offers quality services and experiences. Visitors should rarely face problems in this safe, friendly destination. Accommodation and restaurants *(see pp478–535)* are of international standard, public transport is readily available *(see pp556–63)* and tourist information is plentiful, particularly online. The following pages contain useful information. Personal Security and Health *(see pp548–9)* details recommended precautions, Banking and Local Currency *(see pp550–51)* answers financial queries, and Communication and Media *(see pp552–3)* describes how to stay informed and in touch during a visit.

Skiers enjoying the slopes of Mount Hotham in Eastern Victoria *(see p453)*

When to Go

The northern half of the country lies in a tropical zone and is subject to "wet" and "dry" seasons *(see pp48–9)*. The dry season falls between May and October, and is regarded as the best time to visit this area. During the wet season, conditions are hot and humid, and many areas are inaccessible because of flooding. For those with an interest in wildlife, however, there are areas such as Kakadu National Park *(see pp280–81)* which are particularly spectacular at this time of year.

The southern half of the continent is temperate and the seasons are the opposite to those in Europe and North America. Victoria and Tasmania can be cloudy and wet in winter, but they are very colourful and quite mild in autumn. The vast southern coastline is a popular touring destination during the summer months – the climate is warm to hot, with sea breezes. Avoid the Outback areas during the summer, however, as the temperatures can be extreme.

The popular ski season is between June and September and takes place in both the New South Wales Snowy Mountains *(see p191)* and the Victorian Alps *(see pp452–3)*. In the states of South Australia and Western Australia, there are spectacular wild flower displays between September and December.

Entry Requirements

Visitors to Australia must have a passport valid for longer than the intended period of stay. All visitors, except New Zealand passport holders, must also have a visa issued before arrival. For stays of up to three months the easiest option for most is to get an Electronic Travel Authority (ETA), or an eVisitors, depending on the country of origin. Neither requires a stamp in your passport or has a visa application charge. They can be obtained from travel agents, airlines (usually when you book your flight) or can be applied for online at the **Department of Immigration** website *(see p547)*. Always check the latest entry requirements with the Australian embassy in your country before leaving.

For stays of three to six months, a tourist visa may be applied for in person at the Australian Embassy or by post. Visitors will be asked for proof of a return ticket and of sufficient funds for the duration of their stay. Some visitors, including British nationals, between the ages of 18 and 30 may apply for a 12-month working holiday visa.

Travel Safety

Visitors can get up-to-date travel safety information from the Foreign and Commonwealth Office in the UK, the State Department in the US and the Department of Foreign Affairs and Trade in Australia.

Tourist Information

Tourism Australia is the central tourism body, but each state and territory has its own tourism authority. Travel centres in the capital cities provide abundant information and these are often

Visitor information kiosk and booking centre

◀ Tram at Moseley Square in Adelaide

The platform and view of Sydney Harbour at Circular Quay station, accessible to disabled travellers

the best places to seek advice on specialist tours and to make bookings. Information booths can also be found at airports and tourist sites.

Smaller towns often have tourist offices in general stores, galleries or near a prominent landmark – look for the blue and white information symbol. In remoter areas, national park visitors' centres will provide useful information.

Opening Hours and Admission Prices

Most major tourist sites are open seven days a week, but it is advisable to check first. Many places are closed on Good Friday, Anzac Day (25 April) and Christmas Day. In smaller places, galleries and other sites are often closed for part of the week. Admission prices are generally moderate and, in some cases, free. Exceptions are major touring exhibitions, zoos, theme parks and specialist attractions such as Sovereign Hill in Ballarat (see p437). Make the most of weekdays – locals will be competing for viewing space at weekends at major events and exhibitions.

Etiquette

While Australian society is generally laid-back, there are a few unwritten rules which visitors should follow.

Australians drive on the left and, generally, walk on the left-hand side of a path. They stand on the left of a busy escalator to

allow others to pass. Eating and drinking is frowned upon while on public transport, in taxis and also in many shops and galleries.

Dress codes are casual, particularly in summer when the weather can be hot, but some bars and restaurants require men to wear shirts and place a ban on jeans and trainers.

Topless bathing is accepted in designated areas on some beaches, but it is advisable to see what the locals are doing. While a tiny bikini may go unnoticed on the beach, it is considered polite to cover up when sitting in a café or restaurant.

Continental table manners apply in restaurants. Placing your knife and fork together on the plate indicates to wait staff that you have finished your meal. Tipping is optional; however, 10 per cent of the final bill for good service in a restaurant is appreciated, as is rounding up to the nearest dollar for taxi drivers.

Smoking is prohibited in all public buildings, on public transport, in taxis, stores, sports grounds, cafés, and restaurants, as well as in a wide range of open public spaces. Depending on the state, smoking is also banned in pubs and nightclubs, with many providing a designated outdoor smoking area.

To avoid causing offence, always ask before taking someone's photograph, especially if the person is an Aboriginal Australian. If taking photographs for commercial purposes, permission is required before photographing on private land.

Disabled Travellers

Disabled travellers can generally expect the best in Australia in terms of facilities. Many hotels, restaurants, tourist sites, cinemas, theatres, airports and shopping centres have wheelchair facilities, and guide dogs for the blind are always welcomed.

Traditionally, public transport is a problem for wheelchair users, although most states have adapted their systems more accessible to disabled travellers. Contact the transport authority state by state for more detailed information. Tourist information centres and council offices can provide maps that show sites with wheelchair access.

One of the most useful organizations for disabled travellers is the **National Information Communication Awareness Network (NICAN)** in Canberra. This nationwide database provides information on disabled facilities in different parts of the country and, if they don't have the appropriate information at hand, they will do their best to seek it out. They also have details of many publications written for disabled travellers in Australia.

One particularly good publication is *Easy Access Australia*, written specifically for people with mobility problems. The **Information on Disability and Education Awareness (IDEAS)** website has an extensive listing of disability-friendly accommodation in its travel section.

Mother and child feeding some of Australia's famous marsupials

Travelling with Children

Australia is an ideal destination for children. Most hotels welcome children as guests and can usually provide cots, highchairs and, in some cases, babysitting. However, some smaller bed-and-breakfast places advertise themselves as child-free zones.

Restaurants are also generally welcoming to children and offer children's menus, although it is advisable to check first with the more up-market establishments. City department stores and most major tourist sites have feeding and nappy-changing rooms as standard features. Parents travelling with young children are also encouraged by a range of discounts on transport (see pp554–63).

National laws governing the restraint of children in cars stipulate that children under

seven must be restrained in an appropriate infant or child seat and must not travel in the front seat of a car. As many cars do not have these restraints as standard fixtures, it is essential that prior arrangements are made.

Car hire firms will generally supply car restraints for a small extra charge. **Gillespie's Hire and Sales Service** leases restraints, push-chairs, baby carriers and travel cots. It is illegal to leave children unattended in a car.

Two handy websites for great destinations and child-friendly information are **BYO Kids** and **Holidays with Kids**. Both offer useful tips even if you don't book through them.

Student Travellers

The International Student Identity Card (ISIC) is available

to all students worldwide in full-time study. The ISIC card should be purchased in the student's own country at a Student and Youth Travel office or online from the Student Travel Association (STA) website (www.statravel.com). A similar card for non-students aged under 30 is also available at a slightly higher cost.

Card-holders are entitled to substantial discounts on air travel (see pp554–7), national train and bus services (see pp558–9), as well as discounts on admission to theatres, galleries, museums, cinemas and other establishments.

Gay and Lesbian Travellers

Within inner city areas, the gay and lesbian scene is accepted but you may still find homophobic attitudes across much of Australia, particularly in country areas. The age of consent for homosexual sex varies between states, from 16 to 17. More information can be found on the **Gay and Lesbian Rights Lobby (GLR)** website.

The **Gay and Lesbian Tourism Association (GALTA)** is a not-for-profit organization promoting and listing tolerant businesses for travellers.

Free online magazines and websites for the gay and lesbian community include gaynews network.com.au, lotl.com, starobserver.com.au and qmagazine.com.au.

Budget Travel

Accommodation is more expensive in inner city and tourist areas than in outlying suburbs and country towns. Staying outside the city centre and using public transport to get in is a good, cheap option.

Petrol is more expensive in rural areas and varies from state to state; Queensland is usually the cheapest. Eating out tends to be cheaper outside cities where good-value, reasonable-quality meals are served at local eateries. Groceries, on the other hand, are more expensive in smaller towns.

Australian Time Zones

Australia is divided into three separate time zones: Western Standard Time, Central Standard Time and Eastern Standard Time. Eastern Australia is two hours ahead of Western Australia; Central Australia is one-and-a-half hours ahead. Daylight saving is observed in New South Wales, the ACT, Victoria and South Australia, from October to March, which adds an hour to the time differences.

City and State	Hours + GMT
Adelaide (SA)	+9.5
Brisbane (QLD)	+10
Canberra (ACT)	+10
Darwin (NT)	+9.5
Hobart (TAS)	+10
Melbourne (VIC)	+10
Perth (WA)	+8
Sydney (NSW)	+10

Electrical Appliances

Australia's electrical current is 240–250 volts AC. Electrical plugs have either two or three pins. Most good hotels will provide 110-volt shaver sockets and hair dryers, but a flat, two- or three-pin adaptor will be necessary for other appliances. Buy these from electrical stores.

Bins for all manner of recyclables and general litter on Bondi Beach

Responsible Travel

Most Australians are environmentally aware. Some councils provide designated car-share parking spaces to reduce traffic and on-street parking. Most councils run recycling schemes and encourage the separation of recyclable materials from general rubbish. However, discarded water bottles are a huge environmental problem, and many councils now supply refilling stations to encourage people to reuse their bottles. In some states, including South Australia, Northern Territory and New South Wales, a container-deposit scheme sees a nominal amount, usually 10c, added to the cost of each bottle and can, refunded when the container is returned to a depot or reverse vending machine for recycling.

Respect Australia's wonderfully diverse ecosystem. When bushwalking keep to marked tracks or boardwalks. This is particularly important in coastal areas to prevent beaches from erosion.

Local farmers' markets are increasingly popular and allow visitors to support the local economy and reduce "food miles", the distance produce travels before purchase. Contact the **Australian Farmers' Markets Association (AFMA)** for details of local markets. Most shops offer plastic bags, but shoppers tend to favour reusable fabric bags.

Many accommodation providers, including Melbourne's Alto Hotel, feature energy efficiency, sustainability and waste-reduction initiatives. Organizations like the **Green Building Council of Australia** certify sustainable buildings.

Conversion Chart

Imperial to Metric
1 inch = 2.54 centimetres
1 foot = 30 centimetres
1 mile = 1.6 kilometres
1 ounce = 28 grams
1 pound = 454 grams
1 pint = 0.6 litres
1 gallon = 4.6 litres

Metric to Imperial
1 centimetre = 0.4 inches
1 metre = 3 feet, 3 inches
1 kilometre = 0.6 miles
1 gram = 0.04 ounces
1 kilogram = 2.2 pounds
1 litre = 1.8 pints

DIRECTORY

Immigration

Department of Immigration
Tel 131 881.
w immi.gov.au

Travel Safety

Australia Dept of Foreign Affairs and Trade
w dfat.gov.au
w smartraveller.gov.au

UK Foreign and Commonwealth Office
w gov.uk/foreign-travel-advice

US Department of State
w travel.state.gov

Disabled Travellers

Easy Access Australia
w easyaccessaustralia.com.au

Ideas
Tel 1800 029 904.
w ideas.org.au

Nican

48 Brookes St, Mitchell, ACT 2911. Tel 1800 806 769. w nican.com.au

Travelling with Children

BYO Kids
w byokids.com.au

Gillespie's Hire & Sales Service
13 Elizabeth St, Artarmon, NSW 2064. Tel (02) 9411 2180. w ghss.com.au

Holidays with Kids
w holidayswithkids.com.au

Gay and Lesbian Travellers

Gay and Lesbian Rights Lobby
w glrl.org.au

Gay and Lesbian Tourism Association
w galta.com.au

Tourism Australia

w australia.com

United Kingdom

Australia House, 6th Floor, Melbourne Place, Strand, London WC2B 4LA.
Tel (020) 7379 4334

USA and Canada
6100 Center Drive, Suite 1150, Los Angeles, CA 90045.
Tel (310) 695 3200.

State Tourist Offices

ACT
Regatta Point, Barrine Drive, Parkes, ACT 2600.
w visitcanberra.com.au

New South Wales
Cnr Argyle & Playfair sts, The Rocks, NSW 2000.
w visitnsw.com.au

Northern Territory
Cnr Smith & Bennett sts, Darwin, NT 0800.
Also at: Gregory Terrace, Alice Springs, NT 0870.
w tourismto pend.com.au

Queensland
The Mall, Brisbane, QLD 4001. Also at: Cairns Information Centre, 51 The Esplanade, Cairns, QLD 4870.
w queensland.com

South Australia
9 James Pl, Adelaide, SA 5000. w southaustralia.com

Tasmania
Level 3, 15 Murray St, Hobart, TAS 7000.
w discover tasmania.com.au

Tourism Australia
w tourism.australia.com

Victoria
Federation Square, Melbourne, VIC 3000.
w visitvictoria.com

Western Australia
2 Mill St, Perth, WA 6000.
w westernaustralia.com

Responsible Travel

AFMA
Tel (02) 9360 9380.
w farmersmarkets.org.au

Green Building Council of Australia
w new.gbca.org.au

Personal Security and Health

Australia has a low crime rate and is generally regarded as a safe tourist destination. There is a strong police presence in all the state capitals, and even small towns will have at least one officer. In terms of climate and environment, however, Australia is a tough country, and visitors must observe safety procedures whether travelling to remote areas or merely planning a day at the beach. If you get into trouble, contact one of the national emergency numbers or helplines in the directory opposite.

Police vehicle

Fire engine

Ambulance

What to Be Aware of

Leave valuables and important documents in your hotel safe, and don't carry large sums of cash with you. Credit and debit cards that can be cancelled if lost or stolen is a safe way to go. It is also worth photocopying vital documents in case of loss or theft.

Be on guard against pickpockets in places where big crowds gather. Prime areas for petty theft are tourist attractions, shopping centres, beaches, markets, sporting venues and on peak-hour public transport.

Never carry your wallet in an outside pocket where it is an easy target for a thief. Wear shoulder bags and cameras with the strap across your body and with any clasps fastened. If you have a car, always try to park in well-lit, reasonably busy streets. Lock the vehicle securely and don't leave any valuables or property visible that might attract a thief.

Personal Safety

There are few, if any, off-limit areas in Australian cities. Red-light districts may be a little seedy, but they are often busy and well policed.

Avoid walking alone, especially in poorly lit areas and parks at night. Buses (and trams in Melbourne) are considered safe at night. However, when travelling by train, remember that many stations are not staffed after hours, particularly in suburban areas. Travel in the train carriage nearest the driver or in those marked as being safe for night travel. Taxis are safe and efficient at night. Hitch-hiking is not advisable, and is illegal in some states (*see p562*).

Country towns can shut down fairly early in Australia, which is often a surprise to many visitors. It is advisable to reach a destination before nightfall and avoid wandering around looking for accommodation or a meal after dark. The majority of places are friendly to travellers but in remote areas visitors do stand out and as such are potential targets if a threat exists.

Women Travellers

It is safe for women, generally speaking, to travel throughout Australia, although all the usual rules about personal safety apply. Drink "spiking" sometimes happens, so don't leave drinks unattended and only accept drinks and offers of transport from people you know. Sexual harassment of women can occur; ignoring it, moving away from the area and reporting it to authorities, security or management is a sensible approach.

Medical Matters

Australia's medical services are among the best in the world. Under reciprocal arrangements visitors from the UK, New Zealand, Malta, Italy, Finland, Sweden and Holland are entitled to free hospital and medical treatment provided by Australia's national insurance scheme, Medicare. Medicare does not, however, cover dental work, so dental insurance is worth considering. Visitors from countries other than those mentioned will face prohibitive medical bills if uninsured. Arrangements for adequate medical cover should be made before leaving home.

Park ranger

Policeman

Fire officer

Dial 000 in any part of the country for ambulance assistance. Most public hospitals have an emergency department. For less urgent treatment, wait times can be very long. There are 24-hour medical centres in the major cities, and doctors in or near most towns. A standard consultation with a doctor will cost $75–120. Look in the local Yellow Pages under "Medical Practitioners".

For dental emergencies, go to the emergency department of a public hospital. The government's **Health Direct** service provides health information and details of nearby general practitioner doctors and pharmacies open after hours.

Pharmacies

Pharmacies (or "chemist shops") are plentiful in cities and suburbs, but can be thin on the ground in remote areas. Unrestricted drugs such as over-the-counter painkillers and other goods such as cosmetics, toiletries, suncreams and baby products are standard stock items. Most pharmacies will provide free advice on minor ailments, but foreign prescriptions can only be met if endorsed by a local medical practitioner.

The Health Direct service can advise on after-hours pharmacies.

Environmental Hazards

Paid lifeguards dressed in blue and white, and/or volunteer lifesavers in red and yellow, patrol many beaches in populated areas. Safe swimming areas are indicated by red and yellow flags during spring and summer. However, there are vast stretches of unpatrolled beaches in Australia and many of these are subject to dangerous rips. Rips can often be identified as a darker and calmer stretch of water between the breaking waves. Do not falsely equate calmer water with safe swimming. Certain rips can be so strong that even wading can pose a threat. Follow local advice and,

Surf lifesaving sign indicating a dangerous undertow or "rip"

if in any doubt, do not swim. You should never swim alone.

Even in well-trodden areas of the Australian bush, hikers can lose their way. Always inform someone of your route. Staff at national parks can offer advice and maps, and will keep a note of your intended trip. Take a basic first-aid kit, food and water, a GPS device with coverage, and extra clothing. In many regions, temperatures plummet when the sun sets.

Australia is home to some of the most venomous creatures on earth. Basic precautions such as good boots, thick socks and a wary eye are necessary. Snake-bite victims should be kept calm while emergency help is sought. Try to identify the creature by size and colour so that the appropriate antivenom can be administered.

Crocodiles are fascinating but dangerous creatures. In the northern regions, heed the warning signs and make enquiries before you risk swimming in remote, unpatrolled areas. Box jellyfish and other stingers invade tropical waters between October and May and their sting can be deadly. Again, observe the signs. Light, full-length stinger suits offer good protection, but exposed areas such as face and hands can still be stung.

Bush fires are a fact of life in Australia. When planning a camping trip, ring the **NSW Rural Fire Service** to check on restrictions. Total fire bans are not uncommon during warm,

Tasmania parks logo

dry seasons when campfires and barbecues are restricted and national parks may be closed. Avoid high-risk areas and dial 000 if in immediate danger from fire.

Protecting Your Skin

Australia has the highest rate of skin cancer in the world, caused by harmful ultraviolet rays. The risk of skin damage is high, even on cloudy days. Always use a good SPF 30 to 50+ sunscreen and wear sun protective clothing, a hat and sunglasses. Keep in the shade if possible, especially between 10am and 2pm. The **Cancer Council of Australia** website has more information, and check UV alerts from the Bureau of Meteorology (www. bom.gov.au).

Banking and Local Currency

Branches of national, state and some foreign banks can be found in the central business districts of Australia's state capitals. Suburban shopping centres and country towns will often have at least one branch of a major Australian bank. If travelling to remote areas, find out what banking facilities are available in advance. Banks generally offer the best exchange rates; money can also be changed at bureaux de change, large department stores and hotels. There is no limit to the amount of personal funds that can be taken in or out of Australia, although cash amounts of A$10,000 or more must be declared to customs on arrival or prior to departure.

Using a debit card to pay for goods

High street bank logos

Banks

Banks are usually open 9:30am–4pm Monday–Thursday and until 5pm on Fridays. Some branches are also open Saturday mornings. Major city banks open 8:30am–5pm on weekdays. Outside banking hours, many transactions can be handled online, via phone banking or through automatic teller machines (ATMs). Exchange rates are listed in the windows or foyers of most major banks.

Automatic cash dispenser

Travel Cards and Traveller's Cheques

Traveller's cheques are rarely used. You will need ID such as a passport to cash them at major banks, bureaux de change or major hotels. Pre-paid travel cards or money cards loaded in local currency before you travel are secure and easy for accessing your money through ATMs and making purchases while avoiding excess transaction fees and fluctuating exchange rates.

Credit and Debit Cards

All well-known international credit cards are widely accepted in Australia, as well as debit cards issued by major foreign banks. Visa and MasterCard (Access) are the most widely accepted cards, while American Express is also taken by most retailers and travel providers. Some smaller establishments such as cafés, newsagents and convenience stores do not accept card payments. If your card is linked to a savings account, you can use it as a debit card to both pay for goods and withdraw cash from your account in the same transaction, minimizing ATM fees. Most retailers have "tap-and-go" terminals that use chip readers for card transactions up to A$100, eliminating the need to enter a PIN code. Carry the phone number of your credit card issuer in case your card is lost or stolen.

You should always carry some emergency cash if travelling to remote areas, particularly the Outback, where credit cards may not be accepted at small stores and cafés, and alternatives, such as a 24-hour ATM, may not be available. Most city retailers have "tap and go" terminals that use chip readers for card transactions up to $100, eliminating the need to enter a PIN code.

ATMs

ATMs can be found in most banks, as well as in shopping and tourist areas. In most cases it is possible to access foreign accounts from ATMs by using a linked debit card. Confirm this with your bank, and check what transaction fees will apply. To avoid multiple fees, make a larger cash withdrawal rather than several smaller ones when using an ATM not associated with your card account.

Bureaux de Change

Australian cities and larger towns, particularly tourist favourites, have bureaux de change, usually open Monday to Saturday from 9am to 5:30pm. Some branches also operate on Sundays. While bureaux de change can be a convenient alternative to banks, their commissions and fees are generally higher. Major post offices will also often change foreign money.

DIRECTORY

Foreign Currency Exchange

American Express
Tel 1300 736 659 or 1300 139 060.
W americanexpress.com.au

ANZ Bank
Tel 13 13 14. W anz.com.au

Commonwealth Bank
Tel 13 22 21.
W commbank.com.au

NAB (National Australia Bank)
Tel 13 22 65. W nab.com.au

Travelex
Tel (02) 9978 2871.
W travelex.com.au

Westpac
Tel 13 20 32. W westpac.com.au

Local Currency

The Australian currency is the Australian dollar (A$), which breaks down into 100 cents (c). The decimal currency system now in place has been in operation since 1966.

Single cents may still be used for some prices, but Australian 1c and 2c coins are no longer in circulation, so the total amount to be paid will be rounded up or down to the nearest 5c.

It can be hard to change A$50 and A$100 notes, so avoid using them for low-cost goods in small shops and cafés and when paying for taxi fares. If you do not have change, tell the taxi driver before you start your journey to avoid any misunderstandings. Otherwise, when you arrive at your destination, you may have to find change at the nearest shop or ATM or pay with a credit card, which incurs extra fees.

To improve security, as well as to increase their lifespan, all Australian bank notes are plasticized.

Bank Notes

Australian bank notes are produced in denominations of A$5, A$10, A$20, A$50 and A$100. All bank notes are made of plastic. Paper notes have been phased out and are no longer legal tender.

A$100 note

A$50 note

A$20 note

A$10 note

A$5 note

5 cents (5c)

10 cents (10c)

20 cents (20c)

50 cents (50c)

1 dollar (A$1)

2 dollars (A$2)

Coins

Coins currently in use in Australia are 5c, 10c, 20c, 50c, A$1 and A$2. There are several different 20c, 50c and A$1 coins in circulation; all are the same size and shape, but have different commemorative images on the face. The 10c and 20c coins are useful for local telephone calls (see pp552–3).

Communication and Media

Communications systems in Australia are fast, modern and efficient. Most Australians have mobile phones and home Internet connections, and Internet cafés and Wi-Fi areas are also widely available in cities and large towns.

Postal services within Australia have a two- to three-day delivery time in the same city, with next-day delivery for an extra fee. International mail takes about 10 days to two weeks, but express options are available. Online versions of Australian national newspapers are regularly updated with domestic and international news, while the standard of Australia's television and radio broadcasting is generally high.

Telstra public telephone booths at Bondi Junction, Sydney

Public Telephones

There are about 17,000 **Telstra**-operated public payphones across Australia in city and regional areas. Payment options include coins, prepaid phonecards (available at newsagents, convenience stores and some chemists) and the more expensive operator-assisted calls. Newer Smart Payphones include SMS text messaging and a hearing-aid coupler to assist the hearing impaired. The phone booths display instructions and numbers to call for assistance. Telstra also has an online payphone locator tool (envinsaonline.mapinfo.com.au/ppol).

Payphone Charges

Local calls are untimed and cost 50 cents. Depending on where you are, "local" means the city and its suburbs, or outside the city, a defined country region.

Credit card phones have a A$1.20 minimum fee. Long-distance calls are less expensive if you dial without the help of an operator. The cheapest method of calling long distance is by using a prepaid phonecard. Check which of the available kinds suits your needs. Prepaid phonecards can be bought at newsagents, local shops, post offices and other retail outlets.

Telephone Directories

Each city and region in Australia has two telephone directories: the **White Pages** and the **Yellow Pages**, both of which are easily accessed online. The White Pages lists private and business numbers in alphabetical order. It also has a guide to emergency services and government departments. The Yellow Pages lists businesses under relevant headings such as Dentists, Car Hire and so on.

Mobile Phones

Short-term mobile phone rentals are available for visitors, but if your phone is compatible it may be cheaper to bring it with you and buy a local Sim card once you have arrived. This way you can also avoid paying the high cost of international fees on incoming calls to your mobile.

Optus, Telstra**, Virgin** and **Vodafone** are the main mobile phone service providers. They differ in the coverage and plans they offer, so it is worth looking into each one to find the best deal. All have good coverage in major cities. Telstra has the best network coverage in smaller regional and country areas.

While international texting is relatively cheap, international calls are very expensive from mobile phones in Australia, so using a prepaid phonecard or a plan that includes international minutes to specific countries may be a better option if you need to make a lot of international calls. Making calls while driving is illegal

---

Reaching the Right Number

- To ring Australia from the UK dial **0061**, then the area code, then the local number.
- To ring Australia from the USA or Canada dial **011 61**, then the area code, then the local number.
- For long-distance direct-dial calls outside your local area code, but within Australia (STD calls), dial the appropriate area code, then the number.
- For international direct-dial calls (IDD calls) from a fixed phone line in Australia: dial **0011**, followed by the country code (USA and Canada: 1; UK: 44; Republic of Ireland: 353; New Zealand: 64, South Africa: 27), then the city or area code (omit initial 0) and then the local number.

- Directory information with automatic connection (incurs an additional charge) to local and national destinations: dial **12455**.
- Local and national directory enquiries: dial **1223**.
- Reverse-charge calls to national and mobile numbers: dial **1800 662 274**.
- National and international operator assisted calls: dial **1225**.
- National and international call costs: go online to **telstra.com**.
- Numbers beginning with **1 800** are toll-free numbers.
- Numbers beginning with **13** are charged at the local call rate from anywhere in Australia.
- Ten-digit numbers beginning with **04** are mobiles.
- See also Emergency Services, *p549*.

Standard and express postboxes

and carries a stiff fine. Many places in remote Australia are not on the mobile network.

Internet

Free Wi-Fi is available in numerous hotspots in major cities, and many councils provide free Wi-Fi in local shopping areas and council-run sport and leisure facilities such as swimming centres. Most hotels, cafés, libraries, shopping centres, tourist attractions and transport hubs also provide free access. Some require a password; others just invite you to join the network. As Wi-Fi is widely available and smartphones provide easy ability to connect to mobile data and online services, there are fewer Internet cafés. Those that remain tend to be aimed at gamers, with access to a range of pre-installed games for an hourly rate. Using Wi-Fi-enabled mobile devices to make voice and video calls with apps such as Skype, FaceTime and WhatsApp avoids traditional call costs.

Postal Services

Post offices are open 9am–5pm weekdays and some are open on Saturday mornings. In country towns, the general store often doubles as the post office. Most newsagents also sell stamps.

Standard domestic mail takes two to three business days to be delivered. Priority stamps are available at an extra cost to speed delivery. Post boxes for standard mail are red and can be found outside post offices, in and outside shopping centres, on main streets and scattered throughout suburban streets. Express Post, for which you need to buy the special yellow and white envelopes sold in post offices, guarantees faster, next-day, delivery to capital cities and major regional areas within Australia. Postboxes for Express Post are yellow. Post offices also offer international courier services.

Newspapers

Australia has two national newspapers, *The Australian*, a well-respected broadsheet with excellent national and overseas news coverage, and the *Australian Financial Review*, which largely reports on business and financial matters. Each state capital also has its own daily newspaper. All newspapers have online editions, some free, some subscription. Thenewdaily.com.au and news.com.au are free, while smh.com.au and theage.com.au offer 30 free articles per month.

Television and Radio

The Australian Broadcasting Corporation (ABC) is a state-owned nationwide television

and radio broadcaster which provides excellent news and current affairs coverage, children's programmes and high-quality drama. In addition, the corporation has its own local and national AM and FM radio stations which offer a wide range of services, including news, arts commentary, modern and classical music, indigenous programmes and a nationwide station for the under 30s called Triple J. SBS (Special Broad-casting Service) is Australia's other state-run television and radio network and caters to Australia's many cultures with foreign language programmes. There are also three free-to-view commercial television networks – 7, 9 and 10 – that offer drama, reality shows, sports, news, game shows and other light entertainment on multiple digital channels. Foxtel – and Austar in rural areas – offers the usual wide array of pay television channels.

In all state capitals there is an enormous variety of local FM and AM radio stations. Details of current programming are available on the networks' websites.

ABC
Australian
Broadcasting
Corporation
Logo for the
ABC network

A selection of newspapers available in Australia

TRAVEL INFORMATION

While some visitors to Australia may choose to arrive by sea, the vast majority arrive by air. Once here, flying between locations is also the most popular form of long-distance travel, but there are some other choices, all of which offer the chance to see something of the country along the way. The national rail network links all major cities, while coach routes provide regular services to most provincial and country areas. If you have the time, driving in Australia is an excellent option. Boat travel is best if you want to visit Australia's islands, principally Tasmania, but regular services run to other island destinations such as Rottnest Island off the coast of Western Australia *(see pp312–13)*.

Long-Haul and Green Travel

Given the location and sheer size of the country, and unless you have unlimited time, it is difficult to travel to and within Australia without using long-haul flights. A journey of four hours by plane can take three days by train and, in most cases, a flight is the cheaper option. However, if you can spare the time and money, there are some spectacular long-distance train routes through the country where, especially with the speciality "luxury" operators *(see pp558–9)* the journey can become a worthwhile part of your holiday.

If you plan to hire a car, the Australian government produces a **Green Vehicle Guide** which rates cars according to their carbon emissions and allows useful comparisons between vehicles. Within cities public transport is relatively cheap and efficient, and has the advantage of avoiding costly parking and fuel costs at each destination.

Arriving by Air

Australia is served by around 50 international airlines. The Australian airline Qantas has a worldwide network and offers the most flights in and out of Australia. Qantas, along with Virgin Australia, is one of the main domestic carriers in Australia *(see p556)*. Virgin, Qantas and United Airlines all offer regular flights from the United States, with a variety of stopovers. The large Asian and European carriers including British Airways, Emirates, Singapore Airlines, Cathay Pacific and Japan Airlines, also offer a variety of different routes and stopovers on the Europe–Asia–Australia route. Canadian travellers can fly direct using Air Canada.

International Flights

Flights between Australia and Europe take upwards of 22 hours, and with delays you may be in transit for more than 30 hours. A stopover in Asia is worth considering, especially if travelling with children, as is one in Hawaii or the Pacific islands for visitors from the US. Also, consider arranging flights so that they account for international time differences. Arriving in the afternoon, spending the rest of the day awake, then going to sleep in accordance with local time is a recommended way to help to counteract jet lag.

Australia has several international air terminals so visitors can choose different arrival and departure points. Sydney and Melbourne have major airports servicing flights from all over the world. Sydney's Kingsford Smith Airport is the busiest and can be congested. Melbourne Tullamarine Airport is the second busiest airport in Australia and is consistently voted one of the world's best by travellers for its modern lounges and superior retail facilities. Hobart has flights from New Zealand in the summer months, while Adelaide has direct flights to Singapore and flights to Europe via Sydney or Melbourne. Visitors to the west coast can arrive in Perth from Africa, Asia and the UK. Darwin, Brisbane and Cairns mostly service Asia, but there are a few possibilities for connections from Europe.

Air Fares

Flights to Australia can be expensive, especially during December, the peak season. January to April is slightly cheaper. During the off-peak season, discount fares can often be 30–40 per cent below full economy fares *(see p556)*. Most

International Qantas flight arriving in Sydney

Singapore Airlines 747 taking off at Perth Airport

are non-refundable, stipulate arrival and departure dates and carry cancellation penalties. Round-the-world fares are good value and give the opportunity to break the long journey.

Check with discount travel agents or the airline's website if you can fly at short notice, as any unsold seats are often offered at a discount closer to departure date. In these cases, flexibility isn't usually a feature. A departure tax and various levies are included in the price of a ticket out of Australia.

On Arrival

Just before setting down in Australia you will be given customs documents to fill in. On arrival you will be asked to present your documents, including passport, at Customs. You can then collect your baggage. Even if you have nothing to declare, you may still be questioned and have your baggage checked before you can enter the main area of the airport. Note that Australia has strict quarantine laws. Food, plants and wooden items must be declared at quarantine. Sniffer dogs are common and your bags may be X-rayed on arrival to check for banned goods. Check before departure on allowable goods; there are stiff penalties for non-disclosure.

Larger airports such as Melbourne and Sydney have better services, but most have good shopping, postboxes and information booths. You can hire cars and change money at all airports. Taxis and buses can take you into city centres.

Arrangements for domestic flight connections are usually made when buying your original ticket. Airline staff will advise you how to proceed. In Melbourne's main airport, the domestic and international services are close together but in many places the terminals are separate and

distances can be long – 10 km (6 miles) in the case of Perth. Free shuttle buses run between terminals, but ensure plenty of time to make connections.

DIRECTORY

Airline Carriers

Air New Zealand
Tel 132 476.
W airnewzealand.com.au

British Airways
Tel 1300 767 177. W ba.com

Air Canada
Tel 1300 655 767.
W aircanada.com

Cathay Pacific
Tel 131 747. W cathaypacific.com

Emirates
Tel 1300 303 777.
W emirates.com

Japan Airlines
Tel 1800 802 228. W au.jal.com

Jetstar
Tel 131 538.

Qantas
Tel 13 13 13. W qantas.com.au

Singapore Airlines
Tel 131 011. W singaporeair.com

United Airlines
Tel 131 777.
W unitedairlines.com

Virgin Australia
Tel 136 789.
W virginaustralia.com

Green Travel

Green Vehicle Guide
W greenvehicleguide.gov.au

Airport	Information	Distance from City	Taxi Fare to City	Bus Transfer to City
Sydney	(02) 9667 9111 W sydneyairport.com.au	9 km (6 miles)	A$45	30 mins
Melbourne	(03) 9297 1600 W melbourneairport.com.au	22 km (14 miles)	A$55	30–40 mins
Brisbane	(07) 3406 3000 W bne.com.au	15 km (9 miles)	A$45	30 mins
Cairns	(07) 4080 6703 W cairnsairport.com.au	6 km (4 miles)	A$25	10 mins
Perth	(08) 9478 8888 W perthairport.com.au	15 km (9 miles)	A$50	25 mins
Adelaide	(08) 8308 9211 W adelaideairport.com.au	6 km (4 miles)	A$25	20 mins
Darwin	(08) 8920 1811 W ntapl.com.au	6 km (4 miles)	A$30	15 mins
Hobart	(03) 6216 1600 W hobartairpt.com.au	22 km (14 miles)	A$40	20–30 mins

Domestic Air Travel

Air travel is by far the most practical way of taking in a country the size of Australia, particularly for those with time constraints. The country's main domestic air carriers, **Qantas**, **Virgin Australia**, **Tigerair** and **Jetstar**, concentrate on the high-volume interstate routes, while a host of small operators including Regional Express (Rex) and QantasLink handle air travel within states and to regional and more remote locations. Fares can be expensive, but with the range of discounts available in a deregulated and competitive industry it is unlikely you will ever have to pay the full fare, providing you plan your trips in advance. Speciality aerial tours of distant or hard-to-reach places are also available *(see p539).*

Domestic flight operated by Virgin Australia

The domestic terminal in Brisbane, Queensland

Air Routes and Airlines

Australia's air network is vast, but reasonably streamlined, so arranging flights to even the most remote spots should never be a problem. It is possible to fly direct between most major destinations such as Sydney–Darwin or Melbourne–Perth. However, if you are travelling to smaller centres, you will invariably have to fly first to the capital city in the state before then taking another flight on to your final destination.

Regional airline **QantasLink** is a subsidiary of **Qantas**, which means bookings can be made through Qantas' centralized booking system.

Discounts for Overseas Visitors

Discounted domestic air travel is often offered as part of an international package, so check with your travel agent about booking domestic trips before leaving home.

Qantas offers a Walkabout Pass for visitors to Australia (and New Zealand), with significant savings on domestic flights to more than 60 destinations, when you fly Qantas internationally to and from Australia. You can book your domestic flight at the same time as your international flight or at a later date. Domestic destinations are divided into two zones, based on distance travelled. Surcharges, fees and taxes will be calculated when you make the booking. You need to choose the multi-city option

when booking your international ticket. The pass offers greater convenience than return flights and is usually fairly flexible, but restrictions do apply, so check when booking. You can also manage your booking on the Qantas website.

Other Budget Fares

The cheapest domestic flights are available from the budget, no-frills airline services of **Jetstar**, a subsidiary of Qantas, Virgin Australia and Tigerair, which is owned by Virgin Australia. The best deals are found by booking direct with them online, but flights can occasionally be cancelled at short notice if they are not full. In these instances, you will be offered a seat on the next available flight, or a refund.

All domestic airlines regularly promote sale fares valid for travel during set periods, usually excluding school holidays. Most of the entry-level budget fares are non-refundable, incur hefty fees for any changes (if changes are allowed) and may include only carry-on hand luggage. Be sure you understand the strict conditions before booking.

Plane on the harbourside runway, Hamilton Island *(see p221)*

Fly-Drive Deals

A great way to see Australia is to fly to a destination and then continue on by car. Arrangements can be made for different pick-up and drop-off points for hire vehicles. For example, you could pick up a car in Sydney, drive to Brisbane and drop off the car, fly to Alice Springs and then pick up another car there, although there is an added fee for returning the vehicle to a different destination.

Virgin Australia and Qantas both have affiliations with the major car hire companies, and they offer discounts and loyalty points to passengers travelling on those airlines *(see p560)*.

Baggage Restrictions

Baggage restrictions vary on domestic flights and depend on the type of ticket. Jetstar's cheapest fare class does not allow for any checked-in baggage at all; the next fare class allows for 20 kg (45 lb) of baggage but an additional fee of A$70 is charged for baggage if booked at the airport; and the standard fare allows for 20 kg (45 lb) at no additional cost. Virgin Australia's fares follow a similar structure, allowing 23 kg (50 lb) but an additional charge applies if booked at the airport; and their full-price fare allows 23 kg (50 lb) with no fee. Regardless of the fare, Qantas domestic flights allow 20 kg (45 lb) for checked-in baggage.

Additional baggage fees are charged for any excess baggage; note also that airlines do not guarantee that additional baggage beyond the normal allowance will be carried. The carry-on luggage weight allowance is usually 7 kg (15.5 lb), although it varies depending on the airline and class of travel.

Qantas logo

Checking In

Airlines request that you check in at least 30 minutes before your flight time, and many now offer online seat allocation up to two days before a flight. Check online to ensure that the flight is on time, and be sure to alight at the right terminal – some domestic and international terminals are at separate locations.

DIRECTORY

Domestic Airlines

Jetstar
Tel 131 538. w jetstar.com.au

Qantas
Tel 131 313. w qantas.com.au

Tigerair Australia
Tel 1300 174 266.
w tigerair.com.au

Virgin Australia
Tel 136 789.
w virginaustralia.com

Principal Domestic Air Routes

Domestic flights cover vast distances. Sydney to Perth, for example, is 3,400 km (2,225 miles) and a flight of 5 hours; the 2,600-km (1,615-mile) flight from Adelaide to Darwin is 3.5 hours.

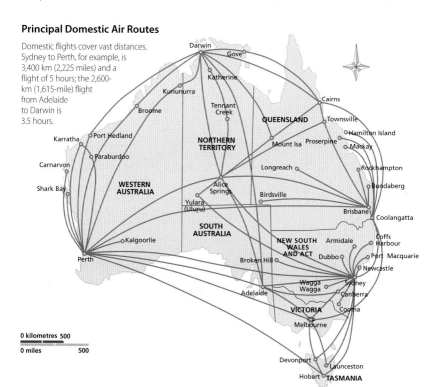

0 kilometres 500
0 miles 500

Travelling by Train and Coach

Australia offers some of the most spectacular train journeys in the world. The vast and diverse continent offers rail travel across red deserts as well as through beautiful rainforests and spectacular coastal scenery; often the journey is as much about enjoying the view as arriving at a destination. However, the train network is not comprehensive – with its small population, Australia has never been able to support an extensive system of long-haul railways. Train journeys are useful for quick trips away from city centres, and regular services link the cities of the east coast. Coaches fill any gaps in overland travel, servicing major centres and remote outposts.

A railway journey across the Australian desert

The Australian Rail Network

The Australian railway system is run by a complex group of several private and state-owned companies. The major tourist-orientated operators include **NSW TrainLink**, **Great Southern Rail** and Traveltrain. Find information and book tickets via the operators' websites.

Due to the availability of inexpensive flights, train travel is no longer cheaper than flying, and journey times are long. The Sydney–Brisbane trip takes 13.5 hours and Sydney–Melbourne takes 10.5 hours.

State governments accept responsibility for providing access to most areas. Queensland has increased its rail services of late, most of which are aimed at the tourist market. Increasingly, however, state-run coach services have replaced under-used railway journeys and, where there is no rail network, such as in Tasmania, there will be an efficient, cheap coach network instead.

Speciality Trips

The chance to take in some of the country's extraordinary landscapes is what makes rail journeys in Australia so special. Standards are high, often with a level of luxury reminiscent of the grand old days of rail travel.

The Indian Pacific route takes three days to cover the 4,352 km (2,700 miles) from Sydney to Perth. The 478-km (300-mile) crossing of the Nullarbor Plain (see p323) is on the world's longest length of straight railway track. The fabled Ghan railway runs between Adelaide and Darwin. A museum in Alice

Springs recounts its history (see p287). The 2,979-km (1,852-mile) trip offers amazing scenery and takes two days.

Two different services run the 1,681 km (1,045 miles) between Brisbane and Cairns: the Sunlander and the Tilt Train. Another Queensland journey is aboard the Gulflander, a 152-km (95-mile) trip through some of Australia's most remote country.

The Overland (Melbourne–Adelaide) and the fast XPI (express passenger trains) services (Brisbane–Sydney–Melbourne) offer a more utilitarian type of train travel.

Travel Classes

There are three types of travel available on most interstate trains. Overnight services, such as Melbourne–Adelaide, offer first-class sleeper, first-class sit-up and economy sit-up. The Indian Pacific, the Ghan and various Queensland trains also offer economy sleepers. All long-distance trains have dining facilities. First-class travel includes meals in the ticket price.

Motorail means you can travel with your car – but the service is expensive, and you are better off hiring a car at your destination.

Tickets and Bookings

Bookings for rail travel can be made with travel agents and at railway stations or via the operators' websites. Long-haul rail operators offer discounts for trips combining multiple journeys and destinations, advance purchase tickets, and pensioners and students with valid identification. Great Southern Rail offers discounts to

Mass Transit Railway Station in Perth

Greyhound coach station in Sydney

DIRECTORY

Rail Companies

Great Southern Rail
Tel 1800 703 357 or (08) 8213 4401.
W greatsouthernrail.com.au

NSW TrainLink
Tel 13 22 32 or (02) 4907 7501.
n nswtrainlink.info

Coach Companies

Greyhound Australia
Tel 1300 473 946.
W greyhound.com.au

Premier Motor Service
Tel 133 410.
P premierms.com.au

backpackers with valid ID, while australianrailpass.com has two passes for unlimited travel within Queensland, and the Discovery Pass for unlimited travel within New South Wales and travel to Brisbane and Melbourne on NSW TrainLink.

Standard rail fares can be high, but there is a good range of discounts available, particularly for advance bookings.

Coach Travel

Coach travel is cheap, efficient and generally safe. The two main operators are **Greyhound Australia** and **Premier Motor Service**. The latter only operates on the east coast.

There are a range of passes that reduce the cost and increase flexibility of any extended travel. The Greyhound KM Pass gives you 12 months to use a pool of kilometres, with complete flexibility to hop on and off at desired destinations. Establish your likely destinations before purchase so you buy the most appropriate option. Other options include flexible Hop On Hop Off passes and the Short Hop pass for shorter journeys. However, bear in mind that this kind of travel involves many days on the road, and nights spent sleeping upright.

There are a range of other companies operating locally – good for trips to particular sights. Tourist information bodies *(see p547)* in each state can advise on services and routes.

Australia's Principal Rail and Coach Routes

In Australia, travel by both rail and coach routes can be easily combined to reach any desired destination.

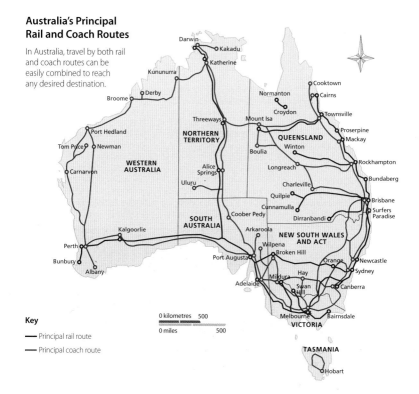

Key

— Principal rail route

— Principal coach route

0 kilometres 500
0 miles 500

Travelling by Car and Four-Wheel Drive

It is well worth considering hiring a car when visiting Australia. Other modes of transport will get you around the cities and from one country town to another, but, once you arrive in a rural area or a small town, you may find it impossible to explore the area other than on foot or with a tour. Australia offers the motorist the chance to meander through areas such as the vineyard regions of South Australia *(see pp342–3)*, the Southern Highlands of New South Wales *(see pp190–91)* and the Great Ocean Road of Victoria *(see pp432–3)*, as well as the experience of Outback travel on near-empty roads.

Driving through the Outback desert in Australia's Red Centre

Driving Licences

Providing your driving licence is in English and you have proof that you are a tourist, there is no need for an additional permit when driving in Australia. If the licence is not in English, you must carry a translation. You must have your licence with you at all times when driving.

Car Hire

Rental cars are available almost anywhere in Australia. They can be picked up at the airport on arrival, or arrangements can be made for delivery to your hotel. The big car rental firms **Avis**, **Budget**, **Hertz** and **Thrifty** have nationwide networks *(see p562)* – an advantage if you are making several different trips across the continent. Check with your travel agent before leaving home about discounts or special fly-drive offers.

Rates vary from around A$35 a day for a small car to more than A$100 a day for larger vehicles. It is invariably more expensive to hire a 4WD vehicle; rates average out at around

A$120 and are more costly in remote areas where demand is high. You can reduce daily rates by hiring over longer periods (usually three days and over). Most deals include unlimited kilometres. Be sure taxes and fees such as levies for collecting a car from an airport are included in the final quote and not added later. Check providers' websites for current offers.

Smaller local operators offer very competitive rates, sometimes as low as A$25 a day, but read the small print carefully; the quote may not include the extras that larger companies consider standard. If travelling with children, make sure the car is

equipped with restraints according to Australian laws *(see p546)*. A Global Positioning System (GPS) can also be hired for around A$11 per day or A$60 per week. Check with the hire-car company whether you will need an electronic tag fitted for road tolls that are common on motorways in major cities, especially Sydney and Melbourne, or if they are billed separately.

Credit cards are the expected method of payment when hiring a car. If paying with cash you will usually be required to pay the full cost of the rental, plus a deposit and provide sufficient identification.

Insurance

For peace of mind it is a good idea to have comprehensive insurance when hiring a car. Check first whether your travel insurance or credit card – particularly American Express if you used it to book your travel – cover car hire claims to avoid paying twice for damage waivers. "Third party fire and theft" insurance is standard and included in the cost of the hire, as is insurance against accidental damage to the car. However, you will have to pay extra to reduce the excess payment. From upwards of A$7 a day, you can bring the excess down from around A$3,000 to A$300. This option is usually only offered by the larger car hire companies.

Personal accident plans are also available, but they may not be necessary, depending on the cover offered with your own travel insurance. Four-wheel

Car and van rental company in Sydney

A Caltex Woolworths petrol station in Sydney

drive vehicles attract a higher excess rate than standard vehicles. Car hire companies will not offer insurance on any off-road driving, regardless of the vehicle type. Higher rates of insurance apply to drivers under the age of 25. Car hire in Australia is often not available to drivers under the age of 21.

Petrol

The typical cost of fuel in urban areas is less than in Europe (though it varies), but prices rise considerably in remote regions. Prices also vary during the week, so watch the prices and fill up when they are lower. Fuel is dispensed by the litre and can be purchased in regular unleaded, premium unleaded, diesel and LPG (liquid petroleum gas) grades. Most petrol stations are self-service, accept major credit cards and have an EFTPOS facility (see p550).

Rules of the Road

Australians drive on the left and give way to the right in all circumstances unless otherwise indicated. Drivers must also give way to emergency vehicles – if possible, pull over to the left when you hear a siren. The speed limit is 40–60 km/h (25–37 mph) in cities, towns and suburban areas and 100–110 km/h (62–68 mph) on major highways. Seat belts are compulsory for drivers and passengers. Baby capsules and child restraints must be used

for all children up to the age of seven. It is illegal to drive a vehicle while using a hand-held mobile phone, even when the vehicle is stopped at traffic lights or in heavy traffic. Drink-driving laws are strictly enforced in Australia. The legal blood alcohol limit is 0.05 per cent. Should you be involved in an accident while over the alcohol limit, your vehicle insurance may be invalidated. Police in country areas are just as vigilant as their city counterparts, and random breath-tests take place in city and country areas.

Any accident involving injury in Australia must be reported to the police within 24 hours. In Western Australia all accidents must be reported and in other states it is advisable to do so if there is considerable property damage. Always get insurance details and a name, licence number and residential address from the other motorist.

The city of Melbourne has two road laws worth noting. First, motorists must stop behind a stationary tram to allow passengers to alight. Second, at certain city intersections motorists intending to turn right must pull over to the left (see pp416–17). Called hook turns, they are designed to prevent traffic queuing across tram tracks.

Road rules are governed by the relevant state authority. Each has a website with traffic reports, highway conditions, road closures and webcams.

Road Conditions

Stretches of multi-lane highways are found on most major routes, with the majority of other routes covered by two-lane highways. All are generally well sealed and signposted. Unsealed dirt roads exist in country regions, but are rarely the only means of getting to a destination. Tollways are restricted to areas in the immediate vicinity of the large cities, such as the Western

Motorway that covers part of the Sydney–Blue Mountains route. Melbourne has an intricate tollway system. All tollways, tunnels and bridges, including Sydney Harbour Bridge, are cashless and require payment by an electronic tag connected to a credit card, or over the phone within three days of the toll being incurred.

Service stations are plentiful along all the well-travelled routes, but are few and far between in the Outback. A particularly Australian and very dangerous road hazard is the prevalence of wildlife crossing country highways. At night danger increases when the nocturnal mammals, such as kangaroos, wallabies and wombats, are more active.

Beware of kangaroos sign

Roadside Assistance

Car hire companies look after breakdowns of their rental cars, sometimes at an extra cost, and, if necessary, arrange for replacements. State-based motoring organizations provide roadside assistance for members around the country (see p562). They also provide maps and guides online and are a great source of information on road rules and conditions, and Outback driving. Members of motoring organizations in Great Britain, Canada and the US usually have reciprocal membership rights with Australian organizations.

Royal Automobile Association vehicle in Adelaide

South approach to the Harbour Bridge in Sydney

Inner-City Driving

If you are planning to drive within any city, a GPS or maps and navigation device is a good idea. If possible, avoid peak-hour traffic (7:30–9:30am and 4:30–7:30pm). Traffic reports are broadcast on radio stations. The larger the city, the more difficult it will be to park in the centre. Parking restrictions are clearly signposted and usually specify an hour or two of metered parking. Most parking meters require credit card payments. Many cities have clearly sign-posted clearway and bus zones that apply at certain times, and parked vehicles will be towed away during the specified times; telephone the local traffic authority or the police to find an impounded vehicle. Car parks are also found in city centres and shopping centres and are signposted with a large white P in a blue rectangle.

Outback Driving

For any Outback travel, first check your route to see if a 4WD is required. Although some Outback areas now have roads of a high enough standard to carry conventional cars, a 4WD is essential in wild and remote areas. Motoring organizations and tourist information centres can provide information about this.

Some basic safety points should be observed. Plan your route and carry up-to-date maps and navigation and commu-nication devices that work in remote areas. If you are travelling between remote destinations, inform the local police of your departure and expected arrival times. Check road conditions before you start, and carry food and water. Find out where you can get petrol, and carry extra supplies if necessary. If you break down, stay with your vehicle – if you fail to arrive at the expected time, a search party will be sent.

The **Royal Flying Doctor Ser-vice of Australia (RFDS)** offers safety advice. You can also hire radio sets with an emergency call button to the RFDS from **BTW Communications**.

Observe important guidelines to protect the land. Native flora and fauna should not be damaged. Stick to vehicle tracks, carry a camping stove and fuel to avoid lighting fires, and don't leave rubbish. Be aware of Aboriginal boundaries and nat-ional parks, and leave gates as you find them: either open or shut.

Hitchhiking

It is not considered safe to hitch-hike in Australia. In Queensland and Victoria it is illegal; their laws do not allow obstructing traffic from the roadside. Elsewhere, pedestrians are not allowed on motorways or freeways but are permitted on highways and other roads where they can find rides.

DIRECTORY

Car Hire Companies

Avis
Tel 136 333. [w] avis.com.au

Budget
Tel 13 27 27. [w] budget.com.au

Hertz
Tel 133 039. [w] hertz.com.au

Thrifty
Tel 1300 367 227.
[w] thrifty.com.au

State Road Departments

Roads and Maritime Services, NSW
Tel 132 213. [w] rms.nsw.gov.au

VicRoads, Victoria
Tel 131 171.
[w] vicroads.vic.gov.au

Motoring Organizations

National Roadside Assistance
Australia-wide breakdown service. **Tel** 131 111

New South Wales and ACT
National Road and Motorist's Association (NRMA). **Tel** 131 122.
[w] mynrma.com.au

Northern Territory
Automobile Association of NT Inc (AANT). **Tel** (08) 8925 5901.
[w] aant.com.au

Queensland
Royal Automobile Club of Queensland (RACQ). **Tel** 13 19 05.
[w] racq.com.au

South Australia
Royal Automobile Association of SA Inc (RAA). **Tel** (08) 8202 4600.
[w] raa.com.au

Tasmania
Royal Automobile Club of Tasmania (RACT). **Tel** 132 722.
[w] ract.com.au

Victoria
Royal Automobile Club of Victoria (RACV). **Tel** 13 11 11 or (03) 8792 4006. [w] racv.com.au

Western Australia
Royal Automobile Club of WA Inc (RACWA). **Tel** 13 17 03. [w] rac.com.au

Outback Driving

BTW Communications
Tel 1800 896 929. [w] btw.com.au

Royal Flying Doctor Service of Australia
Tel (08) 8238 3333.
[w] flyingdoctor.org.au

Driving a 4WD along the Gibb River Road in the Kimberley

Travelling by Ferry and Cruise Boat

For a country with a relatively small population, Australia is one of the world's busiest cruise markets. Domestic cruises up the east coast from Sydney to Queensland, and internationally to Pacific Islands, Southeast Asia and New Zealand are popular. Elsewhere ferries run between the mainland and island destinations such as Rottnest Island, Western Australia *(see pp312–13)*, and Fraser Island, off the Queensland coast *(see p246)*. Large cruise ships mostly sail in and out of Sydney.

Passenger ship berthed at Circular Quay, Sydney *(see pp78–89)*

Arriving by Boat

There is probably no better way of arriving in Australia than to sail into Sydney Harbour aboard a cruise ship. Cruising is expensive, however, and international services to Australia are more limited than domestic cruises. To sail to Australia from the US or Europe, you may have to wait for the next world cruise on **P&O** or **Cunard Line** vessels. Another option is to fly to an Asian city such as Hong Kong and join up with **Princess Cruises**. Sydney is the main port of call for most cruise ships, and there are two passenger terminals, one in the heart of the city and another at White Bay.

Ferries to Tasmania

The *Spirit of Tasmania* takes just over 14 hours to cross the Bass Strait from Melbourne to Tasmania. It runs daily, with day and night sailing options from Port Melbourne and Devonport. The ship has every level of accommodation, from reclining cruise seats and backpacker berths to fully equipped suites. There are restaurants, shops, and entertainment for children. You can book to take a car, too. The price is fair, considering the experience – a double cabin will cost around A$400 return for a couple in off-peak season, less if there is a special offer.

Island Cruises and Ferries

A **Sealink** ferry departs from Cape Jervis, south of Adelaide, for Kangaroo Island *(see p358)*. In Western Australia, **Rottnest Express** runs regular ferries to Rottnest Island from Perth. There are many services between the mainland and the Barrier Reef islands *(see p220)*. A boat also runs between Seisia, Cape York, and Thursday Island, *(see p256)*. Check the **Great Barrier Reef Marine Park Authority** website for a list of certified operators.

DIRECTORY

Shipping Companies

Cunard Line
Sydney. **Tel** 132 441.
W **cunardline.com.au**
Southampton, UK.
Tel (0845) 071 0300.

P&O
Sydney. **Tel** 132 494.
W **pocruises.com.au**
Southampton, UK.
Tel (0843) 374 0111.

Princess Cruises
Sydney. **Tel** 13 24 88.
W **princess.com**

Sealink
Kangaroo Island.
Tel 131 301, (08) 8202 8688.
W **sealink.com.au**

Spirit of Tasmania
Devonport. **Tel** 1800 634 906.
W **spiritoftasmania.com.au**

Tourist Information

Great Barrier Reef Marine Park Authority
W **gbrmpa.gov.au**

Rottnest Express
W **rottnestexpress.com.au**

Rivers and Harbours

Hiring a houseboat is an excellent way of seeing some of Australia's spectacular river scenery. Popular spots include the Hawkesbury River, New South Wales, and the Murray River which runs through New South Wales, Victoria and South Australia. There are tours of Darwin and Sydney harbours, and cruises of the Swan River in Perth and the Yarra River in Melbourne. State tourist authorities can provide details *(see p547)*.

Taking the ferry to Rottnest Island *(see pp312–13)*

General Index

Acknowledgments

Dorling Kindersley would like to thank the following people whose contributions and assistance have made the preparation of this book possible.

Consultant
Helen Duffy is an editor and writer. Since 1992 she has managed and contributed to a range of tourist publications.

Main Contributors
Louise Bostock Lang has worked on a number of Dorling Kindersley Travel Guides.

Jan Bowen is a travel broadcaster and writer. Her travel books include *The Queensland Experience*.

Paul Kloeden lives in Adelaide. A freelance writer and historian, his work ranges from travel articles to government-sponsored heritage surveys.

Jacinta le Plaistrier is a Melbourne-based journalist, poet and librettist.

Sue Neales is a multi-award winning Australian journalist. Her travel articles have appeared in major Australian newspapers and magazines.

Ingrid Ohlsson is a Melbourne-based writer who has contributed to many travel publications.

Tamara Thiessen is a Tasmanian freelance travel writer and photographer.

Additional Contributors
Tony Baker, Libby Lester.

Additional Photography
Simon Blackall, Terry Carter, DK Studio, Geoff Dunn, Jean-Paul Ferrero, Esther Labi, Jean-Marc La Roque, Michael Nicholson, Ian O'Leary, Rob Reichenfeld, William Shaw Carol Wiley, Alan Williams.

Cartography
Lovell Johns Ltd, Oxford, UK; ERA-Maptec Ltd, Dublin, Ireland.

Additional Illustrations
Rockit Design.

Indexer
Hilary Bird.

Senior Revisions Editor
Esther Labi.

Design and Editorial
Duncan Baird Limited
Picture Research: Victoria Peel.
DTP Designer: Rhona Green.
Dorling Kindersley Limited
Senior Managing Editor: Vivien Crump.
Managing Editor: Helen Partington.
Project Editor: Rosalyn Thiro.
Deputy Art Director: Gillian Allan.
Art Editor: Stephen Bere.
Map Co-ordinators: Emily Green, David Pugh.
Production: David Proffit.

Revisions Team
Ross Adams, Emma Anacootee, Jasneet Arora, Rosemary Bailey, Lydia Baillie, Chloe Baker, Kate Berens, Emily Bieber, Uma Bhattacharya, Hanna Bolus, Debbie Brand, Sue Callister, Wendy Canning, Divya Chowfin, Louise Cocks, Sherry Collins, Laura Cook, Lucinda Cooke, Bronwen Davies, Surya Deogun, Stephanie Driver, Angus Duncan, Jonathan Elphick, Mariana Evmolpidou, Alice Fewery, Emer FitzGerald, Fay Franklin, Anna Freiberger, Camilla Gersh, Emma Gregg, Alex Guyver, Vinod Harish, Shobhna Iyer, Gail Jones, Bharti Karakoti, Christine Keilty, Sumita Khatwani, Esther Labi, Maite Lantaron, Stefan Laszczuk, Jude Ledger, Maria Leonardis, Jason Little, Siobhan Mackay, Nicola Malone, Nicolette Martin, Alison McGill, Ciaran McIntyre, Claudine Meissner, Sam Merrell, Jason Mitchell, John Miles, Tania Monkton, Casper Morris, Lee Mylne, Claire Naylor, George Nimmo, Scarlett O'Hara, Ryan Paine, Elizabeth Pallot, Michael Palmer, Catherine Palmi, Manisha Patel, Sangita Patel, Alok Pathak, Susie Peachey, Marianne Petrou, Giles Pickard, Adrian Potts, Rachel Power, Rada Radojicic, Garry Ramler, Marisa Renzullo, Louise Roberts, Ellen Root, Lamya Sadi, Christine Salins, Sands Publishing Solutions, Mark Sayers, Ankita Sharma, Shailesh Sharma, Azeem Siddiqui, Kunal Singh, Rituraj Singh, Beverly Smart, Deborah Soden, Jaynan Spengler, Naomi Stallard, Domenic Stanton, Stuti Tiwari Bhatia, Adrian Tristram, Diana Tucker, Lynda Tyson, Conrad Van Dyke, Nikhil Verma, Ros Walford, Dora Whitaker, Kim Wildman, Carol Wiley, Steve Womersley, Ed Wright.

Special Assistance
Sue Bickers, Perth; Craig Ebbett, Perth; Peter Edge, Met. Office, London; Chrissie Goldrick, The Image Library, State Library of NSW; Cathy Goodwin, Queensland Art Gallery; Megan Howat, International Media & Trade Visits Coordinator, WA Tourist Commission; John Hunter and Fiona Marr, CALM, Perth; Vere Kenny, Auscape International; Selena MacLaren, SOCOG; Greg Miles, Kakadu National Park; Ian Miller, Auslig; Gary Newton, Perth; Murray Robbins, Perth; Ron Ryan, Coo-ee Historical Picture Library; Craig Sambell and Jill Jones, GBRMPA; Norma Scott, Australian Picture Library; Andrew Watts, QASCO; and all state tourist authorities and national park services.

Photography Permissions
Dorling Kindersley would like to thank the following for their kind assistance and permission to photograph at their establishments: Art Gallery of WA; Australian Museum; National Gallery of Australia; Australian War Memorial; Ayers House; Department of Conservation and Land Management (WA); Department of Environment and Natural Resources (Adelaide); Department of Environment (Queensland); Government House (Melbourne); Hermannsburg Historic Precinct; Jondaryan Woolshed Historical Museum; Museum and Art Gallery of NT; Museum of WA; National Gallery of Victoria; National Maritime Museum; National Museum of Australia; National Parks and Wildlife Services (all states); National Trust of Australia (all states); Parliament House (Melbourne); Port Arthur Historic Site; Powerhouse Museum; Rottnest Island Authority; Royal Flying Doctor Service of NT;

Shrine of Remembrance Trustees (Victoria); South Australian Museum; *Spirit of Tasmania*; Supreme Court (Melbourne), Tandanya National Aboriginal Cultural Institute Inc; Victoria Arts Centre Trust; WA Maritime Museum; and all the other sights too numerous to thank individually.

Picture Credits
Key: a - above; b - below/bottom; c - centre; f - far; r - right; t - top.

The publisher would like to thank the following individuals, companies and picture libraries for their kind permission to reproduce their photographs:

123RF.com: Rafael Ben-Ari 548cr; mg1964 276clb; Mykhaylo Palinchak 194; Heewon Seo 180t; Leonard Zhukovsky 548tr. **ABC pool:** 75tl; **Alamy Images:** Bill Bachman 392bl, 411tl; The Art Archive 8-9; Greg Balfour Evans 233crb; Martin Berry 561tl; David Bigwood 186; chris24 163tc, 181bl; Thomas Cockrem 530tr; CulturalEyes - AusGS2; DR Travel 313tl; Foodpix 500cl; Philip Game 448cl, 556cl; amer ghazzal 553bl; Horizon International Images Limited 255tc; JAA 105tl; Bjanka Kadic 153cr; Kennedy Miller Productions / Collection Christophel 25cl; Paul Kingsley 204cl; Jason Knott 269crb; Frans Lanting 298cl; LEDPIX 545t; Chris McLennan 250tl; Robert Mora 403cr; National Geographic Image Collection 469cb; Martin Norris 126bc; Michael Patrick O'Neill 367br; Ozimages 286tr; Wolfgang Pölzer 149br; Radius Images 362; R A Rayworth 520tr; Robertharding 4cr; RosalreneBetancourt 4 237bl; Matt Smith 235br; Andrew Sole 214bc; Richard Sowersby 560br; Dave Stamboulis 302; Steve Vidler 212–3; David Wall 410cla; Rob Walls 120, 501c; Andrew Watson 43cr; John White Photos 264clb; Bosiljka Zutich 108; **Amora Hotel Riverwalk:** 494bl; **ANZ National Bank Ltd:** 550cl Appellation at The Louise: 523tr; **AQWA – The Aquarium of Western Australia:** 310tr; **Ardea London Ltd:** © D Parer & E Parer Cook 220tr; © Francois Gohier 471tr; Jean-Marc La Roque 452cla; Peter Steyn 17ca; © Ron and Valerie Taylor 220cla; **Art Gallery of NSW:** 116tr, *Amitabha Buddha*, 105 x 88 x 65cm 117cl; © Ms Stephenson-Meere 1996, *Australian Beach Pattern* 1940, Charles Meere (1890–1961) oil on canvas, 91.5 x 122cm, 69tl; *Bridge Pattern*, Harold Cazneaux (1878–1953), gelatin silver photography, 29.6 x 21.4cm, gift of the Cazneaux family, 1975, 76bc(d); *Banks of the Marne*, Paul Cézanne (1839-1906), oil on canvas, 65 x 81.3cm 115tl; © Art Gallery of NSW *Sofala* 1947 Russell Drysdale (1912-81), oil on canvas on hardboard, 71.7 x 93.1cm 114clb; *Mars and the Vestal Virgin* 1638, Jacques Blanchard oil on canvas, 130 x 110cm 114cr; © Tiwi Design Executive 1996, *Pukumani Grave Posts, Melville Island* 1958, various artists, natural pigments on wood, 165.1 x 29.2cm, gift of Dr Stuart Scougall 1959, 114cl; *Natives on the Ouse River, Van Diemen's Land* 1838, John Glover oil on canvas, 78 x 115cm 115crb; Art Gallery of NSW Foundation purchase 1990, *A Pair of Tomb Guardian Figures*, late 6th century AD Early, Unknown (China), sculpture earthenware with traces of red and orange pigment, 93 x 82cm, Art Gallery of NSW Foundation Purchase 1990 115cra; *The Golden Fleece – Shearing at Newstead* 1894, Tom Roberts, oil on canvas 104 x 158.7cm 115b; *Curve of the Bridge* 1928–1929, Grace Cossington Smith © Estate of Grace Cossington Smith oil on cardboard, 110.5 x 82.5cm 116cla; ©

Wendy Whitely 1996, *The Balcony 2* 1975, Brett Whitely (1939–92), oil on canvas, 203.5 x 364.5cm 116bl; **Auscape International:** © Kathie Atkinson 30clb; © Nicholas Birks 348bl; © Donna Browning 272br; © John Cancalosi 29clb, 249bl; © Kevin Deacon 29cr; © Jean-Paul Ferrero 27bl, 28tr, 30cla, 163crb, 165cra, 246cl, 265tc, 267tr, 292cla, 459tl/crb; © Jeff & Sandra Foott 29br; © Brett Gregory 172bl, 458bl; © Dennis Harding 31bc; © Matt Jones 281cra/bc; © Mike Langford 31crb; © Wayne Lawler 165crb; © Geoffrey Lea 461b; © Darren Leal 28br, 247tl, 248tr, 249cr; © Reg Morrison 28cb, 246cr, 458tr, 459cl; © Jean-Marc La Roque 22t, 28cr, 31cr, 32–3c, 185tr, 242cla, 243cb, 265br, 284cl, 380tr, 381tr/cb, 389cla, 430cr, 432tr/cl, 434tl; © Jamie Plaza Van Roon 28bl, 29cl, 165tl/cb; © Becca Saunders 29cb, 220–21; **Australian Broadcasting Corporation:** 553crb; **Australian Capital Territory Museums and Galleries:** 21cla; **Australian Museum, Sydney:** www.austmus.gov.au: 34cla, 98cla, 98cl, 98clb, 99cra, 99crb; Nature Focus/John N Cornish; Stuart Humpries 69bl; **Australian National Maritime Museum:** 104cl, 105crb; **Australian Picture Library:** 22c, 24b, 162bl; Adelaide Freelance 371bl; John Baker 24b, 25tr, 175tr, 182cb, 419br, 435t, 445tr; JP & ES Baker 164bl, 475cra; John Carnemolla 19t, 33crb, 42cl, 43cra, 45tr 146b, 162cla, 188tr, 215tl, 266tr, 268cl, 338cb, 355tl, 370bl, 376cl, 556br; Sean Davey 42–3c; R. Eastwood 474tr; Flying Photos 546tl; Evan Gillis 371tr; Owen Hughes 257b; S & B Kendrick 339bc, 358tr; Craig La Motte 215br; Michael Lees 431b; Lightstorm 192bl, 364bc; Johnathan Marks 189cr, 432crb; Aureo Martelli 173cra; Leo Meier 31tr, 254cl, 267clb; PhotoIndex 261br; Fritz Prenzel 432br, 446bl; Oliver Strewe 36cl, 37tr; Neale Winter 372bc; Gerry Withom 173tl; Australian Reptile Park: 176bl; **Australian War Memorial:** 205c. **Bill Bachman:** 30tr, 32cl, 35c, 37tl, 47tl/b, 169b, 249br, 260b, 278tl, 279cr/bl, 280bl, 291b, 300bl, 450tr; **Bamurru Plains Hotel:** 489bl; **Greg Barrett:** 143bc; **Bartel Photo Library:** 175b; **Beccofino Restaurant:** 513t; **Beringer Blass Wine Estates:** 342br; 361cr; © **Mervyn Bishop:** 63cb; **Bistro Dom:** 522tc; **The Boat House by the Lake:** 511tr; **Bodhi Restaurant:** 505tr; **Botanic Gardens Trust, Sydney:** 110cla; **Elise Brennan:** 133br; **Bridgeclimb Sydney:** 85tl; **Bridgeman Art Library London/ New York:** *Bush Plum Dreaming* 1991 (acrylic) by Clifford Possum Tjapaltjarri (b.c.1932), Corbally Stourton Contemporary Art, London © Aboriginal Artists Agency Ltd 37cra; *Men's Dreaming* 1990 (acrylic) by Clifford Possum Tjapaltjarri (b.c.1932), Corbally Stourton Contemporary Art, London © Aboriginal Artists Agency Ltd 34tr; *Kelly in Spring*, 1956 (ripolin on board) by Sidney Nolan (1917–92), Arts Council, London © Lady Mary Nolan 38bl; National Maritime Museum, London 53clb(d); British Museum 55cra; Mitchell Library, State Library of NSW 58tr/bl, 59tl; National Library of Australia 54tr(d), 57tl, cb, 58–9c; *Bush Tucker Dreaming*, 1991 (acrylic) by Gladys Napanangka (b.c.1920) Corbally Stourton Contemporary Art, London, © Aboriginal Artists Agency Ltd 267cr; *The Ashes*, 1883 (The Urn) Marylebone Cricket Club, London, 440bc; **Courtesy of Brisbane Marketing:** 223b, 226tr; 236cr; **Buon Ricordo Restaurant:** 506tl; **The byron at byron:** 483tc.
Canberra Deep Space Communication Complex: D. Paterson 210bl; **Canberra Tourism:** 195b, 538cla; **Cephas Picture Library:** Andy Christodolo 167tl, 342clb, 343c, 382cl; Chris Davis 338cla; Mick Rock 23tr, 40cl, 41cr, 167cr,

178tr/cla, 343c, 345b, 360cla, 361tr; **Chocolate @ No 5:** 524tr; **Peter Clarke:** 406br; **Colorific:** 35tr; Bill Angove 267bl, 297bc; Bill Bachman 261tl, 363b; Penny Tweedie 269tr, 271b; **Coo-Ee Historical Picture Library:** 36–7c, 37br, 39cr, 53tl, 54bc, 55cb, 56crb, 60cr, 61clb, 437cra, 438br, 459bl, 473c; **Coral Sea Resort:** 479t;**Corbis:** Free Agents Limited 453bc; JAI/Walter Bibikow 93crb; Michael Kai 45cl; Frans Lanting 324; Stephane Lemaire 384; Steve Parish 270; Lothar Schulz 262–3; **Sylvia Cordaiy Photo Library Ltd:** © John Farmer 338bl; Nick Rains 300cl, 373tr; **Coterie Restaurant:** 524bl; **Cuisine on Lake Crackenback:** 510bl; **Cumulus Inc Restaurant:** 527br; **Customs House Brisbane:** 512tl; **Customs House Hotel:** 509b.

Rupert Dean: 40br, 360clb/bc, 361cb, 383bl, 502cla, 502crb; **Diamant Hotel:** 485bl; **Dixon Galleries, State Library of NSW:** 84tr; © Domaine Chandon, Australia: 447c; © Ken Done: 38c; **Donovans:** 529tl; **Dreamstime.com:** Allnaturalbeth 540c; Alyssand 174cr; Amarosy 361c; Rafael Ben Ari 70br, 242cb, 254bl, 501tl; Arnab & Manisha Maity 401t; Bbofdon 202cla; Beautifulblossom 358bl; Gordin Bell 385b; Archana Bhartia 305tl; Max Blain 541bl; Dan Breckwoldt 204cr; Byvalet 67crb; John Casey 222; Sam D'cruz 560cla; Ekays 256tr; Darren Falkenberg 344; FiledIMAGE 392tr, 444cl, 544cl; Markus Gann 15t, 334br; Tero Hakala 5tr; Anton Harder 297tr; Fritz Hiersche 339tl; Chris Hill 340bc; Kerry Hill 548tr (1); Inge Hogenbijl 305cr, 537cr; Hotshotsworldwide 2–3; Anujak Jaimook 287tl; Debra James 21b, 218tr; Katerinasamsonova 17bl; Kewuwu 76bl; Lev Kropotov 101tc; Ross Kummer 405bl; Shariff Che Lah 476–7; Chaiwat Leelakajonkij 44cr; Lennykphotography 208c; Lizgiv 306cl; Ralph Loesche 253b; Lucidwaters 239b; Mariagroth 242bl; George Mdivanian 20; Andrey Moisseyev 542-543; Anthony Ngo 96bl; OnAir2 78; Grant Phillips 171tr; Picstudio 341tl; Radmurphy 426; Ralphmaurer 241tr; Uros Ravbar 296clb; Kataca Rix 42tr; Shaun Robinson 464br; Mohd Fuad Salleh 326clb, 547tc; Sburel 26tr; Secondshot 219c; Shaiith 514bl; Kirrily Stewart 383tl; tktktk 46tl; Verdelho 14b; Nils Versemann 438cl, 537clb; Vselenka 44br; Volodymyr Vyshnivetskyy 73br; Robert Winslow 12tl; Marc Witte 285tr; Ian Woolcock 365cl, 472br; Xvaldes 76cl; Ymgerman 339crb; Bin Zhou 27tl. © **DW Stock Picture Library:** 192tr; P Brunotte 561br; **Eleonore's:** 533tl; **Environmental Protection Agency, Queensland:** 244cla; Gollings Photography 386tr; **Fairfax Photo Library:** 62clb/bl, 85crb, 150 cla, 177br(d), 276br; Ken James 143tr; McNeil 124clb; **Falls Creek Alpine Resort:** 453tl; **Falls Wines:** 166cla; **Foragers Field Kitchen:** 520bl; **Forest of Tranquility – Australian Rainforest Sanctuary:** 176cla; **Fotolia:** akjswift 329tr; Nadja 10bl; Stevofarrugia84 11cl.

Getty Images: 44cl, 150bl, 460; Artie Photography 294–5; Pete Atkinson 252; Auscape 369t; Bloomberg 382cl; Tom Cockrem 400tl, 409c; Stuart Hannagan 374–5; Alex Hare 168; Richard I'Anson 268-269c; Daniel Osterkamp 64–5; Peter Parks 401br; Peter Ptschelinzew 264ca; The Sydney Morning Herald 63tl, 72tr; David Wall Photo 160–61; Peter Walton Photography 442, 456–7; WILLIAM WEST 221bl; John White Photos 336–7; David Woolley 550tr; **Glencoe Rural Retreat:** 533br; **Glen Isla House:** 480b, 496bl; **Gorge Wildlife Park:** 356cr/bl; **Government House Perth:** 306clb; © **Great Barrier Reef Marine Park Authority:** 219tr, 221tc/cr; Photo: S Browne 219bl; Photo: W Craik 216bl; Photo: N Collins 216cla; Photo: L

Zell 217bl, 218cla; **Great Southern Rail:** Steve Strike 558cla; **The GreenRoom:** 517br; **Robert Harding Picture Library:** 294–5, 379tl, 587t; © Nick Servian 344, 562tl; **C Moore Hardy:** 142br; **Hood Collection, State Library of NSW:** 85bl; **Horizon:** © Andris Apse 283b; **House of Anvers:** 535br; **Hurricane's Grill Bondi Beach:** 506br; **Hutchison Library:** © R. Ian Lloyd 542–3; © Sarah Murray 558br. **Il Centro Restaurant:** 512br; **Images Colour Library:** 30b, 215cla, 291t, 293br; **The Image Library, State Library of NSW:** 38tr, 40bl, 52tc/clb, 53c, 56bla, 59crb, 62tc, 353br; **Islington Hotel:** 497tr, 534b; iStockphoto.com: John Kirk 214cl; iStockphoto.com: CUHRIG 537tl, kokkai 238, Tom Merton 151bl, ozflash 341bl, RainervonBrandis 218bl; **Ali Kayn:** 396cla; © Dr Ruth Kerr (Commissariat Stores, Brisbane): 226bl; **Kingfisher Bay Resort:** 487tl; **Knee Deep in Margaret River:** Jenny Clark 521tr. **Frank Lane Picture Library – Images of Nature:** 28clb; © Tom & Pam Gardner 29bc, 341clb; © David Hosking 29tr, 341tr/clb; © E & D Hosking 341crb, 459cra/cb; © M Hollings 340crb; © Gerard Lacz 165br; © Martin Withers 172cla, 340clb; **Langham Sydney Hotel:** 479cr; **Lavandula La Trattoria:** 498tl, 531br; **Lion Nathan:** 342ca; **Lochman Transparencies:** © Bill Belson 327cr; © Wade Hughes 300t; © Jiri Lochman 311tr, 312cla; © Marie Lochman 296ca; © Len Stewart 307br; **The Louise:** 491tr. **Marion Bay Tavern:** 526tl; **Lindsay May Pr:** 342cl; **Merlin Entertainments Group Australia:** 102b; © Greg Miles (Environmental Media): 280br; © Mirror Australian Telegraph Publications: 62cr; **Mitchell Library, State Library of NSW:** 52bl; 54–5c, 56b, 85cra, 113tr; **The MONA Pavillions:** 497br, 535tl; **Moorish Cafe:** 517tr; **Mount Baw Baw Alpine Resort:** James Lauritz 452bl; **Multiplex Property Services:** 102tr; **Museum of Contemporary Art, Sydney:** 68cla, 80bl; Alex Davies 82br. **Collection of The National Gallery of Australia, Canberra:** Clarice Beckett, *Sandringham Beach,* c.1933 206crb; Tom Roberts, *In a corner in a Macintyre* 1895, oil on canvas, 73.4 x 88.0cm, 206cl; Margaret Preston; ADAGP, Paris and DACS, London 2011; Aristide Maillol, *The Mountain (La Montagne)* 1937, lead, 167,4 (h) x 193.0 (w) x 82.3 (d)cm 206bl; © ARS, NY and DACS, London 2011, Jackson Pollock, *Blue Poles* 1952, oil enamel and aluminium paint on canvas, 212.0 x 489.0cm, 207tl; © Bula'bula Arts, Ramingining Artists, Ramingining, Central Arnhem Land, NT, *The Aboriginal Memorial* 1998, natural pigments on wood: an installation of 200 hollow log coffins, height 40.0 to 327.0cm, purchased with the assistance of funds from gallery admission charges and commissioned in 1987, 207cr; **National Gallery of Victoria, Melbourne:** 404cla; **National Library of Australia:** 39tl, 50, 53bc (original in possession of the WA Museum), 56ca, 57cra 59cra, 60tl, 201br; Rex nan Kivell Collection 53crb/br, 55crb; ES Theodore, Campaign Director, ALP State of NSW, Trades Hall 60clb; **National Maritime Museum, Sydney:** 55tl, 101cra, 105cra, 105tl, bc; **Nature Focus:** H & J Bestel 458cl; Rob Blakers 458br; John Fields 72bl; Dave Watts 458cr; Babs & Bert Wells 291cra; © Australian Museum 34cla, 36tr, **National Museum of Australia:** © Australia-China Friendship Society, *The Harvest of Endurance Scroll.* The scroll is of 18 segments, ink and colour on paper, mounted on silk and paper 209t, *Untitled* by Charlie Alyungurra, 1970 pigment on composite board 209cra, *The Mermaid Coffin* by Gaynor Peaty, 209br; **National Trust of Australia:** © Christopher Groenhout 408cl, 409tl/bc; **Natural History Photographic Agency:** © A.N.T

28cl, 165cr, 217tl, 299bl/br, 340tr/cra, 458ca/cb, 462tr; © Patrick Faggot 252; © Pavel German 290tl; © Martin Harvey 29ca; © Ralph & Daphne Keller 298cb; **Nautilus Restaurant:** 516bl; Peter Newark's Historical Pictures: 33cr, 54clb; **Tourism NSW:** 182cla/c; **Northern Territory Library:** Percy Brown Collection 268br; N Gleeson Collection 268tr; **Nucolorvue Productions Pty Ltd:** 57br. **Ochre Restaurant:** 515bc; Photography courtesy of the Olympic Co-ordination Authority: Photo: Karl Carlstrom 151clb; © **Open Spaces Photography:** Photo: Andrew Barnes 443b; Photo: Glen Tempest 539cl, 541tc; © **Outback Photographics,** NT: Steve Strike 1994 292tr; Steve Strike 1995 293cla. Palazzo Versace: 514tr; **Paperbark Camp:** 484tl, 510tc; **Park Hyatt Sydney:** 478cl, 499br, 504bl; **Kay Parkin:** 340br; **Parliament House:** The Hon Max Willis, RFD, ED, LLB, MLC, President, Legislative Council, Parliament of NSW. The Hon J Murray, MP, Speaker, Legislative Assembly, Parliament of NSW. Artist's original sketch of the historical painting in oils by Algernon Talmage, RA, *The Founding of Australia.* Kindly loaned to the Parliament of NSW by Mr Arthur Chard of Adelaide, 86tl; **Peppers Mineral Springs Retreat:** 495tr; **Photo Index:** 297cla, 298tr/bl/br, 298–9c, 312tr, 314bc, 317cr, 323tr/c/bl; **Photolibrary:** Geoff Higgins 452tr; Rob Jung 450clb; David Messent 563cla; **Photolibrary.com:** 164cla; © **Phototone Colonial Library:** 59br; **Pictor International:** 222; © **Polygram/ Pictorial Press:** 33tr; **Powerhouse Museum Reproduced courtesy of the Trustees of the Museum of Applied Arts and Sciences, Sydney:** 61bl, 106clb, 106tr, 106bc, 107crb, Marinco Kojdanovski 68br, 106clb; Jean-Francis Lanzarone 106cla; © **Susanna Price:** 431tr. **Qantas:** 60br, 557cla; Collection of The Queensland Art Gallery: R Godfrey Rivers, *Under the Jacaranda,* 1903, oil on canvas, 233c; Russell Drysdale, *Bushfire* 1944, oil and ink on canvas on composition board, 62 × 77cm, Gift of Capt Neil McEacharn through CL Harden 1954, 232cl; © Succession Picasso/DACS London 2011, Pablo Picasso, *La Belle Hollandaise* 1905, gouache on cardboard mounted on wood, 77 × 66.3cm, purchased 1959 with funds donated by Major Harold de Vahl Rubin, 232clb; Rupert Bunny, *Bathers* 1906, oil on canvas, 229.2 × 250cm, purchased 1988, 232tr; **John Oxley Library, State Library of Queensland:** 246br. Ravesi's on Bondi Beach: 499cl, 507br; **Reilly's Cellar Door and Restaurant:** 525tr; **The Rocks Discovery Museum:** 81tl; **The Royal Botanic Garden Sydney:** 110bc; **Royal Mail Hotel Restaurant:** 530bl. **Sand Hills Vineyard:** 166cra; **Science Centre (Brisbane):** 226clb; **Shangri-La Sydney:** 482br; © **Skyscans/Photographer:** David Hancock 277crb, 269c/bl; **Southcorp Wines Europe:** 166tl, 503br; **Southlight Photo Agency:** © Milton Wordley 339cr, 342tr, 343br; **Spectrum Colour Library:** 32bl, 34br,

45crb, 243cr, 290–91c, 373b, 588t; Stan Squire 367tr; **Spice Temple Restaurant:** 505bc; **Spicers Balfour Hotel:** 486bl; **Spicers Clovelly Estate:** 488tl; **St Mary's Cathedral Appeal:** 307cra; © **Tony Stone Images:** 322bl; Gary John Norman 43tl; Fritz Prenzel 26–7c, 235tl; Robin Smith 46br, 171br, 187b; Oliver Strewe 28crb; Penny Tweedie 35bl; Ken Wilson 62bc; **Story Bridge Adventure Club:** Story Bridge Adventure Club 234tl; **Charles Stuart University Winery:** 166bc; **Subo:** Josh Vincent Photography 508tl; **Superstock:** Age Fotostock 282, Dean Fox 90, Minden Pictures / Michael Durham 298c; **Sydney Harbour Foreshore Authority:** 100bc, 101bl; **Sydney Jewish Museum:** 69br; **Sydney Opera House Trust:** 88tr/cla, 89tl/crb/bl; Photography courtesy of the Sydney Organizing Committee for The Olympic Games (SOCOG): 151tl; **Sydney Theatre:** 142cla; **Sydney Tower Eye:** 95br. **The Tahbilk Group:** Four Sisters 382br; **Tali Wiru Restaurant:** 519br; **State Library of Tasmania:** 55tr; **Ten Minutes by Tractor:** 532; **Tenterfield District & Visitors' Information:** 163tr; **Suzie Thomas Publishing:** Thomas O'Flynn bc; **Thorngrove Manor Hotel:** 492bl; **Tolarno Hotel:** 479bl; **Courtesy of Tourism New South Wales:** Phase IX 164tr; **Tourism Victoria:** 409tr; **Transport for NSW:** 133c; **Trip & Artdirectors Photographic Library:** Eric Smith 33bl, 451br; D Silvestris 354bl; **Virgin Australia:** 556tr; **Visions of Victoria:** Peter Dunphy 410br, 417bc; Tim Webster 411c; **Visit Alexandrina:** 357c; Vue de Monde: 528b; Courtesy of **Watermark Press (Sydney):** 61tr; **Whiteman Park:** 311b; © **Wildlight Photo Agency:** Carolyn Jones, 377cra; Tom Keating 301cr/crb; Philip Quirk 23bl, 25bl, 43bl, 185bl; Sean Santos 184bc; Grenville Turner 183cr, 301tl/br; **Wilpena Pound Resort:** 481t; **The Windsor Melbourne:** 493tl; **World Pictures:** 26tr, 27tl, 204cr, 221bl, 254bl, 255tl, 305cra, 444cl; **Yalumba Wine Co.:** 502cra; Zefa: 26cl, 481t. **Young Henrys Brewing & Distilling:** 503cl.

Front Endpaper: Alamy Images: aeropix Rt; David Bigwood Rcrb; Radius Images Lcl; Dave Stamboulis Ltl. **Corbis:** Frans Lanting Ltc; Stephane Lemaire Lb; Steve Parish Rtl. **Dreamstime:** John Casey Rtr; Darren Falkenberg Lbl; Radmurphy Lbc. **Getty Images:** Pete Atkinson Rtc; Alex Hare Rcr; Daniel Osterkamp Rcl; David Wall Photo Rbr; Peter Walton Photography Lbr, Rbl. **Superstock:** Age Fotostock Ltr.

Cover
Front & Spine: **AWL Images:** Tom Mackie
All other images © Dorling Kindersley.
For further information see: www.dkimages.com

Special Editions of DK Travel Guides

DK Travel Guides can be purchased in bulk quantities at discounted prices for use in promotions or as premiums. We are also able to offer special editions and personalized jackets, corporate imprints, and excerpts from all of our books, tailored specifically to meet your own needs.

To find out more, please contact:
(in the United States) **specialsales@dk.com**
(in the UK) **travelguides@uk.dk.com**
(in Canada) w**specialmarkets@dk.com**
(in Australia) **penguincorporatesales@ penguinrandomhouse.com.au**

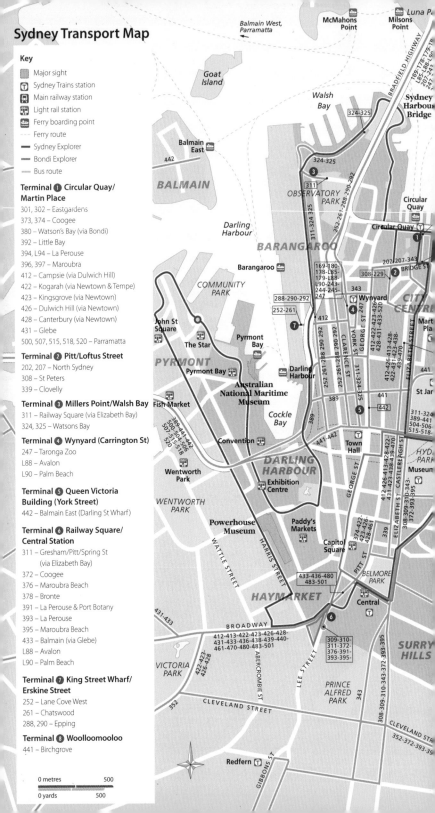